The Elements of Quantitative Investing

Founded in 1807, John Wiley & Sons is the oldest independent publishing company in the United States. With offices in North America, Europe, Australia and Asia, Wiley is globally committed to developing and marketing print and electronic products and services for our customers' professional and personal knowledge and understanding.

The Wiley Finance series contains books written specifically for finance and investment professionals as well as sophisticated individual investors and their financial advisors. Book topics range from portfolio management to e-commerce, risk management, financial engineering, valuation and financial instrument analysis, as well as much more.

For a list of available titles, visit our Web site at www.WileyFinance.com.

The Elements of Quantitative Investing

Giuseppe A. Paleologo

WILEY

Published by John Wiley & Sons, Inc., Hoboken, New Jersey.
Published simultaneously in Canada.

Library of Congress Cataloging-in-Publication Data Applied for:

Print ISBN: 9781394265459
ePDF ISBN: 9781394265473
epub ISBN: 9781394265466

Cover Image: Courtesy of Giuseppe A. Paleologo
Cover Design: Wiley
SKY10099582_030725

To Tofu, again

Contents

	7.4		Interpreting Principal Components	173
		7.4.1	The Clustering View	173
		7.4.2	The Regression View	174
	7.5		Statistical Model Estimation in Practice	176
		7.5.1	Weighted and Two-Stage PCA	176
		7.5.2	Implementing Statistical Models in Production	179
	7.6		★Appendix	181
		7.6.1	Exercises and Extensions to PCA	181
		7.6.2	Asymptotic Properties of PCA	185

Chapter 8 Evaluating Excess Returns 188

	8.1		Backtesting Best Practices	190
		8.1.1	Data Sourcing	190
		8.1.2	Research Process	191
	8.2		The Backtesting Protocol	195
		8.2.1	Cross-Validation and Walk-Forward	195
	8.3		The Rademacher Anti-Serum (RAS)	200
		8.3.1	Setup	200
		8.3.2	Main Result and Interpretation	203
	8.4		Some Empirical Results	208
		8.4.1	Simulations	208
		8.4.2	Historical Anomalies	210
	8.5		★Appendix	214
		8.5.1	Proofs for RAS	214

Chapter 9 Portfolio Management: The Basics 220

	9.1		Why Mean-Variance Optimization?	221
	9.2		Mean-Variance Optimal Portfolios	223
	9.3		Trading in Factor Space	229
		9.3.1	Factor-Mimicking Portfolios	229
		9.3.2	Adding, Estimating, and Trading a New Factor	232
		9.3.3	Factor Portfolios from Sorts?	235
	9.4		Trading in Idio Space	236
	9.5		Drivers of Information Ratio: Information Coefficient and Diversification	237
	9.6		Aggregation: Signals versus Portfolios	240

	9.7	★Appendix	244
		9.7.1 Some Useful Results from Linear Algebra	244
		9.7.2 Some Portfolio Optimization Problems	245
		9.7.3 Optimality of FMPs	245
		9.7.4 Single-Factor Covariance Matrix Updating	247
Chapter 10		Beyond Simple Mean-Variance	250
	10.1	Shortcomings of Naïve MVO	251
	10.2	Constraints and Modified Objectives	254
		10.2.1 Types of Constraints	257
		10.2.2 Do Constraints Improve or Worsen Performance?	261
		10.2.3 Constraints as Penalties	261
	10.3	How Does Estimation Error Affect the Sharpe Ratio?	267
		10.3.1 The Impact of Alpha Error	268
		10.3.2 The Impact of Risk Error	269
	10.4	★Appendix	270
		10.4.1 Theorems on Sharpe Efficiency Loss	270
Chapter 11		Market-Impact-Aware Portfolio Management	276
	11.1	Market Impact	277
		11.1.1 Temporary Market Impact	278
	11.2	Finite-Horizon Optimization	284
	11.3	Infinite-Horizon Optimization	286
		11.3.1 Comparison to Single-Period Optimization	289
		11.3.2 The No-Market-Impact Limit	290
		11.3.3 Optimal Liquidation	290
		11.3.4 Deterministic Alpha	291
		11.3.5 AR(1) Signal	291
	11.4	★Appendix	293
		11.4.1 Proof of the Infinite-Horizon Quadratic Problem	293

Acknowledgments

The following people have proofread, commented on, discussed or supported the development of this book. Some of them are old friends, most are strangers who spontaneously offered to help. Meeting them (usually on X or on LinkedIn) has been an unforeseen pleasure in the writing of the book, and I am grateful for their generosity and the many corrections they sent my way. Unfortunately all the remaining errors are my responsibility.[3]

`@0xfdf`, Rashad Ahmed, Amir Aliev, Sandro C. Andrade, Samuel Babichenko, Ashish Bajpaj, Soumyadipta Banerjee, Rayan Ben Redjeb, Jerome Benveniste, Igor Berman, Jon Beyer, Victor Bomers, David Bonnerot, Thomas Byrne, Ben Chaddha, Yuyao Che, Leif Cussein, Vladimir Cvetkovic, Drake Daly, Alex Darby, Ruolag Deng, Jane Doe, John Doe (Jane's occasionally hostile brother), Saarialho Eero, Bill Falloon, Frank Fan, Marta Filizola, Tom Fleming, Claudio Fontana, Fan Gao, Ernesto Guridi, Touko Haapanen, Victor Haghani, Leila Hardy, Levon Haykazyan, Erik Hellgren, Alex Hermeneanu, Leonhard Hochfilzer, Clint Howard, Jack Huang, Kevin Jacobs,

[3] And my cat's.

Fredrik Jäfvert, Bob Jansen, Amanda Jiménez, Yassine Kachrad, Abhinav R. Kannan, Shahin Khobahi, D. K., Marco Kuhlen, Markku Kurtti, Kofi Kwapong, Jessie Li, Vitoria Lima, `@jesse_livermore`, Samuel Londner, Dustin Lorshbough, Marco Lucchesi, Joseph Maestri, Baridhi Malakar, Emanuel Malek, Paul-Henri Memin, Francesco Mina, Simon Minovitsky, Caroline Moon, Roberto Moura, Abhijit Naik, Graeme Newby, Juntunen Nikolaus, Mikhail Novichkov, Andrew Novotny, Adam Nunes, Tom Ó Nualláin, Yogesh Padmanabhan, Jeff Park, Damon Petersen, Henrik Hiro Pettersson, Saharat Phomthong, Alexis Plascencia, Gabriele Pompa, David Popovic, Akshay Prasadan, Miika Purola, Siddhant Pyasi, Cas Rijnierse, Viktor Salihu, Mateus Sampaio, Ali Sanjari, Douglas Ricardo Sansão, Tanmay Satpathy, Guilherme Saturnino, Abishek Saxena, Christian Schmitz, Maarten Scholl, Timothy Shchetilin, Shawn Sheng, Nakul Shenoy, Marco Signoretto, Ashutosh Singh, Matt Smith, Richárd Süveges, `@systematicls`, Samer Takriti, Gianmario Tamagnone, Xiaolong Tan, Kaspar Thommen, Maxim Tishin, Shahpour Turkian, Nathan Ueda, Carlos Ungil, Sinan Unver, Ricardo Valdez, Derrick VanGennep, Paul Vriend, Jay Vyas, Andrew Wang, Shida Wang, Simon Xiang, Jeremy Young, Alvin Zhang, Howard Zhang, Siqi Zheng.

I owe special thanks to Brandon DiNunno, Denis Dmitriev, Jean-François Fortin, Antoine Liutkus, Dustin Lorshbough, Tom Mainiero, Krutarth Satoskar, and Trent Spears for their deep and wide reading of the manuscript.

G.A.P.

Introduction

This book originates from notes I wrote for two university courses. The first is ORIE5256 - Topics in Risk Management and Portfolio Construction, a course offered in the program for M.S. in Financial Engineering at Cornell University. The second is MATH-GA 2708.001 - Algorithmic Trading & Quantitative Strategies, offered in the Mathematics Department at New York University. When I set out to write this book, my objective was to write the quantitative introduction I had wanted to read at the beginning of my journey in finance. Given the scope and goals of quantitative investing, it is only possible to cover a small fraction of it in a course, or even in a book. To address this problem, I made three choices.

First and most important, I aim for synthesis. A book is, first of all, a knowledge filter. In the preface to his classic (Kelley, 1955), Kelley wrote that he wanted to title his book "What Every Young Analyst Should Know"; that book was barely three hundred pages long. It still feels fresh and necessary today. In order to keep my book of manageable length, my working principle has been to focus on real-world problems and then use the *simplest* techniques that allow me to address the problem at hand. A recurrent theme in the book is that almost everything in it is either linear or quadratic. In the process of writing, I have ruthlessly eliminated topics of secondary importance, material that was too hard for the payoff that it gave the readers, and also topics or ideas that are not sufficiently well-formed, or too experimental. Even if you choose not to read my book, I implore you to internalize the following lesson, learned by practitioners through sweat and tears: *theory is cheap*. There are thousands and thousands of theory papers, in love with technical virtuosity but oblivious of reality. Do not fall into temptation; by applications be driven.[1]

Second, I consider risk management and portfolio management as intrinsically connected. Asset return modeling, volatility estimation, portfolio optimization, *ex-ante* and *ex-post* performance analytics are all linked. For example, hedging belongs to risk and portfolio optimization, and analysis of performance feeds back into portfolio construction. I have avoided redundancy as much as possible. Sections often refer to earlier ones or are linked to later ones. As I was revising my book draft, whenever I found I had introduced some topic (often because I was infatuated with it) and then never used it, I exiled it to a long file made out of "rejected sections" that lives in my laptop. That is the sad part. The happy part: it's surprising how tall a tree can grow with a bit of pruning. Out of metaphor, there is a lot of material in this book, and it gets challenging at times.

Third, I occasionally integrate some standard financial results approaches with tools from the field of statistical learning. The former is applied in fundamental factor modeling, portfolio optimization, and performance attribution. I use the latter for the estimation of statistical models and backtesting. My hope is that the integration of these different approaches is seamless.

The questions that I address in this book are:

1. How do I model returns in a way that allows me to generate risk and return forecasts?
    - (a) What are excess returns?
    - (b) How do I model multivariate returns?
    - (c) How do I describe and forecast risk?
    - (d) How do I test risk forecasts and return forecasts?
    - (e) How do I backtest alphas?

[1] References to "By Demons be Driven" by Pantera and to Warcraft 3 are intentional.

2. How do I monetize these signals?
   (a) How do I optimize a portfolio?
   (b) What is the impact of risk and alpha errors on performance?
   (c) How do I account for transaction costs in portfolio management?
   (d) How do I hedge a portfolio?
3. How do I improve?
   (a) How do I allocate risk over time?
   (b) How do I distinguish skill from luck?

The style of the book is also, I hope, a bit different. I have kept in mind the six values that Italo Calvino (Calvino, 1999) hoped to preserve in the current millennium: Lightness, Quickness, Exactitude, Visibility, Multiplicity, and Consistency. My aversion to advanced mathematics notwithstanding, I must warn the reader that the book is not easy. During my lectures, I have induced more than one student into a comatose stupor. Afterwards, a few students left finance altogether and successfully pursued careers in entertainment. Another student keeps sending me postcards from Ibiza. A handful have become portfolio managers at hedge funds and risk managers. Yet, it is the easiest book I could write for the task at hand, and it is written in the *friendliest* style I am capable of. Also, I would be lying—and conveying the wrong message—if I claimed that the problems I present are now settled, and that the book is the last word on the subject. On the contrary, you and I are in this book together, and together we shall keep a beginner's mind (Suzuki, 1970): a spirit of openness and curiosity, even when facing advanced topics. I will point out the limits of my theories and the open problems for you to work on. If you are old enough to have lived in the seventies and liked punk music, you may remember a cyclostyled zine (Figure 1). On its second page it showed three open chords; below them, a command: "NOW FORM A BAND." May this book be your field guide to being a punk quantitative researcher. It will be a life well lived.

Prerequisites

The book should be accessible to a beginning graduate or advanced undergraduate student in Physics, Mathematics, Statistics, or Engineering. This means having a working relationship, and if possible a romantic one, with advanced linear algebra, probability theory, and statistics. Even more important is to have a deep interest in quantitative modeling of real-life

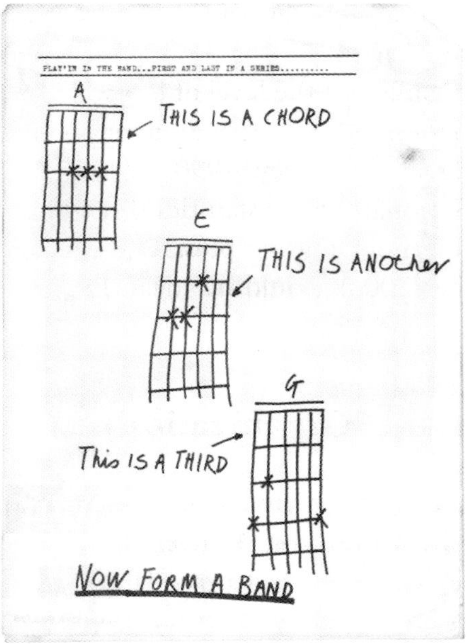

Figure 1 Punk fanzine *Sideburn* #1, page 2 (1977). *Source:* Flickr.com/Dunk.

phenomena. Many readers will be either members of a systematic trading team, or work as quantitative researchers in the central team of a hedge fund or a quantitative asset manager.

The book's material is organized in such a way that you do not need to go through mathematical proofs. You can rely only on informal statements of mathematical results in the main body of the chapters, and that will suffice to understand the main points. The appendices at the end of the chapters contain more rigorous statements, proofs, and background material. If you plan on actively doing research, you should study them, eventually.

Even if you read only the main body, you should be used to thinking in mathematical models. The Book of Nature is written in a mathematical language.[2] Be comfortable with:

---

[2] "Philosophy is written in this grand book, the universe, which stands continually open to our gaze. But the book cannot be understood unless one first learns to comprehend the language and read the letters in which it is composed. It is written in the language of mathematics, and its characters are triangles, circles, and other geometric figures without which it is humanly impossible to understand a single word of it; without these, one wanders about in a dark labyrinth" (Galilei, 1623).

- Working with linear algebra, at least at the level of Strang (2019) and Trefethen and Bau (1997).
- Some applied probability, at the level of Ross (2023). Exposure to some simple control theory and state-space models helps. You can come to this from econometrics (Harvey, 1990; Shumway and Stoffer, 2011), control theory (Simon2006), or statistics (Hyndman et al., 2008).
- Some optimization modeling is a plus. The first few chapters of Boyd and Vandenberghe (2004) would be ideal. However, I will cover the basic theory in an appendix.

Organization

Like Caesar's Gaul, the book is broadly divided into three parts. The first part focuses on returns modeling. I cover the basics of GARCH early on because they are needed for factor modeling, and then I cover factor models because they are necessary for everything. I have separate chapters for fundamental and statistical models. These topics are covered in depth, and both the treatment and some of the modeling approaches are novel. Finally, I cover data snooping/backtesting as a separate chapter, since it is a central element of the investment process.

The second part is devoted to portfolio construction and performance analysis, both *ex ante* and *ex post*. The focus is on mean-variance optimization (MVO). I emphasize the geometric intuition behind much of mean-variance optimization. Rotations, projections, and angles are prevalent throughout. This allows for a synthetic, elegant characterization of performance and for concise proofs. The statistics of the Sharpe Ratio are covered in some detail. The decomposition of payoffs into timing components, factor and idiosyncratic Profit and Loss (PnL), and stock selection versus sizing of positions is rigorously demonstrated. Model error plays an important role in this part. If an optimization problem is Othello, then model error must be Iago: it can drive the optimization insane. Unlike in Shakespeare's tragedies, we can try to rewrite the endings and turn them into comedies.

The third part is the shortest. It contains results about intertemporal volatility allocation and performance attribution. These are essential components of the investment process and belong in a book with the word "Elements" in its title.

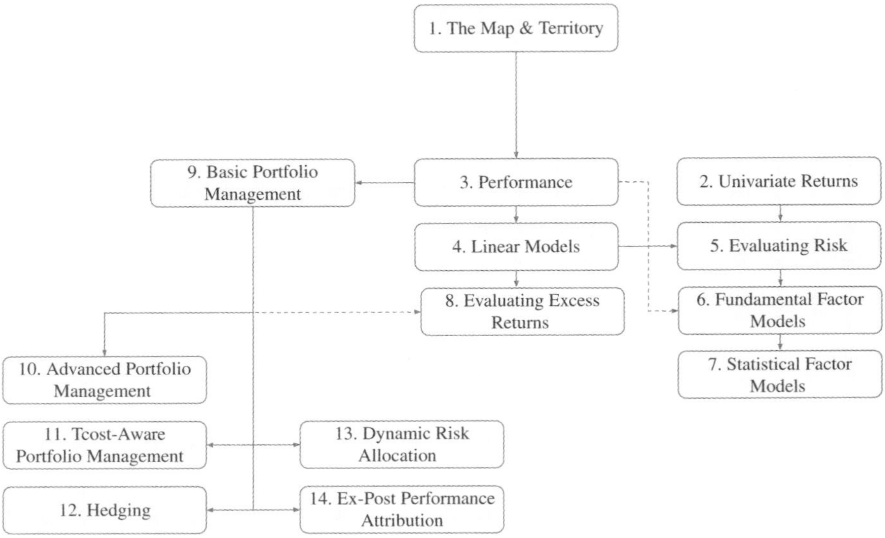

Figure 2 Chapter dependencies.

Each chapter is organized like an onion. The first sections convey the essential ideas using simple quantitative methods and are aimed at a broad audience. Sections marked with a star "★" are more advanced and can be skipped on a first reading. Proofs of new results or basic technical material are relegated to the appendices at the end of the chapters. The goal is not to disrupt the flow of learning. As mentioned at the beginning of this preface, the content of this book was taught first and written later. It is meant to be read aloud and discussed, but it should be suitable for self-study. The dependencies among the chapters are shown in Figure 2.

Giuseppe "gappy" A. Paleologo
Riverdale, New York
March 21, 2025

Notation

$\mathbb{R}$	field of real numbers
$\mathbb{R}^+$	$[0, \infty)$
$\mathbb{N}$	set of natural numbers
$x, y, \ldots$	scalars
$\mathbf{x}, \mathbf{y}, \ldots$	vectors (assumed to be $n \times 1$)
$\mathbf{X}, \mathbf{Y}, \ldots$	matrices
$\mathbf{x}^\top, \mathbf{X}^\top$	vector or matrix transpose
$\mathbf{X}^+$	Moore–Penrose pseudo-inverse
$\mathbf{\Omega}$	covariance matrix
$\mathrm{diag}\left(x_1, \ldots, x_n\right)$	diagonal matrix with scalars $x_1, \ldots, x_n$ on the main diagonal
$[\mathbf{x}]_i, x_i$	ith element of a vector
$[\mathbf{X}]_{i,j}$	element of a matrix on ith row and jth column
$[\mathbf{X}]_{i,\cdot}$ or $\mathbf{x}_i$	ith row of matrix X
$[\mathbf{X}]_{\cdot,j}$ or $\mathbf{x}^j$	jth column of matrix X
$\mathrm{trace}\,(\mathbf{X})$	trace operator: $\mathrm{trace}\,(\mathbf{X}) = \sum_i [\mathbf{X}]_{i,i}$

$\|\mathbf{X}\|$	determinant of a matrix
$\delta_{i,j}$	Kroneker's delta: $\delta_{i,j} = 1$ if $i = j$, 0 otherwise
$\delta(t)$	Dirac's delta function: $\delta(t) = 0$ for $t \neq 0$, and $\int_{-\infty}^{\infty} \delta(t)dt = 1$
$\mathbf{e}$	vector whose elements are all ones: $[\mathbf{e}]_i = 1$ for all i
$\mathbf{1}\{x\}$	indicator function, equal to 1 if x is true, 0 otherwise
$\mathbf{e}_i$	vector whose ith element is 1 and the others are zero: $[\mathbf{e}_i]_j = \delta_{i,j}$
$\mathbf{I}_m$	identity matrix of size $m \times m$
$\|\|\mathbf{x}\|\|_p$	p-norm, for $p \geq 1$: $\left(\sum_{i=1}^{n} \|x_i\|^p\right)^{1/p}$
$\|\|\mathbf{x}\|\|$	2-norm of a vector
$\|\|\mathbf{x}\|\|_{\mathbf{Q}}$	$\sqrt{\mathbf{x}^{\mathsf{T}}\mathbf{Q}\mathbf{x}}$, for a positive-definite matrix $\mathbf{Q}$
$\|\|\mathbf{H}\|\|$	operator norm for a positive-definite matrix $\mathbf{H}$: $\max_{\mathbf{x}} \|\|\mathbf{H}\mathbf{x}\|\| / \|\|\mathbf{x}\|\| := \left(\max_{\mathbf{x}} \mathbf{x}^{\mathsf{T}}(\mathbf{H}^{\mathsf{T}}\mathbf{H})\mathbf{x}/\|\|\mathbf{x}\|\|^2\right)^{1/2}$
$\lfloor x \rfloor$	largest integer that is less than, or equal to, x
$\langle \mathbf{x}, \mathbf{y} \rangle$	scalar product of two vectors, i.e., $\mathbf{x}^{\mathsf{T}}\mathbf{y}$
$\langle \mathbf{A}, \mathbf{B} \rangle$	scalar product of two matrices: $\langle \mathbf{A}, \mathbf{B} \rangle \in \mathbb{R} := \operatorname{trace}\left(\mathbf{A}^{\mathsf{T}}\mathbf{B}\right)$
$S_C(\mathbf{a}, \mathbf{b})$	cosine similarity$S_C(\mathbf{x}, \mathbf{y}) := \langle \mathbf{x}, \mathbf{y} \rangle / (\|\|\mathbf{a}\|\| \, \|\|\mathbf{b}\|\|)$
$\mathbf{x} \circ \mathbf{y} \in \mathbb{R}^n$, $\mathbf{X} \circ \mathbf{Y} \in \mathbb{R}^{m \times n}$	Hadamard (element-wise) product of two vectors (matrices): $[\mathbf{x} \circ \mathbf{y}]_i := x_i y_i$, $[\mathbf{X} \circ \mathbf{Y}]_{i,j} := [\mathbf{X}]_{i,j}[\mathbf{Y}]_{i,j}$
$\xi \perp \zeta$	random variables ξ and ζ are independent
$E(\xi), E(\boldsymbol{\xi})$	expectation of random variables or random vectors
$E_{\xi}(f(\xi))$	expectation of a function f of random variable ξ
$\hat{E}(\mathbf{x})$	average of a vector $\mathbf{x}$: $\hat{E}(\mathbf{x}) := n^{-1} \sum_i x_i$
$\operatorname{var}(x)$	variance of a random variable x
$\mathbf{L}_1 : \mathbb{R}^n \to \mathbb{R}^n$	shift operator: $L_1\mathbf{x} := (x_2, x_3, \ldots, x_n, 0)^{\mathsf{T}}$, i.e., $[\mathbf{L}_1]_{i,j} := \delta_{i,j-1}$
rv	random variables
iid rv	independent, identically distributed random variables
$\stackrel{d}{=}$	equality in distribution of two random variables
$\sim$	rv distributed according to a distribution, e.g., $\xi \sim N(0, 1)$
$\asymp$	of the same order: $n \asymp m$ if $an < m < bn$ for some $0 < a \leq b$
$\Rightarrow$	convergence in distribution
$\equiv$	equivalence of optimization problems: for constants $a > 0$, $b \in \mathbb{R}$ $\max_{\mathbf{x} \in \mathcal{S}} f(\mathbf{x}) \equiv \max_{\mathbf{x} \in \mathcal{S}}[af(\mathbf{x}) + b]$

Chapter 1

The Map and the Territory

The Questions

1. What are the essential components of quantitative investing?
2. What types of securities are involved and how are they traded?
3. Who are the main market participants and what roles do they play?
4. Where do excess returns in investing come from?
5. What are the key elements that form the analytical framework of a quantitative portfolio manager?

This chapter is a guide to the essential components of quantitative investing. When considering the meaning of a word, it's often instructive to go back to its etymology, so let's play this game. Despite being a

Germanic language, English adopted many words from Latin, sometimes by way of French. "Investing" comes from "Investire", which in Latin meant "to cover with a vest", or "to put in a vest". So it should be hardly surprising that two thousand years later, vests would become the favorite garment of hedge fund managers. In the Middle Ages, the verb took on the additional meaning "to surround, to have ownership of". It is also possible that the modern meaning overtook the old because, in ceremonies in which ownership was transferred, the new owner was "invested" with a cloak and other regalia. In Italian—the direct successor to Latin—the old meaning is gone, and "investire" only means "to receive possession of something". As for "quantitative", that is Latin too: "quantum", a noun denoting something that can be measured, increased, and decreased. We will deal with ownership, sold and bought in units that can be measured, increased and decreased. This is, unfortunately, the whole of finance. You can own a house, a painting, a bet on the survival of humankind, or even an idea. Each one of these investment topics deserves its own book, written by a competent author. In writing this book, I have chosen to trade off generality in favor of detail. I have covered each subject with the goal in mind that you would have sufficient information to understand it, implement it, and critique it. However, even an analytical book needs an introduction that puts things in their proper context. In this chapter, I aim to provide that context. You will have a broad understanding of the classes of securities to which these methods apply; and of the way these securities are traded, and by whom. This is a necessary prerequisite to explore fundamental questions: Where are excess returns coming from? What causes these trading opportunities? Finally, I will present the essential components that make up the analytical framework of a quantitative portfolio manager. The underlying message is that to be successful, an investor must understand how things work. A seminal early book on investing is titled "The Intelligent Investor" (Graham, 2006). To double down on Latin, the original meaning of "intelligent" is "to read into something", similar to "insightful" in the English language. Your success will come from reasoning about the behavior of your counterparties, the rules governing the trading of your assets, and the functioning of exchanges. Many budding quants focus on quantitative methods. The fact is that theory is cheap and is often not hard. What is hard is putting the right tool at the service of the right insight.

Finally, this is the only chapter without mathematics. You should enjoy it while it lasts.

1.1 The Securities

We will be concerned with *standardized products* that are *liquid*. We explain these concepts in more detail.

To "own" an object is effectively to own *claims* on that object in the future. If you own a house, you can live in it or rent it out (your claim) and it is yours. This claim is not absolute, however. In most countries, the local or central government may need your property for reasons of public welfare and can require you to exchange your claim for cash at a fair price. If you own a painting, you may enjoy it in the confines of your house, but may not necessarily own its reproduction rights. If you own a bet on the future of humanity, your counterparty may have some *force majeure* clauses that prevent it from paying (e.g., consider a zombie apocalypse scenario). Defining ownership of an "idea" is especially challenging and prone to be treated on an *ad hoc* basis. Compared to the infinite and ever-changing nature of the meaning of property rights, our coverage is very narrow. Specifically, we focus on the subset of contracts that are standardized and liquid. We buy and sell *standardized* claims. These claims come in a few varieties, and their attributes are clearly defined and known to all potential buyers and sellers. Examples are:

- *Equities and Exchange-Traded Funds (ETFs).* These give us partial ownership in companies, or groups of companies, and entitle us to receive future cash payments generated by the economic activities of these companies.
- *Futures.* These contracts deliver a physical commodity or a cash payment contingent on the state of the world at a future date, at a price determined today.
- *Bonds.* These are contracts that allow the transfer of debt claims among parties. An investor lends money to a borrower, in exchange for a fixed cash flow in the future (e.g., periodic interest payments and a final payment). A bond makes this claim transferable to other lenders.
- *Vanilla options.* These are claims that depend on the future value of some underlying asset; for example, you may receive the right (but not the

obligation) to buy a stock at a future date, at a price determined today. The nature of these claims is standardized, hence the term "vanilla".
- *Interest Rate Swaps (IRSs)*. These contracts allow the exchange of a certain, deterministic cash flow stream for an uncertain one, which depends on interest rates at future dates.
- *Credit Default Swaps (CDSs)*. These contracts insure the buyer against the failure of a company at a future date, in exchange for recurring fixed payments.

Further these contracts are *liquid*. For our purposes, a liquid contract is one that can be bought and sold at large enough sizes, and at sufficiently short time horizons, to enable quantitative strategies to be implemented. This means that if we plan to buy or sell a contract, we should be able to do so without incurring a transaction cost so high that our strategy is not economically attractive even for small trading sizes, and that the waiting time due to searching for a counterparty should not be so long as to make the transaction economically unattractive.

The properties of standardization and liquidity are closely intertwined. Increased standardization tends to enhance liquidity by consolidating demand, as it aggregates dispersed demand from bespoke products toward a smaller set of standardized ones. Furthermore, standardization streamlines the trading process, reducing transaction costs and simplifying contracts, thereby fostering investor trust and attracting more participants, thus enhancing liquidity. However, the downside is that customers may sacrifice the ability to trade certain useful product characteristics. Determining the optimal level of customization, even at the expense of liquidity, remains an ongoing process of learning and adaptation. For instance, prior to the 2008 financial crisis, CDSs exhibited greater variety. However, the "Big Bang" initiated by the International Swaps and Derivatives Association (ISDA) on April 8, 2009, simplified contract terms, including standardizing coupon rates (100 bps and 500 bps) and introducing a standard upfront payment, which played a pivotal role in restoring confidence in this asset class (Vause, 2010).

Trading and liquidity are at the core of the book. In order to better understand the trading process and the nature of liquidity, we should describe in some detail how trading on-exchange and over-the-counter happens.

1.2 Modes of Exchange

At any given time, economic agents want to buy or sell contracts. They want to do so quickly, securely, and cheaply. The three options around which trading is currently organized are exchanges, over-the-counter, and dark pools. Exchanges are venues in which the orders of buyers and sellers are anonymized and matched against each other. Orders are characterized by size, the number of contracts, direction (buy or sell), and price. They represent requests to buy or sell a number of contracts. The exchange records such active orders on a ledger, known as the limit-order book (LOB), and employs a set of priority rules to match buy and sell orders in the exchanges—aptly named a matching engine. In order to trade on an exchange, one must be a member of that exchange. Membership entails apparent benefits and less-apparent responsibilities. Market participants must maintain sound governance, risk processes, and capital structure.

Exchanges evolve continuously due to two driving forces. On one side, there is a push toward consolidation, which reduces operating costs and gives the owner pricing power. On the other side, technical and process innovations introduce new competitors into the market. In the United States alone, there are more than a dozen equity stock exchanges. Exchange-traded assets, such as stocks, options, and future contracts (including Forex Futures), are often liquid, although this condition is neither necessary nor sufficient: some exchange-traded assets are traded in minimal volumes and, therefore, are not liquid, and some very liquid products are traded off-exchange.

Other assets are not traded on exchanges, but *over-the-counter (OTC)*. In this case, the buyer or seller transacts through an institutional market participant, the broker-dealer, which is connected to other broker-dealers and facilitates the matching of orders. Bonds, IRSs, Forex spot currencies, Forex Forwards, and CDSs are examples of contracts traded OTC. Some of these, like currencies, are among the world's most liquid contracts. A precondition for liquidity is standardization. Think of a house. "The New York housing market" is very different from the stock market in that each of the 15.4 billion outstanding Apple shares (as of July 2024) is indistinguishable from the other and sells in a matter of seconds. In contrast, a house has many attributes that make it unique: location, size, age, blueprint, and condition. Another characteristic of liquid markets is the large number of participants. When numerous participants are involved in a market, competing for a relatively low number of contracts, transactions become more frequent, and the necessity for bilateral bargaining diminishes. The ability of any individual participant to influence the price is significantly reduced. To illustrate, consider the housing market as a counterpoint: when selling a house, you typically negotiate with one specific buyer (out of a few eligible ones), who may spend many hours searching for the right property and may engage in intense bargaining, sometimes to the point of contention, to secure the best possible price.

Finally, *Dark Pools* (a type of ATS, or Alternative Trading System, which does not make its LOB transparent) are additional venues that are distinct from exchanges (although sometimes owned by them). Dark Pools address the needs of certain institutional investors to execute orders without displaying their trading intentions. By design, Dark Pools hide order details and only make trades details available after execution. As of 2024, approximately 16% of U.S. shares are traded on Dark Pools.

1.3 Who Are the Market Participants?

It is convention to partition traders into the *sell side* and the *buy side*. The former facilitates trading by providing services; the latter receives trade for their own benefit. Below I describe the participant types. For a more detailed description, see Harris (2003).

1.3.1 The Sell Side

The sell side comprises brokers, dealers, and broker-dealers.

- *Dealers*[1] fulfill their clients' demands, thus providing liquidity. They take the opposite side of the trade; they are profitable if, on average, they sell (buy) at a price higher (lower) than what they initially paid to buy (sell) the asset. The difference between buy and sell prices is the *spread*. When dealers interact with clients, they quote the buy price (the *bid price*) and the sell price (the *ask price*) for a contract. They are effectively *making a market*, since these quotes make transactions possible. In OTC markets, dealers are the primary liquidity providers. The most sophisticated among such markets allow the dealers to quote prices,

[1] Ch. 13 in Harris (2003).

quantities, and other attributes continuously. For example, fixed-income products can be traded on Dealerweb or Bloomberg. In order markets or for highly bespoke products, the dealers quote on request, possibly one-sided only, for a specific quantity and with an expiration time. The quote, or the spread if the quote is two-sided, depends on the quantity. Similarly to speculators, dealers trade on their own behalf. Like speculators, they hold a portfolio (or an *inventory* of positions) and face the issue of trading counterparties that may be more informed than themselves. Unlike speculators, dealers are passive traders, in that they respond to their clients. Also, unlike speculators, dealers enjoy special regulatory status. Because dealers observe the demand flow of their clients, they are informed agents, often serving the needs of informed clients. The dealers' profit originates from the realized spread of their trade (which is usually lower than the quoted spread) but also from the specific information the dealer derives from the order flow. One specific type of flow originates from retail investors (who we introduce later in the chapter). These investors access the market indirectly through brokers. Brokers have special arrangements to direct market orders to dealers, who commit to executing them while offering certain price guarantees on the trade.

In summary, dealers are liquidity providers, and they are compensated for services through trading profits.

- *Brokers*[2] trade on behalf of their clients. When the broker receives an order from a client, together with information about the client's time and price preferences, it searches for the most effective channel to execute it in accordance with these preferences. For example, a client sends a broker an order to buy a certain number of shares of a company. The broker is a member of all major exchanges. It splits the large order into smaller orders and routes them to the various markets at times that meet the execution horizon of the client or its expected cost. Unlike dealers, brokers are intermediaries who take no risk by holding contract positions at any given time. The intermediation service they provide is beneficial; however, it comes with its own risks. First, brokers provide exchange access to non-member clients and they provide OTC dealer access to non-institutional clients. Institutional clients, too, may want to enlist a broker when interacting with dealers, since the broker

---

[2] Ch. 7 in Harris (2003).

anonymizes the clients. Further, broker intermediation solves bilateral settlement risk: money is exchanged for contracts after the trade occurs. Clients need to know and trust their counterparty to protect themselves from insolvency, reneging, or non-compliance. There is a small number of brokers compared to the number of traders, so that clients need to approve (and be approved by) only a few counterparties; a reduction in time, cost, and risk. This, of course, does not eliminate counterparty risk. It transfers it to the brokers. The brokers manage it by vetting the clients, and by requiring that clients deposit capital at the broker, which the broker uses in case of client insolvency. The brokers also *clear* and *settle* trades on behalf of the client. In addition to these services, brokers, and especially *prime brokers*, the subclass of brokers servicing hedge funds and other sophisticated investors, offer their clients other services:

- *Custodial services*. Brokers ensure receipt, recording, and safekeeping of securities.
- *Rehypothecation*. Clients may allow the brokers to use their securities for the brokers' own needs in exchange for fees or rebates. For example, brokers may use client securities as collateral for their own transaction or lend them to other clients.
- *Margin loans*. Brokers lend clients short-term capital to buy securities. They charge them SOFR[3] plus a spread.
- *Location of short positions*. Clients may want to *short* stocks (i.e., sell shares first, and buy them back at a later time), with the expectation that future prices will be lower than current ones. Brokers enable these transactions by lending shares from a third party and making them available to clients. The clients then sell them in the open market, buy them back at a later time, and return them to the broker. After the initial sale, but before the buyback, the broker invests the cash proceeds at SOFR plus a spread. The client receives from the broker SOFR minus a spread.
- *Research reports and services*, as well as broker-specific data. These services used to be bundled in broker commissions but after the implementation of MIFID II regulation, they are now charged separately.

[3] Secured Overnight Financing Rate (SOFR) is a measure of the interest rate charged for overnight cash loans.

– *Capital introductions*, in which brokers facilitate the connection between hedge funds and potential investors.

In summary, brokers offer diversified services, the most important of which is to facilitate clients' transactions. They are compensated by commissions, interest on cash balances, interest on lending, and *payment for order flow* (PFOF), which is the compensation brokers receive from market makers for routing orders to them.

Broker-dealers, also called *dual traders*, combine the previous two functions in a single entity. They act both on behalf of the client and on their own behalf. This introduces a tension. The dealer's arm is incentivized to use the broker's information in trading to its advantage. Maybe the simplest action is *front-running*: the dealer is aware of incoming buying or selling demand for a security, and buys it in advance before this demand manifests in the market and is reflected in prices. To mitigate this type of behavior, regulations are in place to safeguard the interest of the client. The most important law regulating brokers, dealers, and broker-dealers is the Securities Exchange Act of 1934 (or "1934 Act").

1.3.2 The Buy Side

The buy side usually trades with the sell side. You (the reader of this book) are likely to be a member of this group, even though certain dealers face quantitative challenges similar to yours. It is important to understand who the actors in the buy-side drama are, because you will continuously interact with them, and your excess returns will be the outcome of this interaction. We could classify the buy-side actors according to several criteria. For example, the sub-industry to which they belong: life insurers, mutual funds, hedge funds, and so on. I opt to classify them (subjectively!) based on the type of investing they perform.

- *Indexers* are passive investors. Their portfolios replicate the compositions of the benchmarks, or indices, generated by data providers like MSCI, S&P, Russell, CRSP, or from exchanges like FTSE 100, TOPIX, and Deutsche Börse. These indices are updated on a quarterly or biannual basis, and they comprise bond indices as well, like the Bloomberg Agg (until 2016 owned by Barclays). Several investment vehicles track indices; mutual funds and exchange-traded funds are the largest in terms of size. Large firms in this group are Blackrock, Vanguard, and State

Street. Indexers make up a large and growing share of the total asset base. According to estimates by Chinco and Sammon (2023), they represent over 37% of the U.S. stock market capitalization as of 2020.

- *Hedgers* are firms participating in markets with the primary objective of reducing financial risk originating from their core businesses. For example, currency risk is faced by any firm doing business internationally. Firms such as airlines and manufacturing companies purchase fossil fuels (gas, Brent, and West Texas Intermediate), whose price variability can be very disruptive. Hedgers primarily participate in derivative markets: futures, swaps, and options. Hedgers differ from other participants who also hedge, such as dealers or hedge funds, in that hedging is the primary activity they perform.
- *Institutional active managers* are firms investing on behalf of their clients. They run strategies that are sometimes benchmarked to commercial indices and hope to beat them. There is some evidence of underperformance of funds serving retail investors; see S&P SPIVA report[4] or the Refinitiv study (Glow, 2023). Both show that over 60% of funds underperform their benchmarks over a one-year trailing basis. The outperformance of funds over one year is not persistent: as of January 2024, 91% of funds trail the performance of the S&P500 over the previous 15 years. On the other side, funds serving institutions seem to beat their benchmarks (Gerakos and Linnainmaa, 2021). The *tracking error* is a measure of the risk they can take when differing from their reference benchmarks. Otherwise stated, their portfolios can be expressed as the sum of the positions in a benchmark, and of discretionary positions of a "tracking portfolio". A large tracking error gives the funds much discretion; a low one places their returns close to the indices, and makes them "index huggers," or "closet indexers" (i.e., index funds in disguise).
- *Asset allocators* manage portfolios composed of securities in multiple asset classes. Within an asset class, the portfolio closely follows a representative benchmark. One can view asset allocators as managers of a portfolio of asset classes. The relative weight of these asset classes in the portfolio is either constant or changes slowly. Common asset classes are equities, bonds, commodities, and cash equivalents.[5] In addition, asset allocators

[4] https://www.spglobal.com/spdji/en/research-insights/spiva/.

[5] *Cash equivalents* are highly liquid assets with low returns, like bank certificates of deposit, short-dated treasuries, or commercial paper.

invest in alternative asset managers like private equity firms, venture capital, hedge funds, and real estate.

- *Informed traders* include primarily hedge funds and principal trading firms. These firms are usually organized as partnerships, although a few are public companies. They face fewer constraints than institutional managers. Whereas principal trading firms only have general partners (GPs, the principals) investing their own money, hedge funds also have limited partners (LPs) who do not invest actively.[6] These firms pursue absolute returns (i.e., not tracking a benchmark), which exhibit low correlation to the indices of major asset classes.[7] Informed traders invest heavily in human capital, technology, and data to achieve this goal. They fulfill two major functions. The first one is *price discovery*. By using all information available to them, they generate estimates of the true value of securities. If the security prices differ from their estimates, they trade to exploit the mispricing. If the price is lower than their estimate, they buy the security. In the process, they increase its price and bring it closer to equilibrium. Mispricing can take many forms. If the same security is offered at different prices on different exchanges, *arbitrageurs* (a subset of informed traders) will try to exploit the difference; of course, this may not be easy to do, so the difference either persists, or disappears very quickly due to technology investment in low-latency trading. The second role of informed traders is *liquidity provisioning*. Supply and demand of certain assets is predictable to a certain degree. I provide examples in Section 1.4; hedge funds and market makers develop specialized strategies that predict imbalances, hold (or short) securities before the liquidity need materializes, and meet the liquidity needs at the event. The range of possible intervals between prediction and event can be vast—from sub-second for high-frequency market makers to weeks or months for hedge funds.
- *Retail investors* trade for their own account via retail brokers. In 2020, retail investors made up approximately 20% of total volume; the share

[6] GPs in hedge funds are both principals (since they invest their own money) and agents (on behalf of the LPs). To resolve this conflict of interest, the SEC regulates the class of investors who can be LPs (high-net-worth, sophisticated investors), and gives LPs special privileges within the fund.

[7] This is not always true in practice because (a) some hedge funds have an explicit market exposure and (b) some hedge funds have an asymmetric exposure to the market (Agarwal and Naik, 2004).

was slightly more than 10% in 2011. Several studies, across different national markets and periods, have shown that retail traders are consistently unprofitable (Barber and Odean, 2013); retail trader flow is uninformed. This is one of the reasons why it is highly sought after by dealers, who will pay the retail brokers for routing it to them (payment for order flow).

1.4 Where Do Excess Returns Come From?

Now that we have introduced the main actors in the play (usually a tragedy, rarely a comedy, and occasionally a farce) of investing, we can discuss the sources of excess returns. The "excess" qualifier means "in excess of portfolio invested in risk-free assets, such as short-dated U.S. treasuries." This topic is central both to academic financial research and to practitioners. Academic finance is primarily concerned with the question of *efficiency*. In the words of Malkiel (1987):

> *A capital market is said to be efficient if it fully and correctly reveals all available information in determining security prices. Formally, the market is said to be efficient with respect to some information set,* ϕ*, if security prices would be unaffected by revealing that information to all participants. Moreover, efficiency with respect to an information set,* ϕ*, implies that it is impossible to make economic profits by trading on the basis of* ϕ.

An exceptionally concise definition, if there ever was one. At its core is the "information set ϕ". This could be, for example, the set of all historical prices of the traded securities. Nowadays, this information can be obtained with *relatively*[8] little effort. A different type of information set is publicly available information,[9] defined in the United States as "any information that you reasonably believe is lawfully made available to the general public from: (i) federal, state, or local government records; (ii) widely distributed media; or (iii) disclosures to the general public that are required to be made by federal, state, or local law." An even finer information set

[8] The "relatively" here denotes a bit of sarcasm. Collecting long time series of good quality, accounting for corporate actions, is hard, expensive, and requires skill.

[9] PRIVACY OF CONSUMER FINANCIAL INFORMATION UNDER TITLE V OF THE GRAMM–LEACH–BLILEY ACT. §163.3 (w) (1).

is the set of *all* information available to *any* investor. Academic research tries to determine the validity of the statement that "security prices would be unaffected by revealing that information to all participants." Note that this does not mean that ϕ is not helpful to predict future prices. Indeed, there is empirical evidence that asset prices are predictable. However, the hypothesis is that current prices may not be affected. We do not trade in the direction of returns, up to the point that the investing opportunity disappears. This is unintuitive. Why would we not take advantage of an informative prediction? One reason is *risk*. Even if we have some information about the future return of an asset, the uncertainty around the prediction is too high for us to take advantage of it. For example, say that, to the best of our knowledge of ϕ, we expect the U.S. market to appreciate 8% next year, while our cash custodied at the broker will return a measly 2%. Does this imply that we will rebalance our portfolio to 100% a market-tracking asset like SPY? Hardly. The reason is that the standard deviation of market returns is 20%, a little too high for comfort. Risk, however, is not the only reason. Another one is *liquidity*. Indeed, the road to hell of an investor is littered with quite accurate predictions of assets that barely trade or do not trade at all. A famous example is the spin-off of Palm (a now-defunct mobile device company) by 3Com (a telecom equipment maker, also defunct) in 2000. 3Com floated on the public market 5% of the shares of Palm, while retaining the other 95%. Right after the initial public offering (IPO), Palm had a market value of $54B, while 3Com had a market capitalization of $28B. The implied value of 3Com assets was –$22B, even though the company had no debt, $1B in cash, and positive cash flow. Either 3Com was dramatically undervalued, or Palm was dramatically overvalued. An investor could have therefore bought 3Com shares and shorted Palm for an equal amount. The portfolio comprising these two assets was a synthetic asset whose return could be predicted. There was a problem, however. Palm shares were in short (pun intended) supply. In order to short a share, the investor must first borrow it, at a rate decided by the lender. If quoted at all, these rates were so high as to make the trade either unattractive or impossible.

Risk and liquidity are not the only two factors limiting the exploitation of information. We list three more. The first one is *funding*. Consider a scenario in which certain assets, or certain portfolios,[10] have lost much

[10] As in the case of the pair 3Com–Palm, we can interpret portfolios as synthetic assets.

of their value due to market distress. We are managing a small hedge fund, which has also lost money in this environment. Based on historical examples, we have a strong belief that such assets will rebound. Such scenarios occur quite regularly, especially in "deleveraging spirals". However, we do not have much capital available to post as margin. In addition, we need a capital buffer in order to withstand a possible additional loss in the very short term. Funding constraints prevent us from buying the asset, in spite of our accurate forecast.

A significant source of excess returns arises from *flow predictability*. Some agents, notably institutional investors and market makers, but not only these, will trade known securities on known dates. Speculators can then take advantage of this information by providing liquidity beforehand.[11] One of the most important instances of this is *index rebalancing*. Several index providers update the weights of their indices on predetermined dates using well-defined rules. Some securities are added to the index, others are removed, and finally most of the remaining ones have an updated weight. The term used for this process is *index reconstitution*. For example, TSLA was added to the NASDAQ 100, effective July 15, 2013. The announcement was made on July 10, 2013; but several investors could have forecasted the event well before that date. These investors would then purchase TSLA shares and sell them at the closing auction of July 15, 2013. The ETF, mutual funds, and bespoke products that track the index have an obligation to buy TSLA on the close of that day, and the resulting demand is likely to push up the stock price. The informed investors providing liquidity do not do so risk-free. They hold the stocks until the effective date, and over these days are exposed to the risk that TSLA may suffer from company-specific or industry-specific losses. Moreover, there is the remote risk that the reconstitution be cancelled or postponed. The size of passive investing is large and its estimate ranges from 17.5% (Novick, 2017) to 38% (Chinco and Sammon, 2023) of total assets under management. The buyer of index products bears the indirect cost of such rebalancing (Li, 2021). This is just one prominent example of predictable flows, but several others exist, usually smaller in size, but also not as widely known as index rebalancing. Their common feature is the existence of

[11] Note that this is not the same as *front running*. The latter also consists of buying or selling a security based on a demand forecast of said security; but in the latter case, the forecast relies on *non-public* information.

institutional or procedural constraints (sometimes driven by internal processes, other times by regulatory requirements) that introduce predictability in the demand of securities.

Finally, we consider a last source of excess returns: *informational advantage*. This means that the investors not only differ by their risk attitude, their tolerance to illiquidity, and their funding level, but also by their information sets, and some investors have better, more accurate forecasts of future prices or returns. This is what is often meant by "statistical arbitrage," the ability to predict returns accurately based on insights our competitors do not have.

In summary, even assuming accurate information owned by participants, some of them cannot exploit this information. We have listed several possible causes of return predictability:

- pure arbitrage;
- heterogeneous risk preferences;
- liquidity;
- funding;
- flow predictability;
- informational advantages.

These categories are not exclusive. For example, flow predictability and liquidity are related, albeit not identical; and the distinction between being compensated for risk-taking and holding an actual information advantage is usually unclear. However, these broad classes can help us reason about one strategy's edge.

1.5 The Elements of Quantitative Investing

The investment process is usually viewed as a highly structured process. There are separate components, the development of which is the responsibility of separate teams. In Figure 1.1, I show a possible organization of these components, which I follow in the organization of the book. I review them below.

- *Data*. The essential inputs to investing are under the "Data" section to the extreme left.

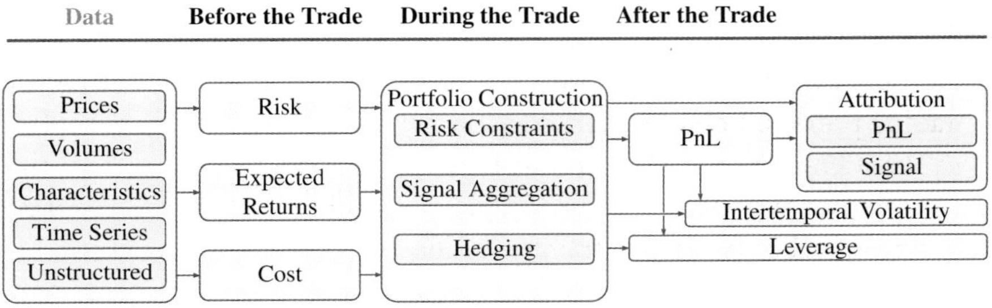

Figure 1.1 The components of the investment process.

- *Prices and trading volumes* are often collected at regular intervals (e.g., every minute, every 5, 10, 15 minutes, or daily). For high-frequency strategies it may be necessary to use order-level exchange data.
- *Characteristics* are numerical vectors associated with a security and a timestamp. Consider them as descriptors of the security. For a stock, a characteristic may be a measure of "quality", like the free cash flow generated by the firm in the most recent quarter, divided by the market capitalization of the firm. Another widely used characteristic is the realized return of the stock over a certain interval, for example the past six months.
- *Time series* differ from characteristics (which are multivariate time series) in that they are not associated with individual securities, but rather provide additional information entering the investment process. Examples of time series are the Consumer Price Index (CPI), which can be used to estimate the inflation rate in the United States; the yield of the 10-year Treasury bond; the Federal Funds Effective Rate, the overnight rate for unsecured lending of reserves among commercial banks; and the VIX, a forward-looking measure of U.S. equities market volatility.
- *Unstructured data* are the dark matter of financial data. Prices, characteristics, and times series are structured data: numerical, categorical, or ordinal (i.e., rankings), and in tabular form. Unstructured data are usually character sequences representing natural language (e.g., earnings transcripts and firm news) or images (e.g., satellite images), video/audio files, or multimodal data (i.e., a combination of all of the above formats).

- *Before the trade.* Data are used to develop three components that enter the portfolio construction during the trade. Because they precede the trading process, I classify their development as being "before the trade".
  - *Risk.* The word "risk" can mean many things. In the context of this book, we will use portfolio volatility as a proxy for risk. Estimating this volatility for an arbitrary portfolio is a challenging task.
  - *Expected returns.* In order to be profitable, a trading strategy needs to have informative predictions of future returns. This is often viewed as the paramount concern of a quantitative investor, and to a large extent it is. In nearly all modern trading systems there is more than one estimate of expected returns. The number of estimates can run into the thousands or millions.
  - *Transaction costs and market impact.* Trading securities is expensive, and these costs are unavoidable when deploying a strategy. Among other things, transaction costs determine whether a predicted return at some horizon can be turned into a profitable strategy or not; and what is the maximum profit that can be extracted from such a strategy.
- *During the trade.* The three components developed in the previous stage are combined in the portfolio construction phase. This happens "during the trade", because the portfolio construction procedure results in real-time trading decisions, and these decisions determine the Profit and Loss (PnL) of the strategy. The decisions taken in the portfolio construction process are:
  - *Incorporation of risk constraints.* A strategy's PnL is a function of the maximum risk that it can take. This is usually represented in the portfolio construction problem either in the form of constraints, or in the form of penalties added to the objective function. Risk constraints and penalties can have a very material impact on the performance of the strategy.
  - *Signal aggregation.* We use the term *signal* for a model of expected returns. As I mentioned above, there can be many signals for the returns of a single asset. A problem encountered in practice is combining such signals into a single signal.
  - *Hedging decisions.* Certain trading strategies have *exposure* to systematic risk. In layman's terms: they can lose money because their returns are correlated to market-wide sources of risk. Some of these sources can

  be *hedged*, which means that such risk can be counterbalanced. This is an important concept in portfolio construction.

- *After the trade.* The trading process generates a time series of PnL, both for the overall portfolio and for its constituents.
  - *Performance attribution.* In the portfolio construction phase we estimate expected returns. This is an *ex-ante* exercise. *Ex post*, we observe the actual PnL of the portfolio. Performance attribution is the practice of tracing back performance to its possible sources, to see what worked and what did not, so that we can learn from the experience. Moreover, performance attribution can also be employed to assess whether we have skill in sizing our bets.
  - *Intertemporal volatility allocation and leverage.* How should we allocate risk across periods? This decision is very consequential to capital growth. A closely related question is that of leverage, defined as the ratio between Gross Market Value (GMV) of the portfolio and Assets under Management (AuM).

I stress that different arrangements are possible; for example, Narang (2024) employs a simpler scheme, and Pedersen (2015) has yet another one. Some of the individual elements I introduce are present in these models of quantitative investing.

The Takeaways

1. Market participants can be broadly classified into sell-side and buy-side participants. The *sell-side participants* are
   - *Dealers*
   - *Brokers*
   - *Broker-dealers*

   The *buy-side participants* are
   - *Indexers*
   - *Hedgers*
   - *Institutional active managers*
   - *Asset allocators*
   - *Informed traders (e.g., hedge funds, principal trading firms)*
   - *Retail investors*
2. *Excess returns* arise from five major sources:
   (a) *Risk*
   (b) *Liquidity*
   (c) *Funding constraints*
   (d) *Predictable flows*
   (e) *Informational advantage* in predicting future returns
3. *Quantitative investing* employs analytical models that can be partitioned into three broad groups:
   (a) *Risk measurement* models and data
   (b) *Market impact models*
   (c) *Models of expected returns*
4. The *investment process* has several stages:
   (a) *Data collection*: Prices, trading volumes, asset characteristics, time series data, and unstructured data
   (b) *Pre-trade analysis*: Risk assessment, expected returns estimation, and transaction cost analysis
   (c) *Portfolio construction*: Aggregation of signals, application of risk constraints, and hedging
   (d) *Post-trade evaluation*: Performance attribution and risk adjustments based on intertemporal volatility and leverage considerations

Chapter 2

Univariate Returns

The Questions

1. What are the definitions and types of returns, including dividend-adjusted and excess returns?
2. What are the stylized facts of stock returns, and why are they important?
3. How do we estimate prices and returns while accounting for market microstructure effects?
4. What are Conditional Heteroskedastic Models (CHMs) and how do they model volatility?
5. How does the GARCH(1, 1) model capture the stylized facts of returns?
6. What is realized volatility and how is it estimated using high-frequency data?
7. How can state-space models and the Kalman filter be used for variance estimation?
8. How does GARCH(1, 1) relate to Exponentially Weighted Moving Averages (EWMAs) in volatility estimation?

We begin with models of univariate returns for two reasons. First, single-asset returns are the basic constituents of portfolios. We cannot hope to understand portfolio behavior without a solid understanding of their building blocks. Therefore, it is necessary to summarize the salient empirical properties of stock returns and the most common processes employed to model them, specifically to model volatility effectively. Second, these models have general applicability and are even more useful when combined with other families of models for multivariate returns. GARCH and exponential moving averages are essential tools for the working modeler. In the process, I introduce models that justify their use. Exponential moving averages find their motivation in linear state-space models, while GARCH is an instance of a non-linear state-space model. These models will be your friends for life. The chapter is organized into four parts. First, we lay out definitions of returns. Second, we summarize some "stylized facts" (empirical features of returns that are ubiquitous and relevant to risk management). As part of basic volatility modeling, we will introduce GARCH models and realized volatility models. Given that these topics are well covered in textbooks, the goal here is to present the essentials, their associated insights, and provide a jumping-off point for the reader. Finally, I will touch on the state-space models for variance estimation.

2.1 Returns

2.1.1 Definitions

We have a set of n assets and a currency, also called the numeraire.[1] Throughout this book, we use dollars as the base currency. It is customary to assume that each of these assets is infinitely divisible. We buy today the equivalent of a unit of currency for asset i. We denote the value of the asset tomorrow (or some future period) $1 + r_i$. An equivalent way to

[1] This word comes to English from the Latin *numerarius*, or "a number", "a unit", through the French *numéraire*.

define returns is from the closing prices of security i on days 0 and 1, which we denote $P_i(0)$ and $P_i(1)$, respectively. The *return*[2] is defined as

$$r_i(1) := \frac{P_i(1) - P_i(0)}{P_i(0)}$$

We extend this definition to the case in which the security pays a dividend. The holder of the asset receives an amount $D_i(1)$. The *dividend-adjusted return* is defined as

$$r_i(1) := \frac{P_i(1) + D_i(1) - P_i(0)}{P_i(0)}$$

In a universe of n assets, the vector of daily returns between times $t-1$ and t is denoted $\mathbf{r}(t) := (r_1(t), \ldots, r_n(t))$. For a portfolio $\mathbf{w} \in \mathbb{R}^n$, where w_i is a monetary amount invested in asset i, the PnL in a single period is given by the change in the value of the portfolio. The number of shares owned in asset i is calculated as $w_i/P_i(0)$. The value of the portfolio in period one is $\sum_i (w_i/P_i(0))P_i(1)$, and the change in value is

$$\sum_i \frac{w_i}{P_i(0)} P_i(1) - \sum_i w_i$$

In vector form, this equals $\mathbf{w}^\top \mathbf{r}$. The *volatility* of a random return is its standard deviation: $\sigma := \sqrt{E[(r - E(r))^2]}$. The *variance* is the square of the volatility. Occasionally, when the approximation $E(r^2) \gg E^2(r)$ holds, we will approximate the volatility by the second moment of the return: $\sigma^2 \simeq E(r^2)$. The *compounded return* is defined as the value of one unit of numeraire after T period, had it been invested in a security yielding returns $r(t)$, i.e.,

$$\begin{aligned} r(1:T) &:= \frac{P(T)}{P_i(0)} - 1 \\ &= \frac{P(T)}{P(T-1)} \frac{P(T-1)}{P(T-2)} \cdots \frac{P(1)}{P(0)} - 1 \\ &= \prod_{t=1}^{T} (1 + r(t)) - 1 \end{aligned}$$

[2] Definitions of returns, log returns, and dividend-adjusted returns are in Connor et al. (2010) and Ruppert and Matteson (2015).

2.1.2 Excess Returns

In the rest of the book, we will not use security returns, but returns minus the *risk-free rate*. If, for example, we model daily returns, the risk-free rate r_f is the interest rate paid by the investor for borrowing cash over the same period, or paid to the investor for cash held in their account.[3] If we hold a security, we pay interest on the cash position of that security. If we are short, we receive interest. Cash is to all effects a security, but a special one, in the sense that it has much lower volatility (for modeling purposes, negligible volatility) than the other risky assets. We borrow or lend an amount equal to the Net Market Value (NMV) of our portfolio, i.e., the sum of the values of each position. The return of a portfolio is

$$\sum_i w_i r_i - \left(\sum_i w_i\right) r_f = \sum_i w_i (r_i - r_f)$$

The formula allows us to eliminate the risk-free asset from the portfolio and provides a natural interpretation of security returns as returns in excess of a rate received in the absence of investing. In the United States, the reference rate is a reference overnight lending rate, like the Secured Overnight Financing Rate (SOFR).[4]

2.1.3 Log Returns

If $\mathbf{r}$ follows a multivariate Gaussian distribution, then so does the portfolio's PnL. The variance of this portfolio can be computed by using just two pieces of information: the portfolio weights and the covariance matrix of the returns.

The question of whether net returns are Gaussian is an empirical one. We at least know that *if* net returns are Gaussian, they are very tractable for analysis at a given point in time. However, they are not easily tractable in time-series analysis. For example, consider the compound return over periods $1, \ldots, T$. If $r_i(t)$ are normally distributed, the cumulative total return is not normally distributed, and its distribution rapidly

[3] The two rates are not exactly the same: when borrowing, the effective rate charged to the borrower by the lending institution is risk-free plus a small spread, and the rate paid by the same institution to a lender is risk-free minus a spread. For modeling purposes, we consider them identical.

[4] https://www.newyorkfed.org/markets/reference-rates/sofr.

diverges from the normal distribution. The variance of the cumulative returns is not a simple function of the single-period variances.

On the other side, *log returns* are additive over time compounding. Let $\tilde{r}_i(t) := \log(1 + r_i(t))$. Then, the log of the compound return is equal to the sum of the log returns in the same period, and if the log return is normal, so is the log of the compound returns. If the returns are independent, the variance of the log returns is equal to the sum of the variances. We can reconcile the two views of returns—raw and log—if the approximation $\log(x) = x - 1 + o(|x - 1|^2)$ is sufficiently accurate, i.e., if net returns are small. In this case, we can make the approximation $\tilde{r}_i \simeq r_i$, which is sufficiently accurate provided the returns are not too large.

A common approximation for the compounded net return of an asset over time is given by

$$\begin{aligned}
\prod_t (r(t) + 1) - 1 &= \exp\left(\sum_t \tilde{r}(t)\right) - 1 \\
&\simeq 1 + \sum_t \tilde{r}(t) - 1 \\
&= \sum_t \tilde{r}(t)
\end{aligned}$$

Always verify the accuracy of the approximation, for example, comparing the estimate of models developed using r and $\tilde{r}$. The approximation is in general optimistic (see Exercise 2.1). When the assets are equities, the approximation is usually considered adequate for daily interval measurements or shorter. For long time intervals (e.g., yearly) or very volatile returns, the approximation is poor.

2.1.4 Estimating Prices and Returns

To estimate return, we need prices. Prices, however, depend crucially on the way a market is designed. OTC markets (Harris, 2003) differ from exchanges that employ limit-order books (Bouchaud et al., 2018). Within a single exchange, the trading mechanism can change over the course of the day, with auctions often taking place at the beginning and at the close of the trading day. As a result of market design, the observation of prices exhibits measurement error. The most conspicuous example of such an error is the bid–ask spread. In limit-order books, the buy orders have a price attribute (the "bidding" price per share the buyer is willing to pay) and a quantity. Similarly, the sell orders have a price attribute, or "asking price," and a quantity. Asking prices are higher than bidding prices, and the difference is called the bid–ask spread. This spread is a multiple of the minimum tick size.[5] For a transaction to occur, a buy order or a sell order must cross the spread; either event can occur. As a result, the transaction price will be either at the top or the bottom of the bid–ask spread interval. Successive transactions will have different price marks due to the randomness of buying and selling transactions. The bid–ask spread bounce is not the only source of measurement error. For example, prices can differ by exchanges, and the selection of price by timestamp depends on the choice of data integration. Then, there may be outright measurement errors. It is important to consider from the outset the fact that prices are imperfectly observed, rather than ignore them and their impact and face unintended consequences. Perhaps the simplest model is the Roll model for asset prices (Roll, 1984). In this model,[6] the "true" price m_t of an asset evolves as an arithmetic random walk, and we imperfectly observe the price p_t. In formulas:

$$\begin{aligned} m_{t+1} &= m_t + \sigma_\epsilon \epsilon_{t+1} && \textit{(evolution)} \\ p_{t+1} &= m_{t+1} + \sigma_\eta \eta_{t+1} && \textit{(observation)} \end{aligned}$$

with ϵ_t, η_t random variables independently distributed (serially and from each other) according to a standard normal distribution.

Before we try to estimate prices, the model presents an immediate and testable consequence: consecutive price differences are negatively correlated. The price difference is

$$\Delta p_{t+1} := p_{t+1} - p_t = \sigma_\epsilon \epsilon_{t+1} + \sigma_\eta (\eta_{t+1} - \eta_t)$$

which is zero in expectation. However,

$$E(\Delta p_{t+1} \Delta p_t) = -\sigma_\eta^2 \tag{2.1}$$

$$E(\Delta p_{t+1} \Delta p_s) = 0, \qquad s < t \tag{2.2}$$

The lag-one autocovariance, Equation (2.1), can also be used to estimate the measurement error. The presence of large non-zero autocorrelations beyond lag one may point to model inadequacy, in the sense that there are actual long-term dependencies in the price process m_t. The model can

[5] As of publication time, the minimum tick size is \$0.01 in U.S. exchanges for shares trading above \$1.

[6] A detailed discussion of the Roll model and its extensions is in Hasbrouck (2007).

be extended to arbitrary lags. An optimal estimator for m_t is provided by the *Kalman filter*. The filter is covered in the Appendix, Section 2.4.1, and specifically in Example 2.1 of Section 2.4.2. The estimator is given by

$$\hat{m}_{t+1|t} = (1 - K)\hat{m}_{t|t-1} + Kp_t$$

where the explicit formula for $K \in (0, 1)$ is given in the Appendix. The smaller the ratio $\sigma_\eta/\sigma_\epsilon$, the higher the K, which makes sense: we do not need to average observations if the price observations are accurate. The gist of the model is that an exponential moving average of prices is preferable to just taking the last price in the measurement period. If we want the daily closing price, for example, we may want to use a weighted average of 5-minute interval prices in the preceding intervals. There is a caveat, however. Suppose we have estimates $\hat{m}_t$, and we use these estimates to compute returns composed of T intervals; i.e., $r_T := \hat{m}_{nT}/\hat{m}_{(n-1)T} - 1$. Because we employ the same observed prices p both in $\hat{m}_{(n-1)T}$ and in $\hat{m}_{nT}$, the two estimates are positively correlated. One should always check that $(1 - K)^T \ll 1$ to alleviate this spurious correlation.

2.1.5 Stylized Facts

Before building the house, we need to look at the bricks, namely, the statistical properties of the single-stock returns. Below we list some "stylized facts" about stock returns and discuss their relevance to risk modeling and management. Returns have a lower bound at -1. We usually characterize the properties of $\tilde{r}(t) := \log(1 + r(t))$. We focus on the properties of $\tilde{r}(t)$, but also $|\tilde{r}(t)|$ and $\tilde{r}^2(t)$, the uncentered volatility of the log returns. Here are some properties. See Cont (2001); Taylor (2007); Zivot (2009); Ratliff-Crain et al. (2023).

1. *Absence of autocorrelations*. Lagged autocorrelations are small unless you observe prices and returns at time scales in which the market microstructure becomes relevant (say, intraday). See Figure 2.1.
2. *Heavy tails*. The *unconditional* distribution of returns shows heavy tail behavior. This will be made more precise in the following section, but the probability of a large return is higher than what would be consistent with any "thin-tailed" distribution with infinite moments. Examples of sample kurtosis are in Table 2.1. The *conditional* (say, conditional on the return's entire history up to time t) distribution of returns may show heavy tail behavior as well, but with lighter tails than the unconditional one.

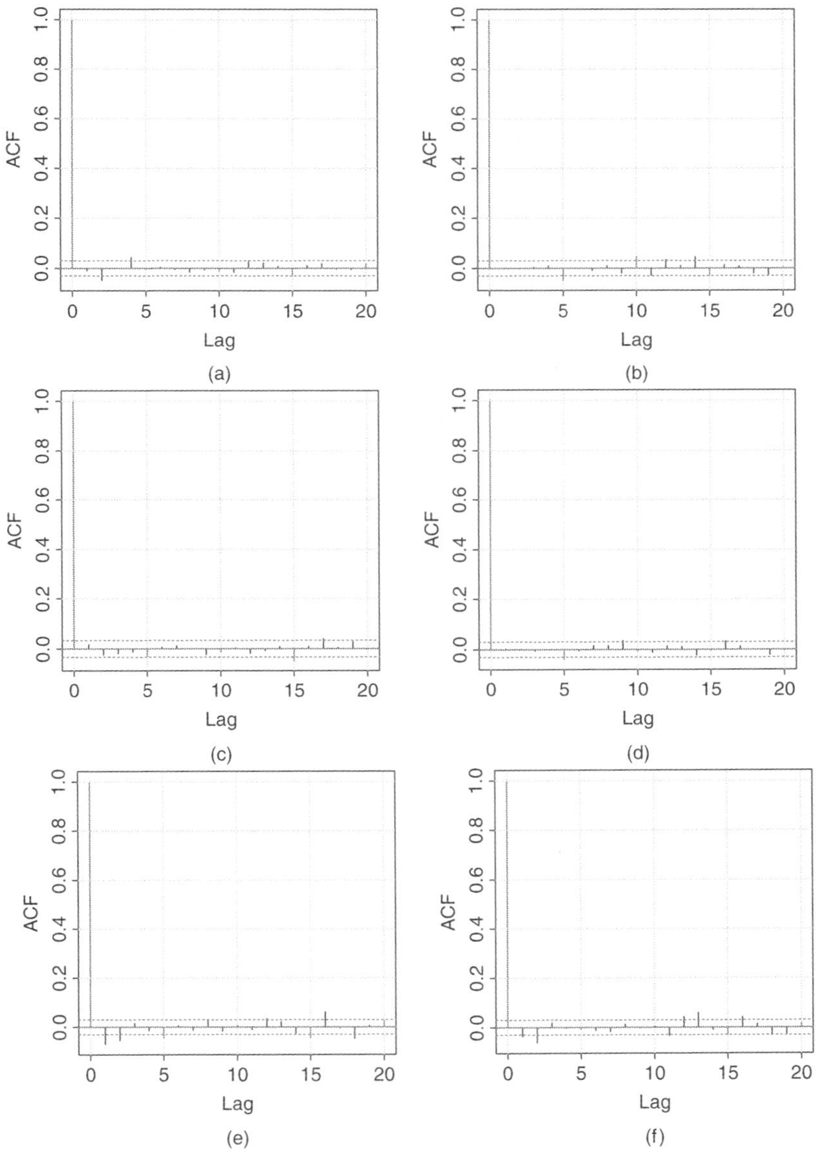

Figure 2.1 Autocorrelation plot of daily log returns (range: 1/3/2000–12/8/2017) for (a) AAPL, (b) IBM, (c) NRG, (d) WAS, (e) SPY, (f) XLK. The horizontal dashed lines delimit the 95% confidence interval for the autocorrelations.

3. *Autocorrelation of absolute returns and second moments.* The time series $|r_i(t)|$ and r_i^2 show strong positive autocorrelation (ACF). The autocorrelation of absolute values is greatest and is called the "Taylor effect"

in the literature (Taylor, 1986; Granger and Ding, 1995). Thus, large realized return movements persist over time, and so do small realized return movements. This phenomenon is sometimes termed *volatility clustering*.

4. *Aggregational Gaussianity*. At longer time scales (say, weekly or monthly returns, as opposed to daily or intraday returns), the distribution of log-returns becomes closer to a Gaussian distribution.

Reality[7] is in stark contrast with simple models of univariate price dynamics like the geometric diffusion process at the core of simple derivative pricing models:

$$\underbrace{\frac{dP(t)}{P(t)}}_{\text{(price change)}} = \underbrace{\mu}_{\text{(drift)}} dt + \underbrace{\sigma dW(t)}_{\text{(noise)}} \tag{2.3}$$

This model predicts Gaussian, independent log returns, which are inconsistent with the empirical evidence. First, returns show little serial autocorrelation. This *does not mean* that returns are independent, nor that returns are unpredictable based on the history of returns or some additional explanatory variables. Regarding the former point: zero autocorrelation does not imply independence. Regarding the latter, *returns*

Table 2.1 Sample skewness and kurtosis of daily log returns and $p = 0.01$ confidence intervals estimated using non-parametric bootstrap with replacement (5000 variates). Range: 1/3/2001–12/8/2017.

	Skewness			**Kurtosis**		
Stock	**Mean**	**Left**	**Right**	**Mean**	**Left**	**Right**
AAPL	−0.2	−0.5	0.2	5.7	3.6	7.8
IBM	0.1	−0.2	0.5	7.1	5.4	8.7
NRG	0.4	−0.5	1.2	14.3	7.9	20.0
WAT	−2.0	−3.3	−0.6	29.8	12.8	48.1
SPY	−0.1	−0.7	0.6	11.4	6.5	16.0

[7] Note, however, that I am not including the leverage effect among the stylized facts. In the words of Cont (2001), "most measures of volatility of an asset are negatively correlated with the returns of that asset". This effect may not sufficiently strong in recent data, as shown by Ratliff-Crain et al. (2023). Whether to take it into account or not is left to the reader, and on the specific application they are considering.

are predictable. This is not only an article of faith of active investors, who usually do a terrible job at it, but also a relatively uncontroversial empirical finding among academics.[8] Nevertheless, even though they are predictable, they are not so trivially predictable.

Regarding heavy tails: for asset returns, we restrict our attention to power-tailed distributions. Then the complement of the cumulative distribution function follows a power law: $\bar{F}(x) := P(r > x) = Cx^{-\alpha}$, with $\alpha > 0$ being the *tail index*. Compare this to Gaussian returns: if F is the cumulative distribution function of the standard Gaussian, then a common approximation (Wasserman, 2004) for the tail probability is

$$\frac{1}{\sqrt{2\pi}}e^{-x^2/2}\left(\frac{1}{|x|} - \frac{1}{|x|^3}\right) \leq F(x) \leq \frac{1}{\sqrt{2\pi}}e^{-x^2/2}\frac{1}{|x|}, \qquad x \leq -2 \quad (2.4)$$

The right-side inequality can be used to bound quantiles on the left tail and the symmetric inequality of the right tail for $0 \leq \delta \leq 0.025$:

$$\bar{F}(x) \leq \frac{1}{\sqrt{2\pi}}e^{-x^2/2} \quad \Rightarrow \quad \bar{F}^{-1}(1-\delta) \leq \sqrt{2\log[(2\sqrt{2\pi}(1-\delta))^{-1}]} \quad (2.5)$$

$$F(x) \geq \frac{1}{\sqrt{2\pi}}e^{-x^2/2} \quad \Rightarrow \quad F^{-1}(\delta) \geq -\sqrt{2\log[(2\sqrt{2\pi}\delta)^{-1}]} \quad (2.6)$$

The approximation is quite accurate. Let the Cumulative Density Function $F(x) = 1 - \bar{F}(x)$. Then we have the bounds

$$-\sqrt{2\log[1/(2\sqrt{2\pi}\delta)]} \leq F^{-1}(\delta) \leq -0.948 \times \sqrt{2\log[1/(2\sqrt{2\pi}\delta)]}$$

for $0 < \delta < 0.025$.

A Gaussian random variable has finite moments of any order. A power-tail random variable with exponent α has finite moments only up to α. A Gaussian random variable has quantiles bounded, up to constants, by $\sqrt{\log(1/\delta)}$, while a power-tail one has a quantile of the form $-(1/\delta)^{1/\alpha}$. It is not controversial that the unconditional log returns have heavy tails. It is still not settled what the exponent α associated with the distribution is. It seems, however, that $\alpha \simeq 4$. This is important for estimation purposes. A sufficient condition for the estimability of the volatility of returns

[8] John Cochrane has written extensively on the subject, e.g., Cochrane (2008) and the blog entry "Predictability and correlation" (https://tinyurl.com/predcochrane).

is that their fourth moment is finite. To see this, recall that the Central Limit Theorem says that, if x_t are iid random variables with mean μ and variance σ^2, then $T^{-1/2}\sum_{t=1}^{T} x_t$ converges in distribution to a Gaussian random variable with mean $\sqrt{T}\mu$ and variance σ^2. The theorem allows us to establish an asymptotic result on $E(r^2)$: assume that r_i are iid. Set $x_t := r_t^2$. If we want to estimate $E(r_t^2)$ using the Central Limit Theorem, then we need finiteness of the variance of the estimator, i.e., $E(r_t^4)$. This seems to be the case. However, a related question is whether the *conditional* return distribution is heavy-tailed. It is possible to model returns as a process with conditional Gaussian returns and heavy-tailed unconditional ones. This family, the Conditional Heteroskedastic Models (CHMs), is rich and the subject of the following subsection. We won't cover models with long-range dependence and/or heavy-tailed conditional returns, like Lévy processes and FARIMA models. No model covers all the empirical features observed in stock returns. GARCH models (and mixture models in general) have the benefit of being easy to interpret, simulate, and estimate.

2.2 Conditional Heteroskedastic Models

This family of models was first proposed in the early 1980s by Engle (1982); Engle and Bollerslev (1986). By the next decade they had been generalized and applied to several economic domains.[9] They are extensively covered in any econometrics book.

The most popular and studied model in this family is the GARCH(1, 1) model. It has good empirical properties, its theoretical properties have been characterized, and it can be estimated efficiently. It also conveys the gist of the large set of models in this family.

---

[9] The literature on GARCH models alone is immense: Zivot and Wang (2003); Lütkepohl (2005); Tsay (2010); Cižek et al. (2011); Ruppert and Matteson (2015) are standard references, and Andersen et al. (2006, 2013) are surveys. The handbook Andersen et al. (2009) has dedicated chapters covering univariate (Teräsvirta, 2009a) and multivariate GARCH (Teräsvirta, 2009b), moments of GARCH models (Lindner, 2009), their detailed extremal properties (Davis and Mikosch, 2009), and multivariate GARCH. For empirical papers on the performance of GARCH, TARCH, EGARCH, and a few other models, see Hansen and Lunde (2005); Brownlees et al. (2011).

The fundamental insight of the model is to make the *parameters* in the model a part of the state of the stochastic process. The laws for GARCH(1, 1) are

$$r_t = h_t \epsilon_t \tag{2.7}$$

$$h_t^2 = \alpha_0 + \alpha_1 r_{t-1}^2 + \beta_1 h_{t-1}^2 \tag{2.8}$$

$$\epsilon_t \sim N(0, 1) \tag{2.9}$$

In the equations above, h_t is the volatility at time t (and h_t^2 the variance) and it determines the size of returns by virtue of Equation (2.7). The parameters $\alpha_0, \alpha_1, \beta_1$ are assumed to be non-negative. The evolution of the process h_t is determined by Equation (2.8). To gain some intuition, let us look at the second equation of the GARCH process when we remove the term $\alpha_1 r_{t-1}^2$. The equation

$$h_t^2 = \alpha_0 + \beta_1 h_{t-1}^2 \tag{2.10}$$

can be rewritten as

$$h_t^2 - h^2 = \beta_1 (h_{t-1}^2 - h^2)$$

where

$$h^2 := \frac{\alpha_0}{1 - \beta_1}$$

The value of h_t^2 converges to h^2 at a geometric rate, so long as $0 < \beta_1 < 1$. High values of the squared return r_t^2 shock the volatility upward, provided that $\alpha_1 > 0$. This in turn increases the probability of large squared returns in the following period, giving rise to a rich dynamic behavior. The increase in volatility cannot continue unabated, because the term $\beta_1(h_{t-1}^2 - h^2)$ will dampen variances that are much greater than the "equilibrium level" h^2. This can be seen through substitution in the second equation of the model:

$$h_t^2 = h^2 + \alpha_1 \sum_{i=1}^{\infty} \beta_1^{i-1} r_{t-i}^2 \tag{2.11}$$

One could replace the true values of $\alpha_0, \alpha_1, \beta_1$ with estimates, and interpret the formula by saying that the variance estimate is an exponential moving average of non-iid squared returns, since they are modulated by h_t, in light of Equation (2.7).

2.2.1 GARCH(1, 1) and Return Stylized Facts

The GARCH model improves on the distributional properties of conditional returns r_t, by making them closer to the Gaussian distribution; see Figure 2.2. How does the GARCH(1, 1) model stack up against the stylized facts?

1. *Absence of autocorrelations.* This property is satisfied (not hard to verify directly).
2. *Heavy tails.* The unconditional returns are leptokurtic (Cont, 2001). In GARCH models (Mikosch and Stărică, 2000), the distribution of the unconditional returns is heavy tailed. In GARCH(1, 1) models estimated from empirical data, the distribution of returns ϵ_t in Equation (2.7) is closer to a Gaussian distribution; see Table 2.2. The tail indices of ϵ_t are also higher than those of r_t; see Table 2.3. These are desirable properties of GARCH processes.
3. *Autocorrelation of absolute and squared returns.* The ACF for GARCH(1, 1) is positive for both absolute and squared returns. For squared returns, it has the form (He and Teräsvirta, 1999; Ruppert and Matteson, 2015)

$$\rho_n = \begin{cases} \dfrac{\alpha_1(1 - \alpha_1\beta_1 - \beta_1^2)}{1 - 2\alpha_1\beta_1 - \beta_1^2} & \text{if } n = 1 \\ \rho_1(\alpha_1 + \beta_1)^{n-1} & \text{if } n > 1 \end{cases}$$

   However, if we look at kurtosis and lag-one autocorrelation for common stock indices, it appears that the autocorrelation predicted by the model for a given observed kurtosis level is *too high* compared to that observed in practice. See Teräsvirta (2009a).
4. *Aggregational Gaussianity.* A GARCH process aggregated over longer horizons is GARCH (with different parameters) and not Gaussian; see Drost and Nijman (1993); Christoffersen et al. (1998). This is consistent with the autocorrelation issue above: roughly, GARCH has a "long-term memory" that is too long, and not completely in agreement with empirical data.

Summing up, some but not all of the stylized facts about log returns are captured by GARCH(1, 1).

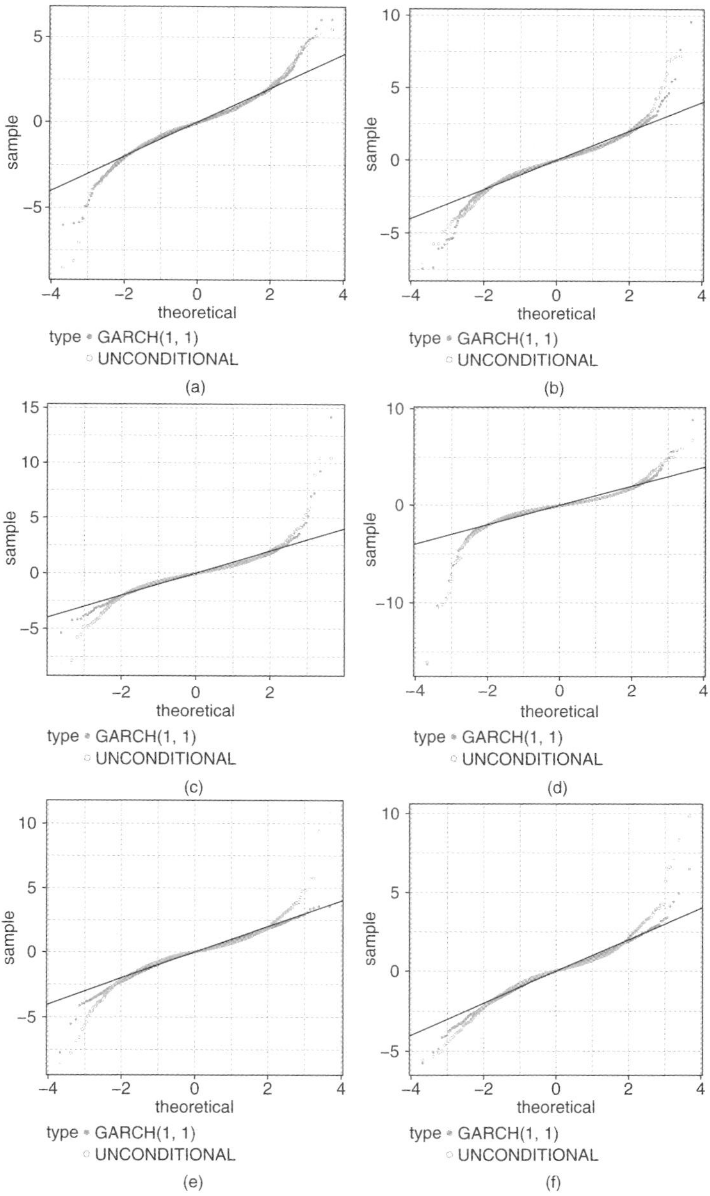

Figure 2.2 Quantile-Quantile plot for daily log returns (light gray dots) and GARCH(1, 1) residuals (dark gray dots) of log returns against the theoretical normal distribution for (a) AAPL, (b) IBM, (c) NRG, (d) WAT, (e) SPY, (f) XLK. Return range: 1/3/2001–12/8/2017.

Table 2.2 Distances between the theoretical normal distribution and the empirical distribution of log residuals of GARCH(1, 1). The distance is reduced in all instances, with the largest improvements for the two proxies for the market (SPY) and the technology sector (XLK). N.B.: We use the Kolmogorov–Smirnov distance. Background on this statistic is adapted from DeGroot and Schervish (2012), Ch. 10.

Stock	Unconditional (r_t)	GARCH(1, 1) (ϵ_t)
AAPL	0.067	0.044
IBM	0.078	0.047
NRG	0.088	0.060
WAT	0.109	0.091
SPY	0.098	0.040
XLK	0.091	0.043

Table 2.3 Estimated α for left and right tail of probability density function $p(x) \propto x^{-\alpha}$. We use the Maximum Likelihood Estimator (MLE) $\hat{\alpha} = 1 + n[\sum_i \log(x_i/x_{\min})]^{-1}$, where n is the number of observations above a cut-off value $x_{\min}$; see Clauset et al. (2009). The value of $x_{\min}$ is set to –2.5% and 2.5%, respectively. The values of α increase sizably for the two indices SPY and XLK.

	Left Tail		Right Tail	
Stock	**Uncond. (r_t)**	**GARCH(1, 1) (ϵ_t)**	**Uncond. (r_t)**	**GARCH(1, 1) (ϵ_t)**
AAPL	4.8	4.6	4.8	4.9
IBM	4.3	3.9	4.2	4.6
NRG	4.0	5.9	3.8	4.1
WAT	3.4	3.2	4.3	4.0
SPY	4.1	5.9	4.2	8.5
XLK	5.0	6.3	4.4	5.9

2.2.2 *GARCH as Random Recursive Equations*

We now look at GARCH(1, 1) through different modeling approaches. First, we could reformulate it as a random iterated function. Rewrite Equation (2.8) as

$$h_t^2 = \alpha_0 + \alpha_1 h_{t-1}^2 \epsilon_{t-1}^2 + \beta_1 h_{t-1}^2 \tag{2.12}$$

Set

$$a_t := \beta_1 + \alpha_1 \epsilon_{t-1}^2$$

The random variables $(a_t)_{t=1}^{\infty}$ are iid. Then

$$h_t^2 = a_t h_{t-1}^2 + \alpha_0$$

This formulation shows that the variance process is Markovian, and also that it is governed by an autoregressive equation with random coefficients a_t. By recursion (Lindner, 2009), we can rewrite the equations as

$$h_t^2 = \left(\prod_{i=0}^{k} a_{t-i} \right) h_{t-k}^2 + \alpha_0 \left(1 + \sum_{i=0}^{k} \prod_{j=0}^{i-1} a_{t-j} \right)$$

This allows us to study the process using the toolkit of random recursive equations.[10]

The distribution of a_i plays the essential role in the convergence of the process. Nelson (1990) characterizes the conditions for convergence. In the case $\alpha_0 = 0$:

1. If $E(\log a_t) > 0$, then $h_t^2 \to \infty$ a.s.
2. If $E(\log a_t) < 0$, then $h_t^2 \to 0$ a.s.
3. If $E(\log a_t) = 0$, then h_t^2 is a driftless random walk.

In the case $\alpha_0 > 0$:

1. If $E(\log a_t) \geq 0$, then $h_t^2 \to \infty$ a.s.
2. If $E(\log a_t) < 0$, then h_t converges to a non-degenerate distribution with a support on $[\alpha_0/(1-\beta_1), \infty)$.

The kurtosis of the process is

$$k = \frac{3(1+\alpha_1+\beta_1)(1-\alpha_1-\beta_1)}{1-\beta_1^2-2\alpha_1\beta_1-3\alpha_1^2} = 3\frac{1-(\alpha_1+\beta_1)^2}{1-(\alpha_1+\beta_1)^2-2\alpha_1^2} > 3$$

---

[10] The convergence properties of Random Recursive Equations (RREs) were studied first by Kesten (1973). Diaconis and Freedman (1999) survey the general recursive equations $x_t = f(x_{t-1}, \epsilon_{t+1})$, where $(\epsilon_t)_{t=1}^{\infty}$ is an iid random sequence, of which RREs are a special case. A monograph on RREs, covering both the univariate and multivariate case, is Buraczewski et al. (2016).

as long as $\alpha_1 > 0$, so that the process is leptokurtic. How about skewness? The unconditional returns are not skewed, because

$$E[(r_\infty - E(r_\infty))^3] = E(h_\infty^3)E(\epsilon_t^3) = 0$$

Finally, we point out that not only are the unconditional returns leptokurtic, but they do in fact have Pareto tails, provided the process is stationary: $P(r_t > x) \sim x^{-\alpha}$, for some $\alpha > 0$; see Mikosch and Stărică (2000); Buraczewski et al. (2016).

2.2.3 ★GARCH(1, 1) Estimation

Although GARCH models are highly general, the vast majority of CHM applications are indeed GARCH(1, 1), so we restrict our analysis to this case for simplicity. Generalization to finite-order processes is straightforward. Define $\boldsymbol{\theta} := (\alpha_0, \alpha_1, \beta_1)$, and let f be the log-density function of the standard normal distribution:

$$\begin{aligned} r_t &= h_t \epsilon_t \\ h_t^2 &= \phi(h_{t-1}^2, r_{t-1}^2, \theta) \end{aligned}$$

where ϕ is defined by the right-hand side in Equation (2.12). By repeated substitution, we can express the unobserved variance h_t^2 as a function of the sequence $r_1, \dots, r_{t-1}$, h_1 and $\boldsymbol{\theta}$. The log-likelihood of the sequence $\epsilon_t = r_t/h_t$ is given by

$$L(\boldsymbol{\theta}) = \sum_{t=1}^{T} f\left(\frac{r_t}{h_t(r_1, \dots, r_{t-1}, \boldsymbol{\theta})}\right)$$

We can then estimate the parameters θ of the model by maximizing the log-likelihood. As an example, consider the GARCH(1, 1) model. The recursive equation for h_t^2 is given by Equation (2.11), so we solve

$$\begin{aligned} &\min \sum_{t=1}^{T} \left(\log h_t^2 + \frac{r_t^2}{h_t^2}\right) \\ &\text{s.t. } h_t = \left(\alpha_0 \frac{1-\beta_1^{t-1}}{1-\beta_1} + \alpha_1 \sum_{i=1}^{t-1} \beta_1^{i-1} r_{t-i}^2\right)^{1/2} \quad t = 1, \dots, T \end{aligned}$$

2.2.4 Realized Volatility

CHMs model the asset volatility as an (unobserved) state of the return stochastic process. Once we have an estimate of the volatility at time t of returns, the rest is trivial. An alternative route would be to estimate directly the volatility from the data, for example with a simple moving-window estimator of the empirical volatility. This approach would not work if the intervals for which we need the estimates are days, and we only have daily data. In recent years, tick-level price data have become widely available; indeed, order-book-level data are also available (with the entire process of order arrivals, fillings, and cancellations). It is now possible to compute one-minute returns, enabling us to estimate the volatility of returns for daily predictions by using these high-frequency data. Below we review some of the statistical properties of realized volatility (RV) measurements. The starting point is Equation (2.3), i.e., a diffusion process for the log price $p(t) = \log P(t)$:

$$dp = \alpha dt + \sigma dW$$

where $W(t)$ is a Brownian process. The scalars $\alpha \in \mathbb{R}$ (the drift) and $\sigma > 0$ (the volatility) are constants. In all applications of interest, the drift is much smaller than the volatility: $|\alpha| \ll \sigma$. The quantity α/σ is termed the *Sharpe Ratio* and will figure prominently in the rest of the book.[11] We observe the process in the interval $[0, 1]$ and measure the state variable p at intervals of length $1/n$. The measured return is $r(j) := p(j/n) - p((j-1)/n)$. Clearly, $r(j)$ are iid random variables, and $r(j) \sim N(\alpha/n, \sigma^2/n)$. The MLEs for drift and moments are

$$\hat{\alpha} = \sum_j r(j) = p(1) - p(0) \tag{2.13}$$

$$\hat{\sigma}_1^2 = \sum_j [r(j) - \hat{\alpha}/n]^2 \tag{2.14}$$

[11] This is the Sharpe Ratio of log returns, which is to a first approximation close to the daily Sharpe Ratio computed on returns.

We also consider the *uncentered* estimator of the volatility[12]

$$\hat{\sigma}_2^2 = \sum_j r^2(j) \tag{2.15}$$

The first remarkable phenomenon is that the MLE for the drift, Equation (2.13), does not depend on the number of intervals n. Moreover, one can show that $\text{var}(\hat{\alpha}) = \text{var}(p(1) - p(0))$, and $p(1) - p(0) \sim N(\alpha, \sigma^2)$, so that $\text{var}(\hat{\alpha}) = \sigma^2$. The estimation error does not depend on the number of intervals either. To estimate the variance of $\hat{\sigma}_2^2$ we need a few formulas. The moments of $r(j)$ are those of a Gaussian random variable with mean α/n and variance σ^2/n:

$$E[r(j)] = \frac{\alpha}{n} \tag{2.16}$$

$$E[r^2(j)] = \left(\frac{\alpha}{n}\right)^2 + \frac{\sigma^2}{n} \tag{2.17}$$

$$E[r^4(j)] = \left(\frac{\alpha}{n}\right)^4 + 6\left(\frac{\alpha}{n}\right)^2\frac{\sigma^2}{n} + 3\left(\frac{\sigma^2}{n}\right)^2 \tag{2.18}$$

so that

$$\text{var}(r^2(j)) = 2\left(\frac{\sigma^2}{n}\right)^2 + 4\left(\frac{\alpha}{n}\right)^2\frac{\sigma^2}{n} \tag{2.19}$$

and

$$E(\hat{\sigma}_2^2) = \sigma^2 + \frac{\alpha^2}{n} \qquad \text{from Equation (2.17)}$$

$$\text{var}(\hat{\sigma}_2^2) = 2\frac{\sigma^4}{n} + 4\left(\frac{\alpha}{n}\right)^2\sigma^2 \qquad \text{from Equation (2.19)}$$

[12] An early analysis of the "vanilla" realized variance estimator is Barndorff-Nielsen and Shephard (2002) and a survey is Andersen and Benzoni (2009). Also useful are the surveys of Andersen et al. (2006, 2013), which situate realized volatility in the context of risk management techniques. Essential readings on realized volatility estimators are Zhang et al. (2005), which presents several estimators and introduces the idea of sub-sampling for RV; the series of papers Barndorff-Nielsen et al. (2008, 2009) on kernel-based estimators; the empirical paper by Liu et al. (2015), comparing several estimators, which includes subsampling and kernel. This list of estimators is not exhaustive. For example, Hansen and Lunde (2006b) analyze an autocorrelation-adjusted estimator introduced in French et al. (1987). Bipower estimators are studied by Podolskij and Vetter (2009) and maximum likelihood ones by Aït-Sahalia et al. (2005). Moreover, these estimators depend on several parameters, like sampling and subsampling intervals, or the choice of kernel.

The estimator $\hat{\sigma}_2^2$ has a small finite-sample bias and is asymptotically consistent.

> **Insight 2.1: *Estimating variance***
>
> Based on Equations (2.17) and (2.19), you can use uncentered returns for variance estimation, since the bias is inversely proportional to n, and the estimator is consistent.

Let us reflect on the steps we took. We discretized the interval over which the price process occurs into n sub-intervals, and retained only the last price within an interval of length $1/n$, assuming the price had no measurement error. We saw that the drift estimator is unbiased, but its variance does not depend on the discretization: we have more estimates of the drift, but they are noisier. Unfortunately, there is no easy way to measure the drift, i.e., the expected return, of a security; otherwise, all statistics undergraduates would be rich. Conversely, we have identified an uncentered estimator of the true variance σ^2. As the number n of intervals approaches infinity, the estimator is unbiased. Its variance decreases like $2\sigma^4/n$, which is good news: in principle, we can estimate to arbitrary accuracy the volatility of the returns at time t; and provided that the true volatility varies very little over time, we can use this estimate to predict the variance at time $t + 1$. If you need volatility estimates over a long time scale for your decisions (e.g., days), but have data over a shorter time scale (e.g., minutes), you do not have to devise a generative model like CHMs or others. What assumptions do not hold in this line of reasoning? Here is a list of issues to consider:

1. We ignored market microstructure. One source of noise is the bid–ask spread (Harris, 2003). When the seller initiates the transaction, she receives the bid price; when the buyer initiates it, he pays the ask price. There is an intrinsic error in the measurement of price, which is approximately equal to half the bid–ask spread. We model this error by assuming that log prices in interval t are $p_t + \epsilon_t$, where the noise terms ϵ_t are independent, identically distributed random variables.
2. Another form of microstructure imperfection is thinly traded securities. If a stock trades less than once every 5 minutes on average, then using 1-minute intervals is probably not a good modeling choice.

3. We assumed that volatility is changing slowly, or is ideally constant. This is not the case in practice. One approach is to impose a model on the time series of realized variances, so that we can produce an error estimate. For example, a simple AR(1) model $\hat{\sigma}_{t+1} = a + b\hat{\sigma}_t + \tau\epsilon_{t+1}$, with $\epsilon_{t+1} \sim N(0, 1)$.
4. We ignored the distinction between open-to-close and close-to-open intervals. Close-to-open returns are often fundamentally driven. Also, we are ignoring the large volatility and bid–ask spreads in the first minutes of the trading day.

For the rest of us, the question is: What to choose? Liu et al. (2015) compare a broad set of estimators, with several choices of parameters, for assets in different asset classes (equities, futures, indices). They use Romano and Wolf's procedure for multiple comparison (Romano and Wolf, 2005) and the "model confidence set" (Hansen et al., 2011). They find that the vanilla RV at 5-minute performs competitively across various assets and asset classes.[13]

2.3 State-Space Estimation of Variance

2.3.1 *Muth's Original Model: EWMA*

A very popular estimator of the expected value of a time series $\{x_s\}$, based on data up to time t, is the *exponentially weighted moving average* (EWMA). It takes the form

$$\hat{x}_t = (1 - K) \sum_{s=0}^{\infty} K^s x_{t-s}$$

for some $0 < K < 1$. We discount the past by giving its observations exponentially decreasing weights, which makes sense, and even more so when we write the estimate as a recursion:

$$\hat{x}_t = (1 - K)x_t + K\hat{x}_{t-1}$$

[13] There are a few cases where this is not true. When higher-frequency measurements are available, this estimator is outperformed by a 1-minute subsampled RV, by 1- and 5-second interval realized kernels (Barndorff-Nielsen et al., 2008). In addition, at lower frequencies, a 5- and 15-minute truncated RV (Mancini, 2009, 2011) also outperforms vanilla RV; see Liu et al. (2015).

A low value of K forgets the past faster. The formula is computationally efficient both in terms of storage and computation. For uncentered variance estimation of a return, this takes the form

$$\hat{\sigma}_t^2 = (1 - K)r_t^2 + K\hat{\sigma}_{t-1}^2 \tag{2.20}$$

Insight 2.2: *GARCH is EWMA with an offset*

Recall Equation (2.11):

$$h_t^2 = \frac{\alpha_0}{1 - \beta_1} + \alpha_1 \sum_{i=1}^{\infty} \beta_1^{i-1} r_{t-i}^2$$

This is, save for an offset, very similar to Equation (2.20):

$$\hat{\sigma}_t^2 = (1 - K) \sum_{i=1}^{\infty} K^{i-1} r_{t-i}^2$$

(we have changed the indexing convention to make it consistent with GARCH). The two are identical when $\alpha_0 = 0$, $\alpha_1 = 1 - K$, and $\beta_1 = K$. Why not use GARCH, then, provided that estimating the parameters per asset is doable? There is no fundamental objection. Commercial models favor simplicity (the half-life in each model, equivalent[a] to choice of K, is shared by all assets) over possible performance increases, perhaps by force of habit, or because the performance improvement is not high enough to justify the additional complexity in parameter estimation and, in the case of commercial models, communication of the model's characteristics to clients.

[a] The half-life τ is such that $K^\tau = 1/2$, i.e., $\tau = -\log 2 / \log K$.

In academic journals, EWMA receives relatively low attention compared to GARCH models (for a rare example, see Ding and Meade (2010)); among practitioners, including major commercial risk model providers like RiskMetrics, Barra, and Axioma, it is the other way around. Aside from these practical considerations, is it possible to motivate the approach based on a model? We devote this section to understanding and extending this simple formula.

We will employ linear state-space models and Kalman filters, which are briefly covered in the Appendix, Section 2.4.1. Rather than giving it a general treatment and then specializing to a specific model, we will jump right in the middle with a relevant example. As it happens, this example is also the simplest non-trivial example of a state-space model. The model (Muth, 1960) posits that there is a scalar *state* x_t that evolves randomly over time with the addition of a Gaussian disturbance to its previous value. We observe the state imperfectly; the *observation* y_t is a noisy measure value x_t. In formulas:

$$\begin{aligned} x_{t+1} &= x_t + \tau_\epsilon \epsilon_{t+1} \\ y_{t+1} &= x_{t+1} + \tau_\eta \eta_{t+1} \\ \epsilon_t &\sim N(0,1) \\ \eta_t &\sim N(0,1) \end{aligned}$$

The innovations and the measurement noises are Gaussian with mean zero, and they are independent of each other: $\epsilon_s \perp \epsilon_t$ $\eta_s \perp \eta_t$ for all $s \neq t$, and $\epsilon_s \perp \eta_t$ for all t and s. I skipped the derivation, which the interested reader can find in the Appendix. Define the ratio of measurement to innovation noise $\kappa := \tau_\eta / \tau_\epsilon$. The stationary $\hat{\sigma}^2_{t+1|t}$ estimate of the variance is given by

$$\hat{\sigma}^2_{t+1|t} = \tau_\epsilon^2 \frac{1 + \sqrt{(2\kappa)^2 + 1}}{2}$$

and the optimal estimation recursion is

$$\begin{aligned} K &:= \frac{\hat{\sigma}^2_{t+1|t}}{\hat{\sigma}^2_{t+1|t} + \tau_\eta^2} \\ \hat{x}_{t+1|t} &= (1 - K)\hat{x}_{t|t-1} + K y_t \end{aligned}$$

The relationship between the measurement/innovation noise and K, is illustrated in Figure 2.3. For $\kappa \gg 1$ the formula simplifies:

$$\hat{x}_{t|t} = \frac{\kappa}{1+\kappa} \hat{x}_{t|t-1} + \frac{1}{1+\kappa} y_t$$

This is an exponential weighted average with a simple interpretation. Imagine that the state does not change at all. Then we want to use all the history we can, since old observations and new ones are drawn from the same distribution. The half-life of EWMA is indeed long. Conversely,

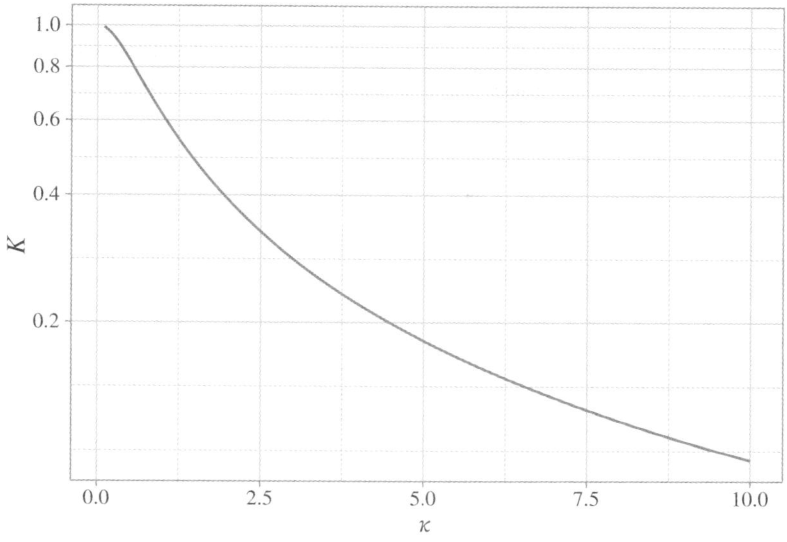

Figure 2.3 Relationship between K and $\kappa := \tau_\eta/\tau_\epsilon$.

when the state changes at a rapid pace, i.e., $\kappa \simeq 0$, then we want to discount the past very aggressively.

According to Muth's original model applied to volatility estimation, the state is the instantaneous variance, and the observation y_t is r_t^2, which is equal to σ_t^2 in expectation.

The model has obvious shortcomings. If returns are normally distributed, then the observation error is not normally distributed. More importantly, the model allows for negative values of the variance, and additionally models the variance evolution as the sum of iid innovations. Over time, the distribution of the variance becomes increasingly spread out: the standard deviation of the distribution grows as the square root of the number of periods. In practice, however, volatility appears to revert to a long-term average.

We cannot directly address the first problem. However, Kalman filters can work well with non-normal innovations and measurement errors, provided that these are not too heavy-tailed. As for the other shortcomings, we can refine the model to accommodate them. For example, we can introduce a mean-reverting model of variance, so that it behaves like an autoregressive process. We slightly extend the state equation by adding a mean-reversion term:

$$x_{t+1} = x_t - \lambda(x_t - \mu) + \tau_\epsilon \epsilon_{t+1}, \qquad \lambda > 0$$

The state reverts to value μ when it is away from this equilibrium value. The stationary distribution of x_t is Gaussian, with the expected value equal to μ and standard deviation equal to $\tau_\epsilon^2/(2\lambda - \lambda^2)$. The optimal variance estimator is still

$$\hat{x}_{t+1|t} = (1 - K)\hat{x}_{t|t-1} + Ky_t$$

However, compared to the first model, the value of K is *smaller*. Otherwise stated, the mean reversion term makes the distribution of the true variance more concentrated around its long-term mean. This implies that we discount the past less. The detailed derivation of these formulas is in the Appendix, Section 2.4.2.

2.3.2 ★The Harvey–Shephard Model

As a final example of the flexibility that linear state-space models can offer, I present the model by Harvey and Shephard (1996), which has several desirable features: it has a closed-form solution; the volatility is by design positive and the distribution of the volatility itself is log-normal, hence right-skewed, as we would expect; and the stock returns are locally log-normal.

The generating process for returns r_t is assumed to be

$$r_t = e^{\beta+\exp(x_t/2)\xi_t} - 1 \tag{2.21}$$

where β is a known constant, and $\xi_t \sim N(0, 1)$; hence returns are, at any point in time, log-normally distributed. Define

$$\begin{aligned} & & u_t &:= \log(1 + r_t) - \beta \\ &\Rightarrow & u_t &= \exp(x_t/2)\xi_t \\ &\Rightarrow & \log u_t^2 &= x_t + \log \xi_t^2 \\ & & &= x_t + \eta_t + \gamma \end{aligned}$$

where $\gamma := E(\log \xi_t^2) \simeq -1.27$, and η_t is a zero-mean random variable with standard deviation given by stdev $(\log \xi_t^2) \simeq 2.22$. Define

$$\begin{aligned} y_t &:= \log u_t^2 - \gamma \\ &= \log[(\log(1 + r_t) - \beta)^2] - \gamma \end{aligned}$$

so that we get an observation equation:

$$y_t = x_t + \eta_t$$

Now, we posit an evolution equation for x_t:

$$x_{t+1} = b + ax_t + \epsilon_t$$

This is the same model as AR(1), from which we obtain an estimate $\hat{x}_t$. If $\beta = 0$, then the formulas take a simple form: $u_t \simeq r_t$ and the state estimate is given by

$$\hat{x}_{t+1|t} = (1 - K)\hat{x}_{t|t-1} + K[\log[(\log(1 + r_t))^2] - \gamma]$$

Since $r_t = \exp(\exp(x_t/2)\xi_t) - 1$ is a log-normal random variable, the estimated standard deviation of r_t is

$$\hat{\sigma}_{t+1|t} = \sqrt{(e^{\exp(\hat{x}_{t+1|t})} - 1)e^{\exp(\hat{x}_{t+1|t})}}$$

A simplified Harvey–Shephard model starts with Equation (2.21), to which it applies the first-order approximation $e^x - 1 \simeq x$, and the parameter $\beta = 0$:

$$r_t = \exp(x_t/2)\xi_t$$

Define

$$\begin{aligned} \log r_t^2 &:= x_t + \log \xi_t^2 \\ &= x_t + \eta_t + \gamma \end{aligned}$$

where γ and η_t are defined as for the Harvey–Shephard model above. The model is completed by the following equations, also from the original model:

$$\begin{aligned} x_{t+1} &= b + ax_t + \epsilon_t \\ y_t &= \log r_t^2 - \gamma \end{aligned}$$

The state and volatility estimates are

$$\begin{aligned} \hat{x}_{t+1|t} &= (1 - K)\hat{x}_{t|t-1} + K[\log r_t^2 - \gamma] \\ \hat{\sigma}_{t+1|t} &= e^{\hat{x}_{t+1|t}/2} \end{aligned}$$

2.4 ★Appendix

2.4.1 The Kalman Filter

This section contains a short treatment of the Kalman filter (KF). The KF in its modern form originates in the early 1960s from work by Kalman (1960) and Kalman and Bucy (1961). At the time of their publication, computers had become available that made calculations feasible in real time. This made the (re)discovery of the filter by Kalman very timely. Rockets used by the Apollo program contained implementations of the KF in 2KB of RAM. Since then, the study of linear control and filtering has flourished. Thousands of papers have been written on it, and there are several monographs covering the KF in detail from different perspectives: control (Whittle, 1996; Simon, 2006), statistical (Harvey, 1990), and econometric (Hansen and Sargent, 2008). I cover the KF because, for somewhat mysterious reasons, the derivation of the KF is often more complicated than it should be. A rigorous yet, I hope, intuitive proof essentially fits in half a page and should save the reader a few hours.

We need the following elementary fact. Let $\mathbf{z} := [\mathbf{x}|\mathbf{y}]^\top$ be a multivariate normal random vector with mean and covariance matrix

$$\mu_{\mathrm{z}} := \begin{bmatrix} \mu_{\mathrm{x}} \\ \mu_{\mathrm{y}} \end{bmatrix} \qquad \mathrm{cov}(\mathbf{Z}) = \begin{bmatrix} \mathbf{\Sigma}_{\mathrm{x,x}} & \mathbf{\Sigma}_{\mathrm{x,y}} \\ \mathbf{\Sigma}_{\mathrm{y,x}} & \mathbf{\Sigma}_{\mathrm{y,y}} \end{bmatrix}$$

The random vector $\mathbf{x}$, conditional on $\mathbf{y} = \mathbf{b}$, is still normally distributed, with conditional mean and covariance matrix equal to

$$E(\mathbf{x}|\mathbf{y} = \mathbf{b}) = \boldsymbol{\mu}_{\mathrm{x}} + \mathbf{\Sigma}_{\mathrm{x,y}}\mathbf{\Sigma}_{\mathrm{y,y}}^{-1}(\mathbf{b} - \boldsymbol{\mu}_{y}) \tag{2.22}$$

$$\mathrm{cov}\,(\mathbf{x}|\mathbf{y} = \mathbf{b}) = \mathbf{\Sigma}_{\mathrm{x,x}} - \mathbf{\Sigma}_{\mathrm{x,y}}\mathbf{\Sigma}_{\mathrm{y,y}}^{-1}\mathbf{\Sigma}_{\mathrm{y,x}} \tag{2.23}$$

This can be verified directly by integration.

Our model has two components. The first is a *state*, represented by a random vector $\mathbf{x}_t$. This vector follows a simple evolution rule: $\mathbf{x}_{t+1} = \mathbf{A}\mathbf{x}_t + \boldsymbol{\epsilon}_{t+1}$. The vector $\boldsymbol{\epsilon}_t$ is random, serially independent (i.e., $\boldsymbol{\epsilon}_s \perp \boldsymbol{\epsilon}_t$ for $s \neq t$), and distributed according to a multivariate normal distribution. The state is not observable directly; the only thing we know is its probability distribution at time 1. We assume it is normal with known mean and covariance matrix. In addition, over time we observe a vector $\mathbf{y}_t$, which is a linear transformation of $\mathbf{x}_t$, corrupted by noise: $\mathbf{y}_{t+1} = \mathbf{B}\mathbf{x}_{t+1} + \boldsymbol{\eta}_{t+1}$.

Once you read Chapter 4, you will note the similarity with the factor model equation:

$$\text{state} \leftrightarrow \text{factor return}$$
$$\text{observation} \leftrightarrow \text{asset return}$$

The vector $\boldsymbol{\eta}_t$ is random, serially independent, independent of $\boldsymbol{\epsilon}_1, \boldsymbol{\epsilon}_2, \ldots$, and distributed according to a multivariate normal distribution.

Summing up, the distributions of $\mathbf{x}_1, \boldsymbol{\epsilon}_t, \boldsymbol{\eta}_t$ are given by

$$\begin{aligned}
&\mathbf{x}_1 \sim N(\hat{\mathbf{x}}_0, \hat{\boldsymbol{\Sigma}}_0) && &&\\
&\boldsymbol{\epsilon}_t \sim N(\mathbf{0}, \boldsymbol{\Sigma}_\epsilon) && \boldsymbol{\epsilon}_t \perp \boldsymbol{\epsilon}_s, \boldsymbol{\epsilon}_t \perp \boldsymbol{\eta}_{s+1} && s \neq t\\
&\boldsymbol{\eta}_t \sim N(\mathbf{0}, \boldsymbol{\Sigma}_\eta) && \boldsymbol{\eta}_t \perp \boldsymbol{\eta}_s, \boldsymbol{\eta}_t \perp \boldsymbol{\epsilon}_{s+1} && s \neq t
\end{aligned}$$

and the linear state-space model is given by

$$\mathbf{x}_{t+1} = \mathbf{A}\mathbf{x}_t + \boldsymbol{\epsilon}_{t+1} \tag{2.24}$$

$$\mathbf{y}_{t+1} = \mathbf{B}\mathbf{x}_{t+1} + \boldsymbol{\eta}_{t+1} \tag{2.25}$$

I denote $\hat{\mathbf{x}}_{t|t-1}$, $\hat{\boldsymbol{\Sigma}}_{t|t-1}$, the conditional estimates for the mean and covariance matrix of the state $\mathbf{x}_t$, based on the information $\mathbf{y}_0, \ldots, \mathbf{y}_{t-1}$. And I denote $\hat{\mathbf{x}}_{t|t}$, $\hat{\boldsymbol{\Sigma}}_{t|t}$ the estimates based on information $\mathbf{y}_0, \ldots, \mathbf{y}_t$.

The vector $\mathbf{z}_t$ is defined as the combination of state and observation:

$$\mathbf{z}_t := \begin{bmatrix} \mathbf{x}_t \\ \mathbf{y}_t \end{bmatrix}$$

Based on information up to time $t-1$, the covariance[14] of $\mathbf{Z}_t$ is

$$\text{cov}(\mathbf{z}_t) = \begin{bmatrix} \hat{\boldsymbol{\Sigma}}_{t|t-1} & \hat{\boldsymbol{\Sigma}}_{t|t-1}\mathbf{B}^\top \\ \mathbf{B}\hat{\boldsymbol{\Sigma}}_{t|t-1} & \mathbf{B}\hat{\boldsymbol{\Sigma}}_{t|t-1}\mathbf{B}^\top + \boldsymbol{\Sigma}_\eta \end{bmatrix}$$

[14] Here and elsewhere in the book (see, e.g., FAQ 4.1) we use the following elementary properties: for random vectors ξ, ζ and a commensurable matrix $\mathbf{B}$, $\text{cov}(\mathbf{B}\xi) = \mathbf{B}\text{cov}(\xi)\mathbf{B}^\top$ and $\text{cov}(\mathbf{B}\xi, \zeta) = \mathbf{B}\text{cov}(\xi, \zeta)$.

We observe $\mathbf{y}_t$. The vector $\mathbf{x}_t$ is normally distributed. We compute the conditional covariance of $\mathbf{x}_t$ given $\mathbf{y}_t$ using Equations (2.22) and (2.23):

$$\begin{aligned}\hat{\mathbf{\Sigma}}_{t|t} &= \hat{\mathbf{\Sigma}}_{t|t-1} - \hat{\mathbf{\Sigma}}_{t|t-1}\mathbf{B}^\top(\mathbf{B}\hat{\mathbf{\Sigma}}_{t|t-1}\mathbf{B}^\top + \mathbf{\Sigma}_\eta)^{-1}\mathbf{B}\hat{\mathbf{\Sigma}}_{t|t-1} && \textit{(update step)}\\ &= [\mathbf{I} - \hat{\mathbf{\Sigma}}_{t|t-1}\mathbf{B}^\top(\mathbf{B}\hat{\mathbf{\Sigma}}_{t|t-1}\mathbf{B}^\top + \mathbf{\Sigma}_\eta)^{-1}\mathbf{B}]\hat{\mathbf{\Sigma}}_{t|t-1} && (2.26)\\ \hat{\mathbf{x}}_{t|t} &= \hat{\mathbf{x}}_{t|t-1} + \hat{\mathbf{\Sigma}}_{t|t-1}\mathbf{B}^\top(\mathbf{B}\hat{\mathbf{\Sigma}}_{t|t-1}\mathbf{B}^\top + \mathbf{\Sigma}_\eta)^{-1}(\mathbf{y}_t - \mathbf{B}\hat{\mathbf{x}}_{t|t-1}) && (2.27)\end{aligned}$$

Once we have the posterior distribution given the observation $\mathbf{y}_t$, the conditional distribution of $\mathbf{x}_{t+1}$ follows from Equation (2.24). $\mathbf{x}_{t+1}$ is Gaussian with the following conditional mean and covariance matrix:

$$\begin{aligned}\hat{\mathbf{\Sigma}}_{t+1|t} &= \mathbf{A}\hat{\mathbf{\Sigma}}_{t|t}\mathbf{A}^\top + \mathbf{\Sigma}_\epsilon && \textit{(prediction step)} \quad (2.28)\\ \hat{\mathbf{x}}_{t+1|t} &= \mathbf{A}\hat{\mathbf{x}}_{t|t} + \mathbf{A}\hat{\mathbf{\Sigma}}_{t|t}\mathbf{B}^\top(\mathbf{B}\hat{\mathbf{\Sigma}}_{t|t}\mathbf{B}^\top + \mathbf{\Sigma}_\eta)^{-1}(\mathbf{y}_t - \mathbf{B}\hat{\mathbf{x}}_{t|t}) && (2.29)\end{aligned}$$

The measurement and time update equations above are the whole of the KF. If we combine Equations (2.26) and (2.28), the covariance matrix evolves according to the equation

$$\hat{\mathbf{\Sigma}}_{t+1|t} = \mathbf{A}(\hat{\mathbf{\Sigma}}_{t|t-1} - \hat{\mathbf{\Sigma}}_{t|t-1}\mathbf{B}^\top(\mathbf{B}\hat{\mathbf{\Sigma}}_{t|t-1}\mathbf{B}^\top + \mathbf{\Sigma}_\eta)^{-1}\mathbf{B}\hat{\mathbf{\Sigma}}_{t|t-1})\mathbf{A}^\top + \mathbf{\Sigma}_\epsilon$$

This is called a *Riccati recursion*. In steady state the covariance matrix does not change in consecutive periods: $\hat{\mathbf{\Sigma}}_{t+1|t} = \hat{\mathbf{\Sigma}}_{t|t-1}$. We can solve for the stationary matrix:

$$\mathbf{X} = \mathbf{A}\mathbf{X}\mathbf{A}^\top - \mathbf{A}\mathbf{X}\mathbf{B}^\top(\mathbf{B}\mathbf{X}\mathbf{B}^\top + \mathbf{\Sigma}_\eta)^{-1}\mathbf{B}\mathbf{X}\mathbf{A}^\top + \mathbf{\Sigma}_\epsilon$$

This is a *discrete-time algebraic Riccati equation.*

The matrix

$$\mathbf{K}_t := \hat{\mathbf{\Sigma}}_{t|t-1}\mathbf{B}^\top(\mathbf{B}\hat{\mathbf{\Sigma}}_{t|t-1}\mathbf{B}^\top + \mathbf{\Sigma}_\eta)^{-1}$$

is called the optimal Kalman gain. The equations become

$$\begin{aligned}\hat{\mathbf{\Sigma}}_{t|t} &= [\mathbf{I} - \mathbf{K}_t\mathbf{B}]\hat{\mathbf{\Sigma}}_{t|t-1} && (2.30)\\ \hat{\mathbf{x}}_{t|t} &= (\mathbf{I} - \mathbf{K}_t\mathbf{B})\hat{\mathbf{x}}_{t|t-1} + \mathbf{K}_t\mathbf{y}_t && (2.31)\\ \hat{\mathbf{\Sigma}}_{t+1|t} &= \mathbf{A}\hat{\mathbf{\Sigma}}_{t|t}\mathbf{A}^\top + \mathbf{\Sigma}_\epsilon && (2.32)\\ \hat{\mathbf{x}}_{t+1|t} &= \mathbf{A}\hat{\mathbf{x}}_{t|t} && (2.33)\end{aligned}$$

2.4.2 Kalman Filter Examples

Example 2.1: *(Muth, 1960)*

$$x_{t+1} = x_t + \tau_\epsilon \epsilon_{t+1} \tag{2.34}$$

$$y_{t+1} = x_{t+1} + \tau_\eta \eta_{t+1} \tag{2.35}$$

This is the simplest possible state-space model. The stationary estimate $\hat{\sigma}_{t+1|t}$ *is given by the solution to the Riccati equation:*

$$\frac{\hat{\sigma}^4_{t+1|t}}{\hat{\sigma}^2_{t+1|t} + \tau^2_\eta} = \tau^2_\epsilon \Rightarrow \hat{\sigma}^2_{t+1|t} = \frac{1}{2}\tau^2_\epsilon(1 + \sqrt{(2\kappa)^2 + 1})$$

$$K = \frac{\hat{\sigma}^2_{t+1|t}}{\hat{\sigma}^2_{t+1|t} + \tau^2_\eta}$$

$$\hat{x}_{t+1|t} = (1 - K)\hat{x}_{t|t-1} + Ky_t$$

where we have introduced the parameter

$$\kappa := \frac{\tau_\eta}{\tau_\epsilon}$$

Loosely, this is a noise-to-signal ratio. It is high when the measurement error is high compared to the typical change of the state per period. For $\kappa \gg 1$ *the formula simplifies:* $K \simeq 1/(\kappa + 1)$.

$$\hat{x}_{t|t} = \frac{\kappa}{1+\kappa}\hat{x}_{t|t-1} + \frac{1}{1+\kappa}y_t$$

Example 2.2: *(AR(1) model) In this model, the state equation is*

$$x_{t+1} = b + ax_t + \tau_\epsilon \epsilon_t \tag{2.36}$$

To have a mean-reverting process, introduce a long-term mean value $\mu > 0$ *and a relaxation constant* $\lambda > 0$*, and set*

$$a := 1 - \lambda \tag{2.37}$$

$$b := \lambda\mu \tag{2.38}$$

Equation (2.36) becomes

$$x_{t+1} = x_t - \lambda(x_t - \mu) + \tau_\epsilon \epsilon_{t+1}$$

The state reverts to value μ *when it is away from this equilibrium value. The stationary distribution of* x_t *is Gaussian, with mean* μ *and standard deviation* $\tau_\epsilon/\sqrt{2\lambda - \lambda^2}$.

Define

$$u_t := x_t - \mu \tag{2.39}$$
$$v_t := y_t - \mu \tag{2.40}$$

We rewrite the equation as

$$\begin{aligned} x_{t+1} - \mu &= x_t - \mu + (a-1)(x_t - \mu) + \tau_\epsilon \epsilon_{t+1} \\ u_{t+1} &= u_t + (a-1)u_t + \tau_\epsilon \epsilon_{t+1} \\ u_{t+1} &= a u_t + \tau_\epsilon \epsilon_{t+1} \end{aligned}$$

The state-space equations are

$$\begin{aligned} u_{t+1} &= a u_t + \tau_\epsilon \epsilon_{t+1} \\ v_{t+1} &= u_{t+1} + \tau_\eta \eta_{t+1} \end{aligned}$$

The Riccati equation is

$$\begin{aligned} (1-a^2)\hat{\sigma}^2_{t+1|t} + \frac{a^2\hat{\sigma}^4_{t+1|t}}{\hat{\sigma}^2_{t+1|t} + \tau^2_\eta} &= \tau^2_\epsilon \\ \Rightarrow \hat{\sigma}^2_{t+1|t} &= \frac{1}{2}\Bigg[(a^2-1)\tau^2_\eta + \tau^2_\epsilon \\ &\quad + \sqrt{(a^2-1)\tau^4_\eta + \tau^4_\epsilon + 2(a^2+1)\tau^2_\eta\tau^2_\epsilon}\Bigg] \\ &= \frac{1}{2}\Bigg[(a^2-1)\tau^2_\eta + \tau^2_\epsilon \\ &\quad + \sqrt{[(a^2-1)\tau^2_\eta + \tau^2_\epsilon]^2 + 4\tau^2_\eta\tau^2_\epsilon}\Bigg] \\ &= \frac{1}{2}\tau^2_\epsilon\left[(a^2-1)\kappa^2 + 1\right] \\ &\quad \times \left[1 + \sqrt{1 + \left(\frac{2\kappa}{(a^2-1)\kappa^2+1}\right)^2}\right] \end{aligned}$$

$$\begin{aligned} K &= \frac{\hat{\sigma}^2_{t+1|t}}{\hat{\sigma}^2_{t+1|t} + \tau^2_\eta} \\ \hat{u}_{t+1|t} &= (1-K)\hat{u}_{t|t-1} + K v_t \end{aligned}$$

Now replace u, v using Equations (2.39) and (2.40):

$$\Rightarrow \hat{x}_{t+1|t} = (1 - K)\hat{x}_{t|t-1} + Ky_t$$

For $a = 1$ the formula is identical to that of Example 2.1. It is straightforward to verify that $\hat{\sigma}^2_{t+1|t}$ is decreasing in a, and consequently also K is decreasing in a. There are two insights to be drawn from this:

1. *The EWMA is still an optimal estimator for a mean-reverting model of volatility.*
2. *In the presence of mean reversion, K decreases, everything else being equal. We discount the past less, because mean reversion causes volatility to be more concentrated. When the volatility is changing less from period to period, past observations become more informative.*

2.5 Exercises

Exercise 2.1: Prove that $\left[\prod_{t=1}^{T}(1 + r_t)\right]^{1/T} - 1 \leq \frac{1}{T}\sum_{t=1}^{T} r_t$.

Exercise 2.2: Provide an example of two random variables that are uncorrelated but dependent.

Exercise 2.3: Provide a second example, employing an entirely different rationale for the lack of correlation from the first one.

Exercise 2.4: With respect to Equation (2.12), prove that if $E(h^2_\infty)$ is finite, i.e., $\alpha_1 + \beta_1 < 1$, then a stationary distribution exists, i.e., $E[\log(\beta_1 + \alpha_1\epsilon_0^2)] < 0$. (Hint: Use Jensen's inequality.)

The Takeaways

1. *Importance of Univariate Models*. Understanding single-asset returns is foundational for modeling portfolios, especially in terms of volatility. GARCH and exponential moving averages are key tools for this.
2. *Types of Returns*. Definitions include simple returns, dividend-adjusted returns, compounded returns, and log returns. Excess returns, adjusted for a risk-free rate, are also essential in portfolio analysis.
3. *Stylized Facts of Returns*. Common features of returns include a lack of autocorrelation, heavy tails, volatility clustering, and aggregational (log-) Gaussianity.
4. *GARCH Models*. GARCH(1, 1) captures some stylized facts like heavy tails and volatility clustering, but it has limitations, such as overly high autocorrelations at longer lags.
5. *Realized Volatility*. Estimating volatility directly using high-frequency data (e.g., tick or minute-by-minute) is effective, though market microstructure issues (e.g., bid–ask spreads) and measurement error must be considered.
6. *EWMA as a Volatility Estimator*. Exponentially weighted moving averages offer a practical, interpretable method for estimating volatility, often used in financial applications.
7. *State-Space Models for Variance*. Kalman filters and state-space models provide a structured way to estimate time-varying volatility, allowing for enhancements like mean reversion in volatility.

Chapter 3

Interlude: What Is Performance?

The Questions

1. What are the key performance metrics for a portfolio manager?
2. How are they related to each other?

A discretionary portfolio manager satisfices; a quantitative portfolio manager optimizes. Maybe such a statement is not entirely fair to discretionary portfolio managers: they instinctively optimize too, the way tiger sharks optimize for food intake or migrating warblers minimize traveling distance to Cuba. On the other side, optimization is part of the job description of a quant. This chapter introduces and justifies the investment metrics that will appear in later chapters. In some cases, the metrics enter the optimization problem as objectives; in others, as constraints. The role played by objectives and constraints is, to some extent, interchangeable.

The performance metrics of a portfolio manager are, by and large, these:

- The expected return of the strategy.
- The volatility of the strategy.
- The Sharpe ratio and the information ratio.
- Capacity.

3.1 Expected Return

The *expected return* of the strategy is defined as the ratio of Profit and Loss (PnL) to Assets under Management (AuM). With the possible exception of Mother Teresa, humans prefer more money to less, and returns are an adequate way to describe this. Returns are preferred to actual money because the normalization makes the measure *stationary*, i.e., having (approximately) the same distribution across different investment periods, and *intensive* (as opposed to extensive), i.e., independent of the amount invested. This allows for better comparison across periods and across funds. Returns can be optimized either over the course of an investment period or over the lifetime of the strategy. In practice, the two problems are separable: we solve a sequence of single-period problems, which we embed in a larger multi-period problem.

3.2 Volatility

We introduced the *volatility* of returns in Chapter 2. The use of volatility in investing is ubiquitous, which, however, does not make it justified. There are, however, several arguments in favor of volatility. The first one is empirical. Cont (2001) reports a tail index for stock returns that is greater than 2 but smaller than 5; only fourth moments of returns may be finite. Therefore volatilities are finite and can be estimated,[1] but there is no assurance that skewness or kurtosis may be estimated. The second reason is related to portfolio optimization. We describe it next.

[1] A sufficient condition for the asymptotic consistency of the variance estimator is that the fourth moment be finite.

Say that the investor solves a one-period utility optimization problem of the form $\max_{\mathbf{w}} E[u(\mathbf{w}^\mathsf{T}\mathbf{R})]$; the utility function describes the preference of the investor and is increasing and concave. Then, one can justify the use of volatility using three different sets of assumptions (Huang and Litzenberger, 1988):

1. The utility function is well approximated by a second-order Taylor expansion centered at the expected payoff, so that $u \simeq aE(\mathbf{w}^\mathsf{T}\mathbf{R}) - bE[(\mathbf{w}^\mathsf{T}\mathbf{R} - E(\mathbf{w}^\mathsf{T}\mathbf{R}))^2]$, and the returns are arbitrarily distributed but with finite variance.
2. The utility takes a specific form (aside from the above quadratic utility):

$$u(\mathbf{w}^\mathsf{T}\mathbf{R}) \equiv \begin{cases} -\exp(-\mathbf{w}^\mathsf{T}\mathbf{R}) \\ -\dfrac{(\mathbf{w}^\mathsf{T}\mathbf{R})^{1-\gamma}}{1-\gamma} & \gamma \in (0,1) \\ \log(\mathbf{w}^\mathsf{T}\mathbf{R}) \end{cases}$$

3. Lastly, one can assume arbitrary utility and returns to be normally distributed.

As we discussed in Chapter 2, there is agreement that returns of many securities have finite variance. The assumption that we can approximate utility with a quadratic function is not unrealistic, since the optimization horizon in quantitative investing is short and the payoffs are small. Globally, utility is not quadratic, and this can be described by the parameters used in the utility approximation formula. A higher value of the ratio b/a can be interpreted as penalizing more the uncertainty of payoffs relative to their expected values, i.e., being more risk-averse. I am not discussing this further, since the topic is covered extensively in textbooks, such as Huang and Litzenberger (1988), and is not essential to the remainder of this book.

3.3 Sharpe Ratio

The *Sharpe Ratio* (SR) is defined as the ratio of expected returns of a strategy to its volatility. It combines the previous two quantities by measuring returns in units of volatility over a certain period of time. The *Information Ratio* (IR) is defined analogously to the Sharpe Ratio but employs a different type of returns: the *idiosyncratic returns* of a strategy. These returns will be introduced in Chapter 4; for now, it suffices to say that the asset idiosyncratic returns describe the "intrinsic" returns of the assets, i.e., the component of total returns that is not driven by common factors affecting all returns at once.

If we assume that the returns[2] of a strategy are identically distributed and independent, the Sharpe Ratio is the same as the t-statistic of the mean of the return distribution. In finance, the Sharpe Ratio is named after William F. Sharpe, one of the authors of the Capital Asset Pricing Model (CAPM). The Sharpe Ratio has drawbacks and advantages. Its drawbacks are two. First, it is not quite justifiable as a metric that ranks uncertain outcomes. Aside from decision-theoretic considerations,[3] the Sharpe Ratio of a portfolio with negative expected return of −5% and volatility 5% is *lower* than the Sharpe Ratio with the same negative return, and volatility 10%. This is unintuitive at best and wrong at worst. Second, it inherits the limitation of volatility as a measure of risk. It is possible to replace the denominator with one's favorite risk measure, of which there is a near-infinite supply.[4] There are advantages, however. First, the Sharpe Ratio is intuitive: return in units of "risk". Second, it comes with a rich arsenal of theoretical results. We have confidence intervals and characterizations of its empirical properties, theoretical results like the relationship between cross-sectional regressions and the Sharpe Ratio. The Sharpe Ratio also implies a bound on the probability of incurring a certain loss. This follows from Cantelli's inequality. For a random variable ξ with mean μ and standard deviation σ, this inequality states that

$$
\begin{aligned}
& P(\xi < \mu - \lambda) \leq \frac{\sigma^2}{\sigma^2 + \lambda^2} \\
\Rightarrow \quad & P(\xi < -\lambda) \leq \frac{\sigma^2}{\sigma^2 + (\lambda + \mu)^2}
\end{aligned}
$$

[2] Or, more commonly, the *excess returns*, i.e., the returns of a strategy in excess of the risk-free rate, often the 3-month Treasury yield. This is the return of holding a self-financed security: we borrow one dollar in the first period at the risk-free rate, and buy one dollar of the security. In the second period, we receive the security return, and pay off the loan.

[3] For these, see Huang and Litzenberger (1988).

[4] See, for example, Bacon (2005) for a list of risk metrics, both theoretically justified and heuristic.

If ξ is the annual return of a strategy, and SR is the annualized Sharpe Ratio of the strategy, and the loss is expressed as a multiple of standard deviations $-L\sigma$, as practitioners often do, then the inequality is

$$P(\xi < -L\sigma) \leq \frac{1}{1 + (L + \text{SR})^2}$$

This holds for *any* distribution of returns with Sharpe Ratio SR. For example, consider an annualized Sharpe Ratio of 3 and an annualized volatility of $50M. The probability of a $100M loss, which is two standard deviations, is not greater than 3.9%. This is a much higher value than we would obtain under the assumption of normal returns. In that case, the probability of a loss would be 2.9E-7.

FAQ 3.1: *What are the dimensions of the Sharpe Ratio?*

Return, volatility, and Sharpe Ratio depend on the time horizon over which they are measured. Daily return r is daily PnL on capital; annualized return, where we assume the same daily PnL over T trading days in a year, is rT. We say that returns have dimension $[\text{time}]^{-1}$. An example: a strategy has a return of 10%/(1 year) = 10%/(T days) = (10%/T)/days. Provided that returns are serially uncorrelated (see Section 2.1.5), variance is also linear in time, because the variance of returns over a year is the sum of T daily variances, so its dimension is $[\text{time}]^{-1}$. Volatility is the square root of variance and has the dimension $[\text{time}]^{-1/2}$. The Sharpe Ratio has the dimension $[\text{return}]/[\text{volatility}] = [\text{time}]^{-1}/[\text{time}]^{-1/2} = [\text{time}]^{-1/2}$. When converting the horizon of a Sharpe Ratio for an equity strategy from a daily horizon to a monthly one, we multiply the daily Sharpe Ratio by $\sqrt{21}$, where 21 is the number of trading days in a month. The conversion factor to an annualized Sharpe Ratio in the United States is[a] $\sqrt{251}$.

[a] The number of trading days depends on the country, the asset class, and the year. In the United States, as of 2024, the stock market is open 251 days a year.

FAQ 3.2: *What is the confidence interval for the Sharpe Ratio?*

Suppose you observe T consecutive returns (or PnL), and estimate the Sharpe Ratio from these data. What is the confidence interval of this estimator? First, the Sharpe Ratio estimator is

$$\hat{\mu} := \frac{1}{T}\sum_{t=1}^{T} r_t \qquad \hat{\sigma} := \sqrt{\frac{1}{T}\sum_{t=1}^{T}(r_t - \hat{\mu})^2}$$

$$\widehat{\mathrm{SR}} := \frac{\hat{\mu}}{\hat{\sigma}}$$

For excess returns r_t that are iid and with finite variance, the estimator is normally distributed in the limit $T \to \infty$, with standard error

$$\mathrm{SE}(\widehat{\mathrm{SR}}) = \sqrt{\frac{1 + \mathrm{SR}^2/2}{T}}$$

Compare this to the case in which we knew in advance the standard deviation of the returns. The Sharpe Ratio is then $\widehat{\mathrm{SR}} := \hat{\mu}/\sigma$, and the SE is $\sqrt{1/T}$.

In the case of autocorrelated returns with $\mathrm{cor}(r_s, r_t) = \rho^{|t-s|}$, the Sharpe Ratio estimator is for small values of $|\rho|$,

$$\widehat{\mathrm{SR}} := \frac{\hat{\mu}}{\hat{\sigma}}\sqrt{\frac{1-\rho}{1+\rho}} \simeq \frac{\hat{\mu}}{\hat{\sigma}}(1-\rho)$$

3.4 Capacity

Whereas the return and the Sharpe Ratio are well known and defined, the *capacity* of a strategy is not unequivocally defined. An informal definition of capacity is "the highest expected PnL that a strategy is able to produce over a certain horizon". You may ask, "but isn't expected PnL just equal to Sharpe Ratio times dollar volatility? Capacity is essentially the maximum volatility at which we can run a strategy". This would be true if the Sharpe Ratio were independent of volatility, and in that case, why not run a strategy to infinite volatility, or at least to the proverbial 11? Sharpe, however, is almost always a decreasing function of volatility. For a large enough volatility, the Sharpe Ratio becomes zero, and beyond this threshold the strategy is unprofitable. The capacity of a strategy can be defined as the maximum PnL that can be attained, subject to a constraint that the Sharpe Ratio exceeds an acceptable level. Alternatively, we could require a minimum bound on the expected return on capital. Defined this way, the capacity is an important parameter for hedge fund managers and portfolio managers alike. A strategy may have attractive return and Sharpe Ratio when run at low volatility. If it can yield only a modest PnL, it will be economically unattractive.

The Takeaways

1. *Expected Return*. Represents profit relative to assets under management; it's stationary and intensive, allowing for comparisons across funds and periods.
2. *Volatility*. A standard measure in portfolio optimization with empirical support for assets with finite variance; used under assumptions about investor utility functions.
3. *Sharpe Ratio*. Represents returns per unit of volatility. Widely adopted but has limitations, such as dependency on risk measure choice and unintuitive outcomes with negative returns.
4. *Capacity*. Refers to the maximum Profit and Loss (PnL) achievable within a strategy's acceptable Sharpe Ratio threshold. Essential for assessing the economic viability of a strategy.

Chapter 4

Linear Models of Returns

The Questions

1. What is a factor model for asset returns, and how is it formulated?
2. What are the different interpretations of factor models (graphical model, superposition of effects, single-asset product)?
3. How do alpha spanned and alpha orthogonal components contribute to asset returns?
4. What transformations can be applied to factor models (rotations, projections, push-outs), and how do they affect the models?
5. What are the practical applications of factor models in finance, such as performance attribution, risk management, portfolio construction, and alpha research?
6. What are the different types of factor models (characteristic, statistical, macroeconomic), and how are they used in practice?

Linear models of asset returns are a cornerstone of this book. They are flexible, interpretable, perform well in applications, and are supported by theory. Furthermore, they fit like a glove with mean-variance optimization and can also be used as a basis for a number of important tasks, like risk management and performance analysis. It is possible that you, the reader, will find this class of models inadequate in some way, at some point. But just because you have outgrown them does not mean that you will find them useless. They will still enable you to reason about the entire investment process, and some of the theory will come in handy.

4.1 Factor Models

We saw in Chapter 2 how to model univariate returns. A direct extension to multivariate returns would be to model each security's return as an independent process. This would not be adequate, however, because the returns are dependent. It is a natural step to model the common dependency among stocks as being generated by a few common sources of randomness, called *factors*, and then to keep a random source of per-security randomness that is independent of the factors. The model for stock returns is called a factor model[1] and takes the form

$$\mathbf{r}_t = \boldsymbol{\alpha} + \mathbf{B}\mathbf{f}_t + \boldsymbol{\epsilon}_t \tag{4.1}$$

where

- $t \in \mathbb{N}$ denotes the discrete time period.
- The random vector $\mathbf{r}_t$ denotes n asset returns minus the risk-free rate (see Section 2.1.2).
- $\boldsymbol{\alpha}$ is an n-dimensional *alpha* vector.
- The random vector $\mathbf{f}_t$ denotes m *factor returns*. m is much smaller than n in most models. Interpret factor returns as pervasive sources of uncertainty in the market, affecting in some ways all asset returns.

[1] Factor models go back to the birth of psychometrics at the turn of the 19th century. Textbook treatments on the subject are Johnson and Wichern (2007), Rencher and Christensen (2012). In finance, factor models were first introduced by Sharpe (1964, 1965, 1966) for the one-factor case, which was extended to multiple factors by Ross (1976). Good introductions to factor models in finance are the survey papers by Connor and Korajczyk (2010), Fan et al. (2016), and the books by Connor et al. (2010) and Connor and Korajczyk (2010), MacKinlay (1995).

- $\mathbf{B}$ is an $n \times m$ *loadings matrix*. The matrix element $[\mathbf{B}]_{i,j}$ is the *loading of asset i with respect to factor j*. Interpret $\mathbf{B}$ as a store of data specifying how factor returns transfer to asset returns.
- $\boldsymbol{\epsilon}_t$ is the random vector of *n idiosyncratic returns*.[2] You can interpret these returns in two ways. The positive interpretation is "returns that are specific to the asset and are uncorrelated with all other returns"; the negative interpretation is "the component of asset returns that are left over after removing the pervasive sources of risk".

If the random vector $\boldsymbol{\epsilon}_t$ had a generic distribution, we would gain nothing in tractability. Instead, we assume that (i) the vector $\boldsymbol{\epsilon}_t$ is independent of the factor returns $\mathbf{f}_s$ for all s; (ii) $E[\boldsymbol{\epsilon}_t] = 0$; (iii) the covariance matrix $\boldsymbol{\Omega}_{\epsilon,t} := \text{var}(\boldsymbol{\epsilon}_t)$ is diagonal, or at least sparse in some sense. Often, models with a diagonal covariance matrix are called *strict* and models with a sparse covariance matrix are called *approximate*. The vector $\boldsymbol{\epsilon}_t$ is the *idiosyncratic component of asset returns*.

We usually refer to the term $\mathbf{Bf}_t$ as the *systematic component of asset returns*. We assume that the pair $(\mathbf{f}_t, \boldsymbol{\epsilon}_t)$ is either identically distributed across periods or has a slowly varying distribution, and that $\mathbf{f}_t$ and $\boldsymbol{\epsilon}_t$ are independent for each t. We denote covariance matrices of $\mathbf{f}_t$ and $\boldsymbol{\epsilon}_t$ with $\boldsymbol{\Omega}_\mathbf{f} \in \mathbb{R}^{m \times m}$ and $\boldsymbol{\Omega}_\epsilon \in \mathbb{R}^{n \times n}$ respectively. With this notation, the covariance matrix of assets is

$$\boldsymbol{\Omega}_\mathbf{r} = \mathbf{B}\boldsymbol{\Omega}_\mathbf{f}\mathbf{B}^\top + \boldsymbol{\Omega}_\epsilon \tag{4.2}$$

This decomposition is at the core of volatility modeling with linear returns and the subject of Chapters 6 and 7.

FAQ 4.1: *Why is the covariance matrix* $\boldsymbol{\Omega}_\mathbf{r} = \mathbf{B}\boldsymbol{\Omega}_\mathbf{f}\mathbf{B}^\top + \boldsymbol{\Omega}_\epsilon$*?*

The covariance matrix $\boldsymbol{\Omega}_\mathbf{r}$ does not depend on the intercept $\boldsymbol{\alpha}$, and the terms $\mathbf{Bf}_t$ and $\boldsymbol{\epsilon}_t$ are independent, so that $\boldsymbol{\Omega}_\mathbf{r} = \text{cov}(\mathbf{Bf}_t) + \boldsymbol{\Omega}_\epsilon$. The factor term is a linear transformation

(*Continued*)

[2] We also use the terms *residual* and *specific* in place of "idiosyncratic".

(*Continued*)
of $\mathbf{f}_t$. For any random vector $\boldsymbol{\xi}$ with covariance $\boldsymbol{\Omega}_\xi$, $\text{cov}(\mathbf{B}\boldsymbol{\xi}) = \mathbf{B}\boldsymbol{\Omega}_\xi\mathbf{B}^\top$, because $[\text{cov}(\mathbf{B}\boldsymbol{\xi})]_{i,j} = \text{cov}(\sum_k [\mathbf{B}]_{i,k}\xi_k, \sum_\ell [\mathbf{B}]_{j,\ell}\xi_\ell) = \sum_{k,\ell}[\mathbf{B}]_{i,k}[\boldsymbol{\Omega}_\xi]_{k,\ell}[\mathbf{B}]_{j,\ell} = [\mathbf{B}\boldsymbol{\Omega}_\xi\mathbf{B}^\top]_{i,j}$.

In this chapter we set aside the very important issue of estimating the parameters of Equation (4.1) from data, and focus instead on its usage and interpretation. Here is the plan for the next few sections. First, we review the *interpretations* of Equation (4.1), of which there are three:

1. As a graphical model.
2. As the superposition of low-dimensional cross-sectional return vectors.
3. As the overlap of the factor return vector with the asset loadings vector.

We then analyze the sources of alpha, namely *alpha spanned* and *alpha orthogonal*. These are fundamental concepts at the core of the research process. Third, we review the *transformations* that can be operated on factor models. There are three of those too:

1. *Rotations* keep the dimension of the model unchanged and its predictions "invariant".
2. *Projections* reduce the dimension of the model.
3. *Push-outs* extend the model by adding factors.

These mathematical operations are versatile tools in the hands of the quantitative manager to reformulate, simplify, or extend a model.
Fourth, we describe the uses of factor models. There are quite a few:

1. *Forecast* and *decompose* volatility, so that we can separate wanted versus unwanted risk.
2. Be a fundamental input to *portfolio construction*.
3. *Understand* performance and separate skill from luck.
4. Serve as a foundation for *alpha research*.

4.2 Interpretations of Factor Models

Before we start interpreting, let us make the factor model more concrete with an example. In Figure 4.1 you see a "typical" loading matrix used in a risk model. A few columns contain *style* loadings.[3] Other columns consist of dummy variables[4] indicating whether the stock belongs to a particular industry. There may be a column for "energy explorers and producers", a column for "biotechnology company", and so on. A stock will have a "1" loading if it belongs to the industry, "0" otherwise. Finally there are columns consisting of dummy variables denoting country classification, similarly to industry. When the factor return for a country or an industry is high, it will move all the stocks in the industry. The factor structure captures comovement among stocks with certain obvious commonalities, as well as less obvious ones.

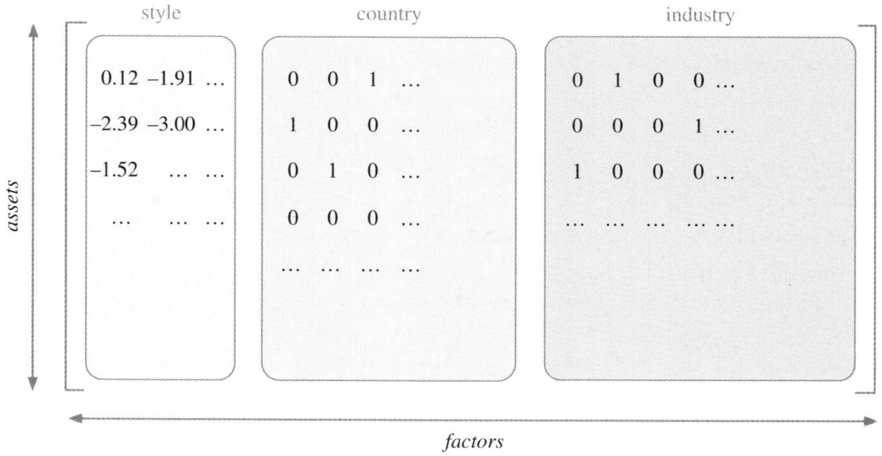

Figure 4.1 A typical loadings matrix, partitioned into different blocks. The style loadings comprise an "intercept" factor (sometimes termed "country" factor). The loadings are all ones, and the intercept factor contribution to total returns is the same for all assets. The other style loadings are often standardized. The country and industry loadings take values equal to 1 if the asset belongs to the country or industry.

---

[3] The use of the term "style" will be clear later, when we associate it with loadings investment styles.

[4] A *dummy variable* is a variable taking binary values (e.g., 0 or 1) or more generally values in a finite set. We will only use binary variables.

Even though Equation (4.1) is older than modern statistics (having really originated in the unpublished work of Gauss), it is surprisingly rich in meaning, and possibly even richer when used in financial applications. First, let's review some interpretations of the equation.

4.2.1 *Graphical Model*

The first one is as a graphical model.[5] Since $\mathbf{r} - \boldsymbol{\alpha} = \mathbf{Bf}$, for each asset i this equation holds:

$$E(r_i - \alpha_i | f) = \sum_j [\mathbf{B}]_{i,j} f_j$$

Each of the many asset returns is dependent on all, or some of, the few factor returns. In a typical regional risk model (say, America, Asia, or Europe) we have up to 10,000 assets and up to 100 factors. In Figure 4.2 we show the relationship visually. A few factors (circles) determine the expected asset returns in excess of $\boldsymbol{\alpha}$ (squares), through the links provided by loadings $\mathbf{B}$ (arrows). When the matrix $\mathbf{B}$ is sparse, the corresponding graph is sparse.

4.2.2 *Superposition of Effects*

The second interpretation is as an overlap of influences on asset returns. A model for the cross-section of returns, i.e., the vector of returns at a

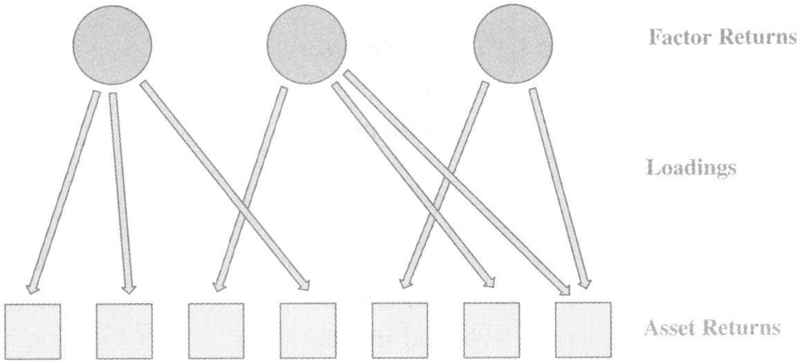

Figure 4.2 Factor models as graphical models.

[5] Graphical models are covered in monographs (Lauritzen, 1996), books on machine learning (Bishop, 2006; Murphy, 2012), and survey papers (Models, 2004).

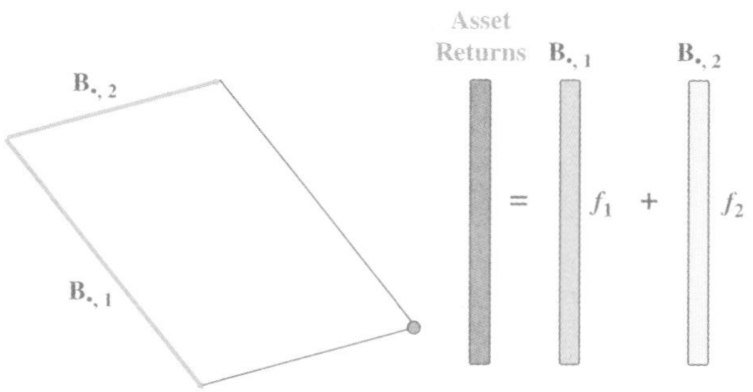

Figure 4.3 A factor model as the superposition of weighted factor loadings.

given point in time. Let $[\mathbf{B}]_{\bullet,j}$ be the jth column of the matrix $\mathbf{B}$. We rewrite $E(\mathbf{r} - \boldsymbol{\alpha}) = \mathbf{Bf}$ as

$$E(\mathbf{r} - \alpha|\mathbf{f}) = \sum_j [\mathbf{B}]_{\bullet,j} f_j$$

The vector of expected excess return is the superposition of a small number of vectors (the loadings $[\mathbf{B}]_{\bullet,j}$ for a specific factor), weighted by the factor return. This makes it clear that the factor component of the cross-section lives in a low-dimensional space: the column subspace of $\mathbf{B}$. This is shown in Figure 4.3.

4.2.3 *Single-Asset Product*

The last interpretation applies to single assets. The expected return of an asset given the factor returns is equal to the scalar product of the asset loadings and the vector of factor returns:

$$E(r_i - \alpha_i|\mathbf{f}) = \langle [\mathbf{B}]_{i,\cdot}, \mathbf{f} \rangle$$

While this formula is rarely used at the asset level, it does show up all the time when we apply it to portfolios. Consider a portfolio $\mathbf{w} \in \mathbb{R}^n$, where w_i is the Net Market Value[6] invested in asset i; for stocks, this is the stock price times the number of shares held long or short. The expected PnL of the portfolio is

[6] Net Market Value (NMV) is the amount invested in the security in the reference currency (numeraire).

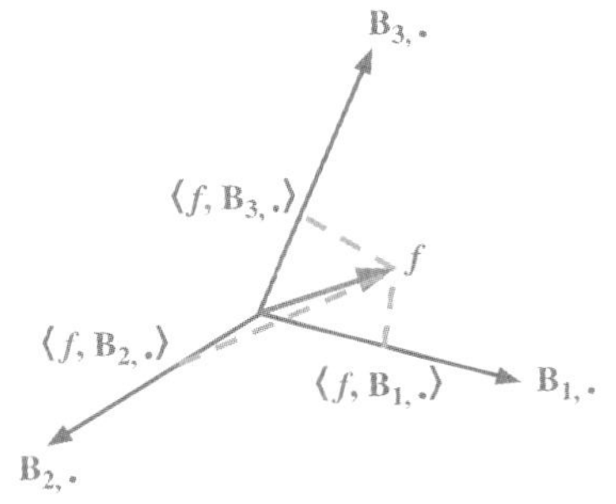

Figure 4.4 Factor models as scalar products of per-stock loadings and factor returns.

$$
\begin{aligned}
E\left(\mathbf{w}^{\top}\mathbf{r}\middle|\,\mathbf{f}\right) &= E\left(\sum_i w_i r_i \middle|\, \mathbf{f}\right) \\
&= \sum_i \left[\alpha_i + \langle [\mathbf{B}]_{i,\cdot}, \mathbf{f}\rangle\right] w_i
\end{aligned}
$$

The relationship is illustrated in Figure 4.4, in the special case of $\alpha_i = 0$. We will have an interpretation of the term $\langle [\mathbf{B}]_{i,\cdot}, \mathbf{f}\rangle w_i$ in Section 4.5.1. This is the PnL attributable to factor returns. We explain this *factor PnL* of a portfolio in terms of a scalar product; and within the scalar product identify the largest contributor, the degree of dispersion of PnL among the factors, and so on. This is the jumping-off point for *performance attribution*, which we will cover extensively later in the book.

4.3 Alpha Spanned and Alpha Orthogonal

Consider the factor equation

$$\mathbf{r}_t = \boldsymbol{\alpha} + \mathbf{B}\mathbf{f}_t + \boldsymbol{\epsilon}_t$$

where $\mathbf{f}_t$ are iid with finite mean and variance, and $\boldsymbol{\epsilon}_t$ are iid (independent on $\mathbf{f}_t$) with zero unconditional mean and finite variance. Decompose $\boldsymbol{\alpha}$ as the sum of its projection on the column subspace of $\mathbf{B}$ (i.e., the image of the operator $\mathbf{B}$) and the orthogonal complement: $\boldsymbol{\alpha} = \mathbf{B}\boldsymbol{\lambda} + \boldsymbol{\alpha}_{\perp}$. By construction, the equality $\mathbf{B}^{\top}\boldsymbol{\alpha}_{\perp} = 0$ holds. So we have $\mathbf{r}_t = \boldsymbol{\alpha}_{\perp} + \mathbf{B}(\boldsymbol{\lambda} + \mathbf{f}_t) + \boldsymbol{\epsilon}_t$. In this relationship, you can see that there is an indeterminacy in the factor model. It is useful to rewrite the model as

$$\mathbf{r}_t = \boldsymbol{\alpha}_{\perp} + \mathbf{B}[\boldsymbol{\lambda} + E(\mathbf{f}_t)] + \mathbf{B}[\mathbf{f}_t - E(\mathbf{f}_t)] + \boldsymbol{\epsilon}_t$$

where $\boldsymbol{\alpha}_{\parallel} := \mathbf{B}[\boldsymbol{\lambda} + E(\mathbf{f}_t)]$. The "alpha" spanned by the columns of $\mathbf{B}$ is indistinguishable from the expected returns of the factors. However, the term $\boldsymbol{\alpha}_{\parallel}$ is independent of how you split the contribution of the $\boldsymbol{\lambda}$ and $E(\mathbf{f}_t)$ terms. In the remainder of the book, we set $\boldsymbol{\lambda} = 0$ and set $\boldsymbol{\mu}_f := E[\mathbf{f}_t]$. Now, for a little prestige: if you choose a portfolio proportional to the alpha vector

$$\mathbf{w} = \frac{\boldsymbol{\alpha}_{\perp}}{\|\boldsymbol{\alpha}_{\perp}\|}$$

its payoff is

$$\begin{aligned}\mathbf{w}^{\top}\mathbf{r}_t &= \frac{1}{\|\boldsymbol{\alpha}_{\perp}\|}\boldsymbol{\alpha}_{\perp}^{\top}\mathbf{r}_t \\ &= \|\boldsymbol{\alpha}_{\perp}\| + \frac{\boldsymbol{\alpha}_{\perp}^{\top}\boldsymbol{\epsilon}_t}{\|\boldsymbol{\alpha}_{\perp}\|}\end{aligned}$$

The expected return and variance of this portfolio are

$$\begin{aligned}E(\mathbf{w}^{\top}\mathbf{r}_t) &= \|\boldsymbol{\alpha}_{\perp}\| \\ \text{var}(\mathbf{w}^{\top}\mathbf{r}_t) &= \frac{\boldsymbol{\alpha}_{\perp}^{\top}\boldsymbol{\Omega}_{\epsilon}\boldsymbol{\alpha}_{\perp}}{\|\boldsymbol{\alpha}_{\perp}\|^2}\end{aligned}$$

There is an upper bound for the variance, given by the operator norm:

$$\frac{\boldsymbol{\alpha}_{\perp}^{\top}\boldsymbol{\Omega}_{\epsilon}\boldsymbol{\alpha}_{\perp}}{\|\boldsymbol{\alpha}_{\perp}\|^2} \leq \left\|\boldsymbol{\Omega}_{\epsilon}\right\|$$

So that

$$\begin{aligned}\text{SR} &= \frac{E(\mathbf{w}^{\top}\mathbf{r}_t)}{\sqrt{\text{var}(\mathbf{w}^{\top}\mathbf{r}_t)}} \\ &\geq \frac{\|\boldsymbol{\alpha}_{\perp}\|}{\sqrt{\left\|\boldsymbol{\Omega}_{\epsilon}\right\|}}\end{aligned}$$

In the case of a diagonal matrix, $\left\|\boldsymbol{\Omega}_{\epsilon}\right\|$ is the largest element on the diagonal. Assume that it has an upper bound.[7] This has interesting implications.

[7] For example, for U.S. equities, the maximum annualized idiosyncratic volatility is approximately 40%.

Consider the case, for example, where the average absolute orthogonal return per asset is positive:

$$\frac{1}{n}\sum_i |[\boldsymbol{\alpha}_\perp]_i| =: \mu > 0, \text{or, equivalently, } \|\boldsymbol{\alpha}_\perp\|_1 = n\mu$$

Now use the simple inequality between 1-norm and Euclidean norm: $\|\mathbf{x}\|_1 \leq \sqrt{n}\,\|\mathbf{x}\|_2$. Hence $\|\boldsymbol{\alpha}_\perp\|_2 \geq \sqrt{n}\mu$. Apply this to the Sharpe Ratio of the alpha orthogonal strategy, and we have a lower bound on the Sharpe Ratio:

$$\text{SR} \geq \frac{\|\boldsymbol{\alpha}_\perp\|}{\sqrt{\|\boldsymbol{\Omega}_\epsilon\|}} \geq \sqrt{n}\frac{\mu}{\sqrt{\|\boldsymbol{\Omega}_\epsilon\|}} \tag{4.3}$$

Let's summarize the assumptions made so far, besides the fact that the factor model is correct. If we assume that:

1. the largest idiosyncratic variance[8] is uniformly bounded in the number of assets, and
2. the average absolute value of the coordinate of $\boldsymbol{\alpha}_\perp$ is bounded below by μ

We have obtained a lower bound on the Sharpe strategy of a portfolio. And if these bounds are uniform for increasing values[9] of n, then we have a sequence of Sharpe Ratios going to infinity! This is highly unlikely in real life, so that at least one of the assumptions we made—factor model, bound on idiosyncratic variances, bound on orthogonal expected returns—is likely incorrect. *Under the assumption that the factor model is correct*, it appears that the assumption of finite idiosyncratic variances holds in practice. This leaves us with the fact that the idiosyncratic orthogonal expected returns are vanishing in n. Let us summarize this result in concrete terms:

- If a linear model is a good approximation of returns, then alpha is either "spanned" or "orthogonal".
- "Alpha orthogonal" is extremely valuable: if you have positive expected alpha at the asset level, then your Sharpe Ratio increases at the rate $\sqrt{n}$, a typical rate that arises when you can diversify risk without giving up on returns.

[8] Or, more generally, the largest eigenvalue of the sparse matrix $\boldsymbol{\Omega}_\epsilon$.

[9] Economists reason in terms of "increasing" economies as a function of the tradeable assets. I believe there is not much to gain from this level of abstraction, so I keep the exposition and the inequalities in finite dimensions.

- There are excess returns, but they are more likely to come from "alpha spanned". This alpha, as we will see in the next chapter, comes with risk that does not diversify away with a large number of assets.

4.4 Transformations

4.4.1 *Rotations*

A factor model is not uniquely identified. Let $\mathbf{C}$ be an $m \times m$ invertible matrix, and define

$$\tilde{\mathbf{B}} = \mathbf{B}\mathbf{C}^{-1}$$
$$\tilde{\mathbf{f}} = \mathbf{C}\mathbf{f}$$

The columns of $\tilde{\mathbf{B}}$ span the same subspace as the columns of $\mathbf{B}$. The model

$$\mathbf{r} = \boldsymbol{\alpha} + \tilde{\mathbf{B}}\tilde{\mathbf{f}} + \boldsymbol{\epsilon}$$

has the same returns as the original model. This is usually termed *rotational indeterminacy* of the factor model.

The covariance matrix of the transformed factors is $\tilde{\boldsymbol{\Omega}}_f = \mathbf{C}\boldsymbol{\Omega}_f\mathbf{C}^\top$. There will be several applications of rotational indeterminacy in the book. Rotations enable us to provide final users with different *views* of the same model. We explore the impact of factor transformations on factor returns for three instructive examples: identity factor covariance, orthonormal loadings, and z-scored loadings.

- *Identity factor covariance matrix*. Sometimes, users of a model would like to see uncorrelated factor returns with unit variances. Under this perspective, exposures of the portfolio can be interpreted directly as factor volatilities, and the factor risk of a portfolio is the sum of the squared exposures, without covariance terms.

  This risk model perspective can be obtained by taking the Singular Value Decomposition (SVD)[10] of $\boldsymbol{\Omega}_f = \mathbf{U}\mathbf{S}\mathbf{U}^\top$ and then setting $\mathbf{C} := \mathbf{S}^{-1/2}\mathbf{U}^\top$. It follows that

$$\tilde{\boldsymbol{\Omega}}_f = \mathbf{C}\boldsymbol{\Omega}_f\mathbf{C}^\top = \mathbf{S}^{-1/2}\mathbf{U}^\top\mathbf{U}\mathbf{S}\mathbf{U}^\top\mathbf{U}\mathbf{S}^{-1/2} = \mathbf{I}$$

[10] See Appendix, Section 4.7.4, for an introduction to the SVD and the square root of a matrix, which we will be using throughout the book.

- *Orthonormal loadings*. We can also choose a rotation so that the loadings are orthonormal $\tilde{\mathbf{B}}^{\mathsf{T}}\tilde{\mathbf{B}} = \mathbf{I}_m$. This means that each column of $\tilde{\mathbf{B}}$ has unit norm (but not unit variance, since the column may have non-zero mean), and is orthogonal to the other. In this case the transformation is $\mathbf{C}^{-1} := \mathbf{V}\mathbf{S}^{-1}$, where $\mathbf{V}$ and $\mathbf{S}$ come from the SVD of $\mathbf{B} = \mathbf{U}\mathbf{S}\mathbf{V}^{\mathsf{T}}$. We get $\tilde{\mathbf{B}} = \mathbf{U}$.
- *z-scored loadings*. The z-scoring of factor loadings is a common procedure. It consists of a linear rescaling of the loadings of one or more factors, so that the new loadings have zero mean and unit variance (since they are zero-mean, they also have unit squared norm). The benefit of the transformation is that it makes the loadings easier to interpret. Is the stock more exposed than the average to the factor, and by how much? What is the average portfolio exposure to the factor on a standardized basis? Is such a linear transformation resulting in an equivalent

FAQ 4.2: *Is z-scoring factor loadings changing a factor model?*

z-scoring the loadings of a model will result in a model that makes the same predictions as the original model with raw loadings only if the unit vector $(1, 1, \ldots, 1)$ can be expressed as a linear combination of the loadings vectors of the original model. A special case is the one where the "country" factor (or "intercept" factor) is among the original factors. If that is not the case, z-scoring factors will result in a model that produces different risk forecasts and performance attributions.

factor model? It is possible to multiply the loadings of factor i by constant κ_i: just consider $\mathbf{C} := \mathrm{diag}\left(\kappa_1^{-1}, \ldots, \kappa_m^{-1}\right)$, which is always invertible. However, in general it is not possible to center the loadings (you can try to find a counterexample in Exercise 4.4). However, assume that the unit vector is in the subspace spanned by the loadings columns, i.e., there is a vector $\mathbf{a} \in \mathbb{R}^m$ such that[11] $\mathbf{e} = \mathbf{B}\mathbf{a}$. In this case,

[11] We use the notation $\mathbf{e} := (1, 1, \ldots, 1)^{\mathsf{T}}$.

the centering is possible. If we want to add constants ν_i to the loadings, then $\tilde{\mathbf{B}} = \mathbf{B} + \mathbf{e}\mathbf{e}^\top \text{diag}(\boldsymbol{\nu}) = \mathbf{B}(\mathbf{I}_m + \mathbf{a}\mathbf{a}^\top \mathbf{B}^\top \text{diag}(\boldsymbol{\nu}))$, hence our transformation is

$$\mathbf{C}^{-1} = \mathbf{I}_m + \mathbf{a}\mathbf{a}^\top \mathbf{B}^\top \text{diag}(\boldsymbol{\nu}) \tag{4.4}$$

This assumption is verified in two common cases. The first one is the use of a "market" (also called a "country") factor, to which all assets have unit exposure. The loadings vector is then **e** by construction. The second case is when there are country or industry loadings, such that for each asset the sum of the loadings across industries is exactly one. In this case $\mathbf{e} = \mathbf{B}\mathbf{a}$ for a vector **a** that has ones in positions corresponding to the industry factors, and zero otherwise.

4.4.2 Projections

Occasionally, we may want to use a risk model with *fewer* factors compared to the original one. At first glance, this operation may seem unjustified. If we trust that our risk model is the most accurate, why would we want to replace it with a different one? The reasons are many. For example, it may be the case that in practice the loadings of one or more factors are changing so fast as to make portfolio management and hedging difficult. Another reason is that we are using a vendor-provided model, and believe that the model is not perfect, i.e., some factors should be pruned from the model. A third reason may be that we want to provide the end user with a "simplified" risk model that is as accurate as possible, while retaining the full model for other uses. For these reasons and more, we need to find a different risk model that is close, in some sense, to the original one.

We have a model $\mathbf{r} = \boldsymbol{\alpha} + \mathbf{B}\mathbf{f} + \boldsymbol{\epsilon}$ and associated covariance matrix $\boldsymbol{\Omega}_\mathrm{r} = \mathbf{B}\boldsymbol{\Omega}_\mathrm{f}\mathbf{B}^\top + \boldsymbol{\Omega}_\epsilon$, but we want to employ a different loadings matrix **A**, in which the range of **A** is contained in the range of **B**. If we model returns as $\mathbf{r} = \boldsymbol{\alpha} + \mathbf{A}\mathbf{g} + \boldsymbol{\eta}$, the covariance matrix would be $\boldsymbol{\Omega}_\mathrm{r} = \mathbf{A}\boldsymbol{\Omega}_\mathrm{g}\mathbf{A}^\top + \boldsymbol{\Omega}_\eta$. What is the value **g** resulting in the best approximation to our original model? Let the distance between the original factor returns **f** and the approximate factor returns **g** be $\left\|\mathbf{B}\mathbf{f} - \mathbf{A}\mathbf{g}\right\|^2$. The distance-minimizing approximate factor returns are $\mathbf{g} = \mathbf{H}\mathbf{f}$, where $\mathbf{H} := (\mathbf{A}^\top\mathbf{A})^{-1}\mathbf{A}^\top\mathbf{B}$. The corresponding value of $\boldsymbol{\Omega}_\mathrm{g}$ is $\boldsymbol{\Omega}_\mathrm{g} = \mathbf{H}\boldsymbol{\Omega}_\mathrm{f}\mathbf{H}^\top$.

FAQ 4.3: *Which projections?*

What types of projections are useful in practice?

1. The columns of the matrix $\mathbf{A}$ are a subset of the columns of $\mathbf{B}$. Thus, we are attributing the maximum risk and performance to a nested factor model derived from the original one. This is by far the main application of projections.
2. The subspace spanned by the columns of $\mathbf{A}$ is not contained in that spanned by the columns of $\mathbf{B}$. In this case, the application is the qualitative ability of the second model to describe the factor risk predictions of the first model.

We call the operator a $\mathbf{H}$ projection because, like geometric projections, they are *idempotent*. An idempotent linear operator $\mathbf{\Pi}$ is such that $\mathbf{\Pi}^2\mathbf{x} = \mathbf{\Pi}\mathbf{x}$. The geometric intuition is that, once you have projected a vector on a plane, projecting the resulting vector again on the same plane does not result in another vector, since the input vector is already on the plane.

4.4.3 Push-Outs

In the previous two sections we introduced a transformation that preserves the number of factors and a transformation that reduces it. The last section focuses on a transformation that *increases* the number of factors. We therefore lift the loadings matrix into a new one, whose column space contains the column space of the old one. Why could this be of interest? A possible scenario that occurs in practice is that our factor model may have been developed on historical data that are not representative of the current regime. As a result, the idiosyncratic returns show some structure, in the sense that they themselves are amenable to be formulated as a different factor model:

$$\epsilon = \mathbf{A}\mathbf{g} + \boldsymbol{\eta}$$

with $\mathbf{A} \in \mathbb{R}^{n\times p}$, $\mathbf{g}$ a random variable (rv) taking values in $\mathbb{R}^p$ and $\boldsymbol{\eta}$ an rv taking values in $\mathbb{R}^n$. The new model becomes

$$\mathbf{r} = \boldsymbol{\alpha}_\perp + \mathbf{B}\mathbf{f} + \mathbf{A}\mathbf{g} + \boldsymbol{\eta} \tag{4.5}$$

with $\boldsymbol{\eta}$ uncorrelated from $\mathbf{f}, \mathbf{g}$. In the specification of the model (4.5), we require that $\mathbf{A}^\top\mathbf{B} = 0$. If not, the factor returns of the original model would have to be modified. To see this, assume that $\mathbf{B}^\top\mathbf{A} \neq 0$. Then we can decompose the columns of $\mathbf{A}$ into the sum of parallel and orthogonal components. In matrix terms, $\mathbf{A} = \mathbf{B}\mathbf{C} + \mathbf{H}$, for some $\mathbf{C} \in \mathbb{R}^{m\times p}$. It follows that the model $\mathbf{r} = \mathbf{B}\mathbf{f} + \mathbf{A}\mathbf{g} + \boldsymbol{\eta}$ can be written as $\mathbf{r} = \mathbf{B}(\mathbf{f} + \mathbf{C}\mathbf{g}) + \mathbf{H}\mathbf{g} + \boldsymbol{\eta}$.

$$\epsilon^\top\mathbf{B}\mathbf{f} = 0 \textit{ (original model orthogonality condition)}$$
$$\eta^\top\mathbf{A}\mathbf{g} = 0 \textit{ (residual model orthogonality condition)}$$
$$\eta^\top(\mathbf{B}\mathbf{f} + \mathbf{A}\mathbf{g}) = 0 \textit{ (final model orthogonality condition)}$$

From the second and third equalities it follows that $\boldsymbol{\eta}^\top\mathbf{B}\mathbf{f} = 0$; the first equality can be rewritten as $0 = (\mathbf{g}^\top\mathbf{A}^\top + \boldsymbol{\eta}^\top)\mathbf{B}\mathbf{f} = \mathbf{g}^\top\mathbf{A}^\top\mathbf{B}\mathbf{f}$ for all realizations of $\mathbf{f}, \mathbf{g}$, hence $\mathbf{A}^\top\mathbf{B} = 0$. The example above assumed that the idiosyncratic returns of each asset have the same volatility (homoskedastic volatilities). In Chapter 9 we will see how to augment a risk model in a characteristic model framework when idiosyncratic returns are heteroskedastic.

Exercise 4.1 ***(Excess Returns and Factor Models)*****:** In the academic literature the standard factor model (4.1) models the *excess* returns, defined as $(r_t)_i - r_f$, as per Section 2.1.2. On the other side, practitioners think in terms of returns, not excess returns.

- When in portfolio management is it incorrect to reason in terms of excess returns? When is it not?
- Show that a model of excess returns could be recast as a model of returns by adding a factor.
- Can you extend the modeling to incorporate sensitivities to interest rates?

4.5 Applications

4.5.1 Performance Attribution

What is the PnL of a portfolio in interval $[t-1, t]$?

$$\begin{aligned}
\textit{(portfolio PnL}_t\textit{)} &= \mathbf{w}_t^\top\mathbf{r}_t \\
&= \mathbf{w}_t^\top\mathbf{B}\mathbf{f}_t + \mathbf{w}_t^\top(\boldsymbol{\alpha}_\perp + \boldsymbol{\epsilon}_t) \\
&= \mathbf{b}_t^\top\mathbf{f}_t + \mathbf{w}_t^\top(\boldsymbol{\alpha}_\perp + \boldsymbol{\epsilon}_t) \qquad (\mathbf{b}_t := \mathbf{B}^\top\mathbf{w}_t)
\end{aligned}$$

The vector $\mathbf{b}_t \in \mathbb{R}^m$ represents the *factor exposures* of the portfolio at time t. The term $[\mathbf{b}_t]_i$ is the sum of the characteristics of factor i of each stock, weighted by the portfolio holdings; keep in mind that the characteristics and the weights can both be negative. The term $\mathbf{b}_t^\top \mathbf{f}_t$ is the factor PnL in time interval t, while the term $\mathbf{w}_t^\top(\boldsymbol{\alpha}_\perp + \boldsymbol{\epsilon}_t)$ is the idiosyncratic PnL. Summing up over a time interval $[1, \ldots, T]$, the PnL of a strategy is

$$\text{PnL} = \textit{(Factor PnL)} + \textit{(Idiosyncratic PnL)}$$

We can also distribute the sum differently:

$$\begin{aligned}
\text{PnL} &= \sum_{t=1}^{T} \textit{(Factor PnL}_t\textit{)} + \textit{(Idiosyncratic PnL}_t\textit{)} \\
&= \sum_{t=1}^{T}\sum_{j=1}^{m}[\mathbf{b}_t]_j[\mathbf{f}_t]_j + \sum_{t=1}^{T}\sum_{i=1}^{n}[\mathbf{w}_t]_i[\boldsymbol{\alpha}_\perp + \boldsymbol{\epsilon}_t]_i \\
&= \sum_{j=1}^{m} \textit{(Factor j PnL)} + \sum_{i=1}^{n} \textit{(Stock i Idiosyncratic PnL)}
\end{aligned}$$

And then, of course, one can partition factors and stocks in groups, to highlight, for example, the performance arising from style factors, from industry factors, or from a specific group of stocks.

4.5.2 Risk Management: Forecast and Decomposition

If we have a covariance matrix (not specifically from a factor model), the variance of a portfolio $\mathbf{w}$ is easy to compute: $\text{var}(\mathbf{r}^\top\mathbf{w}) = \sum_{i,j} \text{cov}(r_i w_i, r_j w_j) = \sum_{i,j} w_i \text{cov}(r_i, r_j) w_j = \mathbf{w}^\top \boldsymbol{\Omega}_\mathbf{r} \mathbf{w}$. We can apply the formula to a covariance matrix associated with a factor model:

$$\begin{aligned}
\text{var}(\mathbf{r}^\top\mathbf{w}) &= \mathbf{w}^\top(\mathbf{B}\boldsymbol{\Omega}_\mathbf{f}\mathbf{B}^\top + \boldsymbol{\Omega}_\epsilon)\mathbf{w} \\
&= \mathbf{b}^\top\boldsymbol{\Omega}_\mathbf{f}\mathbf{b} + \mathbf{w}^\top\boldsymbol{\Omega}_\epsilon\mathbf{w}
\end{aligned}$$

The formula has two applications. The first one is an estimate of a portfolio's *ex-ante* volatility at any point in time. This is an important piece of information for risk managers, since they monitor volatility and allocate risk based on this measure. The second application is the decomposition of variance in factor and idiosyncratic components. Like in the attribution case, the formula is a jumping-off point. For example, a commonly quoted statistic for a strategy is the *percentage of idiosyncratic variance*, defined as 100 × (dollar idiosyncratic variance)/(total variance); the percentage of idiosyncratic variance and factor variance sum to 100, of course. The factor variance can be decomposed further by making factor partitions. The most detailed one has each factor being a singleton, but very common choices are (style group)/(industry group)/(country group), or (subsectors group)/(style group)/(country group). This measure, and the associated sensitivities, are commonly used to monitor strategies. Every partition, either of factors or of assets, induces a covariance matrix $\mathbf{\Omega} \in \mathbb{R}^{p \times p}$ where $\mathbf{\Omega}_{i,j}$ is the covariance between partition group i and j. For example, say that a portfolio has factor exposure $\mathbf{b}$, and we partition the factors into groups $1, \ldots, p$, with group i containing the subset of elements $\mathcal{S}(i)$. Define $\mathbf{b}_{\mathcal{S}(i)}$ as a vector of factor exposures where all the terms not in $\mathcal{S}(i)$ are set equal to zero. Define $\mathbf{\Omega}$ as the covariance matrix of the sets' PnLs:

$$\mathbf{\Omega} = \begin{bmatrix} \mathbf{b}^\top_{\mathcal{S}(1)}\mathbf{\Omega}_{1,1}\mathbf{b}_{\mathcal{S}(1)} & \ldots & \mathbf{b}^\top_{\mathcal{S}(1)}\mathbf{\Omega}_{1,p}\mathbf{b}_{\mathcal{S}(p)} \\ \ldots & \ldots & \ldots \\ \mathbf{b}^\top_{\mathcal{S}(p)}\mathbf{\Omega}_{p,1}\mathbf{b}_{\mathcal{S}(1)} & \ldots & \mathbf{b}^\top_{\mathcal{S}(p)}\mathbf{\Omega}_{p,p}\mathbf{b}_{\mathcal{S}(p)} \end{bmatrix}$$

Then the total factor variance is $v^2_{\text{TOT}} := \mathbf{e}^\top\mathbf{\Omega}\mathbf{e}$, where $\mathbf{e} := (1 \ldots 1)^\top$. The ith group's variance is $v_i^2 := \mathbf{b}^\top_{\mathcal{S}(i)}\mathbf{\Omega}_{i,i}\mathbf{b}_{\mathcal{S}(i)}$.

- *Fraction of total variance* for group i is

$$\begin{aligned} p_i &:= \frac{\textit{(variance of group i + half of covariance contributions)}}{\textit{(portfolio variance)}} \\ &= \frac{\sum_j \mathbf{\Omega}_{i,j}}{v^2_{\text{TOT}}} \\ &= \frac{\text{cov}(\mathbf{r}_i, \mathbf{r}_{\text{TOT}})}{v^2_{\text{TOT}}} \\ &= \beta_i \qquad \textit{(beta of ith factor group's PnL to total PnL)} \end{aligned}$$

So that $\sum_i p_i = 1$. The percentage of variance of a group $\mathcal{S}(i)$ (again, this includes single factors and single assets—perhaps the most commonly used partition!) is simply the beta of returns of the group to the overall portfolio.

- *Marginal contribution to risk* (MCR) of a group $\mathcal{S}(i)$ is defined as

$$
\begin{aligned}
m_i &:= \frac{\textit{(portfolio \$vol change when we buy \$1M vol of set } S(i))}{\$1\text{M}} \\
&= \frac{\partial}{\partial(x_i v_i)} \sqrt{\mathbf{x}^\top \boldsymbol{\Omega} \mathbf{x}} \Big|_{\mathbf{x}=\mathbf{e}} \\
&= \frac{1}{v_i v_{\text{TOT}}} \sum_j [\boldsymbol{\Omega}]_{i,j} \\
&= \rho_i \qquad \textit{(correlation of ith factor group's PnL to total PnL)} \\
&= \frac{v_{\text{TOT}}}{v_i} p_i
\end{aligned}
$$

- *Sharpe Ratio sensitivity*. It is also useful to compute the sensitivity of the Sharpe Ratio to changes in volatility of a group. The total portfolio's *Sharpe Ratio sensitivity* with respect to volatility increase of group i is given by

$$
\begin{aligned}
\frac{\partial}{\partial(v_i x_i)} \frac{E(PnL)}{\text{vol}(PnL)} &= \frac{\text{vol}(PnL) \times \frac{\partial E(PnL)}{\partial(x_i v_i)} - \frac{\partial \text{vol}(PnL)}{\partial(x_i v_i)} \times E(PnL)}{\text{var}\,(PnL)} \\
&= \frac{\text{vol}(PnL) \times \frac{\partial E(PnL)}{\partial(x_i v_i)} - m_i \times \text{SR}_{\text{TOT}} \times \text{vol}(PnL)}{\text{var}\,(PnL)} \\
&= \frac{\text{SR}_{\text{TOT}}}{v_{\text{TOT}}} \left(\frac{\text{SR}_i}{\text{SR}_{\text{TOT}}} - m_i \right)
\end{aligned}
$$

The contribution to total Sharpe Ratio is positive if the Sharpe Ratio of a group exceeds a threshold, which is its marginal contribution to risk times the total Sharpe Ratio.

FAQ 4.4: *Do model rotations affect risk decompositions?*

When we rotate a factor model, we transform the factor loadings and factor covariance matrix as $\tilde{\mathbf{B}} = \mathbf{B}\mathbf{C}^{-1}$ and $\tilde{\boldsymbol{\Omega}}_{\mathrm{f}} = \mathbf{C}\boldsymbol{\Omega}_{\mathrm{f}}\mathbf{C}^\top$ respectively. In the rotated model, the factor exposures of portfolio $\mathbf{w}$ are $\tilde{\mathbf{b}} = \tilde{\mathbf{B}}^\top \mathbf{w} = (\mathbf{C}^\top)^{-1} \mathbf{b}$, and the factor risk is $\tilde{\mathbf{b}}^\top \tilde{\boldsymbol{\Omega}}_{\mathrm{f}} \tilde{\mathbf{b}} = \mathbf{b}^\top \mathbf{C}^{-1} (\mathbf{C}\boldsymbol{\Omega}_{\mathrm{f}}\mathbf{C}^\top)(\mathbf{C}^\top)^{-1} \mathbf{b} = \mathbf{b}^\top \boldsymbol{\Omega}_{\mathrm{f}} \mathbf{b}$. The total factor variance is unchanged. The total (and single-asset) idiosyncratic variance is unchanged too, as it does not depend on rotations. However, the single-factor risk variance is affected by rotations. Rather than being a drawback, this is a plus. It affords us the flexibility to attribute risk to factor groups that are more meaningful (e.g., more intuitive) than others.

FAQ 4.5: *Why not use the empirical covariance matrix?*

Before treating factor model estimation, we address a preliminary question. Given a time series of returns $\mathbf{r}_t$ with population covariance matrix $\Omega_{\mathbf{r}}$, its simplest estimator is the empirical covariance

$$\hat{\boldsymbol{\Omega}}_{\mathbf{r}} = \frac{1}{T}\sum_{t=1}^{T} \mathbf{r}_t \mathbf{r}_t^{\top}$$

or, if we denote $\mathbf{R} \in \mathbb{R}^{n \times T}$ the matrix of returns where $\mathbf{R}_{\cdot,t} = \mathbf{r}_t$, we can write $\hat{\boldsymbol{\Omega}}_{\mathbf{r}} = T^{-1}\mathbf{R}\mathbf{R}^{\top}$. It is well known (and easy to establish) that this estimate maximizes the log-likelihood for a normal multivariate distribution, is asymptotically consistent, and a Central Limit Theorem is available (Anderson, 1963). Why not use this as our estimate for our covariance matrix? The reason is that, when $T \ll n$, the estimator is very inadequate for volatility estimation and portfolio optimization purposes. The covariance matrix has at most rank T. Let $\mathbf{w}_i, i = 1, \ldots, T - n$ be a basis for the null space of $\mathbf{R}^{\top}$, i.e., $\mathbf{R}^{\top}\mathbf{w}_i = 0$. We can interpret these vectors as portfolios. The volatility of portfolio i is $\mathbf{w}_i^{\top}\hat{\boldsymbol{\Omega}}_{\mathbf{r}}\mathbf{w}_i = T^{-1}\left\|\mathbf{R}^{\top}\mathbf{w}_i\right\|^2 = 0$. So, a majority of independent portfolios has zero volatility. The situation is even worse in portfolio optimization. The solution of the mean-variance problem $\max_{\mathbf{w}}[\boldsymbol{\alpha}^{\top} - (2\lambda)^{-1}\mathbf{w}^{\top}\hat{\boldsymbol{\Omega}}_{\mathbf{r}}\mathbf{w}]$ is $\mathbf{w} = \lambda\boldsymbol{\Omega}_{\mathbf{r}}^{-1}\boldsymbol{\alpha}$. In this case, if $\boldsymbol{\alpha}$ is in the null space of $\boldsymbol{\Omega}$, the portfolio is undefined. Choosing an alpha close to the null space yields an arbitrarily large portfolio, and an arbitrarily large Sharpe Ratio.

4.5.3 Portfolio Management

Factor models are useful for portfolio management in several ways. The first one is adjacent to risk management: volatility is the common language spoken by risk managers and portfolio managers, and it is oftentimes generated by a factor model. The second one is the inverse of the covariance matrix, also known as *precision matrix*. This matrix plays a central role in portfolio optimization. As discussed in FAQ 4.5, the empirical covariance matrix is usually not invertible. The factor structure makes it possible to estimate both $\mathbf{\Omega}_\mathbf{r}$ and $\mathbf{\Omega}_\mathbf{r}^{-1}$. The third is the model of the expected asset returns as the sum of two terms: $\boldsymbol{\alpha}$ and $\mathbf{B}^\top E(\mathbf{f})$. These two terms give rise to two qualitatively different classes of expected returns. This makes sense intuitively, since the factor-based returns come with some variability and risk, which is itself captured by the factor covariance matrix $\mathbf{\Omega}_\mathbf{f}$. The alpha term, instead, comes with apparently no risk. How to manage these sources of returns is the concern of *portfolio management*. Lastly, a factor model is *legible*: when applied to a portfolio, it produces factor exposures, risk and performance decompositions, as discussed above. Legibility makes the job of the portfolio managers easier, since it enables them to plan (before the trade), monitor (during the trade), and understand (after the trade) their strategies.

4.5.4 Alpha Research

As volatility is the *lingua franca* spoken by risk managers and portfolio managers, so alpha is what a signal researcher and a portfolio manager both understand. At the cost of excessive generalization, one could say that the signal researcher cares about $\boldsymbol{\alpha}$, the risk manager cares about **Bf**, and the portfolio manager adds trading costs and tries to combine all these terms into a profitable strategy. In reality, there is "risky" alpha worth trading contained in the term **Bf**. I use the language loosely for the time being, with the goal of tightening it in coming chapters. Furthermore, sometimes these people are one and the same, although the roles in sufficiently large and complex strategies are increasingly separated. Alpha research is improved by factor models in two ways. First, **Bf** is important, and for a certain class of investors it is the only thing that matters.[12] Second, the factor-based approach helps separate the two sources of expected returns

[12] A marketing term used for this investment style is *smart beta*.

for a portfolio. One source arises from having factor exposure. These returns come with the associated risk of variable factor returns. The second source is the "true intercept" of returns; i.e., having exposure to the alpha vector.

4.6 Factor Models Types

The model we use from here on is given by Equation (4.1). We have taken the model for granted. But where do the data and parameters of the model come from? In the case of factor models, the answer is especially important, because the meaning attached to the various symbols matters. Practitioners use three broad approaches to identify all the parameters in the equation:

- *Characteristic model.* This is the most common approach. The input data to the model are the time series $\mathbf{r}_t$ and $\mathbf{B}_t$. Factor and idiosyncratic returns are estimated from these data. We define $\mathbf{B}_t$ as a matrix of *asset characteristics* available[13] at the beginning of the interval $[t-1, t]$. The intuition is that these characteristics are partially responsible for the stock return. I cover this in Chapter 6.
- *Statistical model.* In this model, the only primitive is $\mathbf{r}_t$, and $\mathbf{B}_t$, $\mathbf{f}_t$ and $\boldsymbol{\epsilon}_t$ are all estimated. I cover these models in Chapter 7.
- *Macroeconomic model.* In this approach, the primitives are $\mathbf{r}_t$ and $\mathbf{f}_t$, and $\mathbf{B}_t$ and $\boldsymbol{\epsilon}_t$ are estimated. $\mathbf{f}_t$ usually represents a vector of macroeconomic time series.

The relevant methodological issues the modeler must address are:

1. What are the best loss functions to evaluate a model?
2. Once we have estimates (or primitive data) about factor and idiosyncratic returns, how do we estimate the covariance matrices from cross-sectional estimates?
3. What is the best approach within each framework?

---

[13] Important: when using commercial data, always check the data specification to make sure that the time index for the loadings is not off by one. Most vendors use the timestamp t for data available at the end of the interval $[t-1, t]$.

4.7 ⋆Appendix

4.7.1 Linear Regression

Linear models are by far the most widespread class of models in statistics. There are more books on the subject than citizens of the sovereign state of the Vatican.[14] In fact, one could argue there is so much material on linear models that two humans on planet Earth may have completely different interpretations of them. In order to have some common ground, we will describe some less well-known aspects which will be needed later. Our setting is as follows. We are given a pair $(y, \mathbf{x})$, where y is a random variable taking values in $\mathbb{R}$ and $\mathbf{x}$ is a random vector taking values in $\mathbb{R}^m$. The random variables y and $\mathbf{x}$ are in general dependent: knowing the value of a realization of $\mathbf{x}$ tells us something about the values of y and this makes the problem infinitely interesting. Say that we want to provide a forecast of y, which we denote $\hat{y}(\mathbf{x})$. One way to select such forecast is to try to minimize a loss function; we should pay a price for being wrong. One natural choice of loss is the quadratic loss: it is non-negative; it is symmetric; it is differentiable; and it penalizes more for large errors. The problem we face is

$$\min_{\hat{y}} E[(\hat{y}(\mathbf{x}) - y)^2|\mathbf{x}] \tag{4.6}$$

One basic result in statistics[15] and in control theory is that, if $E(y^2|\mathbf{x}) < \infty$, the function that minimizes this expectation is the conditional expectation of y given $\mathbf{x}$. We introduce a new variable ϵ:

$$y = E(y|\mathbf{x}) + \epsilon \tag{4.7}$$

It follows that $E(\epsilon|\mathbf{x}) = E(y|\mathbf{x}) - E(E(y|\mathbf{x})|\mathbf{x}) = 0$. Then we use the following chain:

[14] Not a joke: as of October 2024, the Vatican has 764 citizens; Amazon lists over 1,400 books in the "Probability and Statistics" section with "regression" in their title or subject, the vast majority of them covering linear models.

[15] Linear regression is an inexhaustible topic. Some useful references are, in order of increasing detail, Wasserman (2004), Hastie et al. (2008), Johnson and Wichern (2007), Harrell (2015), Gelman et al. (2022), Hansen (2022).

$$
\begin{aligned}
E[(\hat{y}(\mathbf{x}) - y)^2|\mathbf{x}] &= E[(\hat{y}(\mathbf{x}) - E(y|\mathbf{x}) + E(y|\mathbf{x}) - y)^2|\mathbf{x}] \\
&= E[\epsilon^2|\mathbf{x}] + E[(\hat{y} - E(y|\mathbf{x}))^2|\mathbf{x}] - 2E[\epsilon|\mathbf{x}] \\
&\quad (y - E(y|\mathbf{x})) \\
&= E(\epsilon^2|\mathbf{x}) + E[(\hat{y} - E(y|\mathbf{x})^2|\mathbf{x}] \\
&\geq E(\epsilon^2|\mathbf{x})
\end{aligned}
$$

The equality holds only if $\hat{y} = E(y|\mathbf{x})$. The term $E[\epsilon^2|\mathbf{x}]$ is finite, because

$$
\begin{aligned}
E(\epsilon^2|\mathbf{x}) &\leq 2E(y^2|\mathbf{x}) + 2E[E(y|\mathbf{x})^2|\mathbf{x}] \\
&\leq 2E(y^2|\mathbf{x}) + 2E[E(y^2|\mathbf{x})|\mathbf{x}] && \textit{(Jensen)} \\
&= 4E(y^2|\mathbf{x}) && \textit{(Iterated Expectation)} \\
&< \infty
\end{aligned}
$$

In applications, we have n samples $(y_i, \mathbf{x}_i)$ and we choose a functional form for $\hat{y} = g(\mathbf{x}, \boldsymbol{\theta})$, where $\boldsymbol{\theta}$ is a finite- or infinite-dimensional vector of parameters. We then minimize the *empirical* squared loss $n^{-1} \sum_i (y_i - g(\mathbf{x}, \boldsymbol{\theta}))^2$. The simplest form of g is linear: $g(\mathbf{x}, \boldsymbol{\beta}) = \sum_i \beta_i x_i$. In matrix form, Equation (4.7) becomes

$$\mathbf{y} = \mathbf{X}\boldsymbol{\beta} + \boldsymbol{\epsilon} \tag{4.8}$$

where $\mathbf{y} \in \mathbb{R}^n$, $\mathbf{X} \in \mathbb{R}^{n \times m}$, $\boldsymbol{\beta} \in \mathbb{R}^m$. The integers n and m denote the number of observations and the "features," respectively. We want to estimate the parameters $\boldsymbol{\beta}$, leading to estimates for $\mathbf{X}\boldsymbol{\beta}$. We then minimize the empirical loss

$$\min_{\beta} \left\| \mathbf{y} - \mathbf{X}\boldsymbol{\beta} \right\|^2 \tag{4.9}$$

which is equal to the unweighted sum of squared errors (*Ordinary Least Squares*, OLS)$(y_i - \sum_j [\mathbf{X}]_{i,j} \beta_j)^2$. A different way to arrive at the same problem is to posit that the true model is Equation (4.8), and to further assume that $\boldsymbol{\epsilon} \sim N(0, \sigma^2 \mathbf{I}_n)$. If we fix $\boldsymbol{\beta}$, we have $\boldsymbol{\epsilon} = \mathbf{y} - \mathbf{X}\boldsymbol{\beta}$; and since we know the distribution of $\boldsymbol{\epsilon}$, we can associate to a choice of $\boldsymbol{\beta}$ a *likelihood* $f(\boldsymbol{\epsilon}|\boldsymbol{\beta})$. If we choose the parameter $\boldsymbol{\beta}$ to maximize the likelihood, we end up solving the same problem as Equation (4.9). The choice of maximizing the likelihood is called the *Maximum Likelihood Principle* (MLP).[16]

[16] For a detailed discussion of the MLP, see Robert (2007).

Finally, there is a geometrical interpretation for the regression problem. You can interpret the set $S := \{\mathbf{X}\boldsymbol{\beta} | \boldsymbol{\beta} \in \mathbb{R}^m\}$ as a subspace of $\mathbb{R}^n$. The columns of $\mathbf{X}$ are a (generally non-orthonormal) basis of the subspace. We are then given a point $\mathbf{y} \in \mathbb{R}$ and find the point $\hat{\mathbf{y}} \in S$ that is closest to $\mathbf{y}$. This is the definition of a projection of $\mathbf{y}$ on S. The projection is a linear operator. The minimum distance[17] is attained at

$$\hat{\boldsymbol{\beta}} = (\mathbf{X}^\top\mathbf{X})^{-1}\mathbf{X}^\top\mathbf{y} \tag{4.10}$$

and the estimates $\hat{\mathbf{y}} := E(\mathbf{y}|\boldsymbol{\beta})$ are

$$\begin{aligned} \hat{\mathbf{y}} &= \mathbf{X}\hat{\boldsymbol{\beta}} \\ &= \mathbf{X}(\mathbf{X}^\top\mathbf{X})^{-1}\mathbf{X}^\top\mathbf{y} \end{aligned} \tag{4.11}$$

The matrix $\mathbf{H} = \mathbf{X}(\mathbf{X}^\top\mathbf{X})^{-1}\mathbf{X}^\top$ is called the *hat matrix* or *projection matrix*. The estimated residuals are

$$\hat{\epsilon} = (\mathbf{I} - \mathbf{H})\mathbf{y}$$

Intuitively, the optimal estimates should not change if we change the basis of the subspace. To see this rigorously, transform $\mathbf{X}$ into $\mathbf{XQ}$, where $\mathbf{Q} \in \mathbb{R}^{m \times m}$ is non-singular. The transformed set of predictors spans the same subspace as $\mathbf{X}$. Then

$$\begin{aligned} \hat{\mathbf{y}} &= \mathbf{XQ}((\mathbf{XQ})^\top\mathbf{XQ})^{-1}(\mathbf{XQ})^\top\mathbf{y} \\ &= \mathbf{XQ}(\mathbf{Q}^\top\mathbf{X}^\top\mathbf{XQ})^{-1}\mathbf{Q}^\top\mathbf{X}^\top\mathbf{y} \\ &= \mathbf{XQQ}^{-1}(\mathbf{X}^\top\mathbf{X})^{-1}(\mathbf{Q}^\top)^{-1}\mathbf{Q}^\top\mathbf{X}^\top\mathbf{y} \\ &= \mathbf{X}(\mathbf{X}^\top\mathbf{X})^{-1}\mathbf{X}^\top\mathbf{y} \end{aligned} \tag{4.12}$$

hence $\mathbf{y}$ is independent of base representation.

Another property of the estimate $\hat{\mathbf{y}}$ is that, if we iterate the estimation process on the estimate $\hat{\mathbf{y}}$, we obtain again $\hat{\mathbf{y}}$. This also has a geometric interpretation. Once a point has been projected on a hyperplane, the projection of the projection is unchanged. In algebraic terms, $\mathbf{H}\hat{\mathbf{y}} = \mathbf{H}^2\mathbf{y} = \mathbf{H}\mathbf{y} = \hat{\mathbf{y}}$.

---

[17] The minimum is unique if the rank of $\mathbf{X}$ is m, i.e., if all the columns of $\mathbf{X}$ are linearly independent. In Chapter 6 we will encounter cases of rank-deficient matrices.

Here is another facet of linear regression tying geometric and algebraic interpretations of linear regression. Decompose $\mathbf{X}$ using the SVD: $\mathbf{X} = \mathbf{U}\boldsymbol{\Lambda}\mathbf{V}^{\top}$. $\mathbf{U}$ is an orthonormal basis for the column subspace of $\mathbf{x}$. Then

$$\begin{aligned}\hat{\mathbf{y}} &= \mathbf{U}\boldsymbol{\Lambda}\mathbf{V}^{\top}(\mathbf{V}\boldsymbol{\Lambda}\mathbf{U}^{\top}\mathbf{U}\boldsymbol{\Lambda}\mathbf{V}^{\top})^{-1}\mathbf{V}\boldsymbol{\Lambda}\mathbf{U}^{\top}\mathbf{y}\\ &= \mathbf{U}\mathbf{U}^{\top}\mathbf{y}\end{aligned}$$

So $\mathbf{y}$ is projected on the column space of $\mathbf{U}$.

Replace Equation (4.8) in the beta estimation formula (4.10) to obtain

$$\begin{aligned}\hat{\beta} &= (\mathbf{X}^{\top}\mathbf{X})^{-1}\mathbf{X}^{\top}(\mathbf{X}\beta + \epsilon)\\ &= \beta + (\mathbf{X}^{\top}\mathbf{X})^{-1}\mathbf{X}^{\top}\epsilon\end{aligned}$$

The estimate of beta is unbiased, because $E[(\mathbf{X}^{\top}\mathbf{X})^{-1}\mathbf{X}^{\top}\epsilon] = 0$; and the covariance matrix of $\hat{\boldsymbol{\beta}}$ is

$$\text{var}(\hat{\boldsymbol{\beta}}) = \sigma^2(\mathbf{X}^{\top}\mathbf{X})^{-1} \tag{4.13}$$

Similarly,

$$\text{var}(\hat{y}) = \sigma^2\mathbf{X}(\mathbf{X}^{\top}\mathbf{X})^{-1}\mathbf{X}^{\top}$$

We can write these formulas using the SVD:

$$\text{var}(\hat{\boldsymbol{\beta}}) = \sigma^2\mathbf{V}\boldsymbol{\Lambda}^{-2}\mathbf{V}^{\top} \tag{4.14}$$

$$\text{var}(\hat{\mathbf{y}}) = \sigma^2\mathbf{U}\mathbf{U}^{\top} \tag{4.15}$$

The variance of the estimates $\text{var}(\hat{\boldsymbol{\beta}})$ becomes larger as the columns of X become more collinear. In our interpretation of the matrix $\mathbf{X}$, this occurs when we include factors that overlap heavily with preexisting ones.

The estimation formulas extend directly to the case of *heteroskedastic noise*. In this case we assume that $\boldsymbol{\epsilon} \sim N(0, \boldsymbol{\Omega}_{\epsilon})$, where $\boldsymbol{\Omega}_{\epsilon}$ is a positive-definite matrix. The estimates for $\hat{\boldsymbol{\beta}}$, $\hat{\mathbf{y}}$, and $\text{var}(\hat{\boldsymbol{\beta}})$ can be derived directly from the previous formulas, by left-multiplying by $\boldsymbol{\Omega}_{\epsilon}^{-1/2}$ both sides of Equation (4.8):

$$\boldsymbol{\Omega}_{\epsilon}^{-1/2}\mathbf{y} = \boldsymbol{\Omega}_{\epsilon}^{-1/2}\mathbf{X}\boldsymbol{\beta} + \boldsymbol{\Omega}_{\epsilon}^{-1/2}\boldsymbol{\epsilon}$$

Notice that $\boldsymbol{\Omega}_\epsilon^{-1/2}\boldsymbol{\epsilon}$ is distributed according to a standard normal (exercise), so that the noise is homoskedastic; and we apply the OLS results to obtain the *Weighted Least Squares* (WLS) formulas

$$\hat{\boldsymbol{\beta}} = (\mathbf{X}^\top\boldsymbol{\Omega}_\epsilon^{-1}\mathbf{X})^{-1}\mathbf{X}^\top\boldsymbol{\Omega}_\epsilon^{-1}\mathbf{y} \tag{4.16}$$

$$\text{var}(\hat{\boldsymbol{\beta}}) = (\mathbf{X}^\top\boldsymbol{\Omega}_\epsilon^{-1}\mathbf{X})^{-1} \tag{4.17}$$

$$\hat{\mathbf{y}} = \mathbf{X}(\mathbf{X}^\top\boldsymbol{\Omega}_\epsilon^{-1}\mathbf{X})^{-1}\mathbf{X}^\top\boldsymbol{\Omega}_\epsilon^{-1}\mathbf{y} \tag{4.18}$$

Exercise 4.2: If a matrix $\mathbf{X} \in \mathbb{R}^{n\times m}$ has near collinear columns, then there is a unit-norm vector $\mathbf{u}$ such that $\|\mathbf{Xu}\|^2 = h$ for some small positive h.

1. Show that $\mathbf{u}^\top(\mathbf{X}^\top\mathbf{X})\mathbf{u} = h$.
2. Let λ_i be the eigenvalues of $\mathbf{X}^\top\mathbf{X}$. Show that $\min_i \lambda_i^2 \le h$.
3. From this, show that $\sum_i \text{var}(\hat{\boldsymbol{\beta}}_i)^2 \ge \max_i \lambda_i^{-2} \ge 1/h = \|\mathbf{Xu}\|^{-2}$.

4.7.2 Linear Regression Decomposition

Split Equation (4.8) into two parts:

$$\mathbf{y} = \begin{bmatrix}\mathbf{X}_1 & \mathbf{X}_2\end{bmatrix}\begin{bmatrix}\boldsymbol{\beta}_1\\ \boldsymbol{\beta}_2\end{bmatrix} + \boldsymbol{\epsilon} \tag{4.19}$$

where we have partitioned the predictors $\mathbf{X}$ into two blocks. Equation (4.10) can be rewritten by using block matrices for $\mathbf{X}^\top\mathbf{X}$ and $\mathbf{X}^\top\mathbf{y}$, and the formula for the inverse of block matrices, in order to obtain $\hat{\boldsymbol{\beta}}_1$, $\hat{\boldsymbol{\beta}}_2$. It can be shown that the coefficient $\hat{\boldsymbol{\beta}}_2$ can be estimated by a two-step process. First, regress the columns of $\mathbf{X}_2$ on those of $\mathbf{X}_1$: $\mathbf{X}_2 = \mathbf{X}_1\boldsymbol{\gamma} + \tilde{\mathbf{X}}_2$, where $(\mathbf{X}_2 - \mathbf{X}_1\boldsymbol{\gamma})^\top\tilde{\mathbf{X}}_2 = 0$. The matrix $\tilde{\mathbf{X}}_2$ contains the components of the column vectors of $\mathbf{X}_2$ that are orthogonal to the columns of $\mathbf{X}_1$ (we say that $\tilde{\mathbf{X}}_2$ is the projection on the *orthogonal complement* of the subspace spanned by $\mathbf{X}_1$). The subspace spanned by $[\mathbf{X}_1|\tilde{\mathbf{X}}_2]$ is the same as the subspace spanned by $[\mathbf{X}_1|\mathbf{X}_2]$ (if you do not see it, prove it). Therefore, the estimates $\hat{\mathbf{y}}$ and $\hat{\boldsymbol{\epsilon}}$ in Equation (4.19) are unchanged. Second, regress $\mathbf{y}$ on $\tilde{\mathbf{X}}_2$:

$$\mathbf{y} = \tilde{\mathbf{X}}_2\boldsymbol{\beta}_3 + \boldsymbol{\eta}$$

It can be proven (see, e.g., Hansen (2022), Ch. 2.23; or prove it yourself as an exercise) that the least-squares coefficient of this regression is the same as $\hat{\boldsymbol{\beta}}_2$, i.e., $\hat{\boldsymbol{\beta}}_3 = \hat{\boldsymbol{\beta}}_2$.

4.7.3 *The Frisch–Waugh–Lovell Theorem*

Let us continue along the line of reasoning of the previous section, where we characterized groups of regressors, as in Equation (4.19). As we did above, we remove from the columns of $\mathbf{X}_2$ the component collinear to the columns of $\mathbf{X}_1$ and denote the resulting matrix $\tilde{\mathbf{X}}_2$.

However, this transformation enables us to perform regressions in consecutive stages, where each stage solves a stand-alone linear estimation problem. This insight is formalized in the following theorem.

Theorem 4.1 ***(Frisch–Waugh–Lovell):*** *Denote the reference model*

$$\mathbf{y} = \mathbf{X}_1\boldsymbol{\beta}_1 + \tilde{\mathbf{X}}_2\boldsymbol{\beta}_2 + \boldsymbol{\epsilon} \tag{4.20}$$

whose estimated parameters are $\hat{\boldsymbol{\beta}}_1, \hat{\boldsymbol{\beta}}_2, \hat{\boldsymbol{\epsilon}}$.

Estimate the system in stages. The first-stage model is

$$\mathbf{y} = \mathbf{X}_1\boldsymbol{\gamma}_1 + \boldsymbol{\eta}_1 \tag{4.21}$$

from which we get estimates $\hat{\boldsymbol{\gamma}}_1, \hat{\boldsymbol{\eta}}_1$.

The second-stage model uses $\hat{\boldsymbol{\eta}}_1$ *from the first stage:*

$$\hat{\boldsymbol{\eta}}_1 = \tilde{\mathbf{X}}_2\boldsymbol{\gamma}_2 + \boldsymbol{\eta}_2 \tag{4.22}$$

from which we get estimates $\hat{\boldsymbol{\gamma}}_2, \hat{\boldsymbol{\eta}}_2$. *The following identities hold:*

$$\begin{aligned}
\hat{\boldsymbol{\gamma}}_1 &= \hat{\boldsymbol{\beta}}_1 \\
\hat{\boldsymbol{\gamma}}_2 &= \hat{\boldsymbol{\beta}}_2 \\
\hat{\boldsymbol{\eta}}_2 &= \hat{\boldsymbol{\epsilon}}
\end{aligned}$$

Proof. We use the hat matrix of $\mathbf{X}_1$, $\mathbf{H} = \mathbf{X}_1(\mathbf{X}_1^\top\mathbf{X}_1)^{-1}\mathbf{X}_1^\top$. The operator is a projection, i.e., $\mathbf{H}^2 = \mathbf{H}$ and $(\mathbf{I}_n - \mathbf{H})^2 = \mathbf{I}_n - \mathbf{H}$. First, we characterize the solutions for $\hat{\boldsymbol{\beta}}_1, \hat{\boldsymbol{\beta}}_2$. We use the property that $\mathbf{X}_1^\top\tilde{\mathbf{X}}_2 = \mathbf{X}_1^\top(\mathbf{I}_n - \mathbf{H})\mathbf{X}_2 = (\mathbf{X} - \mathbf{X})\mathbf{X}_2 = 0$.

$$
\begin{aligned}
\mathbf{y} &= \begin{bmatrix} \mathbf{X}_1 & \tilde{\mathbf{X}}_2 \end{bmatrix} \begin{bmatrix} \boldsymbol{\beta}_1 \\ \boldsymbol{\beta}_2 \end{bmatrix} + \epsilon \\
\begin{bmatrix} \hat{\boldsymbol{\beta}}_1 \\ \hat{\boldsymbol{\beta}}_2 \end{bmatrix} &= \begin{bmatrix} \mathbf{X}_1^\top \mathbf{X}_1 & \mathbf{X}_1^\top \tilde{\mathbf{X}}_2 \\ \tilde{\mathbf{X}}_2^\top \mathbf{X}_1 & \tilde{\mathbf{X}}_2^\top \tilde{\mathbf{X}}_2 \end{bmatrix}^{-1} \begin{bmatrix} \mathbf{X}_1^\top \\ \tilde{\mathbf{X}}_2^\top \end{bmatrix} \mathbf{y} \\
\hat{\boldsymbol{\beta}}_1 &= (\mathbf{X}_1^\top \mathbf{X}_1)^{-1} \mathbf{X}_1^\top \mathbf{y} \\
\hat{\boldsymbol{\beta}}_2 &= (\tilde{\mathbf{X}}_2^\top \tilde{\mathbf{X}}_2)^{-1} \tilde{\mathbf{X}}_2^\top \mathbf{y}
\end{aligned}
$$

Now, let us write the outputs $\hat{\boldsymbol{\beta}}_1, \tilde{\mathbf{X}}_2$ of the first stage:

$$
\begin{aligned}
\hat{\boldsymbol{\eta}}_1 &= (\mathbf{I}_n - \mathbf{H})\mathbf{y} \\
\tilde{\mathbf{X}}_2 &= (\mathbf{I}_n - \mathbf{H})\mathbf{X}_2
\end{aligned}
$$

Those are used to generate $\hat{\boldsymbol{\gamma}}_1, \hat{\boldsymbol{\gamma}}_2$. We show that they are identical to $\hat{\boldsymbol{\beta}}_1, \hat{\boldsymbol{\beta}}_2$:

$$
\begin{aligned}
\hat{\gamma}_1 &= (\mathbf{X}_1^\top \mathbf{X}_1)^{-1} \mathbf{X}_1^\top \mathbf{y} \\
&= \hat{\beta}_1 \\
\hat{\gamma}_2 &= (\tilde{\mathbf{X}}_2^\top \tilde{\mathbf{X}}_2)^{-1} \tilde{\mathbf{X}}_2^\top \hat{\eta}_1 \\
&= (\mathbf{X}_2^\top (\mathbf{I}_n - \mathbf{H})^2 \mathbf{X}_2)^{-1} \mathbf{X}_2^\top (\mathbf{I}_n - \mathbf{H})\mathbf{y} \\
&= (\tilde{\mathbf{X}}_2^\top \tilde{\mathbf{X}}_2)^{-1} \tilde{\mathbf{X}}_2^\top \mathbf{y} \\
&= \hat{\beta}_2
\end{aligned}
$$

The equality of $\hat{\boldsymbol{\eta}}_2$ and $\hat{\boldsymbol{\epsilon}}$ follows from Equations (4.20)–(4.22). ■

We close the section with two remarks.

- In Section 4.7.2 we showed that Equation (4.22) yields the same estimate as the regression on the total returns, i.e., that the coefficient estimated using $\hat{\boldsymbol{\eta}}_1 = \tilde{\mathbf{X}}_2 \boldsymbol{\gamma}_2 + \boldsymbol{\eta}_2$ and $\mathbf{r} = \tilde{\mathbf{X}}_2 \boldsymbol{\beta}_3 + \boldsymbol{\eta}$ gives identical estimates: $\hat{\boldsymbol{\gamma}}_2 = \hat{\boldsymbol{\beta}}_3$. This means that, after orthogonalizing the independent variable, we have the option of regressing directly on the total return. However, the estimated residuals $\hat{\boldsymbol{\eta}}_2$ and $\hat{\boldsymbol{\eta}}$ will be different.
- The formulas above hold for the case of identical idiosyncratic volatilities. For the general case, the formula for $\tilde{\mathbf{X}}_2$ becomes

$$\tilde{\mathbf{X}}_2 = (\mathbf{I}_n - \mathbf{X}_1(\mathbf{X}_1^\top \mathbf{\Omega}_\epsilon^{-1} \mathbf{X}_1)^{-1} \mathbf{X}_1 \mathbf{\Omega}_\epsilon^{-1})\mathbf{X}_2$$

Proving this is left as an exercise (whiten the returns by premultiplying by $\mathbf{\Omega}_\epsilon^{-1/2}$, use the results above, and transform back).

Procedure 4.1: *Stagewise linear regression*

1. Estimate the model

$$\mathbf{y} = \mathbf{X}\boldsymbol{\beta}_1 + \epsilon \tag{4.23}$$

to obtain estimates $\hat{\boldsymbol{\beta}}_1$ and $\hat{\epsilon}$.

2. Regress the columns of $\mathbf{Z}$ on $\mathbf{X}$ and take the residuals of each regression. Define $\tilde{\mathbf{Z}}$ as a matrix whose ith column is the residual vector of $[\mathbf{Z}]_{\cdot,i}$ on $\mathbf{X}$.
3. Estimate the model $\hat{\epsilon} = \tilde{\mathbf{Z}}\boldsymbol{\beta}_2 + \boldsymbol{\xi}$ to obtain estimates $\hat{\boldsymbol{\beta}}_2$ and $\hat{\boldsymbol{\xi}}$.

4.7.4 *The Singular Value Decomposition*

The Singular Value Decomposition (SVD) is a fundamental factorization in numerical linear algebra. It powers many numerical computations, as Golub and Van Loan (2012) beautifully explain. In addition, it is extremely insightful in theoretical analysis. Much of this book relies on it. Since it is not always covered in linear algebra courses, this Appendix provides a crash course on the subject. For gentler introductions, see Trefethen and Bau (1997), Horn and Johnson (2012), Strang (2019), and the aforementioned classic book by Golub and Van Loan.

We start by recalling a basic fact of algebra. We are given a square matrix $\mathbf{A}$ that is symmetric and positive semidefinite ($\mathbf{x}\mathbf{A}\mathbf{x}^\top \geq 0$ for all $\mathbf{x}$). Let λ_i, $\mathbf{v}_i$ be the ith eigenvalue and eigenvector of $\mathbf{A}$, i.e., $\mathbf{A}\mathbf{v}_i = \lambda_i \mathbf{v}_i$, where $\mathbf{v}_i$ are unit-norm vectors. Then, the eigenvalues are real, positive, and the eigenvectors are orthonormal, i.e., $\mathbf{v}_i^\top \mathbf{v}_j = \delta_{i,j}$. What can be said about generic rectangular matrices $\mathbf{A} \in \mathbb{R}^{m \times n}$? A possible generalization is to relax the condition that $\mathbf{v}_i$ appears on both sides of the eigenvalue equation. We posit an equation of the form $\mathbf{A}\mathbf{v}_i = s_i \mathbf{u}_i$, with $\mathbf{v}_i \in \mathbb{R}^n$ and $\mathbf{u}_i \in \mathbb{R}^m$. However, we keep the requirement that $\mathbf{v}_i$ be orthonormal and similarly for $\mathbf{U}_i$. Let $r \le \min\{m, n\}$ be the rank of $\mathbf{A}$. The image subspace of $\mathbf{A}$ has dimension r: there are r independent vectors $\mathbf{x}_i$ such that $\mathbf{A}\mathbf{x}_i \neq 0$. The kernel subspace has dimension $n - r$: there are $m - r$ independent vectors $\mathbf{y}_i$ such that $\mathbf{A}\mathbf{y}_i = 0$. We partition $\mathbf{v}_i$ into image and kernel vectors:

$$\mathbf{A}\mathbf{v}_i = s_i\mathbf{u}_i \qquad 1 \le i \le r \tag{4.24}$$

$$\mathbf{A}\mathbf{v}_i = 0 \qquad r < i \le m \tag{4.25}$$

We can write these equations in matrix form:

$$\mathbf{A}\begin{bmatrix} | & & | \\ \mathbf{v}_1 & \dots & \mathbf{v}_n \\ | & & | \end{bmatrix} = \begin{bmatrix} | & & | \\ \mathbf{u}_1 & \dots & \mathbf{u}_m \\ | & & | \end{bmatrix} \begin{bmatrix} s_1 & 0 & \dots & \dots & \dots & 0 \\ 0 & s_2 & \dots & \dots & \dots & 0 \\ 0 & 0 & \dots & \dots & \dots & 0 \\ 0 & 0 & \dots & s_r & \dots & 0 \\ 0 & \dots & \dots & \dots & \dots & 0 \\ 0 & \dots & \dots & \dots & \dots & 0 \end{bmatrix} \tag{4.26}$$

Here, in addition to the vectors $\mathbf{u}_1, \dots, \mathbf{u}_r$, we have completed this orthonormal basis with $\mathbf{u}_{r+1}, \dots, \mathbf{u}_m$ so that it spans $\mathbb{R}^m$. In compact form, Equation (4.26) can be written as $\mathbf{AV} = \mathbf{US}$, where $\mathbf{U}, \mathbf{V}$ are orthonormal matrices, i.e., $\mathbf{U}^\mathsf{T}\mathbf{U} = \mathbf{I}_m$ and $\mathbf{V}^\mathsf{T}\mathbf{V} = \mathbf{I}_n$; and $\mathbf{S} \in \mathbb{R}^{m \times n}$ may have non-zero elements only on the main diagonal. Finally, we rewrite the equation after right-multiplying by $\mathbf{V}^\mathsf{T}$ as

$$\mathbf{A} = \mathbf{USV}^\mathsf{T} \tag{4.27}$$

We show the decomposition visually in Figure 4.5.

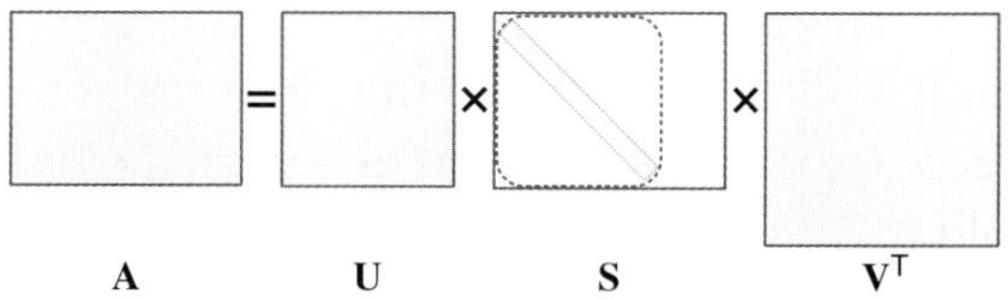

Figure 4.5 Singular Value Decomposition, full form.

We prove Equations (4.24), (4.25) by noting that $\mathbf{A}^\top\mathbf{A}$ is a positive-semidefinite matrix of rank r, so that there are r pairs $(\mathbf{v}_i, \lambda_i)$ satisfying $(\mathbf{A}^\top\mathbf{A})\mathbf{v}_i = \lambda_i\mathbf{v}_i$. Define $s_i := \sqrt{\lambda_i}$ and $\mathbf{u}_i := (\mathbf{A}\mathbf{v}_i)/s_i$. These satisfy Equation (4.24). We prove that the $\mathbf{U}_i$ are orthonormal:

$$\mathbf{u}_i^\top\mathbf{u}_j = \frac{\mathbf{v}_i^\top(\mathbf{A}^\top\mathbf{A}\mathbf{v}_j)}{s_i s_j} = \frac{s_j}{s_i}\mathbf{v}_i\mathbf{v}_j = \delta_{i,j} \tag{4.28}$$

because $\mathbf{v}_1, \ldots, \mathbf{v}_r$ are orthonormal. Now we complete the basis in $\mathbb{R}^n$ by adding orthonormal vectors $\mathbf{v}_{r+1}, \ldots, \mathbf{v}_n$, where $\mathbf{A}\mathbf{v}_i = 0$. These make a basis for the null space of $\mathbf{A}$. Correspondingly, we add orthonormal vectors $\mathbf{u}_{r+1}, \ldots, \mathbf{u}_m$ to complete the basis in $\mathbb{R}^m$. A few observations (among many) on the SVD:

1. If all the singular values are distinct, the first r columns of $\mathbf{U}$ and $\mathbf{V}$ are uniquely determined. However, they are not in the case of identical singular values.
2. The power of a symmetric positive-definite matrix $\mathbf{A}$, and in particular the square root, can easily be defined from the SVD. $\mathbf{A}^a = (\mathbf{U}\mathbf{S}\mathbf{U}^\top)^a = \mathbf{U}\,\mathrm{diag}\left(s_1^a, \ldots, s_n^a\right)\mathbf{U}^\top$. It is easy to show that this definition meets the requirement of exponentiation. For the specific case of the square root, one can show that $\mathbf{A}^{1/2}\mathbf{A}^{1/2} = \mathbf{A}$.
3. Equation (4.27) can be rewritten as

$$\mathbf{A} = \sum_{i=1}^{r} s_i\mathbf{u}_i\mathbf{v}_i^\top \tag{4.29}$$

   The SVD decomposes a matrix into a sum of rank-one matrices.
4. For all $i \leq r$,

$$\mathbf{A}^\top\mathbf{A}\mathbf{v}_i = s_i^2\mathbf{v}_i \tag{4.30}$$

$$\mathbf{A}\mathbf{A}^\top\mathbf{u}_i = \mathbf{A}(\mathbf{A}^\top\mathbf{A}\mathbf{v}_i)/s_i = s_i\mathbf{A}\mathbf{v}_i = s_i^2\mathbf{u}_i \tag{4.31}$$

   In other terms, $\mathbf{A}^\top\mathbf{A}$ and $\mathbf{A}\mathbf{A}^\top$ have the same eigenvalues.
5. The SVD decomposes the operations on an element in $\mathbb{R}^n$ into a rotation, a rescaling of the axes turning a ball into an ellipsoid, followed by another rotation. The net result is that any operator $\mathbf{A}$ maps a point on a ball into a point on a rotated ellipsoid. Figure 4.6 illustrates the steps of the SVD.

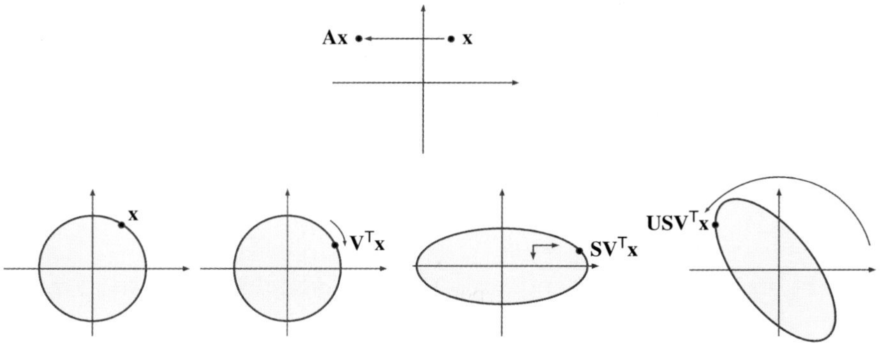

Figure 4.6 Singular Value Decomposition as a sequence of steps: rotation, scaling, rotation.

4.8 Exercises

Exercise 4.3 ***(Portfolio Covariances)***

1. Generalize this result. Let $\mathbf{x}$ be a random vector taking values in $\mathbb{R}^n$ with covariance matrix $\mathbf{\Omega}$. Let A be an $m \times n$ matrix. Prove that the covariance matrix of the random vector $\mathbf{Ax}$ is $\mathbf{A\Omega A}^\intercal$.
2. Say that a random vector $\mathbf{x}$ follows a multivariate normal distribution with covariance matrix $\mathbf{\Omega}$. Let the Singular Value Decomposition of $\mathbf{\Omega}$ be $\mathbf{U\Lambda U}^\intercal$, and define

$$\mathbf{\Omega}^{1/2} = \mathbf{U} \begin{bmatrix} \lambda_1^{1/2} & 0 & \dots & \dots & 0 \\ 0 & \lambda_2^{1/2} & 0 & \dots & 0 \\ \dots & \dots & \dots & \dots & 0 \\ 0 & 0 & 0 & \dots & \lambda_n^{1/2} \end{bmatrix} \mathbf{U}^\intercal$$

Let $\boldsymbol{\xi}$ be a Gaussian distribution with unit covariance matrix. Prove that $\mathbf{\Omega}^{1/2}\boldsymbol{\xi}$ has covariance $\mathbf{\Omega}$.

Exercise 4.4: Provide a counterexample in which it is not possible to center the loadings with a rotation. (Hint: Use a one-factor model.)

Exercise 4.5: Find conditions under which matrix (4.4) is invertible.

The Takeaways

1. *Factor models* express asset returns as a combination of factor contributions and idiosyncratic components. Their general form is

$$\mathbf{r}_t = \boldsymbol{\alpha} + \mathbf{B}\mathbf{f}_t + \boldsymbol{\epsilon}_t$$

2. *Interpretations of Factor Models*
   - *Graphical Model.* Visualizes dependencies between assets and factors using nodes and edges.
   - *Superposition of Effects.* Asset returns are a sum of weighted factor contributions.
   - *Single-Asset Product.* Expected return of an asset is the inner product of its factor loadings and factor returns.

3. *Alpha Components*
   - *Alpha Spanned.* Portion of alpha explained by factors; indistinguishable from expected factor returns.
   - *Alpha Orthogonal.* Portion of alpha unexplained by factors; offers diversification benefits and can enhance Sharpe Ratio.

4. *Transformations of Factor Models*
   - *Rotations.* Change factor representations without altering model predictions (e.g., orthonormal loadings).
   - *Projections.* Reduce the number of factors while approximating the original model.
   - *Push-Outs.* Expand the model by adding new factors to capture additional structure.

5. *Applications of Factor Models*
   - *Performance Attribution.* Decompose portfolio returns into factor and idiosyncratic contributions.
   - *Risk Management.* Forecast and decompose portfolio volatility into systematic and idiosyncratic risk.
   - *Portfolio Construction.* Optimize portfolios using factor risk exposures and expected returns.
   - *Alpha Research.* Identify sources of returns and separate skill from luck by analyzing alpha components.

Chapter 5

Evaluating Risk

The Questions

1. Given the absence of a single performance measure for benchmarking factor models, how should one prioritize and select the best model for a specific use-case?
2. What are the robust loss functions suitable for evaluating volatility predictions in factor models?
3. What are the tests suitable for testing the performance of covariance matrices for portfolio optimization?
4. What are the advantages and limitations of different approaches?
5. What additional tests should we perform to ensure that models can be used in production environments?

There are dozens of papers and documents extolling the virtues of commercial models. Many alternative models. Several asset classes. All combinations of geographies. And, of course, many vendors. However, there are hardly any papers laying out theoretically motivated procedures that test risk properties of factor models that are relevant to practitioners. Testing is hard, it is mundane, it is humble and humbling. In the words of P. J. O'Rourke, "Everybody wants to save the Earth; nobody wants to help Mom do the dishes". This is a chapter about doing dishes. It relies on two simple principles. First, the metrics that we use should be related as much as possible to our applications. We care about accuracy of volatility forecasts, and realized volatility of optimized portfolios, and we strive to measure these quantities in a realistic setting. The second principle follows from the observation that there is not a single performance measure on which we benchmark factor models. It follows that it is possible that a single "best" model may not exist, because it is unlikely that a single model outperforms all the others on all metrics. This should not be viewed necessarily as a curse, but as a blessing. We can concentrate our efforts on our use-case, or at least prioritize for it, and find the best model for the task.

The remainder of the chapter is organized around three families of metrics: those aimed at evaluating the covariance matrix; those aimed at evaluating the precision matrix; and those aimed at evaluating the model usability for secondary tasks.

5.1 Evaluating the Covariance Matrix

5.1.1 Robust Loss Functions for Volatility Estimation

A major application of a factor model is volatility estimation. The quality of volatility predictions is one that has been at the forefront of the early developments of risk models. If a model predicts asset volatilities $\hat{\sigma}_i$ at a certain time t (i.e., the volatility prediction made available at time $t-1$ for time interval $(t-1, t)$), then a measure of the quality of the volatility predictions is given by a loss function

$$\bar{L} := \frac{1}{T} \sum_{t=1}^{n} L(\tilde{\sigma}_t^2, \hat{\sigma}_t^2)$$

where $\tilde{\sigma}_t$ is an empirical estimate of the observed volatility (e.g., the realized volatility metric defined previously). The loss function L is non-negative, and equal to zero if and only if $\hat{\sigma} = \tilde{\sigma}$. In the metric statistic above, we use a volatility proxy $\tilde{\sigma}_t$ instead of the unknown true volatility σ_t. Hansen and Lunde (2006a) introduce a concept of *rank robustness* for losses: if we have two alternative volatility forecasts $\hat{\sigma}_t^{(j)}$, one is better than the other using an unbiased volatility proxy if and only if one is better than the other using the true volatility. That is,

$$\bar{L}(\hat{\sigma}^{(1)}, \sigma) \leq \bar{L}(\hat{\sigma}^{(2)}, \sigma) \Leftrightarrow \bar{L}(\hat{\sigma}^{(1)}, \tilde{\sigma}) \leq \bar{L}(\hat{\sigma}^{(2)}, \tilde{\sigma})$$

Patton and Sheppard (2009) and Patton (2011) completely characterize these loss functions and show that these two are robust:

$$\text{QLIKE}(\hat{\sigma}, r) := \frac{1}{T}\sum_{t=1}^{T}\left(\frac{r_t^2}{\hat{\sigma}_t^2} - \log\left(\frac{r_t^2}{\hat{\sigma}_t^2}\right) - 1\right)$$

$$\text{MSE}(\hat{\sigma}, r) := \frac{1}{T}\sum_{t=1}^{T}\hat{\sigma}_t^2\left(\frac{r_t^2}{\hat{\sigma}_t^2} - 1\right)^2$$

QLIKE is (save for constants) the negative of the log-likelihood of the normal distribution. These two loss functions are increasingly being used in place of the Bias statistic.[1] Their graphs are shown in Figure 5.1.

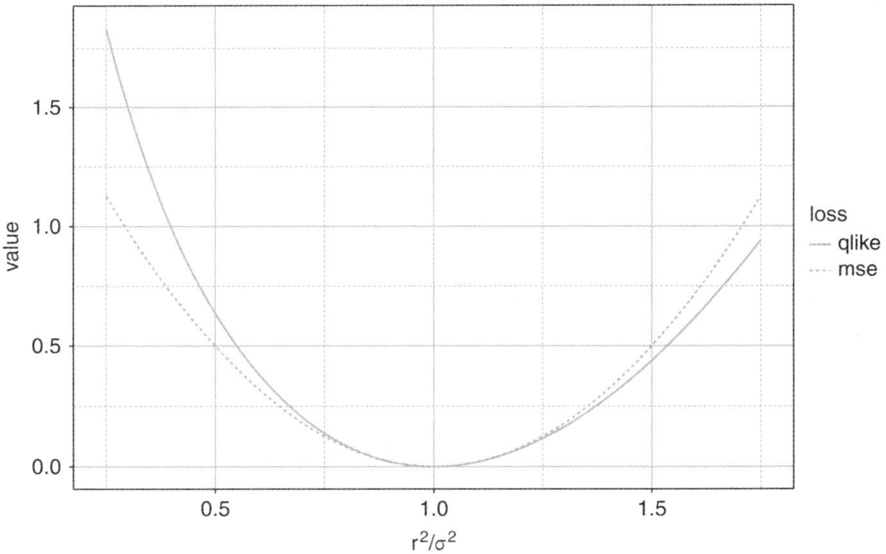

Figure 5.1 QLIKE and MSE comparison. Notice that QLIKE is skewed, with higher losses when the realized variance is smaller than the estimated variance.

[1] The Bias statistic is defined as $T^{-1}\sqrt{\sum_{t=1}^{T} r_t^2/\hat{\sigma}_t^2}$; see Connor et al. (2010).

5.1.2 Application to Multivariate Returns

The loss functions QLIKE and MSE apply to univariate returns, not to covariance matrices. Below are a few ways to adapt the univariate setting to a multivariate one.

Production Strategies. If strategies are already running, a straightforward and necessary test is to evaluate their simulated performance under different factor models. QLIKE and MSE are important and should be checked jointly with metrics that are important for the portfolio manager, like Sharpe Ratio or PnL. It is important that the covariance matrix be the input to the entire production process, i.e., portfolios should be generated on the basis of the factor model themselves. If a portfolio is generated using factor model A and then tested on model B, the test will be marred by this asymmetry.

Average-Case Analysis. An alternative approach is to estimate the expected loss, where the expectation is taken over a distribution of portfolios as well as of asset returns. For the distribution of returns, we use the empirical measure $\hat{P}$ of historical returns; for the distribution of portfolios, we may choose a simple one, like uniform on a sphere (see Procedure 5.1). Then we estimate $E_{\mathbf{w}\sim D,\mathbf{r}\sim\hat{P}}[L((\mathbf{r}^\top\mathbf{w})^2, \mathbf{w}^\top\hat{\mathbf{\Omega}}_\mathbf{r}\mathbf{w})]$. There are a few drawbacks to this approach. First, there is a degree of arbitrariness in choosing a portfolio distribution. The actual distribution of portfolios is almost certainly *not* uniform; and it is not even warranted that the distribution of alphas is uniform. Second, it is computationally expensive. We are simulating in highly dimensional spaces, with $\mathbf{w}$ ranging in size from 1000 assets to tens of thousands. Computational issues, such as simulation schemes and convergence criteria, become important. An approximation is to select a *portfolio basis*, i.e., n portfolios $\mathbf{w}_{1,t}, \ldots, \mathbf{w}_{n,t}$, and then apply an "average"-case analysis to these n portfolios. A special case of this special case is that of *eigenportfolios*: decompose $\mathbf{\Omega}_\mathbf{r} = \mathbf{USU}^\top$, and set the basis portfolios equal to the columns of $\mathbf{U}$. The approach is computationally tractable. One important drawback is that this average loss is not independent of the choice of the portfolios; in fact, it is quite sensitive to it. Even if we restrict our choice to an orthonormal basis, like eigenportfolios, the measured performance still depends on the basis. Since the choice of an appropriate basis cannot be easily justified based on principles, the outcome is arbitrary.

Procedure 5.1: *Random portfolios average variance testing*

1. **Inputs**: candidate covariance matrices $\hat{\mathbf{\Omega}}_{\mathbf{r},t}$ and returns $\mathbf{r}_t$ for $t = 1, \ldots, T$, loss function L.
2. Set $L_{\text{tot}} = 0$, $n_{\text{iter}} = 0$.
3. Set $\mathbf{w} \sim N(0, \mathbf{I}_n)$, $\mathbf{w} \leftarrow \mathbf{w}/\|\mathbf{w}\|$. Choose s uniformly at random in $1, \ldots, T$.
4. Set $L_{\text{tot}} = L_{\text{tot}} + L[(\mathbf{r}_s^{\top}\mathbf{w})^2, \mathbf{w}^{\top}\hat{\mathbf{\Omega}}_s\mathbf{w}]$. Set $n_{\text{iter}} \leftarrow n_{\text{iter}} + 1$.
5. If $L[(\mathbf{r}_s^{\top}\mathbf{w})^2, \mathbf{w}^{\top}\hat{\mathbf{\Omega}}_s\mathbf{w}]/L_{\text{tot}} \geq \epsilon_{\text{tol}}$, go to Step 3.
6. **Output**: $L := L_{\text{tot}}/n_{\text{iter}}$.

Worst-Case Under/Over-Prediction. Yet another approach is to estimate the worst-case loss function:

$$\begin{aligned} &\max\ E_{\mathbf{r}\sim\hat{P}}[L((\mathbf{r}^{\top}\mathbf{w})^2, \mathbf{w}^{\top}\hat{\mathbf{\Omega}}_{\mathbf{r}}\mathbf{w})] \\ &\text{s.t. } \|\mathbf{w}\| \leq 1 \end{aligned}$$

The problem with this approach is that the objective function (be it QLIKE or MSE) is not convex. When the number of assets is large, the problem is not computationally tractable.

Procedure 5.2: *Worst-case variance testing*

1. **Inputs**: candidate covariance matrices $\hat{\mathbf{\Omega}}_{\mathbf{r},t}$ and returns $\mathbf{r}_t$ for $t = 1, \ldots, T$, loss function L.
2. Set $L_{\text{tot}} = 0$, $n_{\text{iter}} = 0$.
3. Set $\mathbf{w} \sim N(0, \mathbf{I}_n)$, $\mathbf{w} \leftarrow \mathbf{w}/\|\mathbf{w}\|$. Choose s uniformly at random in $1, \ldots, T$.
4. Set $\mathbf{w} \leftarrow \mathbf{w} - n_{\text{iter}}^{-1}\nabla_{\mathbf{w}}L[(\mathbf{r}_s^{\top}\mathbf{w})^2, \mathbf{w}^{\top}\hat{\mathbf{\Omega}}_s\mathbf{w})]$. Set $n_{\text{iter}} \leftarrow n_{\text{iter}} + 1$.
5. If $L[(\mathbf{r}_s^{\top}\mathbf{w})^2, \mathbf{w}^{\top}\hat{\mathbf{\Omega}}_s\mathbf{w})]/L_{\text{tot}} \geq \epsilon_{\text{tol}}$, go to Step 3.
6. **Output**: $L := L_{\text{tot}}/n_{\text{iter}}$.

None of the options above dominates the others. Whenever available, production strategies are always being tested against alternative approaches. Average- and worst-case analyses are both computationally very demanding. Moreover, in the case of average-case analysis the result depends on the assumption on portfolio distribution.

Leading-Alpha MVO Portfolios. Another option is to construct portfolios based on the realized leading returns of the securities. This scheme has the advantage to test the predictiveness of the strategy for "relevant" portfolios and is described in Procedure 5.3. After all, volatility prediction matters only if we have alpha in the first place. If we don't, then we have other problems to be worried about.

Procedure 5.3: *Realized alpha variance testing*

1. **Inputs**: candidate covariance matrices $\hat{\mathbf{\Omega}}_{\mathbf{r},t}$ and returns $\mathbf{r}_t$ for $t = 1, \ldots, T$, loss function L, $\tau \in \mathbb{N}^+$.
2. Set $L_{\text{tot}} = 0$.
3. For each $t = 0, \ldots, T - \tau$, let

$$\hat{\boldsymbol{\alpha}}_t := \frac{1}{\tau} \sum_{s=t+1}^{t+\tau} \mathbf{r}_s$$

$$\mathbf{w} := \hat{\mathbf{\Omega}}_{\mathbf{r},t}^{-1} \hat{\boldsymbol{\alpha}}_t$$

$$L_{\text{tot}} := L_{\text{tot}} + L(\mathbf{r}_t^{\mathsf{T}} \mathbf{w}, \mathbf{w}^{\mathsf{T}} \hat{\mathbf{\Omega}}_{\mathbf{r},t} \mathbf{w})$$

4. **Output**: $L := L_{\text{tot}}/(T - \tau + 1)$.

An advantage of this approach is that it can easily be augmented. For example, we could test the performance on portfolios with added noise:

$$\mathbf{w} := \hat{\mathbf{\Omega}}_{\mathbf{r},t}^{-1} (\hat{\boldsymbol{\alpha}}_t + \boldsymbol{\eta}_t), \quad \boldsymbol{\eta}_t \sim N(0, \sigma^2 \mathbf{I}_n)$$

Distribution Likelihood. An alternative that does not depend on the portfolio choice is to use the log-likelihood for the zero-mean multivariate normal distribution, applied to the returns of the estimation universe. Modulo constant terms, the negative log-likelihood[2] is proportional to

$$\text{QDIST} = \sum_t \left(\mathbf{r}_t^\top \hat{\mathbf{\Omega}}_{\mathbf{r},t}^{-1} \mathbf{r}_t + \log \left| \hat{\mathbf{\Omega}}_{\mathbf{r},t} \right| + n \log(2\pi) \right) \tag{5.1}$$

Exercise 5.1: In their survey paper, Patton and Sheppard (2009) propose a multivariate test for $\hat{\mathbf{\Omega}}_{\mathbf{r},t}$ using a proxy estimate for the true covariance matrix $\mathbf{H}_t$. The loss function they propose is

$$L = \sum_t \text{trace}\left(\hat{\mathbf{\Omega}}_{\mathbf{r},t}^{-1} \mathbf{H}_t \right) - \log \left| \hat{\mathbf{\Omega}}_{\mathbf{r},t}^{-1} \mathbf{H}_t \right|$$

Show that, when $\mathbf{H}_t := \mathbf{r}_t \mathbf{r}_t^\top$, L is equivalent to QDIST, i.e., $L = a \times$ **QDIST** $+ b$, for some positive constant a.

5.2 Evaluating the Precision Matrix

5.2.1 Minimum-Variance Portfolios

As we have seen repeatedly throughout the book, the quality of a factor model is reflected in the accuracy of its precision matrix. We propose two methods. The first one is using a well-known test: minimum-variance portfolios. Consider a very simple example: construct a portfolio $\mathbf{w}$ of minimum variance and with unit net market value $\sum_i w_i = 1$. This is the *ex-ante* minimum variance portfolio; the realized variance will differ. The intuition is that a "better" covariance matrix will result in a lower realized variance. We make this intuition rigorous, and generalize to the case where the portfolio has a given exposure to an *arbitrary* factor, i.e., $\sum_i b_i w_i = 1$.

Let $\hat{\mathbf{\Omega}}_{\mathbf{r}} \in \mathbb{R}^{n \times n}$ be a candidate covariance matrix and $\mathbf{\Omega}_{\mathbf{r}}$ be the true covariance matrix. Let $\mathbf{b} \in \mathbb{R}^n$, and solve the risk-minimization problem

$$\begin{aligned} &\min \mathbf{w}^\top \hat{\mathbf{\Omega}}_{\mathbf{r}} \mathbf{w} \\ &\text{s.t. } \mathbf{b}^\top \mathbf{w} = 1 \end{aligned} \tag{5.2}$$

---

[2] A note of caution regarding the computation of QDIST in Equation (5.1): a numerically stable way to compute $\log|\mathbf{A}|$ is to compute the SVD of the argument and exploit the fact that $|\mathbf{A}| = |\mathbf{U}\mathbf{S}\mathbf{V}^\top| = |\mathbf{S}|$, so $\log|\mathbf{A}| = \log|\mathbf{S}| = \sum_i \log s_i$.

and let $\mathbf{w}(\hat{\boldsymbol{\Omega}}_{\mathbf{r}})$ be its solution. Denote the realized variance of the portfolio $\text{var}\,(\mathbf{w}(\hat{\boldsymbol{\Omega}}_{\mathbf{r}}), \boldsymbol{\Omega}_{\mathbf{r}})$. Then, the realized volatility of portfolio $\mathbf{w}(\hat{\boldsymbol{\Omega}}_{\mathbf{r}})$ is greater than that of $\mathbf{w}(\boldsymbol{\Omega}_{\mathbf{r}})$, and the two are identical if and only if $\boldsymbol{\Omega}_{\mathbf{r}} \propto \hat{\boldsymbol{\Omega}}_{\mathbf{r}}$. This is Theorem 5.1 in the Appendix (Section 5.4.1). A way to apply this result is as follows: Set $\mathbf{b} = E[\mathbf{r}]$, the alpha vector. Then the correct covariance matrix results in the best possible Sharpe Ratio, and a natural ranking of covariance models is by the realized Sharpe Ratio for a certain strategy.

We can use all the portfolio-dependent schemes introduced for volatility tests to evaluate the precision matrix. The realized variance acts as a loss function.

5.2.2 *Mahalanobis Distance*

There is another test that is portfolio-independent and that involves the precision matrix only. The *Mahalanobis distance* is defined for a multivariate zero-mean random vector $\mathbf{r}$ and an associated covariance matrix $\boldsymbol{\Omega}_{\mathbf{r}}$ as $d(\mathbf{r}, \boldsymbol{\Omega}_{\mathbf{r}}) := \sqrt{\mathbf{r}^{\top}\boldsymbol{\Omega}_{\mathbf{r}}^{-1}\mathbf{r}}$. For Gaussian returns and under the true covariance matrix, d^2 is distributed according to a chi-squared distribution with n degrees of freedom.[3] One test is then

$$
\begin{aligned}
\nu_t &:= \frac{1}{n_t}\mathbf{r}_t^{\top}\hat{\boldsymbol{\Omega}}_{\mathbf{r},t}^{-1}\mathbf{r}_t \\
\text{MALV} &:= \text{var}(\nu_1, \ldots, \nu_T)
\end{aligned}
$$

The lower the value of $\text{MALV}(\mathbf{r}_{\cdot}, \hat{\boldsymbol{\Omega}}_{\mathbf{r},\cdot})$, the better the performance of the precision matrix. If the variance is very low (say, of the order of $2/n$), then the inverse of the covariance matrix is, save for a multiplicative constant, predicting perfectly. We don't primarily care about the constant in this test, because a volatility test should address that issue. A different way to interpret the result is the following: if returns are Gaussian, then they are distributed as $\boldsymbol{\Omega}_{\mathbf{r},t}^{1/2}\boldsymbol{\xi}_t$, with $\boldsymbol{\xi}$ a multivariate standard normal rv.

---

[3] To prove this, note that the vector $\mathbf{r}$ can be generated by $\mathbf{r} := \boldsymbol{\Omega}_{\mathbf{r}}^{1/2}\boldsymbol{\xi}$, where $\xi \sim N(\mathbf{0}, \mathbf{I}_n)$. Therefore, $\mathbf{r}^{\top}\boldsymbol{\Omega}_{\mathbf{r}}^{-1}\mathbf{r} \sim \sum_i \xi_i^2 \sim \chi_n^2$.

Moreover, $\boldsymbol{\xi}_t^\top \boldsymbol{\xi}_t$ has mean n_t and standard deviation $\sqrt{2n_t}$. For large n_t, $\boldsymbol{\xi}_t^\top \boldsymbol{\xi}_t$ is concentrated at n_t. We rewrite MALV as follows:

$$
\begin{aligned}
\bar{\nu} &:= \frac{1}{T}\sum_t \nu_t \\
\text{MALV} &:= \frac{1}{T}\sum_t \left(\frac{1}{n_t}\boldsymbol{\xi}_t^\top \boldsymbol{\Omega}_{\mathbf{r},t}^{1/2}\hat{\boldsymbol{\Omega}}_{\mathbf{r},t}^{-1}\boldsymbol{\Omega}_{\mathbf{r},t}^{1/2}\boldsymbol{\xi}_t - \bar{\nu}\right)^2 \\
&\simeq \frac{1}{T}\sum_t \frac{1}{n_t^2}\left(\boldsymbol{\xi}_t^\top \boldsymbol{\Omega}_{\mathbf{r},t}^{1/2}\hat{\boldsymbol{\Omega}}_{\mathbf{r},t}^{-1}\boldsymbol{\Omega}_{\mathbf{r},t}^{1/2}\boldsymbol{\xi}_t - \bar{\nu}\boldsymbol{\xi}_t^\top\boldsymbol{\xi}_t\right)^2 \\
&= \frac{1}{T}\sum_t \frac{1}{n_t^2}\left[\boldsymbol{\xi}_t^\top (\boldsymbol{\Omega}_{\mathbf{r},t}^{1/2}\hat{\boldsymbol{\Omega}}_{\mathbf{r},t}^{-1}\boldsymbol{\Omega}_{\mathbf{r},t}^{1/2} - \bar{\nu}\mathbf{I}_n)\boldsymbol{\xi}_t\right]^2
\end{aligned}
$$

The approximate equality comes from the fact that we have replaced $\boldsymbol{\xi}_t^\top \boldsymbol{\xi}_t$ with its expected value. We are testing the closeness of $\boldsymbol{\Omega}_{\mathbf{r},t}^{1/2}\hat{\boldsymbol{\Omega}}_{\mathbf{r},t}^{-1}\boldsymbol{\Omega}_{\mathbf{r},t}^{1/2} - \bar{\nu}\mathbf{I}_n$ to zero by multiplying to the left and right by standard multivariate Gaussian random vectors. In Section 10.3.2 we will see that this matrix difference is also responsible for bounding the Sharpe Ratio efficiency.

5.3 Ancillary Tests

In addition to performance measures on the return covariance matrix $\boldsymbol{\Omega}_\mathbf{r}$ and its inverse, we should verify that the model performs well in tasks that are indirectly related to portfolio optimization and hedging. We consider two specifically. The first one is model turnover. Changes over time in the data we have at hand affect the transaction costs of our strategies. There are three major drivers of such changes. The first one is in our day-to-day forecasts of excess returns, i.e., alpha turnover. We need to model such turnover explicitly, and do so in Chapter 11. The second one is due to changes in the market impact function itself. There are exceptional periods in which trading activity changes very rapidly, and so does the cost of trading. However, in practice, this is the most stable component in portfolio construction and we ignore its short-term variation.[4] The last driver of change is the factor model, which is the subject of the following subsection.

[4] I should note that some researchers do model time variation of execution costs, e.g., by forecasting trading volume. But these approaches are out of the scope of this book.

5.3.1 Model Turnover

Turnover is not an intrinsic property of a model; it is the property of a production trading strategy. However, it may make sense to find a measure that gives us an estimate of strategy turnover. In an ideal setting in which we ignore transaction costs, we may want to target a constant factor exposure level b_i for factor i. In this setting, it is optimal to trade Factor-Mimicking Portfolios (FMPs). The returns of these portfolio are the best approximation to the true factor returns of the model. They are introduced in Section 9.3. The weights of these portfolio are the column vectors of the matrix

$$\mathbf{P}_t := \mathbf{\Omega}_{\epsilon,t}^{-1}\mathbf{B}_t(\mathbf{B}_t^\top\mathbf{\Omega}_{\epsilon,t}^{-1}\mathbf{B}_t)^{-1}$$
$$\mathbf{w}_t := \mathbf{P}_t\mathbf{b}$$

Portfolio turnover is driven by the change in $\mathbf{P}_t$. We then define a simple measure of quadratic turnover as the time-series average

$$\text{turnover}_2 := \frac{1}{T}\sum_{t=1}^{T}\left\|\mathbf{P}_t - \mathbf{P}_{t-1}\right\|_F$$

where $\|\cdot\|_F$ is the Frobenius norm of a matrix. This definition has the advantage of being simple and intuitive. It is possible to refine it, at the cost of losing generality. If we have an indication of the target exposures $\mathbf{b}$ of our strategy, and we have a trading cost function $\text{TC}:\mathbb{R}^n \to \mathbb{R}^+$, then a more accurate measure of turnover would be

$$\text{turnover}_{\text{TC}} := \frac{1}{T}\sum_{t=1}^{T}\text{TC}[(\mathbf{P}_t - \mathbf{P}_{t-1})\mathbf{b}]$$

5.3.2 Testing Betas

A practical application of risk models is to produce predicted beta of investor portfolios to some benchmark. A simple instance is generating the beta for a market portfolio. A slightly less simple example is to generate the beta to an FMP. An even less obvious example is that of beta to a thematic portfolio: for example, a bank has generated a thematic portfolio that describes an industrial or consumption trend that is relevant at that point in time. We want to measure the beta of our portfolio to this thematic portfolio. In all of these instances, we want to make sure that the predicted beta is accurate, in the sense that it exhibits low discrepancy to the realized beta. Therefore, as part of the evaluation of the risk model, we want to include tests on betas. For simplicity, consider the case of a single reference portfolio $\mathbf{w}$ (FMP, or thematic portfolio). The vector of predicted betas of each asset to this reference portfolio is

$$\beta_t(\mathbf{w}) = \frac{\mathbf{\Omega}_{\mathbf{r},t}\mathbf{w}}{\mathbf{w}^\top \mathbf{\Omega}_{\mathbf{r},t}\mathbf{w}}$$

The exponentially weighted empirical covariance matrix $\hat{\mathbf{\Omega}}_{\mathbf{r},t}$ and realized beta vector is given by

$$\hat{\mathbf{\Omega}}_{\mathbf{r},t} := \frac{1 - e^{-T/\tau}}{1 - e^{1/\tau}} \sum_{s=1}^{T} e^{-s/\tau} \mathbf{r}_{t-s}\mathbf{r}_{t-s}^\top$$

$$\hat{\beta}_t(\mathbf{w}) := \frac{\hat{\mathbf{\Omega}}_{\mathbf{r},t}\mathbf{w}}{\mathbf{w}^\top \hat{\mathbf{\Omega}}_{\mathbf{r},t}\mathbf{w}}$$

We measure the beta accuracy as

$$\text{BETAERR}(\mathbf{w}) = \sum_t \left\| \beta_t - \hat{\beta}_t \right\|^2$$

and employ BETAERR as an ancillary measure of accuracy.

5.3.3 *Coefficient of Determination?*

A very popular way to summarize the performance of a factor model is by reporting the average coefficient of determination (or R^2) of the weighted cross-sectional regression. It is defined as 1 minus the ratio of the weighted residual sum of squares and the total sum of squares:

$$R^2 = 1 - \frac{\sum_{t=1}^{T} \left\| \hat{\mathbf{\Omega}}_{\epsilon,t}^{-1/2} (\mathbf{r}_t - \mathbf{B}_t \hat{\mathbf{f}}_t) \right\|^2}{\sum_{t=1}^{T} \left\| \hat{\mathbf{\Omega}}_{\epsilon,t}^{-1/2} \mathbf{r}_t \right\|^2}$$

Since the idiosyncratic covariance matrix $\mathbf{\Omega}_\epsilon$ is not known in advance, a proxy is used in its place, as described in Chapters 6 and 7. The estimated factor returns $\hat{\mathbf{f}}_t$ are the coefficients of the cross-sectional regression in period t. A high coefficient of determination is interpreted as a positive attribute of the model specification, similarly to the case of linear regression.[5] There are important differences, however. First, there is no "out-of-sample" estimate of R^2. We cannot possibly estimate the performance of the model on a holdout sample because the estimated coefficients, the factor returns, must be estimated in every period. This makes the metric amenable to data mining. Even if we keep constant the complexity of the model (the number of factors), it is easy to increase R^2 by successive manipulations and adjustments to the loading matrices $\mathbf{B}_t$. The naïve R^2 is always improved by adding factors (even with random loadings) to an existing model, although the fact that more refined metrics, like AIC and BIC, penalize more for the number of factors is a possible answer to this objection. Another objection to the use of R^2 is that it ignores the rotational invariance of the problem at hand. To illustrate the problem, consider an artificial example. Asset returns follow a simple static factor model $\mathbf{r}_t = \mathbf{B}\mathbf{f}_t + \epsilon_t$, with $\mathbf{B}^\mathsf{T}\mathbf{B} = \mathbf{I}_m$ and $\mathbf{\Omega}_\epsilon = \mathbf{I}_n$. The estimated factor returns are $\hat{\mathbf{f}}_t = \mathbf{B}^\mathsf{T}\mathbf{r}_t$. Now, let us build a new factor model. Let $\mathbf{C}_t \in \mathbb{R}^{m\times m}$ be a sequence of iid random matrices defined as follows:

$$
\mathbf{C}_t = \begin{bmatrix} \xi_{1,t} & 0 & 0 & \dots & 0 \\ 0 & \xi_{2,t} & 0 & \dots & 0 \\ 0 & 0 & \xi_{3,t} & \dots & 0 \\ \dots & \dots & \dots & \dots & \dots \\ 0 & 0 & 0 & \dots & \xi_{m,t} \end{bmatrix}
$$

where $\xi_{i,t}$ take the values 1 or -1 with equal probability. Note that $\mathbf{C}_t^\mathsf{T}\mathbf{C}_t = \mathbf{C}_t\mathbf{C}_t^\mathsf{T} = \mathbf{I}_m$. After some rote calculations, we find that the

[5] We ignore corrections of R^2 for the "degrees of freedom" and alternative measures of quality of fit, like Akaike Information Criterion (AIC) and Bayesian Information Criterion (BIC) (see, e.g., Hastie et al. (2008)), since the main points made in this apply to them as well.

estimated factor returns from this model are $\tilde{\mathbf{f}}_t = (\tilde{\mathbf{B}}_t^\mathsf{T}\tilde{\mathbf{B}}_t)^{-1}\tilde{\mathbf{B}}_t^\mathsf{T}\mathbf{r}_t = \mathbf{C}_t^\mathsf{T}\mathbf{B}^\mathsf{T}\mathbf{r}_t = \mathbf{C}_t\hat{\mathbf{f}}_t$. The coefficient of determination is unchanged:

$$
\begin{aligned}
R^2((\tilde{\mathbf{B}}_t)_{t=1}^T) &= 1 - \frac{\sum_{t=1}^T \left\|(\mathbf{I}_n - \mathbf{B}\mathbf{C}_t\mathbf{C}_t^\mathsf{T}\mathbf{B}^\mathsf{T})\mathbf{r}_t\right\|^2}{\sum_{t=1}^T \left\|\mathbf{r}_t\right\|^2} \\
&= 1 - \frac{\sum_{t=1}^T \left\|(\mathbf{I}_n - \mathbf{B}\mathbf{B}^\mathsf{T})\mathbf{r}_t\right\|^2}{\sum_{t=1}^T \left\|\mathbf{r}_t\right\|^2} \\
&= R^2(\mathbf{B})
\end{aligned}
$$

However, the estimated factor covariance matrix of the rotated model is

$$
\begin{aligned}
[\tilde{\boldsymbol{\Omega}}_\mathbf{f}]_{i,j} &= T^{-1}\sum_{t=1}^{T} \hat{f}_{i,t}\hat{f}_{j,t}\xi_{i,t}\xi_{j,t} \\
&\to \begin{cases} [\tilde{\boldsymbol{\Omega}}_\mathbf{f}]_{i,j} & \text{if } i = j \\ 0 & \text{if } i \neq j \end{cases}
\end{aligned}
$$

When $i = j$, the average is $T^{-1}\sum_{t=1}^T \hat{f}_{i,t}^2$, i.e., it is identical to the variance of the original non-rotated model. When $i \neq j$, the sum approaches 0 in the limit because of the independence of $\hat{f}_{i,t}\hat{f}_{j,t}$, $\xi_{i,t}$ and $\xi_{j,t}$: $\lim_{T\to\infty} T^{-1}\sum_{t=1}^T \hat{f}_{i,t}\hat{f}_{j,t}\xi_{i,t}\xi_{j,t} = E[f_i f_j]E[\xi_i]E[\xi_j] = 0$. The rotations $\mathbf{C}_t$ have had the effect of decorrelating the estimated factor returns. In summary, we have two models: one is the true model, the other is a rotated model with random rotations in every period. The two models are indistinguishable with respect to their coefficient of determination since they are identical. It follows that AIC and BIC are also identical. However, the second model has a very different—and incorrect—covariance matrix. Expert modelers are aware of the shortcomings of R^2 for factor modeling, and resort to heuristics to confirm the effectiveness of the cross-sectional regression. One such heuristic is to check the percentage of periods in which a specific factor's returns meet a significance criterion, i.e., the regression coefficient corresponding to a factor has an absolute t-score greater than two. Another natural check is on the realized Sharpe Ratios of each factor return. These tests confirm that R^2 is inadequate for factor model selection.[6] The recommendation is to rely on the tests we presented earlier in this chapter for risk model performance, and on Chapter 8 for testing risk-adjusted performance.

5.4 ★Appendix

5.4.1 Proof for Minimum-Variance Portfolios

Theorem 5.1: *(Engle and Colacito, 2006) Let $\hat{\mathbf{\Omega}}_r \in \mathbb{R}^{n\times n}$ be a candidate covariance matrix and $\mathbf{\Omega}_r$ be the true covariance matrix. Let $\boldsymbol{\mu} \in \mathbb{R}^n$, and solve the risk-minimization problem*

$$\begin{aligned} &\min \mathbf{w}^\top \hat{\mathbf{\Omega}}_r \mathbf{w} \\ &\text{s.t. } \boldsymbol{\mu}^\top \mathbf{w} = 1 \end{aligned} \tag{5.3}$$

and let $\mathbf{w}(\hat{\mathbf{\Omega}}_r)$ be its solution. Denote the realized variance of the portfolio $var(\mathbf{w}(\hat{\mathbf{\Omega}}_r), \mathbf{\Omega}_r)$.

The realized volatility of portfolio $\mathbf{w}(\hat{\mathbf{\Omega}}_r)$ is greater than that of $\mathbf{w}(\mathbf{\Omega}_r)$, and the two are identical if and only if $\mathbf{\Omega}_r \propto \hat{\mathbf{\Omega}}_r$.

Proof. The solution of Problem (5.3) is $\mathbf{w}(\hat{\mathbf{\Omega}}_r) = (\mu^\top \hat{\mathbf{\Omega}}_r^{-1} \mu)^{-1} \hat{\mathbf{\Omega}}_r^{-1} \mu$. The ratio between realized variance of the portfolios constructed on $\hat{\mathbf{\Omega}}_r$ and on $\mathbf{\Omega}_r$ is

$$\frac{\text{var}(\mathbf{w}(\hat{\mathbf{\Omega}}_r), \mathbf{\Omega}_r)}{\text{var}(\mathbf{w}(\mathbf{\Omega}_r), \mathbf{\Omega}_r)} = \frac{\boldsymbol{\mu}^\top \mathbf{\Omega}_r^{-1} \boldsymbol{\mu}}{\boldsymbol{\mu}^\top \hat{\mathbf{\Omega}}_r^{-1} \boldsymbol{\mu}} \frac{\boldsymbol{\mu}^\top \hat{\mathbf{\Omega}}_r^{-1} \mathbf{\Omega}_r \hat{\mathbf{\Omega}}_r^{-1} \boldsymbol{\mu}}{\boldsymbol{\mu}^\top \hat{\mathbf{\Omega}}_r^{-1} \boldsymbol{\mu}}$$

One can verify directly that if $\hat{\mathbf{\Omega}}_r^{-1} \propto \mathbf{\Omega}_r$ the ratio is one. Let $\hat{\mathbf{\Omega}}_r = \hat{\mathbf{U}}\hat{\mathbf{S}}\hat{\mathbf{U}}^\top$, $\mathbf{\Omega}_r = \mathbf{U}\mathbf{S}\mathbf{U}^\top$. Let $\mathbf{x} := \hat{\mathbf{S}}^{-1/2}\hat{\mathbf{U}}^\top \boldsymbol{\mu}$. Let $\mathbf{H} := \hat{\mathbf{S}}^{1/2}\hat{\mathbf{U}}^\top \mathbf{U}\mathbf{S}^{-1}\mathbf{U}^\top \hat{\mathbf{U}}\hat{\mathbf{S}}^{1/2}$. Then we rewrite the variance ratio as

$$\begin{aligned} \frac{\text{var}(\mathbf{w}(\hat{\mathbf{\Omega}}_r), \mathbf{\Omega}_r)}{\text{var}(\mathbf{w}(\mathbf{\Omega}_r), \mathbf{\Omega}_r)} &= \frac{\mathbf{x}^\top \hat{\mathbf{S}}^{1/2}\hat{\mathbf{U}}^\top \mathbf{U}\mathbf{S}^{-1}\mathbf{U}^\top \hat{\mathbf{U}}\hat{\mathbf{S}}^{1/2}\mathbf{x}}{\|\mathbf{x}\|^2} \frac{\mathbf{x}^\top \hat{\mathbf{S}}^{-1/2}\hat{\mathbf{U}}^\top \mathbf{U}\mathbf{S}\mathbf{U}^\top \hat{\mathbf{U}}\hat{\mathbf{S}}^{-1/2}\mathbf{x}}{\|\mathbf{x}\|^2} \\ &= \frac{\mathbf{x}^\top \mathbf{H}\mathbf{x}}{\|\mathbf{x}\|^2} \frac{\mathbf{x}^\top \mathbf{H}^{-1}\mathbf{x}}{\|\mathbf{x}\|^2} \end{aligned}$$

[6] For another critical perspective on R^2 used as a metric for time-series model, see Lewellen et al. (2010).

Consider now the SVD of $\mathbf{H} = \mathbf{V}\mathbf{D}\mathbf{V}^\top$ and define $\mathbf{y} := \mathbf{V}^\top\mathbf{x}$. We have

$$\frac{\text{var}(\mathbf{w}(\hat{\mathbf{\Omega}}_\mathbf{r}), \mathbf{\Omega}_\mathbf{r})}{\text{var}(\mathbf{w}(\mathbf{\Omega}_\mathbf{r}), \mathbf{\Omega}_\mathbf{r})} = \left(\sum_i \frac{y_i^2}{\sum_j y_j^2} d_i\right)\left(\sum_i \frac{y_i^2}{\sum_j y_j^2} d_i^{-1}\right)$$

The term on the RHS can be interpreted as $E(\xi)E(1/\xi)$, where ξ is a random variable taking value d_i in state i with probability $p_i := y_i^2 / \sum_j y_j^2$. By Jensen's inequality, $E(1/\xi) \geq 1/E(\xi)$ and the result follows. ∎

The Takeaways

1. When evaluating a factor model, we are concerned with three dimensions of performance:
   (a) Accuracy of the *covariance matrix*, since the portfolio's volatility prediction accuracy depends on it.
   (b) Accuracy of the *precision matrix*, since it is used in mean-variance portfolio optimization.
   (c) *Ancillary performance metrics* like turnover and beta prediction since they are important in trading applications.
2. Two principled metrics for volatility estimation are QLIKE and MSE.
3. They can be extended to the multivariate case, allowing for evaluation of models across different strategies (average-case, worst-case, etc.), focusing on realistic portfolio scenarios.
4. For precision matrix accuracy, we use Minimum Variance Portfolios: portfolios with the least predicted variance among all portfolios satisfying a linear constraints. A lower realized variance indicates a better model.
5. Another metric is the Mahalanobis distance test. It is portfolio independent.
6. Ancillary metrics are as follows.
   (a) Turnover: Considers the frequency of model updates and potential transaction costs, with measures such as FMP turnover.
   (b) Beta Accuracy: Compares predicted versus realized betas for portfolios (e.g., thematic, factor-mimicking) to ensure consistency with market exposure.
7. We caution against the use of R^2 for factor model evaluation as it can be manipulated and may not reflect true predictive performance.

Chapter 6

Fundamental Factor Models

The Questions

1. What are the steps involved in the estimation of a fundamental factor model?
2. How do we deal with heteroskedastic returns?
3. Can we estimate a model when we have "redundant" characteristics of the securities in the loadings matrix?
4. What should we be careful about when estimating the factor covariance matrix?
5. Can we make the model more responsive to sudden changes in volatility?
6. How do we estimate off-diagonal terms in the idiosyncratic covariance matrix?
7. How do we link different factor models into a coherent one?
8. How do we model currencies in the model, and how do we change the reference currency?

Fundamental (or characteristic-based) factor models estimate Equation (4.1) using as inputs $\mathbf{r}_t$ and $\mathbf{B}_t$. The outputs of the models are estimates of the factor and idiosyncratic returns $\mathbf{f}_t$, ϵ_t, as well as their covariance matrices $\mathbf{\Omega}_f$, $\mathbf{\Omega}_\epsilon$. Fundamental factor models are perhaps the most popular ones among practitioners. Reasons for their popularity are:

- *Good Performance.* Commercial models are the outcome of a long process of refinement. The first models date back to the mid-1970s. Consequently, some important factors have been identified.
- *Interpretability.* Firm characteristics provide a summary description of individual firms, and exposures based on these characteristics give a summary of a portfolio.
- *Connections to Academic Research.* In the asset pricing literature, multifactor models originate with the Arbitrage Pricing Theory of Ross (1976), and the reference model used by academic researchers to identify pricing anomalies is the three-factor model by Fama and French (1993).
- *Alpha Research.* Fundamental models are the workhorse of alpha research, because they allow the portfolio manager to incorporate almost any data source, to analyze very large datasets, to interpret the outcome of the analysis, and to feed the outcome to a portfolio construction system.

6.1 The Inputs and the Process

There are five major steps needed to identify a factor model. Some of them require sound quantitative methods; others are more art than science. Before we even begin to describe the steps, we should focus on the inputs.

6.1.1 The Inputs

Fundamental model inputs are:

1. A set of returns per asset/date, i.e., the $\mathbf{r}_t$ part.
2. A set of *raw characteristics* per asset/date/characteristic identifier; from these inputs we generate the matrices $\mathbf{B}_t$.

Asset returns. Returns are usually reported over intervals of equal duration. These intervals determine the periodicity of the model. Daily returns may be based on close-to-close prices. Intraday returns may be based on the last transaction price observed in that intraday interval. The interval can range from 30 minutes to a sub-minute interval. It would seem that returns are unambiguously defined, but this is *not* the case. The answer to the question "what is the final price in a time period?" is not easy or unique. Ultimately, models of returns should help the portfolio manager develop a profitable real-life strategy. If prices are such that we could not have executed transactions reliably at their quoted values, then the factor model will not be reliable, and neither will be the strategy built on the model. Consider the closing price. Where does it come from? In many stock exchanges, at the end of the day the limit-order book (LOB) is replaced by a *closing auction* (CA). Without delving into the details of a CA, it suffices to know that a CA is a very liquid event, in which about 7% of the daily volume of a stock is traded.[1] Consequently, *for a liquid stock* the closing price is meaningful, in the sense that it is exploitable by a portfolio manager, at a non-negligible size. Now, compare this scenario to one in which we are interested in modeling a small-cap stock that is a component of the Russell 2000 index. Such a stock would likely qualify to be a member of the risk model estimation universe. However, it could trade at very low volumes. In addition, if we model intraday returns, then we must exercise additional care. What does it mean that the price at the end of a 10-minute interval was $6.93? Maybe the stock did not even transact in that interval, and the period return is zero. Or maybe there were only a handful of trades. What is the correct price, then? The transaction price? That is not obvious. Maybe the transaction happened at the ask, but the transaction just before happened at the bid. Or should we use the mid-price between the bid and the ask? Could our strategy reliably transact at either of these prices in real life? These are just some of the many questions one should ask when developing models based on intra-day return models, but not only. For many asset classes, determining good daily closing prices is a very challenging, important and thankless task. The details are too asset- and data-vendor-specific to be covered in detail; moreover, this is an area where traders accumulate

[1] As of October 2024, in North American markets. It is higher on days when indices are reconstituted.

Intellectual Property that is very material to their success. A few heuristic rules should help. First, the shorter the interval, the harder the problem. We saw this already in Section 2.2.4. You have to model what price is appropriate (bid, ask, mid); whether to explicitly model the noise in price observations; whether time-of-day non-stationarity matters; whether to model close-to-open returns and intraday returns separately. The second recommendation is to think explicitly about the relationship between asset liquidity and model periodicity. Liquidity, for our purposes, could be proxied by trading volume in a fixed interval. Usually, average daily trading volume is available. Liquidity is related to price discovery. The price of a very liquid stock is less prone to observation errors, and it is more tradeable than that of an illiquid stock. Therefore, the choices of model universe and model periodicity are related. Unless you want to model market microstructure explicitly, and want to rely on closing per-period prices, then a shorter period will imply that your model universe will be smaller.

Raw characteristic data. This is the "art", or better, the "dark art" part of the modeling task. "Raw data" can mean almost anything. A possible classification of raw data is in structured and unstructured. The former include numerical data and categorical data that can be associated to a security and to an estimation period. *Categorical* data take only a finite set of values, which do not necessarily have an ordering relationship. Examples are the country and sector of a stock. A slightly less common example is the credit rating of a company, which does admit an order. Unstructured data include any data that do not come directly in such a tabular form. Examples are the earnings transcripts of a company, or its regulatory filings (Forms 10-K, 10-Q, 8-Q); or the web scraping of a firm with information about its products; or the consumer credit card transactions with a firm; or, even more, location data of customers visiting the store of a firm. These few examples give just a taste of the immensity of possible inputs to a model. For asset return modeling purposes, we extract from these vast troves of alternative data some representative statistics that can be interpreted as structured data. For example, from transactional data, we can extract levels (dollars transacted in a quarter by a consumer firm's web portal) and trends (quarterly changes in those levels); or we can extract measures of geographical dispersion. Some of these operations can be automated; some may require the use of machine learning tasks like classification and clustering. One important feature of all these operations, though, is that they entail some form of human expertise. In fact, the task of extracting structured data from unstructured information is perhaps the one that requires the highest amount of human intelligence. A great number of papers have been published on characteristic data. Maybe in the future we will be able to feed such disparate sources of information into a black box and directly predict prices, or even recommend trades. In that event, I'll gladly write a second edition to this book.

6.1.2 The Process

The estimation steps of a characteristic model are:

1. *Data ingestion.* This step encompasses receiving datasets from vendors, checking their integrity, and performing essential data checks. Among them:
   - Ensure that data are of the correct type and not corrupt. This happens with positive probability.
   - Ensure that the set of securities is not substantially different from the previous period.
   - Ensure that the fraction of missing data per asset and characteristic is not substantially different.
   - Identify and report data outliers.
2. *Estimation universe selection.* I introduced issues related to this set earlier in the chapter. The criteria for inclusions are:
   - *Tradeability.* The assets must be sufficiently liquid, because FMPs include them all.
   - *Data quality.* This is closely related to the liquidity of the assets, but for a different goal. We need securities for which prices are *discovered*, i.e., close to their economic fundamental value, since we are using those prices for return calculations and model estimation.
   - *Relevance to investments.* The estimation universe should be overlapping to some extent with the investment universe of the strategy. This is more of an art. There is not (to my knowledge) a rigorous treatment of this problem.
3. *Winsorization.* Identify outliers in returns of the estimation universe and winsorize them.

4. *Loadings generation*. Generate characteristics $\mathbf{B}_t$ by transformations and combinations.
5. *Cross-sectional regression*. For each $t = 1, \ldots, T$, perform a cross-sectional regression of asset returns $\mathbf{r}_t$ against the loadings[2] $\mathbf{B}_t$. The outputs of this step are the vectors $\hat{\mathbf{f}}_t$ and $\hat{\boldsymbol{\epsilon}}_t$.
6. *Time-series estimation*. Using the time series from the previous step, estimate:
   (a) the factor covariance matrix $\hat{\boldsymbol{\Omega}}_{\mathrm{f},t}$;
   (b) the idiosyncratic covariance matrix $\hat{\boldsymbol{\Omega}}_{\epsilon,t}$;
   (c) the risk-adjusted performance of factors returns.

The next three sections cover the essentials of factor models: regression and covariance estimation. We then consider winsorization in Section 6.5. The next section presents an advanced topic on linking multiple factor models coherently, and also considers portfolio assets denominated in multiple currencies. Finally, we offer a preliminary description of identifying the factor characteristics.

6.2 Cross-Sectional Regression

The first step is cross-sectional regression

$$\mathbf{r}_t = \mathbf{B}_t\mathbf{f}_t + \boldsymbol{\epsilon}_t, \qquad t \in \mathbb{N} \tag{6.1}$$

where the parameters to be estimated are $\mathbf{f}_t$ and $\boldsymbol{\epsilon}_t$. This is a case of *random design*: the tuple $(\mathbf{r}_t, \mathbf{B}_t, \mathbf{f}_t, \boldsymbol{\epsilon}_t)$ can be viewed as independent samples drawn from a common distribution. We observe $(\mathbf{r}_t, \mathbf{B}_t)$, and we estimate $(\mathbf{f}_t, \boldsymbol{\epsilon}_t)$.

Several regression approaches are possible. One may minimize the square loss $\left\|\mathbf{r}_t - \mathbf{B}_t\mathbf{f}_t\right\|^2$. The assumptions behind this step are:

1. The matrix $\mathbf{B}_t \in \mathbb{R}^{n\times m}$ has full rank. A necessary but not sufficient condition for this is that $m \leq n$.
2. Residual returns $\epsilon_{t,i}$ have zero mean, are homoskedastic (i.e., have the same variance), and are independent of each other.

[2] A reminder: as explained in Section 4.6, we denote $\mathbf{B}_t$ the loadings available at the end of period $t-1$.

3. Factor returns and residual returns are independent of each other.
4. Factor and residual returns are "well-behaved", in the sense of having at least finite fourth moments.

These assumptions can be relaxed. If the matrix is rank-deficient, the solution to the minimum-norm problem exists but is not unique, and factor returns are not identified. Later in this section we will introduce ways to deal with rank-deficient matrices, in order to have a unique solution. Homoskedasticity is also not a necessary assumption. If residuals have different variances for different assets, we can weight the losses for each asset differently. The intuition is that, if the residual return of an asset has a large variance, we should weight the loss for that asset less, so that this single term does not dominate the sum of losses, and unduly affect the parameters' estimation.

We estimate Model (6.1) by minimizing the sum of a loss function $L : \mathbb{R}^n \to \mathbb{R}^+$:

$$\min L(\mathbf{r}_t - \mathbf{B}_t\mathbf{f}_t)$$

In this section, we choose to minimize the weighted sum of the squared residuals. We know a diagonal, positive matrix $\mathbf{W}$, whose diagonal terms can be interpreted as weights assigned to observation (i.e., asset) i. We then find $\mathbf{f}$ that minimizes

$$L(\mathbf{r}_t - \mathbf{B}_t\mathbf{f}_t) := (\mathbf{r}_t - \mathbf{B}_t\mathbf{f}_t)'\mathbf{W}(\mathbf{r}_t - \mathbf{B}_t\mathbf{f}_t) \tag{6.2}$$

There are good reasons for this choice. If we assume that Model (6.1) is the true model of returns, then least squares gives us the lowest-variance *unbiased* estimate among all the linear models (Hansen, 2022). The lack of bias matters for performance attribution and alpha identification. Even a small bias in factor return estimation (and, consequently, in residual returns) would accumulate over the course of a multi-period performance attribution, thus distorting the results and the insights from the analysis. An additional benefit of weighted least squares regression is that its estimates have a natural interpretation in terms of *Factor-Mimicking Portfolios* (FMPs). We will cover these in detail later. For now, it should suffice to say these are investable portfolios whose returns track as well as possible the true—but unobservable—factor returns. Our recommendation therefore is to use this loss function at least as a starting point, and to run thorough diagnostics to identify its possible shortcomings. To fix ideas, we make the assumption that the model is $\mathbf{r}_t = \mathbf{B}\mathbf{f}_t + \epsilon_t$, with $\mathbf{f}_t \sim N(0, \mathbf{\Omega}_\mathbf{f})$ and $\epsilon_t \sim N(0, \mathbf{\Omega}_\epsilon)$. We address the issue of heteroskedasticity by pre-multiplying both sides of the equation $\mathbf{r}_t = \mathbf{B}_t\mathbf{f}_t + \epsilon_t$ by matrix $\mathbf{\Omega}_\epsilon^{-1/2}$. Now idiosyncratic returns are homoskedastic. We use the Ordinary Least Squares (OLS) loss function $\left\|\mathbf{\Omega}_\epsilon^{-1/2}(\mathbf{r}_t - \mathbf{B}\mathbf{f}_t)\right\|$, which is equivalent to the loss function in Equation (6.2), with a weight matrix $\mathbf{W} = \mathbf{\Omega}_\epsilon^{-1}$.

Factor loadings are assumed to be constant over time. This simplifies the formulas below, but can be relaxed by simply regressing the returns on the time-varying loadings.

Given $\mathbf{B}$, $\mathbf{\Omega}_\epsilon$, the Gaussian likelihood is given by

$$\prod_{t=1}^{T} \frac{1}{(2\pi)^{n/2}|\mathbf{\Omega}_\epsilon|^{1/2}} \exp\left(-\frac{1}{2}(\mathbf{r}_t - \mathbf{B}\mathbf{f}_t)^\intercal \mathbf{\Omega}_\epsilon^{-1}(\mathbf{r}_t - \mathbf{B}\mathbf{f}_t)\right)$$

If we denote the matrix of returns $\mathbf{R} \in \mathbb{R}^{n\times T}$, the log-likelihood is equivalent to $-||\mathbf{R} - \mathbf{B}\mathbf{F}||^2_{\mathbf{\Omega}_\epsilon^{-1}}$. We write the optimization problem as

$$\begin{aligned} \min \quad & \left\|\mathbf{\Omega}_\epsilon^{-1/2}(\mathbf{R} - \mathbf{B}\mathbf{F})\right\|^2 \\ \text{s.t.} \quad & \mathbf{F} \in \mathbb{R}^{m\times T} \end{aligned}$$

We consider first the case of a single period. In this case $\mathbf{R}$ and $\mathbf{F}$ are column vectors. The solution is the OLS solution: $\mathbf{F} = (\mathbf{B}^\intercal\mathbf{\Omega}_\epsilon^{-1}\mathbf{B})^{-1}\mathbf{B}^\intercal\mathbf{\Omega}_\epsilon^{-1}\mathbf{R}$. In the case of multiple periods, the problem is the sum of the single-period problems:

$$||\mathbf{R} - \mathbf{B}\mathbf{F}||^2_{\mathbf{\Omega}_\epsilon^{-1}} = \sum_t \left\|\mathbf{\Omega}_\epsilon^{-1/2}(\mathbf{r}_t - \mathbf{B}\mathbf{f}_t)\right\|^2$$

Each term can be minimized independently. Hence, we have

$$\hat{\mathbf{f}}_t = (\mathbf{B}^\intercal\mathbf{\Omega}_\epsilon^{-1}\mathbf{B})^{-1}\mathbf{B}^\intercal\mathbf{\Omega}_\epsilon^{-1}\mathbf{r}_t \tag{6.3}$$

As a direct extension of the previous formula in matrix form, the problem of minimizing $||\mathbf{A} - \mathbf{B}\mathbf{X}||$ has a closed-form solution:

$$\arg\min_{\mathbf{X}} ||\mathbf{A} - \mathbf{B}\mathbf{X}||^2_F = (\mathbf{B}^\intercal\mathbf{B})^{-1}\mathbf{B}^\intercal\mathbf{A} \tag{6.4}$$

Insight 6.1: *Which idiosyncratic covariance matrix?*

In the cross-sectional regression procedure, we have taken as an input the covariance matrix $\mathbf{\Omega}_\epsilon$. However, this matrix is an *output* of the factor estimation procedure. How to resolve this impasse? We have two options. Underlying both of them is the idea that we need a proxy for the covariance matrix. This proxy won't be the best possible covariance matrix, but it is better than the identity matrix, which corresponds to OLS. The first, and simplest one, is to take advantage of a pre-existing factor model provided by a vendor like MSCI Barra or Axioma. A second approach is to perform a two-stage process. In the first stage, we use the identity matrix as a proxy in the cross-sectional regression, and estimate the idiosyncratic covariance matrix, as explained in Section 6.4. Then, equipped with this matrix, we repeat the entire model estimation process, starting with the cross-sectional regression, and ending with a final idiosyncratic covariance matrix. Finally, there is a variant on this second approach. We can choose the option to run the first-stage estimation process only for a number of periods at the beginning of the history. For example, if we have 20 years of history, we could perform the two-stage process in the first year only. For every day after the first year, we can use as proxy the final estimate of the idiosyncratic covariance matrix estimated for the previous day.

6.2.1 Rank-Deficient Loadings Matrices

In some cases the loadings matrix is rank-deficient: even if there are m factors, the number of independent columns is $p < m$. As concrete (and very common!) examples, consider the following.

- There is a factor with loadings for each asset equal to 1. This is sometimes called a "country", "region," or "universe" factor, since all assets are identically affected by changes in this factor. The interpretation is that this is an "intercept" term in the regression. However, the same loadings matrix contains at the very least industry loadings, which can be interpreted as non-negative weights summing to one. For simplicity, assume that the first factor is the country, and the next $m - 1$ are industries. Then the vector $\mathbf{v} = (1, -1, -1, \ldots, -1)^\top$ is such that $\mathbf{Bv} = 0$. The matrix is rank-deficient.

- In most multi-country models there are industry as well as country loadings. Say the first m_{ind} are industy loadings, followed by m_{ctry} country loadings. The vector $\mathbf{v} = (1, 1, \ldots, 1, -1, -1, \ldots, -1)^\top$, where the first m_{ind} are ones and the remaining m_{ctry} are negative ones, also satisfies $\mathbf{Bv} = 0$.

We generalize this to the case where there are $m - p$ independent vectors $\mathbf{v}_i$ such that $\mathbf{Bv}_i = 0$. Because of this deficiency, $\mathbf{B}^\top\mathbf{B}$ is not invertible and it is not possible to estimate $\hat{\mathbf{f}}$ using Equation (6.1). There are at least three ways to address such an issue.

- The first one is to remove the redundancy. For example, remove one industry and/or a country and/or a country factor. The benefit is that we can reuse the familiar formula for cross-sectional regression. The drawback is that the original loadings matrix is easier to interpret. We would like to know a portfolio exposure to the country *and* to all industries. The country exposure is telling us whether the portfolio is long or short, which is information that the individual industries exposures don't immediately convey. And, of course, all industries are useful. Just ask the portfolio manager whose main covered industry was removed from the model.
- The second one is to add a small quadratic penalty term to $\|\mathbf{r} - \mathbf{Bf}\|^2$, i.e., $\delta\|\mathbf{f}\|^2$. This removes the degeneracy. The factor estimates are no longer unbiased in the linear model, so a careful analysis would be needed before using this method. In the limit $\delta \to 0$, the solution to the regression problem is the *ridgeless regression* one: $\hat{\mathbf{f}} = (\mathbf{B}^\top\mathbf{\Omega}_\epsilon^{-1}\mathbf{B})^\dagger \mathbf{B}^\top\mathbf{\Omega}_\epsilon^{-1}\mathbf{r}_t$, where "†" denotes the Moore–Penrose pseudo-inverse operator.
- Finally, we can add $m - p$ side constraints of the form $\mathbf{C}^\top\mathbf{f} = \mathbf{a}$ (Heston and Rouwenhorst, 1994, 1995) and solve a constrained linear regression problem. This adds some (minor) complexity to the estimation process, but maintains or even enhances the interpretability of factor

returns. For example, we may require that the market-weighted sum of industry factor returns be zero. This would be written as $\mathbf{w}^\mathsf{T}\mathbf{B}_{\text{ind}}\mathbf{f}_{\text{ind}} = 0$, where $\mathbf{B}_{\text{ind}}$ is the column subset of industry factors, $\mathbf{f}_{\text{ind}}$ is the subset of industry factor returns, and $\mathbf{w}$ is a weight vector of asset market caps per asset. The constraint says "the sum across assets of market-weighted industry returns must be 0". If $\mathbf{w}$ are chosen to be the weights of a benchmark portfolio, this can be read as "the benchmark portfolio must have no industry returns".

6.3 Estimating the Factor Covariance Matrix

We have a random vector of factor returns $\hat{\mathbf{f}}_t$, from which we want to estimate $\mathbf{\Omega}_\mathbf{f}$. We assume that the $\mathbf{f}_{t,i}$ have fourth moments, but unlike in Chapter 7 to come, we cannot assume that $\mathbf{\Omega}_\mathbf{f}$ has a special structure. By construction, we do not expect the matrix to be spiked. The number of samples over which we estimate the covariance matrix can be larger than the number of factors; for example, we could estimate a model with 10 factors and 500 days of estimation. The assumptions m constant, $T \to \infty$ seem appropriate.

Let $\mathbf{\Omega}_T^{\text{emp}} := T^{-1}\sum_{t=1}^{T} \hat{\mathbf{f}}_t\hat{\mathbf{f}}_t^\mathsf{T}$. By the Law of Large Numbers, $\mathbf{\Omega}_T^{\text{emp}} \to \mathbf{\Omega}_f$ almost surely. Both eigenvalues and eigenvectors converge to the covariance matrix. See the Appendix, Section 7.6.2. Factor volatilities converge to the true (also denoted *population*) volatilities, and the relative standard error is $\sqrt{2/T}$. The principal components of the factor covariance matrix also converge to their population counterparts, so long as the volatilities of factors are all sufficiently separated. This seems to settle the issue of covariance estimation: just take the empirical covariance matrix. There are several problems, though:

- Oftentimes, the number of factors is not much smaller than the number of observations. In this case, shrinkage may improve the quality of the estimate.
- We will see that factor return estimates are inflated by the estimation process. This is another argument in favor of shrinkage.
- Factor returns are non-stationary, sometimes dramatically so at the onset of a crisis. We need to take this into account.
- Factor returns are mildly autocorrelated. We need to correct that.

6.3.1 *Factor Covariance Matrix Shrinkage*

The first issue lies in the fact that the factor return estimates $\hat{\mathbf{f}}_t$ are just that: estimates. They are the outcome of WLS linear regression estimates, Equation (4.16). The covariance matrix[3] of the estimates $\hat{\mathbf{f}}_t$ is $(\mathbf{B}^\top \mathbf{\Omega}_\epsilon^{-1} \mathbf{B})^{-1}$. This implies that the estimate var $(\hat{\mathbf{f}}_t)$ is biased:

$$\text{var}\,(\hat{\mathbf{f}}_t) = \mathbf{\Omega}_\mathbf{f} + (\mathbf{B}^\top \mathbf{\Omega}_\epsilon^{-1} \mathbf{B})^{-1} \tag{6.5}$$

Insight 6.2: *FMP interpretation of factor covariance shrinkage*

An alternative lens to interpret Equation (6.5) is via factor-mimicking portfolios. The return of FMP $\mathbf{w}_i$ is $\hat{f}_i = f_i + \boldsymbol{\epsilon}^\top \mathbf{w}_i$. The covariance of the returns of FMP i and j, using Equation (9.12), is $\text{cov}(\hat{f}_i, \hat{f}_j) = \text{cov}(f_i, f_j) + [(\mathbf{B}^\top \mathbf{\Omega}_\epsilon^{-1} \mathbf{B})^{-1}]_{i,j}$, which is Equation (6.5). This suggests that we should shrink the empirical covariance matrix in order to obtain an unbiased estimate:

$$\hat{\mathbf{\Omega}}_\mathbf{f} = \text{var}\,(\hat{\mathbf{f}}_t) - (\mathbf{B}^\top \mathbf{\Omega}_\epsilon^{-1} \mathbf{B})^{-1} \tag{6.6}$$

How big is the correction? In the simpler but instructive case where $\mathbf{B}^\top \mathbf{B} = \mathbf{I}_m$ and $\mathbf{\Omega}_\epsilon = \mathbf{I}_n$, the estimated factor returns are $\hat{\mathbf{f}}_t = \mathbf{B}^\top \mathbf{r}_t$, and $\text{var}\,(\hat{\mathbf{f}}_t) = T^{-1} \sum_t \hat{\mathbf{f}}_t \hat{\mathbf{f}}_t^\top = \mathbf{B}^\top \hat{\mathbf{\Omega}}_\mathbf{r} \mathbf{B}$, and therefore

$$\hat{\mathbf{\Omega}}_\mathbf{f} = \mathbf{B}^\top \hat{\mathbf{\Omega}}_\mathbf{r} \mathbf{B} - \mathbf{I}_m \tag{6.7}$$

In applications the number of factors ranges between 1 and 100 and the number of periods ranges between 126 (six months, for daily returns) and 500 (two years of daily returns). Therefore we are not always in the regime $p \ll T$ and the asymptotics of Section 7.6.2 do not apply; neither do results for spiked covariance matrices. A popular shrinkage applied to the covariance matrix is Ledoit–Wolf shrinkage (Ledoit and Wolf, 2003a,b, 2004). It has the advantage of being simple to implement and to tune, and having good performance. The shrunken covariance matrix is

$$\mathbf{\Omega}_{\mathbf{f},\text{shrink}}(\rho) = (1-\rho)\hat{\mathbf{\Omega}}_\mathbf{f} + \rho \frac{\text{trace}\left(\hat{\mathbf{\Omega}}_\mathbf{f}\right)}{m} \mathbf{I}_m$$

[3] See Equation (4.17).

which we combine with Equation (6.6):

$$\Omega_{\mathbf{f},\text{shrink}}(\rho) = (1-\rho)[\text{var}(\hat{\mathbf{f}}_t) - (\mathbf{B}^\top \Omega_\epsilon^{-1} \mathbf{B})^{-1}] + \rho \frac{\text{trace}\left(\text{var}(\hat{\mathbf{f}}_t) - (\mathbf{B}^\top \Omega_\epsilon^{-1} \mathbf{B})^{-1}\right)}{m} \mathbf{I}_m$$

where $\rho \in (0,1)$ is a tunable parameter.

6.3.2 Dynamic Conditional Correlation

An alternative and common approach to estimating the empirical covariance matrix $\text{var}(\hat{\mathbf{f}}_t)$ is to model the factor volatilities and correlations separately. Namely, we decompose the population covariance matrix into the product of a correlation matrix $\mathbf{C}$ and a diagonal matrix $\mathbf{V}$ containing the factor volatilities:

$$\Omega_\mathbf{f} = \mathbf{VCV}$$

Bollerslev (1990) modeled the volatilities as time-varying and the correlation matrix as constant. Practitioners estimate the empirical correlation matrix and the volatility vector using exponential weighted averages with different half-lives:

$$\text{diag}\left(\mathbf{V}_t^2\right) = \kappa_V \sum_{s=0}^{T} e^{-s/\tau_V} \hat{\mathbf{f}}_{t-s} \circ \hat{\mathbf{f}}_{t-s}$$

$$\mathbf{C} := \kappa_C \sum_{s=0}^{T} e^{-s/\tau_C} \mathbf{V}_{t-s}^{-1} \hat{\mathbf{f}}_{t-s} \hat{\mathbf{f}}_{t-s}^\top \mathbf{V}_{t-s}^{-1}$$

where $\tau_C > \tau_V$ are half-lives for factor correlations and variances, respectively, and κ_V, κ_C are normalizing constants. In many equity models estimated using daily returns, the half-lives are set between three months (for exceptionally responsive variance estimations) and two years.

6.3.3 Short-Term Volatility Updating

Estimated factor returns often exhibit large, unanticipated values. Anecdotally, their volatility does not vary smoothly but discontinuously, with regimes of high volatility, followed by a quick transition to low-volatility regimes. This poses two challenges for the modeler. First, a simple exponential weighted estimator will react too slowly to sudden increases in volatility. The very concrete effect of this is that the investors will severely underestimate systemic risk at the time when they need accurate estimates the most. Second, the estimates react too slowly to *reductions* in volatility. By the nature of the weighting scheme, volatilities decay no faster than exponentially, with half-lives of several months. Several approaches have been proposed to address this issue. We mention one that performs well and is simple to implement: Short-Term Volatility Updating (STVU). First, we model the multivariate factor returns so that they are modulated by a latent state variable x_t:

$$\begin{aligned} \mathbf{f}_t &= e^{x_t/2}\mathbf{V}_t\mathbf{C}_t^{1/2}\eta_t \\ \eta_t &\sim N(\mathbf{0}, \mathbf{I}_m) \\ x_{t+1} &= \phi x_t + \sigma\gamma_t \end{aligned} \tag{6.8}$$

In the degenerate case where $x_t = 0$ for all t, the model reduces to one where the factor covariance matrix is $\mathbf{\Omega_f}$.

Define $\mathbf{u}_t := \mathbf{C}_t^{-1/2}\mathbf{V}_t^{-1}\mathbf{f}_t$. Then $x_t = \log\|\mathbf{u}_t\|^2 - \log\|\boldsymbol{\eta}_t\|^2$. This is a linear state-space model. Define

$$\begin{aligned} \kappa &=: E\left(\log\|\boldsymbol{\eta}_t\|^2\right) \\ \epsilon_t &=: \log\|\boldsymbol{\eta}_t\|^2 - \kappa \\ x_t &:= \xi_t \\ y_t &:= \log\|\mathbf{u}_t\|^2 - \kappa \end{aligned}$$

The state-space equation is

$$\begin{aligned} y_t &= x_t + \epsilon_t \\ x_{t+1} &= \phi x_t + \sigma\gamma_t \end{aligned}$$

and the estimate of the state takes the form[4]

$$e^{\hat{x}_t/2} = \exp\left[\frac{1 - e^{-1/\tau_0}}{2}\sum_{s=0}^{\infty} e^{-s/\tau_0}\left(\log\|\mathbf{u}_{t-s}\|^2 - \kappa\right)\right]$$

From the first equation in Model (6.8), the factor covariance matrix is then adjusted by multiplying by the factor $e^{\hat{x}_t}$.

[4] See Section 2.4.2.

Some implementations use the linear approximation of this formula and the approximate equality $\kappa = \log(m) + E\log(\|\boldsymbol{\eta}_t\|^2/m) \simeq \log m$ since $\|\boldsymbol{\eta}_t\|^2/m \to 1$ a.s. for $m \to \infty$.

$$e^{\hat{x}_t/2} \simeq \exp\left[(1 - e^{-1/\tau_0})\sum_{s=0}^{\infty} e^{-s/\tau_0}\left(\frac{\|\mathbf{u}_{t-s}\|}{\sqrt{m}} - 1\right)\right] \tag{6.9}$$

$$\simeq \exp\left[(1 - e^{-1/\tau_0})\left(\sum_{s=0}^{\infty} e^{-s/\tau_0}\frac{\|\mathbf{u}_{t-s}\|}{\sqrt{m}}\right) - 1\right] \tag{6.10}$$

$$\simeq (1 - e^{-1/\tau_0})\sum_{s=0}^{\infty} e^{-s/\tau_0}\frac{\|\mathbf{u}_{t-s}\|}{\sqrt{m}} \tag{6.11}$$

The interpretation of the formula is clearest in the special case of uncorrelated factor returns. In this case, $\mathbf{u}_t$ is the vector of z-scored returns. If $x_t = 1$, they have unit variance. If we view the random variables u_i as iid samples of a random variable, the term $\|\mathbf{u}_{t-s}\|/\sqrt{m}$ gives us an estimate of its standard deviation, and if this estimate exceeds one, then our original estimates for the standard deviations of the factor need to be revised upward. That is what the model does. The half-life τ_0 is typically between 10 and 20 days for daily risk models, in order to incorporate the rapid onset of a shock.

6.3.4 Correcting for Autocorrelation in Factor Returns

Daily factor and asset returns usually exhibit mild, but non-zero, short-term autocorrelation. When the factor covariance matrix is estimated on shorter time intervals, the autocorrelation may be more pronounced. In these cases, adjusting for autocorrelation improves the model's performance. Cohen et al. (1983) build on previous work by Scholes and Williams (1977) and assume that the observed returns follow an autoregressive process of order $l_{\max}$ that is a function of underlying uncorrelated returns. The coefficients in the $AR(l_{\max})$ equation are random, but sum to 1. Let the lagged covariance matrix C_l be defined as

$$[\mathbf{C}_l]_{i,j} := \mathrm{cov}(\mathbf{f}_{t,i}, \mathbf{f}_{t-l,j})$$

Then the autocorrelation-consistent estimator is given by

$$\hat{\boldsymbol{\Omega}}_{\mathrm{f}} = \mathbf{C}_0 + \frac{1}{2}\sum_{l=1}^{l_{\max}}(\mathbf{C}_l + \mathbf{C}_l^{\mathsf{T}})$$

An alternative approach, which is asymptotically consistent in the limit $T \to \infty$, is Newey and West's estimator (Newey and West, 1987):

$$\hat{\boldsymbol{\Omega}}_{\mathrm{f}} = \mathbf{C}_0 + \sum_{l=1}^{l_{\max}}\left(1 - \frac{l}{1 + l_{\max}}\right)(\mathbf{C}_l + \mathbf{C}_l^{\mathsf{T}})$$

6.4 Estimating the Idiosyncratic Covariance Matrix

Next, we need to estimate the covariance matrix $\boldsymbol{\Omega}_\epsilon$ based on the period estimated idiosyncratic returns $\hat{\boldsymbol{\epsilon}}_t$.

6.4.1 *Exponential Weighting*

As in the case of factor volatility, we use exponential weighting for idiosyncratic volatility estimation. Let $\mathbf{E} \in \mathbb{R}^{n\times T}$ be the matrix of estimated idiosyncratic returns, with $[\mathbf{E}]_{i,t} := \epsilon_{i,t}$. The exponential weighting parameter is the half-life τ. The weighting matrix is a diagonal positive-definite matrix $\mathbf{W} \in \mathbb{R}^{T\times T}$. A common choice for the diagonal terms is that of exponential weights $[\mathbf{W}_\tau]_{t,t} = \kappa \exp(-t/\tau)$; the positive constant κ is such that the diagonal terms sum to T. The EWMA empirical idiosyncratic covariance matrix is then $\hat{\boldsymbol{\Omega}}_\epsilon := \mathbf{E}\mathbf{W}\mathbf{E}^{\mathsf{T}}$.

6.4.2 *Visual Inspection*

This matrix should be diagonal, or at least sparse. The sample covariance matrix based on estimated returns does not satisfy these requirements. The sample covariance matrix $\hat{\boldsymbol{\Omega}}_\epsilon$ is neither sparse nor positive-definite, since $T < n$. We (the modelers) could set all the non-diagonal terms to zero, which effectively amounts to a radical shrinkage of the idiosyncratic correlation matrix. This step, however, is not warranted. As a sanity check, I recommend performing a visual inspection of the empirical covariance matrix. Oftentimes, there are striking patterns that can be interpreted as factors that should be added to the model. For example, some Chinese securities are listed both in Mainland China (A and B shares) and in Hong Kong (H shares). These securities have highly correlated but not identical returns, and the correlations will show up in the idiosyncratic covariance matrix. In such a case, rather than assuming that A, B, H shares are identical (they are not), it is more appropriate to add a "share class" factor to the model.

6.4.3 Short-Term Idio Update

Idiosyncratic returns, like factor returns, are subject to sudden changes in volatility that are not captured well by exponential weighting with long half-lifes τ. A very responsive daily return model has $\tau = 126$ trading days, and the shocks may occur over 10 trading days. As a remedy, we reuse the STVU machinery of Section 6.3.3, with one minor but important modification. We use as an example the case of equities, even though the technique is easily applicable to other asset classes. Stocks are likely to receive large shocks in proximity of earnings, either because new information is released before or on earnings date, or because such information becomes fully priced in the following days. We introduce tent-shaped variables $a_{i,t}$. Let $T_{\text{earn},i}$ be the earning date, and τ_{earn} be a time horizon during which earnings information is received. Define the function as

$$a_{i,t} = \begin{cases} 1 - |t - T_{\text{earn},i}|/\tau_{\text{earn}} & \text{if } |t - T_{\text{earn},i}| \leq \tau_{\text{earn}} \\ 0 & \text{otherwise} \end{cases}$$

$a_{i,t}$ ranges from zero to one, when t is within τ_{earn} number of days from the earnings date $t_{i,\text{earn}}$. We use Model (6.8), but restricting our updates to those stocks within the earnings announcement window. The STVU model is somewhat simplified by the fact that the correlation matrix is approximately diagonal. We restrict our attention to the linear approximation: the corrective term is

$$e^{\hat{x}_t/2} = \kappa_0 \sum_{s=0}^{\infty} e^{-s/\tau_0} \sqrt{\frac{\sum_i a_{i,t}(\epsilon_{i,t}/\hat{\sigma}_{i,t})^2}{\sum_i a_{i,t}}}$$

and applies only to the assets affected by earnings:

$$\hat{\sigma}_{i,t}^2 \leftarrow \left[(1 - a_{i,t}) + a_{i,t} e^{\hat{x}_t}\right] \hat{\sigma}_{i,t}^2$$

6.4.4 *Off-Diagonal Clustering*

Finally, we need to identify those assets whose idiosyncratic returns are highly correlated. Two instances are important. The first one is the case of different securities that refer to the same underlying asset. For example, some stocks are listed as different share classes; for example, Berkshire Hathaway trades under BRK.A and BRK.B, with different fractional values. The liquidity of the two securities differs; yet, their returns are highly correlated. Whether to include the two securities in a factor model or not depends on the nature of the trading strategy employing the model itself. If the strategy intends to exploit the temporary small mispricing between two assets, then we should include both assets. If instead we only intend to invest in the company based on fundamental information, then we should only include a security representative of the underlying asset; typically we choose the most liquid asset. The second instance instead has to do with stocks whose dependencies are not described by factors. In order to be identifiable, factors must be pervasive. A factor influencing only a handful of assets is not a factor, and cannot be identified in a large cross-section of assets. The dependency among these stocks is still detectable in the correlation between their idiosyncratic returns. To identify them, we resort to *correlation thresholding*. We transform the correlation elements by applying a simple clipping operator: $\text{thres}_\lambda(\rho_{i,j}) := \rho_{i,j}\mathbf{1}\{|\rho_{i,j}| > \lambda\}$. The optimal threshold λ is $K\sqrt{\log n/T}$ (Cai et al., 2016), for some positive constant K. In practice, however, it is more instructive to explore the clusters emerging for different values of the threshold λ. For some value of λ, the clusters are (a) stable, in the sense that they do not change much for perturbed values of the threshold; (b) interpretable. They are comprised of "similar" stocks, such as stocks in the same sector or industry, and sometimes they have similar style factor loadings as well.[5] It is important to check that, for every level of the threshold, the correlation matrix is symmetric positive-definite (and well-conditioned). As an example, we use the residual returns from a commercial factor model (Axioma US V.4, Short

[5] We could characterize more rigorously this within-cluster similarity as a distance among factor loadings, and given this similarity measure, propose a more systematic thresholding procedure, but it would fall beyond the scope of the book.

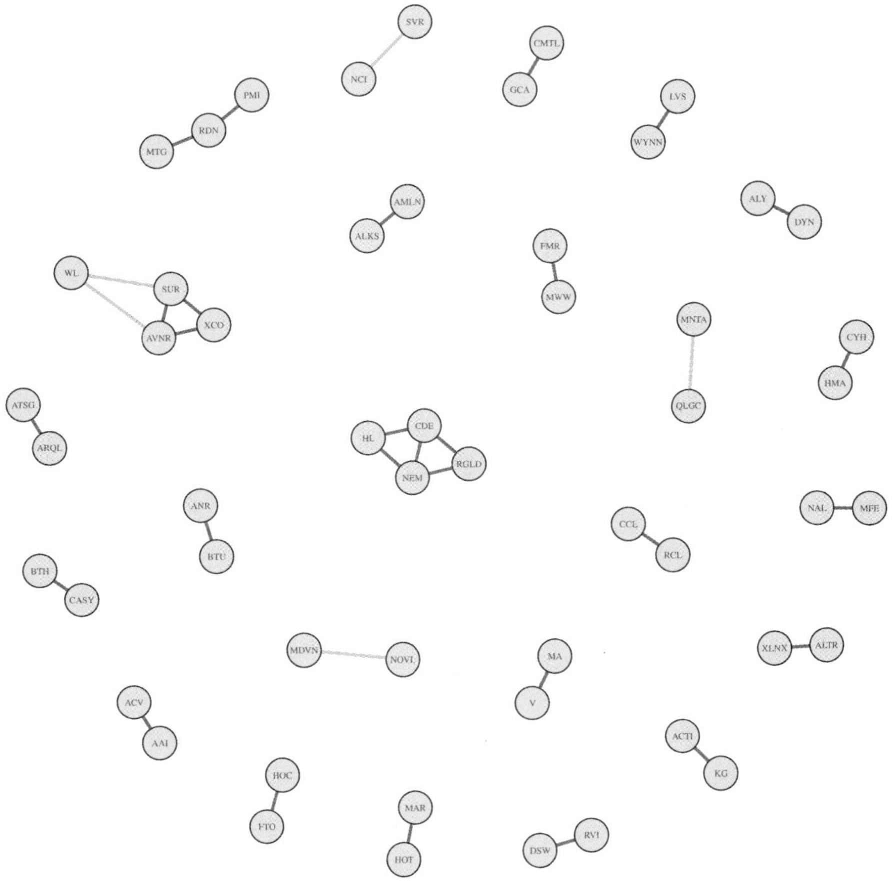

Figure 6.1 Clusters for idiosyncratic matrix.

Horizon, AXUS4SH). We use the residual returns for year 2010. We compute the equal-weighted correlations for continuous constituents of the Russell 3000 index, and threshold their absolute values at 0.55. Figure 6.1 shows the resulting clusters. The number of stocks is small: less than 90, out of a set of nearly 2,900 stocks; about 3%. Table 6.1 lists tickers and associated names. The pairs are quite intuitive: Visa and MasterCard; Wynn and Las Vegas Sands; Peabody Energy and Alpha Natural Resources; and a mining cluster composed of HL, NEM, CDE, RGLD.

Table 6.1 Ticker and company names of cluster components in Figure 6.1

Ticker	Name	Ticker	Name
AAI	AIRTRAN HOLDINGS	HOT	STRW HTL RES WRLWD
ACTI	ACTIVIDENTITY CORP	KG	KING PHARMCUTCL
ACV	ALBERTO CULVER CO NEW	LVS	LAS VEGAS SANDS
ALKS	ALKERMES INC	MA	MASTERCARD INC
ALTR	ALTERA CORP	MAR	MARRIOTT INTL INC NEW
ALY	ALLIS CHALMERS ENERGY INC	MDVN	MEDIVATION INC
AMLN	AMYLIN PHARMACEUTICALS INC	MFE	MCAFEE INC
ANR	ALPHA NATURAL RES	MNTA	MOMENTA PHARMACEUTICALS INC
ARQL	ARQULE	MTG	MGIC INVT CORP WIS
ATSG	AIR TRANSPORT SERVICES GRP I	MWW	MONSTER WORLDWIDE INC
AVNR	AVANIR PHARMACEUTICALS INC	NAL	NEWALLIANCE BANCSHARES INC
BTH	BLYTH INC	NCI	NAVIGANT CONSULTING INC
BTU	PEABODY ENERGY	NEM	NEWMONT MINING CORP
CASY	CASEYS GEN STORES INC	NOVL	NOVELL INC
CCL	CARNIVAL CORP	PMI	PMI GROUP INC
CDE	COEUR D ALENE MINES CORP IDAHO	QLGC	QLOGIC CORP
RCL	ROYAL CARIBBEAN CRUISES LTD	RDN	RADIAN GROUP INC

(*Continued*)

Table 6.1 Ticker and company names of cluster components in Figure 6.1 (*Continued*)

Ticker	Name	Ticker	Name
CMTL	COMTECH TELECOMMUNICATIONS CP	RGLD	ROYAL GOLD INC
CYH	COMMUNITY HEALTH SYS INC NEWCO	RVI	RETAIL VENTURES INC
DSW	DSW-A	SUR	CNA SURETY CORP
DYN	DYNEGY INC DEL	SVR	SYNIVERSE HLDGS INC
FMR	FIRST MERCURY FIN	V	VISA INC
FTO	FRONTIER OIL CORP	WL	WILMINGTON TRUST CORP
GCA	GCA HLDGS	WYNN	WYNN RESORTS
HL	HECLA MNG CO	XCO	EXCO RESOURCES INC
HMA	HEALTH MGMT ASSOC INC NEW	XLNX	XILINX INC
HOC	HOLLY CORP		

6.4.5 *Idiosyncratic Covariance Matrix Shrinkage*

Analogous to the factor covariance shrinkage of Section 6.3.1, we recommend shrinking the idiosyncratic variances toward the identity matrix:

$$\mathbf{\Omega}_{\epsilon,\text{shrink}}(\rho) = (1-\rho)\hat{\mathbf{\Omega}}_{\epsilon} + \rho\frac{\text{trace}\left(\hat{\mathbf{\Omega}}_{\epsilon}\right)}{m}\mathbf{I}_{n}$$

For a diagonal idiosyncratic covariance matrix, this is analogous to shrinking the idiosyncratic variances toward the empirical average of the variances.

6.5 Winsorization of Returns

The issue of outlier detection is, if not central, at least very important both for risk modeling and alpha research. There are many instances of outliers in return data, each one of them responsible for ruining the career of a finance researcher. Before proposing some remedial measures to improve the research process and save a few careers, let us discuss where they come from, and the impact that they may have. The sources of outliers are primarily two. First, the data provider may be providing generally low-quality data. This is, unfortunately, quite common, and good researchers spend a large proportion of their time evaluating and comparing data and questioning providers on the data collection methodology and their applicability. The sources of error are too many to list. In the worst case, prices are not correctly adjusted for stock splits or reverse splits. Data collection may not be synchronous; the ultimate source of the returns may be a broker located in a farming village in New Zealand, and even more unlikely instances. Bad providers are the perfect breeding ground for outliers. Second: authentic outliers do exist. Instances are:

- There are rare stray transactions for a liquid stock.[6]
- Very illiquid stocks exhibit higher volatility, and occasionally large returns, even intraday.

[6] If I can self-indulge in a personal recollection: I was working for Enron in the summer of 2000. One day, at the closing auction, Enron's stock price jumped to $90 after vibrating around $86 all day. And people *on Enron's trading floor* were openly wondering "should we short Enron now?" The stock fell back to mid-80s the day after. Lesson: if traders want to short themselves, then it's a likely outlier of some kind.

- Stocks in the process of being delisted, or entering/exiting bankruptcy, usually trading over-the-counter (OTC) also exhibit very large returns.
- There are genuinely large jumps reflecting new information in the market: surprises in earnings and forward guidance, announcement of market entry by a competitor, merger announcements and news of merger break, accidents or likely new and unforeseen liabilities, and macroeconomic drivers having a large impact on the security's price.

Of these instances, the first one can be dealt with by inspecting price data carefully, i.e., by not only taking the last price of a 5-minute interval, but by inspecting the entire price trace. The second and third can be avoided by choosing the estimation and investment universe carefully. Microcap stocks that are very illiquid should be excluded. The last class of outliers, however large they may be, should *not* be excluded from the estimation process. The main rationale is that this exclusion will make the output of the analysis much less reliable. If we winsorize a large absolute return, we affect the estimated factor returns from the cross-sectional regression. A factor's return is the return of its mimicking portfolio, and by winsorizing returns in the cross-sectional regression, it is effectively the portfolio return using winsorized data. The true portfolio return unfortunately is based on historical returns. This affects the evaluation of the factor returns, as well as of the idiosyncratic returns. Two easy qualitative recommendations that follow from all of this are:

1. Whatever winsorization method you use, make sure to report all the instances of winsorized data in backtest or in production, and examine them one by one.
2. Make sure that your investment universe comprises only liquid, tradeable assets.

For the remaining assets, use a robust outlier detection strategy. There is no ideal and completely justified method. A method that works well enough is to compute at the security level, the robust z-score of return:

$$d_{i,t} = \frac{|\log(1 + r_{i,t})|}{\text{median}(|\log(1 + r_{i,t-1})|, \ldots, |\log(1 + r_{i,t-T})|)}$$

and to winsorize returns exceeding a threshold $d_{\max}$. The threshold depends on asset class, region, and other attributes, and is set by trial-and-error between 5 and 10.

6.6 ⋆Advanced Model Topics

6.6.1 Linking Models

In some applications, you will have an investment universe consisting of securities belonging to different countries. Large hedge funds, for example, invest at least in North America, Europe, and Asia. In other applications, the universe will consist of securities belonging to different asset classes. An example is U.S. equity and corporate credit, but the possibilities are endless. Since the mathematical treatment that will follow is somewhat dry and arduous, it is perhaps worth asking the question: why? What are the uses of an integrated model? Rather subjectively, I think there are two major uses. The first one, and the most common, is for firm-wide (or large business-wide) risk management. We *need* as accurate a measure of firm-wide volatility as possible. Being wrong by 50% in excess or defect on the firm vol is either damaging returns because we believe we have deployed more volatility than we actually have, or it is deadly, because we are running a great deal of unwanted volatility and unwanted risk of a large drawdown. The second use case is—but of course!—that we have a strategy that fundamentally exploits joint properties of heterogenous investment universes. We need a factor model for alpha research and portfolio optimization. In my personal experience, linking models is the last of your problems, except when it is your *only* problem.

In principle, it is possible to build a "model of everything", across asset classes and geographies; Figure 6.2 shows simplified instances of geography and asset-class models. In practice, though, the modeler is faced with three options. The boundaries between them are not perfectly demarcated, the description will target only the idealized cases.

1. You may want to jointly model all the assets. This is not any different from jointly modeling assets belonging to different sectors in equity models. You could include country factors in the models, and do business as usual.
2. You may develop separate models (which we call *local models*) for, say, assets belonging to different geographies and then combine the models in a second stage. The distinguishing feature of this approach is that we want to make sure that the integrated model, when it is applied to portfolios contained in each local model's universe, should be identical to that of the local model.

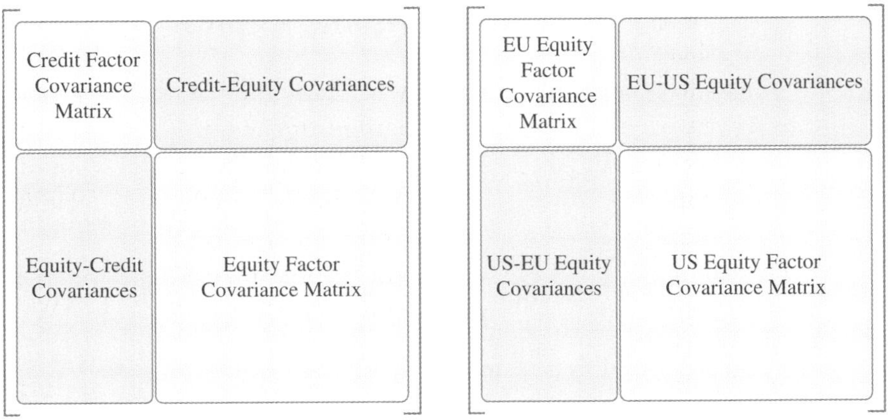

Figure 6.2 Left: credit-equity-linked factor covariance matrix. Right: country-linked factor covariance matrix.

3. You may model the assets jointly in a first stage, and then in a second stage model the residual returns obtained from the first stage in separate models.

We discuss the three approaches, their benefits and drawbacks, below.

1. *Integrated Modeling*. This approach is conceptually straightforward, and has the advantage of giving the model the greatest deal of flexibility when modeling the relationships between securities. For example, in an equity-corporate credit model we may want to create a factor describing Investment Grade versus High-Yield classification. This factor could affect both IG bonds and stocks of companies issuing IG bonds. Such specificity and domain knowledge are best incorporated in an integrated model. Moreover, if the model is used for trading, alphas and factor-mimicking portfolios should be developed and tested for the combined investment universe. There are some complications. One is the asynchronicity in returns due to different time zones, when securities are in multiple countries. Another source of complication comes from the misaligned trading calendars of different markets and asset classes. Trading holidays differ by country, so we have to deal with pairwise incomplete observations in cross-sectional regression, which result in missing factor estimates for country factors on certain days. These, in turn, can result in non-positive-definite factor covariance

matrices. There are strategies to address some of these issues, which we outline below.

- One way to address asynchronicity for daily models is by aggregating returns over multiple days, ranging from two to five. This way, returns become largely overlapping. The number of observations within a time window is reduced accordingly, and the idio volatility scales approximately as sqrt(aggregation window).
- Asynchronicity induces cross-autocorrelation in factor returns. One way to partially address the problem is by applying the Newey-West estimator to the covariance matrix.
- One can also address asynchronicity by explicitly modeling returns in a state-space framework. Such a treatment falls beyond the scope of this book. For an instance of this approach, see Burns et al. (1998).
- Regarding missing returns, one possible approach is to estimate the covariance matrix on complete observations across all local models. The availability of data for all local models on the same dates will ensure that the factor covariance matrix is positive-definite. It is also possible to estimate factor returns (for, e.g., performance attribution) on incomplete observations. This approach has the drawback that factor-mimicking portfolios have potentially high turnover on days when the estimation universe changes due to missing returns for certain local models. Yet another approach is not to drop local models on dates when they are not available but instead to impute returns for their assets. We won't cover it here.[7]
- Regarding missing returns, it is also possible (although slightly unholy) to estimate factor returns on all dates, and then estimate individual factor covariances using pairwise complete observations. The factor covariance matrix will not be necessarily positive-definite, but it may turn into a positive-definite matrix by shrinking the off-diagonal covariances between two local models. We are in uncharted territory; HIC SVNT LEONES.[8]

2. *Separate Modeling*. From the previous item, we know that detailed integrated modeling can be both powerful and dangerous. In the next

---

[7] As a justification for opting not to cover this subject, I note that the technical sophistication involved in imputation of missing data is high, and the return on the effort in this case is comparatively low.

[8] This is the phrase used by medieval cartographers to denote the borders beyond which lay unknown territories.

approach, we seek to keep most of the benefits of the integrated approach, while keeping all the benefits that come with preserving local models. In the analysis below, we have the data of the local models as a starting point. We denote the local factor covariance models $\hat{\boldsymbol{\Omega}}_{\mathbf{f}}^{(1)}, \ldots, \hat{\boldsymbol{\Omega}}_{\mathbf{f}}^{(q)}$. In addition, we have an integrated model, whose factor covariance $\boldsymbol{\Omega}_{\mathbf{f}}^{(I)}$ ("I" is for "Integrated") is estimated using the joint factor returns $\mathbf{f}^{(1)}, \ldots, \mathbf{f}^{(q)}$. We partition its submatrices so that $\mathbf{V}_{i,i}$ is the estimated covariance matrix for the universe of market i, and $\mathbf{V}_{i,j}$ is the matrix of covariances between securities in market i and market j. The idiosyncratic matrix is block-diagonal:

$$\hat{\boldsymbol{\Omega}}_{\mathbf{f}}^{(I)} = \begin{bmatrix} \mathbf{V}_{1,1} & \cdots & \mathbf{V}_{1,q} \\ \cdots & \cdots & \cdots \\ \mathbf{V}_{q,1} & \cdots & \mathbf{V}_{q,q} \end{bmatrix} \qquad \hat{\boldsymbol{\Omega}}_{\epsilon}^{(I)} = \begin{bmatrix} \hat{\boldsymbol{\Omega}}_{\epsilon}^{(1)} & \cdots & 0 \\ \cdots & \cdots & \cdots \\ 0 & \cdots & \hat{\boldsymbol{\Omega}}_{\epsilon}^{(q)} \end{bmatrix}$$

Here is the form of the integrated model:

$$\begin{bmatrix} \mathbf{r}^{(1)} \\ \mathbf{r}^{(2)} \\ \cdots \\ \mathbf{r}^{(q)} \end{bmatrix} = \begin{bmatrix} \mathbf{B}^{(1)} & 0 & \cdots & 0 \\ 0 & \mathbf{B}^{(2)} & \cdots & 0 \\ \cdots & \cdots & \cdots & \cdots \\ 0 & 0 & \cdots & \mathbf{B}^{(q)} \end{bmatrix} \begin{bmatrix} \mathbf{f}^{(1)} \\ \mathbf{f}^{(2)} \\ \cdots \\ \mathbf{f}^{(q)} \end{bmatrix} + \begin{bmatrix} \boldsymbol{\epsilon}^{(1)} \\ \boldsymbol{\epsilon}^{(2)} \\ \cdots \\ \boldsymbol{\epsilon}^{(q)} \end{bmatrix} \tag{6.12}$$

The integrated model's covariance matrix is

$$\hat{\boldsymbol{\Omega}}_{\mathbf{r}}^{(I)} = \mathbf{B}^{(I)} \hat{\boldsymbol{\Omega}}_{\mathbf{f}}^{(I)} (\mathbf{B}^{(I)})^{\top} + \hat{\boldsymbol{\Omega}}_{\epsilon}^{(I)}$$

Let us go back to our challenge. The local models are valuable, because they are estimated using all the information (e.g., all the trading dates for each market) and all the factor-specific information at our disposal. Yet, the cross-market covariances are valuable too to quantify joint risk; that is the point of having a linked model. The idea is to develop a "minimal rotation" $\mathbf{C}$ that transforms $\hat{\boldsymbol{\Omega}}_{\mathbf{f}}^{(I)}$ into a matrix where the main diagonal block covariances are the local model covariances $\hat{\boldsymbol{\Omega}}_{\mathbf{f}}^{(i)}$. It will be sufficient to require the rotation to be block-diagonal $\mathbf{C} := \operatorname{diag}\left(\mathbf{C}^{(1)}, \ldots, \mathbf{C}^{(q)}\right)$, with (this is the clever bit) $\mathbf{C}^{(i)} = \mathbf{V}_{i,i}^{-1/2} (\hat{\boldsymbol{\Omega}}_{\mathbf{f}}^{(i)})^{1/2}$. Note that $\mathbf{C}^{(i)}$ should be close to the identity, because we expect

$\mathbf{V}_{i,i}$ and $\hat{\mathbf{\Omega}}_{\mathrm{f}}^{(i)}$ to be very similar. Let us write the rotation down (the "IR" superscript stands for "Integrated Rotated"):

$$\hat{\mathbf{\Omega}}_{\mathrm{f}}^{(IR)} = \begin{bmatrix} \mathbf{C}_{1,1}^{\mathsf{T}} & \dots & 0 \\ \dots & \dots & \\ 0 & \dots & \mathbf{C}_{q,q}^{\mathsf{T}} \end{bmatrix} \begin{bmatrix} \mathbf{V}_{1,1} & \dots & \mathbf{V}_{1,q} \\ \mathbf{V}_{2,1} & \dots & \mathbf{V}_{2,q} \\ \dots & \dots & \dots \\ \mathbf{V}_{q,1} & \dots & \mathbf{V}_{q,q} \end{bmatrix} \begin{bmatrix} \mathbf{C}_{1,1} & \dots & 0 \\ 0 & \dots & 0 \\ \dots & \dots & \dots \\ 0 & \dots & \mathbf{C}_{q,q} \end{bmatrix}$$
$$= \begin{bmatrix} \hat{\mathbf{\Omega}}_{\mathrm{f}}^{(1)} & \dots & \tilde{\mathbf{V}}_{1,q} \\ \tilde{\mathbf{V}}_{2,1} & \dots & \tilde{\mathbf{V}}_{2,q} \\ \dots & \dots & \dots \\ \tilde{\mathbf{V}}_{q,1} & \dots & \hat{\mathbf{\Omega}}_{\mathrm{f}}^{(q)} \end{bmatrix}$$

Here, $\tilde{\mathbf{V}}_{i,j} := (\mathbf{C}^{(i)})^{\mathsf{T}} \mathbf{V}_{i,j} \mathbf{C}^{(j)}$. Note that we are not transforming $\mathbf{B}^{(I)}$ by post-multiplying it by $\mathbf{C}^{-1}$. Doing so would change the local market loadings, and as a result we would not preserve the local market model. In other words, we are not actually rotating the entire model; we are only perturbing the factor covariance matrix by a small amount, for alignment purposes. The error induced in the $\tilde{\mathbf{V}}_{i,j}$ is small and should be tolerable. Finally, a step that is often performed in this procedure is block shrinkage, so that, for some parameter $\rho > 0$, the final covariance matrix takes the form (the "IRS" superscript stands for "Integrated Rotated Shrunken"):

$$\hat{\mathbf{\Omega}}_{\mathrm{f}}^{(IRS)} = \begin{bmatrix} \hat{\mathbf{\Omega}}_{\mathrm{f}}^{(1)} & \dots & \rho\tilde{\mathbf{V}}_{1,q} \\ \rho\tilde{\mathbf{V}}_{2,1} & \dots & \rho\tilde{\mathbf{V}}_{2,q} \\ \dots & \dots & \dots \\ \rho\tilde{\mathbf{V}}_{q,1} & \dots & \hat{\mathbf{\Omega}}_{\mathrm{f}}^{(q)} \end{bmatrix}$$

3. *Multistage Modeling*. There are use cases in which we would like to have both "global" and "local" factors. The global factors describe the co-movements among securities across all local markets. The local factors are instead affecting only the securities in their markets. The appeal to this approach is that the global factors describe all the dependencies across markets, so that, given the knowledge of these factor returns, the local markets are independent of each other. We describe a way to obtain such a model. As a primitive, we need an integrated model $\hat{\mathbf{\Omega}}_{\mathrm{f}}^{(I)}$, or an integrated and rotated model $\hat{\mathbf{\Omega}}_{\mathrm{f}}^{(IR)}$. In addition, we need

global characteristics $\mathbf{B}^{(G)} \in \mathbb{R}^{n \times m_G}$ ("G" is for "Global"). Examples of these characteristics are:

- a global "country" factor (all loadings equal to one);
- a global market factor;
- global style factors, namely momentum, volatility, and value.

In the first step, we perform cross-sectional regressions on the integrated universe:

$$\begin{bmatrix} \mathbf{r}_t^{(1)} \\ \mathbf{r}_t^{(2)} \\ \dots \\ \mathbf{r}_t^{(q)} \end{bmatrix} = \mathbf{B}^{(G)} \mathbf{g}_t$$

and as an output we obtain global factor returns $\mathbf{g}_t$. We arrange the global factor returns into a matrix $\mathbf{G} \in \mathbb{R}^{m_G \times T}$, whose columns are $\mathbf{g}_t$. In the second step, we regress the local factors against the global factors:

$$\mathbf{f}_t^{(i)} = \mathbf{C}^{(i)} \mathbf{g}_t + \tilde{\mathbf{f}}_t^{(i)}$$

The solution to this regression is given by[9] Equation (6.4):

$$\mathbf{C}^{(i)} = (\mathbf{G}^\top \mathbf{G})^{-1} \mathbf{G}^\top \mathbf{F}^{(\mathbf{i})}$$

In the third step, we replace these formulas in the Integrated Factor Model Equation (6.12):

$$\begin{bmatrix} \mathbf{r}^{(1)} \\ \mathbf{r}^{(2)} \\ \dots \\ \mathbf{r}^{(q)} \end{bmatrix} = \begin{bmatrix} \mathbf{B}^{(1)}\mathbf{C}^{(1)} \\ \mathbf{B}^{(2)}\mathbf{C}^{(2)} \\ \dots \\ \mathbf{B}^{(q)}\mathbf{C}^{(q)} \end{bmatrix} \mathbf{g} + \begin{bmatrix} \mathbf{B}^{(1)} & 0 & \dots & 0 \\ 0 & \mathbf{B}^{(2)} & \dots & 0 \\ \dots & \dots & \dots & \dots \\ 0 & 0 & \dots & \mathbf{B}^{(q)} \end{bmatrix} \begin{bmatrix} \tilde{\mathbf{f}}^{(1)} \\ \tilde{\mathbf{f}}^{(2)} \\ \dots \\ \tilde{\mathbf{f}}^{(q)} \end{bmatrix} + \begin{bmatrix} \epsilon^{(1)} \\ \epsilon^{(2)} \\ \dots \\ \epsilon^{(q)} \end{bmatrix}$$

We must check that the returns vectors $\mathbf{g}_t, \mathbf{f}_t^{(1)}, \dots, \mathbf{f}_t^{(q)}$ are pairwise approximately uncorrelated. In this case, the factor covariance matrix is

$$\text{diag}\left(\text{cov}(\mathbf{g}_t), \text{cov}(\mathbf{f}_t^{(1)}), \dots, \text{cov}(\mathbf{f}_t^{(1)})\right)$$

[9] Note that we are assuming here that the local factor returns $\mathbf{f}_{t,j}^{(i)}$ are homoskedastic. This is generally not the case. However, it is possible to further refine the model in order to allow for heteroskedasticity. Turtles all the way down.

If that is not the case, then we have three options. First, find "better" global factors while keeping m_G constant. Second, add global factors in order to achieve our goal. Third, give up finance altogether.

6.6.2 *Currency Rebasing*

In a multi-country factor model, the return of an asset is usually expressed in a different currency than the one in which the asset is traded. Consider the case of a U.S.-based manager trading a security denominated in Euro. The Dollar/Euro pair is a *currency pair*. In order to purchase a Euro-denominated security, we purchase the currency in which the security is traded (the Euro), also called the *base* currency, and sell Dollars, the *quote* currency. The direct exchange rate is the Dollar amount needed to buy one Euro. More details on usage: when referring to a currency pair, the ordering is base-quoted. In this case: EURUSD.[10] Let us denote the *direct exchange rate* in period t by $p_{\text{EURUSD}}(t)$. The *indirect exchange rate* is the exchange rate of the reversed pair, and it is equal to the reciprocal of the direct exchange rate. The exchange rate return is defined as the return received by holding the base currency in one period, and is equal to $g_{\text{EURUSD}}(t) = [p_{\text{EURUSD}}(t) - p_{\text{EURUSD}}(t-1)]/p_{\text{EURUSD}}(t-1)$. We define the currency return $g_{i,i}$ when the base and quote currencies are the same to be zero.

Let us analyze first the realized return of holding EUR in a simple transaction, in which we buy and sell the currency on consecutive days. We denote by r^f_{USD}, r^f_{EUR} the risk-free return in the interval between the two transaction epochs for the two currencies.

- On day 0, we borrow \$1 and purchase $1/p_{\text{EURUSD}}(0)$ EUR.
- On day 1 the EUR holding is worth $(1 + r^f_{EUR})/p_{\text{EURUSD}}(0)$. We buy back Dollars at the price $p_{\text{EURUSD}}(1)$. The Dollar amount we are left with is

$$
\begin{aligned}
&(1 + r^f_{EUR})p_{\text{USDEUR}}(1)/p_{\text{EURUSD}}(0) \\
&= (1 + r^f_{\text{EUR}})(1 + r_{\text{EURUSD}})
\end{aligned}
$$

[10] The currency codes are identified by three letters. The most common currencies are USD, EUR, GBP (UK Pounds), AUD (Australian Dollars), CAD (Canadian Dollars), CNY (Yuan Renminbi), JPY (Yen).

We then pay our USD loan for an amount $-1 - r^f_{\text{USD}}$. We are left with

$$
\begin{aligned}
(1 + r^f_{\text{EUR}})(1 + g_{\text{EURUSD}}) - 1 - r^f_{\text{USD}} &\simeq g_{\text{EURUSD}} + r^f_{\text{EUR}} - r^f_{\text{USD}} \\
&=: r^{cf}_{\text{EURUSD}}
\end{aligned}
$$

The return r^{cf}_{EURUSD} is the currency return adjusted by the difference in risk-free rates. Let us extend this result. Instead of holding the EUR in a cash account, we invest it in a security with *local* return (in EUR) equal to r^l. Following the same calculations, the return is

$$
\begin{aligned}
r^l + g_{\text{EURUSD}} - r^f_{\text{USD}} &= r^e + r^{cf}_{\text{EURUSD}} \\
r^e &:= r^l - r^f_{\text{EUR}}
\end{aligned}
$$

The return is the sum of two components: the local excess return and the adjusted currency return.

There is yet another identity of interest, which links the currency returns of three (or more) currencies. A no-arbitrage argument along the same lines as above yields $r^{cf}_{j,\ell} = r^{cf}_{j,k} + r^{cf}_{k,\ell}$, from which the identity holds:

$$
r^{cf}_{j,k} := r^{cf}_{j,\ell} - r^{cf}_{k,\ell} \tag{6.13}
$$

In matrix form, we write the identity as

$$
\mathbf{r}^{cf}_{\cdot,k} := (\mathbf{I}_q - \mathbf{A}^{(k)})\mathbf{r}^{cf}_{\cdot,\ell} \tag{6.14}
$$

$$
[\mathbf{A}^{(k)}]_{m,n} := \begin{cases} 0 & \text{if } n \neq k \\ 1 & \text{if } n = k \end{cases} \tag{6.15}
$$

Now we consider the problem of changing numeraire. For example, we want to change the numeraire from USD to GBP:

$$
r^e + r^{cf}_{\text{EURGBP}} = r^e + r^{cf}_{\text{EURUSD}} - r^{cf}_{\text{GBPUSD}} \tag{6.16}
$$

Let us say that our factor model contains securities traded in q currencies. The assets total returns in base currency k can be decomposed into the sum of a local excess return and an exchange-rate return:

$$
\mathbf{r} = \underbrace{\mathbf{B}\mathbf{f} + \boldsymbol{\epsilon}}_{\text{(local factor structure)}} + \underbrace{\mathbf{C}\mathbf{r}^{cf}_{\cdot,k}}_{\text{(currency factor structure)}}
$$

The elements of the matrix $\mathbf{C} \in \mathbb{R}^{n \times q}$ take 0 or 1 values, with $[\mathbf{C}]_{i,j} = 1$ if asset i has reference currency j and 0 otherwise. We rebase from currency k to currency ℓ by way of transforming the currency returns using Equation (6.13):

$$\Rightarrow \mathbf{r} = \mathbf{B}\mathbf{f} + \epsilon + \mathbf{C}(\mathbf{I}_q - \mathbf{A}^{(k)})\mathbf{r}^{cf}_{\cdot,\ell}$$

We close this section with several comments related to modeling extensions and practical implementation:

- We have ignored the question of modeling the joint distribution of the spot currency returns, $\mathbf{g}^{k_0}$. One natural avenue is to model those using a factor model, either fundamental or statistical, so that we can express $\mathbf{g}^{k_0} = \mathbf{H}\boldsymbol{\xi} + \boldsymbol{\eta}$. We need to model the relationship only with respect to one quote currency.
- For simplicity, we have also ignored the covariances between $\mathbf{f}$ and $\mathbf{g}$. The complete model is

$$\mathbf{r} = \begin{bmatrix} \mathbf{B} & \mathbf{C}_{\mathbf{f},\mathbf{g}} \\ \mathbf{C}_{\mathbf{g},\mathbf{g}} & \mathbf{C} \end{bmatrix} \begin{bmatrix} \mathbf{f} \\ \mathbf{g}^{k_0} \end{bmatrix} + \epsilon$$

- Currency risk depends heavily on institutional arrangement of the investment strategy. For example, an investment firm may have fixed capital housed in a different country, and trade using only this capital as collateral. The net exposure is fixed. In this case the foreign currency exposure is given by the capital level, which is usually hedged by currency forward contracts.

6.7 A Tour of Factors

This chapter would not be complete without at least a cursory description of fundamental factors. Because factors should explain cross-sectional returns, they feature prominently in the financial literature exploring return anomalies and extensions to the CAPM or the standard Fama–French three-factor model. The literature on factor anomalies is vast. There are several reviews and introductory books on this subject; a partial list is Singal (2004); Ilmanen (2011); Zack (2011); Berkin and Swedroe (2016); Harvey and Liu (2020a). Cochrane (2011) introduced the term "Factor Zoo" to denote the large set of published factor anomalies introduced until 2011; a set that has greatly expanded since then. Whether these factors represent true, tradeable anomalies is still being debated.

Harvey and his coauthors have developed methodologies and conducted empirical studies, reaching the conclusion that most factor anomalies are false positives (Harvey and Liu, 2019, 2020b). On the other side, Jensen et al. (2023) argues that most anomalies are true. Chen (2024) reconciles the two papers.

Some papers reviewing the large number of factors and attempting to classify them into a smaller set of clusters are Jacobs (2015); Freyberger et al. (2020); Jensen et al. (2023); Swade et al. (2024). The list below is not based on these classifications only, but takes into account the factors included in commercial models.

- *Market.* By far the most pervasive factor in the model, it is usually either the vector e or a vector β of regression coefficients of the asset total return to a "market" factor return (e.g., SPX or RUA in the United States). In the first case, the interpretation is that every return is identically affected by the market, and it is left to other factors to capture the dependence on β.
- *Countries and Industries.* Countries and industries are usually represented as 0/1 variables summing to one for each asset, although non-integer loadings are possible. We consider these factors as homogeneous not only because the information is coded in the same way in the factor loadings, but also because the relative importance of the two has been a subject of intense study both for financial economists and macroeconomists. Aside from the papers by Heston and Rouwenhorst cited above, see also Cavaglia et al. (2000); Berben and Jansen (2005); Brooks and Del Negro (2005); Puchkov et al. (2005); Miralles Marcelo et al. (2013).
- *Momentum.* Stocks that have outperformed (underperformed) their peers over the 3–12 months previous to a given date outperform (underperform) their peers in the future. Jegadeesh and Titman (1993) document this anomaly in the academic literature. They review 20 years of literature in Jegadeesh and Titman (2011); a more recent survey is Wiest (2023).
- *Reversal.* Stocks that have outperformed in the recent past (typically one month or less) underperform. More recent outperformance is more predictive, so the effect is stronger for past-week outperformers than past-month outperformers. See Jegadeesh (1990); Lehmann (1990).

- *Fundamental Valuation.* There are many characteristics descriptive of over/underpricing of firms, based on fundamental data. An early example is Book-to-Price (Fama and French, 1993). Other value-related factors are profitability (Novy-Marx, 2013), quality (Frazzini et al., 2018), and various earnings growth measures, often employing metrics that are customized by the sectors in which the firms operate.
- *Low Beta/Low Vol.* High-beta stocks have lower risk-adjusted performance than low-beta stocks (Baker et al., 2011; Frazzini and Pedersen, 2014); this anomaly is sometimes named *Betting Against Beta*. Similarly, high-volatility stocks have lower risk-adjusted performance than low-volatility stocks (Black, 1972; Haugen and Heins, 1972, 1975). The two effects are related, since the beta of a stock to a benchmark is $\beta_i = (\rho_{b,i}/\sigma_b)\sigma_i$. For possible explanations of the anomaly, see Baker et al. (2011); Blitz et al. (2014); Li et al. (2016); Traut (2023).
- *Liquidity.* Stocks that are more illiquid in recent periods outperform more liquid stocks (Amihud and Mendelson, 1986; Amihud, 2002). A characteristic that describes illiquidity is Amihud's measure:

$$\text{ILLIQ}_{t,i} := \frac{1}{T} \sum_{s=0}^{T-1} \frac{|r_{t,i}|}{\text{VOLD}_{i,t}}$$

  where $r_{i,t}$ is the daily return of stock i on day t and $\text{VOLD}_{i,t}$ is the dollar volume of stock i on the same day. A possible interpretation of the role that (il)liquidity plays in the returns of stocks (and bonds; see Chen et al. (2007)) is that excess returns are a compensation for risk held by investors, especially during the occurrence of "liquidity spirals". These are short intervals in which market participants are forced to liquidate their books due to losses that propagate due to their own liquidation actions; see Mitchell et al. (2007); Brunnermeier and Pedersen (2009). The volume Amihud et al. (2012) collects the literature up to 2012.
- *Crowding.* Forced liquidations are more likely to occur when certain positions are *crowded*, i.e., when many firms with similar trading characteristics hold them. When a position (or, more broadly, a portfolio) is crowded, its liquidation by one of the holders causes an adverse price change that negatively affects the PnL of the other holders. If the loss is large enough, the other holders will reduce or liquidate their positions. By measuring the overlap among portfolios and positions, we can quantify the size of a negative return caused by the liquidation. Since shorting stocks is usually performed by informed traders, short

interest data is a source of crowding information for hedge funds (Boehmer et al., 2010; Jiang et al., 2020). On the long side, Active Manager Holdings are reported at the security and holder level by institutional investors (SEC, 1934).

- *Size*. Small companies are outperforming large ones. First introduced by Banz (1981), the anomaly may be explainable (if true) by the greater risk posed by investing in such firms. Smaller firms are younger than large ones and do not have the same track record; they have higher leverage, and higher earnings variation. There is also a behavioral explanation: small firm stocks are "lottery tickets" (Barberis and Huang, 2008). Risky stocks with positive skewness are preferred by investors; this results in overpricing of the stocks and lower future returns. The mispricing cannot easily be corrected by informed investors, either because they have a mandate not to short stocks, or because shorting shares is expensive due to high borrowing costs.

I close this section with some subjective remarks on the factor literature.

- First, this classification, while broad, is incomplete. For example, I have not included sentiment, and return skewness factors. Researchers continuously publish new factors, sometimes based on interactions among existing factors, sometimes based on increasingly elaborate characteristics. It is unclear that these factors describe true anomalies or are not variants of factors in our list above.
- This brings us to the second issue. Factors are proposed and tested in isolation. Their explanatory power is usually checked only against an elementary model, the Fama–French three-factor model Fama and French (1993) or one of its refinements, such as Fama and French (2015, 2016). As a result, the returns produced by different factors are highly correlated. There is an entire literary sub-genre whose title template is "Factor [X] is explained by factors [Y] and [Z]"; the web of reciprocal explanations is sufficiently dense to believe that Everything is Connected, as in certain New Age self-help manuals.
- The portfolio construction process adopted by most academic literature is simplified. It employs portfolios from sorts and ignores turnover, borrow costs for short positions, and transaction costs.

- Lastly, authors may have tried many variants of a characteristic in order to obtain a positive result. The same historical data are reused many times. This is often called "p-hacking" (Simmons et al., 2013).

The central question is whether the published anomalies are tradeable, profitable factors. My subjective answer is nuanced. First, because of the considerations above, many of the published anomalies are non-existent in the first place, non-tradeable, or arbitraged away post-publication (McLean and Pontiff, 2016). Second, implementation matters. On a personal note, an acquaintance of mine was a phenomenally successful signal researcher before retiring. In their own words, "my top twenty signals were the vast majority of my PnL producers. Each one of them could be described in four lines. It's the details that matter", by which he implied (I believe), signal design, portfolio construction formulation, parameter estimation for impact models, and additional real-time tuning of parameters. All these qualifications leave room for *some* factors to be tradeable and profitable.

The Takeaways

1. Fundamental factor models rely on asset returns and characteristic data to generate factor and idiosyncratic return estimates.
2. Main advantages include interpretability, connections to academic models, and utility in alpha research.
3. There are six major steps in model identification:
   - **(a)** *Data ingestion* and integrity checks.
   - **(b)** *Selection of a universe* of tradeable, liquid assets for estimation.
   - **(c)** *Winsorization of returns* to handle outliers.
   - **(d)** *Generation of factor loadings* from asset characteristics.
   - **(e)** *Cross-sectional regression* of factor returns.
   - **(f)** *Covariance estimation* of factors and idiosyncratic returns.
4. Addressing heteroskedasticity by using weighted least squares improves model reliability.
5. Factor covariance matrix requires shrinkage or dynamic conditional correlation adjustments to account for estimation error and autocorrelation.
6. Idiosyncratic covariance matrix estimation can benefit from short-term updates and clustering to capture residual correlations.
7. Rebasing models for currency adjustments ensures applicability across different geographic regions.
8. Linking different factor models allows integration across regions or asset classes.

Chapter 7

Statistical Factor Models

The Questions

1. How do we estimate factor models when both factor returns and exposures are unknown?
2. How do we employ Principal Component Analysis? What specific adaptations do we need to employ?
3. How can we interpret statistical models, especially when it comes to the loadings that are less interpretable than those in alternative estimation methods?
4. How do we reduce factor model turnover?

In the statistical model framework, we assume that we know neither the factor returns nor the exposures; we estimate both. The estimation relies on Principal Component Analysis (PCA). Starting with

Chamberlain (1983), this approach has been motivated using an asymptotic argument: if the number of factors is finite, say *m*, and if the specific risk stays bounded over bounded portfolios, then when the number of assets is large, there is a clear separation between the *m* largest eigenvalues and the remaining eigenvalues. The PCA solution constitutes then a good approximation and, in the limit, converges to the true model. In applications, one may question the merit of an approach that, unlike the fundamental and macroeconomic ones, ignores additional information about the firm characteristics or the macroeconomic environment. Developing a statistical model is useful for several reasons:

- *Complementarity*. Using several models helps understand the shortcomings of each individual model. We can project an existing model on the statistical model, or augment it with statistical factors.
- *Optimization*. In a portfolio optimization problem, it is often beneficial to compare solutions in which we have bounded the total factor variance using different models; or, we could include *both* variances as constraints.
- *Data*. In certain asset classes, firm characteristics or relevant macroeconomic factors may not be available. When only returns are available, statistical models are the only option.
- *Availability at Short Time Scales*. At certain time scales, such as 1- or 5-minute intervals, fundamental factors may not be as relevant.
- *Performance*. A statistical model may just outperform the alternatives.

The main disadvantage of statistical models is that their loadings are less interpretable than in the case of alternative estimation methods. The first factor is usually easy to interpret as the market. The second and third ones *can* find an interpretation. For example, Litterman and Scheinkman (1991) interpret the first three statistical factors as level, steepness, and curvature of the bond yield curve. The situation is not helpless; in Section 7.4 I describe approaches to interpret statistical models. In the words of Johnson and Wichern (2007): "Analyses of principal components are more of a means to an end rather than an end in themselves because they frequently serve as intermediate steps in much larger investigations". This is perhaps true of all factor models, but is certainly truer with regards to statistical models, because of the possible challenges in interpretation.

This chapter starts with a minimal description of the approach. Then, we take a detour in the real world.

7.1 Statistical Models: The Basics

7.1.1 *Best Low-Rank Approximation and PCA*

Let $\mathbf{R} \in \mathbb{R}^{n\times T}$ be the matrix of observed returns, whose tth column is the vector of returns in period t; the matrices $\mathbf{B} \in \mathbb{R}^{n\times m}$ and $\mathbf{F} \in \mathbb{R}^{m\times T}$ denote a matrix of loadings and of factor returns, respectively. If we wanted to find the loadings and factor returns that minimized the total "unexplained" variation of returns, summed across periods and assets, then we would solve the problem

$$\begin{aligned} \min\ & \|\mathbf{R} - \mathbf{BF}\|_F^2 \\ \text{s.t. } & \mathbf{B} \in \mathbb{R}^{n\times m} \\ & \mathbf{F} \in \mathbb{R}^{m\times T} \end{aligned} \tag{7.1}$$

where $\|\cdot\|_F$ is the Frobenius norm. A matrix of the form **BF** above has rank less than or equal to m. Conversely, every matrix with rank less than or equal to m can be decomposed as **BF** (Exercise 7.1). The problem can be restated as

$$\min_{\text{rank}(\hat{\mathbf{R}})\leq m} \left\|\mathbf{R} - \hat{\mathbf{R}}\right\|^2 \tag{7.2}$$

Here, we have not specified whether the norm is Frobenius. It could be Frobenius, but it could also be any unitarily invariant norm.[1]

We use[2] the *Singular Value Decomposition*[3] of $\mathbf{R} = \mathbf{USV}^\top$, with $\mathbf{U}$, $\mathbf{V}$ square orthonormal matrices of size n and T, respectively, and $\mathbf{S}$ a matrix

---

[1] These are matrix norms that are invariant for left- and right-multiplication by orthonormal matrices: $\|\mathbf{A}\| = \left\|\mathbf{UAV}^\top\right\|$. Spectral, Frobenius, and nuclear norms are unitarily invariant.

[2] This minimization problem was formulated and solved by Eckart and Young (1936) and generalized by Mirsky (1960). Standard references for PCA are Johnson and Wichern (2007), Jolliffe (2010), Pourahmadi (2013), Yao et al. (2015), Jolliffe and Cadima (2016); PCA is also covered in any popular graduate-level textbook on statistical learning, e.g., Bishop (2006), Hastie et al. (2008), Murphy (2012). Skillicorn (2007) is devoted to the interpretation of SVD, PCA, non-negative matrix factorization and its applications.

[3] This is referred to as the full SVD, as opposed to the reduced SVD; see Trefethen and Bau (1997).

of size $n \times T$, which has positive values (called *Singular Values*) on the main diagonal (i.e., $[\mathbf{S}]_{i,i}$) and zero values elsewhere. The solution to Problem (7.2) is given by $\hat{\mathbf{R}} = \mathbf{U}\mathbf{S}_m\mathbf{V}^\intercal$ where $\mathbf{S}_m$ has the singular values in descending order, with singular values after the mth one set to zero. The solution can also be written (Golub and Van Loan, 2012) in compact form as $\hat{\mathbf{R}} = \mathbf{U}_m\mathbf{S}_m\mathbf{V}_m^\intercal$, where $\mathbf{U}_m$ and $\mathbf{V}_m$ are the matrices obtained by taking the first m columns of $\mathbf{U}$ and $\mathbf{V}$, and now $\mathbf{S}_m$ is the square matrix obtained by taking the first m columns and m rows of $\mathbf{S}$. Then, the original Problem (7.1) is solved by setting

$$\mathbf{B} = \mathbf{U}_m \tag{7.3}$$

$$\mathbf{F} = \mathbf{S}_m\mathbf{V}_m^\intercal \tag{7.4}$$

As noted in earlier chapters, there are equivalent "rotated" solutions, of the form $\tilde{\mathbf{B}} = \mathbf{B}\mathbf{C}$, $\tilde{\mathbf{F}} = \mathbf{C}^{-1}\mathbf{F}$, for some non-singular $\mathbf{C} \in \mathbb{R}^{m\times m}$. For example, this is also a solution:

$$\mathbf{B} = \mathbf{U}_m\mathbf{S}_m \tag{7.5}$$

$$\mathbf{F} = \mathbf{V}_m^\intercal \tag{7.6}$$

A related problem, with which many readers are acquainted, is *Principal Component Analysis* (PCA). In this setting, we start with a covariance matrix $\hat{\boldsymbol{\Sigma}} \in \mathbb{R}^{n\times n}$. Our goal is to generate a linear combination of the original vectors $\mathbf{r}^1, \dots, \mathbf{r}^T$, i.e., $\mathbf{w}^\intercal\mathbf{r}^1, \dots, \mathbf{w}^\intercal\mathbf{r}^T$; the vector $\mathbf{w} \in \mathbb{R}^n$ is a vector of weights, normalized to have unit Euclidean norm. We want these random observations $\mathbf{w}^\intercal\mathbf{r}^i$ to have the greatest possible variance. With a little work (which we did in previous chapters; or do Exercise 7.4), you can show that this variance is equal to $\mathbf{w}^\intercal\hat{\boldsymbol{\Sigma}}\mathbf{w}$. The problem then can be stated as

$$\begin{aligned} &\max \mathbf{w}^\intercal\hat{\boldsymbol{\Sigma}}\mathbf{w} \\ &\text{s.t. } \|\mathbf{w}\| \le 1 \end{aligned} \tag{7.7}$$

The vector $\mathbf{w}$ is called the *first principal component* of $\hat{\boldsymbol{\Sigma}}$. You can interpret Problem (7.7) as a financial problem too: find a maximum-variance portfolio, where the sum of the squared net notional positions is less than or equal to 1. The connection between PCA and eigenvalue problems is well known, but it is still useful to highlight it. The Lagrangian of Problem (7.7) is $\nabla_\mathbf{w}(\mathbf{w}^\intercal\hat{\boldsymbol{\Sigma}}\mathbf{w}) + \lambda\nabla_\mathbf{w}(1 - \|\mathbf{w}\|^2) = 2\hat{\boldsymbol{\Sigma}}\mathbf{w} - 2\lambda\mathbf{w}$; a necessary condition for the maximum is that the Lagrangian be zero. This is equal to the eigenvalue equation $\hat{\mathbf{\Sigma}}\mathbf{v} = \lambda\mathbf{v}$. From this equation it follows that $\lambda = \mathbf{v}^{\mathsf{T}}\hat{\mathbf{\Sigma}}\mathbf{v}$. Therefore, the solution is the eigenvector with the highest associated eigenvalue.

Once this maximum-variance portfolio $\mathbf{w}^{(1)}$ has been found, we repeat the process and find another maximum-variance portfolio that is orthogonal to $\mathbf{w}^{(1)}$:

$$\begin{aligned} &\max \ \mathbf{w}^{\mathsf{T}}\hat{\mathbf{\Sigma}}\mathbf{w} \\ &\text{s.t. } \|\mathbf{w}\| \le 1 \\ &\qquad \mathbf{w}^{\mathsf{T}}\mathbf{w}^{(1)} = 0 \end{aligned} \tag{7.8}$$

To see the relationship between PCA and SVD, we write the uncentered covariance matrix using the SVD decomposition:

$$\hat{\mathbf{\Sigma}} = \frac{1}{T}\mathbf{R}\mathbf{R}^{\mathsf{T}} = \frac{1}{T}\mathbf{U}\mathbf{S}^2\mathbf{U}^{\mathsf{T}} \tag{7.9}$$

Replace this decomposition of $\hat{\mathbf{\Sigma}}$ in the optimization problem, Equation (7.7), and notice that $\|\mathbf{U}\mathbf{w}\| = \|\mathbf{w}\|$ because the matrix $\mathbf{U}$ is orthonormal. We are left to solve

$$\begin{aligned} \max \quad & \mathbf{v}^{\mathsf{T}}\mathbf{S}^2\mathbf{v} \\ \text{s.t.} \quad & \|\mathbf{w}\| \le 1 \\ & \mathbf{w} = \mathbf{U}\mathbf{v} \\ & \mathbf{v} \in \mathbb{R}^n \end{aligned} \tag{7.10}$$

The solution is straightforward: $\mathbf{v} = (1, 0, \dots, 0)^{\mathsf{T}}$, and $\mathbf{w}$ equal to the first column of $\mathbf{U}$. If we were to find the first m principal components, we would find that the columns of $\mathbf{U}_m$ solve our problem. These columns, however, are not uniquely identified when two or more eigenvalues are equal. For example you should verify for yourself that, if $\lambda_1 = \lambda_2$, then any vector $\mathbf{v} = (v_1, v_2, 0, \dots, 0)$, with $v_1^2 + v_2^2 = 1$, is indeed a solution. Figure 7.1 gives a geometrical interpretation of this fact.

We call these vectors interchangeably *Principal Components*, *Eigenvectors*, and *Eigenfactors*. The variances of the components are the squared singular values of the SVD of the return matrix $\mathbf{R}$.

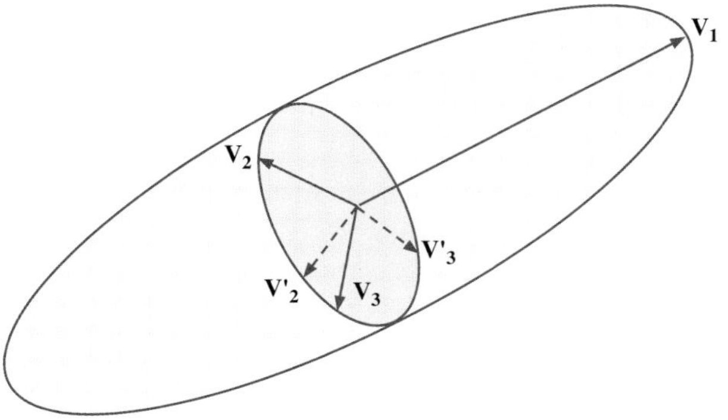

Figure 7.1 The eigenvectors associated with identical eigenvalues are not uniquely identified.

Finally, we note that the Optimization Problem (7.7) can be extended to the case of m eigenvectors:

$$\begin{aligned} \max \quad & \text{trace}\left(\mathbf{W}^\top \hat{\mathbf{\Sigma}} \mathbf{W}\right) \\ \text{s.t.} \quad & \mathbf{W}^\top \mathbf{W} = \mathbf{I}_m \\ & \mathbf{W} \in \mathbb{R}^{n \times m} \end{aligned} \tag{7.11}$$

7.1.2 Maximum Likelihood Estimation and PCA

The statistical model was introduced as a norm-minimization problem, but is not directly related to a factor model formulation:

$$\mathbf{r} = \mathbf{B}\mathbf{f} + \boldsymbol{\epsilon} \tag{7.12}$$

In fact, if we approximated the covariance matrix with a principal component approximation using the top m eigenvalues, we would obtain a singular covariance matrix, which is highly undesirable.

The goal of this section is to establish a first connection between spectral methods and the standard factor model. We consider the model above as a starting point. We assume for simplicity that $\sigma_1, \ldots, \sigma_n$, the asset idiosyncratic volatilities, are all equal to σ. Furthermore we assume, without loss of generality, that $\mathbf{\Sigma}_\mathrm{f} = \mathbf{I}_m$. This is allowed, because rotational invariance affords us this choice of factor covariance matrix. This is the Probability PCA (PPCA) of Bishop (2006).

Under the assumptions $\mathbf{f} \sim N(0, \mathbf{I}_m)$ and $\boldsymbol{\epsilon} \sim N(0, \sigma^2 \mathbf{I}_n)$, the return covariance matrix is $\mathbf{B}\mathbf{B}^\top + \sigma^2 \mathbf{I}_n$. The first m eigenvalues of the covariance matrix are greater than σ^2 (Exercise 7.5). Let $\boldsymbol{\Sigma}_\mathbf{r}$ be the empirical covariance matrix. The log-likelihood function for a zero-mean multivariate normal distribution is (Bishop, 2006; Johnson and Wichern, 2007)

$$\mathcal{L}(\hat{\boldsymbol{\Sigma}}_\mathbf{r}) = -\frac{T}{2}\left[\log|\hat{\boldsymbol{\Sigma}}_\mathbf{r}| + \left\langle \hat{\boldsymbol{\Sigma}}_\mathbf{r}^{-1}, \boldsymbol{\Sigma}_\mathbf{r} \right\rangle + n\log(2\pi)\right] \tag{7.13}$$

where we denote the scalar product of two matrices $\langle \mathbf{A}, \mathbf{B} \rangle :=$ trace $\left(\mathbf{A}^\top \mathbf{B}\right)$. The parameters $\mathbf{B}, \sigma$ can be estimated via maximum likelihood:

$$\max \; -\log|\hat{\boldsymbol{\Sigma}}_\mathbf{r}| - \langle \hat{\boldsymbol{\Sigma}}_\mathbf{r}^{-1}, \boldsymbol{\Sigma}_\mathbf{r} \rangle \tag{7.14}$$

$$\text{s.t.}\; \hat{\boldsymbol{\Sigma}}_\mathbf{r} = \hat{\mathbf{B}}\hat{\mathbf{B}}^\top + \hat{\sigma}^2 \mathbf{I}_n \tag{7.15}$$

The solution to this problem is especially simple and intuitive (Tipping and Bishop, 1999). Decompose $\boldsymbol{\Sigma}_\mathbf{r} = \mathbf{U}\mathbf{S}\mathbf{U}^\top$. Then

$$\begin{aligned} \hat{\mathbf{B}} &= \mathbf{U}_m(\mathbf{S}_m^2 - \hat{\sigma}^2 \mathbf{I}_n)^{1/2} \\ \hat{\sigma}^2 &= \bar{\lambda} \end{aligned} \tag{7.16}$$

where $\bar{\lambda}$ is the average of the last $n - m$ eigenvalues of $\boldsymbol{\Sigma}_\mathbf{r}$. An alternative rotation of this risk model is

$$\mathbf{B} = \mathbf{U}_m \tag{7.17}$$

$$\boldsymbol{\Sigma}_\mathbf{f} = (\mathbf{S}_m^2 - \bar{\lambda}\mathbf{I}_n) \tag{7.18}$$

$$\boldsymbol{\Sigma}_\epsilon = \bar{\lambda}\mathbf{I}_n \tag{7.19}$$

The model offers several insights. First, it links a probabilistic model of returns to the PCA of the empirical covariance matrix. Second, in the model rotation above, the factor covariance matrix is diagonal and the factor variances are equal to the shrinked empirical variances obtained by PCA. Indeed, the PCA solution can be obtained as an asymptotic result. Consider the limit $\hat{\sigma} \downarrow 0$. In this scenario, the idiosyncratic risks are much smaller than the factor risk. In the limit, the formula then simplifies to

$$\mathbf{B} = \mathbf{U}_m \tag{7.20}$$

$$\boldsymbol{\Sigma}_\mathbf{f} = \mathbf{S}_m^2 \tag{7.21}$$

$$\boldsymbol{\Sigma}_\epsilon = 0 \tag{7.22}$$

which is the PCA solution.

We show how PPCA works in a simulated instance. We choose $\sigma = 1$, $T = 250$, n equal to 1000 and 3000 assets, $m = 10$, and factor volatilities equal to $1, 2, \ldots, 10$. For each set of parameters, we run 50 simulations.

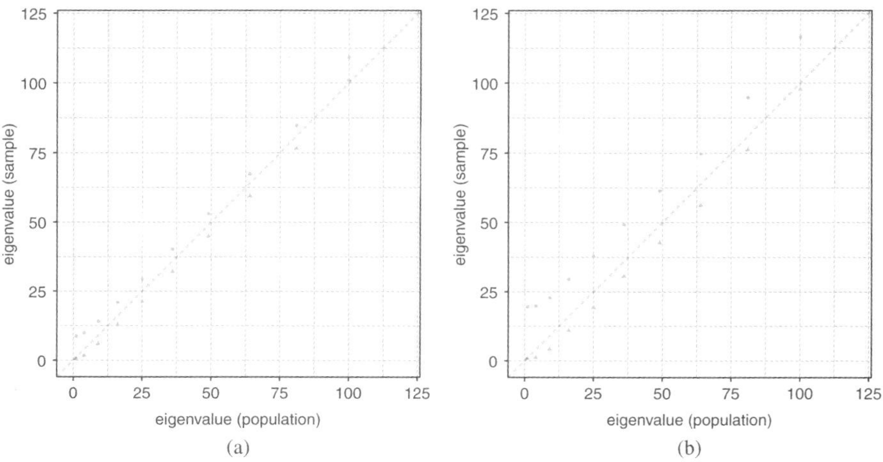

Figure 7.2 (a) Probabilistic PCA for a universe of 1000 assets, with 10 factors with volatilities $1, 2, \ldots, 10$. Circle-shaped points are the sample factor variances against the true variances; triangle-shaped are the shrinked factor variances against the true variances. (b) All parameters are unchanged, with the exception of the number of assets, here equal to 3000.

Figures 7.2 (a), (b) show the true (population) factor variances on the x-axes. On the y-axes we plot the sample factor variances (circles) and the shrinked factor variances (triangles). You can see that, when the ratio between the number of assets and the number of periods is greater, the upward bias of the sample eigenvalues—i.e., of the sample factor variances—is higher. Shrinkage eliminates such bias. However, the shrinked eigenvalues are now biased downwards and, in addition, this downward bias is not constant, which suggests that the optimal shrinkage should not be a constant offset. There are three takeaways from these simulations, which could be confirmed empirically for other choices of the parameters:

- Sample factor eigenvalues are higher than their population counterparts.
- Shrinkage helps, but optimal shrinkage may be more complex than a constant offset.
- Maximum likelihood estimation, which we could solve analytically in this special case, will give in general biased estimates on the factor volatilities.

7.1.3 *Cross-Sectional and Time-Series Regressions via SVD*

A popular approach to PCA is to take the first m principal components of the PCA as factor loadings, and then estimate the factor returns via cross-sectional regression. What are these factor returns? Start by setting $\mathbf{B} = \mathbf{U}_m$. The estimated factor returns are the result of T cross-sectional regressions. We can write the relation as follows:

$$\mathbf{R} = \mathbf{U}_m\hat{\mathbf{F}} + \mathbf{E} \tag{7.23}$$

The least-squares estimate is

$$\hat{\mathbf{F}} = (\mathbf{U}_m^\top \mathbf{U}_m)^{-1}\mathbf{U}_m^\top \mathbf{R} \tag{7.24}$$

or, since $\mathbf{U}$ is orthonormal,

$$\hat{\mathbf{F}} = \mathbf{U}_m^\top \mathbf{R} = \mathbf{U}_m^\top \mathbf{U}\mathbf{S}\mathbf{V}^\top = \mathbf{S}_m\mathbf{V}_m^\top \tag{7.25}$$

Behold, these are the same factor estimates we computed from the SVD in Equation (7.4). If we throw away the factor returns of an SVD, the loadings of the SVD itself allow us to recover them from cross-sectional regressions. Similarly, you can easily prove that, if we only know the estimated factor returns $\hat{\mathbf{F}}$ from Equation (7.25), then we can estimate the loadings using time-series regression of asset returns against these factor returns, and obtain as a result $\hat{\mathbf{B}} = \mathbf{U}_m$. Indeed, the SVD decomposition is the *only* factorization of the returns matrix such that the loadings are the time-series betas of the asset returns to the factor returns, and the factor returns are the cross-sectional betas of the asset returns to the loadings.[4] This is a computational simplification, but also has several applications. It is a useful relationship when we estimate factor loadings for assets with incomplete return data; it helps explain discrepancies in time-series and cross-sectional performance attribution in fundamental factor models; and establishes a connection between statistical and fundamental factor models.

7.2 Beyond the Basics

It is important to understand the behavior of PCA in finite samples, and in settings that are relevant to practitioners. There are a few parameters that intuitively should matter to the portfolio manager. The first two

[4] You can prove all of this! Solve Exercise 7.9.

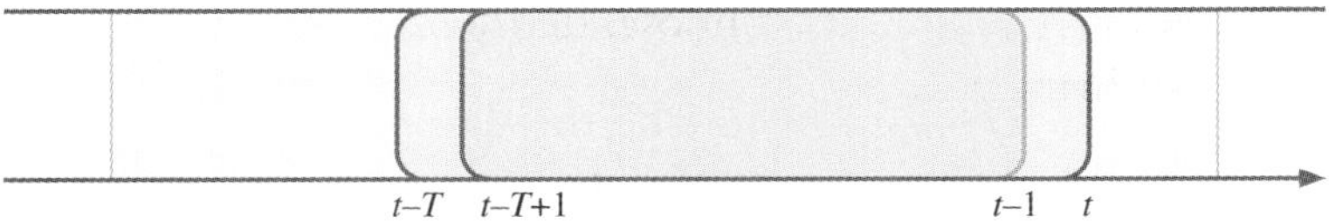

Figure 7.3 We estimate the risk model parameters using data in an interval of width T.

are trivial: the number of assets n and the number of factors m. In addition, we will perform SVD on a rolling window of observations of width T (Figure 7.3). This width is chosen so that the data can be considered broadly stationary (i.e., the cross-section of returns are drawn from the same distribution), but also so that the data has a sufficiently high number of observations to estimate the parameters.

Finally, another important quantity is the gap between the mth and the $(m+1)$th eigenvalues, corresponding to the separation between the smallest variance of a factor and the largest idiosyncratic variance. How do these quantities interact? This question has been at the center of intense research in the past 25 years. PCA, a 120-year-old technique, has witnessed a theory renaissance, which is still far from being concluded. This chapter attempts to give some intuition about the analytical approach; to summarize the state-of-the-art results; to compare them to simulated scenarios; and finally to administer some practical advice in using PCA.

7.2.1 *The Spiked Covariance Model*

Let $\lambda_{T,i}$, with $i = 1, \ldots, n$, be the sorted eigenvalues of the empirical covariance matrix

$$\tilde{\mathbf{\Omega}}_r := T^{-1} \sum_{t=1}^{T} \mathbf{r}_t \mathbf{r}_t^{\mathsf{T}} \tag{7.26}$$

The spiked covariance model posits the following: there is $0 < m < n$ and a positive constant C such that as $T \to \infty$

$$\lambda_i := \lim_{T\to\infty} \lambda_{T,i} \begin{cases} = 1 & \text{for all } i > m \\ \geq Cn & \text{for all } i \leq m \end{cases} \tag{7.27}$$

There is a spectral gap between the largest m eigenvalues and the remaining ones. How does this relate to factor models? Consider the original model specified by Equation (7.4) and choose, like we did in Section 7.1.2, and with $\sigma = 1$, a formulation

$$\mathbf{B}\mathbf{B}^\top + \mathbf{I}_n \tag{7.28}$$

Why should the eigenvalues λ_i grow at least linearly in n? The first m eigenvalues of $\mathbf{B}\mathbf{B}^\top$ are the same as those of $\mathbf{B}^\top\mathbf{B}$. To see this, write the SVD decomposition of $\mathbf{B} = \mathbf{U}\mathbf{S}\mathbf{V}^\top$ and consider the two matrix products $\mathbf{B}\mathbf{B}^\top = \mathbf{U}\mathbf{S}^2\mathbf{U}^\top$ and $\mathbf{B}^\top\mathbf{B} = \mathbf{V}\mathbf{S}^2\mathbf{V}^\top$. The two products have the same first m eigenvalues and different eigenvectors. Instead of analyzing the properties of $\mathbf{B}\mathbf{B}^\top$, we will work on $\mathbf{B}^\top\mathbf{B}$.

A reasonable assumption for $\mathbf{B}$ is that its rows $\mathbf{b}_i$, representing the loadings of a single stock to the factors, are iid samples from a probability distribution D, so that $\mathbf{b}_i \sim P(\mathbb{R}^m)$. We then write $\mathbf{B}^\top\mathbf{B} = \sum_{i=1}^n \mathbf{b}_i^\top\mathbf{b}_i = n(n^{-1}\sum_{i=1}^n \mathbf{b}_i^\top\mathbf{b}_i)$. For large values of n, the term in parentheses converges to an expectation $E_D(\mathbf{b}^\top\mathbf{b})$. We denote μ_i the eigenvalues of this matrix. The eigenvalues of $\mathbf{B}^\top\mathbf{B}$ are then in the limit $n \to \infty$ equal to $n\mu_i$, and the eigenvalues of $\mathbf{B}\mathbf{B}^\top + \mathbf{I}_n$ are $n\mu_i + 1$. This heuristic argument justifies the scaling assumption for the largest eigenvalues for large stock universes, the pervasive (or *spike*) eigenvalues separate for the rest (or *bulk*), and the gap grows linearly in the size of the stock universe.

Let ν_i be the eigenvalues of $\mathbf{B}\mathbf{B}^\top$. The spectrum of the covariance matrix is then given by $\nu_1 + 1, \ldots, \nu_m + 1, 1, \ldots, 1$, so a factor model, after rescaling (so that $\mathbf{\Omega}_\epsilon = \mathbf{I}_n$) and rotation (so that $\mathbf{\Omega}_\mathbf{f} = \mathbf{I}_m$), has an associated spiked covariance matrix. We can see how these conditions translate into practice. In Section 9.3 we will see that the ith factor-mimicking portfolio i is $\mathbf{w}_i = \mathbf{B}(\mathbf{B}^\top\mathbf{B})^{-1}\mathbf{e}_i$. Consider the risk decomposition:

- The factor variance is $\mathbf{w}_i^\top(\mathbf{B}\mathbf{B}^\top)\mathbf{w}_i = \mathbf{e}_i^\top\mathbf{e}_i = 1$.
- The idiosyncratic variance is

$$\begin{aligned}
\mathbf{w}_i^\top\mathbf{w}_i &= \mathbf{e}_i^\top(\mathbf{B}^\top\mathbf{B})^{-1}\mathbf{e}_i \\
&= \mathbf{e}_i^\top\mathbf{V}\mathbf{S}^{-2}\mathbf{V}^\top\mathbf{e}_i \\
&\le \nu_m^{-1}\left\|\mathbf{V}^\top\mathbf{e}_i\right\|^2 \\
&\le \nu_m^{-1}\left\|\mathbf{V}^\top\right\|^2\left\|\mathbf{e}_i\right\|^2 \\
&\le 1/(Cn)
\end{aligned}$$

since the norm of an orthonormal matrix $\mathbf{V}$ is one.

Therefore for large asset universes, i.e., $n \to \infty$, factor-mimicking portfolios have a vanishingly small percentage idiosyncratic variance. They "mimick" the true factor returns well. A different way to state the approximation property is that the idiosyncratic risk "diversifies away" as the number of assets becomes larger; and that there are "factor portfolios" with factor risk that is well above their idiosyncratic risk.

7.2.2 *Spectral Limit Behavior of the Spiked Covariance Model*

The first asymptotic limits for PCA were concerned with large samples: $T \to \infty$ and n constant. In this case, Anderson (1963) showed that the sample eigenvalues and eigenvectors converge to their population counterparts (see Appendix 7.6.2). For modern applications,[5,6] the case where both T and n go to infinity is more relevant, with $\gamma := n/T \in [0, \infty)$. This limit is interesting in applications, because the number of observations is often of the same order of magnitude as the number of variables.

Here, $\mathbf{r}_t$ is a sequence of iid rv taking values in $\mathbb{R}^n$. Assume that

1. the elements of $\mathbf{r}_t$ have finite fourth moments;
2. there are m constants c_i, with $0 < c_1 < c_2 < \cdots < c_m$, such that as $n, T \to \infty$

$$\frac{\gamma}{\lambda_i} \to c_i, \qquad i = 1, \ldots, m \tag{7.29}$$

3. the remaining $n - m$ eigenvalues are equal to one.

---

[5] In the statistical literature, the analysis of this model begins with Johnstone (2001). In a seminal paper, Chamberlain and Rothschild (1983) impose similar conditions, but in an asymptotic setting, by considering an increasing sequence of asset universes (with $n \to \infty$) and risk models in which the diversifiable risk goes to zero.

We have only touched briefly on the asymptotic limit of the spiked model in Section 7.2.2, to give a taste of what happens and give a basis for heuristics. Several papers have characterized the behavior of the model. The first and seminal result is by Baik, Ben Arous and Péché (Baik et al., 2005), and the theorem is named BBP after their initials. Several authors have generalized these results: Baik and Silverstein (2006); Bai and Yao (2008); El Karoui (2008); Mestre (2008); Benaych-Georges and Nadakuditi (2011); Shen et al. (2016); Paul (2017); Wang and Fan (2017). A survey is Johnstone and Paul (2018). General surveys on Random Matrix Theory, with an eye toward finance, are Bun et al. (2017) and Bouchaud and Potters (2020). The line of research concerned with properties of the spectrum in the regime "$p/n \gg 1$" begins perhaps with Johnstone (2001).

[6] The academic literature denotes the number of variables with p and the number of observations with n.

Then the following holds (Shen et al., 2016; Johnstone and Paul, 2018).

1. When $\lambda_i > 1 + \sqrt{\gamma}$:
   - Let $\hat{\lambda}_i$ be the *i*th sample eigenvalue. Then

$$\hat{\lambda}_i \to \mu_i := \lambda_i \left(1 + c_i\right) \qquad \text{a.s.} \tag{7.30}$$

   Because of Equation (7.29), in the limit $n, T \to \infty$, this is the same as

$$\hat{\lambda}_i \to \lambda_i \left(1 + \frac{\gamma}{\lambda_i}\right), \qquad i = 1, \ldots, m \tag{7.31}$$

   The empirical eigenvalues are asymptotically unbiased for large values of λ.
   - Let $\mathbf{u}_i$ denote the population (true) eigenvector and $\hat{\mathbf{U}}_i$ the sample eigenvector. Then, almost surely,

$$|\langle \mathbf{u}_i, \hat{\mathbf{U}}_i \rangle| \to \begin{cases} \dfrac{1}{\sqrt{1 + c_i}} & i \leq m \\ O(1/\sqrt{\gamma}) & i > m \end{cases} \tag{7.32}$$

2. When $\lambda_i \leq 1 + \sqrt{\gamma}$:
   - $\hat{\lambda}_i \to \left(1 + \sqrt{\gamma}\right)^2$ in probability;
   - $|\langle u_i, \hat{u}_i \rangle| \to 0$ a.s.

Even if this strong result only holds asymptotically, it offers a few insights that can be verified experimentally. In addition, there are similar results that extend to the multiple spiked eigenvalue case, albeit with more assumptions. First, let us review the insights:

- Under the spiked model assumptions, the spiked empirical eigenvalues are asymptotically upwardly biased. The bias is higher if λ_1 is closer to the ground eigenvalues; it becomes smaller when λ_1 gets bigger. This makes intuitive sense. When λ_1 is close to one, then the probability that the largest empirical eigenvalue is a "noisy" ground eigenvalue becomes non-negligible. This brings us to the second insight.
- There is a critical threshold at $1 + \sqrt{\gamma}$. For eigenvalues larger than $1 + \sqrt{\gamma}$, it is possible to separate the largest eigenvalue from the spectrum. Indeed, the largest sample eigenvalue is further biased upward.

The sample eigenvector is collinear with the population eigenvector. The larger the first eigenvalue, the better the eigenvector's collinearity.

- Below the threshold, the largest eigenvalue, even if it is larger than 1, cannot easily be identified from data. The associated eigenvector contains no information about the population eigenvector.

In practice, for many applications, the number of assets in a model is in the interval $(10^3, 10^4)$, and the number of observations ranges between 250 and 1000, so that $1 + \sqrt{\gamma}$ ranges between 2 and 7. This is a useful starting point to reason about thresholding eigenvalues, and their associated eigenvector.

7.2.3 *Optimal Shrinkage of Eigenvalues*

We know that the empirical eigenvalues are biased. This means that, should we evaluate portfolios in the subspace spanned by the spike eigenvectors, the predicted variance of the portfolios will be biased upward by γ. Let $\mathbf{a} \in \mathbb{R}^m$ be a unit-norm vector, and let the portfolio be[7] $\mathbf{w} = \mathbf{U}_m\mathbf{a}$. Then the factor variance is biased: $\hat{\sigma}^2_{\mathbf{w}} = \mathbf{a}^\top\hat{\Lambda}\mathbf{a} = \sum_{i=1}^m \hat{\lambda}_i a_i^2 = \sum_{i=1}^m \lambda_i a_i^2 + \gamma = \sigma^2_{\mathbf{w}} + \gamma$. A possible solution to the problem of eigenvalue estimation error is to apply a function to the sample eigenvalues. For example, from Equation (7.30), one could invert λ_i from $\hat{\lambda}_i$ by applying the function

$$\ell(\lambda) = \lambda - \gamma, \quad \lambda \geq 1 + \sqrt{\gamma} \tag{7.33}$$

For large values of λ, this shrinkage function is an offset of the empirical eigenvalues, like the one we first saw in PPCA, Equation (7.19). When we apply this to a diagonal matrix $\mathbf{S}$ filled with eigenvalues, we use the notation $\ell(\mathbf{S})$, which returns a diagonal matrix with the corresponding diagonal terms shrinked using Equation (7.33). However, this is not necessarily the best choice. The choice of the loss function matters. Donoho et al. (2018) characterize the optimal *shrinking* of eigenvalues for a large number of loss functions. Based on what we learned in Chapter 6, we focus only on a few: the operator norm $\|\mathbf{A} - \mathbf{B}\|$ and the operator norm on precision matrix $\left\|\mathbf{A}^{-1} - \mathbf{B}^{-1}\right\|$. For these two losses, the shrinkage formula Equation (7.33) is optimal. For large values of λ, this formula simplifies to $\ell(\lambda) \simeq \lambda + 1 - \gamma$. We subtract a constant offset from each

[7] As in Section 7.1.1, $\mathbf{U}_m$ is the submatrix of $\mathbf{U}$ obtained by taking the first m columns.

eigenvalue. Large eigenvalues are shrunk proportionally less than the small ones. This result is connected to what is perhaps the best-known covariance shrinkage method among practitioners: the Ledoit–Wolf shrinkage.[8] This method starts with finding a matrix of the form

$$\hat{\mathbf{\Sigma}}_r = \rho_1 \tilde{\mathbf{\Sigma}}_r + \rho_2 \mathbf{I}_n \tag{7.34}$$

and identifying ρ_1 and ρ_2 so that $\hat{\Sigma}_r$ minimizes the distance induced by the Frobenius norm from Σ_r:

$$\begin{aligned} &\min \left\|\hat{\mathbf{\Sigma}}_r - \mathbf{\Sigma}_r\right\|_F \\ &\text{s.t. } \hat{\mathbf{\Sigma}}_r = \rho_1 \tilde{\mathbf{\Sigma}}_r + \rho_2 \mathbf{I}_n \end{aligned} \tag{7.35}$$

The space of $n \times n$ matrices is a Hilbert space with scalar product $\langle \mathbf{A}, \mathbf{B} \rangle := \text{trace}\left(\mathbf{A}\mathbf{B}^\top\right)$. The induced norm $\sqrt{\langle \mathbf{A}, \mathbf{A} \rangle}$ is the Frobenius norm. This is then just a special case of the well-known problem of minimum distance of a subspace from a point in a Hilbert space (Luenberger, 1969, Sec 3.3). They assume iid returns, finite fourth moments, and an asymptotic regime in which n is constant and $T \to \infty$. They find that the optimal solution is of the form

$$\hat{\mathbf{\Sigma}}_r = \left(1 - \frac{\kappa}{T}\right) \tilde{\mathbf{\Sigma}}_r + \frac{\kappa}{T} \mathbf{I}_n \tag{7.36}$$

This solution has many interpretations, aside from the geometric one that follows from the solution to Optimization Problem (7.35). While these interpretations may be of independent interest, I will devote some time to justify why this approach is *not* recommended to estimate returns with a spiked covariance. A first issue in using the Frobenius-induced distance is generally not helping to identify the structure of the model, as shown in the previous chapter (Fan et al., 2008). Secondly, because the regime n is fixed, T diverging is not relevant to applications in which $n > T$ or $n \asymp T$. Thirdly, because the condition that the estimate lie in the subspace spanned by $\tilde{\mathbf{\Sigma}}_r$ and $\mathbf{I}_n$ may be overly restrictive. Lastly, because the eigenvalues of the target matrix are of the form $\lambda_i - \kappa T^{-1}(\lambda_i - 1)$. For the

[8] From the very first result on biased asymptotic estimators, a reader may wonder about shrinkage methods. There is an extensive literature on factor model shrinkage. Standard references are Ledoit and Wolf (2003b,a, 2004) on linear shrinkage, and more recent work on non-linear shrinkage by the same authors (Ledoit and Wolf, 2012, 2015, 2020). The paper by Donoho et al. (2018) covers optimal shrinkage functions for a large set of loss functions.

leading eigenvalues, this shrinkage does not match the optimal asymptotic shrinkage of the spiked covariance model.

7.2.4 *Eigenvalues: Experiments versus Theory*

We now compare these theoretical results to simulations. We use the same parameters we used for the Probabilistic PCA in Section 7.1.2: 10 factors with standard deviations ranging between 1 and 10, uniformly spaced; unit idiosyncratic standard deviations; 250 periods, and either 1000 or 3000 assets. In addition to the case of normal returns, I also consider the case of heavy-tailed returns. Specifically, both factor returns and idiosyncratic returns are t-distributed with five degrees of freedom. This choice is meant to simulate returns that have four finite moments, which is a reasonable assumption for daily asset returns.

We simulate 50 instances of each factor model. For each model, we compute the first 10 empirical top eigenvalues, and we shrink them using Equation (7.33) for $\ell(\hat{\lambda})$. The simulation (Figure 7.4) shows that the shrinkage function ℓ works well for normally distributed returns, but not for heavy-tailed returns. In this case, it appears that a better shrinkage approach is to scale the eigenvalues by a common factor. This is a different shrinkage than the ones of Equations (7.18) and (7.33), which are consistent in a constant offsetting term. Combining the empirical observations from simulated data, and theoretical results, it seems at least reasonable to consider a linear shrinkage

$$\ell(\lambda) = \kappa_1 \lambda - \kappa_2$$
$$\kappa_2 \geq \lambda_{\min}$$
$$\kappa_1 \in (0, 1)$$

when identifying a model.

7.2.5 *Choosing the Number of Factors*

In the example above, we assumed that the number of factors was known in advance. This is not the case with applications. An important component of the model definition procedure is the determination of the number

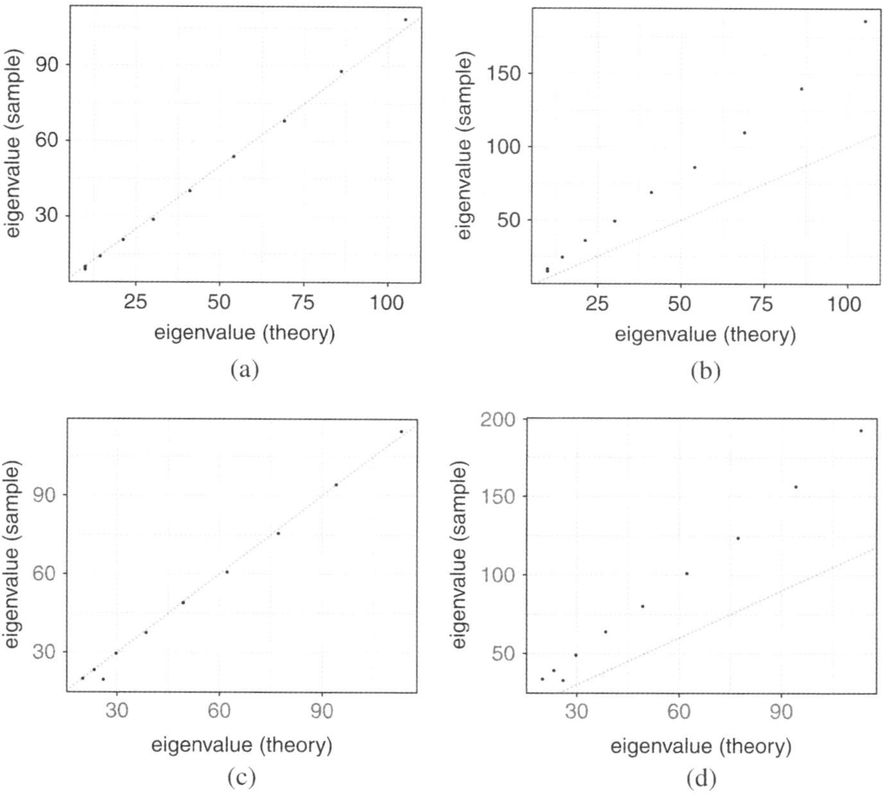

Figure 7.4 (a) 1000 assets, normally distributed returns; (b) 1000 assets, t-distributed returns; (c) 3000 assets, normally distributed returns; (d) 3000 assets, t-distributed returns. The x-axis denotes the population eigenvalues, while the y-axis denotes the shrinked empirical eigenvalues. The dashed line is the line $y = x$.

of factors.[9] There are some criteria motivated by theoretical models, and others that are the outcome of experiments and trial-and-error by generations of practitioners. The theory-based models themselves prescribe different numbers of factors, so we should premise this section with a few considerations. First, finding the *right* factors matters more than finding

[9] For a relatively old survey on methods to select the number of factors, see Ferré (1995); a more recent survey is in Fan et al. (2020). The scree plot method is due to Cattel (1966), and its logarithmic version by Farmer (1971). The scree is the debris that form at the base of a cliff.

their exact right number. By "right", we mean of course the factor loadings with the best "performance", and by performance, we mean one of many metrics introduced in Chapter 5. Because there are many metrics, many of which are not even considered in the theoretical treatments on the number of factors, there is no one-size-fits-all criterion. Second consideration: telling the exact number of factors in practice is either very easy or hopelessly hard. Under the assumptions of pervasive factors, you won't need complex criteria: there is a wide gap between the smallest factor eigenvalue and the largest idiosyncratic one. When the assumption does not hold, eigenvalues will decrease gradually, and a hard rule is unlikely to choose the exact threshold. A final consideration, which is both grounded in theory and in practice, is that one should err on the side of selecting more factors, rather than fewer. The cost of selecting too few factors is that, in portfolio optimization, we will choose portfolios that underestimate their true risk, which can result in steep degradation of the Sharpe Ratio. The cost of choosing too many factors is a slight decrease in the Sharpe Ratio.

After these qualifications, let us review the most common methods.

- **Threshold-Based Methods**. For matrices with ground eigenvalues equal to 1, the results of Section 7.2.2 suggest that we should select as factor eigenvalues those that exceed the threshold $1 + \sqrt{\gamma}$, i.e.

$$m = \max\{k|\hat{\lambda}_k \geq 1 + \sqrt{\gamma}\} \tag{7.37}$$

  An older method is the *scree plot*. This is the best-known method. It consists of plotting the eigenvalues against their rank. The largest eigenvalues dominate and decrease rapidly, to a value where the eigenvalues are small and decrease gradually, usually almost linearly. The method consists of choosing the last eigenvalue preceding this group. A variant of this method plots the logarithm of the eigenvalues.
- **Maximum Change Points**. Associated to the threshold are two additional ones that select the number of factors based on the largest gap between consecutive factor eigenvalues, or consecutive log(eigenvalues):

$$\begin{aligned} m &= \arg \max_{2\leq k\leq k_{\max}} \left(\hat{\lambda}_{k-1} - \hat{\lambda}_k\right) \\ m &= \arg \max_{2\leq k\leq k_{\max}} \left(\log \hat{\lambda}_{k-1} - \log \hat{\lambda}_k\right) \end{aligned} \tag{7.38}$$

  where $k_{\max}$ is a threshold chosen iteratively (Onatski, 2010).

- **Penalty-Based Methods**. We began the chapter with the problem of minimizing the square residual error, Equation (7.2). We can select the number of factors by adding a penalty term, and by making m a decision variable (Bai and Ng, 2008):

$$\min_{k,\text{rank}(\hat{\mathbf{R}})\leq k} \|\mathbf{R} - \hat{\mathbf{R}}\|^2 + kf(n, T) \tag{7.39}$$

$$f(n, T) = \frac{n + T}{nT} \log\left(\frac{nT}{n + T}\right) \tag{7.40}$$

7.3 Real-Life Stylized Behavior of PCA

We now explore a real-life dataset with the goal of comparing the observed behavior of principal components and eigenvalues to the ideal spiked covariance model. We employ daily stock total returns belonging to the Russell 3000 index for the period 2007–2017. Assets that are included in this index must satisfy some essential requirements. As of 2022, on a designated day in May ("rank day"), Russell evaluates eligibility for inclusion in its indices based on several criteria. Among them, the company must be U.S.-based (no ADR/GDRs allowed[10]); the stock price must exceed \$1; the market capitalization must exceed \$30M; and the percentage of float (shares traded on exchange) must exceed 5% of the total shares issued. In addition, some governance requirements and corporate structure must be met; for example, ETFs, trusts, closed-end funds investment companies and REITs are excluded. Out of this eligible set, Russell assigns to R3000 the first 3000 assets by market cap, and effectively changes the composition of the index on the fourth Friday of June. These criteria ensure that the asset characteristics are sufficiently homogeneous (based on geography, revenue source, and corporate governance) and that the returns can be reliably computed based on daily closing prices (based on stock price and market capitalization[11]).

[10] An American Depositary Receipt (ADR) is a foreign company that is listed on a foreign stock exchange, which also offers shares in U.S. exchanges. A Global Depositary Receipt (GDR) is similar to an ADR, but is offered on exchanges in more than one country outside of the primary market.

[11] Note, however, that Russell does not screen stocks based on trading volume, and that the smaller-capitalization companies in R3000 and R2000 may not be sufficiently liquid to be traded in large sizes.

7.3.1 Concentration of Eigenvalues

For our exploration we consider Principal Components based on three types of returns. First, stock total returns. This is the simplest approach. Secondly, we normalize returns by dividing them by their predicted idiosyncratic volatilities. The benefit of this approach is that it should make the spectrum closer to the assumptions we made in the previous sections: the idiosyncratic volatilities of the normalized empirical covariance matrix are all equal to one, and the spike volatilities should be greater than one. Lastly, we normalize returns by their predicted total volatilities. The rationale for this choice is that we study the properties of the empirical *correlation* matrix. It is at least reasonable to hypothesize that the correlation matrix has different properties than the covariance matrix. Correlations may be more stable than covariances; for example, this is the modeling assumption made in Bollerslev (1990), and in Barra's and Axioma's U.S. statistical models. Our procedure is relatively simple. We use one full year of return data, for eight non-overlapping years. When we normalize by idiosyncratic volatilities, we use the data provided by Axioma's U.S. model AXUS Short Horizon. We take this shortcut for one simple reason: although we introduce a self-contained idio volatility estimation process later in the chapter, we did not wait any further to show some empirical data. I will show later that the statistical model idio volatilities are indeed quite close to those of a commercial model, so that this illustrative example is in fact quite close to a self-contained analysis. The raw returns are winsorized at daily returns of (−90%, +100%), and the z-scored returns at returns of (−10, +10), i.e., plus or minus ten standard deviations. Figure 7.5 shows the variances of the first 40 factors, normalized by the variance of the first factor (to make them comparable). Two features are conspicuous. The first one is that there is no obvious gap between variances. The second is that there is a consistent ranking between the spectra of the three covariance matrices. The plot shows the ratio of the variance of lower-order factors to that of the first factor, and this value is smallest for the return/idio volatility covariance matrix, followed by the return/total volatility covariance matrix, and lastly by the covariance matrix of total returns.

This suggests that the first few eigenfactors explain a larger percentage of total variance of the associated covariance matrix. This is confirmed by Figure 7.6. For example, say that we would like to have a number of factors sufficient to capture 50% of the variance of asset returns. For the

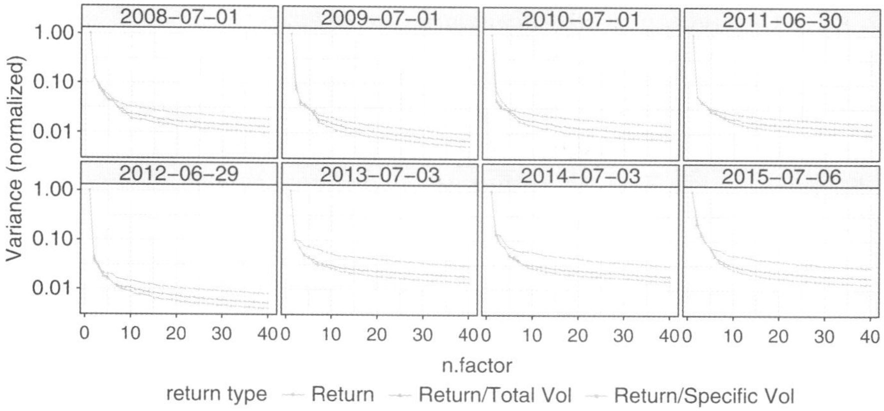

Figure 7.5 Variances of the eigenfactors (normalized to the variance of the first eigenfactor) for the first 40 factors. Note that the scale of the y-axis is logarithmic.

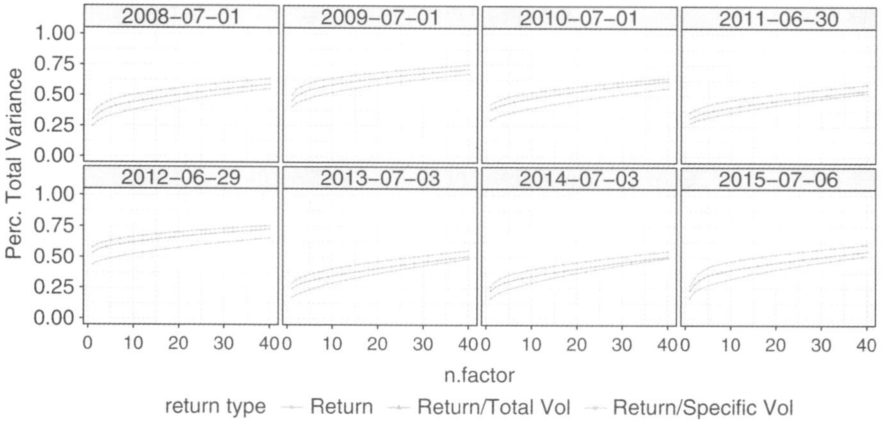

Figure 7.6 Cumulative percentage of variance described by the first n factors, for difference covariance matrices.

period ending on July 1, 2008, we need 30 factors for the raw covariance matrix, 20 factors for the z-scored returns, using total volatility, and only 10 factors for the z-scored returns, using idiosyncratic volatility. This in itself does *not* mean that this choice is preferable, because the performance of a risk model has no direct relationship with this metric. Nonetheless, it suggests that, in this specific instance, a model built on a transformed sequence of returns is more parsimonious.

7.3.2 *Controlling the Turnover of Eigenvectors*

So far, we have focused on the properties of the eigenvalues. Eigenfactors exhibit a distinctive behavior as well. One important property of eigenfactors is their turnover. The turnover for two consecutive portfolios $\mathbf{v}(t-1), \mathbf{v}(t)$ is usually measured as the Gross Market Value (GMV) traded, as a percentage of the GMV of the portfolio: $\text{turnover}_1(\mathbf{v}(t)) := \left\|\mathbf{v}(t) - \mathbf{v}(t-1)\right\|_1$. An alternative is to use as definition the square of the gross notional:

$$\text{turnover}_2(\mathbf{v}(t), \mathbf{v}(t-1)) := \left\|\mathbf{v}(t) - \mathbf{v}(t-1)\right\|^2 \tag{7.41}$$

There are good reasons for this. The first one is that the squared GMV is a fairly good approximation to the transaction costs associated to trading the factor portfolio. A second one is analytical tractability and an associated geometric intuition. For eigenportfolios, recall that $\|\mathbf{v}(t)\| = 1$, and that the numerator $\|\mathbf{v}(t) - \mathbf{v}(t-1)\|^2$ can be rewritten as $2(1 - \mathbf{v}^\intercal(t)\mathbf{v}(t-1))$. The quadratic turnover is therefore related to the cosine similarity. Low-turnover eigenportfolios have high cosine similarity:

$$\text{turnover}_F(\mathbf{v}(t)) = 2[1 - |S_C(\mathbf{v}(t), \mathbf{v}(t-1))|] \tag{7.42}$$

In the equation above we use the absolute value of S_C because the eigenfactors are identified modulo the sign of the vector. In other terms, if $S_C(\mathbf{v}(t), \mathbf{v}(t-1)) < 0$, we can flip the sign of $\mathbf{v}(t)$ in order to have a lower-turnover pair of eigenfactors.

In Figure 7.7 we show the absolute values of the cosine distances over time for the first eight eigenfactors of our three sequences of covariance matrices computed on raw total returns, raw returns normalized by total volatilities, and raw returns normalized by idio volatilities. In Figure 7.8 we show the total distance between subspaces spanned by the first eigenfactors in successive periods; and in Figure 7.9 we show the cumulative returns in the three approaches. The covariance matrix on a given date is computed using the trailing 251 trading days of returns. The number of assets from one day to the next can change slightly as well, because the universe is not fixed. The charts have qualitatively similar behavior. The first eigenfactor is associated to an eigenvalue that has a large gap from the second largest eigenvalue (see Figure 7.5). As a result, the PCA procedure has no issue in identifying it and its weights are very stable throughout the estimation period. This is essentially a "market" portfolio. The

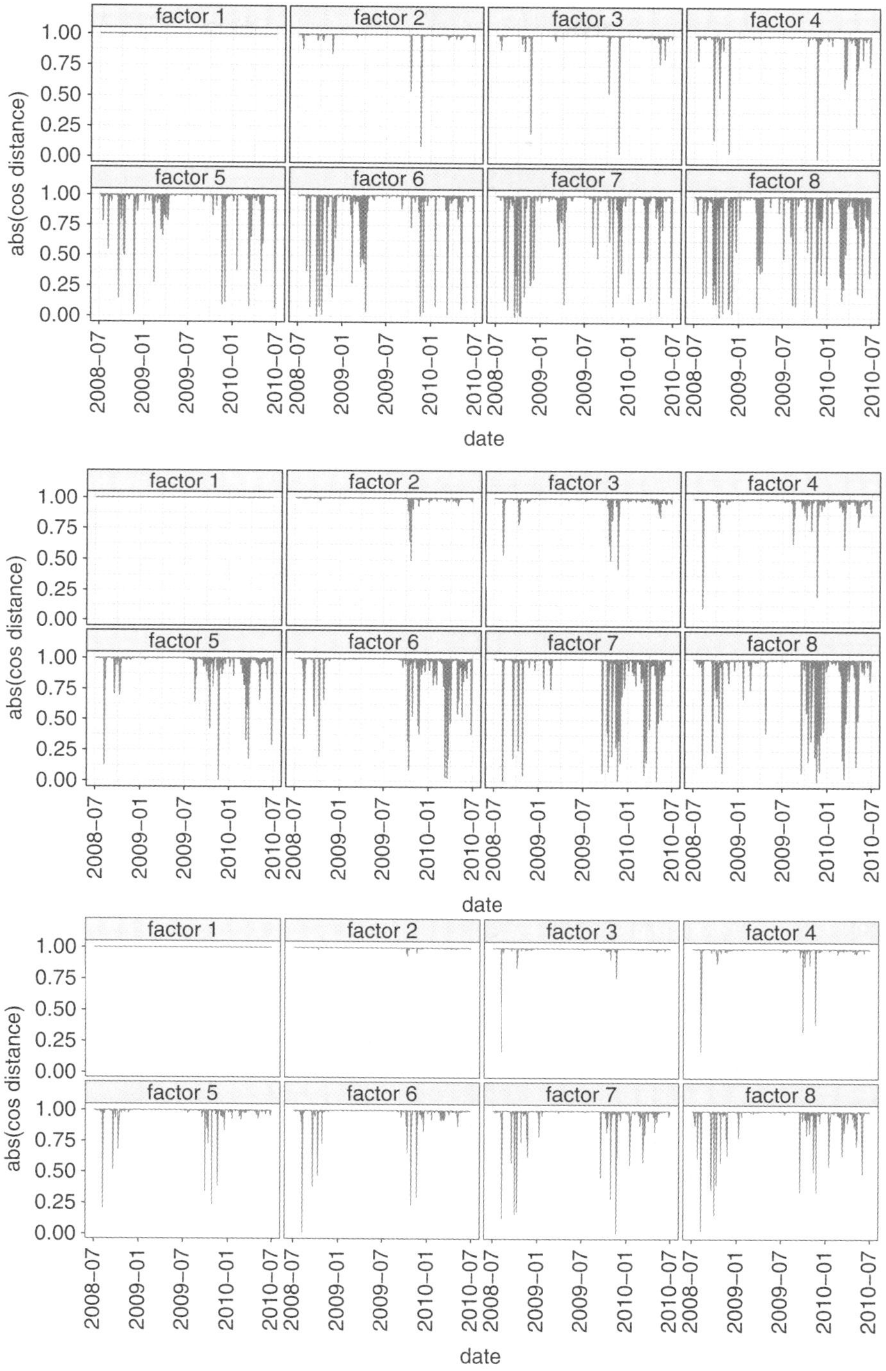

Figure 7.7 Eigenfactor turnover for different covariance matrices. Top: total returns; Middle: total returns/total vol; Bottom: total returns/idio vol.

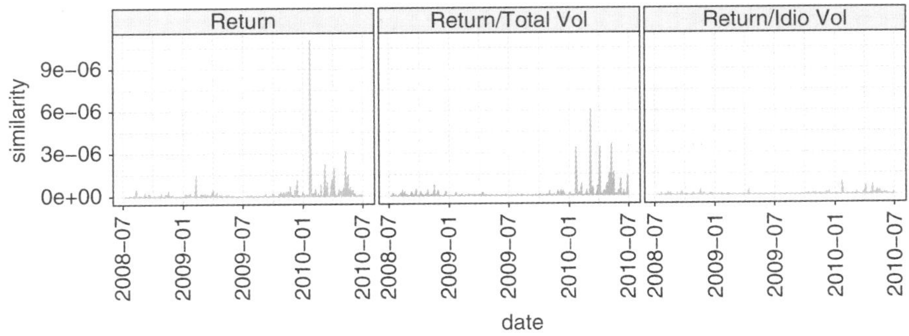

Figure 7.8 Distance between column subspaces of the first eight eigenfactors in consecutive periods. The eigenfactors are generated by PCAs on total returns, total returns/total vol, and total returns/idio vol.

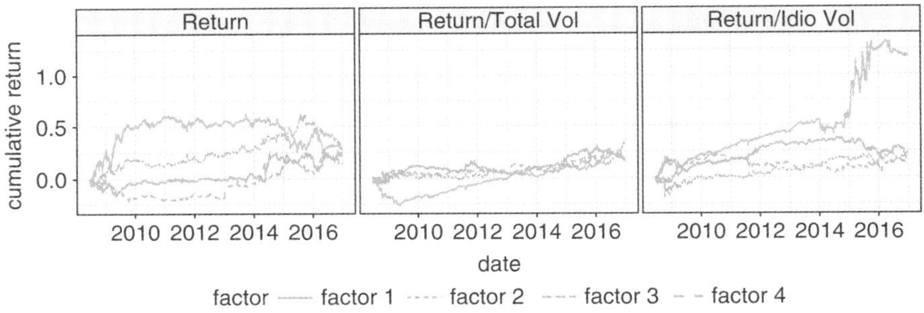

Figure 7.9 Factor returns for the first four eigenvectors. The eigenfactors are generated by PCAs on total returns, total returns/total vol, and total returns/idio vol.

turnover has a more interesting structure for higher-order eigenportfolios. Consider the second eigenportfolio of the (non-normalized) total returns. There are occasional spikes; for example, there are large spikes occurring on October 9, 2009 and November 20, 2009. The second one is so big that the eigenfactors on consecutive dates have a turnover of almost 200%. What is even more puzzling is that immediately before and immediately after the portfolio doesn't turn over at all: it changes dramatically in a single day, to stabilize shortly afterwards. And this behavior qualitatively repeats across covariance matrices and eigenfactors: higher-order eigenfactors transition more often and with larger spikes, but transitions are still relatively rare: even eigenfactor 8 has a cosine similarity below 1/2 only in 6% of the cases. Another qualitative phenomenon is that, as for the case of eigenvalues, standardizing returns seems to reduce turnover incidence and severity; more so for idio volatility normalization. For example, in the latter case, eigenfactor 8 has a cosine similarity below 1/2 only in 1.5% of the cases. How to explain this phenomenon? The cause of the jumps is a direct consequence of the lack of eigenvalue separation. When eigenvalues are close, the addition and removal of an observation of cross-sectional returns, as well as the addition or removal of one or two assets in the estimation universe, is sufficient to affect the numerical solution of the PCA. The distance between the eigenvalues (i.e., variances of the eigenfactors) is within the change of these same eigenvalues from one period to the next due to data updates. Even if the eigenfactors change, the subspace spanned by these eigenfactors may in fact be stable. In Figure 7.7, we show the subspace distance for the three cases above[12] between the column subspaces in consecutive periods. The distances are very small (the largest being just 10^{-5}, for total return factors), and are smaller for idio volatility z-scored returns. This does confirm yet again that statistical models built on normalized returns sequences are more stable, suggesting that the eigenvalues of such models are better separated from each other.

Aside from the quality of the PCA for different choices of covariance matrices, we are faced with an inescapable issue in statistical models. Except for a few high-order factors and variances, most factors in statistical models suffer from a kind of indeterminacy. In consecutive periods, PCA may give us very different loadings, even though the subspaces spanned by these factors are very close to each other. Is this a matter of concern? For most applications, it is not. The reason is that, even if loadings can change a lot from one period to the next, the covariance matrix does not change.[13] This means that a portfolio's volatility prediction does not depend on the orientation of the factor loadings, and therefore that any portfolio optimization problem is also not affected by the choice of loadings, so long as its formulation includes constraints or objective-function penalty terms on the portfolio volatility, or combined factor volatility of the degenerate factors (i.e., factors with identical volatilities). In integrated

[12] For a definition of subspace similarity, see Exercise 7.11.

[13] If you are not convinced, or this statement does not seem obvious, this is a good time to solve Exercise 7.13.

Table 7.1 Summary of impact of high factor turnover

Use	Impact of High Factor Turnover
Volatility Estimation	Not important
Portfolio Optimization/Hedging	Not important
Integrated Stat./Fund. Models	Not important
Performance Attribution	Very high

fundamental/statistical models the indeterminacy of loadings is not affecting the final result, namely the volatility predictions and the performance characteristics of the fundamental factors. In Table 7.1 I summarize the relevance to specific applications.

Essentially only single-factor performance attribution is made irrelevant by eigenvalue quasi-degeneracy. However, single-factor attribution depends on factor turnover. Since model prediction is unaffected by rotations, we can always perform a rotation that minimizes the distance between loadings in consecutive periods; this is a zero-cost operation. In other words, if we have a sequence of loading matrices $\mathbf{B}_t$, we aim for new "rotated" loadings $\tilde{\mathbf{B}}_t$ that have low turnover[14]:

$$
\begin{aligned}
\widetilde{\mathbf{B}}_{t+1} = \arg\min |\mathbf{B}_t - \mathbf{Y}|_F^2 \\
\text{s.t. } \mathbf{Y} = \mathbf{B}_{t+1}\mathbf{X} \\
\mathbf{X}^\top\mathbf{X} = \mathbf{I}_m \\
\mathbf{X} \in \mathbb{R}^{m\times m}
\end{aligned}
\tag{7.43}
$$

First, we prove that the objective is equivalent to maximizing $\langle \mathbf{A}, \mathbf{X}^\top \rangle$, with $\mathbf{A} := \mathbf{B}_t^\top \mathbf{B}_{t+1}$. This follows from the sequence of identities

$$
\begin{aligned}
\left\|\mathbf{B}_t - \mathbf{B}_{t+1}\mathbf{X}\right\|_F^2 &= \text{trace}\left((\mathbf{B}_t^\top - (\mathbf{B}_{t+1}\mathbf{X})^\top)(\mathbf{B}_t - \mathbf{B}_{t+1}\mathbf{X})\right) \\
&= \text{trace}\left(\mathbf{B}_t^\top\mathbf{B}_t\right) + \text{trace}\left((\mathbf{B}_{t+1}\mathbf{X})^\top(\mathbf{B}_{t+1}\mathbf{X})\right) \\
&\quad -\text{trace}\left(\mathbf{B}_t^\top\mathbf{B}_{t+1}\mathbf{X}\right) - \text{trace}\left(\mathbf{X}^\top\mathbf{B}_{t+1}^\top\mathbf{B}_t\right) \\
&\equiv -\text{trace}\left(\mathbf{A}\mathbf{X}\right)
\end{aligned}
$$

The last equality follows from the orthonormality of $\mathbf{B}_t, \mathbf{B}_{t+1}$. Let the SVD of $\mathbf{A}$ be $\mathbf{A} = \mathbf{U}\mathbf{S}\mathbf{V}^\top$. We prove that a solution is given by $\mathbf{X}^\star = \mathbf{V}\mathbf{U}^\top$.

[14] Historical note: this problem is closely related to *Wahba's Problem* (Wahba, 1965).

Let $\mathbf{A} = \mathbf{USV}^\top$ and $\mathbf{X} = \mathbf{VYU}^\top$ for some $\mathbf{Y}$. From orthonormality of $\mathbf{X}$ follows directly $\mathbf{Y}^\top\mathbf{Y} = \mathbf{I}$. We replace these expressions in the objective function: max trace $(\mathbf{AX})$ = max trace $(\mathbf{SY})$. Now for the last step: unitary matrices have all eigenvalues equal to ones and orthogonal eigenvectors $\mathbf{a}_i$. The eigendecomposition of $\mathbf{Y}$ is $\mathbf{Y} = \sum_i \mathbf{a}_i \mathbf{a}_i^\top$ and the objective function is trace $(\mathbf{SY}) = \sum_i s_i [\mathbf{a}_i \mathbf{a}_i^\top]_{i,i}$, which is maximized when $\mathbf{a}_i = \mathbf{e}_i$, and $\mathbf{Y} = \mathbf{I}$, so that the solution is $\mathbf{X} = \mathbf{VU}^\top$.

7.4 Interpreting Principal Components

One criticism that is often leveled against PCA is that its loadings are hard to interpret. The goal of this chapter is to partially dispel this myth. The output of a PCA is interpretable, and in fact sometimes it provides additional non-trivial perspectives for the user.

7.4.1 *The Clustering View*

The first avenue to interpretation is to do no transformation at all. The principal components are uniquely determined up to a change of sign: if $\mathbf{u}$ is an eigenvector associated to eigenvalue λ, so is $-\mathbf{u}$. We show that their loadings can be interpreted as a *clustering membership index* (Ding and He, 2004). In order to make the connection between clustering and PCA, we first introduce the K-means approach. We partition our n assets into K clusters, each characterized by a set membership C_k and centroids $\mathbf{m}_k := \sum_{i \in C_k} \mathbf{r}^i / |C_k|$. The number of clusters K is set in advance. The cluster membership is found by minimizing the sum of squared distances from the centroids:

$$\min \sum_{k=1}^{K} \sum_{i \in C_k} \left\| \mathbf{r}^i - \mathbf{m}_k \right\|^2 \tag{7.44}$$

$$\text{s.t. } \mathbf{m}_k := \sum_{i \in C_k} \mathbf{r}^i / |C_k| \tag{7.45}$$

$$C_i \cap C_j = \emptyset, i \neq j \tag{7.46}$$

$$\bigcup_i C_i = \{1, \ldots, N\} \tag{7.47}$$

We rewrite the objective function as

$$\sum_i \|\mathbf{r}^i\|^2 - \sum_{k=1}^{K} |C_k|^{-1} \sum_{j,\ell \in C_k} (\mathbf{r}^j)^\top \mathbf{r}^\ell \tag{7.48}$$

The first sum is a constant and does not affect the optimization problem. We could represent cluster membership algebraically. Let $\mathbf{h}_k \in \mathbb{R}^n$ and define $[\mathbf{h}_k]_i = 1/\sqrt{|C_k|}$ if asset i is in cluster C_k, zero otherwise. Because an asset needs to belong to exactly one cluster, there is a constraint on the vectors: $\sum_k \sqrt{|C_k|}\mathbf{h}_k = \mathbf{1}$, where $\mathbf{1} \in \mathbb{R}^n$ is a vector of ones. Define $\mathbf{H} = (\mathbf{h}_1, \ldots, \mathbf{h}_K) \in \mathbb{R}^{n\times K}$. Let $\mathbf{g} = (\sqrt{|C_1|}, \ldots, \sqrt{|C_K|})$. The condition that each asset belongs to precisely one cluster can be expressed as $\mathbf{Hg} = \mathbf{1}$. Therefore, to solve a K-clustering problem, we need to solve

$$\max \operatorname{trace}\left(\mathbf{H}^\top \mathbf{R}\mathbf{R}^\top \mathbf{H}\right) \tag{7.49}$$

$$\text{s.t. } [\mathbf{H}]_{i,k} \in \left\{0, |C_k|^{-1/2}\right\} \tag{7.50}$$

Notice that the columns of $\mathbf{H}$ have unit norm and are orthogonal. Then it is natural to relax the discrete requirements on $\mathbf{H}$ and to solve

$$\max \operatorname{trace}\left(\mathbf{H}^\top \mathbf{R}\mathbf{R}^\top \mathbf{H}\right) \tag{7.51}$$

$$\mathbf{H}^\top \mathbf{H} = \mathbf{I}_K \tag{7.52}$$

This is the same formulation as the optimization version of the uncentered PCA, Equation (7.11). The interpretation of the loadings can then be one of approximate cluster membership. The simplest case is when we cluster on the first principal component. We can separate the two clusters based on some clustering method on the loadings; oftentimes, a simple inspection of the loadings distribution will suggest an appropriate cut-off point. When inspecting multiple eigenvectors, a multivariate clustering algorithm will help identify groups.

7.4.2 *The Regression View*

Another way to interpret the loadings of a statistical model is to represent them as sums of vectors, whose weights are intuitive. Qualitatively, we proceed as follows. First, assemble meaningful stock characteristics for a given date. We denote the matrix of characteristics $\mathbf{G} \in \mathbb{R}^{n\times p}$, where each characteristic is a column of the matrix $\mathbf{G}$. We denote $\mathbf{B}$ the matrix of loadings from the statistical model. We regress $[\mathbf{B}]_{\cdot,i}$ on the columns of $\mathbf{G}$, and denote the regression coefficients $\boldsymbol{\beta}^{(i)} \in \mathbb{R}^p$. In formulas, $[\mathbf{B}]_{\cdot,i} = \mathbf{G}\boldsymbol{\beta}^{(i)} + \boldsymbol{\eta}$, where $\boldsymbol{\eta} \in \mathbb{R}^n$ is a vector orthogonal to the column subspace of $\mathbf{G}$. If we are not using a very wide set of characteristics, then the regression weights help interpret the statistical loadings. The approach is, of course, not restricted to statistical models: we could apply this regression approach to any pair of risk models, to interpret one based on information contained in the other.

As a (very simplified) example, we consider a model built on U.S. asset returns normalized by idio vols, for the date of July 6, 2017. In order to gain intuition aboout the eigenfactors, we regress them against style loadings only; we use Axioma AXUS4 as source of these loadings. In Tables 7.2 and 7.3, we report only the most significant loadings.

The first principal component is overwhelmingly explained by the market factor, i.e., the factor of identical loadings all equal to ones. This is usually the case in statistical models. Regarding the second principal component, the most important explanatory variables are a value factor (Dividend Yield), Size, and (with negative coefficient) Short-Term Momentum. The opposite signs for value and momentum are consistent with experience, since the returns of these factors are usually negatively correlated. Size and Dividend Yield loadings are usually *positively*

Table 7.2 Regression coefficients for the first principal component

Term	Estimate	Std.Error	t-Statistic	p Value
Market Intercept	1.7E-02	1.6E-04	1.1E+02	0.0E+00
Volatility	-2.6E-03	1.9E-04	-1.4E+01	8.1E-43
Short-Term Momentum	1.2E-03	1.6E-04	7.6E+00	2.8E-14
Earnings Yield	7.7E-04	1.9E-04	4.1E+00	3.4E-05

Table 7.3 Regression coefficients for the second principal component

Term	Estimate	Std.Error	t-Statistic	p Value
Dividend Yield	4.2E-03	3.3E-04	1.3E+01	8.7E-36
Short-Term Momentum	-3.4E-03	3.3E-04	-1.0E+01	1.1E-24
Size	3.3E-03	3.3E-04	1.0E+01	1.2E-23

correlated, the reason being that large caps are likely to pay higher dividends—or dividends at all—than small caps. For this specific date, the correlation is 0.32. The first factor can be interpreted as a "risk-on" factor, whereas the second factor can be interpreted as a defensive, or "risk-off" factor.

7.5 Statistical Model Estimation in Practice

So far, we have only presented the theory of statistical factor models. The next two sections discuss the issues related to its implementation. PCA is usually applied to matrices (or *panels*) that do not have a time dimension. In contrast, we deal with temporal data; and we cannot assume that these data are drawn in each period from the same probability distribution. We will employ the PCA and SVD *locally*, i.e., at intervals in which the data can be presumed to be approximately stationary. We present two approaches that are used by practitioners and we compare their performance on historical U.S. equity data.

7.5.1 *Weighted and Two-Stage PCA*

A recurring theme in factor estimation is that weighting observations differently helps. Observations in the distant past are less informative than recent ones; observed returns of stocks with high idiosyncratic risk should be downweighted, compared to those of low-idio stocks. There are therefore two basic transformations that we can apply to the raw return matrix. The first one is in the time dimension. We replace the empirical covariance matrix in Equation (7.9) with a weighted one. Let $\mathbf{W}_\tau \in \mathbb{R}^{T\times T}$ be a diagonal matrix with positive diagonal elements. The diagonal terms could be, for example, exponential weights $[\mathbf{W}_\tau]_{t,t} = \kappa \exp(-t/\tau)$; the positive constant κ is such that the squared diagonal terms sum to T. Then the time-weighted empirical uncentered covariance matrix is

$$\hat{\mathbf{\Sigma}} = \frac{1}{T}\mathbf{R}\mathbf{W}_\tau^2\mathbf{R}^\top \tag{7.53}$$

This is the same as first transforming the returns $\tilde{\mathbf{R}} = \mathbf{R}\mathbf{W}$, and then computing the empirical covariance matrix, Equation (7.9), on the transformed returns. In practice, we would not compute the covariance matrix and then perform the PCA, but rather perform the SVD on $\tilde{\mathbf{R}}$, which would be computationally less expensive and give us the same results.

A different type of transformation is cross-sectional reweighting. In Chapter 6 we saw that it is optimal to scale returns by the idiosyncratic volatility, or at least a proxy. As we did in that chapter, we propose a two-step procedure.[15] First, perform an SVD (possibly, time-weighted) on the returns; $\mathbf{R} = \mathbf{USV}^\top$. Take the first p components (say, $p = 5$) and compute the idiosyncratic returns $\mathbf{E} = \mathbf{R} - \mathbf{U}_p S_p \mathbf{V}_p^\top$; a case we also consider is $p = 0$, in which case $\mathbf{E} = \mathbf{R}$. Define the proxy idiosyncratic variances: $\sigma_i^2 = T^{-1} \sum_t [\mathbf{E}]_{i,t}^2$, and $\mathbf{W}_{\boldsymbol{\sigma}} := \text{diag}\left(\sigma_1^{-1}, \dots, \sigma_n^{-1}\right)$. The asset-level reweighted covariance matrix is

$$\hat{\boldsymbol{\Sigma}} = \mathbf{W}_{\boldsymbol{\sigma}} \mathbf{R}\mathbf{R}^\top \mathbf{W}_{\boldsymbol{\sigma}} \tag{7.54}$$

One can perform then a second-stage PCA and a factor model on the reweighted covariance matrix: $\hat{\boldsymbol{\Sigma}} \simeq \mathbf{U}_m \mathbf{S}_m^2 \mathbf{U}_m^\top + \mathbf{I}_n$. Finally, pre- and post-multiply by the idiosyncratic weighting matrices $\mathbf{W}_{\boldsymbol{\sigma}}^{-1}$.

We employ the steps above in the following process. We use two time-series reweightings: one with half-life τ_f (f is for "fast") and τ_s (s is for "slow"). An empirical insight in asset return data is that volatilities and correlations change over different timescales. Volatilities change rapidly; in fact they may change dramatically over the course of a few days. The ratio between the volatility of a stock during a crisis can be four times as large as the volatility of the same asset during a quiet period. On the other side, pairwise correlations are quite stable. Even in the presence of major market stresses, these correlations marginally increase in absolute value. This suggests that we separate volatilities and correlations. Therefore, in the first stage, we use a short half-life to capture adequately changes in volatility. In the second stage, we use a longer half-life to estimate the factor structure of correlations.

[15] The two-step procedure for reweighting the PCA is relatively common; Boivin and Ng (2006) reweights using idio volatilities, and Bollerslev (1990) using total volatilities.

Procedure 7.1: *Statistical model estimation*

1. **Inputs**: $\mathbf{R} \in \mathbb{R}^{n \times T}$, $\tau_s \geq \tau_f > 0$, $p \in \mathbb{N}$, $m > 0$.
2. **Time-Series Reweighting**:

$$\begin{aligned} \mathbf{W}_{\tau_f} &:= \kappa \operatorname{diag}\left(\exp(-T/\tau_f), \ldots, \exp(-1/\tau_f)\right) \\ \widetilde{\mathbf{R}} &= \mathbf{R}\mathbf{W}_{\tau_f} \end{aligned}$$

3. **First-Stage PCA**: $\tilde{\mathbf{R}} := \tilde{\mathbf{U}}\tilde{\mathbf{S}}\tilde{\mathbf{V}}^\top$
4. **Idio Proxy Estimation**:

$$\begin{aligned} \mathbf{E} &= \widetilde{\mathbf{R}} - \widetilde{\mathbf{U}}_p \widetilde{\mathbf{S}}_p \widetilde{\mathbf{V}}_p^\top && \textit{(truncated SVD)} \\ \sigma_i^2 &= \frac{1}{T} \sum_t [\mathbf{E}]_{i,t}^2 && \textit{(idio var proxies)} \\ \mathbf{W}_\sigma &:= \operatorname{diag}\left(\sigma_1^{-1}, \ldots, \sigma_n^{-1}\right) \end{aligned}$$

5. **Idio Reweighting**:

$$\begin{aligned} \mathbf{W}_{\tau_s} &:= \kappa \operatorname{diag}\left(\exp(-T/\tau_s), \ldots, \exp(-1/\tau_s)\right) \\ \hat{\mathbf{R}} &:= \mathbf{W}_\sigma \mathbf{R} \mathbf{W}_{\tau_s} \end{aligned}$$

6. **Second-Stage PCA**: $\hat{\mathbf{R}} := \hat{\mathbf{U}}\hat{\mathbf{S}}\hat{\mathbf{V}}^\top$
7. **Second-Stage Factor Model**: $\hat{\mathbf{r}} = \hat{\mathbf{U}}_m \mathbf{f} + \hat{\epsilon}$

$$\begin{aligned} \text{where: } \mathbf{f} &\sim N\left(0, \operatorname{diag}\left(\ell(s_1^2), \ldots, \ell(s_m^2)\right)\right) \\ \epsilon &\sim N(0, \bar{\lambda}\mathbf{I}_n) \\ \bar{\lambda} &= \frac{1}{n-m} \sum_{i=m+1}^{n} s_i^2 \end{aligned}$$

8. **Output: Final Factor Model**: $\mathbf{r} := \mathbf{B}\mathbf{f} + \epsilon$

$$\begin{aligned} \text{where: } \mathbf{B} &= \mathbf{W}_\sigma^{-1} \hat{\mathbf{U}}_m \\ \mathbf{f} &\sim N\left(0, \operatorname{diag}\left(\ell(s_1^2), \ldots, \ell(s_m^2)\right)\right) \\ \epsilon &\sim N(0, \bar{\lambda}\hat{\mathbf{W}}_\sigma^{-2}) \end{aligned}$$

This procedure is flexible enough to include several PCA-related procedures as special cases, and to serve as a basis for further experimentation. Some examples:

- When $p = 0$, then idio reweighting becomes a z-scoring, so that the second-stage PCA is effectively applied to the correlation matrix.
- The special case of equal-weighted observations in time is obtained in the limit $\tau \to \infty$.
- It is straightforward to use different shrinkage methods in the second-stage factor model step.
- In the second-stage factor model step, we use the PPCA results of Section 7.1.2. The idio reweighting steps approximately "whiten" the idiosyncratic returns, i.e., make them unit-variance, so that PPCA applies. However, we could replace this with a different estimation procedure, like Maximum Likelihood.

7.5.2 Implementing Statistical Models in Production

It is not sufficient to have a procedure that estimates the loadings and the covariance matrix at a point in time. In our applications, factor models are *dynamic*. At time t, we have an estimation universe of stocks, and we use return data up to $T_{\max}$ periods in the past. We apply the two-stage PCA using returns data between $t - T_{\max} + 1$ and t, to obtain:

- Loadings $\mathbf{B}_t$. This is the output loadings matrix.
- Factor returns and idio returns estimate at time t:

$$\hat{\mathbf{f}}_t = (\mathbf{B}_{t-1}^\top \mathbf{W}_{\sigma,t-1}^2 \mathbf{B}_{t-1})^{-1} \mathbf{B}_{t-1}^\top \mathbf{W}_{\sigma,t-1}^2 \mathbf{r}_t \tag{7.55}$$

$$= [\hat{\mathbf{U}}_m]_t^\top \mathbf{W}_{\sigma,t-1} \mathbf{r}_t \tag{7.56}$$

$$\hat{\epsilon}_t = \mathbf{r}_t - \mathbf{B}_t \hat{\mathbf{f}}_t \tag{7.57}$$

We need to address some outstanding problems:

1. Sign indeterminacy of eigenvectors.
2. Time-changing estimation universe.
3. Imputation of loadings for non-estimation universe assets.
4. Imputation of missing values for new or temporarily non-traded assets.

We tackle them in order.

- *Sign indeterminacy of eigenvectors.* Let us begin with a simple observation. In a statistical model, eigenvectors are identified modulo a sign change, i.e., if $\mathbf{u}$ is an eigenvector of matrix $\mathbf{\Sigma}$ and associated eigenvalue λ, then so is $-\mathbf{u}$. When we compute the SVD for adjacent periods, we add and remove observations, which may lead to a sign flip in the loadings. It is important therefore that loadings are collinear, in the sense that the cosine angle between eigenvectors (i.e., their cosine similarity in adjacent periods) is positive. Aside from the straightforward realignment exercise, the turnover of eigenvectors is important in two respects. First, because if we observe that $S_C(\mathbf{u}^i(t), \mathbf{u}^i(t+1)) \simeq 0$, then it is difficult to determine the sign of consecutive eigenvalues. As a result, it is difficult to determine the sign of the factor return $f_i(t)$ over time. Aside from any statistical considerations, high-turnover statistical factors cannot be employed for performance attribution. The second consideration is that a very high-turnover factor results in factor-mimicking portfolios with very high turnover as well, and is therefore a factor that is very difficult to trade, either for hedging or speculation purposes.
- *Time-changing estimation universe.* Similarly to fundamental models, statistical models are estimated on a predetermined set of assets. The rationale for the choice of such a universe is the same as for fundamental models. Assets in the estimation universe should be representative of the investment universe of the trading strategy; they should be sufficiently liquid to be considered tradeable; and, relatedly, they should be sufficiently traded to ensure good price discovery and therefore reliable return calculations. Assets enter and leave the universe over time. We face a dilemma. We cannot use the latest universe composition, because the past returns of recent additions to the index may be unreliable because the asset was illiquid, or be missing altogether. We can still opt to keep these recent additions, provided that their returns are well defined; or alternatively we can use the assets at the intersection of all the universes over the time interval used for estimation. If the time interval used for model estimation is not too long, and if the universe turnover is not too high, we will still have a sufficiently broad panel of assets. It is preferable to employ an estimation universe that

has the lowest possible turnover, and it is important to use a consistent procedure to select the assets to include in the return matrix $\mathbf{R}$.

- *Imputing loadings for non-estimation universe assets.* There are assets that are not in the estimation universe, but that have complete returns. They do not have loadings. We can impute loadings by performing a time-series regression of asset returns against the factor returns. This approach is justified by the results in Section 7.1.3: we can recover loadings from time-series regression, provided that the factor returns we obtained using the estimation universe are close to the true factor returns.
- *Imputation of missing values for new or temporarily non-traded assets.* Some assets do not have sufficient return history to regress their loadings; examples are newly listed assets (IPOs, ADRs), or assets that were either delisted for a long period of time, or had trading volumes considered too low to result in reliable returns. A possible solution is to use additional characteristics of the asset to impute its loadings. The approach is similar to the one we presented in Section 7.4.2 on the interpretation of loadings using regression. In this case, however, we usually are not afforded the luxury to know many of the asset's style characteristics like momentum, beta, liquidity, or profitability. All we have is knowledge of the industry and country of the asset. We regress observed loadings against these two characteristics, and predict the missing loadings. It is common practice to shrink predicted loadings toward zero. We will cover a rationale for this practice in later sections devoted to hedging.

7.6 ★Appendix

7.6.1 Exercises and Extensions to PCA

Exercise 7.1 *(Low-Rank Factorization)*: Prove that a matrix $\mathbf{A} \in \mathbb{R}^{n\times T}$ is of rank $m \leq \min\{n, T\}$ if and only if it can be decomposed into the product of two matrices $\mathbf{B} \in \mathbb{R}^{n\times m}$ and $\mathbf{C} \in \mathbb{R}^{m\times T}$.

Exercise 7.2 *(PCA Solution)*: Prove that the solution $\mathbf{w}^\star$ in Problems (7.7) and (7.10) is unique and that constraint $\|\mathbf{w}\|^2 \leq 1$ is always binding, i.e., $\|\mathbf{w}^\star\| = 1$.

Exercise 7.3 ***(Alternative PCA Formulation):*** Prove that the optimization (7.11) gives the same solution as finding the first m eigenvectors of $\hat{\mathbf{\Sigma}}$, and as finding iteratively k unit-norm vectors $\mathbf{w}_1, \ldots, \mathbf{w}_k$, with $\mathbf{w}_k$ orthogonal to the first $k-1$ vectors $\mathbf{w}_k$, that maximize $\mathbf{w}_k^\top \hat{\mathbf{\Sigma}} \mathbf{w}_k$.

Exercise 7.4 ***(Covariance Matrix of a Linear Transformation):*** Prove that if the random vector $\mathbf{r}$ taking values in $\mathbb{R}^n$ has covariance matrix $\mathbf{\Sigma}$, and if $\mathbf{A} \in \mathbb{R}^{m \times n}$, then the random vector $\mathbf{x} = \mathbf{A}\mathbf{r}$ has covariance matrix $\mathbf{A}\mathbf{\Sigma}\mathbf{A}^\top$.

Exercise 7.5 ***(A Simple Spiked Matrix):*** Let $\mathbf{B} \in \mathbb{R}^{n \times m}$ be an m-rank matrix. Prove that the first m eigenvalues of $\mathbf{B}\mathbf{B}^\top + \sigma^2 \mathbf{I}_n$ are greater than σ^2.

Exercise 7.6: Solve the optimization problem, Equation (7.16).

Exercise 7.7 ***(The Power Method):*** A simple (the simplest?) algorithm for computing the largest eigenvalue of a symmetric p.d. matrix $\mathbf{\Sigma}$ is the following: 1. start with a unit-norm $\mathbf{x}_0$ chosen at random (say, sample the coordinates from a standard normal distribution, then normalize it); 2. iterate: $\mathbf{x}_{i+1} = \mathbf{\Sigma}\mathbf{x}_i / \left\| x_i \right\|$; 3. after the vector converges (say $\left\| x_{i+1} - x_1 \right\|$ is smaller than some tolerance), $\mathbf{x}_{i+1}$ approximates the top eigenvector, and $\mathbf{x}_i^\top \mathbf{\Sigma} \mathbf{x}_i$ the top eigenvalue.

1. Prove the convergence and correctness of the power method. (Hint: $\mathbf{x}_i = \mathbf{\Sigma}^i \mathbf{x}_0 / \left\| \mathbf{\Sigma}^i \mathbf{x}_0 \right\|$.)
2. Let $\delta \in (0, 1)$. Find $f(\delta)$ such that $\mathbf{x}_i^\top \mathbf{\Sigma} \mathbf{x}_i \geq (1-\delta)\lambda_1$ if $i \geq f(\delta)$.
3. How would you extend it to find all the eigenvalues of $\mathbf{\Sigma}$?

Exercise 7.8 ***(Iterated Projections for the SVD):*** A simple (the simplest?) algorithm for computing the largest singular value of a matrix $\mathbf{R} \in \mathbb{R}^{n \times T}$ is the following: 1. start with $\mathbf{x}_0 \in \mathbb{R}^T$ chosen at random (say, sample the coordinates from a standard normal distribution), 2. iterate:

$$\mathbf{y}_{i+1} = \mathbf{R}\mathbf{x}_i \tag{7.58}$$

$$\mathbf{x}_{i+1} = \mathbf{R}^\top \mathbf{y}_{i+1} \tag{7.59}$$

3. after the vectors converge $\mathbf{x}_{i+1}$ approximates the highest left eigenvector, $\mathbf{y}_{i+1}$ the higher right eigenvector, and $\mathbf{y}_{i+1}^\intercal \mathbf{R}\mathbf{x}_{i+1}$ the top singular value.

1. Prove the convergence and correctness of the algorithm. (Hint: power method.)
2. How would you extend it to find the SVD of $\mathbf{R}$? (Hint: Not the same way of the power method.)

Exercise 7.9 ***(Time-Series Regression from the SVD)*:** Let $\mathbf{R} = \mathbf{U}\mathbf{S}\mathbf{V}^\intercal$, and set $\hat{\mathbf{F}} := \mathbf{S}_m \mathbf{V}_m^\intercal$. The vector $\hat{\mathbf{f}}_i$, the ith row of $\hat{\mathbf{F}}$, is the time series of the ith factor return. Prove that the least-squares regression coefficient of the time series $\mathbf{r}_i = \beta_{i,j}\hat{\mathbf{f}}_j + \epsilon$, is $\beta_{i,j} = [\mathbf{U}]_{i,j}$.

Exercise 7.10 ***(Oja's Iterative Algorithm)*:** Let $\mathbf{r}_t$, $t = 1, \ldots, T$ be a time series of returns drawn from a common distribution on $\mathbb{R}^n$ with covariance matrix $\boldsymbol{\Omega}$. Prove that the following algorithm converges to the first eigenvector of $\boldsymbol{\Omega}$:

1. Set $i = 0$ and choose a unit-norm $\mathbf{v}_1 \in B^n$ uniformly at random.
2. Choose column $\pi(i)$ uniformly at random between 1 and T.
3. Update the direction

$$\mathbf{v}_{i+1} = \mathbf{v}_n + i^{-1}(1 - \mathbf{v}_i^\intercal \mathbf{e})(\mathbf{r}_{\pi(i)}^\intercal \mathbf{v}_i)\mathbf{r}_{\pi(i)} \tag{7.60}$$

$$\mathbf{v}_{i+1} \leftarrow \frac{\mathbf{v}_{i+1}}{\left\|\mathbf{v}_{i+1}\right\|} \tag{7.61}$$

4. Set $i \leftarrow i + 1$. If $\left\|\mathbf{v}_{i+1} - \mathbf{v}_i\right\|$ then stop. Otherwise go to Step 2.

Solution (sketch): Let $\mathbf{R} \in \mathbb{R}^{n\times T}$, and $\mathbf{X}$ a random matrix taking values in $\mathbb{R}^{n\times n}$. $\mathbf{X}$ takes one of T values: $\mathbf{r}_i\mathbf{r}_i^\intercal$ with equal probability $1/T$. One can interpret the product $T^{-1}\mathbf{v}^\intercal\mathbf{R}\mathbf{R}^\intercal\mathbf{v}$ as the expectation $E(\mathbf{v}^\intercal\mathbf{X}\mathbf{v})$. The first eigenvalue of $T^{-1}\mathbf{R}\mathbf{R}^\intercal$ is

$$\max_{\|\mathbf{v}\|=1} E\left(\frac{\mathbf{v}^\intercal\mathbf{X}\mathbf{v}}{\|\mathbf{v}\|^2}\right) \tag{7.62}$$

We can apply the stochastic gradient algorithm to the maximum search. Let $f(\mathbf{X}, \mathbf{v}) := (\mathbf{v}^\top \mathbf{X}\mathbf{v})/|\mathbf{v}|^2 - \lambda|\mathbf{v}|^2$. The derivative $\nabla_{\mathbf{v}} f$ for a unit-norm vector $\|\mathbf{v}\|$ is

$$2(1 - \mathbf{v}^\top \mathbf{e})\mathbf{X}\mathbf{v} \tag{7.63}$$

Exercise 7.11 ***(Distance Between Subspaces)***: Let $\mathbf{A}, \mathbf{B} \in \mathbb{R}^{n\times m}$ be orthonormal matrices. If the two column subspaces are "similar", then any unit-norm vector in the column subspace of $\mathbf{A}$ is well-approximated by some unit-norm vector in the column subspace of $\mathbf{B}$. Define similarity between the two subspaces as

$$S(\mathbf{A}, \mathbf{B}) := \frac{1}{2} \max_{\|\mathbf{x}\| \leq 1} \min_{\|\mathbf{y}\| \leq 1} \left\| \mathbf{A}\mathbf{x} - \mathbf{B}\mathbf{y} \right\|^2 \tag{7.64}$$

1. Prove that $S(\mathbf{A}, \mathbf{B})$ is $1 - \sigma_1(\mathbf{A}^\top \mathbf{B})$, where $\sigma_1(\mathbf{A}^\top \mathbf{B})$ is the first singular value of $\mathbf{A}^\top \mathbf{B}$.
2. Prove that $S(\mathbf{A}, \mathbf{B})$ is not a distance because it does not satisfy the triangle inequality.

Exercise 7.12 ***(Angle Between Subspaces)***: Let $\mathbf{A}, \mathbf{B} \in \mathbb{R}^{n\times m}$ be orthonormal matrices. Let the least cosine distance between subspaces be the cosine of the smallest achievable angle between two vectors, one belonging to the column subspace of $\mathbf{A}$, the other belonging to the column subspace of $\mathbf{B}$.

Prove that $S_C(\mathbf{A}, \mathbf{B}) = \sigma_n(\mathbf{A}^\top \mathbf{B})$, where $\sigma_m(\mathbf{A}^\top \mathbf{B})$ is the last singular value of $\mathbf{A}^\top \mathbf{B}$.

Exercise 7.13 ***(Covariance Matrix Invariance for Degenerate Eigenvalues)***: Consider a risk model with the following structure: its loading matrix $\mathbf{B}$ has the form $\mathbf{B} = \mathbf{D}\mathbf{U}$, where $\mathbf{D} \in \mathbb{R}^{n\times n}$ is diagonal positive-definite and $\mathbf{U} \in \mathbb{R}^{n\times m}$, $\mathbf{U}^\top \mathbf{U} = \mathbf{I}_m$; and its factor covariance matrix is proportional to the identity: $\boldsymbol{\Sigma}_f = \bar{\lambda}\mathbf{I}_m$.

1. Prove that if we replace $\mathbf{U}$ with an "equivalent" $\tilde{\mathbf{U}} \in \mathbb{R}^{m\times n}$ spanning the same subspace, the covariance matrix does not change.

2. Extend the result to the case where $\mathbf{\Sigma}_f$ is still diagonal, but with the first p variances being greater than the rest: $\lambda_1 > \lambda_2 > \ldots > \lambda_p > \lambda_{p+1} = \ldots = \lambda_m$, and with

$$\widetilde{\mathbf{U}}_{\cdot,1:p} = \mathbf{U}_{\cdot,1:p}$$
$$\widetilde{\mathbf{U}}^{\mathsf{T}}_{\cdot,(p+1):m}\widetilde{\mathbf{U}}_{\cdot,(p+1):m} = \mathbf{I}_{m-p}$$

7.6.2 *Asymptotic Properties of PCA*

This is a summary of the asymptotic properties of PCA in the regime where the number of variables n is constant and the number of observations T goes to infinity. We have T realizations of iid random vectors $\mathbf{x}_t \sim N(\mathbf{0}, \mathbf{\Sigma})$, from which we want to estimate $\mathbf{\Sigma}$. We assume that the $\mathbf{x}_{t,i}$ have finite fourth moments. Let $\hat{\mathbf{\Sigma}}_T := T^{-1} \sum_{t=1}^{T} \mathbf{x}_t\mathbf{x}_t^{\mathsf{T}}$. By the Strong Law of Large Numbers, $\hat{\mathbf{\Sigma}}_T \to \mathbf{\Sigma}$ almost surely. Both eigenvalues and eigenvectors converge to the covariance matrix. Anderson (1963) proves a Central Limit Theorem for the eigenvalues of the covariance matrix. Decompose the empirical and true covariance matrices into their eigenvalues and eigenvectors:

$$\mathbf{\Sigma} = \mathbf{U}\mathbf{\Lambda}\mathbf{U}^{\mathsf{T}} \tag{7.65}$$

$$\hat{\mathbf{\Sigma}}_T = \hat{\mathbf{U}}\hat{\mathbf{\Lambda}}\hat{\mathbf{U}}^{\mathsf{T}} \tag{7.66}$$

with $\lambda_1 > \lambda_2 > \ldots > \lambda_n$; all eigenvalues are assumed to be distinct. Anderson proves that, as $T \to \infty$,

$$\sqrt{T}(\hat{\boldsymbol{\lambda}} - \boldsymbol{\lambda}) \sim N(\mathbf{0}, 2\mathbf{\Lambda}) \tag{7.67}$$

$$\sqrt{T}(\hat{\mathbf{u}}_i - \mathbf{u}_i) \sim N(\mathbf{0}, \mathbf{E}_i) \tag{7.68}$$

$$\mathbf{E}_i := \mathbf{U} \begin{bmatrix} \frac{\lambda_1\lambda_i}{(\lambda_1 - \lambda_i)^2} & 0 & \ldots & 0 \\ 0 & \frac{\lambda_2\lambda_i}{(\lambda_2 - \lambda_i)^2} & \ldots & 0 \\ 0 & 0 & 0 & 0 \\ \ldots & \ldots & \ldots & \ldots \\ 0 & 0 & \ldots & \frac{\lambda_n\lambda_i}{(\lambda_n - \lambda_i)^2} \end{bmatrix} \mathbf{U}^{\mathsf{T}} \tag{7.69}$$

where the *i*th row has all zeros. Therefore:

1. The standard error on $\hat{\lambda}_i$ is $2\lambda_i/\sqrt{T}$.
2. The standard error on the principal components, defined as $\sqrt{E(\left\|\hat{\mathbf{u}}_i - \mathbf{u}_i\right\|^2)}$, is

$$\frac{1}{\sqrt{T}}\sqrt{\sum_{k=1,k\neq i}^{n} \frac{\lambda_k \lambda_i}{(\lambda_k - \lambda_i)^2}} \tag{7.70}$$

The relative error depends on the separation between eigenvalues.

The Takeaways

- Statistical factor models estimate both factor returns and exposures using return data only, without relying on firm characteristics or macroeconomic data.
- *Advantages*: Complementarity to fundamental models, availability in data-poor environments, including for short-horizon and multi-asset models.
- *Disadvantages:* Interpretability of statistical models is generally lower.
- Principal Component Analysis (PCA) identifies a factor model by minimizing the sum of squared residuals in the factor model.
- Large eigenvalues of the empirical covariance matrix correspond to factor variances, and are separated in magnitude by a bulk of smaller eigenvalues. This is the spiked covariance model.
- The sample factor eigenvalues are larger than the true ones, and should be shrinked.
- Statistical factors can be interpreted. PCA loadings admit a clustering interpretation and a regression interpretation.
- Factor loadings should be rotated in each period in order to reduce turnover.

Chapter 8

Evaluating Excess Returns

The Questions

1. How does reusing historical data impact alpha estimation and backtesting in factor models?
2. What are the best practices we should follow in any backtest?
3. What are the two main backtesting frameworks and what are their drawbacks?
4. What approach could address these limitations?

The task of estimating factor models and testing alphas for systematic strategies usually involves reusing the same historical data. This is somewhat unintuitive. One of the defining features of the past 40 years has been the increased recording of new datasets and their broad dissemination. Investment firms have budgets of tens of millions of dollars allocated to the purchase of market and alternative data, and to the bespoke collection of data (e.g., via web scrapes). And yet, the characteristics of traded assets, and specifically of companies, do not change on a minute-by-minute basis; and investment strategies with relatively long holding times—of the order of a day or longer—do not necessarily employ tick-by-tick data. If we record prices for a broad local investment universe at 5-minute intervals, we collect 60 million numeric data points per year[1]; including a security identifier and a timestamp, the required storage is of the order of gigabytes. History is not *replaceable*, and sometimes it is not *deep*. Not replaceable, in the sense that it is not easy to produce a simulated version of the past that provably reproduces all of its features. Not deep, in the sense that we do not live in a stationary world. The pace at which the real world outside of finance changes is breathtaking and accelerating, and markets are a timid reflection of it. Not even taking such change into account, the introduction of new technology, of new market microstructure designs, of new regulations, and the ongoing collective learning process of all market participants make the investing world of five years ago very different from today's. The fact that we have to rely on historical data poses a major challenge. We cannot design experiments. Our studies are observational and repeated. Financial practitioners do not have a shared protocol for experimental analysis. Even if we had one, it is far from obvious that it is the correct one. Well-established disciplines like medicine and psychology had shared experimental practices accompanied by experimental design, and yet they have undergone a re-evaluation when their practitioners found that most of their results are not replicable (Ioannidis, 2005; Open Science Collaboration, 2015).

This poses a few challenges for us modelers. We have a very large number of signal types, which themselves depend on continuous tuning parameters, and we only have a limited history. This is similar to the situation faced by biostatisticians, who deal with tens of thousands of simultaneous tests in the form of responses from a DNA microarray (Dudoit et al. 2003; Huang et al. 2009). The details are quite different. The "response variable" for a DNA microarray is usually discrete ("polytomous"), and responses are uncorrelated or weakly correlated. In quantitative finance,

[1] Assuming 6.5 trading hours, 251 trading days, and 3000 stocks.

the response variable (be it return or Sharpe) is continuous, and signal correlation plays a decisive role.

This chapter has four sections. First, we list some basic best practices for data preparation and usage. Second, we describe some common backtesting practices and critique them. The third section is entirely devoted to describing a new backtesting protocol, which offers several advantages over the previous ones: it gives finite-sample uniform probabilistic bounds on the Sharpe Ratio of a large set of strategies. The last section applies the theory developed so far to simulated and historical data.

8.1 Backtesting Best Practices

We review a few best practices for backtesting. They do not originate from some comprehensive theory. Unlike Athena, who was born fully formed from the mind of Zeus, it is an ever-incomplete, occasionally shallow body of knowledge that has formed by experimentation. Some references covering these practices are Wang et al. (2014); Arnott et al. (2019); López de Prado (2020).

8.1.1 Data Sourcing

High-quality data are essential to backtesting, and the search for better data is a never-ending task for a researcher. There are several broad areas of concern. The first one is data sourcing. There are multiple vendors offering similar data. When comparing them, ask the following questions:

- *Definition and interpretation.* Perhaps the first and most important question, not only in data sourcing, but in quantitative investing, is *what do the data mean?* What is the exact definition of the data collected? What are their physical units? If the dataset is money-related, it should be unambiguous what is the reference currency (or currencies, for exchange rates). If the data is flow-related (i.e., measuring rates over time), the time unit should be defined. A surprising number of mistakes happen because of unit conversion errors.
- *Provenance.* Where are the data coming from? Does the vendor collect the data themselves (e.g., via web scraping, or internet traffic)? More often, the vendor serves as an intermediary between a data originator and the client. In the former case, what is the collection criterion? Does the vendor sample the data or collect them exhaustively? Is the

population sampling methodology sound? In the latter case, who is originating the data? Are they trustworthy?

- *Completeness.* This leads to the second question: completeness. Are there data that are obviously missing from the dataset such as, for example, intermittently missing prices? Are there data that are non-obviously missing, such as, for example, unrecorded consumer credit card transactions? Some of these questions can be answered by performing exploratory analysis on the data themselves; others need to be addressed with the vendor.
- *Quality assurance.* How does the provider ensure that the data it receives or collects are consistently of good quality? Does it have checks for change points in the data characteristics?
- *Point-in-time versus restated data.* Does the provider offer data collected as of a certain date, without changing them at a later date, based on corrections and company updates? This is an instance of data leakage, which we will cover in more detail later.
- *Transformations.* Data are almost always transformed by the vendor. Examples are: imputation of missing data; winsorization and removal of outliers; end-of-period price calculations (last transaction, mid bid–ask price, weighted average). These transformations should be documented, evaluated, and if possible, verified by the research analyst.
- *Exploring alternatives and complements.* Always ask the following common-sense questions: can we obtain better data, across the following three dimensions. First, are there providers offering larger coverage for the same dataset (e.g., more securities at any point in time, deeper history, more frequent data)? Second, are there providers with better data? For example, if data are collected from broker-dealers, the alternative provider has an agreement with a larger number of participating contributors. Third, can we obtain complementary data? These are datasets that, jointly with the original one, greatly increase its original value. For example, we may obtain transactional data that help us estimate short-term revenues of a company, in addition to data that give us a good estimate of their costs.

8.1.2 Research Process

Every researcher has their own research process. This is part of their competitive advantage; it's indeed part *of what they are*, of thoughts and learned lessons accumulated over a lifetime of experiences and of studying. It would be futile to superimpose the author's overall research philosophy to that of the reader,[2] just in a few pages. However, there are a few steps that are uncontroversial and are part of basic hygiene. Consider these akin to the precept to never leave home without wearing underwear.

- *Data leakage.* The first recommendation is to avoid *data leakage.* The definition of data leakage is the presence in the training data, the data available up to time t, of information contained in the target, i.e., returns in periods $t + 1$ and later. The reference rule is to never use data in a backtest on a certain date that we are not able to use in production on that day. Detecting data leakage is more art than science, and it requires both a deep knowledge of the data (see above) and of the problem at hand. Below are a few examples.
  - *Survivorship bias.* If we backtest the performance of a strategy over an extended period of time, considering only the stocks that have continuously traded during this period, i.e., the surviving stocks at the end of the backtest, we are subject to survivorship bias. Stocks are most often delisted because they experience large losses, trade at low share prices, become illiquid, or do not meet some additional criteria for being listed on an exchange. Removing them biases the investment sample toward outperformers with different characteristics than those of the broader investment universe at a point in time. For example, the survivors' liquidity, momentum, and size are larger than the universe. This is the simplest and most impactful instance of data leakage. The remedy to this issue is to: (a) employ a sensible methodology for inclusion that is applicable at any point in time; (b) specify a realistic and conservative rule in the backtest for the event of a delisting. For example, one could assume that the entire investment is written off. Note that the methodology in (a) should be specified *before* backtests are initiated. Changing the inclusion rules based on the result of backtest is also an instance of data leakage, and it should be avoided. Criteria for inclusion are indeed not straightforward to specify. A common recommendation is to use an investment universe defined by a commercial benchmark, like Russell 1000, Russell 3000, MSCI benchmarks, or commercial factor models investment universes. Note that benchmark components are always

[2] Although, you may argue, this whole book is an exposition of my investment philosophy. Point taken, to an extent. I am providing some building blocks, and you are reshaping and assembling them into something sensible.

announced before ("announcement date") the effective addition date ("reconstitution date"), and the returns of the stocks are affected by the announcement of an inclusion or exclusion. In your backtest, you may want to capture this information, in order to assess how much of the performance of your quantitative strategies is affected by recent changes in the investment universe.

- *Financial statements*. Financial statement information for a given quarter or year should be included in the backtesting data on the day (or the day after) of their public release, not on the last quarter to which the data refer.
- *Point-in-time data*. Financial data used in the backtest on a given date should always be the most recent data available *as of that date*. If a 10Q (a quarterly financial report) is restated because of material error, the backtest should not reflect that. The strategy must be tested by allowing the presence of errors in its input data.
- *Price adjustments*. Shares are regularly split (or reverse-split) into multiple shares. The price of the split share is adjusted accordingly. This occurs when the stock appreciates to the point one share becomes so expensive that it prevents investors from being able to buy it. In order to compute historical returns across long time series, prices and dividend are usually split-adjusted. This introduces a complication. A low stock price in the distant past indicates that the shares have been split several times in the future, likely because of high returns. The price becomes informative of future performance. The recommended remedy is to use adjusted prices only for return calculation. For feature generation, use as-of-date prices.
- *Missingness*. In certain cases (mostly unstructured data instances), data points are missing either because they were not made available as-of-date or because they contain sensitive information and were redacted. In the latter case, missingness may be suffering from look-ahead bias and is informative of future returns.
- *Avoidable mistakes*. The number of silly mistakes (in hindsight) that experienced, effective researchers make never ceases to amaze. For example, a stock characteristic available in a dataset had high Information Coefficient[3] (IC). Upon further investigation, it was a stock

[3] The Information Coefficient is formally defined in Section 8.3.1.

split conversion factor (see the previous bullet point). As another example, because of an erroneous t versus $t + 1$ convention error, a researcher included the next-day return in a three-month momentum factor definition, also causing a false positive.

- *Strategy development.* There are some qualitative recommendations that, while missing a solid foundation, are hard to argue against.
  - *Have a theory (if you can).* It is preferable to have a theory for every anomaly and to pre-register the predictions of the theory before the backtest. For example, in their paper on quality, Asness et al. (2019) propose a theory guiding the development of the factor; so do Frazzini and Pedersen (2014) when they analyze the beta anomaly. With a theory as a guide, it is easier to choose a security characteristic among many, therefore reducing the number of strategies being tested; it is possible to interpret the result and believe in it more, and it is possible to critique and revise the characteristic, which is maybe not desirable (it would be nice if we got it right the first time) but necessary.
  - *Enforce reproducibility.* Document all your strategies and make sure you can reproduce and rerun them at any time.
  - *Use the same setting in backtesting and in production as much as possible.* By this we mean that we should use the same point-in-time data, but also the same optimization formulations, the same market impact model, and the same codebase.
  - *Calibrate the market impact model.* When we perform a backtest, the market impact model has a "descriptive" role. It estimates the losses in efficiency from actual trading. It is not possible, however, to verify the realized market impact on historical data. In order to align backtest performance to live one, it is important not to take a market impact model at face value, especially one provided by a vendor or a partner. Instead, calibrate its parameters against live performance of the current version of your strategy, so that realized and backtested PnL of your current strategy overlap as much as possible.
  - *Include borrow costs.* As part of the effort to align production and simulated PnL, one should take borrow costs[4] for shorted securities into account, since they can have a material impact on the profitability of the short side. This has challenges. Historical borrow rates are not

---

[4] In order to short a security, the investor (or an agent on their behalf, like a broker-dealer) must borrow it first from a lender, who charges interest on the loan.

readily available historically. The researcher may have to approximate them, or predict them on the basis of security characteristics. Another complication, albeit less impactful, is the tax treatment of dividends. When they are received by the investor, they are subject to taxation. When the investor is short the security, the treatment of dividends is more complex. In practice, tax dividend treatment is complex, and does not make a material difference in backtests, so it is not modeled. Still, be aware of it, in case you see discrepancies between accounting and simulated PnL.

- *Define the backtesting protocol beforehand.* A backtesting protocol is the sequence of actions and decisions that lead to assessing the performance of a strategy. It is the subject of the next section. For the sake of this list of folk precepts, it is sufficient to say that the backtesting protocol should be changed (a) rarely, (b) for a good reason, and (c) if it changes, you should rerun and re-evaluate all your strategies under the new protocol.
- *Define the dataset being used beforehand.* If dataset selection is seen as part of the backtesting protocol, the heuristic follows from the previous point. The difference however is that new data become available every day, both in the form of live data, and of extensions to historical dataset. Researchers may be prone to include datasets that confirm their findings, and ignore those that do not. Ignoring new data would be suboptimal, and including them selectively may lead to the wrong conclusions. Use your judgment and research integrity, which no theorems can help.

8.2 The Backtesting Protocol

8.2.1 Cross-Validation and Walk-Forward

Evaluating trading strategies bears similarities with statistical model selection (Hastie et al., 2008). We have a family of strategies (in statistics, a family of models), and a performance measure, such as Sharpe Ratio or return on GMV. The strategies themselves may depend on several parameters. Two evaluation schemes are most common. The first one is cross-validation (Hastie et al. (2008), Ch. 7; Mohri et al. (2018), Ch. 4). The available data is split into a *training dataset* and a *holdout (or validation) dataset*. Sometimes, based on the estimated time dependence in the time series, the training and holdout samples are separated by a "buffer" dataset. The training dataset is split into K equal-sized samples ("folds"). Similarly to the buffer between training and holdout datasets, we may want to separate the folds by a short buffer (for equities, just one or two days) to eliminate dependencies between folds. This eliminates a possible source of look-ahead bias. Then, we perform K estimation-evaluation exercises. The parameters are estimated on each of the possible combinations of $K - 1$ folds, and the performance of the model is evaluated of the remaining fold using the optimized parameter; see Figure 8.1. Then estimate the cross-validation performance as the average of the single-run performances. Finally, performance is checked against the holdout sample; a scheme is shown in Figure 8.2. There are several contraindications to using cross-validation for financial applications. First, the samples are not independent. The time dependence is reflected in the returns themselves. We know that serial dependence of returns is weak and has short memory, while volatility dependence is strong and has long memory. For some time series, it is possible to remedy this by keeping the order intact in the training folds and the errors are serially uncorrelated (Bergmeir et al., 2018; Cerqueira et al., 2023). This is not the only issue faced in financial applications, however. For example, consider the inclusion of security momentum as a predictor. This characteristic uses past returns. Now, if the validation fold precedes temporally the training fold, these past returns are in the validation fold and we are incurring a typical instance of data leakage: the predictors directly contain information about

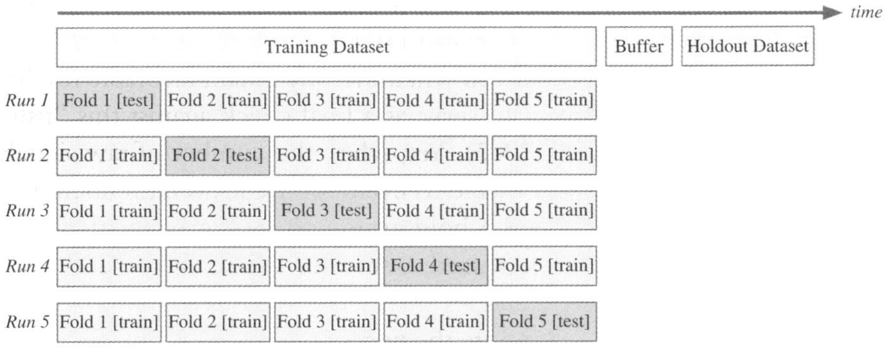

Figure 8.1 A scheme of the cross-validation procedure. Darker boxes are validation folds, while lighter boxes are training folds.

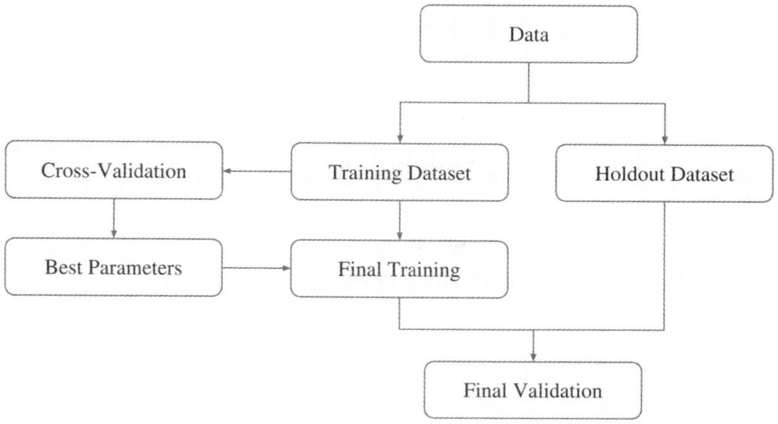

Figure 8.2 A scheme of the cross-validation procedure. Data are split into two sets. Cross-validation is performed on the first one (training dataset), to estimate the expected performance of a strategy. The model is then optimized on the entire training dataset, and validated on the second one (validation dataset).

the target. This is an obvious example, but there are subtle ones as well. For example, we could use forward earnings forecast as a predictor. But forward earnings are usually produced by analysts, who base their judgment on past returns. Like momentum, we may have leaked target data into the training set. Besides the temporal dependencies, there is another practical objection to K-fold cross-validation. In their influential book, Hastie et al. (2008) (Section 7.10.2) make a forceful case that the model should *entirely* be selected by cross-validation. Predictive variables (be they alphas or factors, in our framework) should not be screened in advance. This is often not the case in practice: the predictiveness of signals or fully-fledged strategies is tested separately. Perform cross-validation enough times on different classes of models, and you will inevitably obtain favorable results. The holdout dataset is meant to serve as a final check against this "fishing expedition" (Cochrane, 2005). Yet, when the number of raw signals runs in the millions, it is inevitable to cycle through several refinements and model revisions, so that the holdout sample performance becomes just another variable to be optimized, instead of a performance check to be run only once.

An example may help illustrate the perils of cross-validation. We have $N = 1000$ assets. We simulate iid asset returns with $r_{t,i} \sim N(0, \sigma^2)$, with $\sigma = 0.01$. We introduce p random asset characteristics, also iid drawn at random: $[\mathbf{B}]_{i,j} \sim N(0, 1)$. These random features are by design not predictive of returns. The backtest consists of a fivefold cross-validation, to estimate the performance of the predictors. In each run, we select the best-performing factor, based on in-sample IC, and then compute the IC on the test fold. Then we report the average cross-validated IC. We repeat the process on 1000 simulated datasets. Below are the results for two scenarios:

1. The first one is the "many periods, few predictors" case: we set $T = 5000$ (20 years of daily data) and $p = 2$; two predictors because one would have felt too lonely.
2. The second one is the "not many periods, more predictors" case: we set $T = 1250$ (5 years of daily data) and $p = 500$; not nearly as many as we meet in practice.

The frequency histograms of the simulations are shown in Figure 8.3. Some summary statistics of the simulations are shown in Table 8.1. The averages are close to zero in both cases, with a much larger standard deviation for the many-factor case. The percentage of samples whose Sharpe Ratio passes the 1% significant level is shown in the last column of the table.[5] Frequency histograms for the two simulated scenarios; the conversion IC to Sharpe Ratio is $\text{SR} = \text{IC}\sqrt{251N}$

A remedy to the data leakage issues arising in cross-validation is *walk-forward backtesting* (Pardo, 2007). In this scheme, we use historical data up

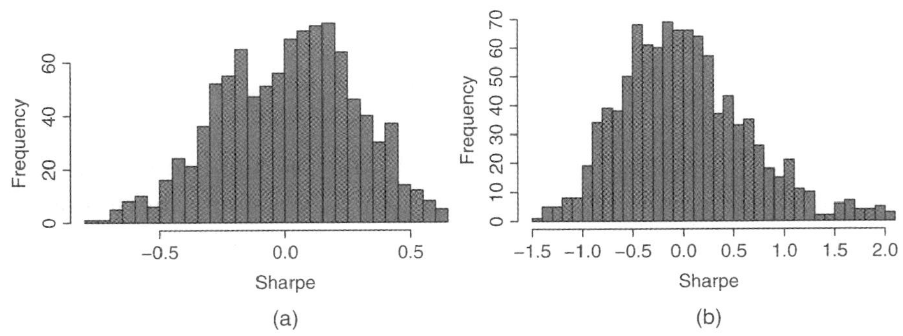

Figure 8.3 Cross-validated Sharpe for (a) Scenario 1, (b) Scenario 2.

[5] This is the percentage of simulation samples for which the condition $\text{SR} > 2.3\sqrt{(1 + \text{SR}^2/2)/T}$

Table 8.1 Frequency histograms for the two simulated scenarios; the conversion IC to Sharpe Ratio is $SR = IC\sqrt{251N}$.

T	p	Mean (SR)	Stdev (SR)	% passing
5000	2	0.07	0.6	1.2
1250	500	0.04	1.4	19

to period t and target returns for period $t + 1$; see Figure 8.4. The scheme is as close as possible to the production process. It addresses two drawbacks of cross-validation for time-series—serial dependence and risk of data leakage—and it also augments naturally the dataset with the arrival of new data. Finally, it is naturally adaptive: it fine-tunes parameters as the environment changes. These advantages are complementary to cross-validation. As a result, it is often the case that signals, or simplified strategies, are first tested using cross-validation, and then tested "out of sample" in a walk-forward test. This is not ideal, however, since it has an opportunity cost caused by the delay in running the strategy in production. Walk-forward has an additional important drawback: it uses less training data than cross-validation. When the set of models and parameters is very large, this limitation could be very severe. On the other side, when the model has been identified, and only a few parameters need to be optimized, then this drawback becomes negligible. Two additional trading settings in which walk-forward does not suffer from data limitations are when (a) data are plenty. This is the case of high-frequency trading. (b) data are very non-stationary. This is the case, to some extent, with every trading strategy, and this very fact suggests that walk-forward backtesting is, in any event, a necessary step in the validation of a strategy, and in its preparation for production.

Summing up, neither cross-sectional nor walk-forward schemes are without flaws. Ideally, we would like a protocol with the following features:

1. *non-anticipative/immune from data leakage*;
2. *taking into account serial dependency*;
3. *using all data*;
4. *allowing for multiple testing of a very large number of signals*;
5. *providing a rigorous decision rule.*

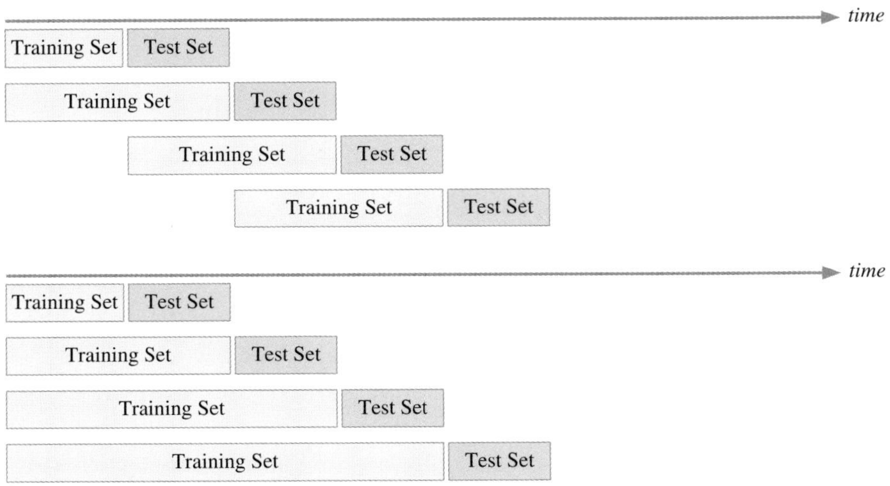

Figure 8.4 Two common walk-forward schemes. The top one uses fixed-length training data, thus keeping the estimation procedures comparable. The bottom one uses all the available data up to a certain epoch, possibly weighting data differently based on the interval from the decision epoch.

Walk-forward meets the first two requirements; cross-validation meets the third. Neither meet the last two. The next section introduces a novel backtesting protocol, the *Rademacher Anti-Serum* (in short, RAS), which meets these requirements.

8.3 The Rademacher Anti-Serum (RAS)

8.3.1 Setup

We will be concerned with testing the performance of strategies and signals.

1. *Strategies* are the time series of the walk-forward simulated returns z-scored by their predicted volatility, which we denote by $x_{t,n}$, so that their average equals the empirical Sharpe Ratio for strategy n. In this respect, the protocol is similar to walk-forward.
2. When we test *signals*, we instead consider the *Information Coefficient* (IC) for the signal n at time t, which is defined as the cosine of the angle

(their *cosine similarity*) between the alpha vector predicted by signal n in period t, and the idiosyncratic returns in the same period.[6]

The definitions are below[7]:

$$x_{t,n} := \frac{\mathbf{w}_{t,n}^{\top}\mathbf{r}_t}{\sqrt{\mathbf{w}_{t,n}^{\top}\Omega_t\mathbf{w}_{t,n}}} \qquad \textit{(Sharpe Ratio)}$$

$$x_{t,n} := \frac{\alpha_{t,n}^{\top}\epsilon_t}{\|\alpha_{t,n}\|\,\|\epsilon_t\|} \qquad \textit{(Information Coefficient)}$$

We also denote $x_{t,n}$ both instances; the interpretation will be clear from the context. In either case, the dataset needed for the analysis is a $T \times N$ matrix $\mathbf{X}$. Rows denote observations as of a certain timestamp and columns denote strategies, whose set we denote S. For notational simplicity, the tth row of $\mathbf{X}$ is denoted by $\mathbf{x}_t$, and the nth column $\mathbf{x}^n$. In the following we make the important assumption that the random vectors $\mathbf{x}_t$ are iid, drawn from a common probability distribution P. We have two justifications for the assumptions. The first one is empirical. Serial dependence is small for returns observed at daily frequencies or lower.[8] The second one is that our framework can be extended to the case of time-dependent returns, at the price of weaker, asymptotic results. We recommend to inspect the autocorrelation plots of the univariate series $\mathbf{x}_t$. If there is sizable autocorrelation up to lag s, then replace the original time series with $\lfloor N/s \rfloor$ non-overlapping, contiguous averages of blocks $(x_{1+ks,n}, \ldots, x_{(k+1)s,n})$. We employ the following notation. We let the joint distribution of $\mathbf{x}_t$ be P. Let $D = \bigotimes_{i=1}^{T} P$ be the joint probability distribution on the space of $T \times N$ matrices in which the element $\mathbf{x}_t \sim P$ has independent, identically distributed (iid) rows, each drawn from P.

The expected value of $\mathbf{x}_t$ is denoted by $\boldsymbol{\theta} \in \mathbb{R}^N$. This is the true vector of strategy/signal performances. Define $\hat{\boldsymbol{\theta}}(\mathbf{X}) \in \mathbb{R}^N$ as the vector of column averages of $\mathbf{X}$:

$$\hat{\theta}(\mathbf{X}) = \frac{1}{T}\sum_{t=1}^{T}\mathbf{x}_t \tag{8.1}$$

which is the expected value of the row of $\mathbf{X}$ according to the bootstrap distribution.

---

6 The IC is featured prominently in Section 9.5.

7 For definitions and uses of $\boldsymbol{\alpha}$, see Sections 4.3 and 9.4.

8 See Chapter 2 and references therein, for example, Cont (2001) and Taylor (2007).

Let a *Rademacher random vector* $\boldsymbol{\epsilon}$ be a T-dimensional random vector whose elements are iid and take values 1 or -1 with probability 1/2. The *Rademacher complexity* of $\mathbf{X}$ is defined as (Mohri et al., 2018):

$$\hat{R} = E_{\epsilon}\left(\sup_n \frac{\boldsymbol{\epsilon}^\top \mathbf{x}^n}{T}\right)$$

Before stating a rigorous result linking this quantity to a bound on performance, we focus our attention on its interpretation. Specifically, we can interpret $\hat{R}$ in at least three ways.

- **As the covariance to random noise**: Consider $\boldsymbol{\epsilon}$ as a random covariate. We can interpret $\hat{R}$ as the expected value of the highest covariance of the performance measure of a strategy to random noise. If, on average, for every set of $+/-1$ indicators, there is at least a strategy that covaries with it, then "we can do no wrong": for every realization of a random vector $\boldsymbol{\epsilon}$, there is a strategy $\mathbf{x}^n$ that would do well matching it, i.e., $\boldsymbol{\epsilon}^\top \mathbf{x}^n / T \simeq 1$. If we interpret the $x_{t,n}$ as predictions for epoch t, then this means that for every sequence of events ϵ_t we have a strategy that predicts them well.
- **As generalized two-way cross-validation**: For sufficiently large T, the sets of positive elements in $\boldsymbol{\epsilon}_t$ concentrate around size $T/2$. We denote S^+ the set of $T/2$ periods where $\epsilon_t = 1$, and S^- the other periods. Rewrite the term inside the sup as

$$\frac{\boldsymbol{\epsilon}^\top \mathbf{x}^n}{T} = \frac{1}{2}\frac{2}{T}\sum_{s \in S+} x_{s,n} - \frac{1}{2}\frac{2}{T}\sum_{s \in S-} x_{s,n} = \frac{1}{2}(\hat{\theta}_n^+ - \hat{\theta}_n^-)$$
$$\hat{\theta}_n^+ := \frac{2}{T}\sum_{s \in S+} x_{s,n}$$
$$\hat{\theta}_n^- := \frac{2}{T}\sum_{s \in S-} x_{s,n}$$

For strategy n, this is the discrepancy in average performance measured on two equal-sized random subsets of the observations. By taking the sup across strategies, we are estimating the worst case: we estimate performance on a subset, and get a very different result on the remaining subset! And if the discrepancy is high for each random subset, this will indicate that performance is not consistent: there's always at least a strategy that performs comparatively well *somewhere* and poorly in the remaining periods. The associated $\hat{R}$ is high, and means that the set of strategies has unreliable performance.

- **As measure of span over possible performances**: We interpret ϵ as a "random direction" chosen at random in $\mathbb{R}^T$. The vector has Euclidean norm equal to $\sqrt{T}$. In the case where the performance measure is the standardized return, $E(\|\mathbf{x}^n\|)$ is also equal to $\sqrt{T}$, and is strongly concentrated around this value. The empirical Rademacher $\hat{R}$ is then approximately equal to

$$E_\epsilon \left(\sup_n \frac{\epsilon^\mathsf{T} \mathbf{x}^n}{\|\epsilon\| \, \|\mathbf{x}^n\|} \right)$$

  This can be interpreted in the following way. We have a set of N vectors $\mathbf{x}^1, \dots, \mathbf{x}^N$. We pick a random direction in the ambient space, and observe the maximum collinearity (expressed as the cosine similarity) of this random direction to our vectors. The expected value of this collinearity measures how much our set of strategy vectors span $\mathbb{R}^T$. If we have n vectors that are copies of the same vector, the answer is: not very well. If, conversely, these vectors are all orthogonal, we have maximum collinearity. The Rademacher complexity is a geometric measure of how much the vectors $\mathbf{x}^n$ "span" $\mathbb{R}^T$.

One interesting characteristic of the Rademacher complexity is that it takes into account dependence among strategies. If, for example, we had a billion strategies to our set of candidate strategies, but they are all identical (hence perfectly correlated), we are not increasing the Rademacher complexity. However, if the strategies are uncorrelated from each other, then the Rademacher complexity is high, indicating higher likelihood of overfitting.

8.3.2 Main Result and Interpretation

The thrust of our protocol is to provide a uniform additive "haircut" (i.e., a term we subtract from the empirical performance) to the performance statistic. In other terms, for each strategy n we have an empirical performance $\hat{\theta}_n$, by Equation (8.1). In the case of z-scored returns, this is the empirical Sharpe Ratio. Then, we can establish a probabilistic guarantee on the true Sharpe Ratio: with high probability, say, greater than $1 - \delta$, the Sharpe Ratio of the strategy is greater than $\hat{\theta}_n$ − "haircut", where the haircut is a function of the Rademacher complexity, the number of samples T, and the parameter δ.

Here, we describe the steps that establish a lower bound for performance. We start with signals. In this case, we have $|x_{t,n}| \leq 1$, because the value is a correlation. For *all* signals, the true performance metric θ_n is bounded below by the empirical performance minus a haircut, with probability greater than $1 - \delta$:

$$\theta_n \geq \hat{\theta}_n - \underbrace{2\hat{R}}_{\text{(data snooping)}} - \underbrace{2\sqrt{\frac{\log(2/\delta)}{T}}}_{\text{(estimation error)}} \tag{8.2}$$

The result is described in Procedure 8.1.

Procedure 8.1: *Rademacher Anti-Serum for signals*

1. Backtest all the strategies using a walk-forward procedure. Let $\mathbf{X} \in \mathbb{R}^{T \times N}$ be the matrix with Information Coefficients of strategy n at time t.
2. Compute $\hat{\theta}(\mathbf{X})$, as defined in Equation (8.1).
3. Compute $\hat{R}(\mathbf{X})$.
4. For all $n \in 1, \ldots, N$

$$\theta_n \geq \hat{\theta}_n - 2\hat{R} - 2\sqrt{\frac{\log(2/\delta)}{T}}$$

with probability greater than $1 - \delta$.

Now, consider the case for Sharpe analysis. The formula is similar, but with a different estimation error:

$$\theta_n \geq \hat{\theta}_n - \underbrace{2\hat{R}}_{\text{(data snooping)}} - \underbrace{3\sqrt{\frac{2\log(2/\delta)}{T}} - \sqrt{\frac{2\log(2N/\delta)}{T}}}_{\text{(estimation error)}} \tag{8.3}$$

The proofs are in the Appendix, Section 8.5.

Procedure 8.2: *Rademacher Anti-Serum for Sharpe*

1. Backtest all the strategies using a walk-forward procedure. Let $\mathbf{X} \in \mathbb{R}^{T \times N}$ be the matrix with Information Ratio of strategy n at time t.
2. Compute $\hat{\theta}(\mathbf{X})$, as defined in Equation (8.1).
3. Compute $\hat{R}(\mathbf{X})$.
4. For all $n \in 1, \ldots, N$

$$\theta_n \geq \hat{\theta}_n - 2\hat{R} - 3\sqrt{\frac{2\log(2/\delta)}{T}} - \sqrt{\frac{2\log(2N/\delta)}{T}}$$

with probability greater than $1 - \delta$.

We focus on the interpretation of the claim. The theorem states that the lower bounds on IC and Sharpe hold *simultaneously* at least with probability $1 - \delta$. Moreover the statement holds for any finite T; no asymptotic approximation is involved. The true expected performance differs from the empirical performance because of two non-negative terms:

- The first is the term $2\hat{R}$. This is the *data-snooping term*. The larger the number of strategies, the higher the $\hat{R}$, because sup is strictly increasing in the number of strategies. Moreover, as we discussed, the higher the dependency among strategies, the lower the $\hat{R}$. In the limit case where we test multiple replicas of the same strategy, $\hat{R}$ is zero. To provide some intuition about the behavior of Rademacher complexity, we consider a set of strategies with normally distributed returns with zero expected returns and a given pairwise correlation among strategy returns. Figure 8.5 displays $2\hat{R}$ as a function of the pairwise correlation. The Rademacher complexity decreases in the correlation, and increases in the number of strategies. Given the data matrix $\mathbf{X}$, the quantity $\hat{R}$ is estimated via simulation. An upper bound for this quantity is given by *Massart's lemma*:

$$\hat{R} \leq \frac{\sqrt{2\log N}}{T}$$

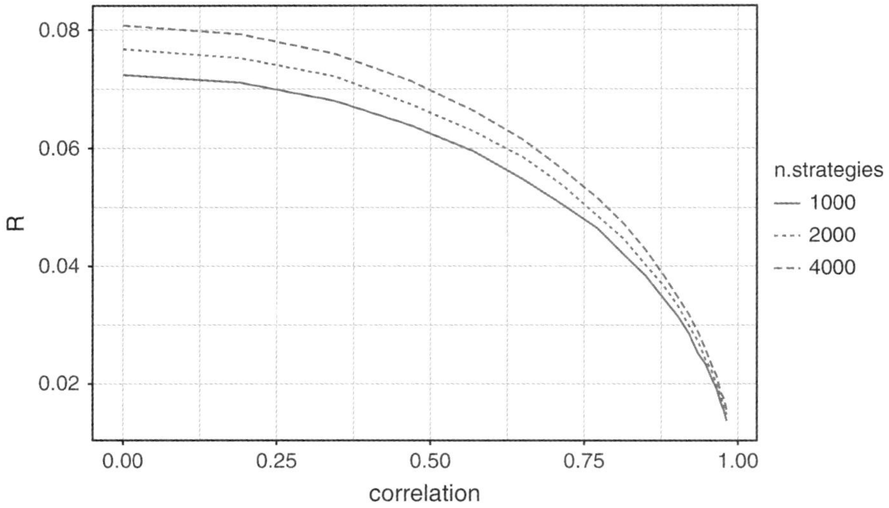

Figure 8.5 Rademacher complexity for 5000 strategies, with iid Gaussian returns and variable pairwise correlation. Estimate based on 2E4 samples.

- The second is the *estimation term*. For some intuition, consider the case of T iid normal random variables θ_t with mean 0 and unit variance. Their average $\hat{\theta}$ is distributed as a normal distribution with standard deviation $1/\sqrt{T}$. What is the δ-quantile of the distribution? There is no closed formula for it, but we can approximate it using Equation (2.6). For a normal distribution with zero mean and standard deviation $1/\sqrt{T}$, and Cumulative Distribution Function F,

$$F^{-1}(\delta) \geq -\sqrt{\frac{2\log[1/(2\sqrt{2\pi}\delta)]}{T}} \tag{8.4}$$

This is similar, up to constants, to the estimation errors in Equations (8.2) and (8.3). In the limit $t \to \infty$, the estimation error in both procedures approaches 0.

The estimation error above is independent of N for bounded distributions and is $\propto \sqrt{\log N}$ for sub-Gaussian ones. An argument for this dependency is the following. Consider the following special case. We have N Gaussian signals with iid returns $N(0, 1)$. The empirical Sharpe

Ratios of the N strategies are also iid, $\hat{\theta}_n \sim N(0, 1/T)$. It can be shown (van Handel, 2016; Kamath, 2020) that

$$\frac{1}{\sqrt{\pi \log 2}}\sqrt{\frac{\log N}{T}} \le E(\max_i \hat{\theta}_i) \le 2\sqrt{\frac{\log N}{T}}$$

When the SR is zero, the maximum (and high quantiles) of the Sharpe Ratio grow as $\sqrt{(\log N)/T}$. In order not to have false positives, the "haircut" on the empirical SR should be equal to $\kappa\sqrt{(\log N)/T}$, for some positive κ. In addition, we should have a term that captures the tail behavior of $\max_i \hat{\theta}_i$. For large N, the dominant term of the estimation error in Equation (8.3) is $\sqrt{2(\log N)/T + 2\log(2/\delta)/T}$, which is majorized by $\sqrt{2(\log N)/T} + \sqrt{2\log(2/\delta)/T}$. The first term is the $\kappa\sqrt{\frac{\log N}{T}}$ growth term, and the second one is the term accounting for the confidence interval that we saw in Equation (8.4).

The procedure is operationally simple: simulate all possible strategies in a walk-forward manner. There should be no look-ahead bias: the strategies should be formulated without looking at the entire dataset and their parameters should be tuned based on past history only. As we mentioned in the "best practices" section, all strategies should be documented and should run in parallel to the production strategy. Then, estimate the Rademacher complexity of matrix **X** by the expectation in the definition of that statistic. The Rademacher complexity is easy to compute for millions (or more) strategies, and can be computed for even larger sets of strategies using tools from numerical analysis.

- The RAS procedure for signals uses the worst case $|x_{t,n}| \le 1$. In practice, however, it is extremely unlikely to observe ICs close to one; IC greater than 0.1 is extremely unlikely. If we assume $|x_{t,n}| \le \kappa < 1$, and apply Theorem 8.3, the estimation term becomes smaller, by a factor κ:

  $$\text{"estimation error"} = 2\kappa\sqrt{\frac{\log(2/\delta)}{T}}$$

  Consider some realistic parameters: $\kappa = 0.02$, $\delta = 0.01$, and $T = 2500$. Then the estimation error is about 0.002.
- In the RAS procedure for strategies, the formula for the estimation error is a rather simple bound and the constant factor could probably be

improved. For realistic parameters, the error is quite large. For example, with $\delta = 0.01$, $T = 2500$, and $N = 1E6$, the estimation error is 0.31, corresponding to an annualized estimation error of 5.1. This seems a loose bound, compared to the standard formula for the standard error of the Sharpe Ratio (Lo, 2002): for a strategy with Sharpe Ratio equal to 3, the estimation error haircut is $F(\delta)\sqrt{(1 + SR^2/2)/T}\sqrt{251} = 1.7$.
- The constant of the data-snooping term is also conservative, since in the proof we rely on a chain of inequalities to obtain a bound.

I will close with the wise words of a former colleague: "the path connecting theory and practice is paved with carefully tuned parameters." The best we can hope from theory is an insightful, interpretable result, which is amenable to be fine-tuned for applications by means of simulation. The bound of Procedure 8.2 will take the form[9]

$$\theta_n - \hat{\theta}_n \geq -a\hat{R} - b\sqrt{\frac{2\log(2/\delta)}{T}}$$

with positive parameters a, b.

8.4 Some Empirical Results

8.4.1 *Simulations*

Let us see how this approach performs in a simulated setting first. We first consider strategies whose returns are normally distributed, are iid (within each strategy) and are cross-sectionally pairwise correlated, with correlation ρ. Specifically, the return of strategy i in period t is given by $r_{i,t} = \rho * f_t + \sqrt{1 - \rho^2} * \epsilon_{i,t}$, with $\epsilon_{i,t} \sim N(0, 1)$ and $f_t \sim N(0, 1)$. We run simulations for different values of the correlation, for different numbers of strategies, and for expected returns (and therefore non-annualized Sharpe Ratios) equal to 0 and 0.1. For each simulation, we report the maximum empirical Sharpe Ratio $\max_i \hat{\theta}_i$, the Rademacher complexity, the estimation error, the percentage of detected positive strategies, i.e., of strategies for which the right-hand side of the Equation (8.2)

[9] In the estimation error of Equation (8.3), for $\delta \geq 0.01$ and $N \leq 1E8$, the term dependent on N is smaller than the term independent of it, i.e., $\sqrt{\frac{2\log(2N/\delta)}{T}} \leq 0.6 \times 33\sqrt{\frac{2\log(2/\delta)}{T}}$, and is very weakly dependent on N.

exceeds 0, and is therefore deemed to have positive Sharpe Ratio. We also report the percentage of "Rademacher positive strategies," i.e., the strategies that exceed the data-snooping haircut alone. In formula:

$$\hat{\theta}_n - 2\hat{R} - 2\sqrt{\frac{\log(2/\delta)}{T}} > 0 \qquad \textit{("positive")} \qquad (8.5)$$

$$\hat{\theta}_n - 2\hat{R} > 0 \qquad \textit{("Rademacher positive")} \qquad (8.6)$$

We perform simulations with returns distributed both according to a Gaussian distribution and to a t-distribution with five degrees of freedom. The latter aims to approximate heavy-tailed returns. The simulations are performed for all possible combinations of the following parameters:

1. *Correlation*: $\rho \in \{0.2, 0.8\}$.
2. *Number of strategies*: $N \in \{500, 5000\}$.
3. *Number of periods*: $T \in \{2500, 5000\}$.
4. *Population Sharpe*: We consider two cases. In the first one, all strategies have SR = 0. In the second one, 80% have SR = 0, and 20% have SR = 0.2 (the Sharpe Ratio is not annualized).

For each of the 16 scenarios, we run eight simulations: we generate a historical return matrix $\mathbf{X}_n$. For each instance, we compute the following outputs:

1. $\max_i \hat{\theta}_i^{(n)}$, the maximum realized Sharpe Ratio across the strategies.
2. $\hat{R}_n$ the Rademacher complexity of $\mathbf{X}_n$.
3. The estimation error for $\delta = 0.05$.
4. The percentage of positive strategies, as per Equation (8.5).
5. The percentage of Rademacher positive strategies, as per Equation (8.6).
6. The percentage of true positive strategies. This percentage is either 0 or 20%.

Tables 8.3 and 8.4 show the results for normally and t-distributed returns, respectively. We interpret the results below.

1. For a fixed distribution of the population Sharpe, the maximum empirical Sharpe Ratio $\max_i \bar{\theta}_i$ is predictably increasing in N, it is decreasing in ρ because the "effective" number of strategies decreases, as the strategies are more correlated, and it is decreasing in T, by the Central Limit Theorem.

Table 8.2 Comparison of $\hat{R}$ and Massart's bound

N	T	$\hat{R}$	**Massart's Bound**
500	2500	0.059	0.070
5000	2500	0.072	0.083
500	5000	0.042	0.049
5000	5000	0.051	0.058

2. Everything else equal, the Rademacher complexity is decreasing in ρ, increasing in N, and is decreasing in T. It is interesting to compare $\hat{R}$ to the bound from Massart's lemma. In Table 8.2, I report the highest $\hat{R}$ from Table 8.3, and Massart's bounds. Massart's bound is at most 19% higher than the observed Rademacher complexity.
3. The data-snooping term and the estimation error term have the same magnitude.
4. In the null Sharpe case (all strategies have zero Sharpe Ratio), the percentage of detected positive cases ("% pos") is zero or nearly zero in all cases; there are no false positives.
5. In the alternative Sharpe case (20% of strategies have Sharpe Ratio equal to 0.2), the percentage of positives is always smaller than the percentage of true positives. All detected positives are in fact true positives: the False Discovery Rate (FDR), defined as the ratio of false positives to all detected positives, is zero. In a few cases the percentage of positives is much lower than the percentage of true positives. The bounds are too conservative.
6. The percentage of Rademacher positives is much closer to the percentage of true positives. The FDR is still zero in this case.

8.4.2 *Historical Anomalies*

It is of independent interest to analyze anomalies published in the academic literature. We consider two sources of returns. In their paper, Jensen et al. (2023) extend a dataset of factor anomalies introduced by Hou et al. (2020), and test their replicability and out-of-sample performance. The dataset contains published characteristics, and it is not possible to know which characteristics were tested prior to publications. In principle, all such variants should be included in the study. Had they been included,

Table 8.3 Simulations for normally distributed returns

ρ	N	T	$\max_i \theta_i$	$\max_i \bar{\theta}_i$	R	Error	% pos	% rad pos	% true pos
0.2	500	2500	0	0.059	0.059	0.109	0.0	0.0	0.0
0.8	500	2500	0	0.050	0.037	0.109	0.0	0.0	0.0
0.2	500	2500	0.2	0.252	0.060	0.109	1.7	20.0	20.0
0.8	500	2500	0.2	0.228	0.037	0.109	14.3	20.0	20.0
0.2	5000	2500	0	0.074	0.072	0.109	0.0	0.0	0.0
0.8	5000	2500	0	0.041	0.044	0.109	0.0	0.0	0.0
0.2	5000	2500	0.2	0.264	0.072	0.109	0.1	19.9	20.0
0.8	5000	2500	0.2	0.242	0.045	0.109	12.3	20.0	20.0
0.2	500	5000	0	0.039	0.042	0.077	0.0	0.0	0.0
0.8	500	5000	0	0.019	0.026	0.077	0.0	0.0	0.0
0.2	500	5000	0.2	0.234	0.042	0.077	19.9	20.0	20.0
0.8	500	5000	0.2	0.221	0.026	0.077	20.0	20.0	20.0
0.2	5000	5000	0	0.051	0.051	0.077	0.0	0.0	0.0
0.8	5000	5000	0	0.037	0.031	0.077	0.0	0.0	0.0
0.2	5000	5000	0.2	0.247	0.051	0.077	18.6	20.0	20.0
0.8	5000	5000	0.2	0.230	0.032	0.077	20.0	20.0	20.0

Table 8.4 Simulations for t-distributed returns

ρ	N	T	$\max_i \theta_i$	$\max_i \bar{\theta}_i$	R	Error	% pos	% rad pos	% true pos
0.2	500.0	2500	0	0.059	0.059	0.109	0.0	0.0	0.0
0.8	500.0	2500	0	0.035	0.036	0.109	0.0	0.0	0.0
0.2	500.0	2500	0.2	0.250	0.060	0.109	1.4	20.0	20.0
0.8	500.0	2500	0.2	0.237	0.037	0.109	16.6	20.0	20.0
0.2	5000.0	2500	0	0.070	0.072	0.109	0.0	0.0	0.0
0.8	5000.0	2500	0	0.045	0.044	0.109	0.0	0.0	0.0
0.2	5000.0	2500	0.2	0.265	0.072	0.109	0.1	19.9	20.0
0.8	5000.0	2500	0.2	0.242	0.045	0.109	11.0	20.0	20.0
0.2	500.0	5000	0	0.047	0.042	0.077	0.0	0.0	0.0
0.8	500.0	5000	0	0.023	0.026	0.077	0.0	0.0	0.0
0.2	500.0	5000	0.2	0.234	0.042	0.077	20.0	20.0	20.0
0.8	500.0	5000	0.2	0.220	0.026	0.077	20.0	20.0	20.0
0.2	5000.0	5000	0	0.051	0.051	0.077	0.0	0.0	0.0
0.8	5000.0	5000	0	0.034	0.031	0.077	0.0	0.0	0.0
0.2	5000.0	5000	0.2	0.247	0.051	0.077	18.5	20.0	20.0
0.8	5000.0	5000	0.2	0.231	0.031	0.077	20.0	20.0	20.0

Table 8.5 Summary data for the factors in Jensen et al.'s database

Country	N	T	$\max_i \bar{\theta}_i$	$\hat{R}$	Error	% pos	% rad pos
AUS	153	3584	0.072	0.040	0.091	0.0	0.0
BRA	141	2823	0.057	0.046	0.102	0.0	0.0
CAN	153	3880	0.043	0.038	0.087	0.0	0.0
CHE	153	3358	0.066	0.042	0.094	0.0	0.0
DEU	153	4475	0.052	0.036	0.081	0.0	0.0
FRA	153	4327	0.055	0.037	0.083	0.0	0.0
GBR	153	4546	0.082	0.036	0.081	0.0	**0.7**
HKG	153	4101	0.100	0.037	0.085	0.0	**6.5**
IND	153	2785	0.091	0.046	0.103	0.0	0.0
JPN	150	2549	0.036	0.047	0.108	0.0	0.0
KOR	148	2560	0.049	0.047	0.107	0.0	0.0
MYS	152	3436	0.084	0.042	0.093	0.0	**0.7**
SAU	139	2925	0.076	0.045	0.100	0.0	0.0
THA	146	2988	0.043	0.044	0.099	0.0	0.0
TWN	151	2899	0.068	0.044	0.101	0.0	0.0
USA	153	13155	0.069	0.020	0.047	0.0	**18.3**
ZAF	151	2676	0.062	0.047	0.105	0.0	0.0

the Rademacher complexity of the dataset would have been higher. As criteria for inclusion, we required that the factors have at least 10 years of trading history, and that they be produced on the last day[10] in the dataset, December 31, 2023. We perform the analysis at the country level. Table 8.5 shows the same columns as the previous two tables, with the exception of the percentage of true positives, which is not known *a priori*. The United Kingdom, United States, and Hong Kong and Malaysia are the only markets where a positive percentage of factors meet the Rademacher bound, Equation (8.6).

[10] Data downloaded on August 15, 2024 from https://jkpfactors.com/.

Table 8.6 Summary data for the factors in Zimmerman and Chen's database

N	T	$\max_i \bar{\theta}_i$	$\hat{R}$	Error	% pos	% rad pos
192	5911	0.126	0.033	0.070	0	**3.1**

Another source of factor return data is curated by Andrew Chen (Chen and Zimmerman, 2022). Among the anomalies,[11] we select those that were available as of the end of 2023 and had at least 5 years of history. The summary results are displayed in Table 8.6. The percentage of strategies that meet the Rademacher bound is above 3%. The smaller percentage is attributable to the fact that the number of periods (days) with complete observations is 5911 (compared to 13,155 for the Jensen, Kelly, and Pedersen dataset) and to the Rademacher complexity being 0.033 (compared to 0.02 for the Jensen, Kelly, and Pedersen dataset).

8.5 ⋆Appendix

8.5.1 Proofs for RAS

We use some essential inequalities in the proofs. Standard references are Boucheron et al. (2013) and Vershynin (2018).

Theorem 8.1 ***(McDiarmid's inequality)*****:** *Let $X_1, \dots, X_n$ be independent random variables, and $f : \mathbb{R}^n \to \mathbb{R}$, such that, for each i,*

$$\sup_{x_i, x_i'} |f(x_1, \dots, x_i, \dots, x_n) - f(x_1, \dots, x_i', \dots, x_n)| \leq c_i$$

Then, for all $\epsilon > 0$,

$$P(|f - Ef| > \epsilon) \leq \exp\left(-\frac{2\epsilon^2}{\sum_i c_i^2}\right)$$

[11] We use the "Predictor" dataset, downloaded from https://www.openassetpricing/ on August 20, 2024.

Specifically, if $c_i = c$*, and with probability greater than* $1 - \delta/2$,

$$f < Ef - \sqrt{\frac{nc^2}{2}\log(\delta/2)}$$

A mean-zero σ-*sub-Gaussian* random variable X is one for which a positive constant σ exists, such that the inequality $P(|X| > \epsilon) \leq 2\exp(-\epsilon^2/(2\sigma^2))$ holds for all positive ϵ. The parameter σ^2 is the proxy variance.

Theorem 8.2 ***(Generalized Hoeffding's inequality):*** *Let* $X_1, \ldots, X_n$ *be iid random variables with finite sub-Gaussian norms and proxy. Then, for all* $\epsilon > 0$,

$$P\left(\frac{1}{n}\sum_{i=1}^{n} X_i - EX > \epsilon\right) \leq \exp\left(-\frac{n\epsilon^2}{2\sigma^2}\right) \tag{8.7}$$

Theorem 8.3 ***(Bounds for bounded berformance metrics):*** *Assume that* $|x_{tn}| \leq a$ *for all* $n = 1, \ldots, N, t = 1, \ldots, T$*. For all* $n \in 1, \ldots, N$,

$$\theta_n \geq \hat{\theta}_n - 2\hat{R} - 3a\sqrt{\frac{2\log(2/\delta)}{T}} \tag{8.8}$$

Proof. The straightforward inequality holds for all $n = 1, \ldots, N$: $\theta_n - \hat{\theta}_n \geq -\sup_n |\hat{\theta}_n - \theta_n|$. Define

$$\Phi := \sup_n |\hat{\theta}_n - \theta_n| \tag{8.9}$$

We claim that with probability greater than $1 - \delta/2$,

$$\Phi \leq E_D\Phi + a\sqrt{\frac{2\log(2/\delta)}{T}} \tag{8.10}$$

This allows one to deal with $E_D \sup_n |\hat{\theta}_n - \theta_n|$, which is easier. To prove the inequality, note that, for all $x_{t,i}, x'_{t,i} \in [-a, a], t = 1, \ldots, T, i = 1, \ldots, N$,

$$|\hat{\theta}_n(\ldots, x_{t,i}, \ldots) - \hat{\theta}_n(\ldots, x'_{t,i}, \ldots)| \leq \frac{2a}{T} \tag{8.11}$$

from which it follows that

$$\sup_{x_{t,n}, x'_{t,n} \in \mathbb{R}^T} |\Phi(\ldots, x_{t,n}, \ldots) - \Phi(\ldots, x'_{t,n}, \ldots)| \leq \frac{2a}{T}$$

We apply McDiarmid's inequality to Φ to obtain the result.

In order to obtain a lower bound on θ_n we need an upper bound on $E_D\Phi$. In the equalities below, we introduce a probability measure D' identical to, and independent from, D:

$$
\begin{aligned}
& E_D \sup_n \left|\hat{\theta}_n - \theta_n\right| \\
&= E_D \sup_n \left|\hat{\theta}_n(\omega) - E_{D'}\hat{\theta}_n(\omega')\right| \\
&= E_D \sup_n \left|E_{D'}\hat{\theta}_n(\omega) - E_{D'}\hat{\theta}_n(\omega')\right| && \textit{(conditioning)} \\
&\leq E_D E_{D'} \sup_n \left|\hat{\theta}_n(\omega) - \hat{\theta}_n(\omega')\right| && \textit{(Jensen)} \\
&\leq \frac{1}{T} E_D E_{D'} \sup_n \left|\sum_t (x_{t,n}(\omega) - x_{t,n}(\omega'))\right| \\
&= (*)
\end{aligned}
$$

We introduce an additional source of noise (the $\boldsymbol{\epsilon}$ Rademacher vector) and we lose a constant of 2, but gain in tractability. We can change the signs of each summand by multiplying by some arbitrary factor $\gamma_t \in \{+1, -1\}$, since the terms are exchangeable:

$$
\begin{aligned}
(*) &= \frac{1}{T} E_D E_{D'} \sup_n \left|\sum_t \gamma_t (x_{t,n}(\omega) - x_{t,n}(\omega'))\right| \\
&= \frac{1}{T} E_D E_{D'} E_\epsilon \sup_n \left|\sum_t \epsilon_t (x_{t,n}(\omega) - x_{t,n}(\omega'))\right| \\
&\leq \frac{1}{T} E_D E_{D'} E_\epsilon \sup_n \left|\sum_t \epsilon_t (x_{t,n}(\omega)\right| + \frac{1}{T} E_D E_{D'} E_\epsilon \sup_n \left|\sum_t \epsilon_t x_{t,n}(\omega')\right| \\
&= \frac{1}{T} E_D E_\epsilon \sup_n \left|\sum_t \epsilon_t x_{t,n}(\omega)\right| + \frac{1}{T} E_D E_\epsilon \sup_n \left|\sum_t \epsilon_t x_{t,n}(\omega)\right| \\
&= \frac{2}{T} E_D \hat{R} \\
&= 2R
\end{aligned}
$$

where we defined R as the expected value of the Rademacher complexity over the distribution of performance realizations.

We now use McDiarmid again: for all $x_{t,i}, x'_{t,i}$,

$$|\hat{R}(\ldots, x_{t,i}, \ldots) - \hat{R}(\ldots, x'_{t,i}, \ldots)| \leq \frac{2a}{T}$$

Hence, with probability greater than $1 - \delta/2$

$$R \leq \hat{R} + a\sqrt{\frac{2\log(2/\delta)}{T}} \tag{8.12}$$

Now we employ the union bound on inequalities (8.10) and (8.12) to obtain the claim. ■

Theorem 8.4 ***(Bounds for sub-Gaussian performance metrics):*** *Assume that $P(|x_{t,n}| > \epsilon) \leq 2e^{-\epsilon^2/2}$ for all $\epsilon > 0$, for all $n = 1, \ldots, N, t = 1, \ldots, T$. Then, for all $n \in 1, \ldots, N$,*

$$\theta_n - \hat{\theta}_n \geq -2\hat{R} - 3\sqrt{\frac{2\log(2/\delta)}{T}} - \sqrt{\frac{2\log(2N/\delta)}{T}}$$

Proof. Let $a > 0$. We split $\theta_n - \hat{\theta}_n$ into the sum of two terms: $\theta_n - \hat{\theta}_n = g(\mathbf{x}^n, a) + h(\mathbf{x}^n, a)$, where

$$\begin{aligned}
\theta_n - \hat{\theta}_n &= g(\mathbf{x}^n, a) + h(\mathbf{x}^n, a) \\
&\geq -\sup_n |g(\mathbf{x}^n, a)| - \sup_n |h(\mathbf{x}^n, a)| \\
g(\mathbf{x}^i, a) &:= E\left[\frac{1}{T}\sum_{t=1}^{T} x_{t,i}\mathbf{1}(|x_{t,i}| \leq a)\right] - \frac{1}{T}\sum_{t=1}^{T} x_{t,i}\mathbf{1}(|x_{t,i}| \leq a) \\
h(\mathbf{x}^i, a) &:= E\left[\frac{1}{T}\sum_{t=1}^{T} x_{t,i}\mathbf{1}(|x_{t,i}| > a)\right] - \frac{1}{T}\sum_{t=1}^{T} x_{t,i}\mathbf{1}(|x_{t,i}| > a)
\end{aligned}$$

We bound $P(\sup_i |h(\mathbf{x}^i, a)| \geq v)$. By symmetrization

$$E|h(\mathbf{x}^i, a)| \leq 2E\sum_{t=1}^{T} |\epsilon_t x_{t,i}\mathbf{1}(|x_{t,i}| > a)|$$

The random variable $|\epsilon_t x_{t,i} \mathbf{1}(|x_{t,i}| > a)|$ is sub-Gaussian, since it is dominated by $|x_{t,i}|$ with probability 1, and it has the same proxy variance as $|x_{t,i}|$. By the general hoeffding inequality,

$$P\left(|\sum_{t=1}^{T} h(x_{t,i})| > v \right) \leq \exp(-Tv^2/2)$$

$$P\left(\sup_i |\sum_{t=1}^{T} h(x_{t,i})| > v \right) \leq N\exp(-Tv^2/2)$$

$$P\left(\sup_i |\sum_{t=1}^{T} h(x_{t,i})| > \sqrt{2\log(2N/\delta)/T} \right) \leq \delta/2$$

By the union bound,

$$\theta_n - \hat{\theta}_n \geq -2\hat{R} - 3\sqrt{\frac{2\log(2/\delta)}{T}} - \sqrt{\frac{2\log(2N/\delta)}{T}} \tag{8.13}$$

■

The Takeaways

1. Strategy performance of systematic strategies is usually validated against historical data. Historical data is often scarce, whereas the number of strategies being tested can be extremely large. We reuse the same data to test each of these strategies.
2. Two prerequisites of an effective backtesting process are:
   (a) perform careful data sourcing;
   (b) conducting the research process so that you avoid data leakage and that the historical simulation reproduces the run of the same strategy in the real world.
3. Common backtesting procedures are cross-validation and walk-forward. Both have drawbacks.
4. We propose an alternative procedure: the Rademacher Anti-Serum (RAS).
   (a) RAS provides a "haircut", i.e., term that is subtracted from the empirical performance metric of every strategy. This haircut depends on a probability $1 - \delta$.
   (b) The reduced performance metric is guaranteed to be greater than or equal to the true performance metric with probability greater than $1 - \delta$.
   (c) The haircut is the sum of a "data-snooping term," function of the set of strategies, and an "estimation term", function of the sampling interval.

Chapter 9

Portfolio Management: The Basics

The Questions

1. Why is Mean-Variance Optimization (MVO) widely used in portfolio construction, and what are its main justifications?
2. How does the structure of the utility function impact investment decisions, specifically in terms of expected return and risk?
3. How do we use factor models in MVO? What does it mean to trade in factor space and in idio space?
4. How do we add a factor to the model?
5. How does the Information Ratio relate to an investor's skill (Information Coefficient) and the diversification benefits of a portfolio?
6. When should a centralized approach to portfolio management be used over a decentralized one, and under what conditions are they equivalent?

This chapter is devoted to the basics of portfolio construction. The common theme throughout the chapter is that we limit ourselves to a single-period optimization setting. This is a chapter for hedgehogs, not for foxes: we set a narrow playing field, but dig a deep hole. The chapter requires knowledge of basic results from optimization theory.[1]

9.1 Why Mean-Variance Optimization?

Investors have objectives, information, and constraints. Besides this generic statement, there is not much in common among them. A large fraction of investment professionals cannot—and would not—articulate a clear objective function; their constraints are sometimes *ad hoc*, vague, or inconsistently enforced. Neither George Soros nor Warren Buffett, nor others among the most successful investors in history, have ever known what the volatility of their portfolios was at any point in time. At the other extreme, academics have developed several normative theories for portfolio construction. In this book I use relevance to applications as a guiding principle. In the vast majority of applications, the optimization formulations are single-period. This is explainable by a combination of the following[2]:

- *Interpretability*. Multi-period optimization problems are vastly more complex to formulate and, once solved, their solutions are also harder to interpret.
- *Data availability*. The amount of data needed for multi-period optimization is larger and more difficult to estimate.
- *Computational tractability*. Single-period optimization problems are solvable by commercial solvers in a matter of seconds.

[1] Extensive treatments of convex optimization are Boyd and Vandenberghe (2004), Bazaraa et al. (2006), and Luenberger and Ye (2008), and finance-oriented optimization textbooks are Cornuéjols et al. (2018); Palomar (2024).

[2] On justifications of the mean-variance approach to portfolio optimization, see Huang and Litzenberger (1988); Cochrane (2005). Both cover the standard cases of exponential and quadratic utilities. A number of textbooks exist covering portfolio construction. A classic is Grinold and Kahn (1999); see also Qian et al. (2007); Isichenko (2021); Chincarini and Kim (2022). On the statistics of the Sharpe Ratio, see Lo (2002) and, for a comprehensive and definitive reference, Pav (2023) and references therein.

- *Short-term investment horizon.* Investors think only about the short term, partly because they heavily discount the future, partly because they do not know how to quantify information uncertainty and rate of change.

The objective function V is a function of the portfolio weights $\mathbf{w}$ and of the returns $\mathbf{r}$. Economic theory interprets V as a utility function, taking different values under different realizations of the future. The expected value of the utility function gives the investor the *ex-ante* value of the bet she would be taking by investing in a portfolio. We assume that the investor has initial wealth W_0, that she knows the distribution of the random vector $\mathbf{r}$, and that she solves the problem

$$\max E\left[V(W_0 + \mathbf{w}^\top \mathbf{r})\right] \tag{9.1}$$

The choice of V is not obvious. Common properties of V are that it must be monotonically increasing (more wealth is better than less) and concave (corresponding to risk aversion, and to decreasing value of a marginal dollar as a function of wealth). One approach, followed by Markowitz (1959), is to consider a polynomial local approximation of the objective function: $V(W_0 + \mathbf{w}^\top \mathbf{r}) \simeq V(W_0) + V'(W_0)\mathbf{w}^\top \mathbf{r} + V''(W_0)(\mathbf{w}^\top \mathbf{r})^2/2$. Taking expectations, we obtain

$$\begin{aligned} E\left[V(W_0 + \mathbf{w}^\top \mathbf{r})\right] &\simeq V(W_0) + V'(W_0)\mathbf{w}^\top \boldsymbol{\mu}_\mathbf{r} + \\ &\quad \frac{V''(W_0)}{2}\left(\mathbf{w}^\top \boldsymbol{\Omega}_\mathbf{r}\mathbf{w} + (\mathbf{w}^\top \boldsymbol{\mu}_\mathbf{r})^2\right) \\ &\simeq V(W_0) + V'(W_0)\mathbf{w}^\top \boldsymbol{\mu}_\mathbf{r} + \\ &\quad \frac{V''(W_0)}{2}\mathbf{w}^\top \boldsymbol{\Omega}_\mathbf{r}\mathbf{w} \end{aligned}$$

We maximize a concave quadratic objective function which is the weighted sum of expected return and variance; hence the name *Mean-Variance Optimization* (MVO) (De Finetti, 1940; Markowitz, 1952):

$$\begin{aligned} \frac{E\left[V(W_0 + \mathbf{w}^\top \mathbf{r})\right] - V(W_0)}{V'(W_0)} &\simeq \mathbf{w}^\top \boldsymbol{\mu}_\mathbf{r} - \frac{\rho}{2}\mathbf{w}^\top \boldsymbol{\Omega}_\mathbf{r}\mathbf{w} \\ \rho &:= -\frac{V''(W_0)}{V'(W_0)} \end{aligned}$$

$\rho > 0$ is called the *coefficient of absolute risk aversion* (CARA). The higher the ρ, the more risk-averse the investor is.

As examples, consider an objective function of the form $V(x) = -\exp(-ax)$. The CARA for this function is constant $\rho = a$: it is independent of the wealth W_0 of the investor, and so are her allocation decisions. The optimization problem is

$$\max_{\mathbf{w}} \mathbf{w}^\top \boldsymbol{\mu}_\mathbf{r} - \frac{a}{2}\mathbf{w}^\top \boldsymbol{\Omega}_\mathbf{r} \mathbf{w}$$

Alternatively, consider the objective function $V(x) = \log(x)$. This function is associated to the *Kelly criterion* for investing. It has unique properties which warrant a dedicated chapter. Here, let us consider its implications for approximate portfolio optimization. The CARA is $\rho = 1/W_0$, so that we solve

$$\max_{\mathbf{w}} \mathbf{w}^\top \boldsymbol{\mu}_\mathbf{r} - \frac{1}{2W_0}\mathbf{w}^\top \boldsymbol{\Omega}_\mathbf{r} \mathbf{w}$$

The wealthier the investor is, the more risk-seeking she becomes.

We have shown that a quadratic utility function implies a mean-variance optimization problem for the investor. This result is standard. Less known is the converse: if an investor selects an investment on the basis of mean and variance only, her utility function is necessarily quadratic (Baron, 1977; Johnstone and Lindley, 2011). Viewed in the context of axiomatic decision theory, portfolio MVO is not satisfactory, because a quadratic utility implies that investors are satiated, and have even a dislike of wealth beyond a certain threshold. As a local approximation, however, MVO is appropriate. Moments of returns (and portfolios) beyond the second one are beyond the realm of what's possible, as seen in Chapter 2. A portfolio manager settled a long discussion on the topic with the laconic statement that "the first two moments should be enough for everybody".

9.2 Mean-Variance Optimal Portfolios

A factor model gives us an asset–asset covariance matrix $\boldsymbol{\Omega}_\mathbf{r} \in \mathbb{R}^{n\times n}$. Given this information, it is straightforward to compute the variance of a portfolio, as we saw in Section 4.5.2 on risk decomposition. The other essential input to the optimization problem is a vector $\boldsymbol{\alpha} \in \mathbb{R}^n$ of expected returns, over the same interval at which we have a volatility forecast. The simplest optimization problem is to maximize expected PnL, subject to a constraint on the maximum tolerable volatility, denoted by $\sigma > 0$. The problem can be stated as

$$\begin{aligned} &\max \boldsymbol{\alpha}^\top \mathbf{w} \\ &\text{s.t. } \mathbf{w}^\top \boldsymbol{\Omega}_\mathbf{r} \mathbf{w} \leq \sigma^2 \end{aligned} \tag{9.2}$$

One of the most important metrics used for the evaluation of strategies is the Sharpe Ratio. If we have covariance matrix and expected returns, we can formulate the Sharpe Ratio optimization thus:

$$\max_{\mathbf{w}} \frac{\boldsymbol{\alpha}^\top \mathbf{w}}{\sqrt{\mathbf{w}^\top \boldsymbol{\Omega}_\mathbf{r} \mathbf{w}}}$$

This optimization, however, is indefinite because the objective function $\text{SR}(\mathbf{w})$ is independent of the portfolio size, i.e., homogeneous of degree 0: $\text{SR}(t\mathbf{w}) = \text{SR}(\mathbf{w})$ for all $t > 0$. We can address this issue by bounding the denominator. This means fixing the portfolio size. The upper bound constraint on the denominator is always binding if there is a portfolio $\mathbf{w}$ such that $\boldsymbol{\alpha}^\top \mathbf{w} > 0$:

$$\begin{aligned} &\max_{\mathbf{w}} \frac{\boldsymbol{\alpha}^\top \mathbf{w}}{\sqrt{\mathbf{w}^\top \boldsymbol{\Omega}_\mathbf{r} \mathbf{w}}} \\ &\text{s.t. } \sqrt{\mathbf{w}^\top \boldsymbol{\Omega}_\mathbf{r} \mathbf{w}} \leq \sigma \\ \text{equivalent to } &\max_{\mathbf{w}} \frac{\boldsymbol{\alpha}^\top \mathbf{w}}{\sigma} \\ &\text{s.t. } \mathbf{w}^\top \boldsymbol{\Omega}_\mathbf{r} \mathbf{w} \leq \sigma^2 \\ \text{equivalent to } &\max_{\mathbf{w}} \boldsymbol{\alpha}^\top \mathbf{w} \\ &\text{s.t. } \mathbf{w}^\top \boldsymbol{\Omega}_\mathbf{r} \mathbf{w} \leq \sigma^2 \end{aligned}$$

Which is Optimization Problem (9.2). The First-Order Necessary Conditions (FONCs) for this problem are

$$\begin{aligned} \nabla_\mathbf{w}(\boldsymbol{\alpha}^\top \mathbf{w} - \lambda \mathbf{w}^\top \boldsymbol{\Omega}_\mathbf{r} \mathbf{w}) &= \boldsymbol{\alpha} - 2\lambda \boldsymbol{\Omega}_\mathbf{r} \mathbf{w} \\ &= 0 \\ \mathbf{w}^\top \boldsymbol{\Omega}_\mathbf{r} \mathbf{w} &\leq \sigma^2 \\ \lambda &\geq 0 \\ \lambda(\mathbf{w}^\top \boldsymbol{\Omega}_\mathbf{r} \mathbf{w} - \sigma^2) &= 0 \end{aligned}$$

The solution to these equations is

$$\mathbf{w}^\star = \frac{\sigma}{\sqrt{\boldsymbol{\alpha}^\top \boldsymbol{\Omega}_\mathrm{r}^{-1} \boldsymbol{\alpha}}} \boldsymbol{\Omega}_\mathrm{r}^{-1} \boldsymbol{\alpha} \tag{9.3}$$

$$\lambda^\star = \frac{\sqrt{\boldsymbol{\alpha}^\top \boldsymbol{\Omega}_\mathrm{r}^{-1} \boldsymbol{\alpha}}}{2\sigma} \tag{9.4}$$

The expected return and the Sharpe Ratio of the portfolio are

$$E(\mathbf{r}^\top \mathbf{w}^\star) = \sigma \sqrt{\boldsymbol{\alpha}^\top \boldsymbol{\Omega}_\mathrm{r}^{-1} \boldsymbol{\alpha}}$$

$$\mathrm{SR}^\star = \sqrt{\boldsymbol{\alpha}^\top \boldsymbol{\Omega}_\mathrm{r}^{-1} \boldsymbol{\alpha}} \tag{9.5}$$

A way to interpret (and derive quickly) the solution is to recall that the optimal portfolio is proportional to $\boldsymbol{\Omega}_\mathrm{r}^{-1} \boldsymbol{\alpha}$, and then to find the proportionality factor so that the variance constraint is met. The optimal portfolio is proportional to the volatility budget: the higher the budget, the bigger the portfolio. However, the portfolio is independent of the magnitude of the alpha vector (it is homogeneous of degree zero in alpha): replacing $\boldsymbol{\alpha}$ with $\kappa\boldsymbol{\alpha}$ gives the same solution. This is interesting.

Insight 9.1: *Miscalibration of alpha size is not catastrophic*

If you have a volatility constraint, a good volatility model, and your *relative* alphas are accurate, then the error in the *absolute* size of the alphas does not matter.

The parameter $\lambda^\star$ also merits special consideration. It is the *shadow price* (or Lagrange multiplier) of the volatility constraint. If we increase the variance budget by one unit, the expected return increases by $\lambda^\star$. In other terms, the shadow price of the variance constraint is the derivative of the objective function with respect to the variance. While this relationship is not very useful in this specific case, it will come in handy for other constraints.

In its simplicity, the solution contains the essential data of the problem: the inverse of the covariance matrix (also called the *precision matrix*) and the vector of expected return. In the next few pages we will interpret, eviscerate, extend this simple formula; and finally, as we start believing it is useful, we will caution you against its unconditional use. Like all the good things in life, MVO is at its most pleasant when it is accompanied by precautionary measures.

Insight 9.2: *MVO from asset Sharpes and correlations*

There is yet another formulation that is equivalent to the previous ones. Oftentimes, we think of portfolio positions not in terms of NMV, but of volatility. We do not invest \$10M in AAPL. The annualized volatility of AAPL is 20%, and therefore we have a \$2M volatility position in the stock. This conveys the position size in terms of its range of dollar movement over the course of a year. Now, we can express the Sharpe-optimal portfolio in terms of volatility in the following way. Let the stock volatilities be $\sigma_1, \ldots, \sigma_n$, and define $\mathbf{V}$ a diagonal matrix with these volatilities on the main diagonal. Denote the asset correlation matrix with $\mathbf{C}$. The covariance matrix is $\mathbf{\Omega_r} = \mathbf{VCV}$. Now let's rewrite the solution to the MVO problem:

$$\mathbf{w}^\star = \frac{1}{2\lambda}(\mathbf{VCV})^{-1}\boldsymbol{\alpha}$$

$$\mathbf{Vw}^\star = \frac{1}{2\lambda}\mathbf{C}^{-1}(\mathbf{V}^{-1}\boldsymbol{\alpha})$$

$$\mathbf{v}^\star = \frac{1}{2\lambda}\mathbf{C}^{-1}\mathbf{s} \tag{9.6}$$

$$\mathrm{SR}^\star = \sqrt{\mathbf{s}^\mathrm{T}\mathbf{C}^{-1}\mathbf{s}} \tag{9.7}$$

In the formula above, $\mathbf{v}^\star := \mathbf{Vw}^\star$ is the vector of optimal dollar volatilities, and $\mathbf{s}$ is the vector of asset-level Sharpe Ratios. Therefore, the optimal dollar volatilities are proportional to the Sharpe Ratios, multiplied by the inverse of the correlation matrix. This is interesting, because dollar volatilities, correlations, and asset Sharpe Ratios are more intuitive quantities than covariances and returns.

First of all, we can derive the same solution when we solve an unconstrained problem:

$$\max \boldsymbol{\alpha}^\top \mathbf{w} - \lambda \mathbf{w}^\top \boldsymbol{\Omega}_\mathrm{r} \mathbf{w} \tag{9.8}$$

$$\text{s.t. } \mathbf{w} \in \mathbb{R}^n \tag{9.9}$$

We have added the constraint to the objective function in the form of a penalty term; the informal term for this operation is *pricing out* the constraint. The objective function is concave, and the solution is given by

$$\mathbf{w}^\star = \frac{1}{2\lambda} \boldsymbol{\Omega}_\mathrm{r}^{-1} \boldsymbol{\alpha}$$

which gives the same solution as the vol-constrained problem when

$$\lambda = \frac{\sqrt{\boldsymbol{\alpha}^\top \boldsymbol{\Omega}_\mathrm{r}^{-1} \boldsymbol{\alpha}}}{2\sigma}$$

The larger the volatility budget, the smaller the penalty coefficient.

Notice that this penalty value is the same as the shadow price in the previous formulation. This is not a coincidence. We obtain the same solution when we price out the constraint and we give the variance a unit price equal to the shadow price of that constraint.

A third equivalent formulation is the one where we minimize volatility, subject to a return constraint:

$$\min \mathbf{w}^\top \boldsymbol{\Omega}_\mathrm{r} \mathbf{w} \tag{9.10}$$

$$\text{s.t. } \boldsymbol{\alpha}^\top \mathbf{w} \geq \mu \tag{9.11}$$

The solution is

$$\mathbf{w}^\star = \frac{\mu}{\boldsymbol{\alpha}^\top \boldsymbol{\Omega}_\mathrm{r}^{-1} \boldsymbol{\alpha}} \boldsymbol{\Omega}_\mathrm{r}^{-1} \boldsymbol{\alpha}$$

Insight 9.3: *Asset correlations, dispersion, and limits to performance*

1. From Equation (9.6) when assets are uncorrelated, the optimal dollar vol allocation is proportional to the asset Sharpe Ratios and the optimal Sharpe Ratio is the length of the vector $(s_1, \ldots, s_n)$,

(Continued)

(*Continued*)

which is not linear in the single-asset Sharpe Ratios; Sharpe Ratios *squared* is what matters.

2. Say that the assets have a pairwise correlation of $\rho \neq 0$. Then[a] the optimal volatility allocated to asset i, in the many-asset case $|\rho n| \gg 0$, is proportional to the *excess* Sharpe Ratio of the asset, compared to the average Sharpe Ratio:

$$v_i \propto s_i - E(\mathbf{s})$$

where we define $E(\mathbf{s}) := \frac{1}{n}\sum_i s_i$. The optimal Sharpe Ratio is

$$\mathrm{SR}^\star = \sqrt{\frac{n}{1-\rho}\mathrm{var}(\mathbf{s}) + \frac{n}{1+(n-1)\rho}E^2(\mathbf{s})}$$

with $\mathrm{var}(\mathbf{s}) := E(\mathbf{s}^2) - E^2(\mathbf{s})$. If all assets have the same Sharpe Ratio s, then

$$\mathrm{SR}^\star = \sqrt{\frac{ns^2}{1+(n-1)\rho}}$$

Finally, in the many-asset limit, we have $\mathrm{SR}^\star = s/\sqrt{\rho}$.

Summing up the results above:

- If there is no dispersion in Sharpe Ratios, then the Sharpe Ratio approaches an upper bound $s/\sqrt{\rho}$.
- However, if there is dispersion in Sharpe Ratios, then the Sharpe Ratio is still proportional to $\sqrt{n}$ and to the dispersion, measured as the cross-sectional standard deviation of the assets' Sharpe Ratios.

---

[a] To prove this, verify directly that the inverse of the correlation matrix is

$$\mathbf{C}^{-1} = \frac{1}{1-\rho}\left(\mathbf{I}_n - \frac{\rho}{1+(n-1)\rho}\mathbf{e}\mathbf{e}^\top\right)$$

Insight 9.4: ★*Reading the entries of the precision matrix*

Is there a way to interpret further the relationship $\mathbf{w}^\star \propto \boldsymbol{\Omega}_{\mathbf{r}}^{-1}\boldsymbol{\alpha}$? The optimal position of asset i is a weighted sum of alphas. The $[\Omega_{\mathbf{r}}^{-1}]_{i,j}$ are proportional to minus the *partial correlations* of the returns of i and j after controlling for the other asset returns. The interpretation of partial correlation is that it captures collinearity between two random variables, after removing the collinearity of these variables with a set of controlling variables. In practice, one follows this procedure: 1. regress the returns of asset i and j on the returns of the other assets; 2. compute the correlation between the residuals from the two regressions, which we denote $\rho_{i,j}$. The formula for the optimal portfolio is

$$w_i \propto [\Omega_{\mathbf{r}}^{-1}]_{i,i}\left(\alpha_i - \sum_{j\neq i} \rho_{i,j}[\Omega_{\mathbf{r}}^{-1}]_{j,j}\alpha_j\right)$$

The diagonal terms of the precision matrix are always positive. The interpretation of this rather convoluted formula is that, whenever the returns of two assets are positively correlated after removing the joint effect of correlations with other variables, the size of the portfolio is reduced, because the collinearity makes the alpha common to both asset i and j.

9.3 Trading in Factor Space

9.3.1 Factor-Mimicking Portfolios

We have a factor model, and we estimate the expected factor returns $\boldsymbol{\lambda}$. Say that we want to generate a portfolio which has the closest possible return to one of the factors. For example, we want to generate a "momentum factor" portfolio. What would it be? The returns of the *Factor-Mimicking Portfolio* (FMP) should be as close as possible to those of the factor: the variance of the difference of the two returns should be minimized. A portfolio $\mathbf{w}$ has an associated factor exposure $\mathbf{b}$. Its returns are $\mathbf{r}^\top \mathbf{w} = \mathbf{b}^\top \mathbf{f} + \mathbf{w}^\top \boldsymbol{\epsilon}$. The tracking variance[3] between f_i and $\mathbf{r}^\top \mathbf{w}$ is $E[((b_i - 1)f_i + \sum_{j \neq i} b_j f_j + \mathbf{w}^\top \boldsymbol{\epsilon})^2]$. This is minimized when $b_i - 1 = 0$, $b_j = 0$ for $j \neq i$, and the portfolio's idio variance is minimized. The optimization formulation is

$$\min \mathbf{w}^\top \boldsymbol{\Omega}_\epsilon \mathbf{w}$$
$$\text{s.t. } \mathbf{B}^\top \mathbf{w} = \mathbf{e}_i$$

The solution is $\mathbf{v}_i = \boldsymbol{\Omega}_\epsilon^{-1} \mathbf{B}(\mathbf{B}^\top \boldsymbol{\Omega}_\epsilon^{-1} \mathbf{B})^{-1} \mathbf{e}_i$. The matrix whose column vectors are the FMPs is ($\mathbf{P}$ is for "portfolios")

$$\begin{aligned}
\mathbf{P} := & \begin{bmatrix} | & | & \cdots & | \\ \mathbf{v}_1 & \mathbf{v}_2 & \cdots & \mathbf{v}_m \\ | & | & \cdots & | \end{bmatrix} \\
= & \boldsymbol{\Omega}_\epsilon^{-1} \mathbf{B}(\mathbf{B}^\top \boldsymbol{\Omega}_\epsilon^{-1} \mathbf{B})^{-1} \begin{bmatrix} | & | & \cdots & | \\ \mathbf{e}_1 & \mathbf{e}_2 & \cdots & \mathbf{e}_m \\ | & | & \cdots & | \end{bmatrix} \\
= & \boldsymbol{\Omega}_\epsilon^{-1} \mathbf{B}(\mathbf{B}^\top \boldsymbol{\Omega}_\epsilon^{-1} \mathbf{B})^{-1} \qquad (9.12)
\end{aligned}$$

We now have factor portfolios as tradeable instruments. The expected return of a factor portfolio is $(\boldsymbol{\alpha}_\perp^\top + \boldsymbol{\lambda}^\top \mathbf{B}^\top)\mathbf{v}_i = \lambda_i$. In practice, we:

1. generate the FMPs compositions over time;
2. compute their per-period PnL;
3. compute their empirical average PnL;
4. apply modifications to the expected PnL, such as penalties[4];
5. optimize in factor space.

We now prove that FMPs emerge naturally from certain assumptions about returns and FMP composition. In the Appendix (Theorem 9.1), we prove that if alpha spanned is zero and if the idiosyncratic variance of the

[3] We ignore the term $\boldsymbol{\alpha}_\perp$, both out of simplicity and because it is very small.

[4] The subject will be covered in Section 10.2.3.

FMPs is small, then the MVO problem reduces to one in which we only trade FMPs. First, we solve the low-dimensional optimization problem

$$\max \boldsymbol{\lambda}^\top \mathbf{u} - \frac{1}{2\gamma}\mathbf{u}^\top \boldsymbol{\Omega}_{\mathrm{f}}\mathbf{u}$$
$$\text{s.t. } \mathbf{u} \in \mathbb{R}^m$$

Say that the solution is $\mathbf{u}^\star$. The optimal portfolio is the weighted sum of the FMPs $\mathbf{w}^\star = \mathbf{P}\mathbf{u}^\star$. A few remarks on the appeal and limitations of the previous result:

- In factor space, the dimensionality of the problem collapses, but we still have an MVO problem, which is usually more interpretable. The possible drawbacks of MVO still hold, but so do the possible remedies, which we present in Chapter 10.
- FMPs make their appearance as the necessary synthetic instruments for trading in factor space. In synthesis, if we perform MVO and factors are sufficiently "pure" (having low idiosyncratic risk), then we *necessarily* trade FMPs. It is an economical, beautiful result.
- Keep in mind that FMPs are associated to the loadings matrix $\mathbf{B}$, and that there are many loadings matrices resulting in equivalent factor models (see Section 4.4.1). Think of FMPs as a vector basis in a finite-dimensional subspace. There are infinitely many such bases, and they don't need to be orthogonal. The subspace, however, is uniquely identified.
- The assumption of small factor idiosyncratic variance can be expressed as $\left\|(\mathbf{B}^\top \boldsymbol{\Omega}_\epsilon^{-1}\mathbf{B})^{-1}\right\| \ll 1$. The matrix inside the norm appears repeatedly in this book—in an ideal world we would like it to be small, but in the real world it is not. The ideal-world solution works well as a sketch of the real world. It tells us the broad shape of the portfolio. When trading, we should include the idiosyncratic variance of the portfolio and not solve for the ideal case.
- In conjunction with the previous point, we have also ignored execution costs. They should not be ignored in applications. Chapter 11 is devoted to the subject.

9.3.2 *Adding, Estimating, and Trading a New Factor*

Let us consider an instructive example, and let us work through the individual steps. In a way, all the steps are implicitly contained in the theory developed so far. The starting point is a factor model with m factors, with parameters $\mathbf{B}, \boldsymbol{\Omega}_{\mathbf{f}}, \boldsymbol{\Omega}_{\epsilon}$. We assume that they are constant through time for notational simplicity; extending the example to time-varying parameters is straighforward. The factors have expected returns $\boldsymbol{\lambda}$. We are exploring a new asset characteristic vector $\mathbf{a} \in \mathbb{R}^n$. We can add the new factor to the existing model without re-estimating the entire model by pushing out the model.

1. *Orthogonalization.* First we orthogonalize the new factor to the existing factors. The orthogonalized factor is given by standard linear regression formulas[5]

$$\mathbf{b}_{m+1} = (\mathbf{I}_n - \mathbf{B}(\mathbf{B}^\top \boldsymbol{\Omega}_\epsilon^{-1} \mathbf{B})^{-1} \mathbf{B}^\top \boldsymbol{\Omega}_\epsilon^{-1})\mathbf{a}$$

2. *Estimation.* Next, we regress in every period the residual returns from the existing model against the orthogonalized factor by using the Frisch–Waugh–Lovell theorem[6]:

$$\epsilon_t = \mathbf{b}_{m+1} \hat{f}_{m+1,t} + \hat{\epsilon}_t \tag{9.13}$$

$$\Rightarrow \hat{f}_{m+1,t} := \frac{\mathbf{b}_{m+1}^\top \boldsymbol{\Omega}_\epsilon^{-1} \boldsymbol{\epsilon}_t}{\mathbf{b}_{m+1}^\top \boldsymbol{\Omega}_\epsilon^{-1} \mathbf{b}_{m+1}} \tag{9.14}$$

$$\hat{\lambda}_{m+1} := \frac{1}{T} \sum_t \hat{f}_{m+1,t} \tag{9.15}$$

$$\hat{\sigma}_{m+1} := \left(\frac{1}{T} \sum_t \hat{f}_{m+1,t}^2 \right) \tag{9.16}$$

$$\widehat{\mathrm{SR}} = \frac{\hat{\lambda}_{m+1}}{\hat{\sigma}_{m+1}} \tag{9.17}$$

In the Appendix (Theorem 9.2), we show that the approximate variance of the new factor is $\hat{\sigma}_{m+1}^2 = (\mathbf{b}_{m+1}^\top \boldsymbol{\Omega}_\epsilon^{-1} \mathbf{b}_{m+1})^{-1}$.

[5] See Section 4.7.1.
[6] See Section 4.7.3.

3. *Risk updating.* We show in Section 9.7.4 that the approximate factor covariance matrix including the new factor is given by

$$\widetilde{\boldsymbol{\Omega}}_{\mathrm{f}} \simeq \begin{bmatrix} \boldsymbol{\Omega}_{\mathrm{f}} & \mathbf{0} \\ \mathbf{0} & (\mathbf{b}_{m+1}^{\top}\boldsymbol{\Omega}_{\epsilon}^{-1}\mathbf{b}_{m+1})^{-1} \end{bmatrix}$$

This result holds only for constant parameters and well-diversified factor portfolios. For time-varying models, we need to resort to numerical estimates for the factor covariance matrix. The analytical results provide a useful approximation.

4. *Trading.* The FMP of the new factor is

$$\mathbf{v}_{m+1} = \frac{\boldsymbol{\Omega}_{\epsilon}^{-1}\mathbf{b}_{m+1}}{\mathbf{b}_{m+1}^{\top}\boldsymbol{\Omega}_{\epsilon}^{-1}\mathbf{b}_{m+1}}$$

This follows from the definition of FMPs, Equation (9.12). A faster route is via the factor return estimation above. The factor return estimate is the same whether we regress using residual returns or total returns[7]:

$$\begin{aligned}\hat{f}_{m+1,t} &= \frac{\mathbf{b}_{m+1}^{\top}\boldsymbol{\Omega}_{\epsilon}^{-1}\hat{\boldsymbol{\epsilon}}_{t}}{\mathbf{b}_{m+1}^{\top}\boldsymbol{\Omega}_{\epsilon}^{-1}\mathbf{b}_{m+1}} \\ &= \frac{\mathbf{b}_{m+1}^{\top}\boldsymbol{\Omega}_{\epsilon}^{-1}\mathbf{r}_{t}}{\mathbf{b}_{m+1}^{\top}\boldsymbol{\Omega}_{\epsilon}^{-1}\mathbf{b}_{m+1}} \\ &= \mathbf{v}_{m+1}^{\top}\mathbf{r}_{t}\end{aligned}$$

Let $\tilde{\boldsymbol{\lambda}} = (\boldsymbol{\lambda} \mid \hat{\lambda}_{m+1})$. Finally, we solve the optimization problem

$$\begin{aligned}&\max \tilde{\lambda}^{\top}\mathbf{u} - \frac{1}{2\gamma}\mathbf{u}^{\top}\widetilde{\boldsymbol{\Omega}}_{\mathrm{f}}\mathbf{u} \\ &\text{s.t. } \mathbf{u} \in \mathbb{R}^{m+1}\end{aligned}$$

whose solution is simple, because of the block structure of the factor covariance matrix

$$\mathbf{u}^{\star} = \gamma \begin{bmatrix} \boldsymbol{\Omega}_{\mathrm{f}}^{-1}\boldsymbol{\lambda} \\ (\mathbf{b}_{m+1}^{\top}\boldsymbol{\Omega}_{\epsilon}^{-1}\mathbf{b}_{m+1})\hat{\lambda}_{m+1} \end{bmatrix}$$

[7] See Sections 4.7.2 and 4.7.3.

So, our investment in the pre-existing factors is unchanged, but we add a position in the new factor, proportional to the expected factor return divided by its variance.

Procedure 9.1: *Adding a new factor to a model and trading it*

1. **Inputs**: a factor model $(\mathbf{b}_t, \mathbf{\Omega}_{\mathrm{f},t}, \mathbf{\Omega}_{\epsilon,t}, \boldsymbol{\epsilon}_t)$, with expected factor returns $\boldsymbol{\lambda}$; raw loadings for the new factor $\mathbf{a}_t$.
2. Orthogonalize the factor:
$$\mathbf{b}_{m+1,t} = (\mathbf{I}_n - \mathbf{b}_t(\mathbf{b}_t^\top \mathbf{\Omega}_\epsilon^{-1} \mathbf{b}_t)^{-1} \mathbf{b}_t^\top \mathbf{\Omega}_\epsilon^{-1})\mathbf{a}_t$$
3. Compute the FMP:
$$\mathbf{v}_{m+1,t} := \frac{\mathbf{\Omega}_{\epsilon,t}^{-1} \mathbf{b}_{m+1,t}}{\mathbf{b}_{m+1,t}^\top \mathbf{\Omega}_{\epsilon,t}^{-1} \mathbf{b}_{m+1,t}}$$
$$\hat{\lambda}_{m+1} := \frac{1}{T} \sum_t \mathbf{v}_{m+1,t}^\top \mathbf{r}_t$$
4. Compute new factor covariance matrix:
$$\tilde{\mathbf{\Omega}}_\mathrm{f} \simeq \begin{bmatrix} \mathbf{\Omega}_{\mathrm{f},t} & \mathbf{0} \\ \mathbf{0} & (\mathbf{b}_{m+1,t}^\top \mathbf{\Omega}_{\epsilon,t}^{-1} \mathbf{b}_{m+1,t})^{-1} \end{bmatrix}$$
5. Compute new weights for FMPs:
$$\mathbf{u}_t^\star = \gamma \begin{bmatrix} \mathbf{\Omega}_{\mathrm{f},t}^{-1} \boldsymbol{\lambda} \\ (\mathbf{b}_{m+1}^\top \mathbf{\Omega}_{\epsilon,t}^{-1} \mathbf{b}_{m+1,t}) \hat{\lambda}_{m+1,t} \end{bmatrix}$$
   and trade portfolio
$$\mathbf{w}_t = \begin{bmatrix} | & | & \cdots & | \\ \mathbf{v}_{1,t} & \mathbf{v}_{2,t} & \cdots & \mathbf{v}_{m+1,t} \\ | & | & \cdots & | \end{bmatrix} \mathbf{u}_t^\star$$

9.3.3 *Factor Portfolios from Sorts?*

A very popular way to form factor portfolios is to sort securities by a given characteristic, and then form a portfolio in which the long positions are top x-quantile positions (say, the top 25% positions) and the shorts are the bottom x-quantile positions. The Net Market Value (NMV) of each position is identical, so that the portfolio is dollar-neutral. For example, we consider book value-to-price (BtP) as the characteristic for a U.S. investment universe of 2000 stocks, and go long $1000 the 500 stocks with the highest value of the ratio, and short $1000 the 500 stocks with the lowest value of the ratio. This approach originates with the paper by Fama and MacBeth (1973), who introduced them to alleviate the problem of estimation error of time-series betas of single securities, by estimating portfolio betas instead. The resulting portfolios are sometimes called *portfolios from sorts* or *characteristic portfolios* (CPs; Daniel et al. (2020)). They are widely used by practitioners to convert a metric that describes a potential mispricing into an investable portfolio. What are the drawbacks of this approach? There are at least four.

1. The characteristic portfolios will have unwanted exposures to other factors. As a result, you may be betting on the characteristic of interest as well as on some other source of systematic risk and return. The unwanted exposures may both increase the overall portfolio risk and reduce the return of the portfolio.
2. The securities in the characteristic portfolio are equally weighted. This is inefficient, since more volatile securities should have a lower weight.
3. Being equal-weighted, the sizes in the characteristic portfolio do not reflect the magnitude of the characteristic. For example, if asset A has twice the book-to-price of asset B, and they are both in the top x-quantile of the distribution, they receive the same weight. This is the same as dichotomizing the characteristic. Dichotomization of data is usually a poor modeling strategy (see, e.g., Harrell (2015)).
4. Over time, characteristics change, and certain securities may be dropped from/added to the portfolio abruptly (from a target weight to zero). This makes trading more expensive and requires some adjustment over the naïve weights.

FAQ 9.1: *What about factor portfolios from sorts?*

Portfolios from sorts (or *characteristic portfolios*) are dollar-neutral portfolios which consist of equal-weighted long positions for securities having the highest values of a certain characteristic, and equal-weighted short positions for an equal number of securities with the lowest value of a characteristic. They hold the intuitive appeal of being a simple implementation of a dollar-neutral portfolio. However, they have many drawbacks: non-optimal volatility weighting, non-optimal characteristic weighting, unwanted exposures to other factors, and high turnover due to abrupt inclusions/exclusions in the portfolio. FMPs are designed to be the most efficient (i.e., lowest risk) portfolios with unit exposure to a characteristic of interest.

9.4 Trading in Idio Space

In Section 4.3 we introduced the concepts of alpha spanned and alpha orthogonal. Alpha spanned are asset expected excess returns attributable to non-zero factor expected returns; alpha orthogonal are not explainable by factor returns. Because of Equation (4.3), Sharpe Ratio scales at least like $\sqrt{n}$. Because of this, alpha orthogonal is the golden currency in investing. How does one build a portfolio that exploits only this alpha? By requiring that the optimal portfolio has no exposures, and therefore no returns, to factors. There are many ways to achieve this, and they are encountered in practice. The first one is to build a portfolio that has an upper bound on volatility, maximizes expected returns, and has no factor exposures. By construction, the portfolio contains "pure alpha" and no factor-related PnL. The formulation is

$$\begin{aligned} \max\ & \alpha_\perp^\top \mathbf{w} \\ \text{s.t. } & \mathbf{B}^\top \mathbf{w} = 0 \\ & \mathbf{w}^\top \boldsymbol{\Omega}_\epsilon \mathbf{w} \le \sigma^2 \end{aligned} \tag{9.18}$$

whose solution[8] is

$$\hat{\boldsymbol{\alpha}}_\perp := (\mathbf{I}_n - \mathbf{B}(\mathbf{B}^\top \boldsymbol{\Omega}_\epsilon^{-1}\mathbf{B})^{-1}\mathbf{B}^\top \boldsymbol{\Omega}_\epsilon^{-1})\boldsymbol{\alpha}_\perp$$

$$\mathbf{w}^\star = \frac{\sigma}{\sqrt{\hat{\boldsymbol{\alpha}}_\perp^\top \boldsymbol{\Omega}_\epsilon^{-1}\hat{\boldsymbol{\alpha}}_\perp}}\boldsymbol{\Omega}_\epsilon^{-1}\hat{\boldsymbol{\alpha}}_\perp$$

In Section 9.3.2, we built an FMP for a new factor through two steps: first, orthogonalization; second, inverse variance weighting. The portfolio construction for an alpha orthogonal portfolio is, indeed, identical: orthogonalization and inverse variance weighting. If all the asset idiosyncratic volatilities are identical, $\boldsymbol{\Omega}_\epsilon$ is proportional to the identity, and the orthogonalization step is superfluous: $\hat{\boldsymbol{\alpha}}_\perp = \boldsymbol{\alpha}_\perp$.

9.5 Drivers of Information Ratio: Information Coefficient and Diversification

What makes a good strategy? Before we are trading (i.e., *ex ante*), we are living the dream, i.e., Equation (9.5):

$$\text{SR}^\star = \sqrt{\boldsymbol{\alpha}^\top \boldsymbol{\Omega}_\mathbf{r}^{-1}\boldsymbol{\alpha}}$$

A substantial part of this and of the next chapter is dedicated to the notion that we do not exist in the dreamtime. Our forecasted returns and risk models are incorrect, and we should incorporate this knowledge in the investment process. A first step is to establish some *ex-post* relationship for the Sharpe Ratio. Start with the solution to the MVO problem, Equation (9.3):

$$\mathbf{w}^\star = \frac{\sigma}{\sqrt{\boldsymbol{\alpha}^\top \boldsymbol{\Omega}_\mathbf{r}^{-1}\boldsymbol{\alpha}}}\boldsymbol{\Omega}_\mathbf{r}^{-1}\boldsymbol{\alpha}$$

and assume that the covariance matrix $\boldsymbol{\Omega}_\mathbf{r}$ is accurate; admittedly a strong assumption. The expected *realized* return is

[8] Derive it as an exercise, or see Section 9.7.2.

$$
\begin{aligned}
E(\mathbf{r}^\mathsf{T}\mathbf{w}^\star) &= \frac{\sigma}{\sqrt{\boldsymbol{\alpha}^\mathsf{T}\boldsymbol{\Omega}_\mathbf{r}^{-1}\boldsymbol{\alpha}}} E(\mathbf{r}^\mathsf{T}\boldsymbol{\Omega}_\mathbf{r}^{-1}\boldsymbol{\alpha}) \\
&= \sigma \frac{E(\mathbf{r}^\mathsf{T}\boldsymbol{\Omega}_\mathbf{r}^{-1}\boldsymbol{\alpha})}{\sqrt{\boldsymbol{\alpha}^\mathsf{T}\boldsymbol{\Omega}_\mathbf{r}^{-1}\boldsymbol{\alpha}}\sqrt{E(\mathbf{r}^\mathsf{T}\boldsymbol{\Omega}_\mathbf{r}^{-1}\mathbf{r})}} \sqrt{\frac{E(\mathbf{r}^\mathsf{T}\boldsymbol{\Omega}_\mathbf{r}^{-1}\mathbf{r})}{n}}\sqrt{n}
\end{aligned}
$$

Recall the *Information Coefficient*, already introduced in Section 8.3.1:

$$
\mathrm{IC} := \frac{E(\mathbf{r}^\mathsf{T}\boldsymbol{\Omega}_\mathbf{r}^{-1}\boldsymbol{\alpha})}{\sqrt{\boldsymbol{\alpha}^\mathsf{T}\boldsymbol{\Omega}_\mathbf{r}^{-1}\boldsymbol{\alpha}}\sqrt{E(\mathbf{r}^\mathsf{T}\boldsymbol{\Omega}_\mathbf{r}^{-1}\mathbf{r})}}
$$

The important thing to know is that the Information Coefficient is a correlation. To see why, we need to transform variables:

$$
\begin{aligned}
\tilde{\mathbf{r}} &= \boldsymbol{\Omega}_\mathbf{r}^{-1/2}\mathbf{r} \\
\hat{\boldsymbol{\alpha}} &= \boldsymbol{\Omega}_\mathbf{r}^{-1/2}\boldsymbol{\alpha}
\end{aligned}
\tag{9.19}
$$

So that the Information Coefficient can be rewritten in a more succinct form

$$
\mathrm{IC}(\hat{\boldsymbol{\alpha}}, \tilde{\mathbf{r}}) := \frac{E(\tilde{\mathbf{r}}^\mathsf{T}\hat{\boldsymbol{\alpha}})}{\sqrt{\hat{\boldsymbol{\alpha}}^\mathsf{T}\hat{\boldsymbol{\alpha}}}\sqrt{E(\tilde{\mathbf{r}}^\mathsf{T}\tilde{\mathbf{r}})}}
$$

which can be interpreted as a cross-sectional uncentered correlation between z-scored alphas and z-scored returns.

We can simplify things further by proving that $E(\mathbf{r}^\mathsf{T}\boldsymbol{\Omega}_\mathbf{r}^{-1}\mathbf{r}) = n$. The random vector $\mathbf{r}$ has the same covariance matrix[9] as $\boldsymbol{\Omega}_\mathbf{r}^{1/2}\boldsymbol{\xi}$, where $\boldsymbol{\xi}$ is a standard multivariate normal:

$$
\begin{aligned}
E(\mathbf{r}^\mathsf{T}\boldsymbol{\Omega}_\mathbf{r}^{-1}\mathbf{r}) &= E(\boldsymbol{\xi}^\mathsf{T}\boldsymbol{\Omega}_\mathbf{r}^{1/2}\boldsymbol{\Omega}_\mathbf{r}^{-1}\boldsymbol{\Omega}_\mathbf{r}^{1/2}\boldsymbol{\xi}) \\
&= \sum_{i=1}^{n} E(\xi_i^2) \\
&= n
\end{aligned}
$$

Putting everything together, the $E(\mathbf{r}^\mathsf{T}\mathbf{w}^\star)/\sigma$ is

$$
\mathrm{SR} = \mathrm{IC}(\hat{\alpha}, \tilde{\mathbf{r}})\sqrt{n}
$$

[9] Prove this step-by-step in Exercise 4.3.

This relationship goes back to Grinold (1989) and Grinold and Kahn (1999), who named it *The Fundamental Law of Active Management*.[10] It is often invoked by practitioners. In practice, users of the formula do not whiten returns and alphas in Equation (9.19). Instead, they apply the law to the active component of a portfolio, so that $\mathbf{\Omega}_\mathbf{r}$ is replaced by the diagonal $\mathbf{\Omega}_\epsilon$ and $\boldsymbol{\alpha}$ by $\boldsymbol{\alpha}_\perp$. Then, IC becomes the cross-sectional correlation between the standardized alphas (expected excess returns in units of volatility) and the standardized idio returns (so that they have unit variance).

The Fundamental Law has several important implications. The first, and most obvious one, is that performance is driven by two factors. The first one is a measure of skill: the Information Coefficient. It is a strength of the predictive strength of the signal. If we have the ability to extend our forecast to a larger panel of stocks without degrading its predictive power, we should do so! This may or not be the case in real life, depending on the specifics of your strategy. Many investors also have a notion of "idea velocity", expressed as the number of forecasts T per year. A higher idea velocity increases, in principle, the Information Ratio. It is really difficult, however, to increase effectively the frequency of *independent* forecasts.

Insight 9.5: *Information Coefficient and predictive regression*

Being a correlation, the IC is also naturally related to the predictive strength of our alphas, as measured by a cross-sectional regression. As an important step in exploring alphas, we perform a cross-sectional weighted least squares regression of residual returns against alpha. We estimate a coefficient x that solves the following minimization problem:

$$\min_b \sum_i \frac{(r_i - \alpha_i b)^2}{\sigma^2_{\epsilon,i}} = \min_b \|\tilde{\mathbf{r}} - \hat{\boldsymbol{\alpha}} b\|^2$$

(*Continued*)

[10] Quite an important name for a "law"! And why not? Nobody had thought of using this title at the time. I can imagine Grinold playing air guitar and singing to an Iron Maiden tune as he was drafting the original 1989 paper.

(*Continued*)

The solution is given by $b^\star = \tilde{\mathbf{r}}^\top \hat{\boldsymbol{\alpha}} / \|\hat{\boldsymbol{\alpha}}\|^2$ and the residual sum of squares is $\|\tilde{\mathbf{r}}\|^2 - (\tilde{\mathbf{r}}^\top \hat{\boldsymbol{\alpha}})^2 / \|\hat{\boldsymbol{\alpha}}\|^2$, while the total sum of squares is $\|\tilde{\mathbf{r}}\|^2$. The coefficient of determination ("R squared") is, in expectation, equal to

$$R^2 = \frac{(\tilde{\mathbf{r}}^\top \hat{\alpha})^2}{\|\hat{\alpha}\|^2 \|\tilde{\mathbf{r}}\|^2} = (\mathrm{IC})^2$$

And we can link the coefficient of determination in predictive regressions to the Information Ratio:

$$\mathrm{IR} = \sqrt{R^2 n}$$

If there are T investment periods in a year, the annualized information has a convenient form as a function of per-period cross-sectional R squared:

$$\mathrm{IR} = \sqrt{R^2 n T} = \mathrm{IC}\sqrt{nT}$$

Otherwise stated, the annualized Information Ratio is equal to the Information Coefficient times the *independent number of return forecasts in a year.*[a]

[a] For the relationship between coefficient of determination and IR, see Chincarini and Kim (2007, 2022).

The Fundamental Law also connects IR to an *ex-post* measure (IC) that is interpretable as a correlation, which can be related to a special kind of regression (as per Insight 9.5).

9.6 Aggregation: Signals versus Portfolios

So far, we have considered the optimization of a single portfolio. That is the situation usually faced by a quantitative portfolio manager, but is far from being the only one. Let us consider two examples. In the first

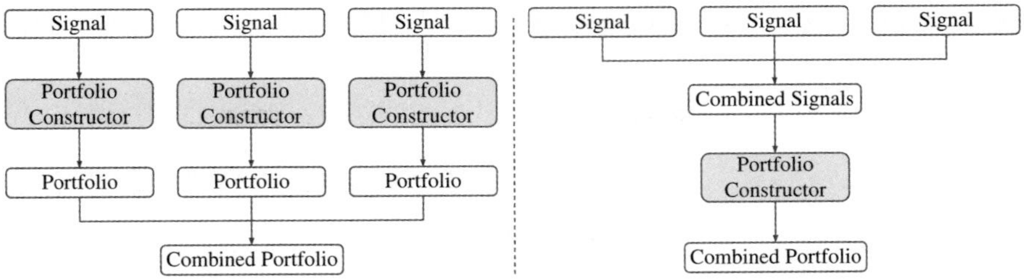

Figure 9.1 Left: the decentralized solution to portfolio combination. Right: the centralized solution.

one, you have a fundamental portfolio manager managing a large team. In order to scale her book, the PM delegates to the analyst trading decisions for the stocks they cover. The portfolio of the entire team is simply the aggregation of the individual portfolios. This is a fully decentralized solution to portfolio management. What would be the alternative? The analysts do their own research, summarize it into a thesis for each stock, and communicate to the PM, who converts them into positions. This is the centralized solution to portfolio management. Now, we produce the second example by going up one level. We have a large number of portfolio managers; the hedge fund has some excess capital it would like to deploy. One option available to the hedge fund is to take the portfolio positions of the individual teams, and increase them by a given percentage, say, 50%. This can be directly performed at the time of an order's submission. This is analogous to the decentralized solution in the first example. There is no need to look inside the box of a team. It's only the output that matters. The predictable alternative is the centralized solution: gather the signals from the teams and construct a portfolio. Figure 9.1 visualizes the two approaches.

A lot of PnL rides on the decision to centralize versus decentralize portfolio construction! How should we organize large teams? How should we deploy spare capital in the most efficient way? The rest of this section is devoted to proving a simple result: under some simple conditions *the two approaches give the same result*. The conditions are, very roughly, that the portfolio constructor is an MVO problem, and there are no transaction costs. Technical details matter, however. The rest of the section spells them out in detail and states the precise result. As for many equivalent results in economic theory,[11] the theorem is interesting because it doesn't hold in practice. It allows us to compare the idealized conditions under which it holds, and the real-world situation, and identify areas where one solution may have the advantage.

Let us formalize the problem. There is an investment universe of n stocks. We have m portfolio managers working under a principal hedge fund manager. Without loss of generality, each one has the same investment coverage of n stocks. Every portfolio manager uses the same asset covariance matrix $\mathbf{\Omega}_\mathbf{r}$, and has a forecast $\boldsymbol{\alpha}_i$.

We model the portfolio managers by assuming that they are mean-variance maximizers. Without loss of generality, PM i produces a unit-volatility portfolio:

$$\mathbf{w}_i = \frac{\mathbf{\Omega}_\mathbf{r}^{-1}\boldsymbol{\alpha}_i}{\sigma_i}$$

$$\sigma_i := \sqrt{\boldsymbol{\alpha}_i^\top \mathbf{\Omega}_\mathbf{r}^{-1}\boldsymbol{\alpha}_i}$$

Correspondingly, we have two solutions.

1. *Decentralized:* PMs trade, the hedge fund manager estimates their Sharpe Ratios and return correlations, and combines their portfolios so as to maximize the overall Sharpe Ratio.
2. *Centralized:* The hedge fund manager receives the signals, simulates their properties (e.g., Sharpe Ratio of the MVO portfolios and return correlations of the portfolios), and then combines the signals and trades a single Sharpe-maximizing portfolio.

We consider the two solutions.

1. *Decentralized solution.* The hedge fund manager observes Sharpe Ratio s_i, for $i = 1, \ldots, m$ for each PM, as well as the correlation matrix $\mathbf{C}$ for the m. Consider Insight 9.2: the optimal dollar volatility allocated to strategy i is $v_i := [\mathbf{C}^{-1}\mathbf{s}]_i$. The portfolios $\mathbf{w}_i$ have unit volatility, hence the aggregated portfolio is

$$\mathbf{w}_{\text{dec}} = \sum_i v_i \mathbf{w}_i = \sum_i [\mathbf{C}^{-1}\mathbf{s}]_i \frac{\mathbf{\Omega}_\mathbf{r}^{-1}\boldsymbol{\alpha}_i}{\sigma_i}$$

---

[11] For example, Modigliani–Miller's theorem and Merton's result on the equivalence of an option claim and a replicating portfolio.

2. *Centralized solution.* The hedge fund manager receives signals and aggregates them: $\boldsymbol{\alpha} = \sum_i u_i \boldsymbol{\alpha}_i$. We need to identify weights u_i. Let $\mathbf{a} := E(\mathbf{r})$. The expected PnL of the portfolio $\boldsymbol{\Omega}_\mathbf{r}^{-1}\boldsymbol{\alpha}$ is

$$\begin{aligned}\mathbf{a}^\top \boldsymbol{\Omega}_\mathbf{r}^{-1} \sum_i u_i \alpha_i &= \sum_i u_i \mathbf{a}^\top \boldsymbol{\Omega}_\mathbf{r}^{-1} \alpha_i \\ &= \sum_i u_i \sigma_i s_i\end{aligned}$$

The covariance of the portfolio is

$$\begin{aligned}(\boldsymbol{\Omega}_\mathbf{r}^{-1} \sum_i u_i \boldsymbol{\alpha}_i)^\top \boldsymbol{\Omega}_\mathbf{r} (\boldsymbol{\Omega}_\mathbf{r}^{-1} \sum_j u_j \boldsymbol{\alpha}_j) &= \sum_i \sum_j \boldsymbol{\alpha}_i^\top \boldsymbol{\Omega}_\mathbf{r}^{-1} \boldsymbol{\alpha}_j u_i u_j \\ &= \sum_i \sum_j [\mathbf{C}]_{i,j} \sigma_i \sigma_j u_i u_j\end{aligned}$$

We find the weights so that the hedge fund manager maximizes the Sharpe Ratio. Define $x_i := \sigma_i u_i$. The maximization problem is

$$\begin{aligned}\max \quad & \frac{\mathbf{s}^\top \mathbf{x}}{\sqrt{\mathbf{x}^\top \mathbf{C} \mathbf{x}}} \\ \text{s.t.} \quad & \mathbf{x} \in \mathbf{R}^m\end{aligned}$$

The solution is $\mathbf{x}^\star = \mathbf{C}^{-1}\mathbf{s}/\sqrt{\mathbf{s}\mathbf{C}^{-1}\mathbf{s}}$, so that

$$\mathbf{w}_{\text{cen}} = \frac{1}{\sqrt{\mathbf{s}\mathbf{C}^{-1}\mathbf{s}}} \boldsymbol{\Omega}_\mathbf{r}^{-1} \sum_i \frac{[\mathbf{C}^{-1}\mathbf{s}]_i}{\sigma_i} \boldsymbol{\alpha}_i$$

The two portfolios $\mathbf{w}_{\text{cen}}$ and $\mathbf{w}_{\text{dec}}$ are identical, save for a multiplicative constant, which is not essential.

This equivalency result is, in a sense, positive, because it suggests that, at least to a first approximation, we can decentralize portfolio construction decisions. What could go wrong? A lot. It is a good point to re-examine the assumptions:

- First, we have ignored execution costs. It is possible that the centralized solution has the advantage, since it would net out opposite-side positions of individual portfolio managers. Optimal execution turns the problem into a multi-period one, so that the analysis in this section does not carry over.

- Second, we have assumed that the portfolio manager solves an MVO problem; the formulation accommodates total return and idio return problems. In real-world implementations, there are side constraints that may differ by portfolio managers. Covariance matrices may also differ among managers, and between them and the hedge fund manager.
- When the individual units are not systematic, but rather discretionary portfolio managers, the portfolios produced by them are not generated by MVO.
- In many cases, the volatility allocation to the signals of the PMs in the centralized solution is not done using MVO. Heuristics, precommitments to individual PMs, and other constraints may play a role.
- Finally, especially in the latter case of discretionary managers, the alpha signal may not be communicated in a timely manner.

In summary, the result suggests that in a real-world setting, provided that transaction costs do not dominate and that agents are MVO optimizers, the centralized solution should not dramatically dominate the decentralized one. The emphasis is on "suggests"; more research is (always) needed.

9.7 ★Appendix

9.7.1 Some Useful Results from Linear Algebra

Spiked covariance matrices are the sum of a full-rank sparse (possibly diagonal) matrix and a low-rank matrix. For this class of matrices, there are useful, computationally cheap ways to compute inverse and determinant: the Woodbury–Sherman–Morrison Lemma and the Matrix Determinant Lemma.

Woodbury–Sherman–Morrison Lemma. Useful to compute the inverse of a matrix (e.g., min-variance portfolio and log-likelihood):

$$(\mathbf{D} + \mathbf{B}\boldsymbol{\Omega}\mathbf{B}^{\top})^{-1} = \mathbf{D}^{-1} - \mathbf{D}^{-1}\mathbf{B}(\boldsymbol{\Omega}^{-1} + \mathbf{B}^{\top}\mathbf{D}^{-1}\mathbf{B})^{-1}\mathbf{B}^{\top}\mathbf{D}^{-1} \tag{9.20}$$

Determinant Lemma. Useful in log-likelihood calculations:

$$\det(\mathbf{D} + \mathbf{B}\boldsymbol{\Omega}\mathbf{B}^{\top}) = \det(\mathbf{D})\det(\Omega)\det(\boldsymbol{\Omega}^{-1} + \mathbf{B}^{\top}\mathbf{D}^{-1}\mathbf{B}) \tag{9.21}$$

9.7.2 Some Portfolio Optimization Problems

Example 9.1 ***(Maximize expected return subject to a vol constraint and linear homogeneous equalities)*****:**

$$\begin{aligned} \max\ & \boldsymbol{\alpha}^{\mathsf{T}}\mathbf{w} \\ \text{s.t. } & \mathbf{B}^{\mathsf{T}}\mathbf{w} = 0 \\ & \mathbf{w}^{\mathsf{T}}\boldsymbol{\Omega}\mathbf{w} \leq \sigma^2 \end{aligned} \tag{9.22}$$

The solution $\mathbf{w}^\star$ *to this problem is given by*

$$\begin{aligned} \boldsymbol{\Pi} &:= \mathbf{I}_n - \mathbf{B}(\mathbf{B}^{\mathsf{T}}\boldsymbol{\Omega}^{-1}\mathbf{B})^{-1}\mathbf{B}^{\mathsf{T}}\boldsymbol{\Omega}^{-1} \\ \tilde{\boldsymbol{\alpha}} &:= \boldsymbol{\Pi}\boldsymbol{\alpha} \\ \mathbf{w}^\star &= \frac{\sigma}{\sqrt{\tilde{\boldsymbol{\alpha}}^{\mathsf{T}}\boldsymbol{\Omega}^{-1}\tilde{\boldsymbol{\alpha}}}}\boldsymbol{\Omega}^{-1}\tilde{\boldsymbol{\alpha}} \end{aligned}$$

Example 9.2 ***(Minimum-variance portfolio subject to linear equalities)*****:**

$$\min \mathbf{w}^{\mathsf{T}}\boldsymbol{\Omega}\mathbf{w} \tag{9.23}$$

$$\text{s.t. } \mathbf{B}^{\mathsf{T}}\mathbf{w} = \mathbf{b} \tag{9.24}$$

The solution is $\mathbf{w}^\star = \boldsymbol{\Omega}^{-1}\mathbf{B}(\mathbf{B}^{\mathsf{T}}\boldsymbol{\Omega}^{-1}\mathbf{B})^{-1}\mathbf{b}$. *Of special interest is the case where* $\boldsymbol{\Omega} = \mathbf{B}\boldsymbol{\Omega}_{\mathrm{f}}\mathbf{B}^{\mathsf{T}} + \boldsymbol{\Omega}_\epsilon$. *In this case the objective is equal to* $\mathbf{b}^{\mathsf{T}}\boldsymbol{\Omega}_{\mathrm{f}}\mathbf{b} + \mathbf{w}^{\mathsf{T}}\boldsymbol{\Omega}_\epsilon\mathbf{w}$. *The first term is constant, so the objective is* $\mathbf{w}^{\mathsf{T}}\boldsymbol{\Omega}_\epsilon\mathbf{w}$, *and the* $\mathbf{w}^\star = \boldsymbol{\Omega}_\epsilon^{-1}\mathbf{B}(\mathbf{B}^{\mathsf{T}}\boldsymbol{\Omega}_\epsilon^{-1}\mathbf{B})^{-1}\mathbf{b} = \mathbf{P}\mathbf{b}$, *where* $\mathbf{P}$ *is the matrix whose columns are the FMPs associated to the factor model. These are introduced in Section 9.3.*

9.7.3 Optimality of FMPs

We now prove that FMPs emerge naturally from certain assumptions about returns and FMP composition, which we use in Section 9.3.

Theorem 9.1: *Consider a sequence of models* $(\mathbf{B}, \boldsymbol{\Omega}_{\mathrm{f}}, \boldsymbol{\Omega}_\epsilon^{(i)})$. *Assume that*

1. *Alpha orthogonal is zero, so that* $\boldsymbol{\alpha} = \mathbf{B}\boldsymbol{\lambda}$, *for some* $\boldsymbol{\lambda} \in \mathbb{R}^m$.
2. *Idiosyncratic variance converges to zero in norm:*

$$\lim_{i\to\infty} \left\| (\mathbf{B}^{\mathsf{T}}(\boldsymbol{\Omega}_\epsilon^{(i)})^{-1}\mathbf{B})^{-1} \right\| = 0$$

Then in the limit, the Sharpe-optimizing portfolio is a weighted sum of the FMPs, and the weights themselves solve an MVO in factor space:

$$\begin{aligned}
\mathbf{w}^\star &= \mathbf{P}\mathbf{u}^\star \\
\textit{where } \mathbf{u}^\star &= \arg\max\{\mathbf{u} \in \mathbb{R}^m | \boldsymbol{\lambda}^\top \mathbf{u} - (1/2\gamma)\mathbf{u}^\top \boldsymbol{\Omega}_\mathrm{f} \mathbf{u}\} \\
&= \gamma \boldsymbol{\Omega}_\mathrm{f}^{-1} \boldsymbol{\lambda}
\end{aligned}$$

for some $\gamma > 0$. The Sharpe Ratio of the optimal portfolio is equal to $SR^\star = \sqrt{\boldsymbol{\lambda}^\top \boldsymbol{\Omega}_\mathrm{f}^{-1} \boldsymbol{\lambda}}$.

The second condition on idiosyncratic variance has a simple interpretation. It is easy to check that the term inside the norm is $\mathbf{P}^\top \boldsymbol{\Omega}_\epsilon^{(i)} \mathbf{P}$, i.e., the covariance matrix of the idiosyncratic PnL of the FMPs. The condition states that the idiosyncratic variance of the FMPs goes to zero.

Proof. Start with the Sharpe-optimizing portfolio problem, Equation (9.8):

$$\begin{aligned}
&\max_{\mathbf{w} \in \mathbb{R}^n} \alpha^\top \mathbf{w} - \frac{1}{2\gamma} \mathbf{w}^\top \boldsymbol{\Omega}_\mathrm{r} \mathbf{w} \\
\Rightarrow \mathbf{w}^\star &= \gamma \boldsymbol{\Omega}_\mathrm{r}^{-1} \mathbf{B} \lambda \\
&= \gamma [(\boldsymbol{\Omega}_\epsilon^{(i)})^{-1} - (\boldsymbol{\Omega}_\epsilon^{(i)})^{-1} \mathbf{B} (\boldsymbol{\Omega}_\mathrm{f}^{-1} + \mathbf{B}^\top (\boldsymbol{\Omega}_\epsilon^{(i)})^{-1} \mathbf{B})^{-1} \mathbf{B}^\top (\boldsymbol{\Omega}_\epsilon^{(i)})^{-1}] \mathbf{B} \lambda
\end{aligned}$$

The second identity is the Woodbury–Sherman–Morrison Lemma.

Now we perform a first-order expansion: Notice that[12]

$$\left\| \boldsymbol{\Omega}_\mathrm{f}^{-1} (\mathbf{B}^\top (\boldsymbol{\Omega}_\epsilon^{(i)})^{-1} \mathbf{B})^{-1} \right\| \leq \left\| \boldsymbol{\Omega}_\mathrm{f}^{-1} \right\| \left\| (\mathbf{B}^\top (\boldsymbol{\Omega}_\epsilon^{(i)})^{-1} \mathbf{B})^{-1} \right\| \to 0, \qquad i \to \infty$$

So we perform a first-order approximation of the inverse[13]:

$$\begin{aligned}
(\boldsymbol{\Omega}_\mathrm{f}^{-1} + \mathbf{B}^\top (\boldsymbol{\Omega}_\epsilon^{(i)})^{-1} \mathbf{B})^{-1} &= [(\boldsymbol{\Omega}_\mathrm{f}^{-1} (\mathbf{B}^\top (\boldsymbol{\Omega}_\epsilon^{(i)})^{-1} \mathbf{B})^{-1} + \mathbf{I}_m)(\mathbf{B}^\top (\boldsymbol{\Omega}_\epsilon^{(i)})^{-1} \mathbf{B})]^{-1} \\
&\simeq (\mathbf{B}^\top (\boldsymbol{\Omega}_\epsilon^{(i)})^{-1} \mathbf{B})^{-1} [\mathbf{I}_m - \boldsymbol{\Omega}_\mathrm{f}^{-1} (\mathbf{B}^\top (\boldsymbol{\Omega}_\epsilon^{(i)})^{-1} \mathbf{B})^{-1}]
\end{aligned}$$

---

[12] Given two square matrices $\mathbf{A}, \mathbf{B}$, the inequality on spectral norms $||\mathbf{AB}|| \leq ||\mathbf{A}||\,||\mathbf{B}||$ holds.

[13] The first-order expansion (from von Neumann's series) is $(\mathbf{I} + \mathbf{A})^{-1} \simeq \mathbf{I} - \mathbf{A}$.

Replace the expression in the solution of $\mathbf{w}^\star$:

$$\begin{aligned}
\mathbf{w}^\star &= \gamma(\boldsymbol{\Omega}_\epsilon^{(i)})^{-1}[\mathbf{B} - \mathbf{B}(\mathbf{B}^\top(\boldsymbol{\Omega}_\epsilon^{(i)})^{-1}\mathbf{B})^{-1}[\mathbf{I}_m - \boldsymbol{\Omega}_\mathrm{f}^{-1}(\mathbf{B}^\top(\boldsymbol{\Omega}_\epsilon^{(i)})^{-1}\mathbf{B})^{-1}] \\
&\quad \mathbf{B}^\top(\boldsymbol{\Omega}_\epsilon^{(i)})\mathbf{B}]\lambda \\
&= \gamma(\boldsymbol{\Omega}_\epsilon^{(i)})^{-1}[\mathbf{B} - \mathbf{B}(\mathbf{B}^\top(\boldsymbol{\Omega}_\epsilon^{(i)})^{-1}\mathbf{B})^{-1}[\mathbf{B}^\top(\boldsymbol{\Omega}_\epsilon^{(i)})\mathbf{B} - \boldsymbol{\Omega}_\mathrm{f}^{-1}]]\lambda \\
&= \gamma(\boldsymbol{\Omega}_\epsilon^{(i)})^{-1}\mathbf{B}(\mathbf{B}^\top(\boldsymbol{\Omega}_\epsilon^{(i)})^{-1}\mathbf{B})^{-1}\boldsymbol{\Omega}_\mathrm{f}^{-1}\lambda \\
&= \mathbf{P}\mathbf{u}^\star
\end{aligned}$$

The expected PnL of the optimal solution is $\gamma\boldsymbol{\lambda}^\top\boldsymbol{\Omega}_\mathrm{f}^{-1}\boldsymbol{\lambda}$. The factor exposure of the optimal solution is $\gamma\boldsymbol{\Omega}_\mathrm{f}^{-1}\boldsymbol{\lambda}$. The factor variance is $\gamma^2\boldsymbol{\lambda}^\top\boldsymbol{\Omega}_\mathrm{f}^{-1}\boldsymbol{\lambda}$. The idiosyncratic variance is

$$\begin{aligned}
(\mathbf{w}^\star)^\top\boldsymbol{\Omega}_\epsilon^{(i)}\mathbf{w}^\star &= \mathbf{P}^\top\boldsymbol{\Omega}_\epsilon\mathbf{P} \\
&= (\mathbf{u}^\star)^\top(\mathbf{B}^\top(\boldsymbol{\Omega}_\epsilon^{(i)})^{-1}\mathbf{B})^{-1}\mathbf{u}^\star \\
&\le \left\|(\mathbf{B}^\top(\boldsymbol{\Omega}_\epsilon^{(i)})^{-1}\mathbf{B})^{-1}\right\| \left\|\mathbf{u}^\star\right\|^2
\end{aligned}$$

and is zero in the limit, per the second assumption. The Sharpe Ratio is $\sqrt{\boldsymbol{\lambda}^\top\boldsymbol{\Omega}_\mathrm{f}^{-1}\boldsymbol{\lambda}}$. ∎

9.7.4 Single-Factor Covariance Matrix Updating

Here we prove a basic result on the updated factor covariance matrix when adding a new factor. The analysis assumes that the parameters $\mathbf{B}, \boldsymbol{\Omega}_\mathrm{f}, \boldsymbol{\Omega}_\epsilon$ of the factor model are constant, and so is the vector $\mathbf{a}$ or characteristics that we are using to augment the factor model. As in Section 9.3.2.

Theorem 9.2: *Let the loadings, factor covariance matrix, and idiosyncratic of a factor model be* $\mathbf{B}, \boldsymbol{\Omega}_\mathrm{f}, \boldsymbol{\Omega}_\epsilon$, *and let* $\mathbf{a} \in \mathbb{R}^n$ *be a vector of characteristic. Define*

$$\mathbf{b}_{m+1} = (\mathbf{I}_n - \mathbf{B}(\mathbf{B}^\top\boldsymbol{\Omega}_\epsilon^{-1}\mathbf{B})^{-1}\mathbf{B}^\top\boldsymbol{\Omega}_\epsilon^{-1})\mathbf{a}$$

The factor covariance matrix associated to the model with loadings $[\mathbf{B}|\mathbf{b}_{m+1}]$ *is given by*

$$\tilde{\boldsymbol{\Omega}}_\mathrm{f} \simeq \begin{bmatrix} \boldsymbol{\Omega}_\mathrm{f} & \mathbf{0} \\ \mathbf{0} & \hat{\sigma}^2_{m+1} \end{bmatrix}$$

Proof. Let the factor return of the new factor be

$$\hat{f}_{m+1,t} = \left(\frac{\mathbf{b}_{m+1}^{\top} \boldsymbol{\Omega}_{\epsilon}^{-1}}{\mathbf{b}_{m+1}^{\top} \boldsymbol{\Omega}_{\epsilon}^{-1} \mathbf{b}_{m+1}} \right) \mathbf{r}_t$$
$$= \mathbf{v}_{m+1}^{\top} \mathbf{r}_t$$

as in Equation (9.14). We assume that the new factor does not have a big impact on the idiosyncratic returns in the sense that $|b_{m+1,i}\hat{f}_{m+1,t}| \ll |\epsilon_{t,i}|$, so that $\boldsymbol{\Omega}_{\epsilon}$ is approximately unchanged by the addition of the new factor. Then the volatility of the new factor is $\hat{\sigma}_{m+1} = (\mathbf{b}_{m+1}^{\top} \boldsymbol{\Omega}_{\epsilon}^{-1} \mathbf{b}_{m+1})^{-1/2}$:

$$\hat{f}_{m+1,t}^2 = \frac{E(\mathbf{b}_{m+1}^{\top} \boldsymbol{\Omega}_{\epsilon}^{-1} \epsilon_t \epsilon_t^{\top} \boldsymbol{\Omega}_{\epsilon}^{-1} \mathbf{b}_{m+1})}{(\mathbf{b}_{m+1}^{\top} \boldsymbol{\Omega}_{\epsilon}^{-1} \mathbf{b}_{m+1})^2}$$

$$\Rightarrow \hat{\sigma}_{m+1}^2 = \frac{\mathbf{b}_{m+1}^{\top} \boldsymbol{\Omega}_{\epsilon}^{-1} \boldsymbol{\Omega}_{\epsilon} \boldsymbol{\Omega}_{\epsilon}^{-1} \mathbf{b}_{m+1}}{(\mathbf{b}_{m+1}^{\top} \boldsymbol{\Omega}_{\epsilon}^{-1} \mathbf{b}_{m+1})^2}$$
$$= (\mathbf{b}_{m+1}^{\top} \boldsymbol{\Omega}_{\epsilon}^{-1} \mathbf{b}_{m+1})^{-1}$$

We show that $\hat{f}_{m+1}$ is approximately uncorrelated to the first m factors. The column vector of the first m factor returns is $\mathbf{P}^{\top}\mathbf{r}_t$:

$$\begin{aligned} E(\mathbf{f}\hat{f}_{m+1}) &= E(\mathbf{P}^{\top}\mathbf{r}_t \mathbf{r}_t^{\top} \mathbf{v}_{m+1}) \\ &= \hat{\sigma}_{m+1}^2 \mathbf{P}^{\top} \boldsymbol{\Omega}_{\mathbf{r}} \boldsymbol{\Omega}_{\epsilon}^{-1} \mathbf{b}_{m+1} \\ &= \hat{\sigma}_{m+1}^2 \mathbf{P}^{\top} (\mathbf{B} \boldsymbol{\Omega}_{\mathbf{f}} \mathbf{B}^{\top} + \boldsymbol{\Omega}_{\epsilon}) \boldsymbol{\Omega}_{\epsilon}^{-1} \mathbf{b}_{m+1} \\ &= \hat{\sigma}_{m+1}^2 (\boldsymbol{\Omega}_{\mathbf{f}} (\mathbf{B}^{\top} \boldsymbol{\Omega}_{\epsilon}^{-1} \mathbf{b}_{m+1}) + \mathbf{P}^{\top} \boldsymbol{\Omega}_{\epsilon}^{-1} \mathbf{b}_{m+1}) \\ &= \mathbf{P}^{\top} \boldsymbol{\Omega}_{\epsilon} \mathbf{v}_{m+1} \end{aligned}$$

The last equality follows from the orthogonality of $\mathbf{b}_{m+1}$. The correlation between FMPs is given by the idiosyncratic component of their returns, which should be small if the factors are diversified. ∎

The Takeaways

1. Mean-Variance Optimization (MVO) is a foundational approach to portfolio construction due to its interpretability, data efficiency, and computational simplicity in single-period settings.
2. Factor models enable systematic decomposition of portfolio risk and return by representing asset covariance through factors, simplifying the optimization process and enhancing interpretability.
3. The Sharpe Ratio is central to portfolio evaluation, representing return in units of risk, and is commonly used in maximizing portfolio efficiency under risk constraints.
4. Factor-Mimicking Portfolios (FMPs) are valuable tools in factor-based investing, enabling efficient trading strategies focused on specific characteristics.
5. The Information Ratio (IR) is influenced by both the quality of forecasts (Information Coefficient, IC) and the degree of diversification, providing a comprehensive measure of performance potential.
6. Centralized portfolio construction can be equivalent to a decentralized approach when both follow MVO principles, but practical differences like transaction costs and constraints may make one approach preferable.

Chapter 10

Beyond Simple Mean-Variance

The Questions

1. When does Mean-Variance Optimization (MVO) suggest shorting an asset with positive returns, and under what conditions is this counterintuitive recommendation justifiable?
2. How do different types of constraints (e.g., on market exposure, trading costs, portfolio turnover) address investor preferences, regulatory requirements, or practical considerations in portfolio construction?
3. What are the potential benefits and drawbacks of using penalties instead of hard constraints in portfolio optimization?
4. How do forecast errors in expected returns affect the realized Sharpe Ratio of an optimal portfolio?
5. In what way does the error in estimating the covariance affect Sharpe Ratio?

10.1 Shortcomings of Naïve MVO

Before introducing more complex optimizations, let's work through a simple example—maybe the simplest instance of the simplest optimization problem—to illustrate the implications of MVO. We have just two assets, with non-negative Sharpe Ratios s_1, s_2. Their returns have correlation ρ. The inverse of the covariance matrix is

$$\mathbf{C}^{-1} = \frac{1}{1-\rho^2}\begin{bmatrix} 1 & -\rho \\ -\rho & 1 \end{bmatrix}$$

So by Equation (9.6), the optimal volatility allocation is

$$v_1^\star = \frac{\kappa}{1-\rho^2}(s_1 - \rho s_2)$$
$$v_2^\star = \frac{\kappa}{1-\rho^2}(s_2 - \rho s_1)$$

where $\kappa > 0$ is a parameter determined by the risk tolerance or by the constraint on maximum portfolio risk. If $s_2/s_1 < \rho$, then we short asset 2. Consider first the case where $s_2 = 0$ and $\rho > 0$. In this case, we always short the asset. Asset 2 acts as *hedge*. Shorting it is beneficial because (a) it has no cost (zero expected return); (b) it reduces the volatility of the portfolio, since it is positively correlated to asset 1. When the Sharpe Ratio of asset 2 is positive, then there is a cost to shorting. A short position in asset 2 reduces volatility, but in order to improve the Sharpe Ratio, the correlation ρ must exceed the threshold s_2/s_1.

Even though the recommendation to short an asset with positive returns is explainable, it is probably at odds with the intuition of many readers. If two assets are very correlated, wouldn't it be preferable to go long both, thus averaging out the signal error? We can make this reasoning more rigorous by assessing the impact of estimation error on expected returns and on the correlation.

Impact of errors in forecasted Sharpe Ratios. We denote the *true* Sharpe Ratios $\tilde{s}_i$, and assume that the error between the true and forecasted Sharpe Ratios is bounded: $||\tilde{\mathbf{s}} - \mathbf{s}|| \leq \epsilon$. We choose optimal dollar volatilities based on forecasted Sharpe Ratios $\mathbf{v}^\star$, and observe performance that is a function of $\tilde{\mathbf{s}}$. The realized expected return is

$$E(\mathrm{PnL}) = \frac{\kappa}{1-\rho^2}[(s_1 - \rho s_2)\tilde{s}_1 + (s_2 - \rho s_1)\tilde{s}_2]$$

Insight 10.1: *A simple linear-quadratic problem*

Let $\mathbf{a}, \mathbf{x}_0 \in \mathbb{R}^n$. The problem $\min \left\{ \langle \mathbf{a}, \mathbf{x} \rangle \middle| \left\| \mathbf{x} - \mathbf{x}_0 \right\|^2 \leq \epsilon^2 \right\}$ has solution

$$\mathbf{x}^\star = \mathbf{x}_0 - \frac{\mathbf{a}}{\|\mathbf{a}\|}\epsilon$$

$$\frac{\langle \mathbf{a}, \mathbf{x}^\star \rangle}{\langle \mathbf{a}, \mathbf{x}_0 \rangle} - 1 = -\frac{\|\mathbf{a}\|}{\langle \mathbf{a}, \mathbf{x}_0 \rangle}\epsilon$$

In the worst case, we solve the problem

$$\begin{aligned} &\min E(\text{PnL}) \\ &\text{s.t. } \|\tilde{\mathbf{s}} - \mathbf{s}\| \leq \epsilon \\ &\tilde{\mathbf{s}} \in \mathbb{R}^2 \end{aligned}$$

I leave the solution as an exercise (also, see Insight 10.1); the relative reduction in PnL is

$$-\frac{\sqrt{(s_1 - \rho s_2)^2 + (s_2 - \rho s_1)^2}}{(s_1 - \rho s_2)s_1 + (s_2 - \rho s_1)s_2}\epsilon$$

This is also the relative loss in Sharpe, since the volatility of the portfolio is unaffected by return forecast error. Figure 10.1 shows numerical results for two assets, assuming an error $\epsilon = 0.5$ and varying levels of correlation. An error of 0.5 is perhaps conservative; actual differences in forecasted versus realized Sharpe Ratios are higher. Notice that high correlation makes things worse. In all scenarios, the percentage in efficiency is significant. It is of course lower for higher Sharpes (because the relative forecasting error is smaller); and is higher for higher correlations. In all cases it exceeds 10% and can be as high as 50%.

Impact of errors in correlation among assets. We repeat the analysis, but allowing for error in the assets' correlation ρ. We denote the true correlation $\tilde{\rho}$ and assume that the estimation error is bounded: $|\tilde{\rho} - \rho| \leq \epsilon$. The error in estimated correlation affects the volatility; the return is not

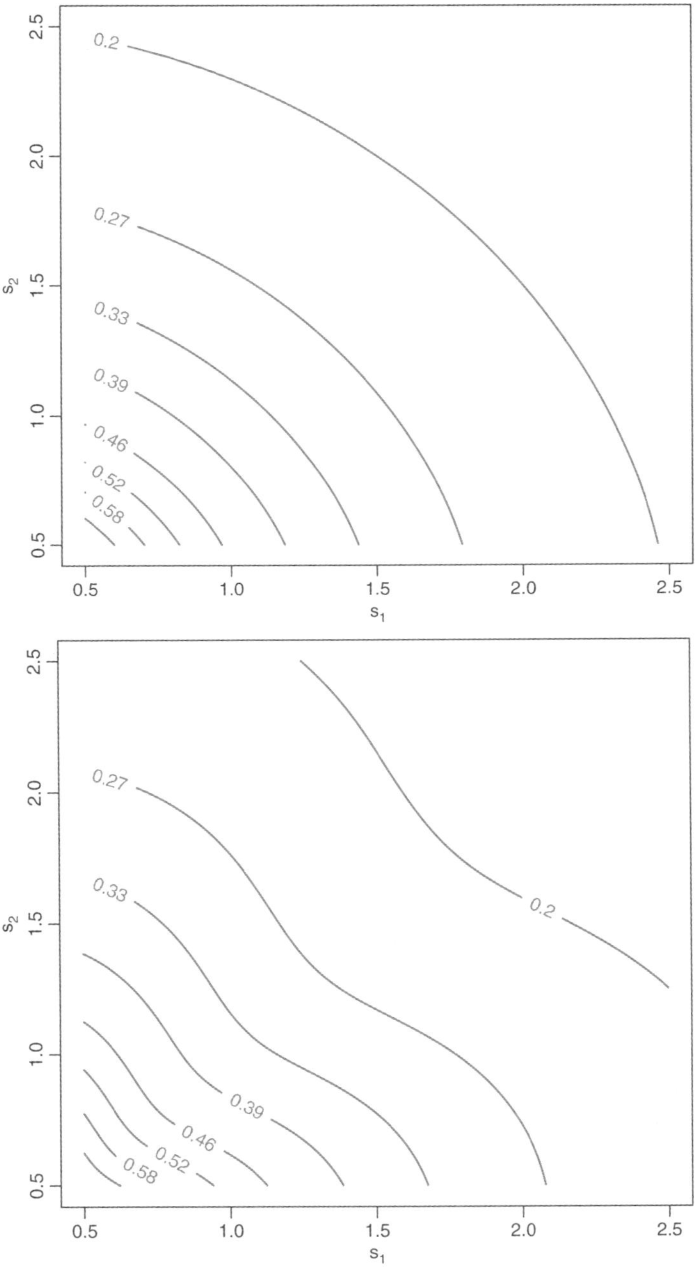

Figure 10.1 Level plots of the loss of PnL (and Sharpe Ratio) as a function of the Sharpe Ratio of two assets, assuming a maximum error ϵ in the Sharpe Ratio norm. Parameters: $\epsilon = 0.5$; Correlation: $\rho = 0.1$ (top), $\rho = 0.5$ (bottom).

affected. The Sharpe Ratio is minimized when the realized volatility is maximized:

$$\begin{aligned} &\max\ (\mathbf{V}^\star)^\top \widetilde{\mathbf{C}}\mathbf{V}^\star \\ &\text{s.t. } |\tilde{\rho} - \rho| \le \epsilon \\ &\rho \in \mathbb{R} \end{aligned}$$

In this case the worst-case realized relative volatility (exercise!) is

$$\sqrt{(\mathbf{V}^\star)^\top \mathbf{C}\mathbf{V}^\star + 2\epsilon|v_1^\star v_2^\star|}$$

and the associated relative loss in Sharpe Ratio is

$$\sqrt{\frac{(\mathbf{V}^\star)^\top \mathbf{C}\mathbf{V}^\star}{(\mathbf{V}^\star)^\top \mathbf{C}\mathbf{V}^\star + 2\epsilon|v_1^\star v_2^\star|}} - 1$$

We show the impact of the error in Figure 10.2, for a reasonable error in correlation estimate of 0.1. However, in periods of crisis, the error can be larger (albeit not dramatically so). In Figure 10.3 I show the impact of correlation error on Sharpe.

Insight 10.2: *Degradation in performance due to forecasting error*

When we use naïve MVO optimization, the degradation in Sharpe Ratio arising from forecasted (*ex-ante*) parameters for volatilities and returns versus realized values (*ex post*) can easily range in the 10–50%.

10.2 Constraints and Modified Objectives

Equation (9.2) is the starting point for more complex optimization problems. They reflect the detailed preferences of the investors, short-term concerns, regulatory constraints, and implementation considerations.

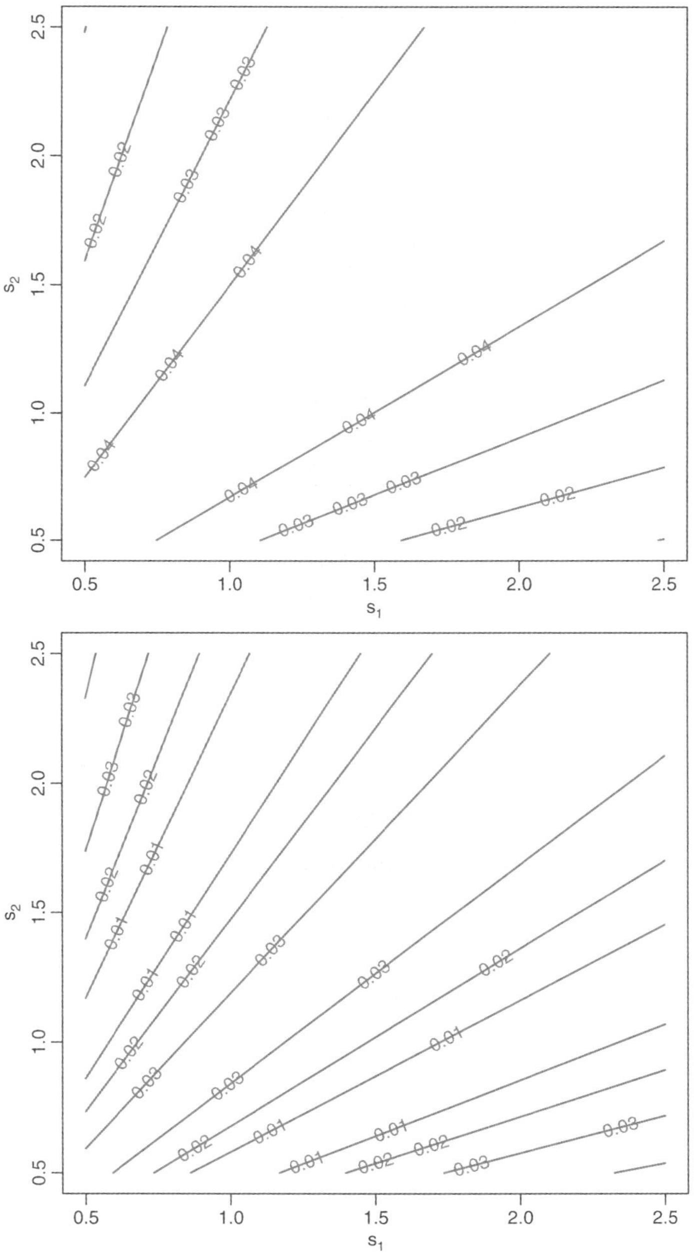

Figure 10.2 Level plots of the loss of PnL (and Sharpe Ratio) as a function of the Sharpe Ratio of two assets, assuming a maximum error ϵ in the correlation. Parameters: $\epsilon = 0.1$; Correlation: $\rho = 0.1$ (top), $\rho = 0.5$ (bottom).

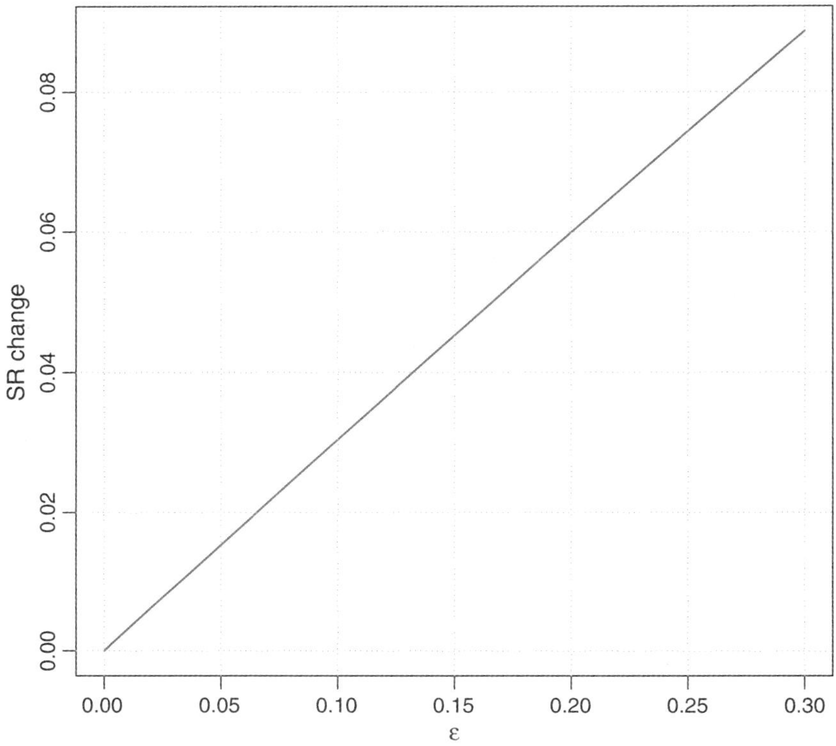

Figure 10.3 Fraction loss in Sharpe Ratio for two strategies with Sharpe Ratios of 3 and 2, return correlation $\rho = 0.3$, and error ϵ ranging from 0 to 0.3.

In applications, optimization formulations differ widely because they address a wide range of concerns.

- *Investor's preferences*: "Keep medium-term momentum exposure exactly equal to zero."
- *Tactical considerations*: "Don't trade this stock because it could be acquired tomorrow" or "liquidate this stock because it could be acquired tomorrow"; both are valid, if incompatible, concerns.
- *Regulatory considerations*: "The portfolio must be long only".
- *Fiduciary considerations*: "The portfolio must *track* a benchmark, i.e., the difference in returns between the portfolio's returns and the benchmark's cannot exceed a certain *tracking volatility*".
- *Implementation considerations*: "The objective function must include the trading costs."

From a modeling viewpoint, constraints can take several forms. We introduce those first, and then we map them to the applications at hand. The "mapping" part will be either instructive if you have never been exposed to it, or terminally boring if you have worked in portfolio management for a few years. Rejoice with the former group, and commiserate with the latter.

10.2.1 Types of Constraints

Although one can imagine infinite types of constraints, some of them are much more common than others. We review them below.

- *Linear constraints.* These can be inequality or equality constraints:

$$\begin{aligned} \mathbf{A}^{\mathsf{T}}\mathbf{w} &\leq \mathbf{c} \quad \textit{(Inequality constraints)} \\ \mathbf{A}^{\mathsf{T}}\mathbf{w} &= \mathbf{c} \quad \textit{(Equality constraints)} \end{aligned} \tag{10.1}$$

  These are perhaps the most common constraints in financial optimization, because they are used to address several of the concerns listed at the beginning of the section. For example, some strategies are required to be *long-only*. The constraint is simply

$$\mathbf{w} \geq 0 \qquad \textit{(Long-Only constraint)}$$

  Extending this to a bound on maximum short and long size for a single position is only a small step. The main rationales for such constraints are many. There are natural limits due to maximum institutional ownership of a stock (say, no more than 5% of the outstanding stocks); or to the maximum risk concentration in a stock: the idiosyncratic variance of a stock may not exceed a certain percentage of the total idiosyncratic variance, which translates to a linear constraint. Furthermore, we may impose a maximum liquidation cost requirement on all stocks; which also becomes a constraint on single position size.

  A slightly more complex constraint, which does not seem linear at first sight, is on GMV: $\sum_i |w_i| \leq G$. This constraint may originate on limits on financial leverage that the fund can apply to its managed assets. The constraint may be turned into a linear one[1] by introducing

[1] Before rediscovering the wheel, know that some financial optimization packages abstract the modeling of the GMV constraint, so that you just have to specify it.

ancillary variables representing the long and short side of a position, and additional constraints:

$$\mathbf{x} \geq 0 \qquad \textit{(long positions)} \tag{10.2}$$

$$\mathbf{y} \geq 0 \qquad \textit{(short positions)} \tag{10.3}$$

$$\mathbf{w} = \mathbf{x} - \mathbf{y} \qquad \textit{(portfolio)} \tag{10.4}$$

$$\sum_i (x_i + y_i) \leq G \qquad \textit{(GMV constraint)} \tag{10.5}$$

A similar constraint is on the long versus short ratio.[2] If we want the long/short ratio to be equal to a certain value, then the constraint is $\sum_i x_i = K \sum_i y_i$. This constraint is the same as the GMV constraint, with the exception of Equation (10.5), which we replace with

$$\sum_i x_i = K \sum_i y_i \qquad \textit{(Long/Short ratio constraint)}$$

Yet another class of constraint is that on factor model exposures, and on exposures to other asset characteristics not in the model. An example is the constraint on historical market betas β_i. The constraint then is $\sum_i \beta_i w_i = b_0$. The general form of factor exposure is *verbatim* that of Equation (10.1).

A constraint on maximum portfolio turnover takes a similar form to the previous constraints that use absolute values. I am leaving it as an exercise to the reader. The turnover constraint may be either (poorly) justified to control costs, or by fiduciary requirements on portfolio turnover. A better way to model execution costs takes us in the domain of non-linear constraints.

- *Non-linear constraints*. A constraint of a different nature is trading-related. Trading occurs over many periods, and one approach to control excessive trading is to limit the traded capital, possibly weighted to account for asset-specific trading cost, in each portfolio rebalancing. This is equivalent to assuming linear transaction costs. We generalize this at little cost, and model trading costs as superlinear in the traded amount but

[2] For example, a few years ago, *130/30 portfolios* were popular. These strategies managed net-long portfolios, with 30% of NMV invested in shorts and 130% invested in longs.

growing at a quadratic rate or less: $c_i|\Delta w_i|^\gamma$, where $\gamma \in [1, 2]$ and $c_i > 0$. The constraint takes the form

$$\sum_i c_i|w_i - w_i^{\text{start}}|^\gamma \leq C \qquad \textit{(Trading cost constraint)}$$

where $\mathbf{w}^{\text{start}}$ is the portfolio held at the beginning of the period. The constraint is convex, so that the portfolio optimization problem has a unique solution.

Quadratic constraints appear naturally when we want to control risk at a finer resolution than that on total variance. For example, let $\mathbf{\Omega_f}^{\text{style}}$ be the principal submatrix in the factor covariance matrix, and let $\mathbf{b}^{\text{style}} = (\mathbf{B}^{\text{style}})^\intercal \mathbf{w}$ be the vector of style-factor exposures. Then a constraint on the maximum style-factor risk becomes

$$\mathbf{b}^{\text{style}} = (\mathbf{B}^{\text{style}})^\intercal \mathbf{w}$$
$$(\mathbf{b}^{\text{style}})^\intercal \mathbf{\Omega_f}^{\text{style}} \mathbf{b}^{\text{style}} \leq \sigma^2_{\text{style}} \qquad \textit{(Style-factor vol constraint)}$$

Risk constraints are often not only applied to the positions of a portfolio, but to the *active* positions of the portfolio itself. For example, consider a long-only portfolio with a GMV of \$1B, and let $\mathbf{w}^{\text{bench}}$ be the positions of a portfolio with the same GMV, with weights proportional to those of the S&P500 benchmark. The *active holdings* are $\mathbf{w}^{\text{a}} = \mathbf{w} - \mathbf{w}^{\text{bench}}$. *Tracking error* is the volatility of the active portfolio, and is a measure of the freedom the portfolio manager has in selecting stocks. A constraint on the tracking error is

$$(\mathbf{w}^a)^\intercal \mathbf{\Omega_r} \mathbf{w}^a \leq \sigma_a^2 \qquad \textit{(Tracking error constraint)}$$

- *Non-convex constraints*. Finally, there are a few constraint types that lead to a non-convex feasible region. Finding a global optimum is in general NP-hard. Convex solvers may either not accept such constraints,[3] or may not converge. I would argue that, in most cases, these constraints should *not* be used on grounds of sensible modeling. I am presenting them both for completeness and as a cautionary tale.

  The first constraint type is on the maximum number N_{max} of assets in the portfolio. This is usually implemented by introducing 0/1 variables

[3] Some solvers are able to understand from the description of the problem whether it is convex or not.

x_i, and by setting a maximum (large) absolute position size M. The constraint becomes

$$|w_i| \leq Mx_i \qquad i = 1, \ldots, n \qquad \textit{(Max number of positions)} \tag{10.6}$$

$$\sum_{i=1}^{n} x_i \leq N_{\text{max}} \tag{10.7}$$

$$x_i \in \{0, 1\} \qquad i = 1, \ldots, n \tag{10.8}$$

The rationale for this constraint is that a very broad portfolio may be too burdensome to trade or manage. This combinatorial constraint can be handled by some commercial solvers for realistic problem instances with thousands of assets. However, its utility is limited. It is usually preferable to model trading costs directly, and either not include a constraint at all, or have a threshold for trading below which the trades of the optimal solution are set to zero. This usually has a negligible impact on optimality.

A very different type of constraint is on the minimum idio variance as a percentage of the total variance. We have mentioned this metric in Section 4.5.2. It is tempting to include a constraint of the form

$$\mathbf{w}^\top \mathbf{\Omega}_\epsilon \mathbf{w} \geq p_{\text{idio}} \mathbf{w}^\top \mathbf{\Omega}_\mathbf{r} \mathbf{w} \tag{10.9}$$

or, equivalently,

$$\mathbf{w}^\top [p_{\text{idio}} \mathbf{B} \mathbf{\Omega}_\mathbf{f} \mathbf{B}^\top - (1 - p_{\text{idio}}) \mathbf{\Omega}_\epsilon] \mathbf{w} \leq 0 \tag{10.10}$$

The problem is that the matrix $p_{\text{idio}} \mathbf{B} \mathbf{\Omega}_\mathbf{f} \mathbf{B}^\top - (1 - p_{\text{idio}}) \mathbf{\Omega}_\epsilon$ is in general not positive-definite, and therefore the constraint is not convex (exercise: prove it by providing an example).

A constraint type with a similar objective is to require a minimum idiosyncratic dollar volatility: $\mathbf{w}^\top \mathbf{\Omega}_\epsilon \mathbf{w} \geq \sigma^2_{\text{idio}}$. This is obviously a non-convex constraint, and its proponents should be excommunicated from the Orthodox Church of Optimization. A sensible approach is to simply upper bound the factor variance, or impose bounds of factor exposures, and test the impact of the bound on the portfolio's performance.

Yet another excommunicable offense is imposing a lower bound on total volatility. I would not mention it, had I not witnessed actual humans proposing it.

In the same spirit, i.e., the goal of ensuring that the portfolio meets a minimum size, is a lower bound on GMV. The answer to these constraints is that they are usually ill-conceived. If, after accounting for excess return forecasts, trading costs, and risk constraints, the optimal portfolio is small, then maybe it should stay small. And if one really wants to make it bigger (again, not advisable), one could loosen the upper bounds on risk or underestimate the transaction costs.

10.2.2 Do Constraints Improve or Worsen Performance?

The naïve answer to the title of this section is that—of course!—they worsen performance. If you reduce the feasible region of your optimization problem by adding a constraint, you will not get a better optimum. Specifically, if we maximize the Sharpe Ratio, adding constraints will degrade the Sharpe Ratio.[4] This is true if the data in the problem, i.e., covariance matrix and expected returns, are estimated correctly. If we take estimation error into account, however, constraints may help. The next section interprets constraints as regularization terms for parameters entering in the optimization.[5]

10.2.3 Constraints as Penalties

One alternative way to interpret a constraint in portfolio optimization is as a penalty term added to the objective function: given a problem

$$\begin{aligned} &\max f(\mathbf{x}) \\ &\text{s.t. } g(\mathbf{x}) \leq a \end{aligned}$$

with optimal solution $\mathbf{x}^\star(a)$, there is a $\lambda^\star(a) > 0$ such that

$$\max f(\mathbf{x}) - \lambda^\star(a) g(\mathbf{x})$$

has the same solution $\mathbf{x}^\star(a)$. We used this result at the beginning of the chapter. The parameter $\lambda^\star(a)$ can also be interpreted as a sensitivity to the constraint's right-hand-side parameter a. The variable λ is the marginal change in the optimum when we increase (or "relax") a: $df(\mathbf{x}^\star(a))/da = \lambda(a)$. Since a commercial solver returns both $\mathbf{x}^\star$ and $\lambda^\star$, this means that we

[4] For example, see Clarke et al. (2002).

[5] The academic literature on this subject is not very large. See Jagannathan and Ma (2003) for an early contribution to the analysis of long-only constraints; the work by DeMiguel et al. (2009a,b) on trading penalties; Fan et al. (2012) on GMV constraints and Ceria et al. (2012); Saxena and Stubbs (2013) on penalties on the factor covariance matrix.

get sensitivities at zero additional cost. This result also opens up a different modeling approach. What if we converted constraints into penalties? We now know that the outcome, for the appropriate penalizing coefficient, is the same. Does this mean that the approaches are equivalent? The answer is no, and the remainder of this section is devoted to illustrating the difference.

First, let us focus our attention on the meaning of constraints and penalties. There are constraints that are commensurable with the objective, and that are naturally expressed as penalties. For example, you could put a constraint on maximum trading costs. However, costs and expected PnL in the objective have the same unit (dollar) and it makes more sense to express the objective function as the difference of PnL and trading cost. The penalty parameter is simply one. What about risk? If we fix the time interval, the variance constraint has the dimension of dollar squared, and is therefore not commensurable to PnL in the objective. What we could add to the objective function is $\sqrt{\mathbf{w}^\top \mathbf{\Omega}_r \mathbf{w}}$. This is possible in some optimization packages.[6] However, if we know the approximate value σ_0 of final volatility, we can choose a penalty parameter such that the adding a volatility term or a variance one gives a similar result. We do so by linearizing in the region of the optimum portfolio:

$$-\lambda\sqrt{\sigma_0^2 + (\mathbf{w}^\top \mathbf{\Omega}_r \mathbf{w} - \sigma_0^2)} \simeq -\frac{\lambda\sigma_0}{2} - \frac{\lambda}{2\sigma_0}\mathbf{w}^\top \mathbf{\Omega}_r \mathbf{w}$$

The constant term is irrelevant to the optimization problem, and the volatility is locally approximated by a variance.

A second class of constraints does not have an obvious interpretation. Should we add the constraint on GMV as a penalty? Or long-only constraints? The answer, somewhat surprisingly, is that adding those constraints as a penalty may actually help the performance of the optimized portfolio, when the parameters in the model are not accurately estimated.

Let us start with an augmented version of Problem (9.8):

$$\begin{aligned} &\max\ \boldsymbol{\alpha}^\top \mathbf{w} - \lambda \mathbf{w}^\top \mathbf{\Omega}_r \mathbf{w} \\ &\text{s.t. } \|\mathbf{w}\|^2 \leq G \end{aligned} \tag{10.11}$$

[6] A volatility constraint or penalty is in practice computationally more burdensome to solve than a variance constraint or penalty.

whose penalized version is

$$\max \boldsymbol{\alpha}^\top \mathbf{w} - \lambda \mathbf{w}^\top \boldsymbol{\Omega}_\mathbf{r} \mathbf{w} - \nu \|\mathbf{w}\|^2 \tag{10.12}$$

This problem can interpreted in many different ways. The first one is a simple rewriting of the quadratic terms as $\lambda \mathbf{w}^\top(\boldsymbol{\Omega}_\mathbf{r} + (\nu/\lambda)\mathbf{I}_n)\mathbf{w} =: \mathbf{w}^\top \tilde{\boldsymbol{\Omega}}_\mathbf{r} \mathbf{w}$. The problem then is an MVO with a modified covariance matrix. The correlations $\rho_{i,j}$ of the original covariance matrix have been reduced by a factor $(1 + \nu/\lambda\sigma_i)^{-1}(1 + \nu/\lambda\sigma_j)^{-1}$. The asset variances have been increased, and are more similar to each other; in the limit $\nu \to \infty$ they are identical. The norm constraint therefore has a "regularizing" effect on the solution. There are different optimization formulations that lead to the same solution of the Optimization Problem (10.12).

1. *Uncertain alpha* (Stubbs and Vance, 2005). Let us start with the assumption that the vector $\boldsymbol{\alpha}$ is not known with accuracy. We make the assumption that the vector is distributed according to a multivariate Gaussian: $\boldsymbol{\alpha} \sim N(\boldsymbol{\alpha}_0, \tau^2 \mathbf{I}_n)$. We still solve an MVO, taking into account alpha uncertainty:

   $$\text{var}(\mathbf{r}^\top \mathbf{w}) = \text{var}(\boldsymbol{\alpha}^\top \mathbf{w}) + \text{var}[(\mathbf{r} - \boldsymbol{\alpha})^\top \mathbf{w}] = \mathbf{w}^\top(\tau^2 \mathbf{I}_n + \boldsymbol{\Omega}_\mathbf{r})\mathbf{w}$$

   The MVO formulation is again the same as that of Equation (9.8), but with a modified covariance matrix. As in the case of Equation (10.12), the variances are made more equal, and correlations are shrunk toward zero.
2. *Robust alpha* (Pedersen et al., 2021). Instead of modeling alphas' imperfect estimation by assuming that we know their distribution, we model their error deterministically, and adversarially: we know that the true alphas are within a certain distance d from our estimate and, as we did at the beginning of the chapter, we look at the worst case, i.e., the realized alpha is the worst possible one among the admissible realizations. In formulas, we solve

   $$\max \mathbf{a}^\top \mathbf{w} - \lambda \mathbf{w}^\top \boldsymbol{\Omega}_\mathbf{r} \mathbf{w} \tag{10.13}$$
   $$\text{s.t. } \mathbf{a} = \arg\min_{\mathbf{x}} \{\mathbf{x}^\top \mathbf{w} \mid \|\mathbf{x} - \boldsymbol{\alpha}\|^2 \le d^2\} \tag{10.14}$$

   We know the solution to the nested Problem (10.14): from Insight 10.1, it is equal to $\mathbf{a} = \boldsymbol{\alpha} - d\mathbf{w}/\|\mathbf{w}\|$. Hence we solve

   $$\max \boldsymbol{\alpha}^\top \mathbf{w} - \lambda \mathbf{w}^\top \boldsymbol{\Omega}_\mathbf{r} \mathbf{w} - d\|\mathbf{w}\| \tag{10.15}$$

This is similar, but not identical, to Equation (10.12): the norm penalty term is not squared. The same argument can be made to show that the norm and the norm squared are interchangeable, once the penalty constant d is rescaled: $d\|\mathbf{w}\| \simeq (d/\|\mathbf{w}_0\|)\|\mathbf{w}\|^2$, for a $\|\mathbf{w}_0\|$ close to $\|\mathbf{w}\|$ of the final solution.

3. *Robust factors* (Ceria et al., 2012). We consider another instance of constrained optimization. A recurrent theme in this book is model misspecification. Factor models can be misspecified (both in their factor structure and in their expected returns), but they also offer remedies. Consider the case of an omitted factor. As a special case of misspecification, its effect is to worsen the Sharpe Ratio of the MVO portfolio. In order to reduce the impact, let us consider again an adversarial approach. Assume that there is a hidden factor, whose loadings we do not know, but whose volatility τ is given. We use this as a parameter to quantify the importance of the omitted factor.

   The new factor model contains an additional factor loading $\mathbf{v}$ orthogonal to $\mathbf{B}$. The covariance matrix is

$$\tilde{\mathbf{\Omega}}_{\mathbf{r}} = \mathbf{\Omega}_{\mathbf{r}} + \tau^2 \mathbf{v}\mathbf{v}^{\top}$$

   We solve

$$\max_{\mathbf{w}} \min_{\|\mathbf{v}\|\le 1} \boldsymbol{\alpha}^{\top}\mathbf{w} - \lambda \mathbf{w}^{\top}(\mathbf{\Omega}_{\mathbf{r}} + \tau^2 \mathbf{v}\mathbf{v}^{\top})\mathbf{w}$$

$$\max_{\mathbf{w}} \boldsymbol{\alpha}^{\top}\mathbf{w} - \lambda \mathbf{w}^{\top}\left(\mathbf{\Omega}_{\mathbf{r}} + \frac{\tau^2}{\|\mathbf{w}\|^2}\mathbf{w}\mathbf{w}^{\top}\right)\mathbf{w}$$

$$\max_{\mathbf{w}} \boldsymbol{\alpha}^{\top}\mathbf{w} - \lambda \mathbf{w}^{\top}(\mathbf{\Omega}_{\mathbf{r}} + \tau^2 \mathbf{I}_n)\mathbf{w}$$

   So, yet again, we are solving an optimization problem with a penalized covariance matrix.

4. *Robust asset correlations* (Boyd et al., 2016). Here we have another case of adversarial modeling that is expressed as a penalization term. Assume that we estimate the asset correlation matrix terms with some error independent of the asset pair, so that the difference between the estimated correlation and the true correlation is at most $|\rho_{i,j} - \hat{\rho}_{i,j}| \le d$. The adversarial model looks for a solution to the MVO problem, where

an adversary ("Nature") chooses the covariance matrix with the highest variance compatible with the error bound:

$$\max \mathbf{a}^{\mathsf{T}}\mathbf{w} - \lambda\sigma^2 \tag{10.16}$$

$$\text{s.t. } \sigma^2(\mathbf{w}) = \arg \max_{\Delta \in \mathbb{R}^{n\times n}} \mathbf{w}^{\mathsf{T}}(\boldsymbol{\Omega}_{\mathbf{r}} + \boldsymbol{\Delta})\mathbf{w} \tag{10.17}$$

$$\text{s.t.} |[\boldsymbol{\Delta}]_{i,j}| \le d\sqrt{[\boldsymbol{\Omega}]_{i,i}[\boldsymbol{\Omega}]_{j,j}},\ i, j = 1, \ldots, n \tag{10.18}$$

The objective of the nested problem is equivalent to

$$\mathbf{w}^{\mathsf{T}}\boldsymbol{\Delta}\mathbf{w} = \sum_{i,j} w_i w_j \sqrt{[\boldsymbol{\Omega}]_{i,i}[\boldsymbol{\Omega}]_{j,j}}\rho_{i,j} \tag{10.19}$$

Every term is maximized when $\rho_{i,j} = d \times \operatorname{sgn}\left(w_i w_j\right)$, and the objective function value is

$$(\mathbf{w}^{\star})^{\mathsf{T}}\boldsymbol{\Delta}\mathbf{w}^{\star} = d\sum_{i,j} |w_i w_j|\sqrt{[\boldsymbol{\Omega}]_{i,i}[\boldsymbol{\Omega}]_{j,j}} \tag{10.20}$$

$$= d\left(\sum_{i} |w_i|\sqrt{[\boldsymbol{\Omega}]_{i,i}}\right) \tag{10.21}$$

$$= d\,\|\mathbf{V}\mathbf{w}\|_1 \tag{10.22}$$

where $\mathbf{V}$ is a diagonal covariance matrix whose ith diagonal term is the volatility of asset i. Let us plug this back in the original problem:

$$\max\ \mathbf{a}^{\mathsf{T}}\mathbf{w} - \lambda\mathbf{w}^{\mathsf{T}}\boldsymbol{\Omega}_{\mathbf{r}}\mathbf{w} - \lambda d\,\|\mathbf{V}\mathbf{w}\|_1 \tag{10.23}$$

And we have yet again a penalization term, which is, in this case, the square of an L1 norm of the portfolio weights. The function $\|\mathbf{V}\mathbf{w}\|_1^2$ is concave, so the optimization problem is convex. I summarize the penalization approaches in the table in Exercise 10.1.

5. *Robust covariance matrix* (Ledoit and Wolf, 2004). Consider a different starting point to model robust covariance optimization. We assume that the adversary has a budget for the maximum cumulative squared error of the asset covariances: $\sum_{i,j} [\boldsymbol{\Delta}]_{i,j}^2 \le d^2$. This is the same as a bound on the Frobenius norm of the error, $\|\boldsymbol{\Delta}\|_F$. The robust problem formulation is similar to the previous one:

$$\max \mathbf{a}^{\mathsf{T}}\mathbf{w} - \lambda\mathbf{w}^{\mathsf{T}}\boldsymbol{\Omega}_{\mathbf{r}}\mathbf{w} - \lambda\sigma^2$$
$$\text{s.t. } \sigma^2 = \arg\max_{\Delta}\left\{\mathbf{w}^{\mathsf{T}}\boldsymbol{\Delta}\mathbf{w} \,|\, \|\boldsymbol{\Delta}\|_F^2 \le d^2\right\}$$

The strategy to solve this problem is similar to previous cases: the adversary maximizes a linear objective function with a norm constraint; see Insight 10.1 for the solution. In this case, $(\sigma^\star)^2 = d\|\mathbf{w}\|^2$, yet again, and the problem becomes an MVO with a quadratic penalization term.

Exercise 10.1: Define the norm $\|\mathbf{x}\|_{\Lambda,p} := \left\|\Lambda^{-1}\mathbf{x}\right\|_p$. Extend Problem (10.12) to this norm. Read Olivares-Nadal and DeMiguel (2018) for additional interpretations of this penalty, and discuss their applicability to real-world settings.

Approach	Penalty	Parameter Interpretation
Uncertain Alpha	$\tau^2\|\mathbf{w}\|^2$	std. error of $\hat{\boldsymbol{\alpha}}$
Robust Alpha	$d\,\|\mathbf{w}\|$	max distance $\|\boldsymbol{\alpha} - \hat{\boldsymbol{\alpha}}\|$
Robust Factor	$\lambda\tau^2\|\mathbf{w}\|^2$	volatility of a missing factor
Robust Correlations	$\lambda d\|\mathbf{V}\mathbf{w}\|_1^2$	max distance $\lvert\rho_{i,j} - \hat{\rho}_{i,j}\rvert$
Robust Covariance	$\lambda d\|\mathbf{w}\|^2$	max distance $\|\boldsymbol{\Omega}_{\mathbf{r}} - \hat{\boldsymbol{\Omega}}_{\mathbf{r}}\|$

Insight 10.3: *The distinction between constraints and penalties*

Although they can yield the same optimal portfolio, the constrained and penalty version differ in two important ways. The first one is that the shadow price of the constraint is not known before the optimization is run. This means that the solution can be very sensitive to the choice of the right-hand side of the constraint: we don't know the trade-off between constraint limit and optimum value. This is not the case with a penalty: we *set* the price, and the price has often a straightforward interpretation (like the price for risk). In successive optimizations, this price is unchanged, making comparisons easier. When the interpretation is clear, penalties are preferable. The second difference is almost a corollary of the first one: in the constrained formulation, we may have no feasible solution, which is, in a loose sense, like saying that the price of the constraint is infinite. This is never the case with a penalized formulation, which is always feasible.

10.3 How Does Estimation Error Affect the Sharpe Ratio?

An investor starts with estimates of expected returns and of the covariance matrix.[7] We denote them with $\hat{\boldsymbol{\alpha}}$ and $\hat{\boldsymbol{\Omega}}_r$ respectively. The MVO portfolio is proportional to $\hat{\boldsymbol{\Omega}}_r^{-1}\hat{\boldsymbol{\alpha}}$; the proportionality constant is irrelevant for the Sharpe Ratio. The realized Sharpe Ratio, however, is a function of the true expected returns and covariance matrix $\boldsymbol{\alpha}, \boldsymbol{\Omega}_r$:

$$\mathrm{SR}(\hat{\boldsymbol{\alpha}}, \hat{\boldsymbol{\Omega}}_r) = \frac{\boldsymbol{\alpha}^{\mathsf{T}}(\hat{\boldsymbol{\Omega}}_r^{-1}\hat{\boldsymbol{\alpha}})}{\sqrt{(\hat{\boldsymbol{\Omega}}_r^{-1}\hat{\boldsymbol{\alpha}})^{\mathsf{T}}\boldsymbol{\Omega}_r(\hat{\boldsymbol{\Omega}}_r^{-1}\hat{\boldsymbol{\alpha}})}}$$

We compare the realized Sharpe Ratio to the best Sharpe Ratio, based on the true values of $\boldsymbol{\alpha}$ and $\boldsymbol{\Omega}_r$, given by Equation (9.5):

$$\frac{\mathrm{SR}(\hat{\boldsymbol{\alpha}}, \hat{\boldsymbol{\Omega}}_r)}{\mathrm{SR}(\boldsymbol{\alpha}, \boldsymbol{\Omega}_r)}$$

We call this the *Sharpe Ratio Efficiency* (SRE). It is important to study this quantity, because we want to know, at all times, whether we are losing a great deal of performance from inaccurate parameter estimation or large transaction costs. We will ask a few qualitative and quantitative questions, and see how far the analysis can take us.[8]

First, we prove an intuitive fact: incorrect estimates worsen performance.

Theorem 10.1: *The Sharpe Ratio Efficiency is less than or equal to one, and is equal to one if and only if* $\boldsymbol{\Omega}_r^{-1/2}\boldsymbol{\alpha}$ *and* $\boldsymbol{\Omega}_r^{1/2}\hat{\boldsymbol{\Omega}}_r^{-1}\hat{\boldsymbol{\alpha}}$ *are collinear.*

Proof. The SRE is

$$\frac{\mathrm{SR}(\hat{\boldsymbol{\alpha}}, \hat{\boldsymbol{\Omega}}_r)}{\mathrm{SR}(\boldsymbol{\alpha}, \boldsymbol{\Omega}_r)} = \frac{\boldsymbol{\alpha}^{\mathsf{T}}\hat{\boldsymbol{\Omega}}_r^{-1}\hat{\boldsymbol{\alpha}}}{\sqrt{\hat{\boldsymbol{\alpha}}^{\mathsf{T}}\hat{\boldsymbol{\Omega}}_r^{-1}\boldsymbol{\Omega}_r\hat{\boldsymbol{\Omega}}_r^{-1}\hat{\boldsymbol{\alpha}}}}\frac{1}{\sqrt{\boldsymbol{\alpha}^{\mathsf{T}}\boldsymbol{\Omega}_r^{-1}\boldsymbol{\alpha}}} \qquad (10.24)$$

---

[7] The third leg of the trading stool is a model for trading cost. We will cover this in later chapters.

[8] Early papers on model estimation error, and the relative impact of alpha and estimation error, are Michaud (1989); Chopra and W. Ziemba (1993); Shephard (2009).

Let[9]

$$\mathbf{a} := \mathbf{\Omega}_{\mathbf{r}}^{-1/2}\boldsymbol{\alpha} \tag{10.25}$$

$$\mathbf{b} := \mathbf{\Omega}_{\mathbf{r}}^{1/2}\hat{\mathbf{\Omega}}_{\mathbf{r}}^{-1}\hat{\boldsymbol{\alpha}} \tag{10.26}$$

so that

$$\frac{\mathrm{SR}(\hat{\boldsymbol{\alpha}}, \hat{\mathbf{\Omega}}_{\mathbf{r}})}{\mathrm{SR}(\boldsymbol{\alpha}, \mathbf{\Omega}_{\mathbf{r}})} = \frac{\mathbf{a}^{\top}\mathbf{b}}{\|\mathbf{a}\|\,\|\mathbf{b}\|}$$

The Sharpe Ratio Efficiency is always less than one because of the Cauchy–Schwartz inequality,[10] unless $\mathbf{\Omega}_{\mathbf{r}}^{-1/2}\boldsymbol{\alpha}$ and $\mathbf{\Omega}_{\mathbf{r}}^{1/2}\hat{\mathbf{\Omega}}_{\mathbf{r}}^{-1}\hat{\boldsymbol{\alpha}}$ are collinear. ∎

10.3.1 The Impact of Alpha Error

It is more useful to derive lower bounds on performance inefficiency, based on the estimation error of either expected returns or covariance.

We need to introduce a few basic results. Let the norm of a matrix be defined as the operator norm. Define the relative alpha error as

$$\left\| \frac{\boldsymbol{\alpha}}{\|\boldsymbol{\alpha}\|} - \frac{\hat{\boldsymbol{\alpha}}}{\|\hat{\boldsymbol{\alpha}}\|} \right\| \le \delta_{\text{alpha}}$$

In the Appendix (Section 10.4.1) I prove the following result:

$$\frac{\mathrm{SR}(\hat{\boldsymbol{\alpha}}, \hat{\mathbf{\Omega}}_{\mathbf{r}})}{\mathrm{SR}(\boldsymbol{\alpha}, \mathbf{\Omega}_{\mathbf{r}})} \ge 1 - 2\left\|\mathbf{\Omega}_{\mathbf{r}}^{-1}\right\| \|\mathbf{\Omega}_{\mathbf{r}}\|\, \delta_{\text{alpha}}^{2}$$

The damage made by alpha error is magnified by the term $\left\|\mathbf{\Omega}_{\mathbf{r}}^{-1}\right\| \|\mathbf{\Omega}_{\mathbf{r}}\|$, which is equal to (easy exercise) the ratio of the largest eigenvalue to the smallest eigenvalue of the matrix $\mathbf{\Omega}_{\mathbf{r}}$, or the ratio of the largest variance to the smallest variance associated to eigenfactors. The ratio is the *condition number* of a matrix. If we are operating in idio space (all alphas are orthogonalized to factor exposures), then we have a diagonal covariance matrix, and the condition number is the ratio of the largest asset idiosyncratic variance to the smallest asset idiosyncratic variance.

---

[9] Let $\mathbf{H}$ be a symmetric positive-definite matrix and let $\mathbf{V}\mathbf{\Lambda}\mathbf{V}^{\top}$ be its SVD. Define $\mathbf{H}^{1/2} := \mathbf{V}\mathbf{\Lambda}^{1/2}\mathbf{V}^{\top}$. Then $\mathbf{H}^{1/2}\mathbf{H}^{1/2} = \mathbf{H}$ and $\left\|\mathbf{H}^{1/2}\right\|_{\text{op}}^{2} = \|\mathbf{H}\|_{\text{op}}$.

[10] Which can be found in almost any linear algebra book. If $\mathbf{x}, \mathbf{y} \in \mathbb{R}^{n}$, then $|\mathbf{a}^{\top}\mathbf{b}| \le \sqrt{\mathbf{a}^{\top}\mathbf{a}}\sqrt{\mathbf{b}^{\top}\mathbf{b}}$, with the equality holding only if $\mathbf{a} = \kappa\mathbf{b}$.

10.3.2 *The Impact of Risk Error*

If there is $\kappa > 0$ such that

$$\left\| \boldsymbol{\Omega}_{\mathrm{r}}^{1/2} \hat{\boldsymbol{\Omega}}_{\mathrm{r}}^{-1} \boldsymbol{\Omega}_{\mathrm{r}}^{1/2} - \kappa \mathbf{I} \right\| \leq \delta_{\mathrm{risk}} \tag{10.27}$$

then

$$\frac{\mathrm{SR}(\hat{\boldsymbol{\alpha}}, \hat{\boldsymbol{\Omega}}_{\mathrm{r}})}{\mathrm{SR}(\boldsymbol{\alpha}, \boldsymbol{\Omega}_{\mathrm{r}})} \geq 1 - \frac{2\delta_{\mathrm{risk}}}{\kappa + \delta_{\mathrm{risk}}} \tag{10.28}$$

This formula follows directly from Equation (10.24). At first sight, what is interesting about this result is how weak it is. Let us consider a few special cases. We define $\mathbf{H} := \boldsymbol{\Omega}_{\mathrm{r}}^{1/2} \hat{\boldsymbol{\Omega}}_{\mathrm{r}}^{-1} \boldsymbol{\Omega}_{\mathrm{r}}^{1/2}$.

1. If the estimated covariance matrix is biased, but uniformly so, i.e., $\hat{\boldsymbol{\Omega}}_{\mathrm{r}} = \kappa \boldsymbol{\Omega}_{\mathrm{r}}$, then $\mathbf{H} = \kappa^{-1}\mathbf{I}$, and there is no efficiency loss. We knew this already from the previous chapter. What happens in practice is that we would deploy a portfolio with the highest Sharpe Ratio, but incorrect volatility.
2. Say, however, that we *really* estimate the covariance matrix incorrectly, so that $\mathbf{H} \not\propto \mathbf{I}$. It can still happen that we have an SRE of one! This will happen if $\hat{\boldsymbol{\alpha}}$ is proportional to an eigenvector of $\mathbf{H}$ with a positive eigenvalue. Say the associated eigenvalue is γ. Then, use directly Equation (10.24):

$$\mathrm{SRE} = \frac{\hat{\boldsymbol{\alpha}}^{\mathsf{T}}(\gamma \hat{\boldsymbol{\alpha}})}{\|\hat{\boldsymbol{\alpha}}\|^2} \sqrt{\frac{\|\hat{\boldsymbol{\alpha}}\|^2}{\hat{\boldsymbol{\alpha}}^{\mathsf{T}}(\gamma^2 \hat{\boldsymbol{\alpha}})}} = \mathrm{sgn}\,(\gamma)$$

Even more pathologically, though, this also implies that if our $\hat{\boldsymbol{\alpha}}$ is proportional to an eigenvector with *negative* eigenvalue, then the Sharpe Ratio Efficiency is -1. Incidentally, $\mathbf{H}$ is neither necessarily symmetric nor positive-definite, so a negative eigenvalue is indeed a possibility.
3. But, you may argue, this is an exceptional circumstance. Consider a simpler but instructive case. We make the assumption that $\hat{\boldsymbol{\Omega}}_{\mathrm{r}}$ has the same eigenvectors (aka eigenfactors) as $\boldsymbol{\Omega}_{\mathrm{r}}$. In other words, the SVDs only differ because of the singular values:

$$\boldsymbol{\Omega}_{\mathrm{r}} = \mathbf{U}\boldsymbol{\Lambda}\mathbf{U}^{\mathsf{T}}$$
$$\hat{\boldsymbol{\Omega}}_{\mathrm{r}} = \mathbf{U}\hat{\boldsymbol{\Lambda}}\mathbf{U}^{\mathsf{T}}$$

so that $\mathbf{H} = \mathbf{U}\boldsymbol{\Lambda}^{1/2}\mathbf{U}^{\mathsf{T}}\mathbf{U}\hat{\boldsymbol{\Lambda}}^{-1}\mathbf{U}^{\mathsf{T}}\mathbf{U}\boldsymbol{\Lambda}^{1/2}\mathbf{U}^{\mathsf{T}} = \mathbf{U}\boldsymbol{\Lambda}\hat{\boldsymbol{\Lambda}}^{-1}\mathbf{U}^{\mathsf{T}}$; a great simplification. Denote the eigenvalue ratio $\nu_i := \lambda_i/\hat{\lambda}_i$. What is the lower bound on the SRE in this case? We solve for κ:

$$\begin{aligned}
\delta &:= \min_\kappa \left\| \mathbf{U}(\boldsymbol{\Lambda}\hat{\boldsymbol{\Lambda}}^{-1} - \kappa \mathbf{I})\mathbf{U}^\top \right\| \\
&= \min_\kappa \sqrt{\max_i (\nu_i - \kappa)^2} \\
&= \frac{1}{2}(\max_i \nu_i - \min_i \nu_i)
\end{aligned}$$

and the optimal point is $\kappa^\star = (\max_i \nu_i + \min_i \nu_i)/2$. We use these values in Equation (10.28) to obtain

$$\text{SRE} \geq 1 - \frac{\max_i \nu_i - \min_i \nu_i}{\max_i \nu_i} = \frac{\min_i \nu_i}{\max_i \nu_i}$$

Hence the loss in efficiency arises from the fact that we estimate unevenly the volatilities of the eigenvectors of the asset covariance matrix. If we underestimate them (or overestimate them) by the same constant, then we lose nothing, as noted in the first point above. Let us think of an adverse case. Say we estimate all volatilities exactly ($\nu_i = 1$) except for one, which we underestimate by 50%. Then the worst-case loss in Sharpe Ratio can be 50%.

10.4 ★Appendix

10.4.1 *Theorems on Sharpe Efficiency Loss*

These theorems are informally introduced in Section 10.3.

We recall that

$$\left\| \mathbf{H}^{-1} \right\|^{-1} \|\mathbf{x}\| \leq \|\mathbf{Hx}\| \leq \|\mathbf{H}\| \, \|\mathbf{x}\|$$

and

$$\|\mathbf{Hy}\| \leq \|\mathbf{Hx}\| + \|\mathbf{H}(\mathbf{y} - \mathbf{x})\| \leq \|\mathbf{Hx}\| + \|\mathbf{H}\| \, \|\mathbf{x} - \mathbf{y}\|$$

so that

$$| \, \|\mathbf{Hx}\| - \|\mathbf{Hy}\| \, | \leq \|\mathbf{H}\| \, \|\mathbf{x} - \mathbf{y}\|$$

Also, use the cosine rule:

$$\left\|\frac{\mathbf{a}}{\|\mathbf{a}\|}-\frac{\mathbf{b}}{\|\mathbf{b}\|}\right\|^2=2\left(1-\frac{\mathbf{a}^\top\mathbf{b}}{\|\mathbf{a}\|\,\|\mathbf{b}\|}\right)$$

$$\Rightarrow\frac{\mathrm{SR}(\hat{\boldsymbol{\alpha}},\hat{\boldsymbol{\Omega}}_{\mathbf{r}})}{\mathrm{SR}(\boldsymbol{\alpha},\boldsymbol{\Omega}_{\mathbf{r}})}=\frac{\mathbf{a}^\top\mathbf{b}}{\|\mathbf{a}\|\,\|\mathbf{b}\|}$$

$$=1-\frac{1}{2}\left\|\frac{\mathbf{a}}{\|\mathbf{a}\|}-\frac{\mathbf{b}}{\|\mathbf{b}\|}\right\|^2$$

where $\mathbf{a},\mathbf{b}$ are defined by Equations (10.25) and (10.26).

Lemma 10.1: *Let* $\mathbf{H}$ *be symmetric positive-definite,* $\mathbf{x},\mathbf{y}\in\mathbb{R}^n$*, and*

$$\left\|\frac{\mathbf{x}}{\|\mathbf{x}\|}-\frac{\mathbf{y}}{\|\mathbf{y}\|}\right\|\le\delta$$

Then

$$\left\|\frac{\mathbf{Hx}}{\|\mathbf{Hx}\|}-\frac{\mathbf{Hy}}{\|\mathbf{Hy}\|}\right\|\le 2\min\left\{\|\mathbf{H}\|\left\|\mathbf{H}^{-1}\right\|\delta,1\right\}$$

Proof. Let $\mathbf{a},\mathbf{b}\in\mathbb{R}^n$.

$$\left\|\frac{\mathbf{Ha}}{\|\mathbf{Ha}\|}-\frac{\mathbf{Hb}}{\|\mathbf{Hb}\|}\right\|=\left\|\frac{\|\mathbf{Hb}\|\,\mathbf{Ha}-\|\mathbf{Ha}\|\,\mathbf{Hb}}{\|\mathbf{Ha}\|\,\|\mathbf{Hb}\|}\right\|$$

$$=\left\|\frac{\|\mathbf{Hb}\|\,\mathbf{H}(\mathbf{a}-\mathbf{b})-(\|\mathbf{Ha}\|-\|\mathbf{Hb}\|)\mathbf{Hb}}{\|\mathbf{Ha}\|\,\|\mathbf{Hb}\|}\right\|$$

$$\le\frac{1}{\|\mathbf{Ha}\|}\left(\|\mathbf{H}(\mathbf{a}-\mathbf{b})\|+\big|\,\|\mathbf{Ha}\|-\|\mathbf{Hb}\|\,\big|\right)$$

$$\le\frac{1}{\|\mathbf{Ha}\|}\left(\|\mathbf{H}(\mathbf{a}-\mathbf{b})\|+\|\mathbf{H}\|\,\|\mathbf{a}-\mathbf{b}\|\right)$$

$$\le\frac{1}{\|\mathbf{Ha}\|}\left(\|\mathbf{H}\|\,\|(\mathbf{a}-\mathbf{b})\|+\|\mathbf{H}\|\,\|\mathbf{a}-\mathbf{b}\|\right)$$

$$=\frac{2}{\|\mathbf{Ha}\|}\|\mathbf{H}\|\,\|(\mathbf{a}-\mathbf{b})\|$$

$$\left(\mathbf{a}:=\frac{\mathbf{x}}{\|\mathbf{x}\|},\mathbf{b}:=\frac{\mathbf{y}}{\|\mathbf{y}\|}\right)=\frac{2}{\left\|\mathbf{H}\frac{\mathbf{x}}{\|\mathbf{x}\|}\right\|}\|\mathbf{H}\|\left\|\frac{\mathbf{x}}{\|\mathbf{x}\|}-\frac{\mathbf{y}}{\|\mathbf{y}\|}\right\|$$

$$\le 2\,\|\mathbf{H}\|\left\|\mathbf{H}^{-1}\right\|\delta$$

This bound is tight, up to a constant. For example, consider the case of diagonal[11] $\mathbf{H} := \operatorname{diag}(\lambda_1, \dots, \lambda_n)$, $\mathbf{x} := \epsilon \mathbf{e}_1 + \mathbf{e}_n$, $\mathbf{y} := \mathbf{e}_n$, with $\epsilon \leq \lambda_n / \lambda_1$. We have

$$\left\| \frac{\mathbf{x}}{\|\mathbf{x}\|} - \frac{\mathbf{y}}{\|\mathbf{y}\|} \right\| \leq \sqrt{\frac{3}{2}} \epsilon =: \delta$$

$$\begin{aligned}
\left\| \frac{\mathbf{Hx}}{\|\mathbf{Hx}\|} - \frac{\mathbf{Hy}}{\|\mathbf{Hy}\|} \right\| &= \left\| \frac{\lambda_n \mathbf{e}_n + \epsilon \lambda_1 \mathbf{e}_1}{\sqrt{\lambda_n^2 + \epsilon^2 \lambda_1^2}} - \mathbf{e}_n \right\| \\
&= \sqrt{\left(\frac{\lambda_n}{\sqrt{\lambda_n^2 + \epsilon^2 \lambda_1^2}} - 1 \right)^2 + \frac{(\epsilon \lambda_1)^2}{\lambda_n^2 + \epsilon^2 \lambda_1^2}} \\
&\geq \sqrt{2 \frac{-\lambda_n^2 (\epsilon \lambda_1 / \lambda_n)^2 / 2 + (\epsilon \lambda_1)^2}{\lambda_n^2 + (\epsilon \lambda_1)^2}} \\
&\geq \sqrt{\frac{(\epsilon \lambda_1)^2}{\lambda_n^2 + (\epsilon \lambda_1)^2}} \\
&\geq \frac{1}{\sqrt{2}} \frac{\lambda_1}{\lambda_n} \epsilon \\
&= \frac{1}{\sqrt{3}} \|\mathbf{H}\| \left\| \mathbf{H}^{-1} \right\| \delta
\end{aligned}$$

Theorem 10.2 ***(Misspecification of alpha):*** *If*

$$\left\| \frac{\boldsymbol{\alpha}}{\|\boldsymbol{\alpha}\|} - \frac{\hat{\boldsymbol{\alpha}}}{\|\hat{\boldsymbol{\alpha}}\|} \right\| \leq \delta$$

then

$$\frac{\mathrm{SR}(\hat{\boldsymbol{\alpha}}, \hat{\boldsymbol{\Omega}}_{\mathbf{r}})}{\mathrm{SR}(\boldsymbol{\alpha}, \boldsymbol{\Omega}_{\mathbf{r}})} \geq 1 - 2 \left\| \boldsymbol{\Omega}_{\mathbf{r}}^{-1} \right\| \|\boldsymbol{\Omega}_{\mathbf{r}}\| \, \delta^2$$

[11] We use the notation $\mathbf{e}_1, \dots, \mathbf{e}_n$ for the standard basis in $\mathbb{R}^n$.

Proof. From Lemma 10.1:

$$\left\| \frac{\boldsymbol{\Omega}_{\mathbf{r}}^{-1/2}\boldsymbol{\alpha}}{\left\|\boldsymbol{\Omega}_{\mathbf{r}}^{-1/2}\boldsymbol{\alpha}\right\|} - \frac{\boldsymbol{\Omega}_{\mathbf{r}}^{-1/2}\hat{\boldsymbol{\alpha}}}{\left\|\boldsymbol{\Omega}_{\mathbf{r}}^{-1/2}\hat{\boldsymbol{\alpha}}\right\|} \right\| \leq 2\left\|\boldsymbol{\Omega}_{\mathbf{r}}^{-1/2}\right\|\left\|\boldsymbol{\Omega}_{\mathbf{r}}^{1/2}\right\|\delta$$

$$= 2\sqrt{\left\|\boldsymbol{\Omega}_{\mathbf{r}}^{-1}\right\|\,\|\boldsymbol{\Omega}_{\mathbf{r}}\|}\,\delta$$

Then

$$\frac{\mathrm{SR}(\hat{\boldsymbol{\alpha}}, \hat{\boldsymbol{\Omega}}_{\mathbf{r}})}{\mathrm{SR}(\boldsymbol{\alpha}, \boldsymbol{\Omega}_{\mathbf{r}})} = 1 - \frac{1}{2}\left\| \frac{\boldsymbol{\Omega}_{\mathbf{r}}^{-1/2}\boldsymbol{\alpha}}{\left\|\boldsymbol{\Omega}_{\mathbf{r}}^{-1/2}\boldsymbol{\alpha}\right\|} - \frac{\boldsymbol{\Omega}_{\mathbf{r}}^{-1/2}\hat{\boldsymbol{\alpha}}}{\left\|\boldsymbol{\Omega}_{\mathbf{r}}^{-1/2}\hat{\boldsymbol{\alpha}}\right\|} \right\|^2$$

$$\geq 1 - 2\left\|\boldsymbol{\Omega}_{\mathbf{r}}^{-1}\right\|\,\|\boldsymbol{\Omega}_{\mathbf{r}}\|\,\delta^2$$

■

Theorem 10.3 ***(Misspecification of risk)***: *If there is $\kappa > 0$ such that*

$$\left\|\boldsymbol{\Omega}_{\mathbf{r}}^{1/2}\hat{\boldsymbol{\Omega}}_{\mathbf{r}}^{-1}\boldsymbol{\Omega}_{\mathbf{r}}^{1/2} - \kappa\mathbf{I}_n\right\| \leq \delta \tag{10.29}$$

then

$$\frac{\mathrm{SR}(\hat{\boldsymbol{\alpha}}, \hat{\boldsymbol{\Omega}}_{\mathbf{r}})}{\mathrm{SR}(\boldsymbol{\alpha}, \boldsymbol{\Omega}_{\mathbf{r}})} \geq 1 - \frac{2\delta}{\kappa + \delta} \tag{10.30}$$

Proof. Let $\mathbf{H} := \boldsymbol{\Omega}_{\mathbf{r}}^{1/2}\hat{\boldsymbol{\Omega}}_{\mathbf{r}}^{-1}\boldsymbol{\Omega}_{\mathbf{r}}^{1/2}$ and let $\hat{\boldsymbol{\alpha}} := \boldsymbol{\Omega}_{\mathbf{r}}^{-1/2}\boldsymbol{\alpha}$. Using this notation, the SRE Equation (10.24) and Condition (10.29) are

$$\frac{\mathrm{SR}(\boldsymbol{\alpha}, \hat{\boldsymbol{\Omega}}_{\mathbf{r}})}{\mathrm{SR}(\boldsymbol{\alpha}, \boldsymbol{\Omega}_{\mathbf{r}})} = \frac{\hat{\boldsymbol{\alpha}}^{\mathsf{T}}\mathbf{H}\hat{\boldsymbol{\alpha}}}{\|\hat{\boldsymbol{\alpha}}\|^2}\sqrt{\frac{\|\hat{\boldsymbol{\alpha}}\|^2}{\hat{\boldsymbol{\alpha}}^{\mathsf{T}}\mathbf{H}^2\hat{\boldsymbol{\alpha}}}}$$

$$\left\|\mathbf{H} - \kappa\mathbf{I}_n\right\| \leq \delta$$

Let $\lambda_1 \geq \lambda_2 \geq \cdots \geq \lambda_n$ be eigenvalues of $\mathbf{H}$. The condition $\left\|\mathbf{H} - \kappa \mathbf{I}_n\right\| \leq \delta$ is equivalent to $|\lambda_i - \kappa| \leq \delta$ for all $i = 1, \ldots, n$:

$$\frac{\hat{\boldsymbol{\alpha}}^{\mathsf{T}} \mathbf{H} \hat{\boldsymbol{\alpha}}}{\|\hat{\boldsymbol{\alpha}}\|^2} \geq \lambda_n \geq \kappa - \delta$$

$$\frac{\hat{\boldsymbol{\alpha}}^{\mathsf{T}} \mathbf{H}^2 \hat{\boldsymbol{\alpha}}}{\|\hat{\boldsymbol{\alpha}}\|^2} \leq \lambda_1^2 \leq (\kappa + \delta)^2$$

$$\Rightarrow \frac{\hat{\boldsymbol{\alpha}}^{\mathsf{T}} \mathbf{H} \hat{\boldsymbol{\alpha}}}{\|\hat{\boldsymbol{\alpha}}\|^2} \sqrt{\frac{\|\hat{\boldsymbol{\alpha}}\|^2}{\hat{\boldsymbol{\alpha}}^{\mathsf{T}} \mathbf{H}^2 \hat{\boldsymbol{\alpha}}}} \geq \frac{\kappa - \delta}{\kappa + \delta} = 1 - \frac{2\delta}{\kappa + \delta}$$

■

The Takeaways

1. Mean-Variance Optimization (MVO) can suggest shorting assets with positive expected returns if their correlation with other assets is high relative to their Sharpe Ratios.
2. Errors in forecasted Sharpe Ratios and correlations can substantially reduce realized Sharpe Ratios, with higher asset correlations worsening performance loss due to estimation error.
3. Estimation errors in expected returns degrade portfolio performance, especially when errors are high relative to the accuracy of risk estimates.
4. Constraining portfolio allocations (e.g., long-only, gross exposure limits) can reduce sensitivity to estimation error, often improving robustness but potentially lowering maximum achievable Sharpe Ratio.
5. Non-linear and quadratic constraints, such as those on factor exposure or tracking error, allow for more tailored risk control in portfolio construction.
6. Penalties can serve as a flexible alternative to constraints, especially when risk tolerance or trading costs need to be controlled within feasible limits.
7. Robust optimization, which models uncertainty in alpha and covariance estimates, helps mitigate performance loss by introducing penalties that account for estimation risk.
8. Shrinking or regularizing asset correlations and variances can improve realized Sharpe Ratios when covariances are uncertain, reducing sensitivity to estimation error.
9. Constraints on turnover and trading costs can reduce portfolio drift and control rebalancing expenses, particularly in markets with high transaction costs.
10. The optimal approach often combines constraints and penalties to balance estimation error tolerance with implementation feasibility, allowing for adaptable portfolio construction.

Chapter 11

Market-Impact-Aware Portfolio Management

The Questions

1. What are the main sources of trading costs, and how do they affect the profitability of a trading strategy?
2. How can we model and quantify market impact, specifically temporary market impact, in the context of trading?
3. How does market impact propagate over time, and what functional forms are commonly used to describe this propagation?
4. How can finite-horizon optimization be structured to manage expected returns, market impact, and transaction costs over multiple periods?
5. How does an infinite-horizon optimization framework differ from finite-horizon models, and when is it appropriate to use each approach?

Trading can *possibly* make money, but it *surely* costs money. When we execute a trade, we incur costs of all sorts: financing costs when we leverage our portfolio; borrowing costs when we short securities; commission costs to exchanges and other counterparties. In addition to all of the above, we pay an indirect cost: our actions move prices. It appeals to our intuition that, when we purchase a security, we somewhat push its price upward, which in turn makes the additional purchase of a security more expensive. What is less intuitive, however, is that this "price impact" can turn a strategy that is potentially profitable into a very unprofitable one. We are then faced with two important questions. The first one is to adequately describe the laws governing price impact dynamics. The second is to use these laws to optimize the performance of our trading strategy. These two questions inform the organization of the chapter: in the next section, we provide a quick description of market impact models. Then we descend into the infernal circles of optimal execution.[1]

11.1 Market Impact

A synthetic definition of market impact is the following (Velu et al., 2020): "Market impact is the cumulative market-wide response of the arrival of new order flow". The underlying process is complex and results from the joint contribution of several factors:

- First, there is a direct reduction in inventory of the securities being bought or sold, causing a price movement.
- Second, there is an informational effect: initiating a transaction may reveal private beliefs about the future price of that security, as well as be informative of future transactions in the near future.
- Third, there is a mimetic effect, where participants, in the absence of information, imitate each other's behavior, leading to temporary run-ups or draw-downs.
- Finally, there is a strategic aspect. Even in the absence of information leakage, participants trade so as to exploit potential arbitrages arising from price impact.

[1] The academic literature on optimal execution is vast, and growing rapidly. This chapter offers a selective treatment of portfolio optimization. Reference texts are Guéant (2016); Bouchaud et al. (2018); Bacidore (2020); Velu et al. (2020); Webster (2023).

Each one of these phenomena is complex, and hard to model. The total transaction cost associated to a trade is usually decomposed into three components:

$$\text{Expected Transaction Cost} = \textit{(spread cost)} + \textit{(temporary market impact)} + \textit{(permanent market impact)}$$

The *spread costs* reflect the difference between the bid and the ask price. A market order "crosses" the spread, i.e., is executed at the best price offered by the counterparty. This order reduces the inventory available for transactions, and thus removes liquidity. On the other side, a limit order has an associated execution price[2] and adds liquidity. The average cost incurred in a trade is modeled as a fraction of the bid–ask spread, and assumed to be independent from other transactions. It is usually modeled as an asset-dependent percentage of the dollar traded.

The *permanent impact* is the price change that persists long after the order has been executed.

The *temporary impact* (also called "slippage") is the price change that occurs during order execution and immediately afterwards, until price reaches equilibrium.

In the rest of the chapter, we focus on temporary impact, and effectively ignore both spread costs and permanent impact, although these are both interesting areas of research. The rationales for this choice are modeling priorities and brevity. From the vantage point of a modeler specifically concerned with portfolio optimization, as opposed to one interested in understanding the mechanisms underlying price impact, spread costs and temporary impact are by far the most important concerns because of their magnitude compared to permanent impact. Even our discussion of temporary impact is kept as short as possible, but not shorter.

11.1.1 Temporary Market Impact

We want to submit a large order, usually called a *parent order* or a *meta-order*. Depending on the asset class, we have different options for execution. For example, we could split the parent order into smaller "child"

---

[2] There are at least two classes of costs associated with it. First, there are opportunity costs. If the price moves away, we may be forced to reprice the order and pay a higher price than the market order we could have submitted. Second, our counterparty is typically an informed trader who is forecasting a price change in the opposite direction to our order.

orders and execute them on exchange. In other cases, OTC or alternate trading systems are available. It is remarkable that, despite the broad array of trading venues and matching mechanisms, the expected market impact is described well by a common formula. Let x_t denote the net number of shares traded up to time t and with $\dot{x}_t$ the trading rate, i.e., the number of shares traded per unit time, at time t. We now introduce two functions: the instantaneous market impact $f : \mathbb{R} \to \mathbb{R}^+$ and the propagator $G : \mathbb{R}^+ \to \mathbb{R}^+$. We also have a positive constant term κ, which is a function of the security characteristics. The expected temporary market impact is given by the formula

$$E(P_T) - P_0 = \kappa \int_0^T f(\dot{x}_t) G(T - t) dt \tag{11.1}$$

For an interpretation, consider the case of a marketable order[3] single-buy trade, a short "pulse" occurring at time t_0. Then the market impact for $T \geq t_0$ is proportional to $G(T - t_0)$: an instantaneous price change occurs at time t_0, and is followed by a "relaxation" back to an equilibrium level. The function G is monotonically decreasing, thus reflecting the long-term convergence to an equilibrium level (see Figure 11.1). The function f should intuitively be monotonically increasing: the higher the trading rate, the higher the instantaneous impact. The interpretation of Equation (11.1) is then as a linear superposition of pulse trades, each one having an impact that relaxes back to equilibrium over time. The big question is then what is the functional form of f and G. Below are a few alternatives.

- (Almgren et al., 2005) The functions are

$$f(\dot{x}) = \sigma \operatorname{sgn}(\dot{x}) \left| \frac{\dot{x}}{v} \right|^{\beta}$$
$$G(t) = \delta(t)$$

  where $\beta \approx 0.6$, σ is the security's volatility, v is the total number of shares traded per unit interval by all market participants, and $\delta(\cdot)$ is the Dirac delta function.[4]

[3] A marketable order is one that executes immediately at the best available price offered by a counterparty, and that therefore removes inventory.
[4] $\delta(\cdot)$ is a "pulse" generalized function, zero everywhere except the origin, and whose integral is 1.

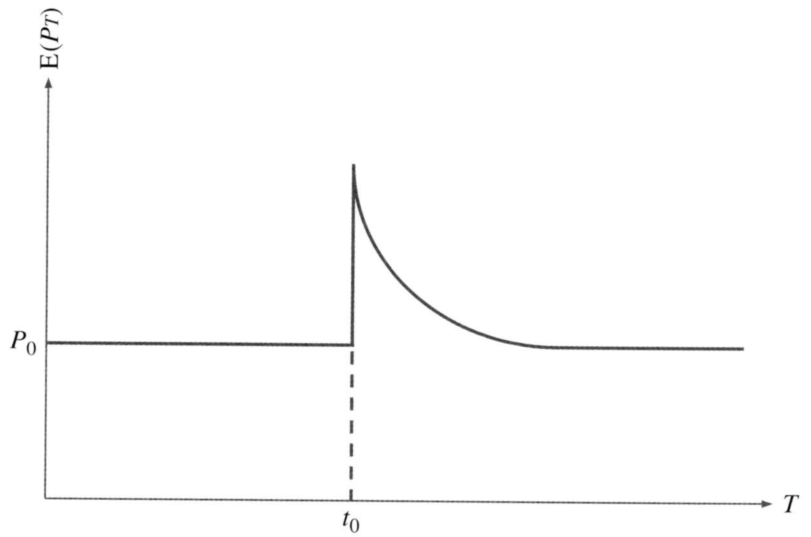

Figure 11.1 Market impact over time for a single trade executed at time t_0. The decay after t_0 is proportional to G.

We consider here and in the remainder of this a buy order, i.e., $\dot{x} > 0$. The trading cost is

$$\begin{aligned} C[x] &= \kappa\sigma \int_0^T d t \dot{x}_t \int_0^t ds \left(\frac{\dot{x}_s}{v}\right)^\beta \delta(t-s) \\ &= \frac{\kappa\sigma}{v^\beta} \int_0^T d t \dot{x}_t^{1+\beta} \end{aligned}$$

As an important example, we trade share quantity Q at constant rate in $[0, T]$ and the total traded volume in the market in the same period is $V = vT$. The ratio Q/V is usually referred to as the *participation rate* or *PoV* (Percentage of Volume). From the formula above, the total and unit costs are

$$\begin{aligned} C &= \kappa\sigma \left(\frac{Q}{V}\right)^\beta Q \\ c &= \kappa\sigma \left(\frac{Q}{V}\right)^\beta \end{aligned}$$

The unit cost is decreasing in the execution time. By replacing $V = vT$, we have $c \propto T^{-\beta}$.

There is an argument made on the basis of physical dimensions[5] that suggests that $\beta = 1/2$. Pohl et al. (2017) propose an argument for the universality of the Almgren market impact. They assume that there are only three quantities that matter:

- Q, which we interpret as the dollar value traded during a period.
- V, which we interpret as the dollar value traded by all participants during the same period.
- σ, the security's volatility during the same period. Volatility has the physical unit of the inverse square root of time.

The transaction cost c is dimensionless and invariant in the units chosen for currency and time. If the argument is a polynomial of the input quantities above, we write

$$c(Q, \sigma, V, T) = F(V^a Q^b \sigma^c)$$
$$[\text{number}] = \left(\frac{[\text{currency}]}{[\text{time}]}\right)^a [\text{currency}]^b \left(\frac{1}{[\text{time}]^{1/2}}\right)^c$$

From which $0 = a + b$ and $-a - c/2 = 0$. Set, without loss of generality, $a = -1/2$. It follows that the cost is a function of $V^{-1/2}Q^{1/2}\sigma$: $c(Q, \sigma, V) = F(V^{-1/2}Q^{1/2}\sigma)$.

- (Kyle, 1985; Huberman and Stanzl, 2004) This model is a special case of Almgren-Chriss's model and precedes it historically. The functions are

$$f(\dot{x}) = \sigma\left(\frac{\dot{x}}{v}\right)$$
$$G(t) = \delta(t)$$

  The model is interesting in two regards. First, it is robust to price manipulation: a round-trip trade where an agent starts and ends flat, and is expected to extract a profit from the market impact they generate (Huberman and Stanzl, 2004; Gatheral, 2010). Second, it is analytically tractable. We will use this model in Section 11.3, where we present a model of infinite-horizon trading.

- (Obizhaeva and Wang, 2013) The functions are

$$f(\dot{x}) = \frac{\dot{x}}{v}$$
$$G(t) = e^{-t/\tau}$$

[5] For background on dimensional analysis, see Bluman and Kumei (1989); Barenblatt (2003); Gibbins (2011); Mahajan (2014).

The trading cost is

$$C[x] = \kappa \int_0^T dt\dot{x}_t e^{-t/\tau} \int_0^t ds \frac{\dot{x}_s}{v} e^{s/\tau}$$

Consider again the constant-rate trade of Q shares over an interval $[0, T]$. The trading cost is

$$\begin{aligned} C &= \kappa \left(\frac{Q}{T}\right)^2 \frac{1}{v} \int_0^T dte^{-t/\tau} \int_0^t dse^{s/\tau} \\ &= \kappa \left(\frac{Q}{T}\right)^2 \frac{1}{v} \tau[T - \tau(1 - e^{-T/\tau})] \\ c &= \kappa\tau \left[1 - \frac{\tau}{T}(1 - e^{-T/\tau})\right] \left(\frac{Q}{V}\right) \end{aligned} \tag{11.2}$$

Consider the two cases where timescales of execution and relaxation separate: "slow" execution $\tau \ll T$ and "fast" execution $\tau \gg T$:

$$c \simeq \begin{cases} \kappa\tau \left(\dfrac{Q}{V}\right) & \text{if } \tau \ll T \\ \dfrac{\kappa T}{2} \left(\dfrac{Q}{V}\right) & \text{if } \tau \gg T \end{cases}$$

For the slow execution case, the unit cost is inversely proportional to execution time, whereas it is independent of T when $T \ll \tau$. The overall market impact time series is shown in Figure 11.2. The Obizhaeva and Wang model (OW henceforth) has a dynamic formulation. Let $Q : [0, T]+ \rightarrow \mathbb{R}$ be the cumulative traded notional, and $q := \dot{Q}$. The OW market impact is modeled as

$$\dot{I}_t = \frac{\kappa}{v} q_t - \frac{1}{\tau} I_t$$

With an initial condition $I(0) = 0$, and with constant rate of execution $q = Q_T/T$, this differential equation has a simple solution:

$$I_t = \frac{\kappa}{v\lambda} q(1 - e^{-t/\tau})$$

and the trading cost is given by

$$\begin{aligned} C &= \int_0^T dtI_t q \\ &= \frac{\kappa\tau T}{v} q^2 \left[1 - \frac{\tau}{T}(1 - e^{-T/\tau})\right] \\ &= \kappa\tau \left[1 - \frac{\tau}{T}(1 - e^{-T/\tau})\right] \left(\frac{Q_T}{V}\right) Q_T \end{aligned}$$

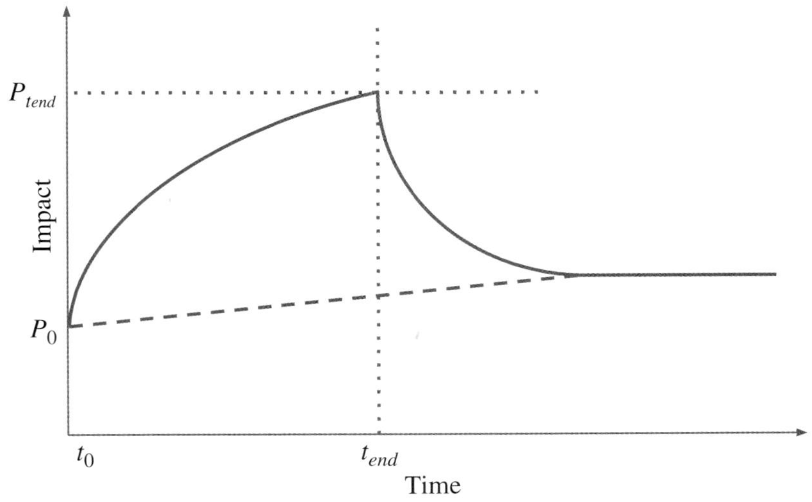

Figure 11.2 Market impact over time. The dashed line is the permanent market impact. The solid line is the sum of temporary and permanent market impacts.

The formula of $c = C/Q_T$ is the same form as Equation (11.2).

- (Gatheral, 2016) The functions are

$$f(\dot{x}) = \sigma \operatorname{sgn}(\dot{x}) \left| \frac{\dot{x}}{v} \right|^{1/2}$$
$$G(t) = \frac{1}{\sqrt{t}}$$

The trading cost is

$$C = \kappa\sigma \int_0^T dt\dot{x}_t \int_0^t ds \left(\frac{\dot{x}_s}{v}\right)^{1/2} \frac{1}{\sqrt{t-s}}$$

Assuming constant-rate trading of Q shares over an interval $[0, T]$, i.e., $\dot{x}_s = Q/T$, yields our final result:

$$C = \frac{4}{3}\kappa\sigma\sqrt{\frac{QT}{V}}Q$$
$$c = \frac{4}{3}\kappa\sigma\sqrt{\frac{QT}{V}}$$

The unit execution cost is $c \propto \sigma\sqrt{Q/v}$, and independent of T.

11.2 Finite-Horizon Optimization

We have a large class of models to choose from. Which one to use is a question that can be settled empirically. In the following, we use the general form of Equation (11.1) for market impact, and a term proportional to trade size for transaction costs.

Let us focus on a single security. The market-impact-related trading cost is, after integrating by parts,

$$\int_0^t x_s \dot{p}_s ds = x_t p_t - x_0 p_0 - \int_0^t \dot{x}_s p_s ds$$

The term $x_0 p_0$ is not a decision variable, so we can ignore it in the optimization process. As a boundary condition on the optimization, we assume that we end flat, i.e., $x_t = 0$. The overall trading cost becomes $-\int_0^t \dot{x}_s p_s ds$. Now, let us write the expected costs from trading for a single asset:

$$\text{Cost}_{\text{trade}} = \underbrace{-p \int_0^t |\dot{x}_s| ds}_{\text{(transaction cost)}} \underbrace{- \kappa \int_0^t ds \int_0^u du \dot{x}_s f(\dot{x}_u) G(s-u)}_{\text{(impact)}}$$

The idea behind multi-period optimization is to use the current forecast for excess returns over time, and plan trades for the entire horizon. Only the front-end of the trade is executed. In the next trading period, we develop or receive a new forecast, and we optimize again, using the updated portfolio as initial condition. This approach has both advantages and drawbacks. The main advantage is its flexibility. First, we can employ any market impact function, and the formulation will allow us to account for the decay in impact. In addition, we can also include as many side constraints as we want. In this section, we only include linear constraints, since they are very flexible and cover the vast majority of use cases; but non-linear constraints (e.g., on maximum factor risk) are also possible. What are the drawbacks, then? There are three. The first one is that we have to solve numerically an optimization, whose execution time may introduce delays in trading and therefore adversely affect profitability. The second one is that the convergence properties of the program depend on its structure. Specifically, one has to ensure that the objective function is concave. This depends on the choice of market impact, which can make the problem non-concave. The third one is that we are incorporating the change in expected returns as a function of the horizon, but are not incorporating in the problem the dynamics of updates in our return forecast from one period to the next.

We split the trading periods into intervals delimited by timestamps T_i. We use the convention

$$
\begin{aligned}
0 &= T_0 < T_1 < \cdots < T_m \\
\Delta_i &:= T_i - T_{i-1}
\end{aligned}
$$

For example, Δ_1 could be 10 minutes; Δ_2 could be one hour; Δ_3 could be one day; Δ_4 could be one week; and Δ_5 could be four weeks. At time T_i we hold x_i dollars of the security. In interval $[T_{i-1}, T_i)$ we have expected return μ_i, and trade at rate z_i. The relationship between $x_.$ and $z_.$ is $x_{T_i} = x_{T_{i-1}} + z_i(T_i - T_{i-1})$. At time $t \in [T_{i-1}, T_i)$, we hold $x_t = x_{T_{i-1}} + z_i(t - T_{i-1})$ dollars in the security. In this equation, we are not adjusting our holdings with price changes. The correct formula would be $\dot{x}_t = z_t + x_t\dot{p}_t$. In the words of Boyd et al. (2016), we are ignoring "second-order terms" in the holdings. This seems reasonable on two grounds. First, for short-enough intervals, $|\dot{p}_t| \ll 1$. Second, because the error introduced by ignoring return adjustment is smaller than other errors already present in the model. For example, we replaced the realized market impact with the expected impact. The initial condition x_0 and the trading rates z_i determine x_t. We can then express $\text{PnL}_{\text{trade}}$ as a function of z_i and add this term to the objective function. The rest is (nasty) details:

$$
\begin{aligned}
\textit{(transaction cost)} &= -p\sum_{i=1}^{m}\Delta_i|z_i| \\
\textit{(impact cost)} &= -\kappa\sum_{i=1}^{m}\sum_{j=1}^{m} a_{i,j} z_i f(z_j) \\
a_{i,j} &:= \mathbf{1}\{j \le i\} \int_{T_{i-1}}^{T_i}\left(\int_{T_{j-1}}^{T_j \wedge s} G(s-u)du\right) ds
\end{aligned}
$$

The variance penalty is integrated over a time interval:

$$
\begin{aligned}
\text{Var}(\mathbf{x}_t) &= \int_0^t \mathbf{x}_s^{\mathsf{T}}\mathbf{\Omega}\mathbf{x}_s ds \\
&= \sum_{i=1}^{m}\left[\Delta_i \mathbf{x}_{T_{i-1}}^{\mathsf{T}}\mathbf{\Omega}\mathbf{x}_{T_{i-1}} + \Delta_i^2 \mathbf{x}_{T_{i-1}}\mathbf{\Omega}\mathbf{z}_i + (\Delta_i^3/3)\mathbf{z}_i^{\mathsf{T}}\mathbf{\Omega}\mathbf{z}_i\right]
\end{aligned}
$$

Now we can write the optimization formulation. We use the following notation: $\mathbf{x}_i := (x_{T_i,1}, \ldots, x_{T_i,n})$, $\mathbf{f}(\mathbf{x}) := (f_1(x_1), \ldots, f_n(x_n))$. We also introduce $m-1$ pairs of matrices and vectors $\mathbf{H}_i \in \mathbb{R}^{q \times 2n}$, $\mathbf{b}_i \in \mathbb{R}^q$. These objects store linear constraints on holdings and portfolios for each stage of the optimization problem:

$$\begin{aligned}
\max \quad & \frac{1}{2}\sum_{i=1}^{m} \boldsymbol{\mu}_i^\top(\mathbf{x}_{i-1} + \mathbf{x}_i) && \textit{(expected PnL)}\\
& - \sum_{i=1}^{m} \Delta_i \mathbf{p}^\top |\mathbf{z}_i| && \textit{(trading cost)}\\
& -\kappa \sum_{k=1}^{n}\sum_{i=1}^{m}\sum_{j=1}^{m} a_{i,j} z_{i,k} f(z_{j,k}) && \textit{(impact cost)}\\
& -\frac{\rho}{2}\sum_{i=1}^{m}\left[\Delta_i \mathbf{x}_{i-1}^\top \boldsymbol{\Omega}\mathbf{x}_{i-1} + \Delta_i^2 \mathbf{x}_{i-1}\boldsymbol{\Omega}\mathbf{z}_i + (\Delta_i^3/3)\mathbf{z}_i^\top \boldsymbol{\Omega}\mathbf{z}_i\right] && \textit{(variance penalty)}\\
\text{s.t.} \quad & \mathbf{x}_i - \mathbf{x}_{i-1} - \mathbf{z}_{i-1}\Delta_i = 0 && \textit{(flow conservation)}\\
& \mathbf{H}_i \begin{bmatrix} \mathbf{x}_i \\ \mathbf{z}_i \end{bmatrix} \le \mathbf{b}_i \qquad i = 1, \ldots, m-1 && \textit{(side constraints)}\\
& \mathbf{x}_i \in \mathbb{R}^n \qquad i = 1, \ldots, m-1 &&\\
& \mathbf{z}_i \in \mathbb{R}^n \qquad i = 1, \ldots, m-1 &&
\end{aligned}$$

We impose that the initial portfolio $\mathbf{x}_0$ is given, and usually (but not necessarily), we set a final holding condition $\mathbf{x}_m = 0$. The "not necessarily" qualification depends on the parameters used in the problem. For example, if we set $\boldsymbol{\mu}_m = 0$, the optimization will attempt to reduce the size of the portfolio in the last stage, since holding the positions yields a risk cost. For large variance penalties and low execution costs, the solution will yield a value of $\mathbf{x}_m$ that is close to zero, without the need of boundary condition.

11.3 Infinite-Horizon Optimization

We now present an infinite-horizon optimization model, introduced by Ritter et al. (2022). Compared to the finite-horizon optimization model of the previous section, the model allows only for quadratic costs and cannot accommodate generic side constraints.[6] On the other side, it is flexible with respect to alpha processes.

[6] Linear equality constraints can be priced in the objective function, but linear inequality constraints can't.

We maximize a mean-variance objective, inclusive of transaction costs.

$$\max_{\mathbf{x}} E \int_0^{\infty} \left(\boldsymbol{\mu}_t^{\mathsf{T}} \mathbf{x}_t - \frac{1}{2} \dot{\mathbf{x}}_t^{\mathsf{T}} \mathbf{C} \dot{\mathbf{x}}_t - \frac{1}{2} \rho \mathbf{x}_t^{\mathsf{T}} \boldsymbol{\Omega} \mathbf{x}_t \right) dt \tag{11.3}$$

where:

1. The asset expected returns are described by a non-anticipative[7] stochastic process $\boldsymbol{\mu}_t$ taking values in $\mathbb{R}^n$, defined over a probability space $(\Omega, P, \mathcal{F})$.
2. The cost matrix $\mathbf{C}$ is positive-definite and diagonal.[8] The cost rate from trading asset i at time t is $[\mathbf{C}]_{i,i} \dot{x}_{i,t}^2$.
3. The return covariance matrix $\boldsymbol{\Omega}$ is positive-definite, with positive penalty factor ρ.

The optimal trading policy is described in Procedure 11.1.

Procedure 11.1: *Infinite-horizon optimal trading policy*

1. **Input:**
   (a) symmetric positive-definite cost matrix $\mathbf{C} \in \mathbb{R}^{n \times n}$;
   (b) symmetric positive-definite return covariance matrix; $\boldsymbol{\Omega} \in \mathbb{R}^{n \times n}$;
   (c) expected return process $\boldsymbol{\mu}_t$ taking values in $\mathbb{R}^n$;
   (d) initial portfolio $\mathbf{x}_0 \in \mathbb{R}^n$.

(Continued)

[7] A loose description of such a process is that the value of $\boldsymbol{\mu}_t$ is known based on the information available at time t. The rigorous definition of non-anticipative (or adapted) process is beyond the scope of this book; see a graduate-level textbook on probability theory, such as Durrett (2019).

[8] We make the assumption of diagonal cost matrix because it is intuitive and most relevant to applications. It can be relaxed to model *cross-market impact* among securities. Many such models use quadratic costs. See, e.g., Mastromatteo et al. (2017); Min et al. (2022).

(*Continued*)

2. Define

$$\mathbf{\Gamma} := (\rho \mathbf{C}^{-1}\mathbf{\Omega})^{1/2}$$

$$\mathbf{b}_t := \int_t^\infty e^{\mathbf{\Gamma}(t-s)}\mathbf{C}^{-1}E_t\boldsymbol{\mu}_s ds$$

3. Output:

(a) Optimal trading policy:

$$\mathbf{x}_t = e^{-\mathbf{\Gamma}t}\left(\mathbf{x}_0 + \int_0^t e^{\mathbf{\Gamma}s}\mathbf{b}_s ds\right)$$

$$\dot{\mathbf{x}}_t = -\mathbf{\Gamma}\mathbf{x}_t + \mathbf{b}_t$$

(b) Optimum:

$$f^\star = \int_0^\infty \left(\boldsymbol{\mu}_t^\top \mathbf{x}_t - \frac{1}{2}\dot{\mathbf{x}}_t^\top \mathbf{C}\dot{\mathbf{x}}_t - \frac{1}{2}\rho \mathbf{x}_t^\top \mathbf{\Omega}\mathbf{x}_t\right) dt$$

Let us try to interpret the (rather magical) objects we have introduced.

- The ith term of the vector $\mathbf{b}_t$ is a discounted expected return of asset i, where the discount factor is determined by the matrix $\mathbf{\Gamma}$.
- Consider the special case of uncorrelated asset returns, so that $[\mathbf{\Gamma}]_{i,i} = \sqrt{\rho\sigma_i}/\sqrt{c_i}$. The greater the volatility or the risk aversion, the more we discount future returns.
- On the other side, the higher the trading costs, described by c_i, the less we discount the future. Why? Because if trading is expensive, we want to weight future returns more, so that we do not chase only short-horizon performance.
- What is being discounted in $\mathbf{b}_t$ is not quite the future expected returns, but the cost-normalized expected returns $\mathbf{C}^{-1}E_t\boldsymbol{\mu}_t$. If unit costs are higher, we have smaller future adjusted returns being discounted. However, we have a smaller $\mathbf{\Gamma}$, hence we discount the future less. These are two competing effects. In Exercise 11.1, you will assess their relative impact in a few special cases.

- The discretized version of the optimal trading policy is

$$\begin{aligned} \mathbf{b}_t &:= \sum_{s=t}^{\infty} \delta t e^{\delta t \boldsymbol{\Gamma}(t-s)} \mathbf{C}^{-1} E_t(\mu_s) \\ \mathbf{x}_{t+1} &= (\mathbf{I} - \delta t \boldsymbol{\Gamma})\mathbf{x}_t + \delta t \mathbf{b}_t \end{aligned} \tag{11.4}$$

The optimal trading policy is recursive. The next optimal portfolio is a linear combination of the existing portfolio, discounted using matrix $\boldsymbol{\Gamma}$, and of the "alpha-to-go" $\mathbf{b}_t$.

Exercise 11.1 ***(The Impact of Costs on Trading)*:** Consider the following simple problem. There is only one asset with volatility σ and cost parameter c. Consider two cases:

1. The signal's strength is exponentially decreasing over time: $E_0\mu_s = e^{-\lambda s}$, with $\lambda > 0$.
2. The signal strength is constant in interval $[0, 1]$.

Prove that $b_0(c)$ is a decreasing function of c in both cases. Generalize this result.

11.3.1 Comparison to Single-Period Optimization

Let us solve the single-period problem. Define

$$\max\,(E_t\boldsymbol{\mu}_{t+1})^{\mathsf{T}}\mathbf{x}_{t+1} - \frac{1}{2}(\mathbf{x}_{t+1} - \mathbf{x}_t)^{\mathsf{T}}\mathbf{C}(\mathbf{x}_{t+1} - \mathbf{x}_t) - \frac{1}{2}\rho\mathbf{x}_{t+1}\boldsymbol{\Omega}\mathbf{x}_{t+1} \tag{11.5}$$

$$\max\,(E_t\boldsymbol{\mu}_{t+1} + \mathbf{C}\mathbf{x}_t)^{\mathsf{T}}\mathbf{x}_{t+1} - \frac{1}{2}\mathbf{x}_{t+1}(\rho\boldsymbol{\Omega} + \mathbf{C})\mathbf{x}_{t+1} \tag{11.6}$$

$$\mathbf{x}_{t+1} = (\mathbf{I} + \rho\mathbf{C}^{-1}\boldsymbol{\Omega})^{-1}\mathbf{x}_t + (\mathbf{I} + \rho\mathbf{C}^{-1}\boldsymbol{\Omega})^{-1}\mathbf{C}^{-1}E_t\boldsymbol{\mu}_{t+1} \tag{11.7}$$

In the case $\|\rho\mathbf{C}^{-1}\boldsymbol{\Omega}\| \ll 1$, we can approximate

$$\simeq (\mathbf{I} - \rho\mathbf{C}^{-1}\boldsymbol{\Omega})\mathbf{x}_t + (\mathbf{I} - \rho\mathbf{C}^{-1}\boldsymbol{\Omega})\mathbf{C}^{-1}E_t\boldsymbol{\mu}_{t+1} \tag{11.8}$$

The solution is similar to multi-period, in that it is a combination of the existing portfolio and an alpha-related term. If we assume that $E_t\boldsymbol{\mu}_s = 0$ for $s > t + 1$, and assuming again $\|\rho\mathbf{C}^{-1}\boldsymbol{\Omega}\| \ll 1$, we approximate the first term only of $\mathbf{b}_t$ and the multi-period solution is

$$\mathbf{x}_{t+1} \simeq (\mathbf{I} - \delta t(\rho\mathbf{C}^{-1}\boldsymbol{\Omega})^{1/2})\mathbf{x}_t + (\mathbf{I} - \delta t(\rho\mathbf{C}^{-1}\boldsymbol{\Omega})^{1/2})\mathbf{C}^{-1}E_t\boldsymbol{\mu}_{t+1} \tag{11.9}$$

The two are identical, except that a square-root term appears in the multi-period approximation.

11.3.2 The No-Market-Impact Limit

Consider the case of vanishing market impact. We set $\mathbf{C} := \kappa\mathbf{C}_0$, and let $\kappa \downarrow 0$. When $||\boldsymbol{\Gamma}|| \gg 1$, from Equation (11.4) we have

$$\mathbf{b}_t := \int_t^\infty e^{\boldsymbol{\Gamma}(t-s)}\mathbf{C}^{-1}E_t\boldsymbol{\mu}_s ds \tag{11.10}$$

$$\simeq \int_0^\infty e^{-s\boldsymbol{\Gamma}}\mathbf{C}^{-1}\boldsymbol{\mu}_t ds \tag{11.11}$$

$$= -\boldsymbol{\Gamma}^{-1}e^{-s\boldsymbol{\Gamma}}\mathbf{C}^{-1}\boldsymbol{\mu}_t\Big|_{s=0}^\infty \tag{11.12}$$

$$= -\boldsymbol{\Gamma}^{-1}(e^{-s\boldsymbol{\Gamma}} - \mathbf{1})\mathbf{C}^{-1}\boldsymbol{\mu}_t \tag{11.13}$$

$$\simeq \boldsymbol{\Gamma}^{-1}\mathbf{C}^{-1}\mu_t \tag{11.14}$$

and

$$\dot{\mathbf{x}}_t = -\boldsymbol{\Gamma}\mathbf{x}_t + \mathbf{b}_t \tag{11.15}$$

$$= \kappa^{-1/2}\left[-(\rho\mathbf{C}_0^{-1}\boldsymbol{\Omega})^{1/2}\mathbf{x}_t + (\rho\mathbf{C}_0^{-1}\boldsymbol{\Omega})^{-1/2}\mathbf{C}_0^{-1}\boldsymbol{\mu}_t\right] \tag{11.16}$$

In the limit $\kappa \downarrow 0$, a solution exists if

$$\mathbf{x}_t = (\rho\mathbf{C}_0^{-1}\boldsymbol{\Omega})^{-1}\mathbf{C}_0^{-1}\boldsymbol{\mu}_t$$
$$= \rho^{-1}\boldsymbol{\Omega}^{-1}\boldsymbol{\mu}_t$$

This is the solution to the single-period MVO problem in the absence of transaction costs. The optimal solution is to rebalance instantaneously to the MVO allocation, depending on the instantaneous alpha prediction. We have recovered the result from conventional single-period optimization.

11.3.3 Optimal Liquidation

Suppose that we hold a portfolio $\mathbf{x}_0$, and have no forward-looking alpha: $\boldsymbol{\mu}_t = 0$ a.s. for $t \geq 0$. What is the optimal trading policy? In this case, $\mathbf{b}_t = 0$ and the optimal trade-out policy is the solution to the equation $\dot{\mathbf{x}}_t = -\boldsymbol{\Gamma}\mathbf{x}_t$, i.e., $\mathbf{x}_t = e^{-t\boldsymbol{\Gamma}}\mathbf{x}_0$. We reduce the positions at an exponential rate, with the rate of liquidation depending on the matrix $\boldsymbol{\Gamma}$. The larger the coefficient of risk aversion ρ and the volatility, the faster the liquidation. The higher the cost, the slower the liquidation.

11.3.4 Deterministic Alpha

Say that the future returns are a deterministic function $\boldsymbol{\mu}_t$. The function $\mathbf{b}_t$ is also deterministic and given by the integral (11.26). The solution to the Ordinary Differential Equation (ODE) (11.29) is

$$\mathbf{b}_t = \int_t^\infty e^{\boldsymbol{\Gamma}(t-s)}\mathbf{C}^{-1}\boldsymbol{\mu}_s ds$$

$$\begin{aligned}\mathbf{x}_t &= e^{-\boldsymbol{\Gamma}t}\left(\mathbf{x}_0 + \int_0^t e^{\boldsymbol{\Gamma}s}\mathbf{b}_s ds\right)\\ &= e^{-\boldsymbol{\Gamma}t}\left(\mathbf{x}_0 + \int_0^t e^{\boldsymbol{\Gamma}s}\left(\int_s^\infty e^{\boldsymbol{\Gamma}(s-u)}\mathbf{C}^{-1}\boldsymbol{\mu}_u du\right) ds\right)\end{aligned}$$

It is useful to present an indicative case of a "spiked" alpha: $\boldsymbol{\mu}_t := \boldsymbol{\mu}_0\delta(t-t_0)$. In this case the function $\mathbf{b}_t$ takes a simple form:

$$\mathbf{b}_t = \mathbf{1}(t_0 - t)e^{\boldsymbol{\Gamma}(t-t_0)}\mathbf{C}^{-1}\boldsymbol{\mu}_0$$

For $t \le t_0$,

$$\begin{aligned}\mathbf{x}_{t_0} &= e^{-\boldsymbol{\Gamma}t}\left(\mathbf{x}_0 + \int_0^t e^{2\boldsymbol{\Gamma}s}e^{-\boldsymbol{\Gamma}t_0}\mathbf{C}^{-1}\boldsymbol{\mu}_0 ds\right)\\ &= e^{-\boldsymbol{\Gamma}t}\left(\mathbf{x}_0 + \boldsymbol{\Gamma}^{-1}e^{\boldsymbol{\Gamma}t}\cosh(\boldsymbol{\Gamma}t)e^{-\boldsymbol{\Gamma}t_0}\mathbf{C}^{-1}\boldsymbol{\mu}_0\right)\end{aligned}$$

In the formula above, we have introduced a direct extension of the hyperbolic cosine to square matrices, i.e., $\sinh(\mathbf{X}) := (e^{\mathbf{X}} - e^{-\mathbf{X}})/2$.

When $t = t_0$, the optimal portfolio position is

$$\mathbf{x}_{t_0} = e^{-\boldsymbol{\Gamma}t_0}\left(\mathbf{x}_0 + \boldsymbol{\Gamma}^{-1}\cosh(\boldsymbol{\Gamma}t_0)\mathbf{C}^{-1}\boldsymbol{\mu}_0\right)$$

For $t > t_0$, the portfolio is liquidated in the absence of alpha:

$$\mathbf{x}_t = e^{-\boldsymbol{\Gamma}t}\left(\mathbf{x}_0 + \boldsymbol{\Gamma}^{-1}\cosh(\boldsymbol{\Gamma}t_0)\mathbf{C}^{-1}\boldsymbol{\mu}_0\right)$$

11.3.5 AR(1) Signal

Let us consider first the case of autoregressive expected returns:

$$\boldsymbol{\mu}_{t+1} = \boldsymbol{\Phi}\boldsymbol{\mu}_t + \boldsymbol{\eta}_t \tag{11.17}$$

$$\mathbf{r}_t = \boldsymbol{\mu}_t + \boldsymbol{\epsilon}_t \tag{11.18}$$

where

- $\mathbf{\Phi}$ is a diagonal matrix with $[\mathbf{\Phi}]_{i,i} \in (0, 1)$;
- $\boldsymbol{\eta}_t \sim N(0, \mathbf{\Omega}_\eta)$, with $\mathbf{\Omega}_\eta$ diagonal and positive-definite;
- $\boldsymbol{\epsilon}_t \sim N(0, \mathbf{\Omega}_\epsilon)$;
- $\boldsymbol{\eta}_t$, $\boldsymbol{\epsilon}_t$ are jointly independent and serially independent, i.e., $\boldsymbol{\eta}_s \perp \boldsymbol{\epsilon}_t$ for all s, t and $\boldsymbol{\eta}_s \perp \boldsymbol{\eta}_t$, $\boldsymbol{\epsilon}_s \perp \boldsymbol{\epsilon}_t$, for all $s \neq t$.

By repeated substitution we have

$$\boldsymbol{\mu}_{t+s} = \mathbf{\Phi}^s \boldsymbol{\mu}_t + \sum_{i=0}^{s-1} \mathbf{\Phi}^{s-i} \boldsymbol{\eta}_{t+i} \tag{11.19}$$

$$E_t \boldsymbol{\mu}_{t+s} = \mathbf{\Phi}^s \boldsymbol{\mu}_t \tag{11.20}$$

The long-term covariance matrices of $\boldsymbol{\mu}_t$ and $\mathbf{r}_t$ are $\mathbf{\Omega}_\eta(\mathbf{I} - \mathbf{\Phi})^{-1}$ and $\mathbf{\Omega}_\epsilon + \mathbf{\Omega}_\eta(\mathbf{I} - \mathbf{\Phi})^{-1}$ respectively.

The continuous-time solution is

$$\begin{aligned} \mathbf{\Gamma} &:= \left[\rho \mathbf{C}^{-1}(\mathbf{\Omega}_\epsilon + \mathbf{\Omega}_\eta(\mathbf{I} - \mathbf{\Phi})^{-1})\right]^{1/2} \\ \mathbf{b}_t &:= \int_t^\infty e^{\mathbf{\Gamma}(t-s)} \mathbf{C}^{-1} \mathbf{\Phi}^{s-t} \mu_t ds && (\textit{from Equation } (11.26)) \\ &= \int_0^\infty e^{-v\mathbf{\Gamma}} \mathbf{C}^{-1} \mathbf{\Phi}^v \mu_t dv && (v := s - t) \end{aligned}$$

Define $\mathbf{\Gamma} = \mathbf{USV}^\top$ and $\mathbf{A} := \mathbf{V}^\top \mathbf{C}^{-1}$. We rewrite $\mathbf{b}_t$ as

$$\mathbf{b}_t = \mathbf{U}\left(\int_0^\infty \text{diag}\,(e^{-vs_1}, \ldots, e^{-vs_n})\, \mathbf{A}\mathbf{\Phi}^v dv\right) \boldsymbol{\mu}_t \tag{11.21}$$

$$\begin{aligned} \left[\int_0^\infty \text{diag}\,(e^{-vs_1}, \ldots, e^{-vs_n})\, \mathbf{A}\mathbf{\Phi}^v dv\right]_{i,j} &= a_{i,j} \int_0^\infty (e^{-s_i}\phi_j)^v dv \\ &= \frac{a_{i,j}}{s_i - \log(\phi_j)} \\ &< \infty \end{aligned}$$

Define a matrix $\mathbf{H}$ by $[\mathbf{H}]_{i,j} := (s_i - \log(\phi_j))^{-1}$. Then $\mathbf{b}_t = \mathbf{U}[(\mathbf{V}^\top\mathbf{C}^{-1}) \circ \mathbf{H}]\boldsymbol{\mu}_t$. The optimal trading policy at time t, given portfolio $\mathbf{x}_t$ and predicted returns $\boldsymbol{\mu}_t$, is

$$\delta\mathbf{x}_t = (\underbrace{-\boldsymbol{\Gamma}\mathbf{x}_t}_{(liquidation)} + \underbrace{\mathbf{K}\boldsymbol{\mu}_t}_{(investment)})\delta t \tag{11.22}$$

$$\mathbf{K} := \mathbf{U}[(\mathbf{V}^\top\mathbf{C}^{-1}) \circ \mathbf{H}] \tag{11.23}$$

Equation (11.22) has an intuitive interpretation. In the absence of expected returns, liquidate the book using a trading rate proportional to position size. With non-zero expected returns, we combine the liquidation with a trade that is a linear function of the expected return.

11.4 ★Appendix

11.4.1 Proof of the Infinite-Horizon Quadratic Problem

We need a few definitions:

$$\begin{aligned}
\langle \mathbf{x}, \mathbf{y} \rangle &:= E\left[\int_0^\infty \mathbf{x}_s^\top \mathbf{y}_s ds\right] \\
\|\mathbf{x}\|^2 &:= \langle \mathbf{x}, \mathbf{x} \rangle \\
(K\mathbf{x})_t &:= \int_0^t \mathbf{x}_s ds
\end{aligned}$$

The adjoint operator of K is such that $\langle K^*\mathbf{x}, \mathbf{y}\rangle = \langle \mathbf{x}, K\mathbf{y}\rangle$. In formulas:

$$\begin{aligned}
\langle \mathbf{x}, K\mathbf{y} \rangle &= E\left[\int_0^\infty \mathbf{x}_s^\top \left(\int_0^s \mathbf{y}_t dt\right) ds\right] \\
&= E\left[\int_0^\infty \mathbf{x}_t dt \int_0^\infty \mathbf{y}_{s'} ds' - \int_0^\infty \left(\int_0^{t'} \mathbf{x}_t dt\right) \mathbf{y}_{t'} dt'\right] \\
&= E\left[\int_0^\infty \left(\int_t^\infty \mathbf{x}_{t'} dt'\right) \mathbf{y}_t dt\right] \\
&= E\left[\int_0^\infty E_u\left(\int_u^\infty \mathbf{x}_{u'} du'\right) \mathbf{y}_u du\right] \\
\Rightarrow (K^*\mathbf{x})_t &= E_t \int_t^\infty \mathbf{x}_u du
\end{aligned}$$

We solve Problem (11.3):

$$\max_{\mathbf{x}} E \int_0^\infty \left(\boldsymbol{\mu}_t^\mathsf{T} \mathbf{x}_t - \frac{1}{2} \dot{\mathbf{x}}_t^\mathsf{T} \mathbf{C} \dot{\mathbf{x}}_t - \frac{1}{2} \rho \mathbf{x}_t^\mathsf{T} \boldsymbol{\Omega} \mathbf{x}_t \right) dt$$

Introduce the variable $\mathbf{u}$ such that $\mathbf{x} := K\mathbf{u}$:

$$\max_{\mathbf{u}} E \int_0^\infty \left[\boldsymbol{\mu}_t^\mathsf{T} (K\mathbf{u})_t - \frac{1}{2} \mathbf{u}_t^\mathsf{T} \mathbf{C} \mathbf{u}_t - \frac{1}{2} \rho (K\mathbf{u})_t^\mathsf{T} \boldsymbol{\Omega} (K\mathbf{u})_t \right] dt$$

$$F[\mathbf{u}] := \langle \boldsymbol{\mu}, K\mathbf{u} \rangle - \frac{1}{2} \langle \mathbf{u}, \mathbf{C}\mathbf{u} \rangle - \frac{1}{2} \rho \langle K\mathbf{u}, \boldsymbol{\Omega} K\mathbf{u} \rangle$$

$$\text{FONC on functionals} \quad \nabla F = K^* \boldsymbol{\mu} - \mathbf{C}\mathbf{u} - \rho K^* \boldsymbol{\Omega} K \mathbf{u} = 0$$

$$K^* \boldsymbol{\mu} = \mathbf{C} \dot{\mathbf{x}} + \rho K^* \boldsymbol{\Omega} \mathbf{x} \tag{11.24}$$

This is a linear system. Some definitions:

- $E_s(\mathbf{x}) := E(\mathbf{x}|\mathcal{F}_s)$. The tower property of expectation is $E_s E_t = E_{s\wedge t}$.
- For some $\mathbf{x}$, $t_0 \le t$, let $\mathbf{x}_{t_0,t} := E_{t_0} \mathbf{x}_t$. From the definition $\mathbf{x}_{t_0,t}$, $E_t \mathbf{x}_t = \mathbf{x}_t(\omega)$.

Apply E_{t_0} to Equation (11.25):

$$E_{t_0} E_t \int_t^\infty \boldsymbol{\mu}_s ds = \mathbf{C} \frac{d}{dt} E_{t_0} \mathbf{x}_t + \rho E_{t_0} \int_t^\infty \boldsymbol{\Omega} \mathbf{x}_s ds$$

$$E_{t_0} \int_t^\infty \boldsymbol{\mu}_s ds = \mathbf{C} \frac{d}{dt} E_{t_0} \mathbf{x}_t + \rho \boldsymbol{\Omega} E_{t_0} \int_t^\infty \mathbf{x}_s ds$$

$$\frac{d}{dt} E_s \int_t^\infty \boldsymbol{\mu}_s ds = -E_{t_0} \boldsymbol{\mu}_t = \mathbf{C} \frac{d^2}{dt^2} E_{t_0} \mathbf{x}_t - \rho \boldsymbol{\Omega} E_{t_0} \mathbf{x}_t$$

$$\frac{d^2}{dt^2} \mathbf{x}_{t_0,t} = -\mathbf{C}^{-1} \boldsymbol{\mu}_{t_0,t} + \rho \mathbf{C}^{-1} \boldsymbol{\Omega} \mathbf{x}_{t_0,t}$$

This is a linear ODE in $\mathbf{x}_{t_0,t}$, which we can solve analytically. First, define

$$\boldsymbol{\Gamma} := (\rho \mathbf{C}^{-1} \boldsymbol{\Omega})^{1/2} \tag{11.25}$$

$$\mathbf{b}_t := \int_t^\infty e^{\boldsymbol{\Gamma}(t-s)} \mathbf{C}^{-1} E_t \boldsymbol{\mu}_s ds \tag{11.26}$$

The solution that satisfies $\lim_{t\to\infty} \mathbf{x}_{t_0,t} = 0$ is

$$\mathbf{x}_{t_0,t} = e^{-\boldsymbol{\Gamma}(t-t_0)} \mathbf{x}_{t_0,t_0} + \frac{1}{2} \mathbf{C}^{-1} \int_{t_0}^t dse^{-\boldsymbol{\Gamma}(t-s)} \int_s^\infty dze^{-\boldsymbol{\Gamma}(z-s)} \boldsymbol{\mu}_{t_0,z} \tag{11.27}$$

From which it follows directly

$$\left.\frac{d}{dt}\mathbf{x}_{t_0,t}\right|_{t=t_0} = -\boldsymbol{\Gamma}\mathbf{x}_{t_0,t_0} + \mathbf{b}_{t_0} \tag{11.28}$$

Finally, from $d\mathbf{x}_{t_0,t}/dt = \dot{\mathbf{x}}_{t_0}$ and $\mathbf{x}_{t_0,t_0} = \mathbf{x}_{t_0}$, the law for the optimal trading policy follows:

$$\dot{\mathbf{x}}_t = -\boldsymbol{\Gamma}\mathbf{x}_t + \mathbf{b}_t \tag{11.29}$$

$$\mathbf{x}_t = e^{-\boldsymbol{\Gamma}t}\left(\int_0^t e^{\boldsymbol{\Gamma}s}\mathbf{b}_s ds + \mathbf{x}_0\right) \tag{11.30}$$

$$f^\star = \int_0^\infty \left(\boldsymbol{\mu}_t^\top \mathbf{x}_t - \frac{1}{2}\dot{\mathbf{x}}_t^\top \mathbf{C}\dot{\mathbf{x}}_t - \frac{1}{2}\rho\mathbf{x}_t^\top \boldsymbol{\Omega}\mathbf{x}_t\right) dt \tag{11.31}$$

$$= \int_0^\infty \left(\boldsymbol{\mu}_t^\top \mathbf{x}_t - \frac{1}{2}(-\boldsymbol{\Gamma}\mathbf{x}_t + \mathbf{b}_t)^\top \mathbf{C}(-\boldsymbol{\Gamma}\mathbf{x}_t + \mathbf{b}_t) - \frac{1}{2}\rho\mathbf{x}_t^\top \boldsymbol{\Omega}\mathbf{x}_t\right) dt \tag{11.32}$$

$$= \int_0^\infty \left((\boldsymbol{\mu}_t^\top + \mathbf{b}_t^\top \mathbf{C}\boldsymbol{\Gamma})\mathbf{x}_t - \frac{1}{2}\mathbf{x}_t^\top(\rho\boldsymbol{\Omega} + \boldsymbol{\Gamma}^\top \mathbf{C}\boldsymbol{\Gamma})\mathbf{x}_t - \frac{1}{2}\mathbf{b}_t^\top \mathbf{C}\mathbf{b}_t\right) dt \tag{11.33}$$

The Takeaways

1. Trading incurs various costs, including market impact, which can turn profitable strategies unprofitable.
2. Market impact is the cumulative market response to new order flow, influenced by inventory reduction, informational effects, mimetic effects, and strategic trading.
3. Total transaction costs comprise spread costs, temporary market impact, and permanent market impact.
4. Spread costs arise from the bid–ask spread; market orders cross the spread and remove liquidity.
5. Permanent impact is the long-term price change post-execution; temporary impact occurs during and immediately after execution.
6. Temporary market impact is modeled using functions f (instantaneous impact) and G (propagator), representing price impact dynamics.
7. Models like Almgren–Chriss, Kyle, Obizhaeva–Wang, and Gatheral use specific forms of f and G to describe impact.
8. Finite-horizon optimization plans trades over multiple periods, accounting for market impact and transaction costs.
9. Multi-period optimization is flexible but may require complex numerical solutions and has convergence concerns.
10. Infinite-horizon optimization provides analytical optimal trading policies by maximizing a mean-variance objective with transaction costs.
11. The optimal policy balances expected returns, costs, and risk, depending on volatility, risk aversion, and costs.
12. Special cases like no-market-impact limit and optimal liquidation illustrate the policy under different conditions.

Chapter 12

Hedging

The Questions

1. What is the purpose of hedging in a portfolio, and what are the different types of hedges available?
2. How does a simple hedging model, with no transaction costs or parameter uncertainty, apply to real-world portfolio management?
3. How does the inclusion of parameter uncertainty affect optimal hedging strategies?
4. What are the implications of execution costs in multi-period hedging?
5. How can factor models be used in constructing hedging strategies, especially when managing factor exposures?
6. In what scenarios is it beneficial to hedge with FMPs, liquid assets, or futures, and how do these impact portfolio risk and return?

Hedging is the process of reducing the risk of a pre-existing portfolio by means of augmenting the portfolio with additional investments, whose returns are negatively correlated to the existing portfolio. The most common forms of hedging are market hedging and currency hedging, but there are at least three additional cases of practical relevance to portfolio managers. The first is hedging by means of Factor-Mimicking Portfolios (FMPs) obtained from a fundamental factor model. The second one is hedging by means of a future or liquid asset capturing equity and non-equity risk. This includes energy and interest rate futures, and liquid ETFs and ETNs describing market (e.g., SPY, a very liquid ETF tracking the S&P500), sector (e.g., XLK, an ETF tracking the stocks in the technology sector), or style (e.g., MTUM, an ETF reproducing the behavior of the momentum factor) risk. The last application of interest is the creation of thematic tradeable baskets by banks. One can buy these baskets to hedge or speculate on political risk (e.g., elections) or thematic risks (e.g., Citi has a global thematic engine with 80+ industry trends).

The chapter is broadly organized into three sections. The first part covers vanilla hedging. There are no villains in this story—no transaction costs, no parameter uncertainty, and a single period. Yet, such a simple model is still widely used in many applications. In the second part we explore the impact of parameter error and how it affects optimal hedging. Lastly, we look at multi-period hedging in the presence of execution costs.

12.1 Toy Story

In its simplest form, we have the following ingredients:

- We have two decision dates t_0, t_1, and one realized return between them. We make investment decisions at t_0, and observe realized returns at t_1.
- We have two assets, which we denote *core* and *hedge,* with returns r_c, r_h, expected returns $\mu_c \neq 0, \mu_h = 0$, volatilities $\sigma_c, \sigma_h > 0$, and return correlation between the two equal to $\rho_{c,h}$.

We decide the size of the hedging instrument in order to maximize the Sharpe Ratio of the combined portfolio. You already see how similar this problem is to the two-asset Mean-Variance Optimization (MVO) instance we saw in Section 10.1. In that problem, we decided the optimal positions of both assets; not a major difference. The MVO optimization problem

$$\max_{x_h \in \mathbb{R}} \mu_c x_c - \frac{\lambda}{2}(\sigma_c^2 x_c^2 + \sigma_h^2 x_h^2 + 2\rho_{c,h}\sigma_h\sigma_c x_c x_h)$$

has solution

$$x_h^\star = -\frac{\rho_{c,h}\sigma_c x_c}{\sigma_h} \tag{12.1}$$

$$\frac{x_h^\star}{x_c} = -\frac{\rho_{c,h}\sigma_c}{\sigma_h} = -\beta(r_c, r_h) \tag{12.2}$$

The ratio $|x_h^\star/x_c|$ is the *optimal hedge ratio* and is equal to the beta of the core portfolio's return to the hedging portfolio's return.

The unhedged variance is $\sigma_c^2 x_c^2$; after hedging, it is $(1 - \rho_{c,h}^2)\sigma_c^2 x_c^2$. The improvement in Sharpe Ratio is equal to the improvement in volatility:

$$\frac{\text{SR(hedged)}}{\text{SR(native)}} = \frac{1}{\sqrt{1 - \rho_{c,h}^2}} \tag{12.3}$$

The parameter β is estimated either via time-series regression or by using a return covariance matrix, such as one supplied by a factor model. Define $\mathbf{w}_c, \mathbf{w}_h$ the core and hedge portfolios; the model beta is

$$\beta(r_c, r_h) = \frac{\mathbf{w}_c^\top \mathbf{\Omega}_\mathbf{r} \mathbf{w}_h}{\mathbf{w}_h^\top \mathbf{\Omega}_\mathbf{r} \mathbf{w}_h} \tag{12.4}$$

From that, Equation (12.2) gives the relative size of the hedge, and Equation (12.3) the improvement in Sharpe Ratio from hedging.

In their simplicity, Equations (12.1)–(12.3) are applied widely. A typical application involves the use of a single hedging instrument that is very liquid and inexpensive to trade, and whose expected return is negligible compared to that of the native portfolio. Examples are e-mini S&P500 futures and the SPY, IVV, and VOO ETFs, which also track the S&P500 index. We perform intraday or end-of-day hedging in order to remove the associated risk.

Exercise 12.1 ***(Comparing a Market FMP and Benchmark as Hedging Instruments)*****:** For this exercise, you will need test portfolios (maybe for a live strategy), an equity factor model, and the weights of several benchmarks.

1. Compute the risk decompositions of the benchmarks and of the market FMP. What is their idiosyncratic variance as a percentage of total variance? What are their exposures (this applies to benchmarks only)?
2. Now, hedge the test portfolios using the FMP and the benchmark. What is the reduction in factor variance in the two cases? Benchmarks will have exposures to non-market factors. Are these partially hedged out? Are they material?

Perform the analysis over a number of years to verify whether the findings are stable.

Procedure 12.1: *Simple single-asset hedging*

1. **Inputs**: Core portfolio NMV x_c with returns r_c. Hedging asset with return r_h. Parameter $\beta(r_h, r_c)$, obtained by means of time-series regression, or of an asset covariance matrix and Equation (12.4).
2. **Output**: Hedge NMV $x_h^\star = -\beta(r_h, r_c)x_c$.

Hedging in this specific instance rests on several implicit and explicit assumptions:

- We assume that the beta of the core portfolio to the hedging instrument can be estimated accurately.
- We assume that there is a single trading instrument.
- We assume that trading costs are negligible.
- We assume that the hedging instrument has negligible expected return.

In the remainder of this chapter we re-examine these hypotheses and relax them.

12.2 Factor Hedging

12.2.1 The General Case

We have made recurrent use of factor models in this book, and unsurprisingly they matter for hedging as well. In principle, portfolio construction should take into account the predicted risk arising from factor exposures and idiosyncratic bets, and generate a portfolio that meets our investment goals. In practice, there are situations in which this is not possible. An important instance is when the core portfolio is the outcome of a portfolio construction process outside of our control. For example, we may have several groups of independent discretionary portfolio managers trading stocks based on their fundamental outlook. The sum of their individual portfolios constitutes a core portfolio that is not optimized, and that exhibits undesired systematic risk. In this case, the hedging process takes $\mathbf{w}_c$ as an input, and seeks to reduce the unwanted risk from factor exposures.[1] We defined factor-mimicking portfolios in Chapter 9, Equation (9.12): they are the columns of matrix $\mathbf{P}$, and have unit exposure to factor i. One way to hedge factor risk would be Procedure 12.2.

Procedure 12.2: ***A simple factor hedging procedure***

1. Compute the core portfolio factor exposure $\mathbf{b}_c = \mathbf{B}^{\mathsf{T}}\mathbf{w}_c$.
2. "Trade out" the core exposure by buying an amount of factor exposure $-\mathbf{b}_c$. We do this by buying a hedge portfolio $-\mathbf{P}\mathbf{b}_c$.

We have achieved zero factor exposure. The solution is simple, elegant, and unfortunately unrealistic. We have ignored two essential aspects of the hedging problem. First, factors have non-zero expected returns. Second, trading factors is expensive. However, we can change the

[1] We are assuming, again, that the returns of the factors we want to hedge are zero, or negligible.

formulation to include these modeling concerns. Let us begin with accounting for the non-zero expected return of the hedging portfolio. To this end, we need to go back to Section 4.3, which introduced the definition of alpha orthogonal and alpha spanned. In formulas: the expected return of a portfolio $\mathbf{w}$ is equal to $(\boldsymbol{\alpha}_\perp^\top + \boldsymbol{\mu}^\top \mathbf{B}^\top)\mathbf{w}$. Regarding the execution costs, we can include them in the optimization formulation, using a square-root impact model, or a quadratic model, as seen in Chapter 11. We denote the expected trading cost of a portfolio $\mathbf{w}$ from a starting portfolio $\mathbf{w}_0$ as $f(\mathbf{w} - \mathbf{w}_0)$. The coefficient of risk aversion is ρ. In a single-period setting, we then write the problem as

$$
\begin{aligned}
\max\ & \boldsymbol{\alpha}_\perp^\top(\mathbf{w}_c + \mathbf{w}_h) + \boldsymbol{\mu}^\top \mathbf{b} - \frac{1}{2}\rho(\sigma_{fac}^2 + \sigma_{idio}^2) - f(\mathbf{w}_h - \mathbf{w}_{h,0}) \\
\text{s.t. } & \mathbf{b} = \mathbf{B}^\top(\mathbf{w}_c + \mathbf{w}_h) \\
& \sigma_{fac}^2 = \mathbf{b}^\top \boldsymbol{\Omega}_\mathbf{f} \mathbf{b} \\
& \sigma_{idio}^2 = (\mathbf{w}_c + \mathbf{w}_h)^\top \boldsymbol{\Omega}_\epsilon (\mathbf{w}_c + \mathbf{w}_h) \\
& \mathbf{w}_h \in \mathbb{R}^n
\end{aligned}
\tag{12.5}
$$

I leave it as an exercise to prove that if execution costs are zero, orthogonal and spanned alphas are zero, and factor portfolios have zero idiosyncratic variance, then *of course* we would hedge out exposure. Not a single one of these assumptions holds, and it's worth spending some time commenting on them.

- Some of the factors do have zero expected returns,[2] some don't. Hedging them can in fact be counterproductive because the gains in Sharpe Ratio are countered by expected PnL losses.
- The hedging portfolio may also have non-zero alpha orthogonal exposure. This must be taken into account, especially when alpha orthogonal is indeed what the profitability of the strategy depends on, more than on alpha spanned.
- Even if we traded the pure FMPs of Procedure 12.2, we would add idiosyncratic risk to our core portfolio. This additional idiosyncratic risk reduces the benefits of factor risk reduction. The optimization

[2] Sometimes these are referred to as *unpriced factors*, because we receive no reward for holding their associated risk.

formulation takes this into account. In fact, the following exercise asks you to work out the details and show that the optimal hedging is not equal to $-\mathbf{b}_c$.

Exercise 12.2: Assume that:
1. factor portfolios have zero expected returns;
2. we hedge using only factor portfolios;
3. we have no transaction costs.

Prove that the optimal hedging policy is

$$\begin{aligned}\mathbf{x}^\star &= -(\mathbf{\Omega}_f + (\mathbf{B}^\top \mathbf{\Omega}_\epsilon^{-1}\mathbf{B})^{-1})^{-1}(\mathbf{B}^\top \mathbf{\Omega}_\epsilon^{-1}\mathbf{B})^{-1}\mathbf{b}_c \\ &= -[\mathbf{I}_m + (\mathbf{B}^\top \mathbf{\Omega}_\epsilon^{-1}\mathbf{B})\mathbf{\Omega}_f]^{-1}\mathbf{b}_c\end{aligned}$$

Under what condition is the optimal hedging size smaller than the perfect factor neutralization of Procedure 12.2?

The solution is in the Appendix. Meanwhile, here is a much easier problem to get you started.

Exercise 12.3: For simplicity, consider the case where asset returns are described by a one-factor model, and there is a hedging portfolio that has exposure to that factor. Starting with Equation (12.4), show that it is optimal not to hedge entirely the exposure of the core portfolio to that factor.

- In the simplistic hedging procedures of the first part of this chapter, we could ignore our investment objective, because volatility reduction was a zero-cost improvement: no execution concerns, no expected factor returns, no idiosyncratic volatility increase. But reality is complicated. The parameter ρ quantifies our risk tolerance and determines where we want to be on the curve, trading off volatility for expected costs. *This is a good thing*. In practice, we should explore this trade-off and determine the optimal operating point.
- In the special case of quadratic costs, Optimization Problem (12.5) can be rewritten as a multi-period optimization problem and solved using the techniques presented in Chapter 11 and specifically in Procedure 11.3.

Exercise 12.4: Extend Optimization Problem (12.5) to the multi-period setting. Discuss the implementation complexity and propose some simplifying assumptions.

12.3 Hedging Tradeable Factors with Time-Series Betas

A relatively common use case for hedging is the following. There are non-equity tradeable and liquid instruments that are associated with macroeconomic movements; for example, energy or metal commodity futures; or fixed-income futures. Because of their ability to capture broad macroeconomic themes and their liquidity, we would like to use these instruments for hedging. To fix our ideas further, consider the case of a portfolio composed of energy stocks, and of gas and crude future contracts, which are among the most liquid in the world. It stands to reason that the energy portfolio is correlated to energy prices, and at the same time that the portfolio manager or the trading algorithm does not have a view on the future energy price movements. A possible approach is to estimate time-series betas $\hat{\beta}_i := \beta(r_i, r_h)$, and then hedge the exposure $\hat{\boldsymbol{\beta}}^\top \mathbf{w}_c$ using Procedure 12.1. Would this approach work? Surprisingly, in more than one real-world instance, the realized risk of the *hedged* portfolio was worse than the realized risk of the core portfolio. This is somewhat counterintuitive. In this section, we aim to shed some light on hedging for this particular scenario.

As in the previous sections, we denote the return of the tradeable instrument r_h, with variance σ_h^2. We model the estimated betas as $\hat{\beta}_i = \beta_i + \eta_i$. In other words, we do not ignore the estimation error in the model. We denote by $\boldsymbol{\eta}$ the random vector of estimation error with covariance matrix $\boldsymbol{\Omega}_\eta$, and $\boldsymbol{\beta}$ the vector of true betas. In order to see what could go wrong, let us hedge with the "optimal" hedge ratio

$$x_h^\star = -\hat{\boldsymbol{\beta}}^\top \mathbf{w} = -(\boldsymbol{\beta} - \boldsymbol{\eta})^\top \mathbf{w}$$

The covariance matrix, augmented with the hedging instrument, is

$$\begin{pmatrix} \boldsymbol{\Omega}_{\mathbf{r}} & \sigma_h^2 \boldsymbol{\beta} \\ \sigma_h^2 \boldsymbol{\beta}^\top & \sigma_h^2 \end{pmatrix}$$

Let us compute the variance of the hedged portfolio:

$$\begin{aligned}
\mathrm{var}\,(\mathbf{r}^{\mathsf{T}}\mathbf{w} + r_h x_h^{\star}) &= E_{\eta}\left[E\left[(\mathbf{r}^{\mathsf{T}}\mathbf{w} + r_h x_h^{\star})^2 |\boldsymbol{\eta}\right]\right] \\
&= E_{\eta}\left[\mathbf{w}^{\mathsf{T}}\boldsymbol{\Omega}_{\mathbf{r}}\mathbf{w} - 2\sigma_h^2\boldsymbol{\beta}\mathbf{w}(\boldsymbol{\beta} - \boldsymbol{\eta})^{\mathsf{T}}\mathbf{w} + (\sigma_h(\boldsymbol{\beta} - \boldsymbol{\eta})^{\mathsf{T}}\mathbf{w})^2\right] \\
&= \mathbf{w}^{\mathsf{T}}\boldsymbol{\Omega}_{\mathbf{r}}\mathbf{w} - (\sigma_h\boldsymbol{\beta}^{\mathsf{T}}\mathbf{w})^2 + \sigma_h^2\mathbf{w}^{\mathsf{T}}\boldsymbol{\Omega}_{\eta}\mathbf{w}
\end{aligned}$$

The variance of the hedged portfolio exceeds the unhedged variance when $\mathbf{w}^{\mathsf{T}}\boldsymbol{\Omega}_{\eta}\mathbf{w} > (\boldsymbol{\beta}^{\mathsf{T}}\mathbf{w})^2$. The left-hand side of the inequality is the squared estimation error of the portfolio's beta. The right-hand side is the portfolio beta-related variance.

Between the non-hedged and the fully-hedged portfolio, maybe there is a hedging level that improves on both. We consider the case where we apply a positive *hedging shrinkage factor* γ_h to the optimal hedging: $x_h = -\gamma_h\hat{\boldsymbol{\beta}}^{\mathsf{T}}\mathbf{w}$. We estimate the variance of $(\mathbf{r}^{\mathsf{T}}\mathbf{w} + x_h r_h)$, and then we minimize it with respect to γ_h. The formula for the variance is similar to the one we performed above:

$$\begin{aligned}
E(\mathbf{r}^{\mathsf{T}}\mathbf{w} + r_h x_h)^2 &= E_{\eta}\left[E\left[(\mathbf{r}^{\mathsf{T}}\mathbf{w} + r_h x_h)^2 |\boldsymbol{\eta}\right]\right] \\
&= \mathbf{w}^{\mathsf{T}}\boldsymbol{\Omega}_{\mathbf{r}}\mathbf{w} - \gamma_h(\boldsymbol{\beta}^{\mathsf{T}}\mathbf{w})^2\sigma_h^2 + \gamma_h^2\sigma_h^2\mathbf{w}^{\mathsf{T}}\boldsymbol{\Omega}_{\eta}\mathbf{w}
\end{aligned}$$

which we minimize to find the optimal shrinkage factor and hedge ratio:

$$\gamma_h^{\star} = 1 - \frac{\mathbf{w}^{\mathsf{T}}\boldsymbol{\Omega}_{\eta}\mathbf{w}}{(\mathbf{w}^{\mathsf{T}}\hat{\boldsymbol{\beta}})^2} \tag{12.6}$$

$$x_h^{\star} = -\hat{\boldsymbol{\beta}}^{\mathsf{T}}\mathbf{w} + \frac{\mathbf{w}^{\mathsf{T}}\boldsymbol{\Omega}_{\eta}\mathbf{w}}{\mathbf{w}^{\mathsf{T}}\hat{\boldsymbol{\beta}}} \tag{12.7}$$

Let's sense-check this formula:

- The shrinkage factor $\gamma_h^{\star}$ is independent of the units of the portfolio. If we measure the portfolio in cents or in dollars, we get the same value of $\gamma_h^{\star}$. Otherwise stated: if we hedge a portfolio 10 times the size of our current one, the fraction is unchanged, and the best hedge is 10 times the hedge of the original portfolio.
- If there are no estimation errors in the betas, then $\boldsymbol{\Omega}_{\eta} = 0$ and $\gamma_h^{\star} = 1$: we use the optimal hedge ratio.

- The numerator is a weighted sum of the estimation errors. The larger the error, the smaller the shrinkage factor.
- The ratio in Equation (12.6) can be loosely interpreted as the square of the aggregate noise-to-signal ratio of the betas. The higher the ratio, the smaller the scaling factor.
- Consider the edge case where the true betas are all zero and errors are independent. Then $\hat{\boldsymbol{\beta}} = \boldsymbol{\eta}$ and the expected value[3] of the denominator is $E[(\mathbf{w}^\intercal \hat{\boldsymbol{\beta}})^2] = \mathbf{w}^\intercal \boldsymbol{\Omega}_\eta \mathbf{w}$. In expectation, numerator and denominator are equal, and $\gamma_h^\star = 0$. On average, we do not hedge, which is the correct course of action.

In practice, we recommend the following steps:

1. Estimate the time-series $\hat{\beta}_i$ and its standard error τ_i. Define $\boldsymbol{\Omega}_\eta$ as the diagonal matrix whose ith term is τ_i^2.
2. Compute $\gamma_h^\star$ using Equation (12.6).
3. Buy $x_h^\star = -(\gamma_h^\star)^+ \times (\hat{\boldsymbol{\beta}}^\intercal \mathbf{w})$ of the hedging instrument. The lower bound at zero is meant to avoid the situation where we hedge in the opposite direction.
4. (optional). It is difficult to estimate the correlations between estimation errors, especially in periods of market stress. You can simulate their impact by assuming constant correlations between them and then defining

$$\boldsymbol{\Omega}_\eta = \begin{bmatrix} \tau_1 & 0 & \dots & \dots \\ 0 & \tau_2 & \dots & \dots \\ \dots & \dots & \dots & \dots \\ \dots & \dots & \dots & \tau_n \end{bmatrix} \begin{bmatrix} 1 & \rho & \dots & \rho \\ \rho & 1 & \dots & \rho \\ \dots & \dots & \dots & \dots \\ \rho & \dots & \dots & 1 \end{bmatrix} \begin{bmatrix} \tau_1 & 0 & \dots & \dots \\ 0 & \tau_2 & \dots & \dots \\ \dots & \dots & \dots & \dots \\ \dots & \dots & \dots & \tau_n \end{bmatrix}$$

   and testing the sensitivity for different values of ρ. The hedging ratio decreases linearly as ρ increases.

[3] Informally, if the number of assets is large, we should expect the variance of $(\mathbf{w}^\intercal \hat{\boldsymbol{\beta}})^2$ to be small, so that the expected value is a good proxy for $(\mathbf{w}^\intercal \hat{\boldsymbol{\beta}})^2$.

5. (simplifying Equations (12.6) and (12.7). Assume that the terms w_i^2 are cross-sectionally uncorrelated with τ_i^2. Then[4]

$$\begin{aligned}\mathbf{w}^{\mathsf{T}}\mathbf{\Omega}_{\eta}\mathbf{w} &= \sum_i w_i^2\tau_i^2 \\ &= \frac{1}{n}\sum_i w_i^2 \sum_i \tau_i^2 + n\text{cov}((w_1^2,\ldots,w_n^2),(\tau_1^2,\ldots,\tau_n^2)) \\ &= \|\mathbf{w}\|^2 \hat{E}(\boldsymbol{\tau}^2)\end{aligned}$$

An analogous simplification occurs for the denominator. Then the formula for the optimal hedge ratio becomes

$$\gamma^{\star} = 1 - \frac{\hat{E}(\boldsymbol{\tau}^2)\|\mathbf{w}\|^2}{(\hat{\boldsymbol{\beta}}^{\mathsf{T}}\mathbf{w})^2} \tag{12.8}$$

Higher standard errors τ_i imply greater shrinkage. Lower dollar exposure to the tradeable factor also means greater shrinkage. Finally, to simplify things dramatically, consider the case where all $\hat{\beta}_i$ are identical, and the portfolio is long only. The shrinkage factor simplifies further:

$$\gamma_h^{\star} = 1 - \underbrace{\hat{\beta}^{-2}\hat{E}(\boldsymbol{\tau}^2)}_{\textit{(squared noise-to-signal)}} \times \underbrace{H(\mathbf{w})}_{\textit{(portfolio concentration)}}$$

The ratio $H(\mathbf{w}) := \|\mathbf{w}\|_2^2/\|\mathbf{w}\|_1^2$ is a measure of portfolio concentration.[5] A portfolio that has maximum diversification has n positions with identical NMV, and has $H(\mathbf{w}) = 1/n$, while a maximally concentrated portfolio has all NMV concentrated in a single stock, so that $H(\mathbf{w}) = 1$. The interpretation here is that the shrinkage factor is smaller when the portfolio is more concentrated. The intuition is that the estimation error of the beta averages out more in diversified portfolios.

12.4 Factor-Mimicking Portfolios of Time Series

A problem related to hedging a portfolio using a tradeable security is that of trading a portfolio that is close to a *non-tradeable* security. Such time series abound in real life. A quantitative portfolio manager may be

---

[4] For a vector $\mathbf{x}$, define $\hat{E}(\mathbf{x})$ the average of the values $x_1, \ldots, x_n$.

[5] The Herfindahl Index is usually defined for a set of n non-negative numbers x_i that sum to one: $H := \sum_i x_i^2$. It can be extended to arbitrary sets of numbers y_i, by defining $x_i := |y_i|/\sum_j |y_j|$ and applying the original definition.

interested in trading them for a few reasons. First, the time series may show high correlation to the securities in her investment universe and therefore the time series could serve as a useful hedging instrument. Another use case is that of the macroeconomic systematic investor[6] who has some well-informed reason to trade a theme. Developing a tradeable portfolio that "tracks" the time series has real value for her. Lastly, just verifying how well we can track a time series is interesting in itself. It shows us whether the time series is of concrete use. The occasional analysts that hawk non-tradeable themes are full of sound and fury, usually signifying sell-side research fees.

We introduced the ingredients for our problem earlier in the chapter. We have n assets with returns r_i, and a time-series with return r_h; we keep the original subscript, since subscripts should not be multiplied beyond necessity. In its simplest form, we have the following ingredients:

- Two periods and one realized return. Investment decisions are made in period one, profits are realized in period two.
- n assets with returns r_i, with covariance matrix $\mathbf{\Omega}_\mathbf{r}$.
- n loadings $\hat{\beta}_i = \beta_i + \eta_i$ where η_i is the estimation error of β_i, with $E(\eta_i^2) = \tau_i^2$. We denote $\mathbf{\Gamma} := \text{diag}\left(\tau_1^2, \ldots, \tau_n^2\right)$.

The problem asks to minimize the tracking error between the time series and a portfolio: $\min_\mathbf{w} E\left[(\mathbf{r}^\mathsf{T}\mathbf{w} - r_h)^2\right]$. We condition on $\boldsymbol{\eta}$, as we did earlier in the chapter:

$$\begin{aligned}
E\left[(\mathbf{r}^\mathsf{T}\mathbf{w} - r_h)^2\right] &= E_{\boldsymbol{\eta}}\left[E[(\mathbf{r}^\mathsf{T}\mathbf{w} - r_h)]^2 + \text{var}\,(\mathbf{r}^\mathsf{T}\mathbf{w} - r_h)|\boldsymbol{\eta}]\right] \\
&= E_{\boldsymbol{\eta}}[E[((\boldsymbol{\beta} - \boldsymbol{\eta})\mu_h + \boldsymbol{\epsilon})^\mathsf{T}\mathbf{w} - r_h)]^2 \\
&\quad + \mathbf{w}^\mathsf{T}\mathbf{\Omega}_\mathbf{r}\mathbf{w} - 2\sigma_h^2(\boldsymbol{\beta} - \boldsymbol{\eta})^\mathsf{T}\mathbf{w} + \sigma_h^2] \\
&= \mu_h^2(\boldsymbol{\beta}^\mathsf{T}\mathbf{w} - 1)^2 + \mu_h^2\mathbf{w}^\mathsf{T}\mathbf{\Gamma}\mathbf{w} + \mathbf{w}^\mathsf{T}\mathbf{\Omega}_\mathbf{r}\mathbf{w} - 2\sigma_h^2\boldsymbol{\beta}^\mathsf{T}\mathbf{w} + \sigma_h^2 \\
&= \mathbf{w}^\mathsf{T}(\mathbf{\Omega}_\mathbf{r} + \mu_h^2\mathbf{\Gamma} + \mu_h^2\boldsymbol{\beta}\boldsymbol{\beta}^\mathsf{T})\mathbf{w} - 2(\mu_h^2 + \sigma_h^2)\boldsymbol{\beta}^\mathsf{T}\mathbf{w} + \mu_h^2 + \sigma_h^2
\end{aligned}$$

[6] A species I have ignored in this book, because I have not been lucky enough to meet its members in the wild.

And the first-order condition on this unconstrained problem gives the optimal portfolio, which we transform by means of the Woodbury–Sherman–Morrison Lemma of the inverse matrix (see Equation (9.20)):

$$
\begin{aligned}
\mathbf{w}^\star &= (\mu_h^2 + \sigma_h^2)(\mathbf{\Omega}_\mathbf{r} + \mu_h^2\mathbf{\Gamma} + \mu_h^2\boldsymbol{\beta}\boldsymbol{\beta}^\top)^{-1}\boldsymbol{\beta} \\
&= (\mu_h^2 + \sigma_h^2)\left(\mathbf{I} - \frac{(\mathbf{\Omega}_\mathbf{r} + \mu_h^2\mathbf{\Gamma})^{-1}\boldsymbol{\beta}\boldsymbol{\beta}^\top}{\mu_h^{-2} + \boldsymbol{\beta}^\top(\mathbf{\Omega}_\mathbf{r} + \mu_h^2\mathbf{\Gamma})^{-1}\boldsymbol{\beta}}\right)(\mathbf{\Omega}_\mathbf{r} + \mu_h^2\mathbf{\Gamma})^{-1}\boldsymbol{\beta}
\end{aligned}
$$

Having done most of the heavy lifting, we close with a few remarks:

- The beta estimation error $\mathbf{\Gamma}$ serves as a regularizer for the covariance matrix. The larger the expected returns, the higher the importance of the regularization term.
- When $\mathbf{\Gamma} = 0$ (no estimation error), and $\mu_h = 0$ (zero return), the optimal portfolio is $\mathbf{w}^\star = \sigma_h^2\mathbf{\Omega}_\mathbf{r}^{-1}\boldsymbol{\beta}$, which is, up to a scaling factor, the minimum-variance portfolio. A minor point: it seems that the scaling factor is σ_h^2, which would make no sense. The covariance matrix does contain σ_h, though, so that dependency is effectively linear.
- When $|\boldsymbol{\mu}_h| \to \infty$, the optimal portfolio approaches, up to a constant, $\mathbf{\Gamma}^{-1}\boldsymbol{\beta}$.
- Once we have the optimal portfolio $\mathbf{w}^\star$, hedging is straightforward, in the sense that we can employ Equation (12.4) to reduce the core portfolio's risk.

Exercise 12.5: Describe how you would hedge to a time-series factor (or an FMP of a time-series) on top of equity FMPs for a pre-existing model (Hint: Orthogonalization.)

12.5 ⋆Appendix

Proof. [Proof of Exercise 12.2] We replace the decision variable $\mathbf{w}_h = \mathbf{P}\mathbf{x}$. From the definition of $\mathbf{P}$, it follows that $\mathbf{B}^\top\mathbf{P}\mathbf{x} = \mathbf{x}$, and $\mathbf{x}^\top\mathbf{P}^\top\mathbf{\Omega}_\epsilon\mathbf{P}\mathbf{x} = \mathbf{x}^\top(\mathbf{B}^\top\mathbf{\Omega}_\epsilon^{-1}\mathbf{B})^{-1}\mathbf{x}$.

It follows that the Optimization Problem (12.5) can be rewritten

$$
\begin{aligned}
\max\ & \boldsymbol{\alpha}_\perp^\mathsf{T}(\mathbf{w}_c + \mathbf{w}_h) - \frac{1}{2}\rho(\sigma_f^2 + \sigma_i^2) - f(\mathbf{w}_h - \mathbf{w}_{h,0}) \\
\text{s.t. } & \mathbf{b} = \mathbf{b}_c + \mathbf{x} \\
& \sigma_f^2 = \mathbf{x}^\mathsf{T}\boldsymbol{\Omega}_\mathrm{f}\mathbf{x} \\
& \sigma_i^2 = \sigma_{\epsilon,c}^2 + \mathbf{x}^\mathsf{T}(\mathbf{B}^\mathsf{T}\boldsymbol{\Omega}_\epsilon^{-1}\mathbf{B})^{-1}\mathbf{x} + \mathbf{b}_c^\mathsf{T}(\mathbf{B}^\mathsf{T}\boldsymbol{\Omega}_\epsilon^{-1}\mathbf{B})^{-1}\mathbf{x} + \mathbf{w}_c^\mathsf{T}\boldsymbol{\Omega}_\epsilon\mathbf{y} \\
& \mathbf{w}_h \in \mathbb{R}^n
\end{aligned}
$$

Assume that $\mathbf{y} = 0$, $\boldsymbol{\mu} = 0$ and transaction costs equal 0. The objective function becomes

$$
\begin{aligned}
& \boldsymbol{\alpha}_\perp^\mathsf{T}\mathbf{w}_c - \frac{1}{2}\rho(\mathbf{x}^\mathsf{T}\boldsymbol{\Omega}_\mathrm{f}\mathbf{x} + \sigma_{\epsilon,c}^2 + \mathbf{x}^\mathsf{T}(\mathbf{B}^\mathsf{T}\boldsymbol{\Omega}_\epsilon^{-1}\mathbf{B})^{-1}\mathbf{x} + \mathbf{b}_c^\mathsf{T}(\mathbf{B}^\mathsf{T}\boldsymbol{\Omega}_\epsilon^{-1}\mathbf{B})^{-1}\mathbf{x}) \\
& \equiv -\frac{1}{2}\rho[\mathbf{x}^\mathsf{T}(\boldsymbol{\Omega}_\mathrm{f} + (\mathbf{B}^\mathsf{T}\boldsymbol{\Omega}_\epsilon^{-1}\mathbf{B})^{-1})\mathbf{x} + \mathbf{b}_c^\mathsf{T}(\mathbf{B}^\mathsf{T}\boldsymbol{\Omega}_\epsilon^{-1}\mathbf{B})^{-1}\mathbf{x}]
\end{aligned}
$$

which is minimized at

$$
\begin{aligned}
\mathbf{x}^\star &= -(\boldsymbol{\Omega}_\mathrm{f} + (\mathbf{B}^\mathsf{T}\boldsymbol{\Omega}_\epsilon^{-1}\mathbf{B})^{-1})^{-1}(\mathbf{B}^\mathsf{T}\boldsymbol{\Omega}_\epsilon^{-1}\mathbf{B})^{-1}\mathbf{b}_c \\
&= -[\mathbf{I} + (\mathbf{B}^\mathsf{T}\boldsymbol{\Omega}_\epsilon^{-1}\mathbf{B})\boldsymbol{\Omega}_\mathrm{f}]^{-1}\mathbf{b}_c
\end{aligned}
$$

■

The Takeaways

1. Hedging reduces portfolio risk by adding negatively correlated investments.
2. Common hedging methods include market and currency hedging.
3. Additional hedging techniques involve:
   - Using FMPs from fundamental factor models.
   - Hedging with futures or liquid assets capturing equity and non-equity risk (e.g., energy futures, sector ETFs).
   - Employing thematic tradeable baskets offered by banks to hedge or speculate on specific risks.
4. In a simple hedging scenario we have two assets: core (with expected return μ_c) and hedge (with expected return $\mu_h = 0$) and want to maximize the Sharpe Ratio of the combined portfolio. The optimal hedge position is $x_h^{\text{optimal}} = -\beta x_c$, with $\beta := \frac{\rho_{c,h}\sigma_c}{\sigma_h}$.
5. In practice, we remove the assumptions in simple hedging: accurate beta estimates, single trading instrument, negligible trading costs, hedging instrument with negligible expected return.
6. In both cases, we will hedge less than the optimal hedge ratio of the simple hedging case.

Chapter 13

Dynamic Risk Allocation

The Questions

1. What are the limitations of single-period portfolio optimization for long-term investment strategies?
2. How does the Kelly criterion provide both descriptive and prescriptive value in multi-period investment decisions?
3. In what ways can different capital allocation strategies impact the growth rate and cumulative returns of a portfolio?
4. How do parameter uncertainty and fractional Kelly allocation strategies improve risk management for investors?
5. What are the mathematical properties of Kelly strategies that make them desirable for long-term growth?
6. How are stop-loss policies related to the Kelly criterion?

So far we have focused exclusively on single-period portfolio optimization. This may be appropriate for one-off investment decisions, but is inadequate for long-term investment strategies. There is a rich academic literature on intertemporal choice theory, which aims at modeling the interplay between consumption and investment in the long run, both at the level of the individual consumer and at the aggregate level. Much of the literature has been ignored by asset managers, for a few possible reasons we conjecture below. First, these models require the specification of a principled utility function and of an intertemporal trade-off (in the form of a discount factor for future utility), something that no investment manager would or could specify. If quadratic utility had been the main justification of MVO, it would probably have never been adopted. Second, these models don't capture well the institutional setting of asset managers. "Consumption" for asset managers corresponds to outflows, and asset managers don't receive any utility from it. Moreover, outflows do not bear a direct relationship to the principals' utilities (i.e., those who provide the investment capital to the managers). The reason for this is that inflows and outflows occur at low rates (they are "sticky"), due to inertia of the principals (who resist changing their asset allocations) and to contractual obligations with the asset managers (who require long advance notice for capital withdrawal).

Even if hedge fund managers do not read the academic literature while driving their Ferraris (don't read and drive), they still have to make decisions about the risk they want to take the next day, week, and month. There is one line of research, initiated by electrical engineers and mostly developed by researchers not employed by economics departments, which is relevant to investors. It is broadly known as the *Kelly criterion*, Kelly Investing, Kelly Gambling, Universal Portfolios, Optimal Growth Portfolios, or Optimal Growth Investing. It has both descriptive power, since it is followed by many successful investors, and prescriptive value, in that it is based on first principles and has attractive properties. The rest of this chapter is devoted to presenting the basics of the theory. We start with a description and motivation of the Kelly criterion. Then we link it to the familiar concepts of Mean-Variance Optimization and Sharpe Ratio. The way that vodka is not suitable as a dinner drink, "Pure" Kelly is not suitable for investing. *Fractional Kelly* is to Kelly what Chardonnay is to vodka: more sustainable, better tasting, and ultimately more fun. Finally, we introduce a time-varying version of fractional Kelly, which helps manage the occurrence of drawdowns.

13.1 The Kelly Criterion

To introduce the ideas behind the Kelly criterion,[1] we consider first a very simple example. You have one risky asset in which to invest, which returns +100% or −50% with equal probability. The single-period expected return of the asset is 1/4, and its volatility is 3/4. You have to decide how to invest your initial capital in this asset. Consider two alternatives:

1. *(Constant Capital Allocation)* Every day you allocate the same amount of capital to the risky asset. This approach is consistent with solving an MVO problem in each period. The problem faced in every period is

$$\max_{w} \frac{5}{4}w - \frac{\lambda}{2}\frac{9}{16}w^2 \Rightarrow w^* = \frac{20}{9\lambda} \tag{13.1}$$

   where w is the net amount allocated to the risky asset and is independent of the period.
2. *(Static Allocation)* On day 0, you allocate a fraction x of your capital to the risky asset, and then you let it run. This is consistent with solving an MVO in period 0, and letting it run.
3. *(Dynamic Allocation)* Every day, you allocate a fraction x of your capital *on that day* to the risky asset. We have no motivation for this (yet). The intuition, however, is that it seems reasonable to have a volatility proportional to the available capital in each period. The ratio of the strategy's volatility to capital in each period is equal to $3x/4$ and is indeed constant in this approach.

Figure 13.1 shows the cumulative returns under the three approaches. The constant capital allocation shows low growth. Independently of x, the static allocation has poor performance, even though the risky asset has positive expected return. Conversely, the dynamic allocation exhibits a variety of behaviors. Its growth rate (equal to the slope of the curve) is not monotonically increasing with x. Risk-adjusted performance is good for low values of x, but the average returns are low. The most profitable strategy corresponds to $x = 1/2$. Higher values detract from performance.

[1] For an intuitive treatment of the Kelly criterion, with plenty of examples and applications, see Haghani and White (2023). Markku Kurtti's blog "Outcast Beta" is also bridging the world of applications and the mostly academic literature.

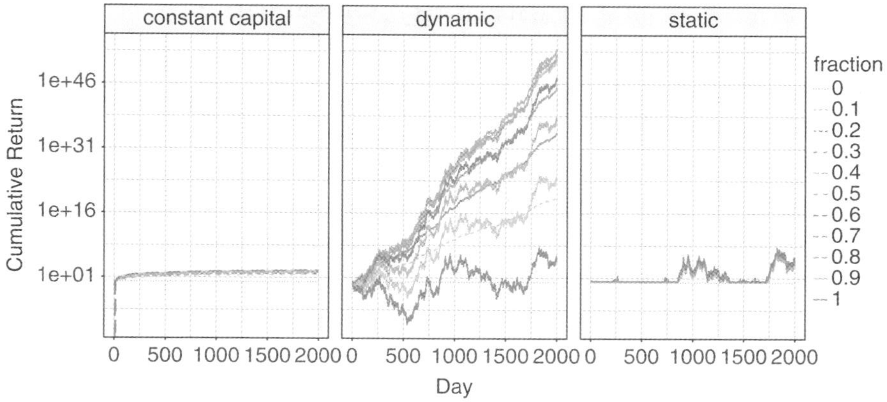

Figure 13.1 Cumulative returns under the dynamic and static policies. All the curves are based on the same realization of returns of the risky asset. The returns are plotted on a logarithmic scale.

What is remarkable is that, for each strategy, and for each period, the Sharpe Ratio is identical and equal to 1/3, because in each period the portfolio, being the combination of a risk-free asset and a risky asset, is mean-variance efficient. This numerical example should warn about the subtleties of using the Sharpe Ratio as a performance measure. We have been able to compute the Sharpe Ratio exactly, thus abstracting away any complication due to performance measurement, and we obtained the same value for all the strategies in our example. Yet, the behavior of the cumulative returns differs wildly among the strategies! We can interpret this as follows: the single-period Sharpe Ratio, defined as expected mean return/standard deviation in a single period, is a measure of *investor skill*, but not of *strategy performance*. Averaging the Sharpe Ratio over the life of a strategy can give us a better estimate of skill, but is not telling us much about the risk-adjusted performance of the strategy over its lifetime. If we chose the cumulative returns over the strategy lifetime as a metric—and ignored any drawdown concern—then the dynamic strategy with $x^* = 1/2$ would be the clear favorite.

A second observation is that skill alone, defined as the ability to select a high-Sharpe portfolio in any given period, is necessary but not sufficient to be a successful investor. The size of the overall portfolio over time plays a major role in the long term. Yet, this topic does not receive much attention among academics or practitioners.

To understand where the value $x = 1/2$ comes from, let $r_t(x)$ be the random return of the dynamic allocation strategy in period t. It is

$$1 + r_t(x) = \begin{cases} 1 + x & p = 1/2 \\ 1 - x/2 & p = 1/2 \end{cases} \tag{13.2}$$

The total return of the strategy is $\prod_{t=1}^{T}(1 + r_t(x))$. The average growth rate of the strategy $g_T(x)$ is such that

$$\prod_{t=1}^{T}(1 + r_t(x)) = \exp(Tg_T(x))$$
$$\text{where } g_T(x) := \frac{1}{T}\sum_{t=1}^{T}\log(1 + r_t(x))$$

For a fixed number of periods T, if we wanted to maximize the expected growth rate of the strategy, we would solve the problem $\max_x g_T(x)$. For $T \to \infty$, because returns are iid rvs, by the Law of Large Numbers, $g_T(x) \to E[\log(1 + r_1(x))]$ a.s. The solution to the problem

$$\max_x E\left[\log(1 + r_1(x))\right] \tag{13.3}$$

is asymptotically equivalent to maximizing the expectation (13.3). The objective function is maximized when the investment fraction x is equal to 1/2 (see Figures 13.2 and 13.3).

From Figure 13.1, it appears that this strategy performs decidedly better than other strategies with lower investment fractions. By simulation (or from Figure 13.2) one can see that any strategy in which $x > 1$ performs even worse; this corresponds to borrowing money to invest in the risky asset. Summing up, it appears that long-term returns are maximized not by maximizing the expected returns, but by maximizing the expected growth rate, which is mathematically equivalent to maximizing an expected utility, with a logarithmic utility function.

Let's work out in detail an important example.

Example 13.1 ***(The Kelly Allocation to a Single Security)*****:** *We have only two assets: a risk-free asset and a risky asset. Let the excess return of the risky asset be r with mean μ and variance σ^2. One way to interpret this asset in real-world*

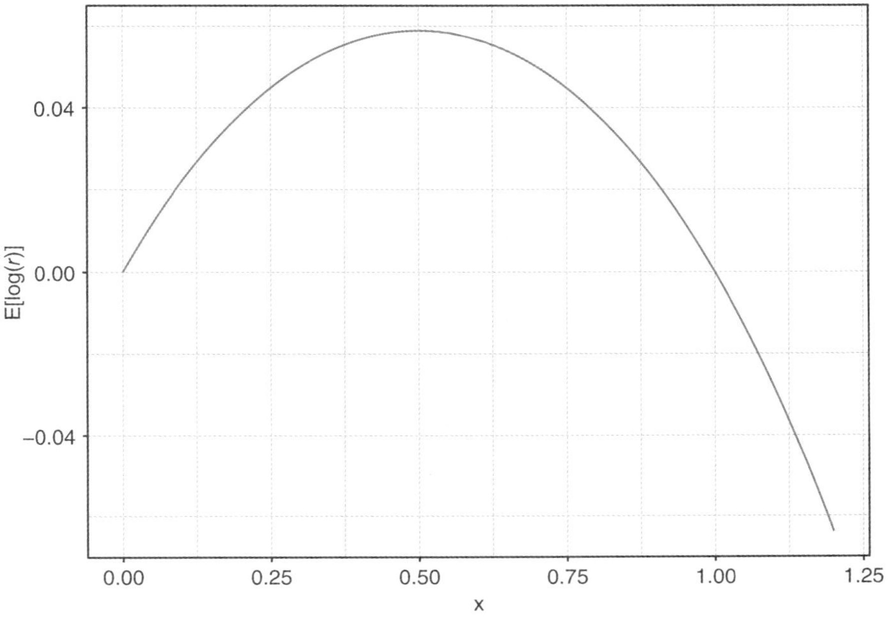

Figure 13.2 Expected value of the log of the single-period growth, which is maximized at $x^\star = 1/2$.

application is as a portfolio manager to which we need to allocate capital. If we were to maximize the expected growth of the portfolio, then we would solve the problem

$$\max_x g(x) := \max_x E\left[\log(1 + rx)\right] \tag{13.4}$$

In addition to an exact numerical solution, we also produce an approximate solution based on the quadratic approximation of the logarithm:

$$\log(1 + x) = x - \frac{x^2}{2} + o(x^3) \tag{13.5}$$

Then a quadratic approximation is

$$\max_x E\left[\log(1 + rx)\right] \simeq \max_x \mu x - \frac{1}{2}(\sigma^2 + \mu^2)x^2 \tag{13.6}$$

and a further approximation, in which we assume $\mu \ll \sigma$, is

$$\max_x E\left[\log(1 + rx)\right] \simeq \max_x \mu x - \frac{1}{2}\sigma^2 x^2 \tag{13.7}$$

from which

$$\text{(exact result)}: \begin{cases} x^\star = \arg\max_x E\left[\log(1 + rx)\right] \\ g(x^\star) = E\left[\log(1 + rx^\star)\right] \end{cases} \tag{13.8}$$

$$\text{(quadratic approximation)}: \begin{cases} x_1^\star \simeq \dfrac{\mu}{\mu^2 + \sigma^2} \\ g(x_1^\star) \simeq \dfrac{1}{2}\dfrac{\text{SR}^2}{\text{SR}^2 + 1} \end{cases} \tag{13.9}$$

$$\text{(assuming that } \mu \ll \sigma): \begin{cases} x_2^\star \simeq \dfrac{\text{SR}}{\sigma} \\ g(x_2^\star) \simeq \dfrac{1}{2}\text{SR}^2 \end{cases} \tag{13.10}$$

This approximate result is reliable when the typical fluctuations of xr are smaller than 1. A heuristic is to require that the volatility of $x^* r$ be smaller than 1: $|x^*\sigma| \ll 1$, i.e., $|\text{SR}| \ll 1$.

Let us consider in some more detail the accuracy of the approximations $x_1^\star, x_2^\star$. We consider daily Gaussian returns. The approximation $x_1^\star$ is accurate (relative error $|x_1^\star - x^\star|/x^\star \leq 2\%$) for daily Sharpe Ratios up to 0.24 (annualized Sharpe Ratio of 4). The approximation $x_2^\star$ is accurate (relative error $|x_2^\star - x^\star|/x^\star \leq 2\%$) for daily Sharpe Ratios up to 0.15 (annualized Sharpe Ratios up to 2.4). The crucial assumption in these calculations is the rebalancing interval. If we rebalance at shorter horizons, the volatility of returns in that horizon is smaller, and the quadratic approximation is more accurate. If we rebalanced capital at shorter horizons than daily, the approximation would hold for higher values of the annualized Sharpe Ratio.

Another way to read this result is that *the optimal ratio between dollar volatility and capital is equal to the Sharpe Ratio*. The volatility deployed is $W_0 x^\star \sigma$. Hence the (dollar volatility)/(capital) ratio is

$$\frac{\text{(dollar volatility)}}{\text{(capital)}} = \frac{(W_0 x_2^\star)\sigma}{W_0} = \text{SR} \tag{13.11}$$

Note that the formulas above hold for volatilities and Sharpe Ratio measured at the same timescale. For example: if we deploy \$1B of capital, and have an annualized Sharpe Ratio of 2, then we should deploy approximately \$2B of dollar volatility to run a Kelly-optimal strategy.

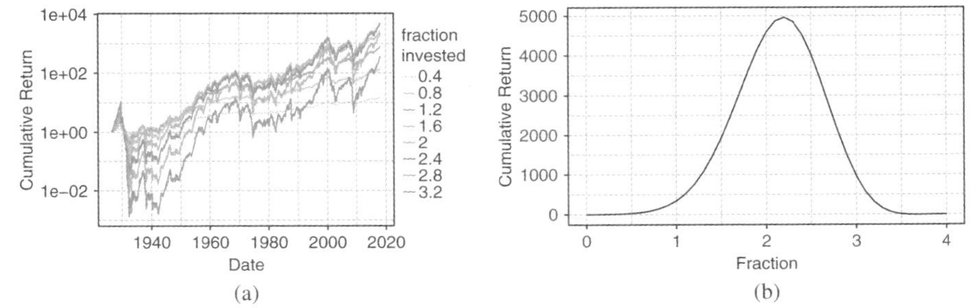

Figure 13.3 (a) Time series of cumulative returns for different fractions of the capital invested in the U.S. market benchmark (cap-weighted average of NYSE, AMEX, and NASDAQ-listed companies). Monthly excess returns of the benchmark for the period February 1926–March 2018 are from Ken French's data library site. (b) Cumulative returns as a function of the fraction invested in the U.S. market benchmark. The optimal Kelly fraction under the two approximations (Equations (13.9) and (13.10)) is $x_1^\star = 1.88$ and $x_2^\star = 2.2$.

Another observation: according to Equation (13.11), the Kelly-optimal expected return is

$$\textit{(expected strategy return)} = \text{SR} \times \frac{\textit{(dollar volatility)}}{\textit{(capital)}} = \text{SR}^2$$

Example 13.2 ***(The Kelly Allocation to the U.S. Market)*****:** *We can specialize the analysis above to the important case in which the risky asset is the U.S. market benchmark. This asset is available to retail investors in the form of low-management fees mutual funds and ETFs, both of which track the U.S. market accurately. Futures for the U.S. markets are also available to sophisticated investors. The Sharpe Ratio computed on the returns of the S&P500 in excess of 3-month Treasury bills is a function of starting and ending dates.*[2] *We assume a Sharpe Ratio of 0.42 and an annualized volatility of 19%. Based on the observed realization of the historical daily returns, the optimal total return is maximized at* $x_1^\star = 1.88$ *(Equation (13.9)) and* $x_2^\star = 2.2$ *(Equation (13.10)). A chart of the cumulative returns*[3] *of the S&P500 is shown in Figure 13.3. This example suggests that, if our goal was to maximize our long-term returns, then it would be optimal to leverage our capital. In practice, there are*

[2] A. Damoradan maintains a page (https://tinyurl.com/spdamor) with S&P500 and Treasury returns.

[3] Before January 1957, the S&P500 had 90 components. The returns for 1926–1956 use this S&P90 index.

borrowing constraints and the live behavior of a Kelly strategy has drawbacks: the historical plot shows how a larger fraction invested results in much more volatile PnL and in larger drawdowns. However, this example illustrates that the invested fraction can have a very dramatic impact on capital appreciation.

The S&P500 example shows the attractive features, but also the drawbacks of Kelly strategies.

Example 13.3 ***(Sizing a Bet)*****:** *Consider a bet with a binary outcome: if we invest \$1, we receive a payoff equal to $r_w > 0$ with probability p and $-r_l < 0$ with probability $q = 1 - p$. The optimization problem is*

$$\max_x \; p\log(1 + xr_w) + q\log(1 - xr_l)$$

$$\frac{pr_w}{1 + x^\star r_w} - \frac{qr_l}{1 - x^\star r_l} = 0 \qquad \textit{(first-order condition)}$$

$$\Rightarrow \quad x^\star = \frac{p}{r_l} - \frac{q}{r_w}$$

Introduce the win-loss ratio p/q, and the winning skew r_w/r_l:

$$x^\star = \frac{p}{r_l}\left(1 - \frac{1}{\textit{(win-loss ratio)}}\frac{1}{\textit{(winning skew)}}\right)$$

The higher the win-loss ratio and the winning-skew, the higher the size of the bet. If both win-loss ratio and winning skew are smaller than one, the optimal size cannot be positive.

We close this section with a more advanced example.

Example 13.4 ***(Optimal Strategy for a Geometric Diffusion)*****:** *Consider a strategy with expected excess return r in a single period and volatility σ in the same period, which we can lever by a factor $x(t) > 0$. The strategy has return and volatility equal to $x(t)r$ and $x(t)\sigma$. We start with capital W_0. Over the interval $[0, \infty)$, the continuous-time process governing the capital accumulation at time t is*

$$dW_t = x(t)\mu W_t dt + x(t)\sigma W_t dB_t$$

Here, B_t is a standard Brownian process. It can be shown that the distribution at time t is given by

$$W_T = W_0 \exp\left[\int_0^T \left(x(t)\mu - \frac{1}{2}x^2(t)\sigma^2\right) dt + \int_0^T x(t)\sigma dB_t\right]$$

Hence

$$g_T(x) = \frac{1}{T}\int_0^T \left(x(t)\mu - \frac{1}{2}x^2(t)\sigma^2\right) dt + \frac{1}{T}\int_0^T x(t)\sigma dB_t$$

For $T \to \infty$ the second integral converges to zero a.s. (for intuition: B_t scales like $\sqrt{t}$). The first integral is maximized when the integrand is maximized for all t, which occurs when $x(t) = \mu/\sigma^2 = \mathrm{SR}/\sigma$. We have recovered Equation (13.10).

In our presentation, we have ignored two important features:

- The Sharpe Ratio is a decreasing function of the capital x allocated to the active strategy. Modeling this dependency explicitly is challenging, and to my knowledge there is no analysis where μ is a function of x. The formula $x^\star = \mathrm{SR}/\sigma$ does not hold any longer. *At the very least*, we should acknowledge this dependency in the ideal formula, and solve for the allocation that solves the equation $x = \mathrm{SR}(x)/\sigma$.
- There are transaction costs even in the case of a static $x^\star$. Whenever the active strategy has a positive PnL, in order to maintain a fraction $x^\star$ in the active strategy, we need to partially trade out of the policy and allocate to the risk-free asset. The dollar amount we need to trade in order to maintain the fraction $x^\star$ is

$$\frac{W_t x^\star(1 + r_t) + \delta_t}{W_t[x^\star(1 + r_t) + (1 - x^\star)]} = x^\star \Rightarrow \delta_t = \frac{1 - x^\star}{1 + r_t} W_t r_t$$

  Trading costs are super-linear in δ_t, and therefore super-linear in W_t, and become dominant as wealth grows. HIC SVNT LEONES.

The next section is devoted to describing the attractive mathematical properties of Kelly strategies.

13.2 Mathematical Properties

We limit our attention to the case in which we can choose in each period among a set of strategies Θ, and the associated returns $r_t(\theta)$ are independent of $r_{t'}(\theta)$, for all $t' < t$. These results were proved first by Breiman (1961) and Dubins and Savage (1965) for iid returns, and the results that follow apply to this case. Some of them have also been established for dependent random variables; see Algoet and Cover (1988).

Let X_t, Y_t be the cumulative returns of the Kelly strategy, and of an alternative strategy with lower expected growth rate.

1. The first property is that the Kelly strategy grows faster than any other strategy. Let X_t, Y_t be the cumulative returns of the Kelly strategy and alternative strategy, respectively. Then, with probability 1,

$$\lim_{t\to\infty} \frac{X_t}{Y_t} = \infty \tag{13.12}$$

2. The second property characterizes the long-term growth of a strategy based on the expected value of its log returns. Let $g := E[\log(1 + r_1)]$ and X_t the associated cumulative return process. Then, with probability 1:
   (a) $g > 0 \Rightarrow X_t \to \infty$;
   (b) $g < 0 \Rightarrow X_t \to -\infty$;
   (c) $g = 0 \Rightarrow \limsup_t X_t = \infty, \liminf_t X_t = -\infty$.
3. The expected time to reach capital level C is equal to $\log C/g$ in the limit $C \to \infty$, and it is shortest for the Kelly strategy.

Insight 13.1: *The intuition behind Kelly strategies*

The Kelly criterion for sizing has several intuitive and attractive features.

- *Goal*: The allocation strategy achieves the highest long-term capital growth.
- *Simplicity*: The optimal strategy is simple, since it allocates a constant fraction of total capital to the risky strategy.
- *Lower and Upper Bound on Risky Allocation*: The fraction of capital allocated to a risky strategy should be high enough to ensure growth $g > 0$, and at most equal to $x^\star$.
- *Sharpe-Proportional*: To a first approximation, the optimal fraction of invested capital and the volatility/capital ratio are proportional to the Sharpe Ratio of the strategy.

What these results say is that a Kelly strategy has many very desirable features. In the long run, it beats almost surely any other strategy that has a different expected growth rate. It also reaches a certain cumulative return faster than any other strategy; and the approximate time needed to reach this return can be expressed as a function of g. Finally, a positive expected growth rate is a necessary and sufficient condition for any strategy to have a growing cumulative return over time.[4]

What the results *don't say* is that a Kelly strategy is maximizing the Sharpe Ratio, even if we were able to compute it exactly from knowledge of the true expected return and volatility of the strategy. Nor does it guarantee any lower bound on the maximum drawdowns, which can be severe, as seen in the simulations above. In Example 13.2, as the fraction x invested increases from 0 to the growth-maximizing level x^*, both the growth rate and the size of the drawdowns increase with x. The scale of the y-axis is logarithmic. The excursion of the returns is therefore proportional to the drawdown percentage. Above the optimal level, the growth rate diminishes (as expected) and the drawdowns increase further. For fractions of the invested wealth lower than x^*, there is a trade-off between expected log returns and volatility of the log returns: we get lower returns, in exchange for lower risk. We explore this trade-off next.

13.3 The Fractional Kelly Strategy

The *fractional Kelly strategy* consists of investing in a strategy with iid return r_t a fraction $x^\star_{\text{frac}}$ of the available capital smaller than $x^\star$, but still such that $E[\log(1 + r_1 x^\star_{\text{frac}})] > 1$. It can be interpreted in several ways:

- *Combination of risk-free asset and full Kelly*. Fractional Kelly is a combination of two investments: a risk-free asset and the full Kelly strategy. The percentage volatility of the strategy is $\sigma x^\star_{\text{frac}}$. This is the line of analysis pursued by MacLean et al. (1992). They show (MacLean et al., 2004, 2010a) that the fractional Kelly strategy does indeed trade off growth for security. Assume, for example, that in each period we cannot tolerate a percentage volatility greater than some value p. This threshold is related to the maximum drawdown per period that we can

[4] There are other properties of the Kelly strategy. See MacLean et al. (2010a) for a review, and Part IV of the book MacLean et al. (2010b) for a diversity of views.

accept. From Equation (13.11), $x\sigma \leq p$. We choose the minimum of the $x^\star = \min\{p/\sigma, \mathrm{SR}\}$.

Example 13.5: *We deploy \$1B of capital, and have a Sharpe Ratio of 2. The strategy has a percentage volatility of 5%. We can lose at most 1% of our capital in a week. Say that 3 × (weekly dollar volatility) = 0.01 × (capital), i.e.,*

$$p = \frac{\text{(weekly dollar volatility)}}{\text{(capital)}} = 0.01/3$$

So that $p/\sigma = 0.11$. *This is smaller than the weekly Sharpe Ratio* $2/\sqrt{52} \approxeq 0.27$, *which corresponds to the optimal Kelly fraction.*

- *Higher risk aversion.* We start from Equation (13.6), which approximates the log objective function with a linear-quadratic one. We modify the approximate objective function by overweighting the quadratic penalty:

$$\max_x \mu x - \frac{\lambda}{2}(\sigma^2 + \mu^2)x^2, \qquad \theta > 1$$

The optimization point is

$$x^\star_{\text{frac}} = \frac{x^\star}{\lambda}$$

Fractional Kelly is then a modified Kelly strategy for investors who are more risk-averse than logarithmic utility would suggest.[5]

- *Parameter uncertainty.* Thorp (2006) makes the case that uncertainty about the properties of returns should result in fractional Kelly. Indeed, being wrong can have terrible consequences. Imagine, for example, that we have a strategy with a volatility of 19%, and an estimate of Sharpe Ratio equal to 0.84. The Kelly fraction is 4.4. We over-leverage the strategy and go bankrupt (see Figure 13.3, bottom panel, for a historical simulation based on the returns of the market).

  We have introduced parameter uncertainty already in Section 10.2.2, in the context of MVO. Here we model parameter uncertainty as follows. Per-period returns are $r_t = r(\omega_t, \theta_t)$, where r_t is a function of two iid random variables ω_t (the sample in the probability space Ω_t, with probability measure P_ω) and θ_t (a random parameter taking values in a set Θ, with probability measure P_Θ). The

[5] The relationship between this mean-variance approximation and power utility function $u(x) \propto u^\gamma$, for $\gamma > 0$, is explored by Pulley (1981).

interpretation is that in every period we have a noisy estimate of the true parameter $\bar{\theta} := E_\theta(\theta_t)$. We make the assumptions that $r(\omega_t, \theta_t)$ is twice differentiable in θ_t and that $\partial^2 r/\partial\theta_t^2 \leq 0$. The log total return is

$$
\begin{aligned}
g_T(x) &:= \frac{1}{T}\sum_{t=1}^{T} \log(1 + xr(\omega_t, \theta_t)) \\
g(x) &:= \lim_{T\to\infty} g_T(x) \\
&= E_{\omega,\theta}[\log(1 + xr(\omega, \theta))] \qquad \text{a.s.}
\end{aligned}
$$

The expectation is taken with respect to the random variables $\omega \sim P_\omega$ and $\theta \sim P_\theta$. We want to maximize $g(x)$. The first-order condition is $g'(x) = 0$:

$$
\begin{aligned}
g'(x) &= E_\omega E_\theta \left[\frac{r(\omega, \theta)}{1 + xr(\omega, \theta)}\right] \\
g(x^\star_{\text{uncert}}) &= 0
\end{aligned}
$$

As a function of r, the function $h(r) := r/(1 + xr)$ is increasing and strictly concave. Then it follows that, as a function of θ, $h(r(\theta))$ is concave, because

$$
\frac{\partial^2 h(r(\theta))}{\partial\theta^2} = h''(r)r^2 + h'(r)\frac{\partial^2 r}{\partial\theta^2} \leq 0
$$

By Jensen's inequality,

$$
E_\theta\left[\frac{r(\omega, \theta)}{1 + xr(\omega, \theta)}\right] < \frac{r(\omega, \bar{\theta})}{1 + xr(\omega, \bar{\theta})}
$$

And therefore, taking expectations over ω,

$$
g'(x) = E_\omega E_\theta \left[\frac{r(\omega, \theta)}{1 + xr(\omega, \theta)}\right] < E_\omega \left[\frac{r(\omega, \bar{\theta})}{1 + xr(\omega, \bar{\theta})}\right] =: g_0(x)
$$

The function on the left-hand side is the derivative of the expected log return in the presence of parameter uncertainty. The function on the right-hand side is the derivative of the expected log return when the parameter is known. It follows that $x^\star_{\text{uncert}} \leq x^\star$. Figure 13.4 visually illustrates the location of the two solutions.

Let us consider two examples that have some general application: uncertainty about a strategy's expected return and about its variance.

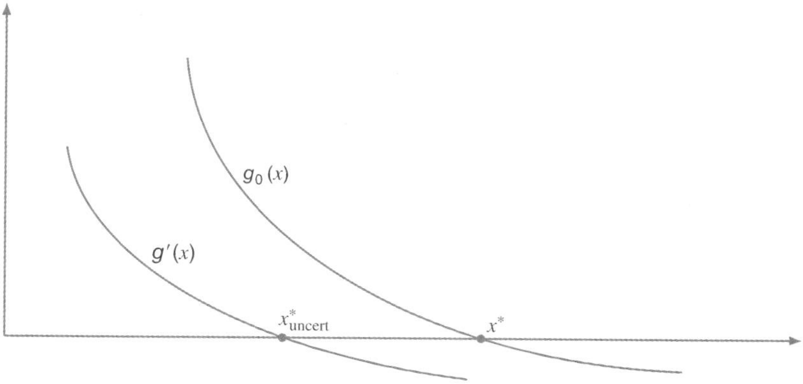

Figure 13.4 The optimal Kelly size in the presence of parameter uncertainty is always smaller than the optimal size when parameters are known.

Example 13.6 ***(Strategy with Uncertain Expected Return):*** *Let $r = \theta + \sigma\xi$, where ξ is an rv with zero mean and unit variance, and θ is random, with $E(\theta) = \mu$ and $var(\theta) = \tau^2$. We assume that ξ and θ are independent. In this case $\partial^2 r/\partial\theta^2 = 0$.*

$$E[\log(1 + rx)] \simeq \mu x - \frac{1}{2}(\mu^2 + \sigma^2 + \tau^2)x^2$$

so that the Kelly fraction is

$$x_1^\star \simeq \frac{\mu}{\mu^2 + \sigma^2 + \tau^2}$$

Let us use the S&P500 rough market estimates from previous examples: $\sigma = 0.19$, $\mu = 0.08$, and $\tau = 0.04$. We get $x_1^\star = 1.81$, compared to an estimate of 1.88 in the absence of estimation error.

Example 13.7 ***(Strategy with Uncertain Volatility):*** *Let $r = \mu + (\sigma + \tau\theta)\xi$, where $\tau > 0$ and ξ, θ are rvs with mean zero and unit variance. We assume that ξ and θ are independent. Also in this case $\partial^2 r/\partial\theta^2 = 0$.*

$$\begin{aligned} E[\log(1 + rx)] &\simeq \mu x - \frac{1}{2}[\mu^2 + E((\sigma + \tau\theta)^2\xi^2)]x^2 \\ &= \mu x - \frac{1}{2}(\mu^2 + \sigma^2 + \tau^2)x^2 \end{aligned}$$

so that the Kelly fraction is again

$$x_1^\star \simeq \frac{\mu}{\mu^2 + \sigma^2 + \tau^2}$$

Let us use the S&P500 rough market estimates from previous examples: $\sigma = 0.19$, $\mu = 0.08$, and $\tau = 0.1$ for the market return. We get $x_1^\star = 1.52$, compared to an estimate of 1.88 in the absence of estimation error.

Insight 13.2: *All reasonable investors use fractional Kelly without knowing*

All reasonable investors allocate capital to a risky strategy so that the volatility/capital ratio is constant, or slowly varying. This is in line with the first justification we gave to fractional Kelly strategies. In other words, they want to allocate as much capital as possible, compatibly with the drawdowns that their investors can bear. In a series of papers (Part VI of MacLean et al. (2010b) collects the contributions on this subject), Ziemba and coauthors provide anecdotal evidence that successful investors follow Kelly allocations. The likely reason is not that investors are aware of the Kelly criterion, but rather that they use the simple constant vol/capital heuristic, which turns out to be equal to fractional Kelly.

13.4 Fractional Kelly and Drawdown Control

In an influential paper, Grossman and Zhou (1993) address a question related to that of identifying a growth-optimal strategy and of controlled growth-optimal optimization. In the Grossman–Zhou formulation (GZ henceforth), the investor wants to maximize the long-term growth and with probability one avoids reaching a drawdown threshold. As formulated in their original paper, the model only considers a risk-free asset and a risky one following a geometric diffusion with mean μ and volatility σ. We introduced this model in Example 13.4. In order to formulate the policy, we define the *high watermark* of the wealth process W_t as $M_t = \max\{W_s : s \in [0, t]\}$. Let d_t be the current drawdown percentage from the high watermark: $d_t := 1 - W_t/M_t$. Let the maximum allowed percentage drawdown be D. The optimal policy gives the optimal fraction invested in the risky asset and is given by

$$f_t = \frac{\mu}{\sigma^2}\left(1 - \frac{1-D}{1-d_t}\right) \tag{13.13}$$

This policy is elegant and intuitive. For some intuition, fix first $D = 1$; i.e., we can tolerate infinite drawdown. Then the strategy is the one we identified in Equation (13.6): invest a fixed fraction $x^* = \mu/\sigma^2$. If $0 < D < 1$, then the optimal strategy is to invest a fraction x^*D when we are at the high watermark $d_t = 0$. This means that we are more prudent than in the simple Kelly scenario, and we are more prudent if our threshold is conservative; a "dynamic fractional Kelly" with maximum fraction D of the optimal Kelly. The less tolerant we are of drawdowns, the smaller the fraction. Moreover, we decrease the invested fraction as we approach the drawdown threshold, and we liquidate the risky asset. Figure 13.5 shows the optimal fraction as a function of the threshold. The reduction rate is nearly constant over the range of allowed drawdowns.

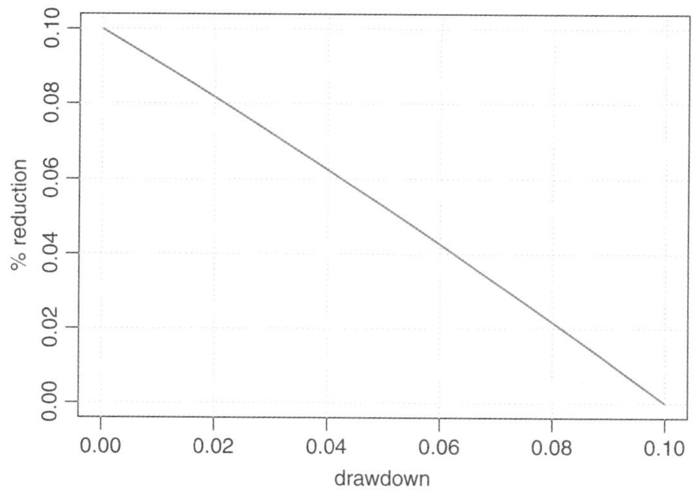

Figure 13.5 Percentage reduction factor $1 - (1 - D)/(1 - d_t)$.

Insight 13.3: *Modulating volatility reduces the Sharpe Ratio*

The GZ criterion changes capital allocation, and hence volatility, over time. Changing the volatility of a strategy *when the volatility* is independent of the expected return of the strategy is Sharpe-reducing. To gain intuition about this fact, consider the simple example of a strategy with Sharpe Ratio equal to s. Half of the year we deploy a volatility $\sigma/2$, and half of the year a volatility $(3/2)\sigma$. The expected PnL for the entire year is $((1/2)s\sigma + (3/2)s\sigma)/2 = s\sigma$. The annualized volatility is $\sqrt{(\sigma/2)^2/2 + (\sigma(3/2))^2/2} = \sqrt{11/8}\sigma$. The Sharpe Ratio is $\sqrt{8/11}s$. Compare to the case in which we had kept the volatility constant at the value $\sqrt{11/8}\sigma$. The Sharpe Ratio would have been s. This example can be generalized, and shows that drawdown control doesn't come for free.

The strategy is a continuous version of the *stop-loss policies* employed by many hedge funds and successful investors. In the presence of a large drawdown, a portfolio manager operating autonomously within the fund is required to partially or completely liquidate her portfolio. The strategy has many interpretations. One interpretation of a stop-loss policy is a tail insurance policy on the strategy itself. View the policy as a synthetic asset, whose price is W_t. Imagine that we hold an out-of-the-money put on strategy.

To understand the trade-offs between optimizing for variance control and optimizing for drawdown control, it is useful to compare the GZ and fractional Kelly strategies in a numerical example. Specifically, we consider the case of a risky asset with independent, identically distributed returns. Its expected daily return is 0.08% and its daily volatility is 1%, corresponding to a Sharpe Ratio of 1.27. The two strategies are parametrized by the Kelly fraction and the drawdown threshold, respectively, i.e.,

$$f_t(p) = p\frac{\mu}{\sigma^2} \qquad \textit{(fractional Kelly)} \qquad (13.14)$$

$$f_t(D) = \frac{\mu}{\sigma^2}\left(1 - \frac{1-D}{1-d_t}\right) \qquad \textit{(Grossman–Zhou)} \qquad (13.15)$$

with $p \in (0, 1), D \in (0, 1)$. I then simulate the performance of the two strategies over a 100-year period (i.e., 25,200 days) and compare the realized volatility and the maximum drawdown for strategies having the same expected log-return. Figure 13.6 shows the results. As expected, the fractional Kelly strategy has a better profile than GZ in the mean-volatility plane, and a worse one in the mean-maximum drawdown one. In this numerical example, the reduction in drawdown of GZ seems more marked than the associated increase in volatility.

For example, consider a max tolerated drawdown of 30%. GZ achieves an average daily return of approximately 0.09%, while fractional Kelly achieves an average daily return of 0.075%, a 20% increase. More importantly, GZ controls the maximum drawdown *ex ante*, with probability one and independently of misspecification of the problem. In the fractional Kelly approach, we can at best provide a probabilistic bound on the drawdown; moreover, if the parameters in the optimization problem are incorrect, this bound will be incorrect as well. These considerations

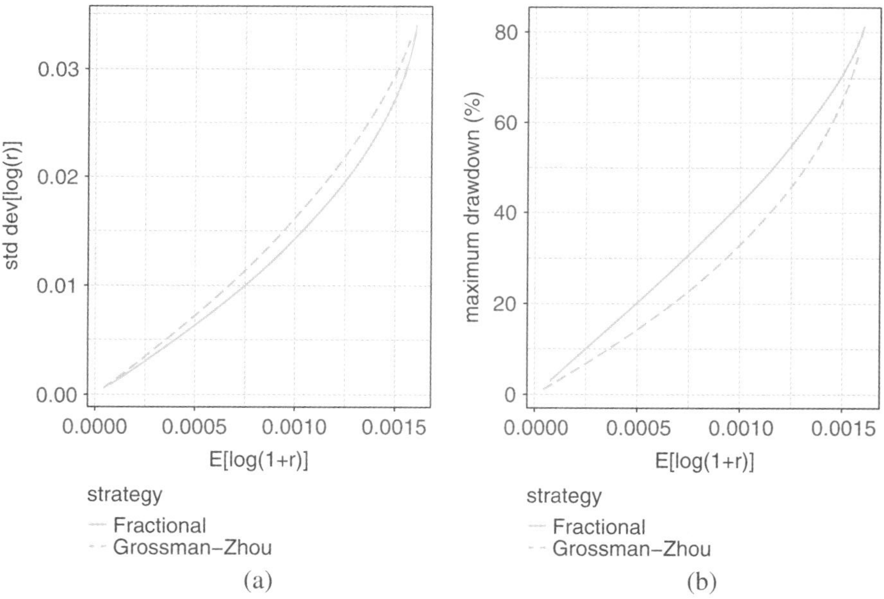

Figure 13.6 Comparison of fractional Kelly and Grossman-Zhou strategies. Both strategies' performance measures are estimated over the same sequence of 25,200 returns, but with different parameters p, D. (a) Standard deviation of daily log-returns versus mean log-return. (b) Maximum drawdown.

suggest that the GZ strategy may be preferable. There is an important qualification to this statement. Throughout this chapter, we have ignored the role played by transaction costs. As we mentioned above, a static fractional Kelly policy requires the continuous allocation of capital to/from a risk-free asset and the active strategy. In GZ, the fraction allocated to the strategy itself is varying over time, sometimes very rapidly in the event of a sudden drawdown, since we may force a complete liquidation of the risky asset when we reach the threshold. This in turn may affect the profitability of the strategy and make the approach less attractive. It is beyond the scope of this chapter to extend the analysis to the case of transaction costs which, in the absence of analytical results, may only be tractable with numerical experiments. These objections notwithstanding, GZ is a useful heuristic that can be used as an overlay to a Kelly-like strategy.

The Takeaways

1. The policy that generates the highest capital growth in the long run is the Kelly criterion.
2. The Kelly criterion prescribes that we allocate a constant fraction of our capital over time to our active strategy that is equal to the Sharpe Ratio of the strategy, divided by its percentage volatility.
3. The Kelly criterion has the undesirable property of incurring large drawdowns over time.
4. To alleviate this problem, we can adopt the fractional Kelly criterion, which allocates a constant, smaller fraction of capital to our active strategy. It trades off growth for higher security.
5. Parameter uncertainty is another way to justify the fractional Kelly criterion.
6. It is further possible to modify the Kelly criterion, so that the fraction of capital is a function of the maximum tolerable drawdown, and this fraction is linearly decreasing as a function of the drawdown size. The strategy trades off further growth in exchange for a deterministic guarantee on the experienced drawdown.
7. Many successful investors naturally follow a fractional Kelly with drawdown control.
8. All of these simple strategies are valid in the absence of transaction costs, and need to be simulated and calibrated in real-world applications, in order to account for such costs.

Chapter 14

Ex-Post Performance Attribution

The Questions

1. Is portfolio performance primarily due to skill or luck?
2. What is the breakdown of PnL between factor-driven and idiosyncratic sources?
3. In idiosyncratic space, is asset selection or sizing a more significant contributor to PnL?
4. How can factor-driven PnL be analyzed in a concise and meaningful way?
5. What are effective methods for decomposing portfolio performance in dynamic and complex markets?
6. How does uncertainty in model parameters affect performance attribution accuracy?

"After the leaves have fallen, we return/To a plain sense of things". So begins a famous poem[1] which describes well the spirit of this chapter. Out of metaphor, the "rain" is the realized performance of our strategy, and the plain sense of things is our ability to understand what happened after the fact, namely:

- Is our performance due to luck or skill?
- How did we make or lose money? What is the contribution of factor PnL and idiosyncratic PnL?
- In idiosyncratic space, what drove our PnL? Asset selection or sizing? The first is being on the right side of a bet; the second is the ability to size appropriately asset bets that yield higher returns.
- How can we explain factor PnL concisely and insightfully, i.e., using only factors that are of interest to us?

Performance attribution offers numerous advantages. First, it provides the portfolio manager with a much-needed reality check. If she lost money, maybe she can explain the source of the loss, and identify countermeasures to apply going forward; sometimes the remedies are straightforward and contained in the output of the performance attribution itself. If she made money, maybe she did so as the result of unintended bets on factors that were not included in the strategy's scope. "The first principle is that you must not fool yourself—and you are the easiest person to fool." This statement, made by Richard Feynman in his 1974 CalTech commencement address, holds true for scientists and traders alike. Secondly, performance attribution empowers the *principal* to reward an agent appropriately. The principal may be the hedge fund manager and the agent the portfolio manager, or, descending one step down in the decision-making hierarchy, the principal may be the portfolio manager and the agent may be the analyst who works in the portfolio manager's team. There are other benefits. A portfolio manager is bound to use a specific factor model for *ex-ante* portfolio construction. No *ex-post* limitation exists after the trade, though: she can look at her performance under the magnifying glass of different risk models. For example, a global risk model, sometimes unsuited for country-specific investing, could reveal cross-country exposures. We can also use statistical models in addition to fundamental models.

[1] W. Stevens, "The Plain Sense of Things", in Stevens (1990).

Performance attribution is conceptually simple but it is not trivial. The remainder of this chapter is broadly organized into two parts. First, we introduce *characteristics-based performance attribution* (also known as *holdings-based*), and then review the concept of *time-based* attribution.

14.1 Performance Attribution: The Basics

Recall the short introduction to performance attribution in Section 4.5.1: the PnL can be decomposed into the sum of factor and idiosyncratic components. The performance decomposition *process* is slightly more involved. Trading time is not discrete, whereas performance attribution occurs in discrete time. To reconcile the two views, the time axis is partitioned into intervals delimited by epochs τ_i. Denote with PnL_i the PnL in interval $[\tau_{i-1}, \tau_i]$, and $\mathbf{r}_i$, $\mathbf{f}_i$, and $\boldsymbol{\epsilon}_i$ the total returns, factor returns, and idiosyncratic returns, respectively. Also, define, as we have done previously, $\mathbf{b}_i := \mathbf{B}^\top \mathbf{w}_i$. Then we can isolate the *trading PnL* with the decomposition

$$
\begin{aligned}
\text{PnL} &= \sum_t (\text{PnL}_t - \mathbf{r}_t \mathbf{w}_t) + \mathbf{r}_t \mathbf{w}_t \\
&= \underbrace{\sum_t (\text{PnL}_t - \mathbf{r}_t \mathbf{w}_t)}_{\textit{trading PnL}} + \underbrace{\underbrace{\sum_t \mathbf{b}_t^\top \mathbf{f}_t}_{\textit{factor PnL}} + \underbrace{\sum_t \boldsymbol{\epsilon}_t^\top \mathbf{w}_t}_{\textit{idiosyncratic PnL}}}_{\textit{position PnL}}
\end{aligned}
$$

The sum of factor and idiosyncratic PnL is sometimes referred to as *position PnL*. This is the PnL we would experience if we could instantaneously trade, with no transaction costs, so that the PnL is resulting from the application to the portfolio of the interval's total returns. To fix ideas on the interpretation of the trading PnL, it is helpful to consider the case of an idealized high-frequency trader (HFT). Let the epochs be the close of trading days. The HFT ends the day flat[2]: $\mathbf{w}_t = 0$. The accounting PnL is zero, but the trading PnL is not. It originates from three terms: intraday alpha, i.e., "price discovery"; compensation for providing liquidity by submitting limit orders and receiving a fraction of the bid–ask spread; and costs incurred by taking liquidity by submitting market orders.

---

[2] Non-idealized HFTs do not necessarily close the day flat, but instead rebalance the book and/or partially hedge it.

The factor PnL can be decomposed into separate time series for the contribution of each factor:

$$\text{Factor PnL} = \sum_{j=1}^{m} \left(\sum_{t=1}^{T} [\mathbf{b}_t]_j [\mathbf{f}_t]_j \right) \tag{14.1}$$

This could be the end of a simple story: take portfolio snapshots at each epoch, decompose PnL into three terms, and then dive into the contribution of individual factors and of individual securities to idiosyncratic PnL. Reality, however, is more complex. First, we need to unveil the illusion of certainty that comes with the simple decomposition of Equation (14.1).

14.2 Performance Attribution with Errors

14.2.1 *Two Paradoxes*

To motivate the importance of having a more nuanced view of factor-based performance attribution, we introduce two paradoxical facts, both related to FMPs:

- *Factor-Mimicking Portfolios have idiosyncratic risk but not PnL.* Each FMP $\mathbf{v}_i$ has by necessity a non-zero idiosyncratic variance $\sigma^2_{\mathbf{v}_i} := \mathbf{v}_i^\top \mathbf{\Omega}_\epsilon \mathbf{v}_i$. However, the FMP has no idiosyncratic PnL whatsoever. This can be seen intuitively by the fact that the return of the factor is the return of the portfolio itself. More rigorously, let $\mathbf{P}$ be the matrix whose columns are the FMPs, as defined in Equation (9.12). Then their idio PnL is

$$\mathbf{P}^\top \epsilon = \mathbf{B}(\mathbf{B}^\top \mathbf{\Omega}_\epsilon^{-1} \mathbf{B})^{-1} \mathbf{B}^\top \mathbf{\Omega}_\epsilon^{-1} (\mathbf{I}_n - \mathbf{B}(\mathbf{B}^\top \mathbf{\Omega}_\epsilon^{-1} \mathbf{B})^{-1} \mathbf{B}^\top \mathbf{\Omega}_\epsilon^{-1}) \mathbf{r} = 0$$

  and therefore the idio PnL is null. This holds for *all* factor portfolios, including those that have an idiosyncratic variance percentage close to 50%, and for all periods. This is especially concerning given that factor model performance is often evaluated on factor portfolios.
- *Factor-Neutral Portfolios.* On the other side, consider a portfolio $\mathbf{w}$ with no factor exposures, i.e., $\mathbf{B}^\top \mathbf{w} = 0$. Hence, its entire variance is its idiosyncratic variance $\sigma^2_{\mathbf{w}} := \mathbf{w}^\top \mathbf{\Omega}_\epsilon \mathbf{w}$. Now, consider the portfolio $\mathbf{w} + \lambda \mathbf{v}$, where $\mathbf{v}$ is an FMP and $\lambda \in \mathbb{R}$. The idiosyncratic PnL of this portfolio is the same for any value of λ, since

$\mathbf{v}$ has no idio PnL. However, the idiosyncratic volatility of $\mathbf{w} + \lambda\mathbf{v}$ depends on λ, and is equal to $\sigma_{\mathbf{w}}^2 + \lambda^2\sigma_{\mathbf{v}}^2 + 2\lambda\mathbf{w}^\intercal\mathbf{\Omega}_\epsilon\mathbf{v}$. Hence we have *exactly* the same sequence of residual PnL generated by a continuum of portfolios with possibly very different volatilities. We can make the realized idiosyncratic volatility of the portfolio arbitrarily different than the predicted idiosyncratic volatility, thus greatly undermining the credibility of the model. How can this be?

One could object that in practice, factor portfolios do not have zero idiosyncratic PnL. This is due primarily to the non-stationarity of the process, so that factor portfolios as of time t are slightly stale when applied to time $t+1$. This criticism doesn't address the concerns exemplified by the paradoxes for two reasons. First, because even in the ideal case in which the model is stationary, and we have accurately estimated its parameters, we do have these paradoxes. Second, because the idiosyncratic PnL would be in any event much smaller than what would be compatible with the idiosyncratic volatility predicted by the model.

In the next three sections I present a possible solution to these paradoxes. The overall takeaway in the analysis is that the returns of the FMPs are *estimates* of the true factor returns from the model. Factor portfolios have, according to *any*[3] factor model, non-zero idiosyncratic volatility, and they have idiosyncratic returns in addition to their true factor returns. Once we account rigorously for the estimation error, the factor PnL and idiosyncratic PnL can be characterized as random variables whose first and second moments can be obtained from model and portfolio data. The next section lays out some basic facts about model estimation; the last section derives the main formulas. We then give explanations for the paradoxes.

14.2.2 Estimating Attribution Errors

Let us rewrite the attribution equations, but paying attention to the fact that we are using factor and idiosyncratic return estimates $\hat{\mathbf{f}}_t, \hat{\boldsymbol{\epsilon}}_t$.

[3] By "any", we mean that the return covariance matrix can be decomposed into the sum of a dense low-rank matrix and a sparse full-rank one.

We consider the case of a time-independent factor model. Recall from Section 6.3.1 that the factor returns can be written as

$$\hat{\mathbf{f}}_t = \mathbf{f}_t + \boldsymbol{\eta}_t \qquad \boldsymbol{\eta}_t \sim N(0, (\mathbf{B}^\top \boldsymbol{\Omega}_\epsilon^{-1} \mathbf{B})^{-1})$$

Analogously, for the idiosyncratic returns, we have

$$\begin{aligned} \hat{\epsilon}_t &= \mathbf{r}_t - \mathbf{B}\hat{\mathbf{f}}_t \\ &= \epsilon_t - \mathbf{B}\eta_t \qquad \mathbf{B}\eta_t \sim N(0, \mathbf{B}(\mathbf{B}^\top \boldsymbol{\Omega}_\epsilon^{-1} \mathbf{B})^{-1} \mathbf{B}^\top) \end{aligned}$$

$$\begin{aligned} \textit{(estimated factor PnL)}_t &= \mathbf{w}_t^\top \mathbf{B}\hat{\mathbf{f}}_t \\ &= \textit{(true factor PnL)}_t + \mathbf{w}_t^\top \mathbf{B}\boldsymbol{\eta}_t \\ \textit{(estimated idiosyncratic PnL)}_t &= \mathbf{w}_t^\top \hat{\boldsymbol{\epsilon}}_t \\ &= \textit{(true idiosyncratic PnL)}_t - \mathbf{w}_t^\top \mathbf{B}\boldsymbol{\eta}_t \\ \mathbf{w}_t^\top \mathbf{B}\boldsymbol{\eta}_t &\sim N(0, \mathbf{b}_t^\top (\mathbf{B}^\top \boldsymbol{\Omega}_\epsilon^{-1} \mathbf{B})^{-1} \mathbf{b}_t) \end{aligned}$$

When we attribute the PnL over multiple periods, we have

$$\textit{(true factor PnL)} = \textit{(estimated factor PnL)} - \sum_t \mathbf{w}_t^\top \mathbf{B}\boldsymbol{\eta}_t$$

$$\textit{(true idiosyncratic PnL)} = \textit{(estimated idiosyncratic PnL)} + \sum_t \mathbf{w}_t^\top \mathbf{B}\boldsymbol{\eta}_t$$

Finally, this gives us two useful results. First, it provides confidence intervals around the attributed PnL:

$$\textit{(true factor PnL)} \sim N\left(\sum_t \mathbf{b}_t^\top \hat{\mathbf{f}}_t, \sum_t \mathbf{b}_t^\top (\mathbf{B}^\top \boldsymbol{\Omega}_\epsilon^{-1} \mathbf{B})^{-1} \mathbf{b}_t\right)$$

$$\textit{(true idiosyncratic PnL)} \sim N\left(\sum_t \mathbf{w}_t^\top \hat{\epsilon}_t, \sum_t \mathbf{b}_t^\top (\mathbf{B}^\top \boldsymbol{\Omega}_\epsilon^{-1} \mathbf{B})^{-1} \mathbf{b}_t\right)$$

If, for example, we observe a negative idiosyncratic PnL over a given time interval, we can determine whether $0 falls inside the 95% confidence interval or not. The same applies to factor PnL. An additional result is that the time series of factor and idiosyncratic PnLs are in general negatively correlated. Take the case of a constant portfolio, and constant factor exposures **b**. The covariance between factor and idiosyncratic PnL is given by $-\mathbf{b}^\top (\mathbf{B}^\top \boldsymbol{\Omega}_\epsilon^{-1} \mathbf{B})^{-1} \mathbf{b}$. This is sometimes observed in practice.

14.2.3 Paradox Resolution

We first discuss the paradoxes introduced in the first section.

- *Factor Portfolios.* Factor portfolio i has exposure vector $\mathbf{b}_i = (0, \ldots, 0, 1, 0, \ldots, 0)$, where the 1 is in the ith position, so $\left\|\mathbf{b}_t\right\| = 1$. Therefore

$$\text{(true factor PnL)} \sim N\left(\sum_{t=1}^{T} \hat{f}_{t,i}, T[(\mathbf{B}^{\mathsf{T}}\mathbf{\Omega}_{\epsilon}^{-1}\mathbf{B})^{-1}]_{i,i}\right)$$

$$\text{(true idiosyncratic PnL)} \sim N\left(0, T\,[(\mathbf{B}^{\mathsf{T}}\mathbf{\Omega}_{\epsilon}^{-1}\mathbf{B})^{-1}]_{i,i}\right)$$

  So the factor portfolio has a random zero-mean idiosyncratic PnL whose variance grows linearly in T.
- *Factor-Neutral Portfolios.* Let $\mathbf{w}$ be a portfolio with no exposure to any factor, i.e., $\mathbf{B}^{\mathsf{T}}\mathbf{w} = 0$. The portfolio $\mathbf{w} + \lambda\mathbf{v}_i$ (where $\mathbf{v}_i$ is the first FMP) has exposure $\mathbf{b}_i = (0, \ldots, \lambda, \ldots, 0)$. The factor and idiosyncratic PnLs are

$$\text{(true factor PnL)} \sim N\left(\lambda\sum_{t=1}^{T} \hat{f}_{t,i}, \lambda^2 T[(\mathbf{B}^{\mathsf{T}}\mathbf{\Omega}_{\epsilon}^{-1}\mathbf{B})^{-1}]_{i,i}\right) \tag{14.2}$$

$$\text{(true idiosyncratic PnL)} \sim N\left(\sum_{t=1}^{T} \mathbf{w}^{\mathsf{T}}\hat{\epsilon}_t, \lambda^2 T[(\mathbf{B}^{\mathsf{T}}\mathbf{\Omega}_{\epsilon}^{-1}\mathbf{B})^{-1}]_{i,i}\right) \tag{14.3}$$

  The idiosyncratic PnL is no longer independent of the hedge $\lambda\mathbf{v}_i$. A greater hedge makes the idiosyncratic attribution more uncertain, and the uncertainty is linear in the hedge.

Insight 14.1: *Reporting standard errors for attributions*

When reporting factor-based performance attributions, always include (either graphically, or in tabular form), the standard errors of the factor and idiosyncratic PnLs, using the volatilities from Equations (14.2) and (14.3). This will help the portfolio manager better understand the uncertainty associated with her attributed performance.

Summing up, the current factor-based attribution methodology universally assigns a numeric factor and idiosyncratic PnL to a strategy; these are deterministic functions of the portfolios over time, the stock returns, and additional available data, such as asset characteristics. Ignoring the estimation error of these attributions leads to inconsistencies. These inconsistencies are not edge cases. Attributing performance of factor portfolios and hedged portfolios is central to the practice of risk management and to understanding the performance of a strategy. As a simple resolution to these paradoxes, we saw that, even if we are employing the true factor model, the returns of the FMPs are unbiased estimates of the actual factor returns, and we can characterize the estimation error. Given this characterization, one can propagate its impact in the performance attribution process, and view the factor and idiosyncratic PnLs as random variables for which we have the full distributions (under the assumption of normality of returns) and the confidence intervals.

14.3 Maximal Performance Attribution

A different way to summarize the previous section is: do performance attribution, but use caution. The coming section admits a similarly concise summary: do performance attribution, but try to reduce confusion. If we had to attempt a parallel to real life, performance attribution is like falling in love: fundamentally *good*, but certainly dangerous, and potentially confusing. Where does the confusion come from? Consider the following scenario. A portfolio manager has positive momentum exposure and loses a large sum due to a negative momentum return. He then cuts momentum exposure to zero, as a defensive measure. The day after, the factor has a very large negative return. We ask: is the portfolio's *expected* PnL equal to zero? The answer is no. Another way to state this fact is that the relationship between asset performance and factor returns is mediated by betas, not exposures. The beta of a portfolio to momentum is given by the covariance between portfolio returns and the factor's returns, divided by the factor's variance. In formulas[4]:

$$\beta(\mathbf{w}^\top \mathbf{r}, f_i) \simeq \frac{\mathbf{b}^\top \boldsymbol{\Omega}_f \mathbf{e}_i}{\sigma_i^2}$$

[4] We use the notation $\mathbf{e}_i$ for the vector having a 1 in the ith position: $(0, \ldots, 1, \ldots, 0)$. We also assume that the factor portfolio has negligible idiosyncratic variance.

The beta is in general non-zero, even if $b_i = 0$, because $\beta = \sum_{k\neq 0} \rho_{k,i} b_k(\sigma_k/\sigma_i)$. Factors other than momentum, but that are correlated to it, are responsible for the transmission of the shock.

Let us go through another example. You are developing a risk model with a country factor (whose loadings are all ones) and a historical beta factor. You have the option of z-scoring the historical beta loadings. The choice to z-score does not affect the performance of the risk model, i.e., z-scoring is a model rotation if a country factor is present, and aggregated factor risk does not change if you z-score or not; nor does the aggregate performance attribution. However, PnL attributions of the individual beta and country factors change. The z-scoring makes attribution in the beta factor much smaller. What is the "right" choice? What criteria should we use? This is relevant for *ex-post* analysis. If a portfolio has a large factor drawdown, it is possible that the PnL be spread across multiple factors and that no factor stands out. It is also possible that all these factor losses may be correlated. For example, losses in many industries could be "explained" as momentum losses, or crowding losses. The problem is not only associated with performance analysis. The *ex-ante* risk associated with a factor depends on the representation of the factor itself in the risk model. By this, we mean that the information contained in a given set of factors can be represented in different ways. The same factor may have zero correlation to other factors in one representation, and positive correlation in another. The central question is then: is there a single, non-ambiguous way to assign performance attribution and risk to a subset of factors, such that it explains the PnL and the risk of the portfolio as much as possible?

The answer is in the affirmative: there is a procedure to assign unequivocally maximum risk and PnL to a subset of factors. There are four different ways to formulate and model the problem, all yielding the same result.

We introduce some notation. Denote the sets

$$\begin{aligned}
\mathcal{U} &:= \{1, \ldots, m\} \\
\mathcal{S} &:= \{1, \ldots, p\} \\
\bar{\mathcal{S}} &:= \{p+1, \ldots, m\}
\end{aligned}$$

so we write $\mathbf{f}_{\bar{\mathcal{S}}}$ instead of $\mathbf{f}_{(p+1):m}$ or $\mathbf{\Omega}_{\mathcal{U},\bar{\mathcal{S}}}$ instead of $\mathbf{\Omega}_{1:m,(p+1):m}$.

1. *Maximal Cross-Sectional Return Explanation.* Consider the problem of describing the asset returns as a function of the returns of factors $\mathcal{S}$ as well as possible, i.e.,

$$\mathbf{r} = \boldsymbol{\beta}\mathbf{f}_{\mathcal{S}} + \boldsymbol{\eta} \tag{14.4}$$

where $\boldsymbol{\beta} \in \mathbb{R}^{n \times p}$ and $\boldsymbol{\eta}$ is uncorrelated with $\mathbf{f}_{\mathcal{S}}$. By construction, this is the maximum amount of returns we can attribute to factors $\mathcal{S}$. Once we identify beta, the return attributed to the factors is $\boldsymbol{\beta}^{\mathsf{T}}\mathbf{f}_{\mathcal{S}}$, which is in general different than $\mathbf{B}_{\cdot,\mathcal{S}}\mathbf{f}_{\mathcal{S}}$. We solve the problem

$$\begin{aligned} \min\ & E\|\boldsymbol{\eta}\|^2 \\ \text{s.t.}\ & \mathbf{r} = \mathbf{B}\mathbf{f} + \epsilon \\ & \mathbf{r} = \boldsymbol{\beta}\mathbf{f}_{\mathcal{S}} + \boldsymbol{\eta} \\ & \boldsymbol{\beta} \in \mathbb{R}^{n \times p} \end{aligned} \tag{14.5}$$

This is equivalent to

$$\min_{\beta} E\left\|\mathbf{B}\mathbf{f} - \boldsymbol{\beta}\mathbf{f}_{\mathcal{S}}\right\|^2$$

which is solved by $\boldsymbol{\beta} = \mathbf{B}\boldsymbol{\Omega}_{\mathcal{U},\mathcal{S}}\boldsymbol{\Omega}_{\mathcal{S},\mathcal{S}}^{-1}$. Then the attribution using factor set $\mathcal{S}$ is given by

$$\begin{aligned} \mathbf{w}^{\mathsf{T}}\mathbf{r} &= \mathbf{w}^{\mathsf{T}}\boldsymbol{\beta}\mathbf{f}_{\mathcal{S}} + \textit{(PnL independent of } \mathbf{f}_{\mathcal{S}}) \\ \mathbf{w}^{\mathsf{T}}\boldsymbol{\beta}\mathbf{f}_{\mathcal{S}} &= \mathbf{b}^{\mathsf{T}}\boldsymbol{\Omega}_{\mathcal{U},\mathcal{S}}\boldsymbol{\Omega}_{\mathcal{S},\mathcal{S}}^{-1}\mathbf{f}_{\mathcal{S}} \\ &= \mathbf{b}_{\mathcal{S}}^{\mathsf{T}}\boldsymbol{\Omega}_{\mathcal{S},\mathcal{S}}\boldsymbol{\Omega}_{\mathcal{S},\mathcal{S}}^{-1}\mathbf{f}_{\mathcal{S}} + \mathbf{b}_{\bar{\mathcal{S}}}^{\mathsf{T}}\boldsymbol{\Omega}_{\bar{\mathcal{S}},\mathcal{S}}\boldsymbol{\Omega}_{\mathcal{S},\mathcal{S}}^{-1}\mathbf{f}_{\mathcal{S}} \\ &= \mathbf{b}_{\mathcal{S}}^{\mathsf{T}}\mathbf{f}_{\mathcal{S}} + \mathbf{b}_{\bar{\mathcal{S}}}^{\mathsf{T}}\boldsymbol{\Omega}_{\bar{\mathcal{S}},\mathcal{S}}\boldsymbol{\Omega}_{\mathcal{S},\mathcal{S}}^{-1}\mathbf{f}_{\mathcal{S}} \end{aligned} \tag{14.6}$$

The term $\mathbf{w}^{\mathsf{T}}\boldsymbol{\beta}\mathbf{f}_{\mathcal{S}}$ is the *maximal* attribution to factors in $\bar{\mathcal{S}}$. When factors in $\mathcal{S}$ are uncorrelated to factors in $\bar{\mathcal{S}}$, the factor covariance matrix has a blockwise structure, with $\boldsymbol{\Omega}_{\mathcal{S},\bar{\mathcal{S}}} = 0$ and $\boldsymbol{\beta} = \mathbf{B}_{\cdot,\mathcal{S}}$, so that standard performance attribution and maximal attribution are the same. But in general, the factors in $\mathcal{S}$ and in $\bar{\mathcal{S}}$ are correlated and $\boldsymbol{\Omega}_{\mathcal{S},\bar{\mathcal{S}}} \neq 0$. Maximal attribution shifts the PnL attributable to factors in $\mathcal{S}$ from the other factors.

2. *Conditional Expectation.* There is another way to interpret these formulas, based on conditional distribution of the multivariate Gaussian

distribution. Given returns $\mathbf{f}_{\mathcal{S}}$, the conditional expected returns of factors in $\bar{\mathcal{S}}$ are known analytically and are given by the vector

$$E(\mathbf{f}_{\bar{\mathcal{S}}}|\mathbf{f}_{\mathcal{S}}) = \mathbf{\Omega}_{\bar{\mathcal{S}},\mathcal{S}}\mathbf{\Omega}^{-1}_{\mathcal{S},\mathcal{S}}\mathbf{f}_{\mathcal{S}} \tag{14.7}$$

The formula for the normal performance attribution is

$$\mathbf{b}^{\mathsf{T}}_{\mathcal{S}}\mathbf{f}_{\mathcal{S}} + \mathbf{b}^{\mathsf{T}}_{\bar{\mathcal{S}}}E(\mathbf{f}_{\bar{\mathcal{S}}}|\mathbf{f}_{\mathcal{S}}) = \mathbf{b}^{\mathsf{T}}_{\mathcal{S}}\mathbf{f}_{\mathcal{S}} + \mathbf{b}^{\mathsf{T}}_{\bar{\mathcal{S}}}\mathbf{\Omega}_{\bar{\mathcal{S}},\mathcal{S}}\mathbf{\Omega}^{-1}_{\mathcal{S},\mathcal{S}}\mathbf{f}_{\mathcal{S}}$$

and this is identical to the maximal attribution term in Equation (14.6).

3. *Maximal Portfolio PnL Explanation.* Start with the factor PnL of the portfolio $\mathbf{w}^{\mathsf{T}}$, with factor exposure $\mathbf{b}$. Try to explain as much of this PnL by means of the returns of factors in set $\mathcal{S}$. In formulas, we solve the problem

$$\min_{\tilde{\mathbf{b}}\in\mathbb{R}^p} E\left\|\mathbf{b}^{\mathsf{T}}\mathbf{f} - \tilde{\mathbf{b}}^{\mathsf{T}}\mathbf{f}_{\mathcal{S}}\right\|^2 = \min_{\tilde{\mathbf{b}}\in\mathbb{R}^p} \mathbf{b}^{\mathsf{T}}\mathbf{\Omega}_{\mathcal{U},\mathcal{U}}\mathbf{b} + \mathbf{x}^{\mathsf{T}}\mathbf{\Omega}_{\mathcal{S},\mathcal{S}}\mathbf{x} - 2\mathbf{b}^{\mathsf{T}}\mathbf{\Omega}_{\mathcal{U},\mathcal{S}}\tilde{\mathbf{b}}$$
$$\Rightarrow \tilde{\mathbf{b}} = \mathbf{\Omega}^{-1}_{\mathcal{S},\mathcal{S}}\mathbf{\Omega}_{\mathcal{S},\mathcal{U}}\mathbf{b}$$

and the PnL attribution is $\tilde{\mathbf{b}}^{\mathsf{T}}\mathbf{f}_{\mathcal{S}} = \mathbf{b}^{\mathsf{T}}\mathbf{\Omega}_{\mathcal{U},\mathcal{S}}\mathbf{\Omega}^{-1}_{\mathcal{S},\mathcal{S}}\mathbf{f}_{\mathcal{S}}$, which is, again, what we obtain in Equation (14.6).

This suggests an interpretation of the vector $\tilde{\mathbf{b}}$ as the *adjusted-dollar betas* of the portfolio to factors in set $\mathcal{S}$.

4. *Uncorrelated Factor Rotation.* We have seen in Section 4.4.1 that factor models are not uniquely determined. One can transform the loadings matrix by right-multiplying it by a non-singular square matrix $\mathbf{C}$, and correspondingly transform the factor returns by left-multiplying them by $\mathbf{C}^{-1}$. The resulting risk model has factor covariance matrix $\mathbf{C}^{-1}\mathbf{\Omega}(\mathbf{C}^{-1})^{\mathsf{T}}$. It makes the same predictions as the original risk model, in the sense that the factor variance predicted by the two models is identical, and so is the total factor PnL attribution. However, the PnL attributed to the individual factors will change. $[\mathbf{w}^{\mathsf{T}}\mathbf{B}]_i f_i$ is not the same as $[\mathbf{w}^{\mathsf{T}}\mathbf{BC}]_i[\mathbf{C}^{-1}\mathbf{f}]_i$. We ask whether there is an equivalent model that yields the above "maximal attribution" for the first p factors, and what is its interpretation. The answer to the first question is simple, given the previous derivations. We need to find $\mathbf{C}$ such that

$$\sum_{i\in\mathcal{S}}[\mathbf{b}^{\mathsf{T}}\mathbf{C}]_i[\mathbf{C}^{-1}\mathbf{f}]_i = \mathbf{b}^{\mathsf{T}}\mathbf{\Omega}_{\mathcal{U},\mathcal{S}}\mathbf{\Omega}^{-1}_{\mathcal{S},\mathcal{S}}\mathbf{f}_{\mathcal{S}} \tag{14.8}$$

Define the matrix $\mathbf{A} := \mathbf{\Omega}_{\mathcal{U},\mathcal{S}}\mathbf{\Omega}^{-1}_{\mathcal{S},\mathcal{S}}$ and the rotation matrix $\mathbf{C}$ as

$$\mathbf{C} := \begin{bmatrix} \mathbf{I}_{\mathcal{S},\mathcal{S}} & 0 \\ \mathbf{A} & \mathbf{I}_{\bar{\mathcal{S}},\bar{\mathcal{S}}} \end{bmatrix}$$

$$\Rightarrow \quad \mathbf{C}^{-1} = \begin{bmatrix} \mathbf{I}_{\mathcal{S},\mathcal{S}} & 0 \\ -\mathbf{A} & \mathbf{I}_{\bar{\mathcal{S}},\bar{\mathcal{S}}} \end{bmatrix}$$

Direct calculation shows that

$$[\mathbf{b}^{\top}\mathbf{C}]_{\mathcal{S}} = \mathbf{b}^{\top}_{\mathcal{S}} + \mathbf{b}^{\top}_{\bar{\mathcal{S}}}\mathbf{\Omega}_{\mathcal{U},\mathcal{S}}\mathbf{\Omega}^{-1}_{\mathcal{S},\mathcal{S}} = \mathbf{b}^{\top}\mathbf{\Omega}_{\mathcal{U},\mathcal{S}}\mathbf{\Omega}^{-1}_{\mathcal{S},\mathcal{S}}\mathbf{f}_{\mathcal{S}} \tag{14.9}$$

which is the same as Equation (14.6). In the rotated risk model the covariance matrix is

$$\begin{aligned} \mathbf{C}^{-1}\mathbf{\Omega}(\mathbf{C}^{-1})^{\top} &= \begin{bmatrix} \mathbf{I}_{\mathcal{S},\mathcal{S}} & 0 \\ \mathbf{A} & \mathbf{I}_{\bar{\mathcal{S}},\bar{\mathcal{S}}} \end{bmatrix} \begin{bmatrix} \mathbf{\Omega}_{\mathcal{S},\mathcal{S}} & \mathbf{\Omega}_{\mathcal{S},\bar{\mathcal{S}}} \\ \mathbf{\Omega}_{\bar{\mathcal{S}},\mathcal{S}} & \mathbf{\Omega}_{\bar{\mathcal{S}},\bar{\mathcal{S}}} \end{bmatrix} \begin{bmatrix} \mathbf{I}_{\mathcal{S},\mathcal{S}} & 0 \\ -\mathbf{A} & \mathbf{I}_{\bar{\mathcal{S}},\bar{\mathcal{S}}} \end{bmatrix} \\ &= \begin{bmatrix} \mathbf{\Omega}_{\mathcal{S},\mathcal{S}} & 0 \\ 0 & \mathbf{\Omega}_{\bar{\mathcal{S}},\bar{\mathcal{S}}} - \mathbf{\Omega}_{\bar{\mathcal{S}},\mathcal{S}}\mathbf{\Omega}^{-1}_{\mathcal{S},\mathcal{S}}\mathbf{\Omega}_{\mathcal{S},\bar{\mathcal{S}}} \end{bmatrix} \end{aligned} \tag{14.10}$$

The interpretation of the transformation is that it makes the first p factors independent from the remaining ones. The returns and volatilities of the first p factors are unchanged, and the volatilities of the remaining ones are reduced. This is unintuitive at first sight, but has a simple interpretation: we have orthogonalized the factors in the set $\bar{\mathcal{S}}$, and pushed the explanatory power in the first p ones. The dollar exposures of a portfolio for the first p factors, on the other side, are *changing* from $\mathbf{b}$ to $\mathbf{C}^{\top}\mathbf{b}$, as per Equation (14.9), so that the volatility and the performance attributable to them is increasing as well.

Let us go through an example. We have a sector strategy for which we run daily factor performance attribution, which is shown in Figure 14.1 (top). We select as maximal factors the market, momentum, and crowding factors. After rotating the remaining factors, the performance attribution changes significantly and is shown in Figure 14.1 (bottom). The market is responsible for a higher loss; crowding losses are also steeper than in the regular attribution, whereas growth is responsible for a smaller loss.

We close this section with two observations. First, we focused on the "maximal attribution" factors. Alternatively, we could focus on the factors in the set $\bar{\mathcal{S}}$. If the performance attributable to these factors is small, then

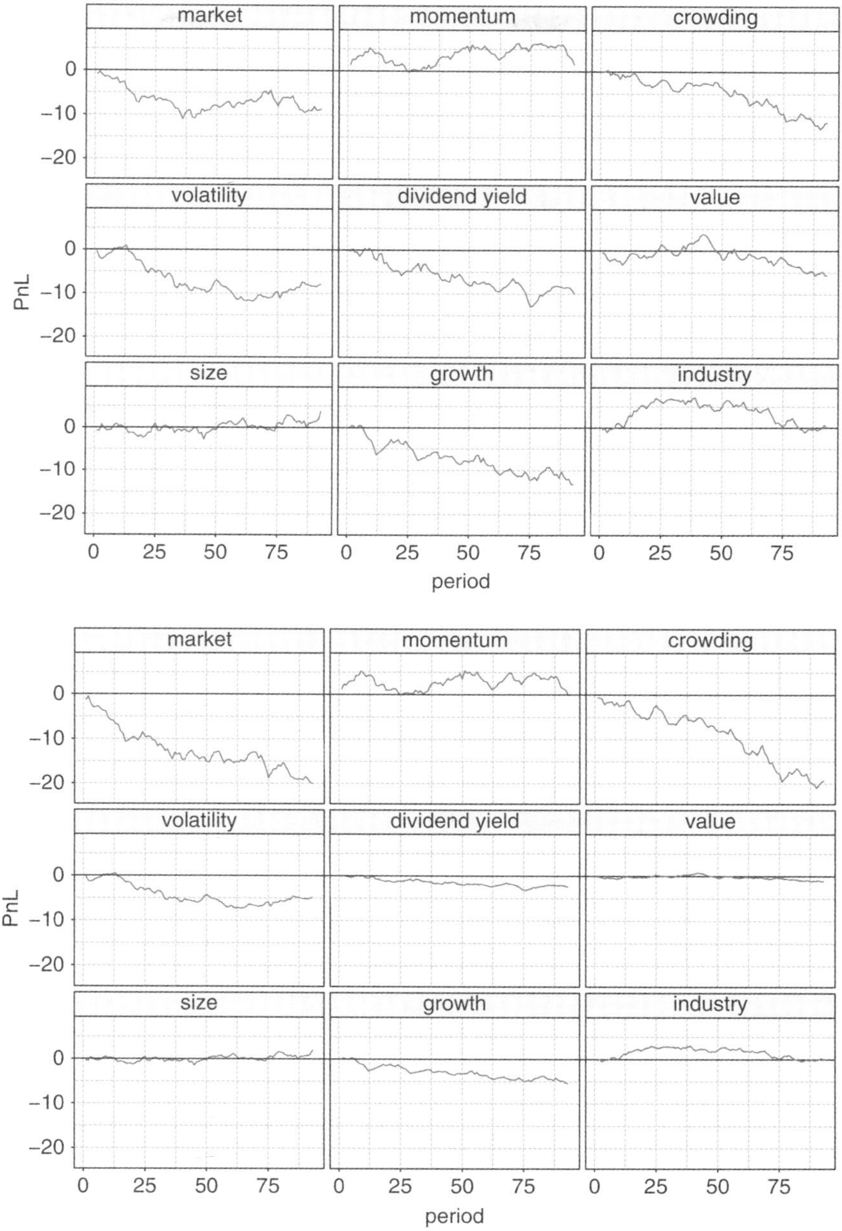

Figure 14.1 Top: PnL base factor performance attribution. Bottom: Maximal attribution on three factors: market, momentum, and crowding.

we have identified "minimal attribution" factors. The model has been rotated so that the portfolio performance has been described by a smaller dimensional space.

Second, we can perform a *nested* maximal performance attribution. Instead of having a "maximal attribution" set and a "minimal attribution" set, we extend the approach to a partition of the factor set $\{1, \dots, m\}$ by factor sets $\mathcal{S}_i$. Factor set $\mathcal{S}_1$ gets the maximal attribution; set $\mathcal{S}_2$ gets the maximal attribution of the remaining PnL; and so on. The most granular instance is where $\mathcal{S}_i = \{i\}$, so that we orthogonalize the model sequentially one factor at a time. In practice, however, it may be more sensible to create a coarser partition, every element of which describes a common theme. For example, we may have a "market factor" set composed of country, market, and volatility factors; then a "value factor" set composed of earnings yield, earning variation, dividend yield, book-to-price, and quality; a "sentiment factor" set, an "industry" set, and so on. The steps involved in simple maximal attribution and nested attribution are described in Procedures 14.1 and 14.2.

Procedure 14.1: *Maximal attribution*

1. **Inputs**: Factor covariance matrix $\mathbf{\Omega} \in \mathbb{R}^{m \times m}$; loadings matrix $\mathbf{B} \in \mathbb{R}^{n \times p}$, factor universe $\mathcal{U} := \{1, \dots, m\}$; sets $\mathcal{S}$, $\bar{\mathcal{S}} := \mathcal{U}/\mathcal{S}$; portfolio $\mathbf{w}$.
2. Set

$$\mathbf{b} := \mathbf{B}^\top \mathbf{w}$$
$$\mathbf{A} := \mathbf{\Omega}_{\mathcal{U},\mathcal{S}} \mathbf{\Omega}^{-1}_{\mathcal{S},\mathcal{S}}$$
$$\mathbf{C} := \begin{bmatrix} \mathbf{I}_{\mathcal{S},\mathcal{S}} & 0 \\ \mathbf{A} & \mathbf{I}_{\bar{\mathcal{S}},\bar{\mathcal{S}}} \end{bmatrix}$$

3. **Output**:
Per-factor maximal PnL: $\text{PnL}_k = [\mathbf{b}^\top \mathbf{A}]_k f_k$, for all $k \in \mathcal{S}$.
Rotated factor covariance matrix: $\tilde{\mathbf{\Omega}} := \mathbf{C}^{-1} \mathbf{\Omega} (\mathbf{C}^{-1})^\top$

Procedure 14.2: *Nested maximal attribution*

1. **Inputs**: Factor covariance matrix $\mathbf{\Omega} \in \mathbb{R}^{m \times m}$; $\mathcal{U} := \{1, \ldots, m\}$; set partition $\mathcal{S}_1, \ldots, \mathcal{S}_p$ of $\mathcal{U}$; portfolio $\mathbf{w}$.
2. For $i = 1, \ldots, p$:
   (a) Perform maximal attribution (Procedure 14.1) on $\mathbf{\Omega}$, $\mathbf{B}$, $\mathcal{U}$, $\mathcal{S}_i$, $\mathbf{w}$.
   (b) Set $\mathbf{\Sigma}^{(i)} := \mathbf{\Omega}_{\mathcal{S}_i,\mathcal{S}_i}$, $\mathcal{U} \leftarrow \mathcal{U}/\mathcal{S}_i$, $\mathbf{B} \leftarrow \mathbf{B}_{\cdot,\mathcal{U}}$, $\mathbf{\Omega} \leftarrow \tilde{\mathbf{\Omega}}_{\mathcal{U},\mathcal{U}}$.
3. Return PnL_k, for $k \in \mathcal{U}$, and the rotated risk model

$$\begin{bmatrix} \mathbf{\Sigma}^{(1)} & 0 & \ldots & 0 & 0 \\ 0 & \mathbf{\Sigma}^{(2)} & \ldots & 0 & 0 \\ \ldots & \ldots & \ldots & \ldots & \ldots \\ 0 & \ldots & \ldots & \mathbf{\Sigma}^{(p-1)} & 0 \\ 0 & \ldots & \ldots & 0 & \mathbf{\Omega} \end{bmatrix}$$

14.4 Selection versus Sizing Attribution

In factor-based attribution, the idiosyncratic PnL of a strategy is the most crucial performance term, representing the PnL that cannot be explained by factor exposure. While factor-based attribution identifies the non-idiosyncratic portion of the PnL, it fails to explain the source of idiosyncratic performance. Portfolio managers often consider asset selection and sizing as the primary sources of their skills. Selection skill refers to the ability to be long on stocks with positive returns and short on those with negative returns. Sizing skill means being more profitable when right than when wrong. These skills have practical implications for portfolio construction and can lead to improved risk-adjusted performance. Quantitative analysts have developed "hitting" and "slugging" metrics to quantify selection and sizing. Hitting is the percentage of profitable single-asset investments, while slugging is the ratio between the average PnL of profitable and unprofitable investments. Despite their intuitive appeal, these measures have two drawbacks: they lack a direct relationship with profitability measures like the Information Ratio, and do not provide clear guidance for portfolio managers.

This section aims to address these problems. We show how a new selection-sizing decomposition achieves two objectives:

1. It links through an analytical, interpretable formula the IR of a strategy to the selection, sizing, and breadth of a portfolio.
2. It provides guidance for portfolio managers, both in the case that the strategy has positive sizing skill and that it has negative sizing skill.

The IR is the expected value of the idiosyncratic PnL divided by its standard deviation. If we restrict our attention to a single period, an estimate of the IR is

$$\widehat{\text{IR}}_t = \frac{(\textit{Idio PnL})_t}{(\textit{Idio Vol})_t}$$

An estimate for the IR that employs the available time series of portfolios in epochs $1, 2, \dots, T$ is

$$\widehat{\text{IR}} = \frac{1}{T}\sum_{t=1}^{T} \widehat{\text{IR}}_t$$

The IR can be expressed as a simple combination of intuitive terms. The decomposition is

$$\widehat{\text{IR}} = \frac{1}{T}\sum_{t=1}^{T} \left[(\textit{selection})_t \times (\textit{diversification})_t + (\textit{sizing})_t \right]$$

The terms in the identity are[5]

- A *selection* skill

$$(\textit{selection})_t := \frac{1}{n}\sum_{i=1}^{n} \tilde{\epsilon}_{t,i}\text{sgn}\left(w_{t,i}\right)$$

We z-score the idiosyncratic return $\epsilon_{t,i}$ of an asset to obtain $\tilde{\epsilon}_{t,i} := \epsilon_{t,i}/\sigma_i$ and multiply it by the sign of that asset's holding. If holding and return have the same sign, the portfolio manager was on the right side of a security bet in a specific period and the contribution to selection is

[5] We refer the reader to the Appendix, Section 14.5.1 for derivations of the formulas below.

positive. The z-scoring puts assets with different volatility on the same scale, so that selection does not reward the magnitude of the return.

- *Diversification*. Instead of reasoning about the notional value of positions, we use the dollar volatility of each position, defined as $\tilde{w}_{t,i} := \sigma_i w_{t,i}$. Then we define

$$\textit{(diversification)}_t := \frac{\|\tilde{\mathbf{w}}_t\|_1}{\|\tilde{\mathbf{w}}_t\|_2}$$

When all the dollar volatilities are identical, then the portfolio diversification is $\sqrt{n}$. At the other end, if the portfolio has a single position, then the portfolio diversification is 1. The diversification squared ranges between 1 and n, and can be interpreted as the effective number of assets. This diversification term has a well-known connection to the Herfindahl Index, which is a measure of concentration. To be more specific, define weights $x_i := |\tilde{w}_{t,i}| / \sum_j |\tilde{w}_{t,j}|$. The Herfindahl Index is defined as $H := \sum_i x_i^2$. The relationship is then $\textit{(diversification)}_t = 1/\sqrt{H}$. The relationship between diversification and portfolio construction was first explored by Bouchaud et al. (1997).

- The last term is *sizing*. It is equal to

$$\text{SIZING}_t = \frac{\sqrt{n}}{\sqrt{\mathbf{w}_t^\intercal \boldsymbol{\Omega} \mathbf{w}_t}} \hat{\boldsymbol{\Omega}}(\tilde{\epsilon}_t \circ \text{sgn}(\mathbf{w}_t), |\tilde{\mathbf{w}}_t|) \tag{14.11}$$

$$= \sqrt{n} \widehat{\text{cor}}(\tilde{\boldsymbol{\epsilon}}_t \circ \text{sgn}(\mathbf{w}_t), |\tilde{\mathbf{w}}_t|) \tag{14.12}$$

Here, $\widehat{\text{cov}}$ is a cross-sectional covariance, where we treated the quantities associated to individual assets as empirical observations.[6] The interpretation of sizing is that it measures the correlation between being on the right side of a bet $\tilde{\epsilon}_{t,i}\text{sgn}(w_{t,i})$, and the bet size $|\sigma_i w_{t,i}|$. Sizing is positive if, when the portfolio manager is right about the *side* of a position, she is right about its *size* by having a relatively large position. In formulas, we first define

$$\textit{(sizing)}_t := \frac{n}{\|\tilde{\mathbf{w}}_t\|} \widehat{\text{cov}}(\underbrace{\tilde{\boldsymbol{\epsilon}}_t \circ \text{sgn}(\tilde{\mathbf{w}}_t)}_{\textit{(right-side index)}}, \underbrace{|\tilde{\mathbf{w}}_t|}_{\textit{(bet size)}})$$

[6] More rigorously, for two vectors $\mathbf{x}, \mathbf{y} \in \mathbb{R}^n$, $\widehat{\text{cov}}(\mathbf{x}, \mathbf{y}) := n^{-1} \sum_i x_i y_i - n^{-2} \sum_j x_j \sum_k y_k$.

This equation can be used in several ways. To achieve a higher IR, a portfolio manager has the following three options:

- *Increase diversification.* Markowitz famously said that diversification is the only free lunch in investing. This equation shows that benefits from diversification are accrued via selection skill, i.e., selection is the marginal benefit obtained by increasing diversification. This reasoning is not entirely correct, however. Managers can increase diversification in two ways. The first one is by making portfolio positions more equal. This does not require additional effort.[7] Alternatively, the portfolio manager could add stocks to the investment universe. This operation is not costless, since it would involve spending less time on each stock, and possibly cover less desirable stocks not in the primary universe. When increasing diversification, the manager may want to consider the impact on stock selection from this decision.
- *Improve selection skill.* The decomposition helps by providing a simple measure, which makes use of the entire dataset at a manager's disposal: daily positions, PnL, and idiosyncratic risk of the individual positions. Once selection can be measured, several actions are possible. For example, the portfolio manager can track the selection skill at the sub-industry or at the thematic level; or the portfolio manager can compare performance during earnings versus outside earnings. Improving portfolio selection is not easy, but is possible.
- *Improve sizing skill.* There is value already in having portfolio managers assess their sizing skill relative to selection; most portfolio managers overestimate their sizing skill, and find the low sizing skill, or even the absence thereof, instructive. If their sizing skill is *negative*, the portfolio manager should not differentiate positions according to size. In doing so, they will eliminate the drag from negative sizing and magnify the benefit of stock selection, by maximizing breadth. If there is *positive* sizing skill, the portfolio manager can optimize the size of the high-conviction positions to maximize the IR. This is the subject of the next subsection.

---

[7] The analysis presented here does not take into account transaction costs. This is a reasonable approximation for small portfolios. A more comprehensive model is possible, but outside of our scope.

14.4.1 Connection to the Fundamental Law of Active Management

The IR decomposition bears some resemblance to Grinold and Kahn's Fundamental Law of Active Management (Grinold and Kahn, 1999). That formula stated that the IR is the product of the Information Coefficient and the breadth of the portfolio $\sqrt{n}$. This formula uses a different portfolio breadth—the effective breadth—which treats not all positions as equal. For example, a portfolio of 100 stocks with a gross notional of \$10,000 in each of them does not have the same breadth as a portfolio of 100 stocks where one position is \$999,901 in one stock and \$1 in the remaining 99. In their seminal article, Bouchaud et al. (1997) present a modified mean-variance portfolio formulation that puts a lower bound on our definition of diversification. This results in using a shrinked covariance matrix. The same approach has been advocated using robust portfolio construction models (Stubbs and Vance, 2005; DeMiguel et al., 2013; Pedersen et al., 2021) and penalized covariance estimation methodologies (Ledoit and Wolf, 2003a).

14.4.2 Long–Short Performance Attribution

The selection component of our performance attribution is linear, and therefore lends itself naturally to be further partitioned in different performance subclasses. A natural partition is long versus short; that is, the fraction of selection skill that arises from being on the right side of returns when positions are long versus when positions are short. The decomposition follows from the chain of equalities below:

$$
\begin{aligned}
(\textit{selection})_t &= \frac{1}{n}\sum_{i:w_{t,i}>0} \tilde{\epsilon}_{t,i}\operatorname{sgn}\left(w_{t,i}\right) + \frac{1}{n}\sum_{i:w_{t,i}<0} \tilde{\epsilon}_{t,i}\operatorname{sgn}\left(w_{t,i}\right) \\
&= \frac{n_{\text{long}}}{n}\frac{1}{n_{\text{long}}}\sum_{i:w_{t,i}>0} \tilde{\epsilon}_{t,i}\operatorname{sgn}\left(w_{t,i}\right) + \frac{n_{\text{short}}}{n}\frac{1}{n_{\text{short}}}\sum_{i:w_{t,i}<0} \tilde{\epsilon}_{t,i}\operatorname{sgn}\left(w_{t,i}\right) \\
&= q_{\text{long}} \times (\textit{selection})_{L,t} + q_{\text{short}} \times (\textit{selection})_{S,t}
\end{aligned}
$$

where n_{long}, n_{short} are the number of long and short positions, and q_{long}, q_{short} are the fraction of the total portfolio positions that are long and short, respectively.

Summing up, in Figure 14.2 we show the dependency tree of the decomposition terms.

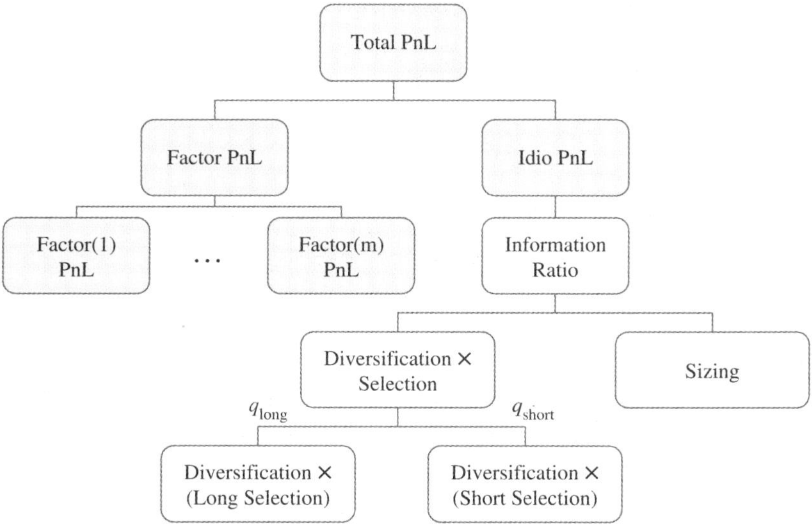

Figure 14.2 A taxonomy of performance attribution.

14.5 Appendix⋆

14.5.1 Proof of the Selection versus Sizing Decomposition

Theorem 14.1: *Consider a portfolio sequence $\mathbf{w}_t \in \mathbb{R}^n$, and a sequence of iid idiosyncratic returns $\boldsymbol{\epsilon}_t$ taking values in $\mathbb{R}^n$, with $cov(\boldsymbol{\epsilon}_t) = \boldsymbol{\Omega}$. Define the empirical Information Ratio:*

$$\widehat{IR} = \frac{1}{T}\sum_{t=1}^{T} \frac{(Idio\ PnL)_t}{(Idio\ Vol)_t}$$

Then the identity holds

$$\widehat{IR} = \frac{1}{T}\sum_{t=1}^{T} \left[(selection)_t \times (diversification)_t + (sizing)_t \right] \tag{14.13}$$

where the terms in the equation above are defined as follows:

$$\tilde{\mathbf{w}}_t := \mathbf{\Omega}^{1/2}\mathbf{w}_t$$
$$\tilde{\mathbf{u}}_t := \sqrt{n}\frac{\tilde{\mathbf{w}}_t}{\left\|\tilde{\mathbf{w}}_t\right\|}$$
$$\tilde{\boldsymbol{\epsilon}}_t := \mathbf{\Omega}^{-1/2}\boldsymbol{\epsilon}_t$$

$$\textit{(selection)}_t := \hat{E}(\tilde{\boldsymbol{\epsilon}}_t \circ sgn\,(\tilde{\mathbf{u}}_t))$$
$$\textit{(diversification)}_t := \sqrt{n}\hat{E}(|\tilde{\mathbf{u}}_t|) = \frac{\left\|\tilde{\mathbf{w}}_t\right\|_1}{\left\|\tilde{\mathbf{w}}_t\right\|_2}$$
$$\textit{(sizing)}_t := \sqrt{n}\widehat{\text{cov}}(\tilde{\boldsymbol{\epsilon}}_t \circ sgn\,(\tilde{\mathbf{u}}_t), |\tilde{\mathbf{u}}_t|) = \frac{n}{\left\|\mathbf{w}_t\right\|}\widehat{\text{cov}}(\tilde{\boldsymbol{\epsilon}}_t \circ sgn\,(\tilde{\mathbf{w}}_t), |\tilde{\mathbf{w}}_t|)$$

Proof. In period t, the risk-adjusted PnL of the portfolio at time t is given by

$$\widehat{\text{IR}}_t = \frac{\mathbf{w}_t^{\mathsf{T}}\boldsymbol{\epsilon}_t}{\sqrt{\mathbf{w}_t^{\mathsf{T}}\mathbf{\Omega}\mathbf{w}_t}}$$

Set $\tilde{\mathbf{w}}_t := \mathbf{\Omega}^{1/2}\mathbf{w}_t$, and $\tilde{\boldsymbol{\epsilon}}_t := \mathbf{\Omega}^{-1/2}\boldsymbol{\epsilon}_t$. The vector $\tilde{\mathbf{w}}_t$ has a familiar interpretation. It is a portfolio whose positions are not expressed as NMV but rather as dollar volatilities of each asset. The return vector $\tilde{\boldsymbol{\epsilon}}_t$ contains the z-scored asset returns. Its covariance matrix is the identity. With these transformations, the sample IR takes a simpler form:

$$\widehat{\text{IR}}_t = \frac{\tilde{\mathbf{w}}_t^{\mathsf{T}}\tilde{\boldsymbol{\epsilon}}_t}{\left\|\tilde{\mathbf{w}}_t\right\|}$$

This follows from the fact that the numerator is

$$\mathbf{w}_t^{\mathsf{T}}\boldsymbol{\epsilon}_t = \sum_i w_{t,i}\epsilon_{t,i} = \sum_i(\sigma_i w_{t,i})(\epsilon_{t,i}/\sigma_i) = \sum_i \tilde{w}_{t,i}\tilde{\epsilon}_{t,i}$$

and the denominator is

$$\sqrt{(\mathbf{w}_t^{\mathsf{T}}\boldsymbol{\Omega}^{1/2})(\boldsymbol{\Omega}^{1/2}\mathbf{w}_t)} = \|\boldsymbol{\Omega}^{1/2}\mathbf{w}_t\| = \left\|\tilde{\mathbf{w}}_t\right\|$$

We can further simplify the formula by considering a breadth-rescaled percentage of the total dollar volatility:

$$\begin{aligned}
\widehat{\mathrm{IR}}_t &= \sum_i \tilde{\epsilon}_i \frac{\tilde{w}_i}{\|\tilde{\mathbf{w}}\|} \\
&= \sum_i \tilde{\epsilon}_i \operatorname{sgn}\left(\tilde{w}_i\right) \frac{|\tilde{w}_i|}{\|\tilde{\mathbf{w}}\|} \\
&= \sqrt{n}\frac{1}{n} \sum_i \tilde{\epsilon}_i \operatorname{sgn}\left(\tilde{w}_i\right) \frac{\sqrt{n}|\tilde{w}_i|}{\|\tilde{\mathbf{w}}\|} \\
&= \sqrt{n}\frac{1}{n} \sum_i \tilde{\epsilon}_i \operatorname{sgn}\left(\tilde{u}_i\right) |\tilde{u}_i|
\end{aligned}$$

where we set

$$\tilde{\mathbf{u}}_t := \sqrt{n}\frac{\tilde{\mathbf{w}}_t}{\left\|\tilde{\mathbf{w}}_t\right\|}$$

We denote the *cross-sectional empirical average* and the *cross-sectional empirical covariance*

$$\begin{aligned}
\hat{E}(\mathbf{x}) &:= n^{-1} \sum_i x_i \\
\widehat{\mathrm{cov}}(\mathbf{x}, \mathbf{y}) &:= \hat{E}[(\mathbf{x} - \hat{E}\mathbf{x})^2(\mathbf{y} - \hat{E}\mathbf{y})^2]
\end{aligned}$$

The formula becomes

$$\widehat{\mathrm{IR}}_t = \sqrt{n}\hat{E}(\tilde{\boldsymbol{\epsilon}}_t \circ \operatorname{sgn}\left(\tilde{\mathbf{u}}_t\right) \circ |\tilde{\mathbf{u}}_t|)$$

where we have used the notation "$\circ$" to denote the element-wise (Hadamard) product of two vectors, i.e., $(\mathbf{x} \circ \mathbf{y})_i := x_i y_i$. Finally, in the last step we use the identity $\hat{E}(\mathbf{x} \circ \mathbf{y}) = \widehat{\mathrm{cov}}(\mathbf{x}, \mathbf{y}) + \hat{E}(\mathbf{x})\hat{E}(\mathbf{y})$ with $\mathbf{x} = \tilde{\boldsymbol{\epsilon}}_t \circ \operatorname{sgn}\left(\tilde{\mathbf{u}}_t\right)$ and $\mathbf{y} = |\tilde{\mathbf{u}}_t|$. It follows that

$$\widehat{\mathrm{IR}}_t = \sqrt{n}\left[\hat{E}(\tilde{\boldsymbol{\epsilon}}_t \circ \operatorname{sgn}(\tilde{\mathbf{u}}_t))\hat{E}(|\tilde{\mathbf{u}}_t|) + \widehat{\mathrm{cov}}(\tilde{\boldsymbol{\epsilon}}_t \circ \operatorname{sgn}(\tilde{\mathbf{u}}_t), |\tilde{\mathbf{u}}_t|)\right]$$

A possible interpretation of the above formula is as a sample of the realized IR over a single observation, or period. An estimate of the IR over the period 1, …, T is then given by its time-series average:

$$\widehat{\text{IR}} = \frac{1}{T}\sum_{t=1}^{T} \frac{\tilde{\mathbf{w}}_t^\top \tilde{\boldsymbol{\epsilon}}_t}{\left\|\tilde{\mathbf{w}}_t\right\|}$$

$$= \sqrt{n}\left[\frac{1}{T}\sum_{t=1}^{T} \hat{E}(\tilde{\boldsymbol{\epsilon}}_t \circ \text{sgn}\,(\tilde{\mathbf{u}}_t))\hat{E}(|\tilde{\mathbf{u}}_t|) + \frac{1}{T}\sum_{t=1}^{T} \widehat{\text{cov}}(\tilde{\boldsymbol{\epsilon}}_t \circ \text{sgn}\,(\tilde{\mathbf{u}}_t), |\tilde{\mathbf{u}}_t|)\right]$$

This is equal to Equation (14.13) once we define

$$\textit{(selection)}_t = \hat{E}(\tilde{\boldsymbol{\epsilon}}_t \circ \text{sgn}\,(\tilde{\mathbf{u}}_t))$$

$$\textit{(diversification)}_t = \sqrt{n}\hat{E}(|\tilde{\mathbf{u}}_t|) = \frac{\sum_{i=1}^{n} |\tilde{w}_{t,i}|}{\sqrt{\sum_{i=1}^{n} \tilde{w}_{t,i}^2}}$$

$$\textit{(sizing)}_t = \sqrt{n}\widehat{\text{cov}}(\tilde{\boldsymbol{\epsilon}}_t \circ \text{sgn}\,(\tilde{\mathbf{u}}_t), |\tilde{\mathbf{u}}_t|) = \frac{n}{\sqrt{\sum_{i=1}^{n} \tilde{w}_{t,i}^2}}\widehat{\text{cov}}(\tilde{\boldsymbol{\epsilon}}_t \circ \text{sgn}\,(\tilde{\mathbf{w}}_t), |\tilde{\mathbf{w}}_t|)$$

■

The Takeaways

- Performance attribution helps determine if results are due to luck or skill and identifies sources of profit or loss.
- Decomposing PnL into factor PnL and idiosyncratic PnL provides deeper insights into portfolio performance.
- *Two paradoxes in performance attribution:*
  - *Factor-Mimicking Portfolios:* They have idiosyncratic risk but no idiosyncratic PnL, which is counterintuitive.
  - *Factor-Neutral Portfolios:* They can have the same idiosyncratic PnL despite varying idiosyncratic volatility.
- These paradoxes highlight the need to consider estimation errors in performance attribution models.
- Accounting for estimation errors allows factor and idiosyncratic PnLs to be characterized as random variables.
- *Maximal Performance Attribution:* Assigns as much PnL as possible to selected factors for clearer insights.
- Methods for maximal attribution include cross-sectional return explanation, conditional expectation, and model rotation.
- Nested maximal attribution allows sequential attribution to different sets of factors, enhancing analysis granularity.
- Selection versus sizing attribution decomposes idiosyncratic PnL into stock selection (right asset choice) and sizing (position size) components.
- The Information Ratio (IR) links to selection skill, diversification, and sizing skill, providing a measure of performance.
- Improving diversification increases the marginal benefits of selection skill in a portfolio.
- Enhancing selection and sizing skills can lead to better risk-adjusted returns and overall portfolio performance.

Chapter 15

A Coda about Leitmotifs

It seems almost impolite to abruptly close a book with a chapter on performance attribution. In "*The Return of the King*", the coda of the movie lasted 30 minutes, enough to make us forget the satisfying spectacle of Mordor's fall. I promise this one will be shorter. There are some recurrent themes in the book. By highlighting them, I hope to provide the quantitative researcher and strategy developer with some principles to inspire them in their daily endeavor.

1. *Use legible methods*. With few exceptions, the mathematics used in the book is more than 60 years old. The exceptions are Rademacher complexity, which dates back to the work of Vapnik and Chervonenkis in the early 1970s; and the spectral properties of spiked covariance matrices, which go back to the turn of the century. Using established methods makes the theory *legible*: at any time you know what is going on. Calvino speaks of *visibility*. Good math makes the invisible visible. What is visible can be communicated, inspected, critiqued, and improved.

2. *Use the simplest possible methods.* Theory is cheap. You can make theory infinitely complicated. The hard part is to summon from the void the simplest tools that answer your question. Everything in the book is linear and quadratic. Don't restrict yourself to these families; however, if some new idea does not show some promise in a toy model, it is unlikely that it will deliver in a very complex one.
3. *Think deeply of simple things.* Start with simple questions, possibly identifying them within a more complex system. And then solve them from first principles as much as you can. For example, do not make up performance metrics about hitting and sizing. Link performance metrics to the Sharpe Ratio. Or link backtesting overfit to the complexity of your space of strategies.
4. *Take errors into account from the start.* "Certainty is beautiful, but uncertainty is more beautiful still".[1] All investment is the heavenly marriage of expectation and error. Parameter error is important in portfolio optimization, in intertemporal volatility allocation, in backtesting. Modeling uncertainty from the start is sound theoretically and addresses the shortcomings of known methods, like mean-variance optimization.
5. *Justify heuristics from first principles.* So many processes we have advocated resonate deeply with our everyday decision-making process. Exponential weighting: update what you learned so far by mixing with new evidence. Shrinkage: incorporate uncertainty by downweighting your estimates. Myopic optimization: approximate a multi-period complex decision with a simple single-period one. Over and over, successful researchers are the ones that achieve *principled simplicity*.

[1] I am borrowing a verse from "Love at first sight", a poem by W. Szymborska (Szymborska, 2016).

References

V. Agarwal and N. Y. Naik. Risks and portfolio decisions involving hedge funds. *The Review of Financial Studies*, 17(1):63–98, 2004.

Y. Aït-Sahalia, P. A. Mykland, and L. Zhang. How often to sample a continuous-time process in the presence of market microstructure noise. *Review of Financial Studies*, 18(2):351–416, 2005.

P. H. Algoet and T. M. Cover. Asymptotic optimality and asymptotic equipartition properties of log-optimum investment. *Annals of Probability*, 16(2):876–898, 1988.

R. Almgren, C. Thum, H. L. Hauptmann, and H. Li. Equity market impact. *Risk*, pages 57–62, July 2005.

Y. Amihud. Illiquidity and stock returns: Cross-section and time-series effects. *The Journal of Financial Markets*, 5(1):31–56, 2002.

Y. Amihud and H. Mendelson. Asset pricing and the bid–ask spread. *Journal of Financial Economics*, 17(2):223–249, 1986.

Y. Amihud, H. Mendelson, and L. H. Pedersen. *Market Liquidity*. Cambridge University Press, 2012.

T. G. Andersen and L. Benzoni. Realized volatility. In T. G. Andersen, R. A. Davis, J.-P. Kreiss, and T. Mikosch, editors, *Handbook of Financial Time Series*, pages 555–575. Springer, 2009.

T. G. Andersen, T. Bollerslev, P. F. Christoffersen, and F. X. Diebold. Volatility and correlation forecasting. In G. Elliott, C. W. J. Granger, and A. Timmermann, editors, *Handbook of Economic Forecasting*, volume 1, chapter 15, pages 777–878. Elsevier, 2006.

T. G. Andersen, R. A. Davis, J.-P. Kreiss, and T. Mikosch, editors., *Handbook of Financial Time Series*. Springer, 2009.

T. G. Andersen, T. Bollerslev, P. F. Christoffersen, and F. X. Diebold. Financial risk measurement for financial risk management. In G. M. Constantinides, M. Harris, and R. M. Stulz, editors, *Handbook of the Economics of Finance*, volume 2, part B, chapter 17, pages 1127–1220. Elsevier, 2013.

T. W. Anderson. Theory for principal component analysis. *The Annals of Mathematical Statistics*, 34(1):122–148, 1963.

R. Arnott, C. R. Harvey, and H. Markowitz. A backtesting protocol in the era of machine learning. *The Journal of Financial Data Science*, 1(1):64–74, 2019.

C. S. Asness, A. Frazzini, and L. H. Pedersen. Quality minus junk. *Review of Accounting Studies*, 24:34-112, 2019.

J. M. Bacidore. *Algorithmic Trading: A Practitioner's Guide*. TBG Press, 2020.

C. R. Bacon. *Practical Portfolio Performance Measurement and Attribution*. Wiley, 2005.

Z. Bai and S. Ng. Large dimensional factor analysis. *Foundations and Trends in Econometrics*, 3(2):447–474, 2008.

Z. Bai and J. Yao. Central limit theorems for eigenvalues in a spiked population model. *Annales de l'Institut Henri Poincaré*, 44(3):447–474, 2008.

J. Baik and J. W. Silverstein. Eigenvalues of large sample covariance matrices of spiked population models. *Journal of Multivariate Analysis*, 97:1382–1408, 2006.

J. Baik, G. Ben Arous, and S. Péché. Phase transition of the largest eigenvalue for nonnull complex sample covariance matrices. *Annals of Probability*, 33(5):1643–1697, 2005.

M. Baker, B. Bradley, and J. Wurgler. Benchmarks as limits to arbitrage: Understanding the low-volatility anomaly. *Financial Analysts Journal*, 67(1):40–54, 2011.

R. Banz. The relationship between return and market value of common stock. *Journal of Financial Economics*, 9(1):3–18, 1981.

B. M. Barber and T. Odean. *Handbook of the Economics of Finance*, volume 2(B), chapter The Behavior of Individual Investors, pages 1533–1570. Elsevier, 2013.

N. Barberis and M. Huang. Stocks as lotteries: The implications of probability weighting for security prices. *American Economic Review*, 98(5):2066–2100, 2008.

G. I. Barenblatt. *Scaling*. Cambridge University Press, 2003.

O. E. Barndorff-Nielsen and N. Shephard. Estimating quadratic variation using realized variance. *Journal of Applied Econometrics*, 17(5):457–477, 2002.

O. E. Barndorff-Nielsen, P. R. Hansen, A. Lunde, and N. Shephard. Designing realized kernels to measure the ex post variation of equity prices in the presence of noise. *Econometrica*, 76(6):1481–1536, 2008.

O. E. Barndorff-Nielsen, P. R. Hansen, A. Lunde, and N. Shephard. Realized kernels in practice: Trades and quotes. *Econometrics Journal*, 12:C1–C32, 2009.

D. P. Baron. On the utility theoretic foundations of mean-variance analysis. *Journal of Finance*, 32(5):1683–1697, 1977.

M. S. Bazaraa, H. D. Sherali, and C. M. Shetty. *Nonlinear Programming: Theory and Algorithms*. Wiley, 3rd edition, 2006.

F. Benaych-Georges and R. R. Nadakuditi. The eigenvalues and eigenvectors of finite, low rank perturbations of large random matrices. *Advances in Mathematics*, 227(1):494–521, 2011.

R.-P. Berben and W. J. Jansen. Comovement in international equity markets: A sectoral view. *Journal of International Money and Finance*, 24(5):832–857, 2005.

C. Bergmeir, R. J. Hyndman, and B. Koo. A note on the validity of cross-validation for evaluating autoregressive time series prediction. *Computational Statistics & Data Analysis*, 120:70–83, 2018.

A. L. Berkin and L. E. Swedroe. *Your Complete Guide to Factor-Based Investing*. Buckingham, 2016.

C. M. Bishop. *Pattern Recognition and Machine Learning*. Springer, 2006.

F. Black. Capital market equilibrium with restricted borrowing. *The Journal of Business*, 45(3):444–455, 1972.

D. Blitz, E. Falkenstein, and P. van Vliet. Explanations for the volatility effect: An overview based on the CAPM assumptions. *Journal of Portfolio Management*, 40(3):61–76, 2014.

G. W. Bluman and S. Kumei. *Symmetries and Differential Equations*. Springer, 1989.

E. Boehmer, Z. R. Huszar, and B. D. Jordan. The good news in short interest. *Journal of Financial Economics*, 91(1):80–97, 2010.

J. Boivin and S. Ng. Are more data always better for factor analysis? *Journal of Econometrics*, 132(1):169–194, 2006.

T. Bollerslev. Modelling the coherence in short-run nominal exchange rates: A multivariate generalized ARCH model. *The Review of Economics and Statistics*, 72(3):498–505, 1990.

J.-P. Bouchaud and M. Potters. *A First Course in Random Matrix Theory*. Cambridge University Press, 2020.

J.-P. Bouchaud, M. Potters, and J.-P. Aguilar. Missing information and asset allocation. cond-mat/9707042, 1997.

J.-P. Bouchaud, J. Bonart, J. Donier, and M. Gould. *Trades, Quotes and Prices*. Cambridge University Press, 2018.

S. Boucheron, G. Lugosi, and P. Massart. *Concentration Inequalities: A Nonasymptotic Theory of Independence*. Oxford University Press, 2013.

S. Boyd and L. Vandenberghe. *Convex Optimization*. Cambridge University Press, 2004.

S. Boyd, E. Busseti, S. Diamond, R. N. Kahn, K. Koh, P. Nystrup, and J. Speth. Multi-period trading via convex optimization. *Foundations and Trends in Optimization*, 3(1):1–76, 2016.

L. Breiman. Optimal gambling systems for favorable games. In J. Neyman, editor, *Fourth Berkeley Symposium on Mathematical Statistics and Probability*, pages 65–78. University of California Press, 1961.

R. Brooks and M. Del Negro. Country versus region effects in international stock returns. *Journal of Portfolio Management*, 31(4):67–72, 2005.

C. Brownlees, B. Engle, and B. Kelly. A practical guide to volatility forecasting through calm and storm. *Journal of Risk*, 14(2):3–22, 2011.

M. K. Brunnermeier and L. H. Pedersen. Market liquidity and funding liquidity. *Review of Financial Studies*, 22(6):2201–2238, 2009.

J. Bun, J.-P. Bouchaud, and M. Potters. Cleaning large correlation matrices: Tools from random matrix theory. *Physics Reports*, 666:1–109, 2017.

D. Buraczewski, E. Damek, and T. Mikosch. *Stochastic Models with Power-Law Tails*. Springer, 2016.

P. Burns, P. Engle, and J. Mezrich. Correlations and volatilities of asynchronous data. University of California, San Diego, discussion paper 97-30R, 1998.

T. T. Cai, Z. Ren, and H. H. Zhou. Estimating structured high-dimensional covariance and precision matrices: Optimal rates and adaptive estimation. *Electronic Journal of Statistics*, 10:1–59, 2016.

I. Calvino. *Six Memos for the Next Millennium*. Harvard University Press, 1999.

R. B. Cattel. The scree test for the number of factors. *Multivariate Behavioral Research*, 1(2):245–276, 1966.

S. Cavaglia, C. Brightman, and M. Aked. The increasing importance of industry factors. *Financial Analysts Journal*, 56(5):41–54, 2000.

S. Ceria, A. Saxena, and R. A. Stubbs. Factor alignment problems and quantitative portfolio management. *Journal of Portfolio Management*, 28(2):29–43, 2012.

V. Cerqueira, L. Torgo, and C. Soares. Model selection for time series forecasting an empirical analysis of multiple estimators. *Neural Processing Letters*, 55:10073–10091, 2023.

G. Chamberlain. A characterization of the distributions that imply mean-variance utility functions. *Journal of Economic Theory*, 29:184–201, 1983.

G. Chamberlain and M. Rothschild. Arbitrage, factor structure, and mean-variance analysis of large asset markets. *Econometrica*, 51(5):1281–1305, 1983.

A. Y. Chen. Most claimed statistical findings in cross-sectional return predictability are likely true, 2024.

A. Y. Chen and Y. Zimmerman. Open source cross-sectional asset pricing. *Critical Finance Review*, 27(2):207–264, 2022.

L. Chen, D. A. Lesmond, and J. Z. Wei. Corporate yield spreads and bond liquidity. *Journal of Finance*, 62(1):119–149, 2007.

L. B. Chincarini and D. Kim. Another look at the information ratio. *Journal of Asset Management*, 8(5):284–295, 2007.

L. B. Chincarini and D. Kim. *Quantitative Equity Portfolio Management*. McGraw Hill, 2nd edition, 2022.

A. Chinco and M. Sammon. The passive-ownership share is double what you think it is, 2023. https://www.alexchinco.com/double-what-you-think-it-is.pdf.

V. K. Chopra and W. Ziemba. The effect of errors in means, variances, and covariances on optimal portfolio choice. *Journal of Portfolio Management*, 19(2):6–11, 1993.

P. F. Christoffersen, F. X. Diebold, and T. Schuermann. Horizon problems and extreme events in financial risk management. *FRBNY Economic Policy Review*, 4(3):109–118, 1998.

P. Cižek, W. K. Härdle, and R. Weron. *Statistical Tools for Finance and Insurance*. Springer, 2nd edition, 2011.

R. Clarke, H. de Silva, and S. Thorley. Portfolio constraints and the fundamental law of active management. *Financial Analysts Journal*, 58(5):48–66, 2002.

A. Clauset, C. R. Shalizi, and M. E. J. Newman. Power-law distributions in empirical data. *SIAM Review*, 51(4):661–703, 2009.

J. H. Cochrane. *Asset Pricing*. Princeton University Press, 2005.

J. H. Cochrane. The dog that did not bark: A defense of stock return predictability. *The Review of Financial Studies*, 21(4):1533–1575, 2008.

J. H. Cochrane. Discount rates. *Journal of Finance*, 66(4):1047–1108, 2011.

K. J. Cohen, G. A. Hawawini, S. F. Maier, R. A. Schwartz, and D. K. Whitcomb. Friction in the trading process and the estimation of systematic risk. *Journal of Financial Economics*, 12:263–278, 1983.

G. Connor and R. A. Korajczyk. Factor models of asset returns. In R. Cont, editor, *Encyclopedia of Quantitative Finance*. Wiley, 2010.

G. Connor, L. R. Goldberg, and R. A. Korajczyk. *Portfolio Risk Analysis*. Princeton University Press, 2010.

R. Cont. Empirical properties of asset returns: Stylized facts and statistical issues. *Quantitative Finance*, 1:223–236, 2001.

G. Cornuéjols, J. Peña, and R. Tütüncü. *Optimization Methods in Finance*. Cambridge University Press, 2nd edition, 2018.

K. Daniel, L. Mota, S. Rottke, and T. Santos. The cross-section of risk and returns. *The Review of Financial Studies*, 33(5):1927–1979, 2020.

R. A. Davis and T. Mikosch. Extreme value theory for GARCH processes. In T. G. Andersen, R. A. Davis, J.-P. Kreiss, and T. Mikosch, editors, *Handbook of Financial Time Series*, pages 187–200. Springer, 2009.

B. De Finetti. Il problema dei pieni. *Giornale dell'Istituto Italiano degli Attuari*, 11: 1–88, 1940.

M. H. DeGroot and M. J. Schervish. *Probability and Statistics*. Addison-Wesley, 4th edition, 2012.

V. DeMiguel, L. Garlappi, F. J. Nogales, and R. Uppal. A generalized approach to portfolio optimization: Improving performance by constraining portfolio norms. *Management Science*, 55(5):798–812, 2009a.

V. DeMiguel, L. Garlappi, and R. Uppal. Optimal versus naive diversification: How inefficient is the 1/n portfolio strategy? *Review of Financial Studies*, 22(5):1915–1953, 2009b.

P. Diaconis and D. Freedman. Iterated random functions. *SIAM Review*, 41(1):45–76, 1999.

C. Ding and X. He. K-means clustering via principal component analysis. In *Proceedings of the Twenty-First International Conference on Machine Learning*, 2004.

J. Ding and N. Meade. Forecasting accuracy of stochastic volatility, GARCH and EWMA models under different volatility scenarios. *Applied Financial Economics*, (10):1742–1778, 2010.

D. L. Donoho, M. Gavish, and I. M. Johnstone. Optimal shrinkage of eigenvalues in the spiked covariance model. *Annals of Statistics*, 46(4):1742–1778, 2018.

F. C. Drost and T. E. Nijman. Temporal aggregation of GARCH processes. *Econometrica*, 61(4):909–927, 1993.

L. Dubins and L. J. Savage. *How to Gamble if You Must: Inequalities for Stochastic Processes*. McGraw-Hill, 1965.

S. Dudoit, J. Popper Shaffer, and J. C. Boldrick. Multiple hypothesis testing in microarray experiments. *Statistical Science*, 18(1):71–103, 2003.

R. Durrett. *Probability: Theory and Examples*. Cambridge University Press, 5th edition, 2019.

G. Eckart and G. Young. The approximation of one matrix by another of lower rank. *Psychometrika*, 1(3):211–218, 1936.

N. El Karoui. Spectrum estimation for large dimensional covariance matrices using random matrix theory. *Annals of Statistics*, 36(6):2757–2790, 2008.

R. Engle and R. Colacito. Testing and valuing dynamic correlations for asset allocation. *Journal of Business and Economic Statistics*, 24(2):238–253, 2006.

R. F. Engle. Autoregressive conditional heteroscedasticity with estimates of the variance of United Kingdom inflation. *Econometrica*, 50:987-1007, 1982.

R. F. Engle and T. Bollerslev. Modelling the persistence of conditional variances. *Econometric Reviews*, 5(1):1–50, 1986.

E. F. Fama and K. R. French. The cross-section of expected stock returns. *Journal of Finance*, 47(2):427–465, 1993.

E. F. Fama and K. R. French. A five-factor asset pricing model. *Journal of Financial Economics*, 116(1):1–22, 2015.

E. F. Fama and K. R. French. Dissecting anomalies with a five-factor model. *The Review of Financial Studies*, 29(1):69–103, 2016.

E. F. Fama and J. D. MacBeth. Risk, return, and equilibrium: Empirical tests. *Journal of Political Economy*, 81(3):607–636, 1973.

J. Fan, Y. Fan, and J. Lv. High dimensional covariance matrix estimation using a factor model. *Journal of Econometrics*, 147:186–197, 2008.

J. Fan, J. Zhang, and K. Yu. Vast portfolio selection with gross-exposure constraints. *Journal of the American Statistical Association*, 107(498):592–606, 2012.

J. Fan, Y. Liao, and H. Liu. An overview of the estimation of large covariance and precision matrices. *The Econometrics Journal*, 16:C1–C32, 2016.

J. Fan, R. Li, C.-H. Zhang, and H. Zou. *Statistical Foundations of Data Science*. CRC Press, 2020.

S. A. Farmer. An investigation into the results of principal component analysis of data derived from random numbers. *Statistician*, 20(4):63–72, 1971.

L. Ferré. Selection of components in principal component analysis: A comparison of methods. *Computational Statistics & Data Analysis*, 19(19):669–682, 1995.

A. Frazzini and L. H. Pedersen. Betting against beta. *Journal of Financial Economics*, 111(1):1–25, 2014.

A. Frazzini, D. Kabiller, and L. H. Pedersen. Buffett's alpha. *Financial Analysts Journal*, 74(4):35–55, 2018.

K. R. French, G. W. Schwert, and R. F. Stambaugh. Expected stock returns and volatility. *Journal of Financial Economics*, 19(1):3–29, 1987.

J. Freyberger, A. Neuhierl, and M. Weber. Dissecting characteristics nonparametrically. *Review of Financial Studies*, 33(5):2326–2377, 2020.

G. Galilei. *Il Saggiatore*. 1623.

J. Gatheral. No-dynamic-arbitrage and market impact. *Quantitative Finance*, 10(7):749–759, 2010.

J. Gatheral. Three models of market impact. 2016.

A. Gelman, J. Hill, and A. Vehtari. *Regression and Other Stories*. Cambridge University Press, 2022.

J. Gerakos and J. T. Linnainmaa. Asset managers: Institutional performance and factor exposures. *Journal of Finance*, 76(4):2035–2075, 2021.

J. C. Gibbins. *Dimensional Analysis*. Springer, 2011.

Detlef Glow. Monday morning memo: Performance review – relative performance equity funds 2023, 2023. https://tinyurl.com/3br2swyk.

G. H. Golub and C. F. Van Loan. *Matrix Computations*. Johns Hopkins University Press, 4th edition, 2012.

B. Graham. *The Intelligent Investor*. Harper Business, 2006.

C. W. J. Granger and Z. Ding. Some properties of absolute return: An alternative measure of risk. *Annales d"Economie et de Statistique*, 40:67–91, 1995.

R. C. Grinold. The fundamental law of active management. *Journal of Portfolio Management*, 15(3):30–37, 1989.

R. C. Grinold and R. N. Kahn. *Active Portfolio Management*. McGraw-Hill Education, 2nd edition, 1999.

S. J. Grossman and Z. Zhou. Optimal investment strategies for controlling drawdowns. *Mathematical Finance*, 3(3):241–276, 1993.

O. Guéant. *The Financial Mathematics of Market Liquidity*. Chapman & Hall/CRC, 2016.

V. Haghani and J. White. *The Missing Billionaires*. Wiley, 2023.

B. Hansen. *Econometrics*. Princeton University Press, 2022.

L. P. Hansen and T. J. Sargent. *Robustness*. Princeton University Press, 2008.

P. R. Hansen and A. Lunde. A forecast comparison of volatility models: Does anything beat a $GARCH(1,1)$. *Journal of Applied Econometrics*, 20(7):873–889, 2005.

P. R. Hansen and A. Lunde. Consistent ranking of volatility models. *Journal of Econometrics*, 131(1-2):97–121, 2006a.

P. R. Hansen and A. Lunde. Realized variance and market microstructure noise. *Journal of Business and Economic Statistics*, 24(2):127–161, 2006b.

P. R. Hansen, A. Lunde, and J. M. Nason. The model confidence set. *Econometrica*, 79(2):453–497, 2011.

F. E. Harrell. *Regression Modeling Strategies*. Springer, 2nd edition, 2015.

L. Harris. *Trading and Exchanges*. Oxford University Press, 2003.

A. C. Harvey. *Forecasting, Structural Time Series Models and the Kalman Filter*. Cambridge University Press, 1990.

A. C. Harvey and N. Shephard. Estimation of an asymmetric stochastic volatility model for asset returns. *Journal of Business & Economic Statistics*, 14(4):429–424, 1996.

C. H. Harvey and Y. Liu. A census of the factor zoo. *preprint*, 2020a.

C. R. Harvey and Y. Liu. Lucky factors. *preprint*, 2019.

C. R. Harvey and Y. Liu. False (and missed) discoveries in financial economics. *Journal of Finance*, 75(5):2503–2553, 2020b.

J. Hasbrouck. *Empirical Market Microstructure*. Oxford University Press, 2007.

T. Hastie, R. Tibshirani, and J. Friedman. *The Elements of Statistical Learning*. Springer, 2nd edition, 2008.

R. A. Haugen and A. J. Heins. On the evidence supporting the existence of risk premiums in the capital market. *manuscript*, 1972.

R. H. Haugen and A. J. Heins. Risk and the rate of return on financial assets: Some old wine in new bottles. *Journal of Financial and Quantitative Analysis*, 10(5):775–784, 1975.

C. He and T. Teräsvirta. Fourth moment structure of the GARCH(p, q) process. *Econometric Theory*, 15(6):824–846, 1999.

S. L. Heston and K. G. Rouwenhorst. Does industrial structure explain the benefits of industrial diversification? *Journal of Financial Economics*, 36:3–27, 1994.

S. L. Heston and K. G. Rouwenhorst. Industry and country effects in international stock returns. *The Journal of Portfolio Management*, 21(3):53–58, 1995.

R. A. Horn and C.R. Johnson. *Matrix Analysis*. Cambridge University Press, 2nd edition, 2012.

K. Hou, C. Xue, and L. Zhang. Replicating anomalies. *Review of Financial Studies*, 33(5):2019–2133, 2020.

C.-F. Huang and R. H. Litzenberger. *Foundations for Financial Economics*. Prentice-Hall, 1988.

D. W. Huang, B. T. Sherman, and R. A. Lempicki. Bioinformatics enrichment tools: Paths toward the comprehensive functional analysis of large gene lists. *Nucleic Acids Research*, 37(1):1–13, 2009.

G. Huberman and W. Stanzl. Price manipulation and quasi-arbitrage. *Econometrica*, 74(4):1247–1276, 2004.

R. Hyndman, A. B. Koehler, J. K. Ord, and R. D. Snyder. *Forecasting with Exponential Smoothing: The State Space Approach*. Springer, 2008.

A. Ilmanen. *Expected Returns*. Wiley, 2011.

J. P. A. Ioannidis. Why most published research findings are false. *PLOS Medicine*, 2(8):696–701, 2005.

M. Isichenko. *Quantitative Portfolio Management*. Wiley, 2021.

H. Jacobs. What explains the dynamics of 100 anomalies? *Journal of Banking and Finance*, 57:65–85, 2015.

R. Jagannathan and T. Ma. Risk reduction in large portfolios: Why imposing the wrong constraints helps. *Journal of Finance*, 58(4):1651–1683, 2003.

N. Jegadeesh. Evidence of predictable behavior of security returns. *Journnal of Finance*, 45(3):881–898, 1990.

N. Jegadeesh and S. Titman. Returns to buying winners and selling losers: Implications for stock market efficiency. *Journal of Finance*, 48(1):65–91, 1993.

N. Jegadeesh and S. Titman. Momentum. *Annual Review of Financial Economics*, 3(1):493–509, 2011.

T. I. Jensen, B. Kelly, and L. H. Pedersen. Is there a replication crisis in finance? *Journal of Finance*, 78(5):2465–2518, 2023.

H. Jiang, A. Habib, and M. M. Hasan. Short selling: A review of the literature and implications for future research. *European Accounting Review*, 31(1–31), 2020.

R. A. Johnson and D. W. Wichern. *Applied Multivariate Statistical Analysis*. Pearson, 6th edition, 2007.

D. J. Johnstone and D. V. Lindley. Elementary proof that mean–variance implies quadratic utility. *Theory and Decision*, 70(2):149–155, 2011.

I. M. Johnstone. On the distribution of the largest eigenvalue in principal components analysis. *Annals of Statistics*, 29:295–327, 2001.

I. M. Johnstone and D. Paul. PCA in high dimensions: An orientation. *Proceedings of the IEEE*, 106(8):1277–1292, 2018.

I. T. Jolliffe. *Principal Component Analysis*. Springer, 2nd edition, 2010.

I. T. Jolliffe and J. Cadima. Principal component analysis: A review and recent developments. *Philosophical Transactions of the Royal Society A*, 374 (2065):20150202, 2016.

R. E. Kalman. A new approach to linear filtering and prediction problems. *Journal of Basic Engineering*, 82(1):35–45, 1960.

R. E. Kalman and R. S. Bucy. New results in linear filtering and prediction theory. *Journal of Basic Engineering*, 83(1):95–108, 1961.

G. Kamath. Bounds on the expectation of the maximum of samples from a gaussian. Technical report, University of Waterloo, 2020.

R. L. Kelley. *General Topology*. Van Nostrand, 1955.

H. Kesten. Random difference equations and renewal theory for products of random matrices. *Acta Mathematica*, 131:207–248, 1973.

A. S. Kyle. Continuous auctions and insider trading. *Econometrica*, 54(6):1315–1335, 1985.

S. L. Lauritzen. *Graphical Models*. Oxford Science Publications, 1996.

O. Ledoit and M. Wolf. Improved estimation of the covariance matrix of stock returns with an application to portfolio selection. *Journal of Empirical Finance*, 10:603–621, 2003a.

O. Ledoit and M. Wolf. Honey, I shrunk the sample covariance matrix: Problems in mean-variance optimization. *Journal of Portfolio Management*, 30:110–119, 2003b.

O. Ledoit and M. Wolf. A well-conditioned estimator for large-dimensional covariance matrices. *Journal of Multivariate Analysis*, 88:365–411, 2004.

O. Ledoit and M. Wolf. Nonlinear shrinkage estimation of large-dimensional covariance matrices. *Annals of Statistics*, 40(2):1024–1060, 2012.

O. Ledoit and M. Wolf. Spectrum estimation: A unified framework for covariance matrix estimation and PCA in large dimensions. *Journal of Multivariate Analysis*, 139:360–384, 2015.

O. Ledoit and M. Wolf. Analytical nonlinear shrinkage of large-dimensional covariance matrices. *Annals of Statistics*, 48(5):3043–3065, 2020.

B. N. Lehmann. Fads, martingales and market efficiency. *Quarterly Journal of Economics*, 105(1):1–28, 1990.

J. Lewellen, S. Nagel, and J. Shanken. A skeptical appraisal of asset pricing tests. *Journal of Financial Economics*, 96:175–194, 2010.

S. Li. Should passive investors actively manage their trades?, 2021. https://papers.ssrn.com/sol3/papers.cfm?abstract_id=3967799.

X. Li, R. N. Sullivan, and L. Garcia-Feijóo. The low-volatility anomaly: Market evidence on systematic risk vs. mispricing. *Financial Analysts Journal*, 72(1):36–47, 2016.

A. M. Lindner. Stationarity, mixing, distributional properties and moments of GARCH(p, q)-processes. In T. G. Andersen, R. A. Davis, J.-P. Kreiss, and T. Mikosch, editors, *Handbook of Financial Time Series*, pages 43–70. Springer, 2009.

R. Litterman and J. Scheinkman. Common factors affecting bond returns. *The Journal of Fixed Income*, 1(1):54–61, 1991.

L. Y. Liu, A. J. Patton, and K. Sheppard. Does anything beat 5-minute rv? a comparison of realized measures across multiple asset classes. *Journal of Econometrics*, 187(1):293–311, 2015.

A. W. Lo. The statistics of Sharpe ratios. *Financial Analysts Journal*, 58(4):36–52, 2002.

M. López de Prado. *Machine Learning for Asset Managers*. Cambridge University Press, 2020.

D. G. Luenberger. *Optimization by Vector Space Methods*. Wiley, 1969.

D. G. Luenberger and Y. Ye. *Linear and Nonlinear Programming*. Springer, 3rd edition, 2008.

H. Lütkepohl. *New Introduction to Multiple Time Series Analysis*. Springer, 2005.

A. C. MacKinlay. Multifactor models do not explain deviations from CAPM. *Journal of Financial Economics*, 38(1):3–28, 1995.

L. C. MacLean, W. T. Ziemba, and G. Blazenko. Growth versus security in dynamic investment analysis. *Management Science*, 38(11):1562–1585, 1992.

L. C. MacLean, R. Sanegre, Y Zhao, and W. T. Ziemba. Capital growth with security. *Journal of Economic Dynamics and Control*, 28:937–954, 2004.

L. C. MacLean, E. O. Thorp, and W. T. Ziemba. Good and bad properties of the Kelly criterion. In L. C. MacLean, E. O. Thorp, and W. T. Ziemba, editors, *The Kelly Capital Growth Investment Criterion*, pages 563–574. World Scientific, 2010a.

L. C. MacLean, E. O. Thorp, and W. T. Ziemba, editors. *The Kelly Capital Growth Investment Criterion*. World Scientific, 2010b.

S. Mahajan. *The Art of Insight in Science and Engineering*. MIT Press, 2014.

B. Malkiel. *The New Palgrave Dictionary of Economics*, chapter Efficient Market Hypothesis, pages 1–7. Palgrave MacMillan, 1987.

C. Mancini. Non-parametric threshold estimation for models with stochastic diffusion coefficient and jumps. *Scandinavian Journal of Statistics*, 36(2):270–296, 2009.

C. Mancini. The speed of convergence of the threshold estimator of integrated variance. *Stochastic Processes and their Applications*, 121(4):845–855, 2011.

H. M. Markowitz. Portfolio selection. *Journal of Finance*, 7(1):77–91, 1952.

H. M. Markowitz. *Portfolio Selection: Efficient Diversification of Investments*. Basil Blackwell, 2nd edition, 1959.

I. Mastromatteo, M. Benzaquen, Z. Eisler, and J.-P. Bouchaud. Trading lightly: Cross-impact and optimal portfolio execution. *Risk*, July 2017:78–83, 2017.

R. D. McLean and J. Pontiff. Does academic research destroy stock return predictability? *Journal of Finance*, 71(1):5–32, 2016.

X. Mestre. Improved estimation of eigenvalues and eigenvectors of covariance matrices using their sample estimates. *IEEE Transactions on Information Theory*, 54(11):5113–5129, 2008.

R. O. Michaud. The Markowitz optimization enigma: Is 'optimized' optimal? *Financial Analysts Journal*, 45(1):31–42, 1989.

T. Mikosch and C. Stărică. Limit theory for the sample autocorrelations and extremes of a GARCH(1, 1) process. *Annals of Statistics*, 28(5):1427–1451, 2000.

S. Min, C. Maglaras, and C. C. Moallemi. Cross-sectional variation of intraday liquidity, cross-impact, and their effect on portfolio execution. *Operations Research*, 70(2):830–846, 2022.

J. L. Miralles Marcelo, J. L. Miralles Quirós, and J. L. Martins. The role of country and industry factors during volatile times. *Journal of International Financial Markets, Institutions and Money*, 26:273–290, 2013.

L. Mirsky. Symmetric gauge functions and unitarily invariant norms. *The Quarterly Journal of Mathematics*, 11(1):50–59, 1960.

M. Mitchell, L. H. Pedersen, and T. Pulvino. Slow moving capital. *American Economic Review*, 92(2):215–220, 2007.

M. I. Jordan. Graphical models.*Statistical Science*, 19(1):140–155, 2004.

M. Mohri, A. Rostamizadeh, and A. Talwalkar. *Foundations of Machine Learning*. MIT Press, 2nd edition, 2018.

K. P. Murphy. *Machine Learning*. MIT Press, 2012.

J. F. Muth. Optimal properties of exponentially weighted forecasts. *Journal of the American Statistical Association*, 55(290):299–306, 1960.

R. K. Narang. *Inside the Black Box*. Wiley, 3rd edition, 2024.

D. R. Nelson. Stationarity and persistence in the GARCH(1, 1) model. *Econometric Theory*, 6:318–334, 1990.

W. K. Newey and K. D. West. A simple, positive semi-definite, heteroskedasticity and autocorrelation consistent covariance matrix. *Econometrica*, 55(3):703–708, 1987.

B. Novick. Index investing supports vibrant capital markets. *Blackrock Viewpoint*, 2017. https://www.blackrock.com/corporate/literature/whitepaper/viewpoint-index-investing-supports-vibrant-capital-markets-oct-2017.pdf.

R. Novy-Marx. The other side of value: The gross profitability premium. *Journal of Financial Economics*, 108:1–28, 2013.

A. A. Obizhaeva and J. Wang. Optimal trading strategy and supply/demand dynamics. *Journal of Financial Markets*, 16(1):1–32, 2013.

A. V. Olivares-Nadal and V. DeMiguel. Technical note—a robust perspective on transaction costs in portfolio optimization. *Operations Research*, 66(3):733–739, 2018.

A. Onatski. Determining the number of factors from empirical distribution of eigenvalues. *Review of Economics and Statistics*, 92(4):1004–1016, 2010.

Open Science Collaboration. Estimating the reproducibility of psychological science. *Science*, 349(6251):aac4716, 2015.

D. P. Palomar. *Portfolio Optimization*. Cambridge University Press, 2024.

R. Pardo. *The Evaluation and Optimization of Trading Strategies*. Wiley, 2nd edition, 2007.

A. J. Patton. Volatility forecast comparison using imperfect volatility proxies. *Journal of Econometrics*, 160:246–256, 2011.

A. J. Patton and K. Sheppard. Evaluating volatility and correlation forecasts. In T. G. Andersen, R. A. Davis, J.-P. Kreiss, and T. Mikosch, editors, *Handbook of Financial Time Series*, pages 801–838. Springer, 2009.

D. Paul. Asymptotics of sample eigenstructure for a large dimensional spiked covariance model. *Statistica Sinica*, 17:1617–1642, 2017.

S. E. Pav. *The Sharpe Ratio*. Chapman & Hall/CRC, 2023.

L. H. Pedersen. *Efficiently Inefficient: How Smart Money Invests and Market Prices are Determined*. Princeton University Press, 2015.

L. H. Pedersen, A. Babu, and A. Levine. Enhanced portfolio optimization. *Financial Analysts Journal*, 77(2):124–151, 2021.

M. Podolskij and M. Vetter. Bipower-type estimation in a noisy diffusion setting. *Stochastic Processes and their Applications*, 119(9):2803–2831, 2009.

M. Pohl, A. Ristig, W. Schachermayer, and L. Tangpi. The amazing power of dimensional analysis: Quantifying market impact. *Market Microstructure and Liquidity*, 3(4):1850004, 2017.

M. Pourahmadi. *High-Dimensional Covariance Estimation*. Wiley, 2013.

A. V. Puchkov, D. Stefek, and M. Davis. Sources of return in global investing. *Journal of Portfolio Management*, 31(2):12–21, 2005.

L.B. Pulley. A general mean-variance approximation to expected utility for short holding periods. *The Journal of Financial and Quantitative Analysis*, 16(3):361–363, 1981.

E. E. Qian, R. H. Hua, and E. H. Sorensen. *Quantitative Equity Portfolio Management*. Chapman & Hall/CRC, 2007.

E. Ratliff-Crain, C. M. Van Oort, J. B. Matthew T. K. Koehler, and B. F. Tivnan. Revisiting stylized facts for modern stock markets, 2023.

A. C. Rencher and W. F. Christensen. *Methods of multivariate analysis*. Wiley, 2012.

G. Ritter, B. Baldacci, and E. Benveniste. Optimal turnover, liquidity, and autocorrelation. 2022.

C. P. Robert. *The Bayesian Choice*. Springer, 2nd edition, 2007.

R. Roll. A simple implicit measure of the effective bid-ask spread in an efficient market. *Journal of Finance*, 39(4):1127–39, 1984.

J. P. Romano and M. Wolf. Stepwise multiple testing as formalized data snooping. *Econometrica*, 73(4):1237–1282, 2005.

S. A. Ross. The arbitrage theory of capital asset pricing. *Journal of Economic Theory*, 13(3):341–360, 1976.

S. M. Ross. *Introduction to Probability Models*. Academic Press, 13th edition, 2023.

D. Ruppert and D. S. Matteson. *Statistics and Data Analysis for Financial Engineering*. Springer, 2nd edition, 2015.

A. Saxena and R. A. Stubbs. The alpha alignment factor: A solution to the underestimation of risk for optimized active portfolios. *Journal of Risk*, 15(3):3–37, 2013.

M. Scholes and J. Williams. Estimating beta from nonsynchronous data. *Journal of Financial Economics*, 5(3):309–327, 1977.

SEC. Form 13f: Information required of institutional investment managers pursuant to section 13(f) of the securities exchange act of 1934 and rules thereunder, 1934. https://www.sec.gov/pdf/form13f.pdf.

W. F. Sharpe. Capital asset prices: A theory of market equilibrium under conditions of risk. *Journal of Finance*, 19(3):425–442, 1964.

W. F. Sharpe. The valuation of risk assets and the selection of risky investments in stock portfolios and capital budgets. *Review of Economics and Statistics*, 47(1):13–37, 1965.

W. F. Sharpe. Equilibrium in a capital asset market. *Econometrica*, 34(4):768–783, 1966.

D. Shen, H. Shen, H. Zhu, and J. S. Marron. The statistics and mathematics of high dimension low sample size asymptotics. *Statistica Sinica*, 26:1747–1770, 2016.

P. G. Shephard. Second order risk, 2009.

R. H. Shumway and D. S. Stoffer. *Time Series Analysis and Its Applications*. Springer, 2011.

J. P. Simmons, L. D. Nelson, and U. Simonsohn. Life after p-hacking. Volume paper presented at the 14th Annual Meeting of the Society for Personality and Social Psychology, New Orleans, LA, 2013.

D. Simon. *Optimal State Estimation: Kalman, H_∞, and Nonlinear Approaches*. Wiley, 2006.

V. Singal. *Beyond the Random Walk*. Oxford University Press, 2004.

D. Skillicorn. *Understanding Complex Datasets: Data Mining with Matrix Decompositions*. Chapman & Hall/CRC, 2007.

W. Stevens. *The Collected Poems*. Vintage, 1990.

G. Strang. *Linear Algebra and Learning from Data*. Wellesley - Cambridge Press, 2019.

R. A. Stubbs and P. Vance. Computing return estimation error matrices for robust optimization. Technical Report 1, Axioma Research Paper, 2005.

S. Suzuki. *Zen Mind, Beginner's Mind*. Weatherhill, 1970.

A. Swade, M. X. Hanauer, H. Lorde, and D. Blitz. Factor zoo (.zip). *The Journal of Portfolio Management*, 50(3):11–31, 2024.

W. Szymborska. *Map: Collected and Last Poems*. Ecco, 2016.

S. J. Taylor. *Modelling Financial Time Series*. Wiley, 1986.

S. J. Taylor. *Asset Price Dynamics, Volatility, and Prediction*. Princeton University Press, 2007.

T. Teräsvirta. An introduction to univariate GARCH models. In T. G. Andersen, R. A. Davis, J.-P. Kreiss, and T. Mikosch, editors, *Handbook of Financial Time Series*, pages 17–42. Springer, 2009a.

T. Teräsvirta. Multivariate GARCH models. In T. G. Andersen, R. A. Davis, J.-P. Kreiss, and T. Mikosch, editors, *Handbook of Financial Time Series*. Springer, 2009b.

E. O. Thorp. The Kelly criterion in blackjack sports betting, and the stock market. In S. A. Zenios and W. Ziemba, editors, *Handbook of Asset and Liability Management*, volume 1. Elsevier, 2006.

M. E. Tipping and C. M. Bishop. Probabilistic principal component analysis. *Journal of the Royal Statistical Society Series B*, 61(3):611–622, 1999.

J. Traut. What we know about the low-risk anomaly – a literature review. *Financial Markets and Portfolio Management*, 37(3):297–324, 2023.

L. Trefethen and D. Bau. *Numerical Linear Algebra*. SIAM, 1997.

R. S. Tsay. *Analysis of Financial Time Series*. Wiley, 3rd edition, 2010.

A. DeMiguel, V. Martin-Utrera, and F. J. Nogales. Size matters: Optimal calibration of shrinkage estimators for portfolio selection. *Journal of Banking and Finance*, 37(8):3018–3034, 2013.

R. van Handel. Probability in high dimensions. Technical report, 2016.

N. Vause. Counterparty risk and contract volumes in the credit default swap market. *BIS Quarterly Review*, 2010.

R. Velu, M. Hardy, and D. Nehren. *Algorithmic Trading and Quantitative Strategies*. CRC Press, 2020.

R. Vershynin. *High-Dimensional Probability*. Cambridge University Press, 2018.

G. Wahba. A least squares estimate of satellite attitude. *SIAM Review*, 7(3):384, 1965.

S. Wang, Y. Luo, M.-A Alvarez, J. Jussa, A. Wang, and G. Rohal. Seven sins of quantitative investing. Technical report, Deutsche Bank, 2014.

W. Wang and J. Fan. Asymptotics of empirical eigenstructure for high dimensional spiked covariance. *Annals of Statistics*, 45(3):1342–1374, 2017.

L. Wasserman. *All of Statistics*. Springer, 2004.

K. T. Webster. *Handbook of Price Impact Modeling*. Chapman & Hall/CRC, 2023.

P. Whittle. *Optimal Control. Basics and Beyond*. Wiley, 1996.

T. Wiest. Momentum: What do we know 30 years after Jegadeesh and Titman's seminal paper? *Financial Markets and Portfolio Management*, 37:95–114, 2023.

J. Yao, S. Zheng, and Z. Bai. *Large Sample Covariance Matrices and High-Dimensional Data Analysis*. Cambridge University Press, 2015.

L. Zack. *The Handbook of Equity Market Anomalies*. Wiley, 2011.

L. Zhang, P. A. Mykland, and Y. Aït-Sahalia. A tale of two time scales: Determining integrated volatility with noisy high-frequency data. *Journal of the American Statistical Association*, 100(472):1394–1411, 2005.

E. Zivot. Practical issues in the analysis of univariate GARCH models. In T. G. Andersen, R. A. Davis, J.-P. Kreiss, and T. Mikosch, editors, *Handbook of Financial Time Series*, pages 113–155. Springer, 2009.

E. Zivot and J. Wang. *Modeling Financial Time Series with S-Plus*. Springer, 2003.

Index